HISTORY OF ART

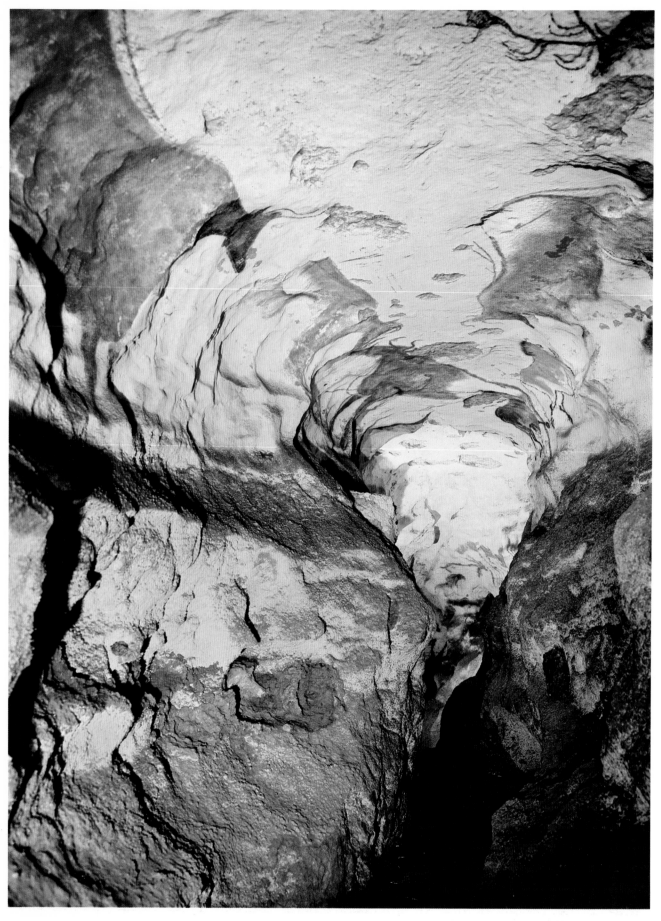

AXIAL GALLERY, LASCAUX CAVES, FRANCE
15,000–10,000 B.C. (figure 31)

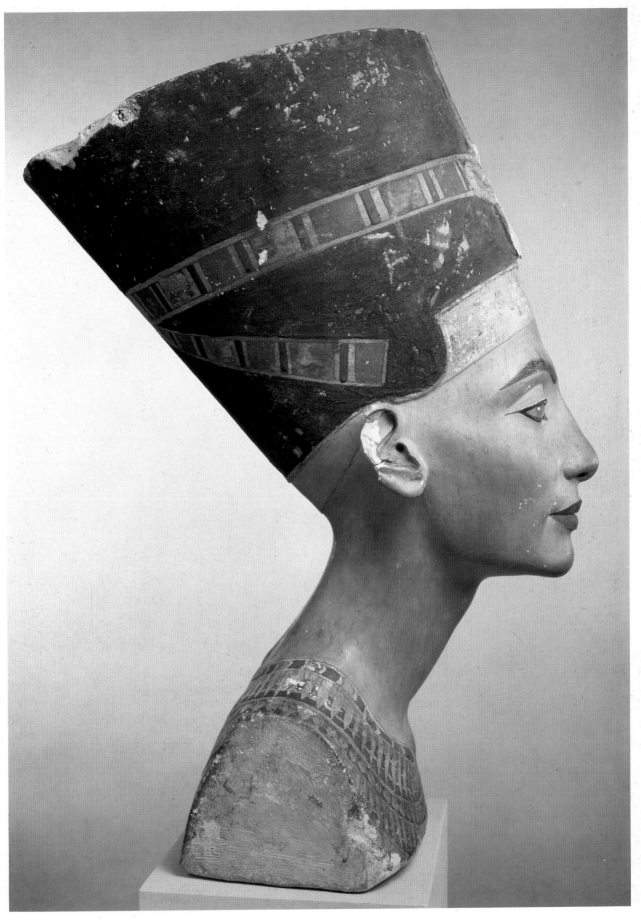

QUEEN NOFRETETE, FROM EGYPT
c. 1360 B.C. (figure 101)

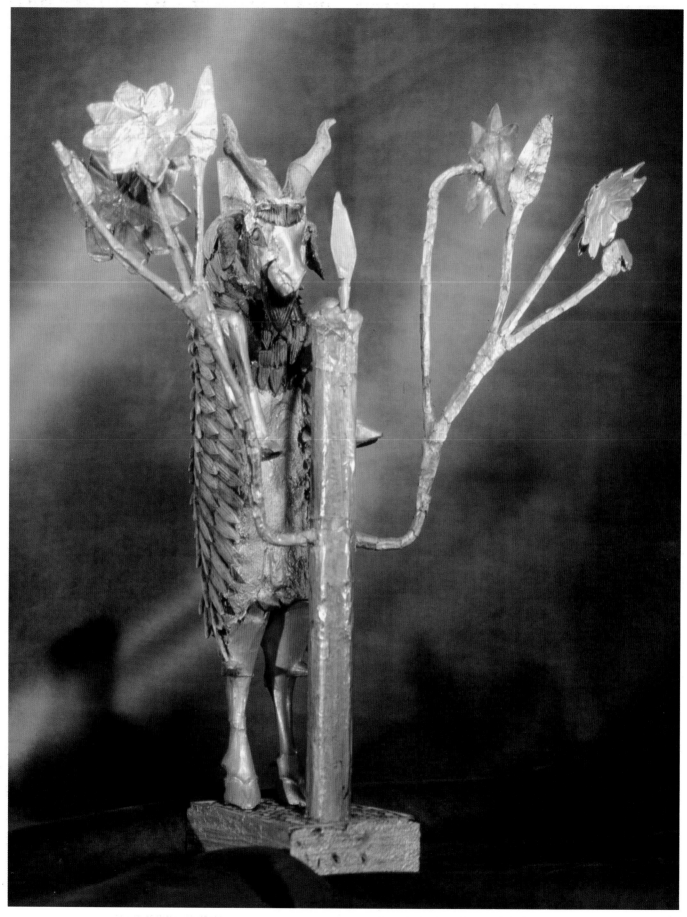

RAM AND TREE, FROM UR IN SUMER
c. 2600 B.C. (figure 112)

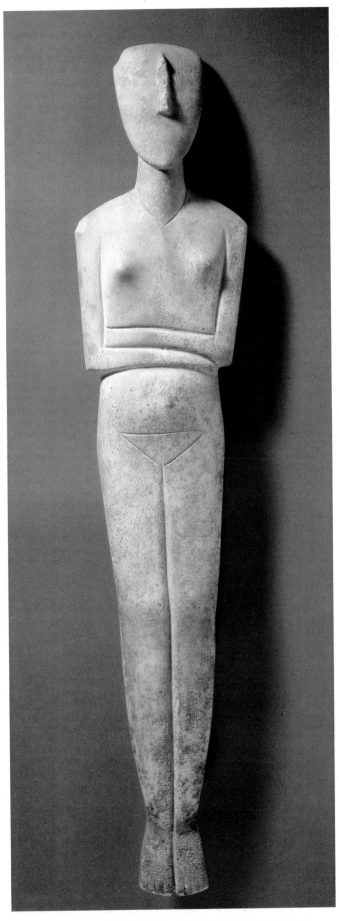

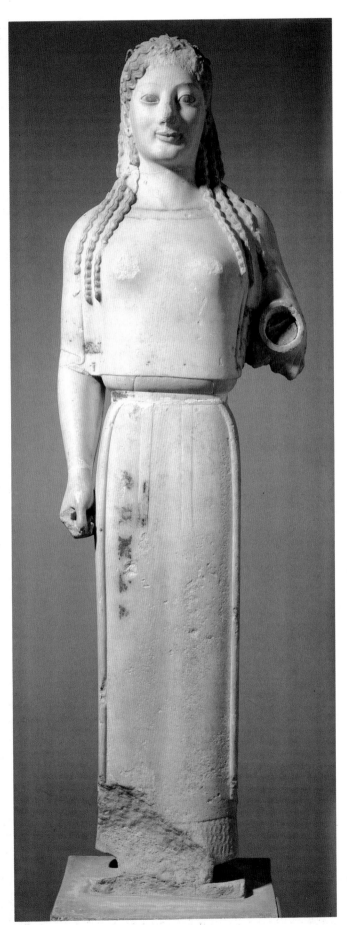

CYCLADIC STATUE, FROM AMORGOS IN THE CYCLADES
2500–1100 B.C. (figure 137)

ARCHAIC GREEK KORE
c. 530 B.C. (figure 171)

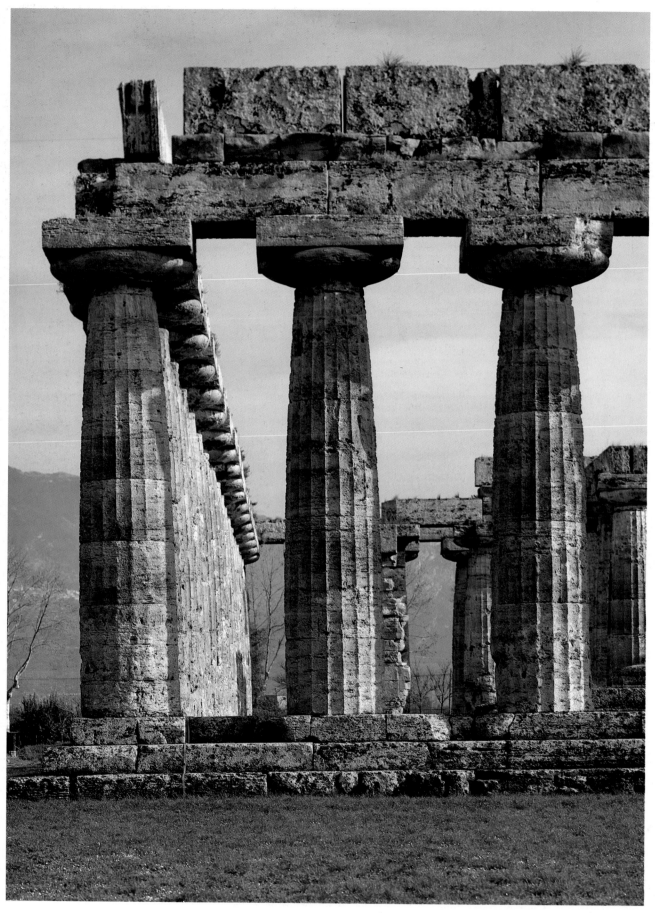

THE "BASILICA," A DORIC GREEK TEMPLE IN PAESTUM, ITALY
c. 550 B.C. (figure 184)

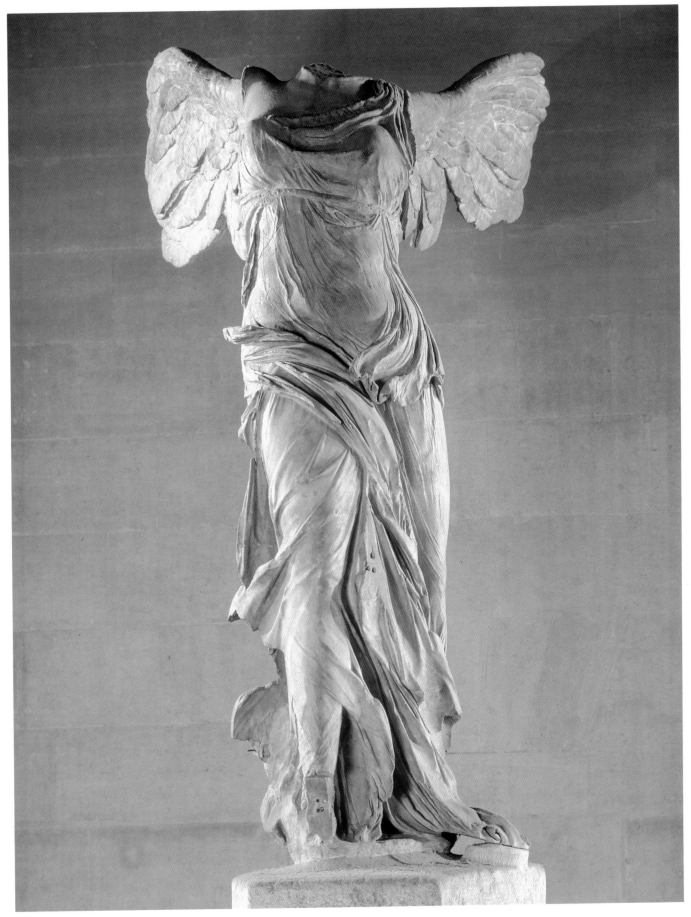

NIKE OF SAMOTHRACE, A HELLENISTIC SCULPTURE
c. 200–190 B.C. (figure 229)

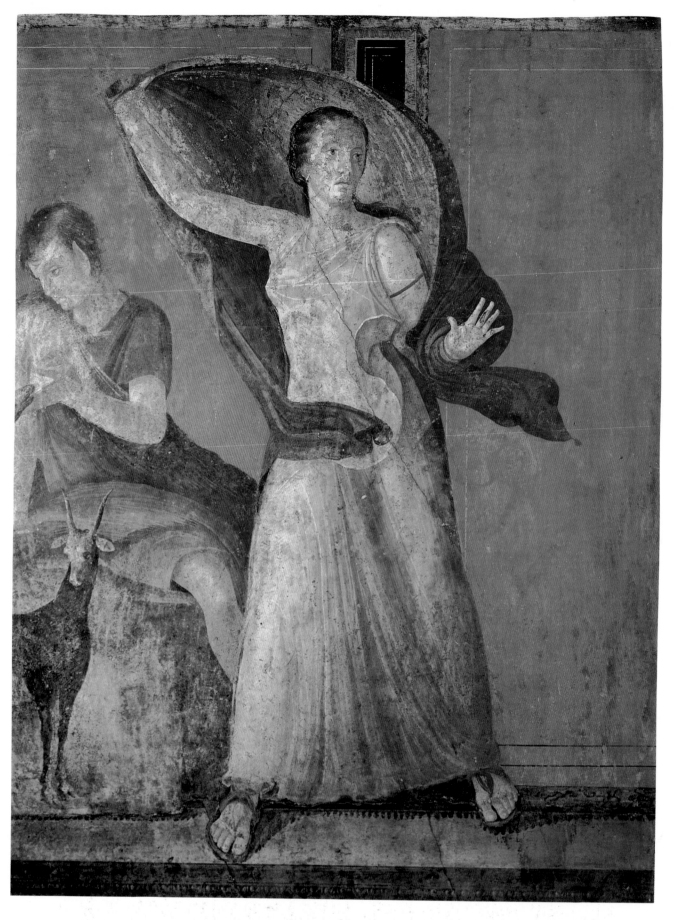

WOMAN WITH A VEIL, FROM A ROMAN WALL PAINTING IN POMPEII, ITALY
c. 50 B.C. (figure 311)

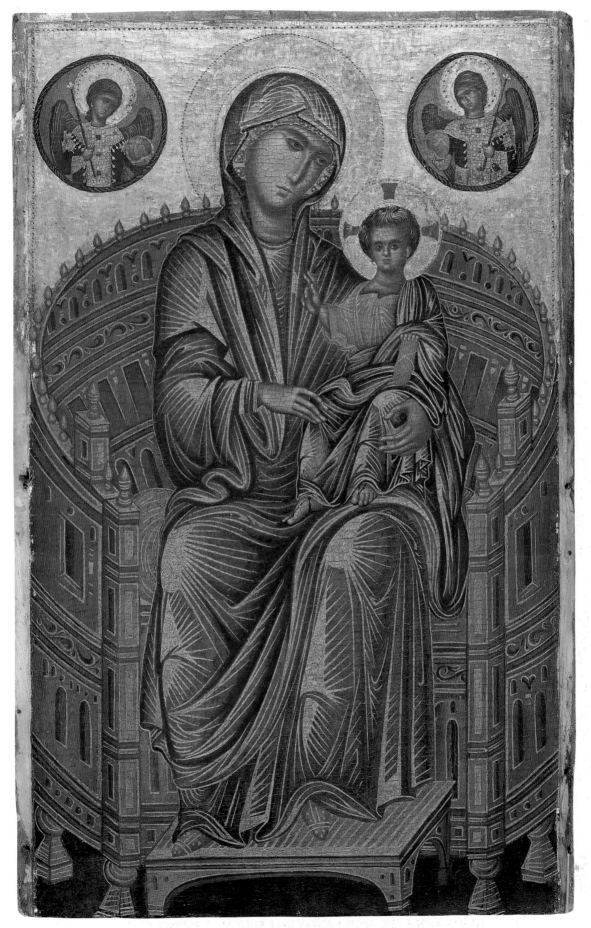

MADONNA ENTHRONED, A BYZANTINE PANEL PAINTING
Late 13th century (figure 358)

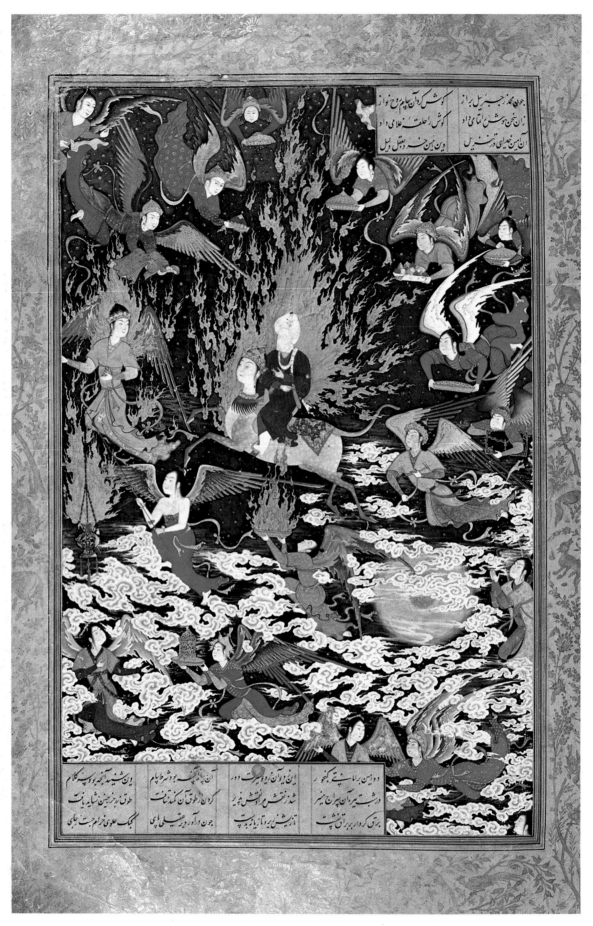

THE ASCENSION OF MOHAMMED, FROM A PERSIAN MANUSCRIPT
1539–43 (figure 383)

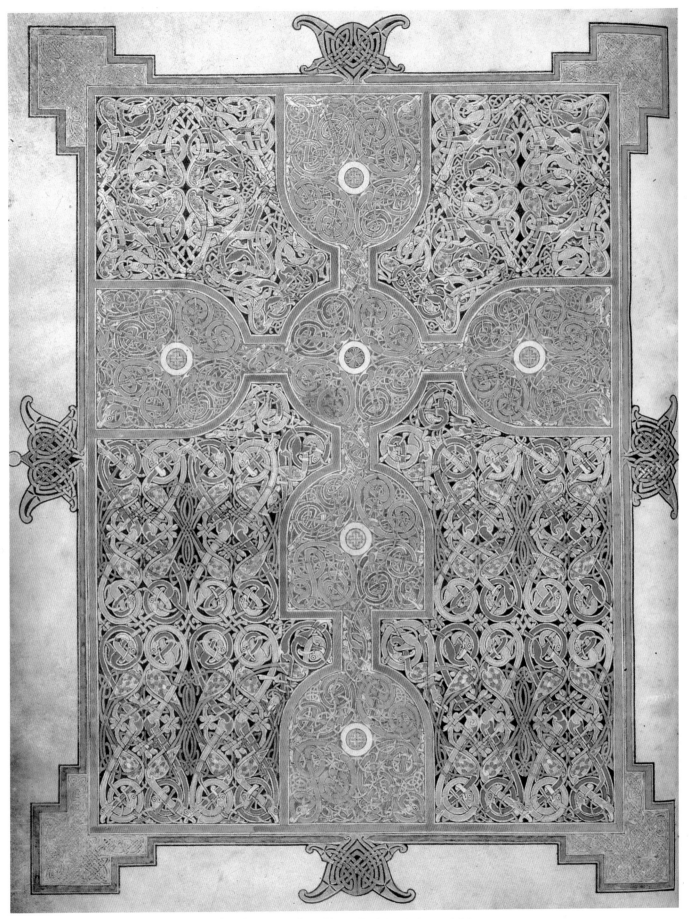

CROSS PAGE, FROM THE HIBERNO-SAXON LINDISFARNE GOSPELS
c. 700 (figure 387)

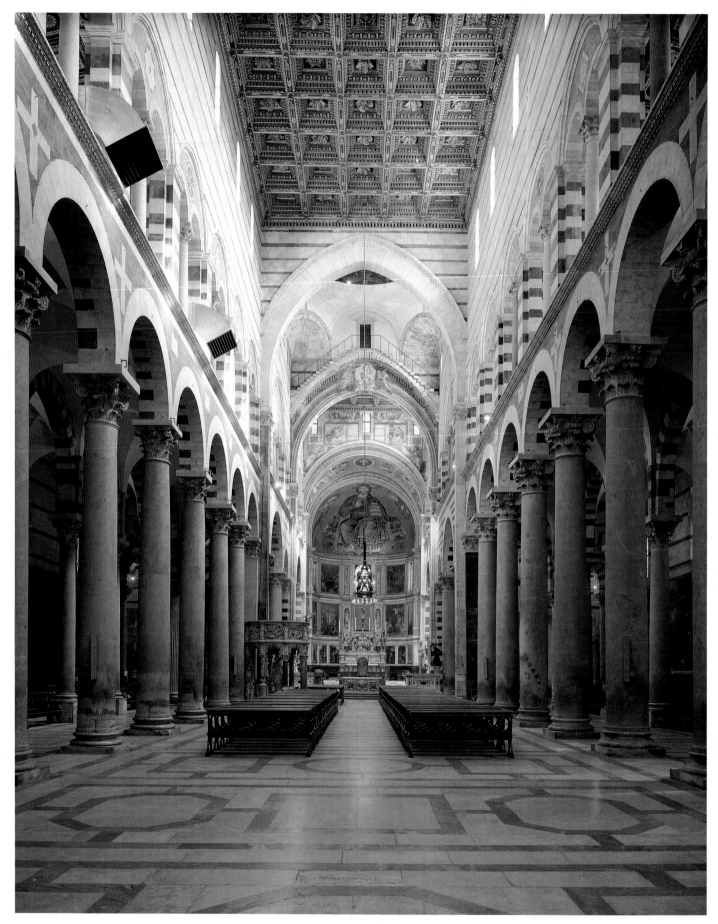

PISA CATHEDRAL
1053–1272 (figure 430)

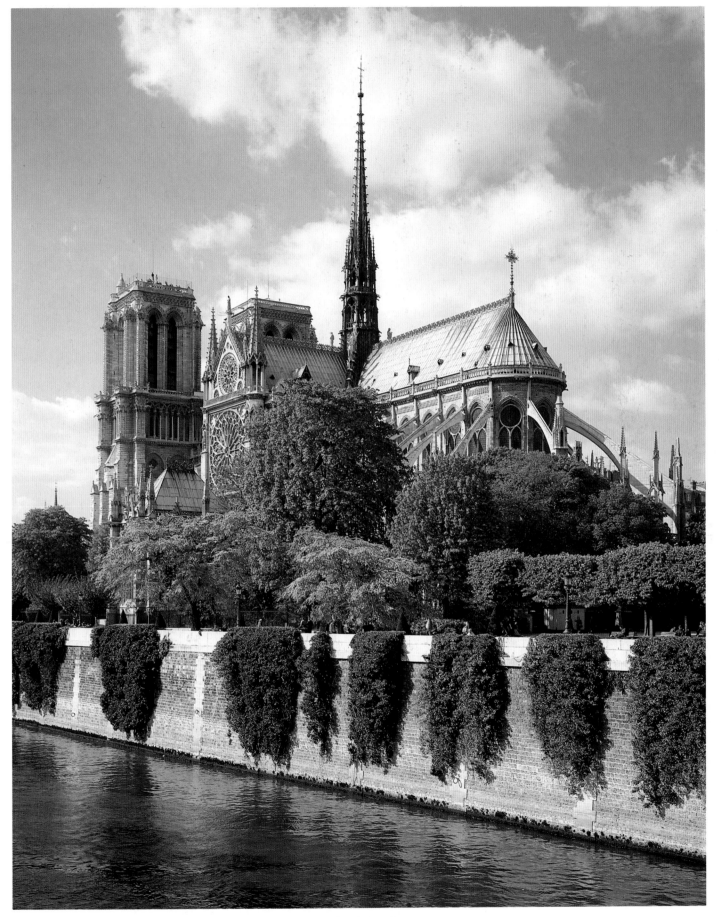

NOTRE-DAME CATHEDRAL, PARIS
1163–c. 1250 (figure 455)

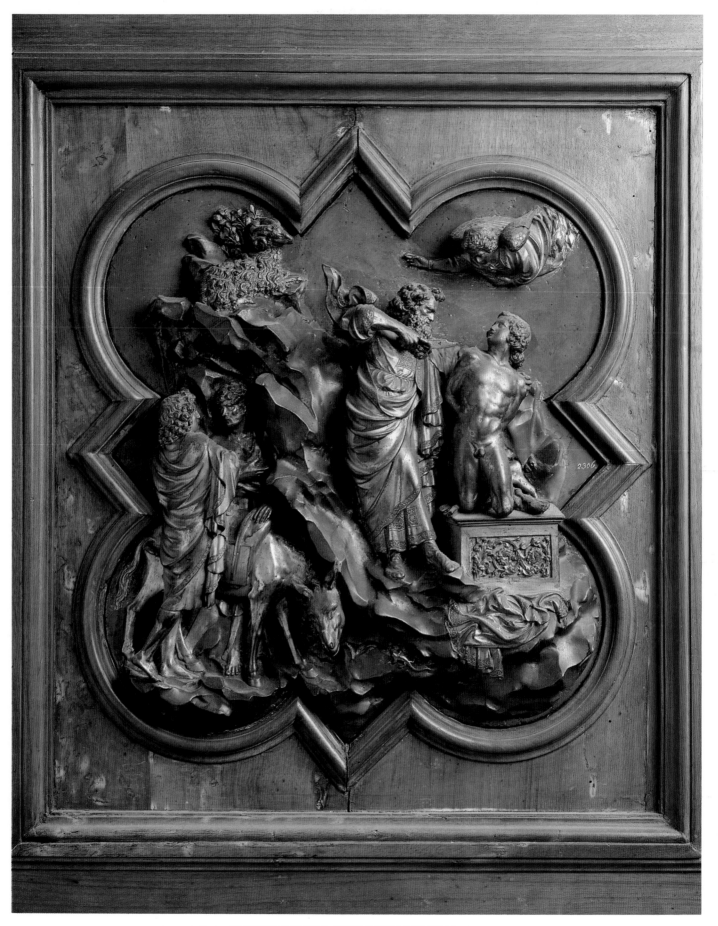

LORENZO GHIBERTI. THE SACRIFICE OF ISAAC
1401–02 (figure 516)

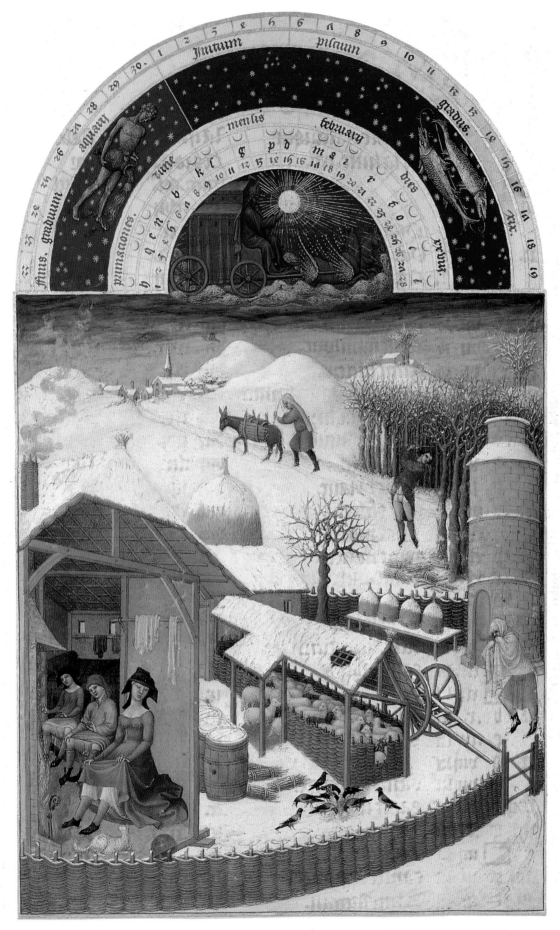

THE LIMBOURG BROTHERS. FEBRUARY, FROM LES TRÈS RICHES HEURES DU DUC DE BERRY
1413–16 (figure 542)

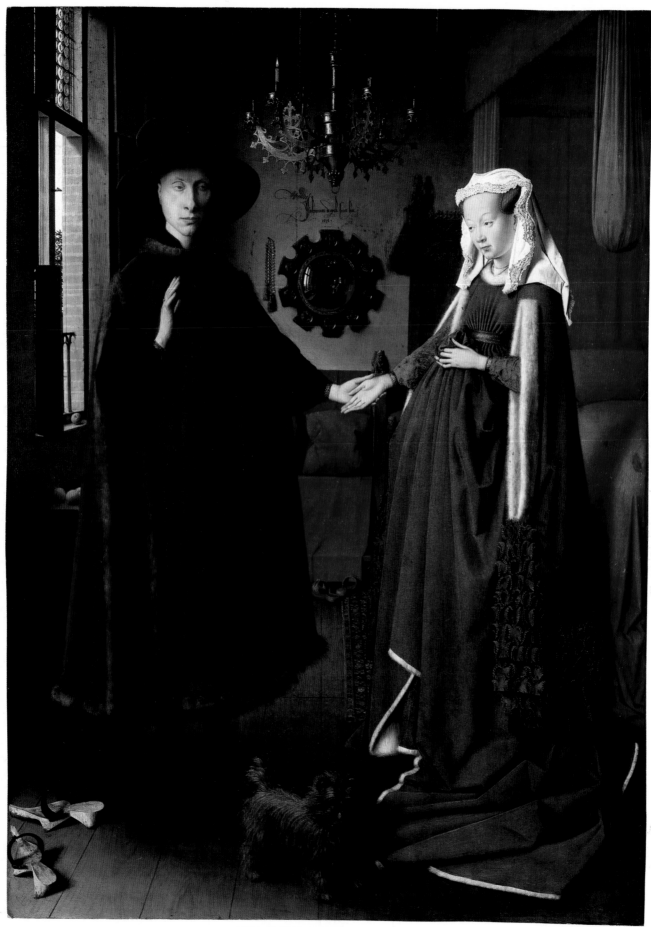

JAN VAN EYCK. WEDDING PORTRAIT
1434 (figure 553)

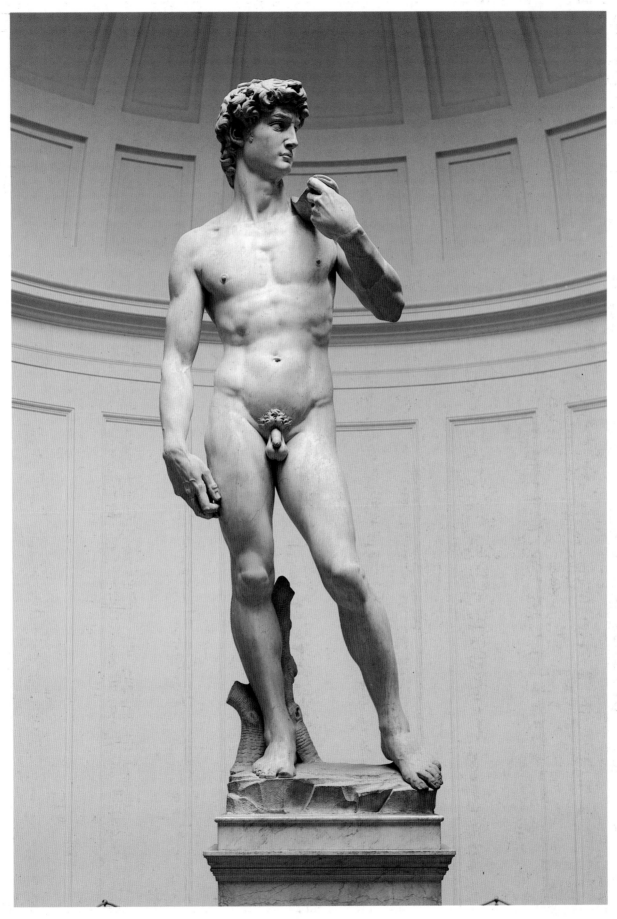

MICHELANGELO. DAVID
1501–04 (figure 652)

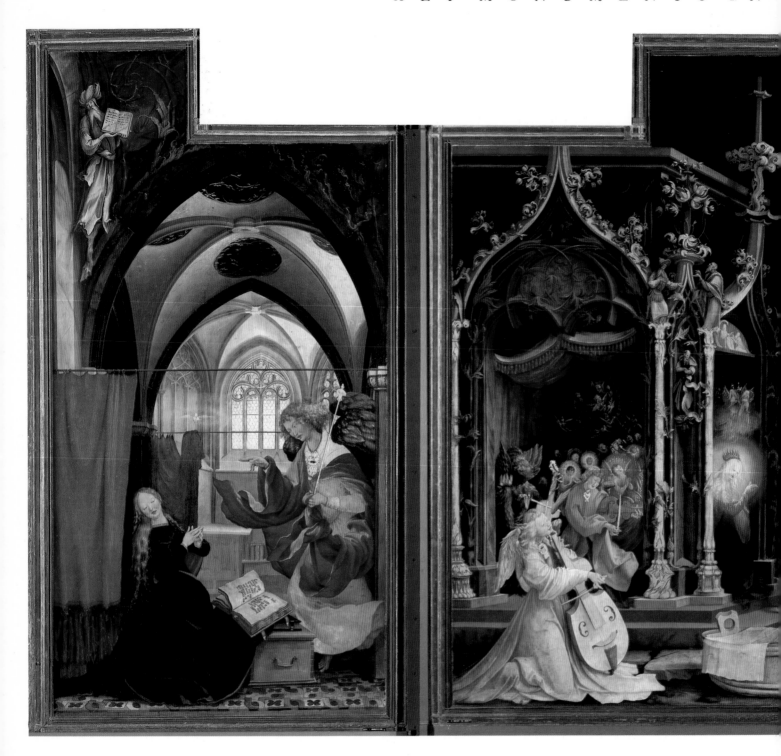

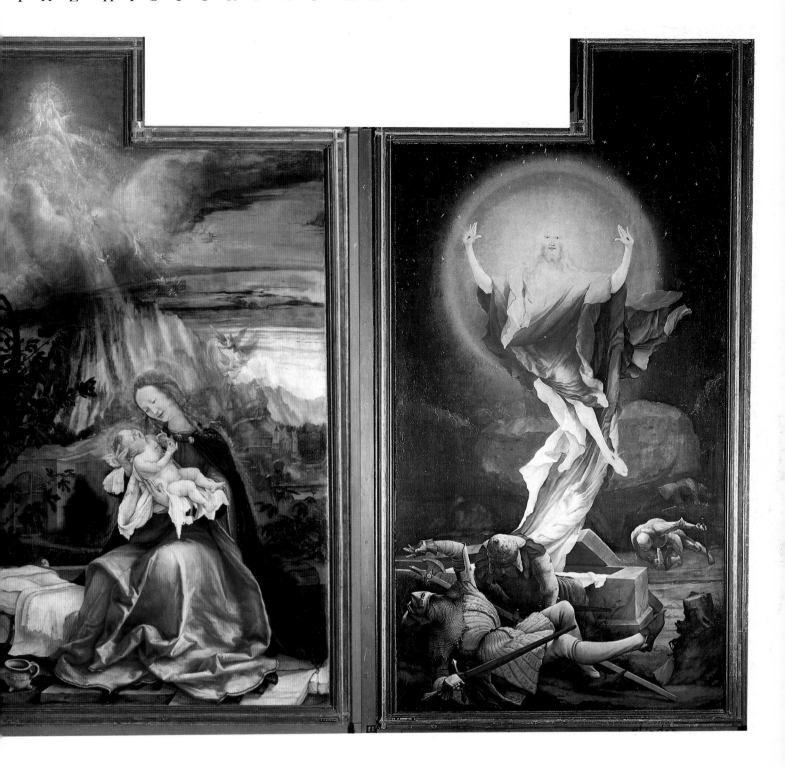

MATTHIAS GRÜNEWALD. ISENHEIM ALTARPIECE, SECOND VIEW
c. 1510–15 (figure 711)

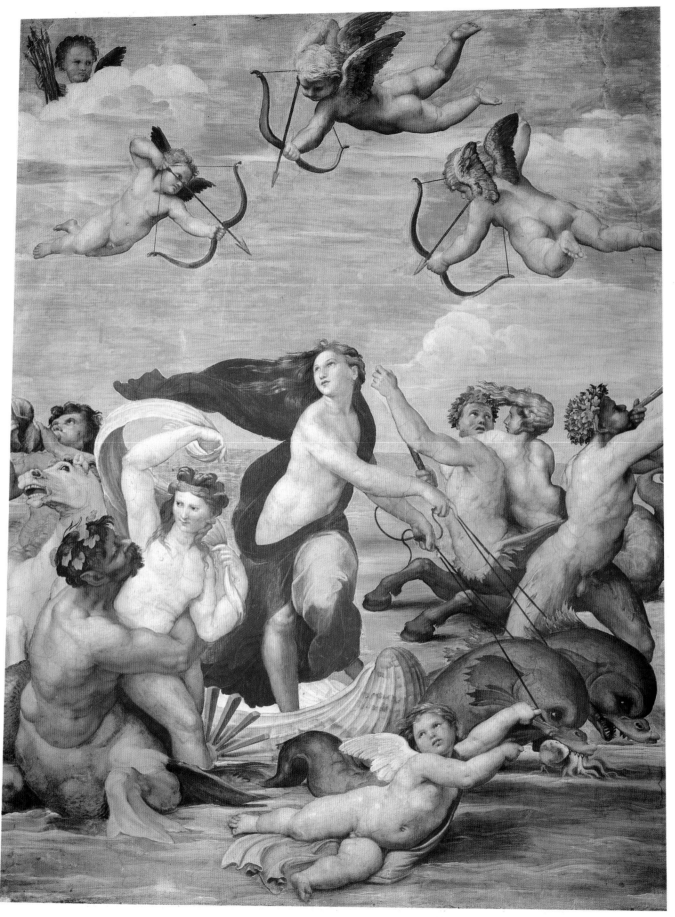

RAPHAEL. GALATEA
1513 (figure 673)

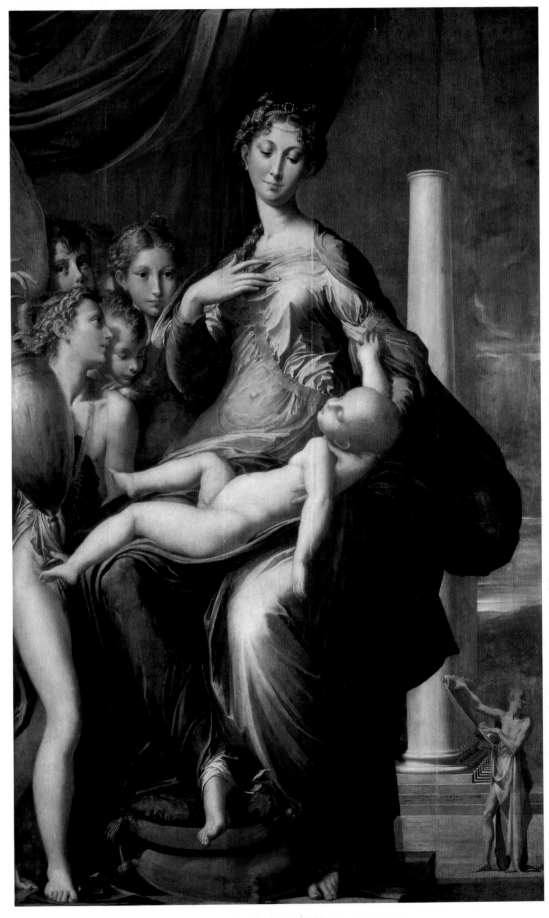

PARMIGIANINO. THE MADONNA WITH THE LONG NECK
c. 1535 (figure 684)

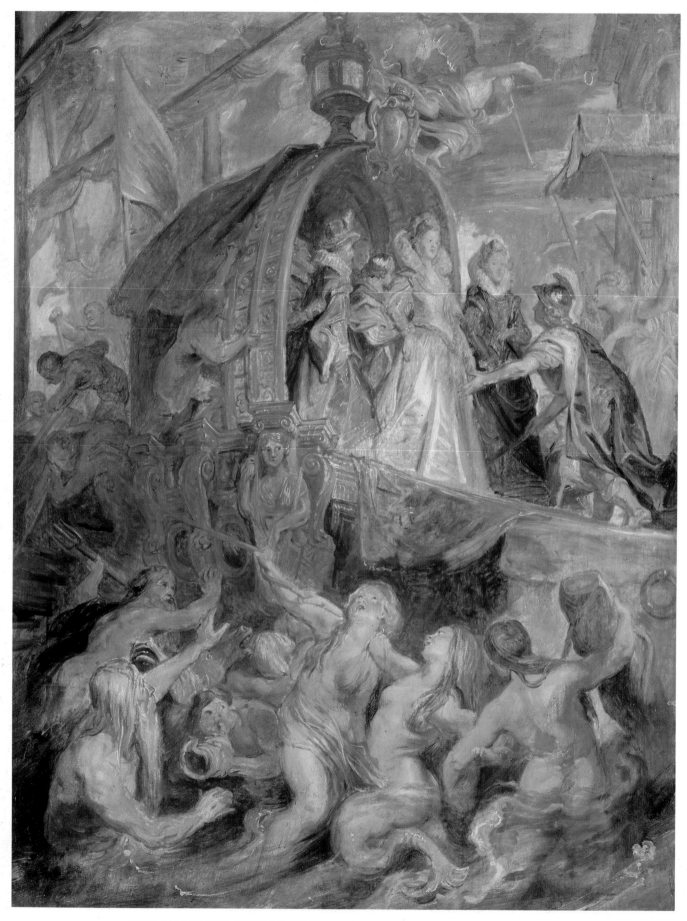

PETER PAUL RUBENS. MARIE DE'MEDICI, QUEEN OF FRANCE, LANDING IN MARSEILLES
1622–23 (figure 774)

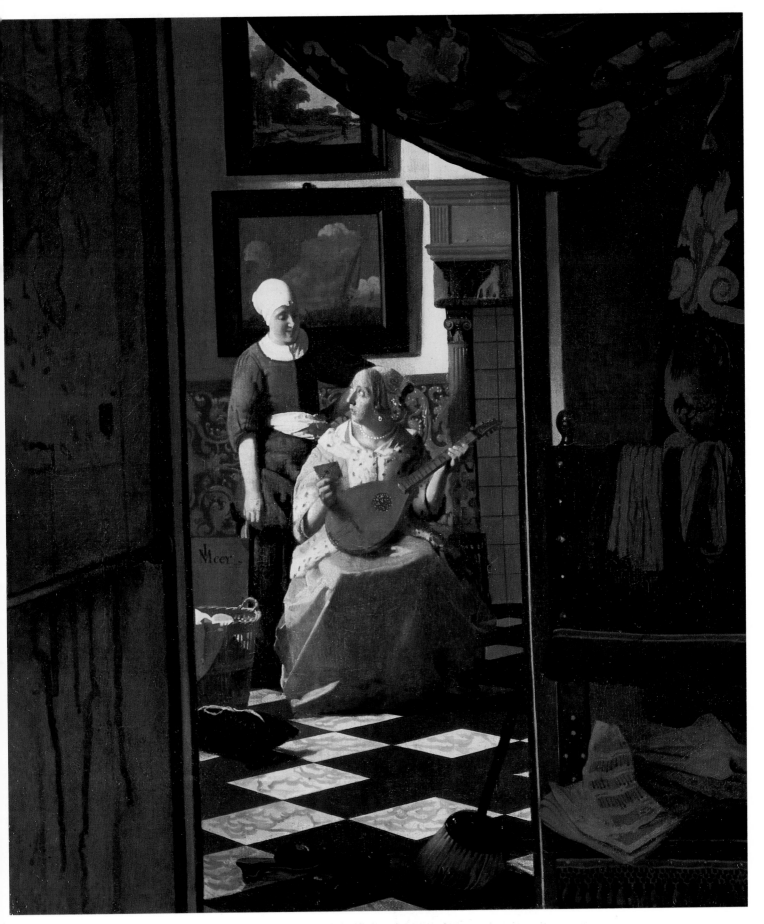

JAN VERMEER. THE LETTER
1666 (figure 794)

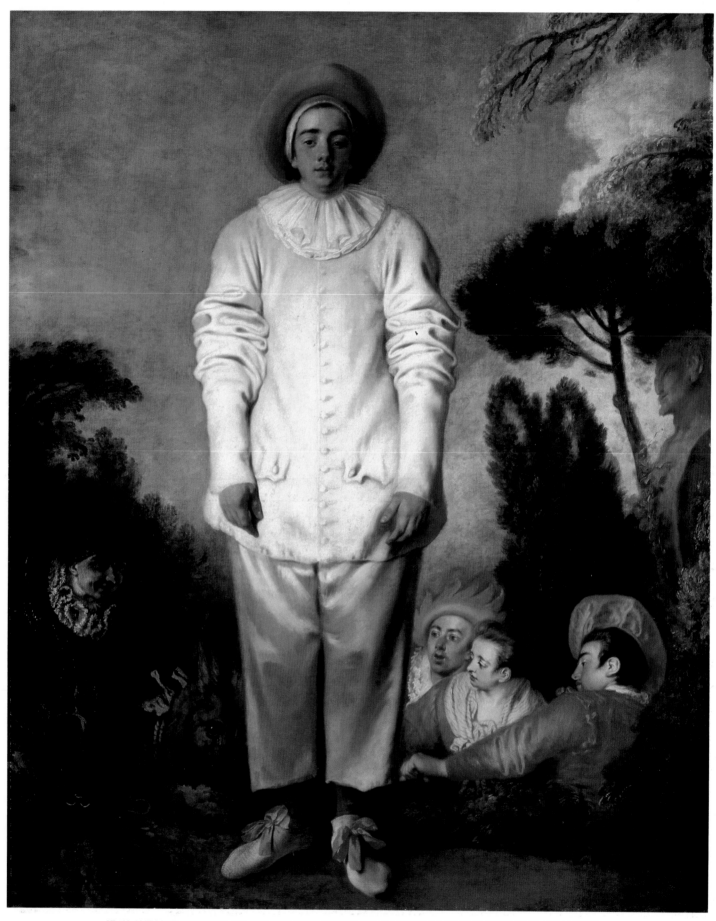

JEAN-ANTOINE WATTEAU. GILLES AND FOUR OTHER CHARACTERS FROM THE COMMEDIA DELL'ARTE
c. 1719 (figure 819)

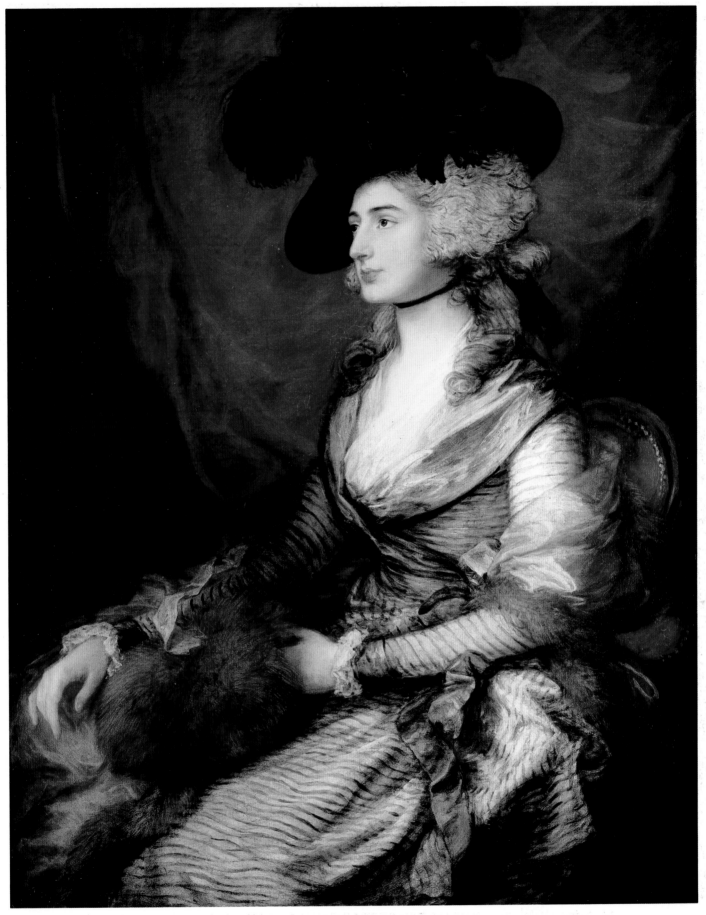

THOMAS GAINSBOROUGH. MRS. SIDDONS
1785 (figure 834)

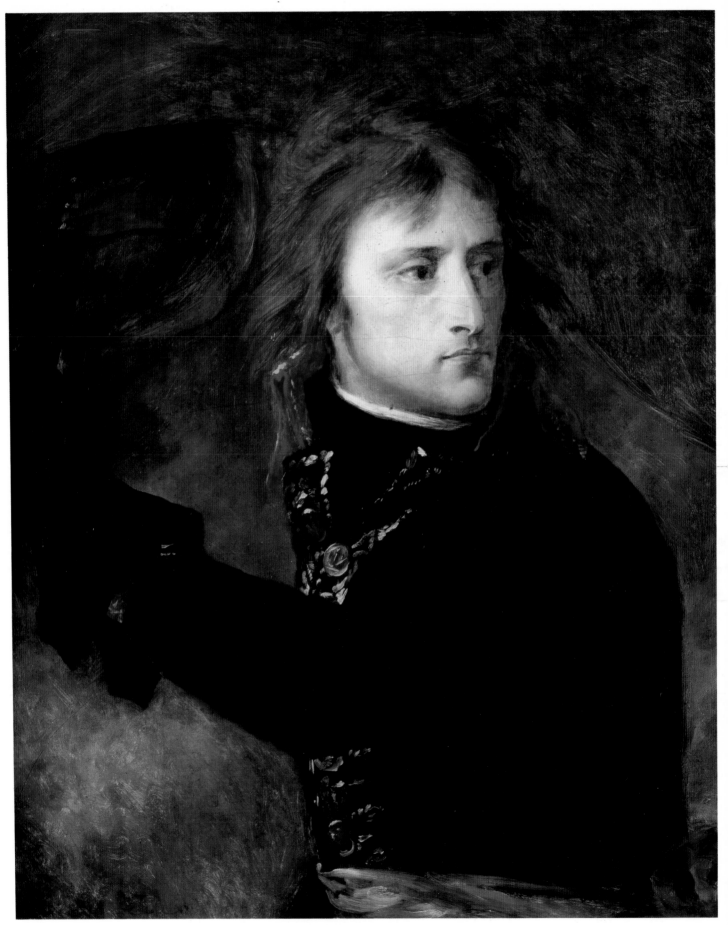

ANTOINE-JEAN GROS. NAPOLEON AT ARCOLE
1796 (figure 859)

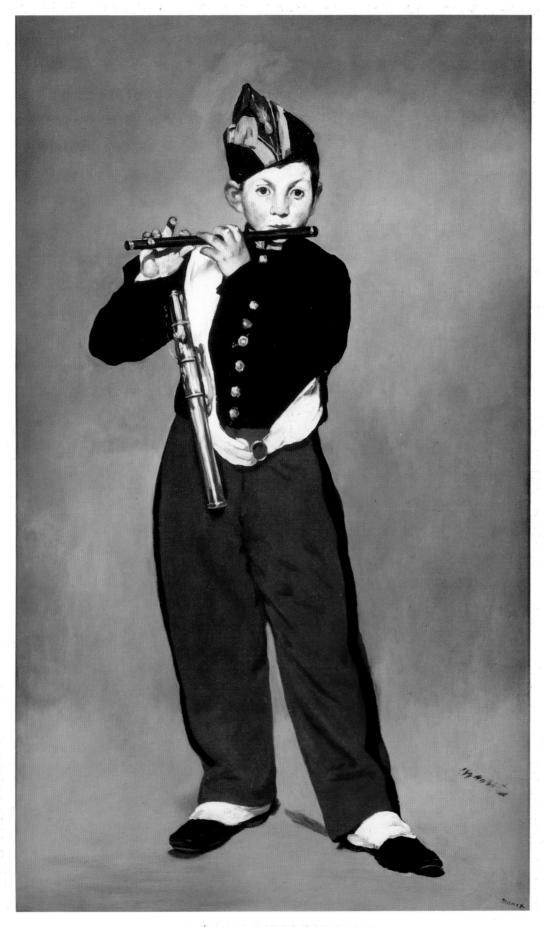

ÉDOUARD MANET. THE FIFER
1866 (figure 912)

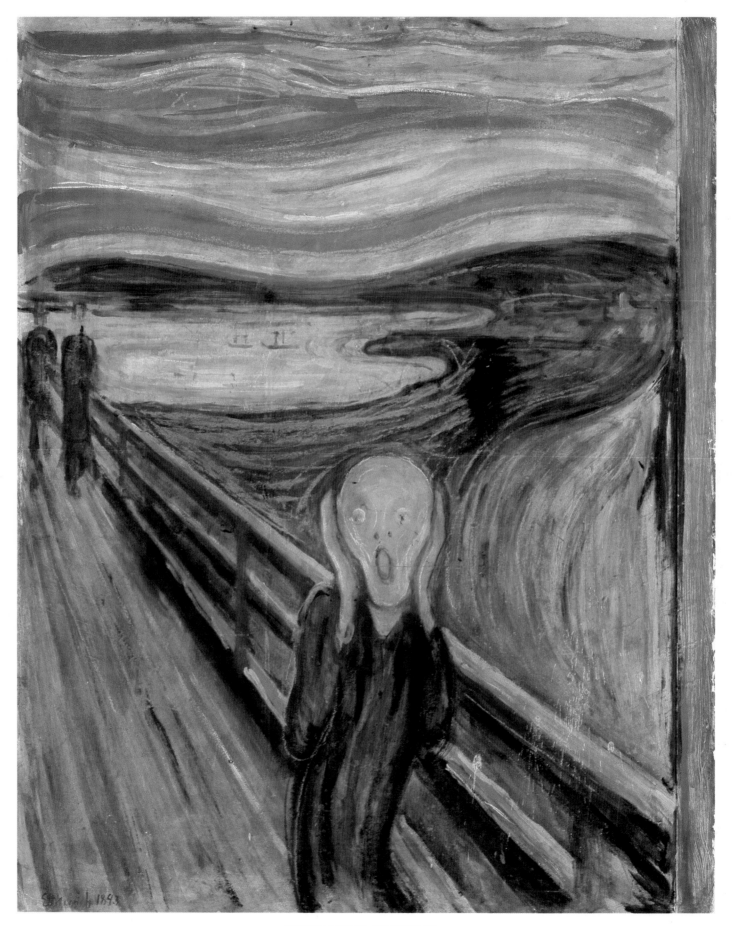

EDVARD MUNCH. THE SCREAM
1893 (figure 958)

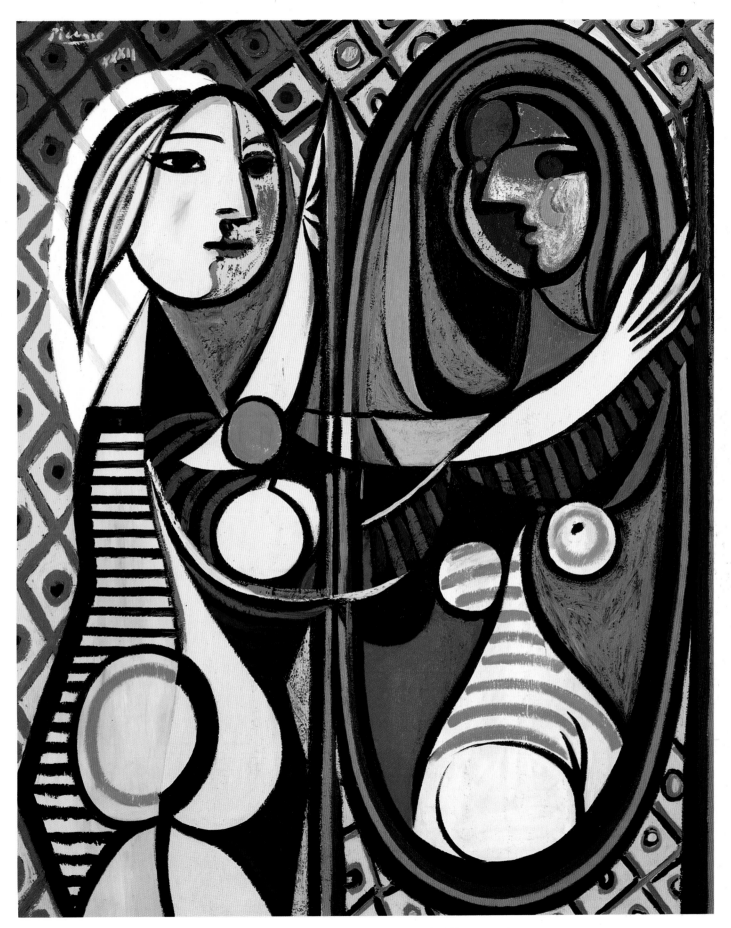

PABLO PICASSO. GIRL BEFORE A MIRROR
1932 (figure 12)

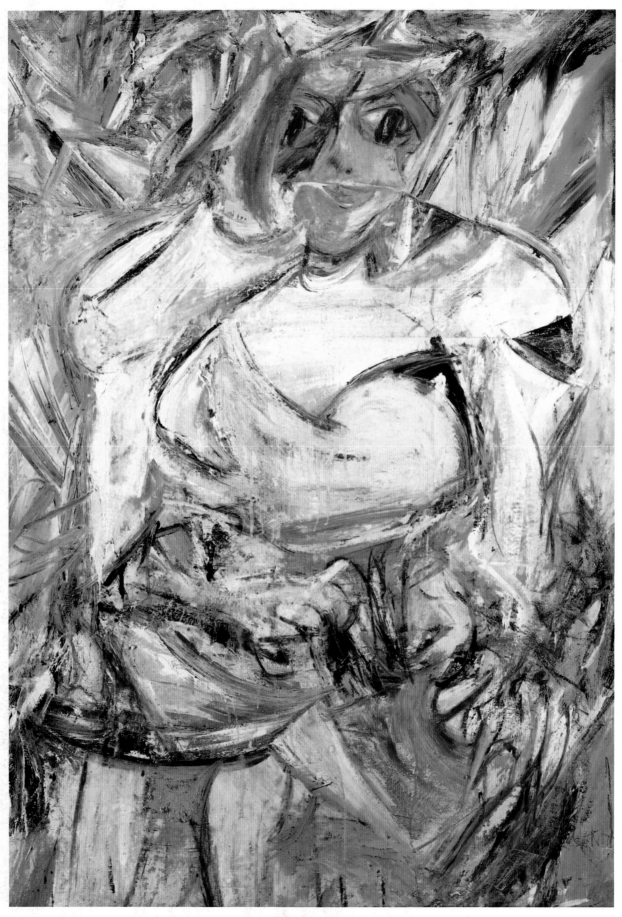

WILLEM DE KOONING. WOMAN II
1952 (figure 1037)

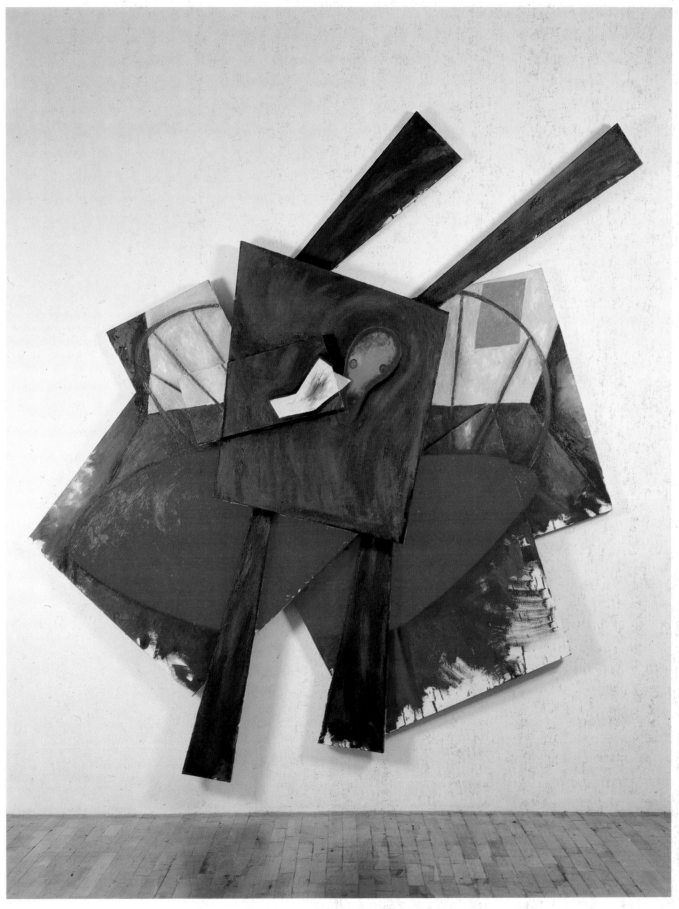

ELIZABETH MURRAY. MORE THAN YOU KNOW
1983 (figure 1063)

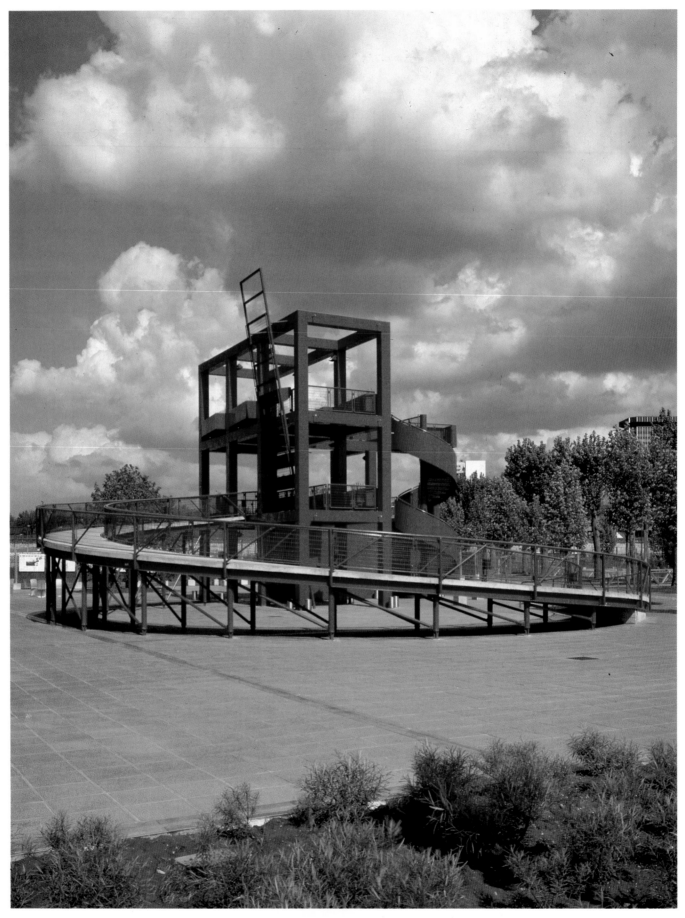

BERNARD TSCHUMI ARCHITECTS. FOLIE P6, PARC DE LA VILLETTE, PARIS
Designed 1983 (figure 1118)

VOLUME TWO

HISTORY OF ART

FOURTH EDITION

H. W. JANSON

HISTORY

HARRY N. ABRAMS, INC.

REVISED AND EXPANDED BY

ANTHONY F. JANSON

OF ART

VOLUME
TWO

PRENTICE HALL, INC.

Project Managers: Sheila Franklin Lieber, Julia Moore
Editor: Julia Moore
Designer: Bob McKee
Rights and Reproductions/
Picture Researcher: Jennifer Bright

On the front cover: AUGUSTE RENOIR. *Le Moulin de la Galette* (detail)
1876. Oil on canvas, 51½×69″ (130.7×175.3 cm)
Musée d'Orsay, Paris (fig. 915)
On the back cover: NANCY GRAVES. *Trace.* 1979–80
Bronze, steel, patina, and paint
107×115×59″ (271.8×292.1×149.7 cm)
Private collection (fig. 1088)

Library of Congress Cataloging-in-Publication Data
Janson, H. W. (Horst Woldemar), 1913–
History of art / by H. W. Janson.—4th ed. / revised and expanded
by Anthony F. Janson.
p.   cm.
Includes bibliographical references and index.
ISBN 0-13-388448-1 (Prentice-Hall : pbk. : v. 1). —ISBN
0-13-388455-4 (Prentice-Hall : pbk. : v. 2).
1. Art—History.   I. Janson, Anthony F.   II. Title.
N5300.J3   1991
709—dc20   90-7405
CIP

Prentice Hall, Inc.
A Simon & Schuster Company
Englewood Cliffs, New Jersey 07632

Printed and bound in Japan

Note on the Picture Captions
Each illustration is placed as close as possible to its first
discussion in the text. Measurements are given throughout,
except for objects that are inherently large: architecture, architectural
sculpture, interiors, and wall paintings. Height precedes width.
A probable measuring error of more than one percent is
indicated by "c." Titles of works are those designated by the museums
owning the works, where applicable, or by custom. Dates are
based on documentary evidence, unless preceded by "c."

First Edition 1962
Revised and Enlarged in 1969
Second Edition 1977
Third Edition 1986
Fourth Edition 1991

CONTENTS

PREFACE AND ACKNOWLEDGMENTS
TO THE FIRST EDITION

The title of this book has a dual meaning: it refers both to the events that *make* the history of art, and to the scholarly discipline that deals with these events. Perhaps it is just as well that the record and its interpretation are thus designated by the same term. For the two cannot be separated, try as we may. There are no "plain facts" in the history of art—or in the history of anything else, for that matter; only degrees of plausibility. Every statement, no matter how fully documented, is subject to doubt, and remains a "fact" only so long as nobody questions it. To doubt what has been taken for granted, and to find a more plausible interpretation of the evidence, is every scholar's task. Nevertheless, there is always a large body of "facts" in any field of study; they are the sleeping dogs whose very inertness makes them landmarks on the scholarly terrain. Fortunately, only a minority of them can be aroused at the same time, otherwise we should lose our bearings; yet all are kept under surveillance to see which ones might be stirred into wakefulness and locomotion. It is these "facts" that fascinate the scholar.

I believe they will also interest the general reader. In a survey such as this, the sleeping dogs are indispensable, but I have tried to emphasize that their condition is temporary, and to give the reader a fairly close look at some of the wakeful ones. I am under no illusion that my diagnosis is up to date in every case; the field is too vast for anyone to encompass all of it with equal competence. If the shortcomings of my account have been kept within tolerable limits, this is due to the many friends and colleagues who have permitted me to tax their kindness with inquiries, requests for favors, or discussions of doubtful points. I am particularly indebted to the following: Richard Ettinghausen, M. Ş. İpşiroğlu, Wolfgang Lotz, Richard Krautheimer, and Meyer Schapiro, who reviewed various aspects of the book; and Max Loehr, Florentine Mütherich, Ernest Nash, and Halldor Soehner, for generous help in securing photographic material. I must also record my gratitude to the American Academy in Rome, which made it possible for me, as art historian in residence during the spring of 1960, to write the chapters on ancient art under ideal conditions; and to the Academy's indefatigable librarian, Nina Langobardi. Irene Gordon, Celia Butler, and Patricia Egan have improved the book in countless ways. Patricia Egan also deserves the chief credit for the reading list. I should like, finally, to acknowledge the admirable skill and patience of Philip Grushkin, who is responsible for the design and layout of the volume; my thanks go to him and to Adrianne Onderdonk, his assistant.

H. W. J.
1962

PREFACE AND ACKNOWLEDGMENTS
TO THE FOURTH EDITION

This, the fourth edition of H. W. Janson's *History of Art,* preserves most of the text of the previous one. At the same time, it presents a number of major changes and additions. There are now more than 550 illustrations in color—three times the number of the previous edition—and all illustrations are integrated with the text. In addition, a special color section, Key Monuments in the History of Art, sets the stage for our survey by presenting thirty-one masterpieces of painting, sculpture, and architecture that eloquently show how great artists from the Old Stone Age to the present have responded to that most human of impulses, the urge to create art. New illustrations show works *in situ,* adding a new dimension of visual context to the narrative of art history. There are diagrams and architectural drawings that have never appeared in *History of Art,* as well as many improved diagrams and plans.

Less immediately apparent perhaps, but no less important, is the complete reorganization of Part Four, devoted to the modern world. The distinction between Neoclassicism and Romanticism is now drawn more clearly. Twentieth-century painting now has a more straightforward chronological organization. A separate chapter is devoted to sculpture since 1900, which has followed a rather different path from painting. Modern architecture begins with Frank Lloyd Wright, while its antecedents, including the Chicago School and Art Nouveau, have been placed in earlier chapters where they properly belong. I have also taken the opportunity throughout to make numerous adjustments in the text and headings; to bring the record of art history up-to-date; and to add a number of artists, including half again as many women as were in the previous edition. In this connection, it should be noted that the masculine gender is used in referring collectively to artists and some other groups of people only to avoid awkward circumlocutions and repetitive language.

The expanded Introduction now includes a brief discussion of line, color, light, composition, form, and space. This section is intended to help the beginner become more sensitive to visual components of art. The decision to incorporate basic elements of art appreciation—a subject that lies outside the traditional scope of art history—is based on the conviction that one must first learn how to look at art in order to understand it, since the works of art themselves remain the primary document. Most people who read this book do so to enhance their enjoyment of art, but often feel uneasy in looking at individual works of art. The new material addresses that obstacle by providing some general observations on viewing art, without resorting to formulaic guidelines that too often get in the way.

In making these revisions, I am mindful that changing anything in a book that has become an institution is not a task to be undertaken lightly. My primary aim has been to preserve the humanism that provided the foundation of this book and to integrate my own approach and writing style as seamlessly as possible into *History of Art* as it has evolved over almost thirty years. Further, I am quite aware that asserting the traditional value of the aesthetic experience runs counter to the "new art history," which sees art essentially as a conveyor of meaning determined by social context. The influence of the semiotic approach—an interest of mine that goes back more than a decade—can be detected in the Introduction's reference to language and meaning. Nevertheless, it is arguably more suited to the written word than to the visual arts, stemming as it does largely from French literary criticism and linguistics. Moreover, it can be seen as embodying a distinctly Post-Modernist sensibility (discussed toward the end of the book), in which the artist and his creation are relegated to secondary considerations. The book's traditional approach is based on my belief that ignoring the visual and expressive qualities of a work in order to make it conform to a theoretical construct risks depriving us of much of art's pleasure, purpose, and inherent worth by turning its study into a scholastic exercise.

I am greatly indebted to two former colleagues: Michael McDonough for his helpful suggestions on modern architecture and Joseph Jacobs for his stimulating ideas about contemporary art. At Harry N. Abrams, Inc., I have been fortunate to have the collaboration of Senior Editor Julia Moore, who was responsible for editing and for tracking the myriad revisions. Project Manager Sheila Franklin Lieber provided strong support and made consistently helpful suggestions early in the revision process. Bob McKee redesigned the entire book with intelligence and aplomb. Jennifer Bright worked miracles in the herculean task of securing hundreds of new photographs. In finding solutions to the complex problems of integrating color—without sacrificing the high quality production for which this book is known—Shun Yamamoto performed with the greatest professionalism. I am especially grateful to Paul Gottlieb for his unfailing support, sound advice, and good humor. Lastly, it is only fitting that this edition be dedicated to the memory of Fritz Landshoff, whose impact on me was so profound.

A. F. J.
1990

INTRODUCTION

ART AND THE ARTIST

"What is art?" Few questions provoke such heated debate and provide so few satisfactory answers. If we cannot come to any definitive conclusions, there is still a good deal we can say. Art is first of all a *word*—one that acknowledges both the idea and the fact of art. Without it, we might well ask whether art exists in the first place. The term, after all, is not found in every society. Yet art is *made* everywhere. Art, therefore, is also an object, but not just any kind of object. Art is an *aesthetic object*. It is meant to be looked at and appreciated for its intrinsic value. Its special qualities set art apart, so that it is often placed away from everyday life—in museums, churches, or caves. What do we mean by aesthetic? By definition, aesthetic is "that which concerns the beautiful."

Of course, not all art is beautiful to our eyes, but it is art nonetheless. And no matter how unsatisfactory, the term will have to do for lack of a better one. Aesthetics is, strictly speaking, a branch of philosophy which has occupied thinkers from Plato to the present day. Like all matters philosophical, it is inherently debatable. During the last hundred years, aesthetics has also become a field of psychology, a field which has come to equally little agreement. Why should this be so? On the one hand, people the world over make much the same fundamental judgments, since our brains and nervous systems are the same. On the other hand, taste is conditioned solely by culture, which is so varied that it is impossible to reduce art to any one set of precepts. It would seem, therefore, that absolute qualities in art must elude us, that we cannot escape viewing works of art in the context of time and circumstance, whether past or present. How indeed could it be otherwise, so long as art is still being created all around us, opening our eyes almost daily to new experiences and thus forcing us to readjust our understanding?

Imagination

We all dream. That is imagination at work. To imagine means simply to make an image—a picture—in our minds. Human beings are not the only creatures who have imagination. Even animals dream. A cat's ears and tail may twitch as he sleeps, and a sleeping dog may whine and growl and paw the air, as if he were having a fight. Even when awake, animals "see" things. For no apparent reason a cat's fur may rise on his back as he peers into a dark closet, just as you or I may get goose bumps from phantoms we neither see nor hear. Clearly, however, there is a profound difference between human and animal imagination. Humans are the only creatures who can tell one another about imagination in stories or pictures. The urge to make art is unique to us. No other animal has ever been observed to draw a recognizable image spontaneously in the wild. In fact, their only images have been produced under carefully controlled laboratory conditions that tell us more about the experimenter than they do about art. There can be little doubt, on the other hand, that people possess an aesthetic faculty. By the age of five every normal child has drawn a moon pie-face. The ability to make art is one of our most distinctive features, for it separates us from all other creatures across an evolutionary gap that is unbridgeable.

Just as an embryo retraces much of the human evolutionary past, so the budding artist reinvents the first stages of art. Soon, however, he completes that process and begins to respond to the culture around him. Even children's art is subject to the taste and outlook of the society that shapes his or her personality. In fact, we tend to judge children's art according to the same criteria as adult art—only in appropriately simpler terms—and with good reason, for if we examine its successive stages, we find that the youngster must develop all the skills that go into adult art: coordination, intellect, personality, imagination, creativity, and aesthetic judgment. Seen this way, the making of a youthful artist is a process as fragile as growing up itself, and one that can be stunted at any step by the vicissitudes of life. No wonder that so few continue their creative aspirations into adulthood.

Given the many factors that feed into it, art must play a very special role in the artist's personality. Sigmund Freud, the founder of modern psychiatry, conceived of art primarily in terms of sublimation outside of consciousness. Such a view hardly does justice to artistic creativity, since art is not simply a negative force at the mercy of our neuroses but a positive expression that integrates diverse aspects of personality. Indeed, when we look at the art of the mentally ill, we may be struck by its vividness; but we instinctively sense that something is wrong, because the expression is incomplete.

Artists may sometimes be tortured by the burden of their genius, but they can never be truly creative under the thrall of psychosis. The imagination is one of our most mysterious facets. It can be regarded as the connector between the conscious and the subconscious, where most of our brain activity takes place. It is the very glue that holds our personality, intellect, and spirituality together. Because the imagination responds to all three, it acts in lawful, if unpredictable, ways that are determined by the psyche and the mind. Thus, even the most private artistic statements can be understood on some level, even if only an intuitive one.

The imagination is important, as it allows us to conceive of all kinds of possibilities in the future and to understand the past in a way that has real survival value. It is a fundamental part of our makeup. The ability to make art, in contrast, must have been acquired relatively recently in the course of evolution. The record of the earliest art is lost to us. Human beings have been walking the earth for some two million years, but the oldest prehistoric art that we know of was made only about 35,000 years ago, though it was undoubtedly the culmination of a long development no longer traceable. Even the most "primitive" ethnographic art represents a late stage of development within a stable society.

Who were the first artists? In all likelihood, they were shamans. Like the legendary Orpheus, they were believed to have divine powers of inspiration and to be able to enter the underworld of the subconscious in a deathlike trance, but, unlike ordinary mortals, they were then able to return to the realm of the living. Just such a figure seems to be represented by our *Harpist* (fig. 1) from nearly five thousand years ago. A work of unprecedented complexity for its time, it was

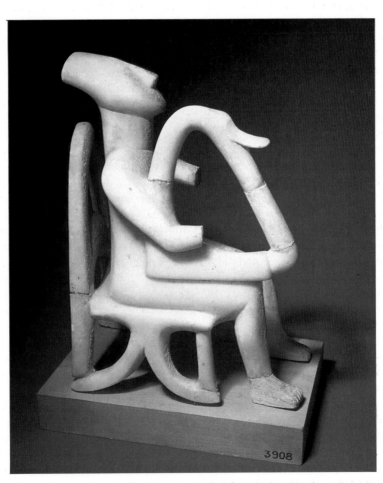

1. *HARPIST,* so-called Orpheus. Marble statuette from Amorgos
in the Cyclades. Latter part of the 3rd millennium B.C.
Height 8½″ (21.5 cm). National Archeological Museum, Athens

carved by a remarkably gifted artist who makes us feel the visionary rapture of a bard as he sings his legend. With this artist-shaman's unique ability to penetrate the unknown and his rare talent for expressing it through art, he gained control over the forces hidden in human beings and nature. Even today the artist remains a magician whose work can mystify and move us—an embarrassing fact to civilized people, who do not readily relinquish their veneer of rational control.

In a larger sense art, like science and religion, fulfills our innate urge to comprehend ourselves and the universe. This function makes art especially significant and, hence, worthy of our attention. Art has the power to penetrate to the core of our being, which recognizes itself in the creative act. For that reason, art represents its creator's deepest understanding and highest aspirations; at the same time, the artist often plays an important role as the articulator of our shared beliefs and values, which he expresses through an ongoing tradition to us, his audience. A masterpiece, then, is a work that contributes to our vision of life and leaves us profoundly moved. Moreover, it can bear the closest scrutiny and withstand the test of time.

Creativity

What do we mean by making? If, in order to simplify our problem, we concentrate on the visual arts, we might say that a work of art must be a tangible thing shaped by human hands. This definition at least eliminates the confusion of treating as works of art such natural phenomena as flowers, seashells, or sunsets. It is a far from sufficient definition, to be sure, since human beings make many things other than works of art. Still, it will serve as a starting point. Now let us look at the striking *Bull's Head* by Picasso (fig. 2), which seems to consist of nothing but the seat and handlebars of an old bicycle. How meaningful is our formula here? Of course the materials used by Picasso are fabricated, but it would be absurd to insist that Picasso must share the credit with the manufacturer, since the seat and handlebars in themselves are not works of art.

While we feel a certain jolt when we first recognize the ingredients of this visual pun, we also sense that it was a stroke of genius to put them together in this unique way, and we cannot very well deny that it is a work of art. Yet the handiwork—the mounting of the seat on the handlebars—is ridiculously simple. What is far from simple is the leap of the imagination by which Picasso recognized a bull's head in these unlikely objects; that, we feel, only he could have done. Clearly, then, we must be careful not to confuse the making of a work of art with manual skill or craftsmanship. Some works of art may demand a great deal of technical discipline; others do not. And even the most painstaking piece of craft does not deserve to be called a work of art unless it involves a leap of the imagination.

But if this is true are we not forced to conclude that the real making of the *Bull's Head* took place in the artist's mind? No, that is not so, either. Suppose that, instead of actually putting the two pieces together and showing them to us, Picasso merely told us, "You know, today I saw a bicycle seat and handlebars that looked just like a bull's head to me." Then there would be no work of art and his remark would not even strike us as an interesting bit of conversation. Moreover, Picasso himself would not have felt the satisfaction of having created something on the basis of his leap of the imagination alone. Once he had conceived his visual pun, he could never be sure that it would really work unless he put it into effect.

Thus the artist's hands, however modest the task they may have to perform, play an essential part in the creative process. Our *Bull's Head* is, of course, an ideally simple case, involving only one leap of the imagination and a manual act in response to it—once the seat had been properly placed on the handlebars (and then cast in bronze), the job was done. The leap of the imagination is sometimes experienced as a flash of inspiration, but only rarely does a new idea emerge full-blown like Athena from the head of Zeus. Instead, it is usually preceded by a long gestation period in which all the hard work is done without finding the key to the solution to the problem. At the critical point, the imagination makes connections between seemingly unrelated parts and recombines them.

Ordinarily, artists do not work with ready-made parts but with materials that have little or no shape of their own; the creative process consists of a long series of leaps of the imagination and the artist's attempts to give them form by shaping the material accordingly. The hand tries to carry out the commands of the imagination and hopefully puts down a brushstroke, but the result may not be quite what had been expected, partly because all matter resists the human will, partly because the image in the artist's mind is constantly shifting and changing, so that the commands of the imagination cannot be very precise. In fact, the mental image begins to come into focus only as the artist "draws the line somewhere." That line then becomes part—the only fixed part—of the image; the rest of the image, as yet unborn, remains fluid. And each time the artist adds another line, a new leap of the imagination is needed to incorporate that line into his ever-growing mental image. If the line cannot be incorporated, he discards it and puts down a new one.

In this way, by a constant flow of impulses back and forth between his mind and the partly shaped material before him, he gradually defines more and more of the image, until at last all of it has been given visible form. Needless to say, artistic creation is too subtle and intimate an experience to permit an exact step-by-step description; only the artist himself can observe it fully, but he is so absorbed by it that he has great difficulty explaining it to us.

The metaphor of birth comes closer to the truth than would a description of the process in terms of a transfer or projection of the image from the artist's mind, for the making of a work of art is both joyous and painful, replete with surprises, and in no sense mechanical. We have, moreover, ample testimony that the artist himself tends to look upon his creation as a living thing. Perhaps that is why creativity was once a concept reserved for God, as only He could give material form to an idea. Indeed, the artist's labors are much like the Creation told in the Bible; but this divine ability was not realized until Michelangelo described the anguish and

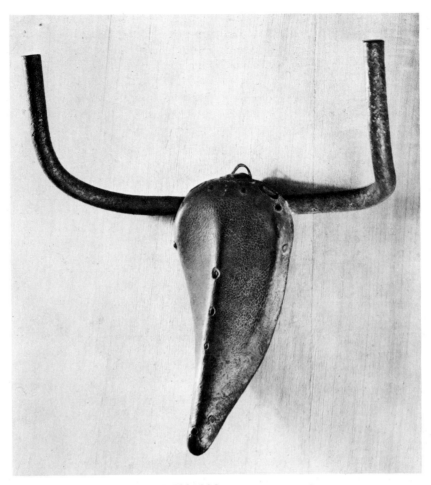

2. PABLO PICASSO. *BULL'S HEAD.* 1943.
Bronze cast bicycle parts, height 16⅛″ (41 cm).
Musée Picasso, Paris

glory of the creative experience when he spoke of "liberating the figure from the marble that imprisons it." We may translate this to mean that he started the process of carving a statue by trying to visualize a figure in the rough, rectilinear block as it came to him from the quarry. (At times he may even have done so while the marble was still part of the "living" rock; we know that he liked to go to the quarries and pick out his material on the spot.)

It seems fair to assume that at first Michelangelo did not see the figure any more clearly than one can see an unborn child inside the womb, but we may believe that he could see isolated "signs of life" within the marble—a knee or an elbow pressing against the surface. To get a firmer grip on this dimly felt, fluid image, he was in the habit of making numerous drawings, and sometimes small models in wax or clay, before he dared to assault the "marble prison" itself. For that, he knew, was the final contest between himself and his material. Once he started carving, every stroke of the chisel would commit him more and more to a specific conception of the figure hidden in the block, and the marble would permit him to free the figure whole only if his guess as to its shape was correct.

Sometimes he did not guess well enough—the stone refused to give up some essential part of its prisoner, and Michelangelo, defeated, left the work unfinished, as he did with his *Captive* (fig. 3), whose very gesture seems to record the vain struggle for liberation. Looking at the block, we may get some inkling of Michelangelo's difficulties here. But could he not have finished the statue in *some* fashion? Surely there is enough material left for that. Well, he probably could have, but perhaps not in the way he wanted, and in that case the defeat would have been even more stinging.

Clearly, then, the making of a work of art has little in common with what we ordinarily mean by "making." It is a strange and risky business in which the maker never quite knows what he is making until he has actually made it; or, to put it another way, it is a game of find-and-seek in which the seeker is not sure what he is looking for until he has found it. (In the case of the *Bull's Head* it is the bold "finding" that impresses us most; in the *Captive*, the strenuous "seeking.") To the non-artist, it seems hard to believe that this uncertainty, this need-to-take-a-chance, should be the essence of the artist's work. We all tend to think of "making" in terms of the craftsman or manufacturer who knows exactly what

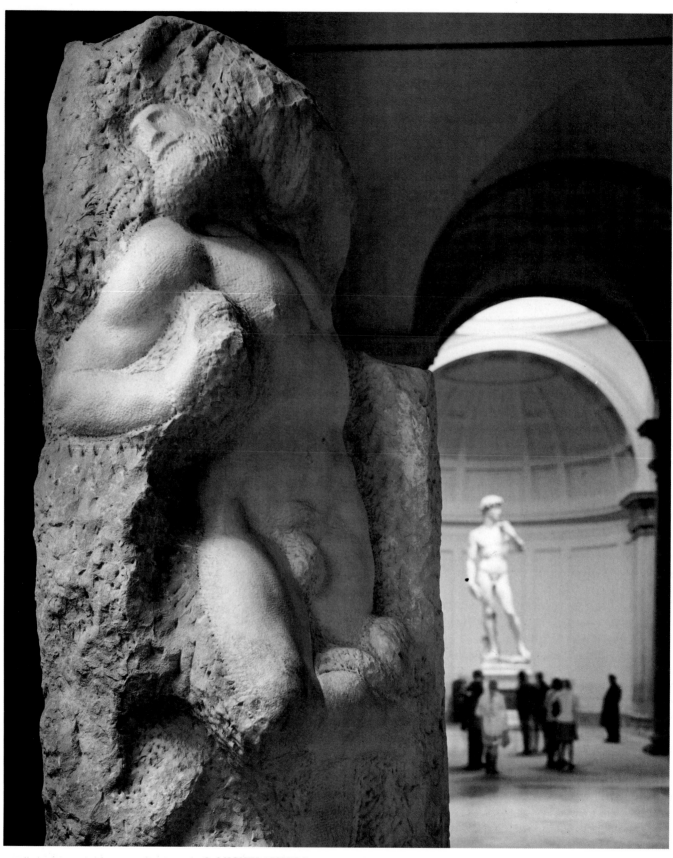

3. MICHELANGELO. *CAPTIVE* (foreground). 1506.
Marble, height 8′11″ (2.7 m).
Galleria dell'Accademia, Florence

he wants to produce from the very outset, picks the tools best fitted to the task, and is sure of what he is doing at every step. Such "making" is a two-phase affair: first the craftsman makes a plan, then he acts on it. And because he—or his customer—has made all the important decisions in advance, he has to worry only about the means, rather than the ends, while he carries out his plan. There is thus comparatively little risk, but also little adventure, in his handiwork, which as a consequence tends to become routine. It may even be replaced by the mechanical labor of a machine.

No machine, on the other hand, can replace the artist, for with him conception and execution go hand in hand and are so completely interdependent that he cannot separate the one from the other. Whereas the craftsman attempts only what he knows to be possible, the artist is always driven to attempt the impossible—or at least the improbable or unimaginable. Who, after all, would have imagined that a bull's head was hidden in the seat and handlebars of a bicycle until Picasso discovered it for us; did he not, almost literally, "make a silk purse out of a sow's ear"? No wonder the artist's way of working is so resistant to any set rules, while the craftsman's encourages standardization and regularity. We acknowledge this difference when we speak of the artist as *creating* instead of merely *making* something, although the word has been done to death by overuse, and every child and fashion designer is labeled "creative."

Needless to say, there have always been many more craftsmen than artists among us, since our need for the familiar and expected far exceeds our capacity to absorb the original but often deeply unsettling experiences we get from works of art. The urge to penetrate unknown realms, to achieve something original, may be felt by every one of us now and then; to that extent, we can all fancy ourselves potential artists—mute inglorious Miltons. What sets the real artist apart is not so much the desire to *seek*, but that mysterious ability to *find*, which we call talent. We also speak of it as a "gift," implying that it is a sort of present from some higher power; or as "genius," a term which originally meant that a higher power—a kind of "good demon"—inhabits the artist's body and acts through him.

One thing we can say about talent is that it must not be confused with aptitude. Aptitude is what the craftsman needs; it means a better-than-average knack for doing something. An aptitude is fairly constant and specific; it can be measured with some success by means of tests that permit us to predict future performance. Creative talent, on the other hand, seems utterly unpredictable; we can spot it only on the basis of *past* performance. And even past performance is not enough to ensure that a given artist will continue to produce on the same level: some artists reach a creative peak quite early in their careers and then "go dry," while others, after a slow and unpromising start, may achieve astonishingly original work in middle age or even later.

Originality

Originality, then, ultimately distinguishes art from craft. We may say, therefore, that it is the yardstick of artistic greatness or importance. Unfortunately, it is also very hard to define; the usual synonyms—uniqueness, novelty, freshness—do not help us very much, and the dictionaries tell us only that an original work must not be a copy. Thus, if we want to rate works of art on an "originality scale," our problem does not lie in deciding whether or not a given work is original (the obvious copies and reproductions are for the most part easy enough to eliminate) but in establishing exactly *how* original it is. To do that is not impossible. However, the difficulties besetting our task are so great that we cannot hope for more than tentative and incomplete answers. This does not mean that we should not try; quite the contrary. For whatever the outcome of our labors in any particular case, we shall certainly learn a great deal about works of art in the process.

A straightforward copy can usually be recognized as such on internal evidence alone. If the copyist is a conscientious craftsman rather than artist, he will produce a work of craft; the execution will strike us as pedestrian and thus out of tune with the conception of the work. There are also likely to be small slipups and mistakes that can be spotted in much the same way as misprints in a text. But what if one great artist copies another? In using another work as his model, the artist does not really copy it in the accepted sense of the word, since he does not try to achieve the effect of a duplicate. He does it purely for his own instruction, transcribing it accurately yet with his own inimitable rhythm. In other words, he is not the least constrained or intimidated by the fact that his model, in this instance, is another work of art. Once we understand this, it becomes clear to us that the artist *represents* (he does not *copy*) the other work, and that his artistic originality does not suffer thereby.

A relationship as close as this between two works of art is not as rare as one might think. Ordinarily, though, the link is not immediately obvious. Édouard Manet's famous painting *Luncheon on the Grass* (fig. 4) seemed so revolutionary a work when first exhibited more than a century ago that it caused a scandal, in part because the artist had dared to show an undressed young woman next to two men in fashionable contemporary dress. People assumed that Manet had intended to represent an actual event. Not until many years later did an art historian discover the source of these figures: a group of classical deities from an engraving after Raphael (fig. 5). The relationship, so striking once it has been pointed out to us, had escaped attention, for Manet did not *copy* or *represent* the Raphael composition—he merely *borrowed* its main outlines while translating the figures into modern terms.

Had his contemporaries known of this, the *Luncheon* would have seemed a rather less disreputable kind of outing to them, since now the hallowed shade of Raphael could be seen to hover nearby as a sort of chaperon. (Perhaps the artist meant to tease the conservative public, hoping that after the initial shock had passed, somebody would recognize the well-hidden quotation behind his "scandalous" group.) For us, the main effect of the comparison is to make the cool, formal quality of Manet's figures even more conspicuous. But does it decrease our respect for his originality? True, he is "indebted" to Raphael; yet his way of bringing the forgotten old composition back to life is in itself so original and creative that he may be said to have more than repaid his

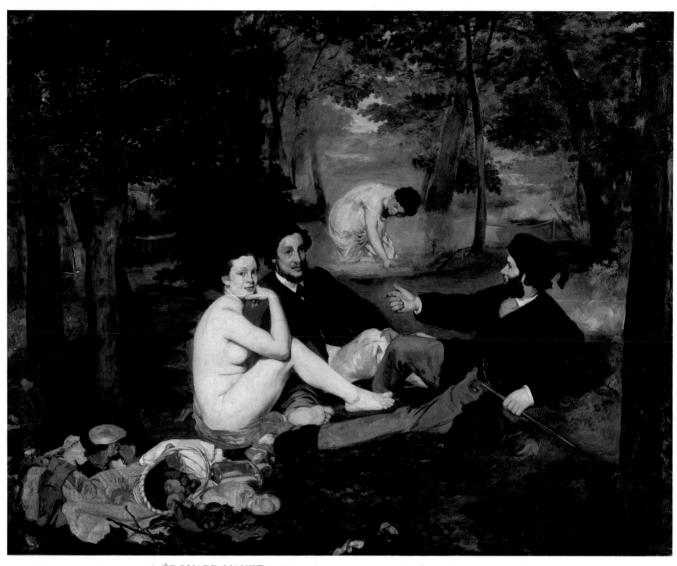

4. ÉDOUARD MANET. *LUNCHEON ON THE GRASS (LE DÉJEUNER SUR L'HERBE).*
1863. Oil on canvas, 7′ × 8′10″ (2.1 × 2.6 m).
Musée d'Orsay, Paris

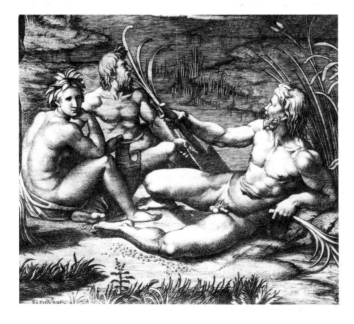

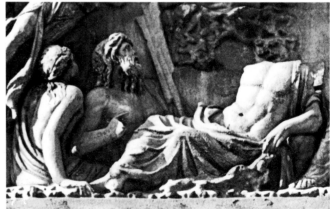

5. *(left)* MARCANTONIO RAIMONDI, after RAPHAEL
THE JUDGMENT OF PARIS (detail). c. 1520. Engraving

6. *(above) RIVER GODS.* Detail of Roman sarcophagus.
3rd century A.D. Villa Medici, Rome

debt. As a matter of fact, Raphael's figures are just as "derivative" as Manet's; they stem from still older sources which lead us back to ancient Roman art and beyond (compare the relief of *River Gods* (fig. 6).

Thus Manet, Raphael, and the Roman river gods form three links in a chain of relationships that arises somewhere out of the distant past and continues into the future—for the *Luncheon on the Grass* has in turn served as a source of more recent works of art. Nor is this an exceptional case. All works of art anywhere—yes, even such works as Picasso's *Bull's Head*—are part of similar chains that link them to their predecessors. If it is true that "no man is an island," the same can be said of works of art. The sum total of these chains makes a web in which every work of art occupies its own specific place; we call this *tradition*. Without tradition—the word means "that which has been handed down to us"—no originality would be possible; it provides, as it were, the firm platform from which the artist makes a leap of the imagination. The place where he lands will then become part of the web and serve as a point of departure for further leaps.

And for us, too, the web of tradition is equally essential. Whether we are aware of it or not, tradition is the framework within which we inevitably form our opinions of works of art and assess their degree of originality. Let us not forget, however, that such assessments must always remain incomplete and subject to revision. For in order to arrive at a definitive view, we should be able to survey the entire length of every chain. And that we can never hope to achieve.

If originality distinguishes art from craft, tradition serves as the common meeting ground of the two. Every budding artist starts out on the level of craft by imitating other works of art. In this way, he gradually absorbs the artistic tradition of his time and place until he has gained a firm footing in it. But only the truly gifted ever leave that stage of traditional competence and become creators in their own right. None of us, after all, can be taught how to create; we can only be taught how to go through the motions of creating. If the aspiring artist has talent, he will eventually achieve the real thing. What the apprentice or art student learns are skills and techniques—established ways of drawing, painting, carving, designing; established ways of *seeing*.

Nevertheless, one of the attributes that distinguishes great artists is their consummate technical command. This superior talent is recognized by other artists, who admire their work and seek to emulate it. This is not to say that facility alone is sufficient. Far from it! Ample warning against such a notion is provided by the academic painters and sculptors of the nineteenth century, who were as a group among the most proficient artists in history—as well as the dullest. Still, complete technical command is a requisite of masterpieces, which are distinguished by their superior execution.

If the would-be artist senses that his gifts are not large enough for him to succeed as a painter, sculptor, or architect, he may take up one of the countless special fields known collectively as "the applied arts." There he can be fruitfully active in less risky work—illustration, typographic design, industrial design, and interior design, for example.

All these pursuits stand somewhere between "pure" art and "traditional" craft. They provide some scope for originality to their more ambitious practitioners, but the flow of creative endeavor is cramped by such factors as the cost and availability of materials or manufacturing processes, accepted notions of what is useful, fitting, or desirable; for the applied arts are more deeply enmeshed in our everyday lives and thus cater to a far wider public than do painting and sculpture. Their purpose, as the name suggests, is to beautify the useful—an important and valued end, but limited in comparison to art pure-and-simple.

Nevertheless, we often find it difficult to maintain the distinction between fine and applied art. Medieval painting, for instance, is to a large extent "applied," in the sense that it embellishes surfaces which serve other, practical purposes as well—walls, book pages, windows, furniture. The same may be said of much ancient and medieval sculpture. Greek vases, as we shall see, although technically pottery, were sometimes decorated by artists of very impressive talent. And in architecture the distinction breaks down altogether, since the design of every building, from country cottage to cathedral, reflects external limitations imposed upon it by the site, by cost factors, materials, technology, and by the practical purpose of the structure. (The only "pure" architecture is imaginary, unbuilt architecture.) Thus architecture is, almost by definition, an applied art, but it is also a major art (as against the other applied arts, which are often called the "minor arts").

The graphic arts form a special case of their own. Drawings are original works of art; that is, they are entirely by the artist's own hand. With prints, however, the relationship between artist and image is more complex. Prints are not unique images but multiple reproductions made by mechanical means. Perhaps the distinction between original and copy is not so critical in printmaking after all. The printmaker must usually copy onto his plate a composition that was first worked out in a drawing, whether his own or someone else's. From the beginning, most prints have been made, at least in part, by craftsmen whose technical skill is necessary to ensure the outcome. Woodcuts and engraving in particular were traditionally dependent on craftsmanship, which may explain why so few creative geniuses have made them and have generally been content to let others produce prints from their designs. Although it does not require the artist's intervention at every step of the way, printmaking usually involves the artist's supervision and even active participation, so that we may think of the process as a collaborative effort.

Meaning and Style

Why do we create art? Surely one reason is an irresistible urge to adorn ourselves and decorate the world around us. Both are part of a larger desire, not to remake the world in our image but to recast ourselves and our environment in *ideal* form. Art is, however, much more than decoration, for it is laden with meaning, even if that content is sometimes slender or obscure. Art enables us to communicate our understanding in ways that cannot be expressed otherwise. Truly a painting (or sculpture) is worth a thousand words, not only in its descriptive value but also in its symbolic significance. In art, as in language, we are above all inventors of symbols that convey complex thoughts in new ways. We must think of art not in terms of everyday prose but of poetry, which is free to rearrange conventional vocabulary and syntax in order to convey new, often multiple, meanings and moods. A work of art likewise suggests much more than it states. And like a poem, the value of art lies equally in what it says and how it says it: it communicates partly by implying meanings through pose, facial expression, allegory, and the like.

But what is the *meaning* of art—its iconography? What is it trying to say? Artists often provide no clear explanation, since the work is the statement itself. (If they could say what they mean in words, they would surely be writers instead.) Fortunately, certain visual symbols and responses occur so regularly over time and place that they can be regarded as virtually universal. Nevertheless, their exact meaning is specific to each particular culture, giving rise to art's incredible diversity.

The meaning, or content, of art is inseparable from its formal qualities, its *style*. The word *style* is derived from *stilus*, the writing instrument of the ancient Romans; originally, it referred to distinctive ways of writing—the shape of the letters as well as the choice of words. Nowadays, however, style is used loosely to mean the distinctive way a thing is done in any field of human endeavor. It is simply a term of praise in most cases: "to have style" means to have distinction, to stand out. But something else is implied, which comes to the fore if we ask ourselves what we mean when we say that something "has no style." Such a thing, we feel, is not only undistinguished but also undistinguishable; in other words, we do not know how to classify it, how to put it into its proper context, because it seems to point in several directions at once. Of a thing that *has style*, then, we expect that it not be inconsistent within itself—that it must have an inner coherence, or unity, that it possess a sense of wholeness, of being all of a piece. These are the qualities we admire in things that have style, for style has a way of impressing itself upon us even if we do not know what particular *kind* of style is involved.

In the visual arts, style means the particular way in which the forms that make up any given work of art are chosen and fitted together. To art historians the study of styles is of central importance; it not only enables them to find out, by means of careful analysis and comparison, when and where (and by whom) a given work was produced, but it also leads them to understand the artist's intention as expressed through the style of his work. This intention depends on both the artist's personality and the setting in which he lives and works. Accordingly, we speak of "period styles" if we are concerned with those features which distinguish, let us say, Egyptian art as a whole from Greek art. And within these broad period styles we in turn distinguish the styles of particular phases, such as the Old Kingdom; or, wherever it seems appropriate, we differentiate national or local styles within a period, until we arrive at the personal styles of individual artists. Even these may need to be subdivided further into the various phases of an artist's development. The ex-

tent to which we are able to categorize effectively depends on the degree of internal coherence, and on how much of a sense of continuity there is in the body of material we are dealing with.

Thus art, like language, requires that we learn the style and outlook of a country, period, and artist if we are to understand it properly. We are so accustomed to a naturalistic tradition of accurate reproductions that we expect art to imitate reality. But illusionism is only one vehicle for expressing an artist's understanding of reality. Truth, it seems, is indeed relative, for it is a matter not only of what our eyes tell us but also of the concepts through which our perceptions are filtered.

There is, then, no reason to place a premium on realistic representation for its own sake. Instead, style need only be appropriate to the intent of the work. The advantage of realism at face value is that it *seems* easier to understand. The disadvantage is that representational art, like prose, is always bound to the literal meaning and appearance of the everyday world, at least to some extent. Actually, realism is exceptional in the history of art and is not even necessary to its purposes. We must remember that any image is a separate and self-contained reality which has its own ends and responds to its own imperatives, for the artist is bound only to his creativity. Even the most convincing illusion is the product of the artist's imagination and understanding, so that we must always ask why he chose this subject and made it this way rather than some other way. Understanding the role of self-expression may provide some answers.

Self-Expression and Audience

Most of us are familiar with the famous Greek myth of the sculptor Pygmalion, who carved such a beautiful statue of the nymph Galatea that he fell in love with it and embraced her when Venus made his sculpture come to life. The myth has been given a fresh interpretation by John De Andrea's *The Artist and His Model* (fig. 7), which tells us a good deal about creativity by reversing the roles. Now it is the artist, lost in thought, who is oblivious to the statue's gaze. Clearly based on a real woman rather than an ideal conception, the model is still in the process of "coming to life"; the artist has not finished painting her white legs. The illusion is so convincing that we wonder which figure is real and which one is dreaming of the other, the artist or the sculpture? De Andrea makes us realize that to the artist, the creative act is a "labor of love" that brings art to life through self-expression. But can we not also say that it is the work of art which gives birth to the artist?

The birth of a work of art is an intensely private experience (so much so that many artists can work only when completely alone and refuse to show their unfinished pieces to anyone), yet it must, as a final step, be shared by the public in order for the birth to be successful. The artist does not create merely for his own satisfaction, but wants his work validated by others. In fact, the creative process is not completed until the work has found an audience. In the end, works of art exist in order to be liked rather than to be debated.

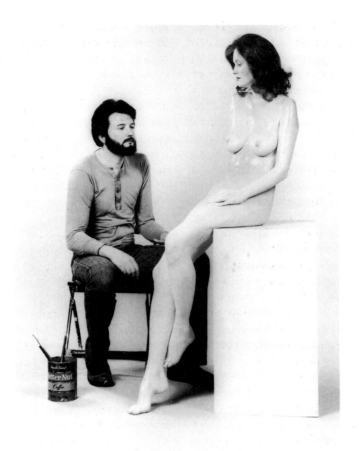

7. JOHN DE ANDREA. *THE ARTIST AND HIS MODEL.* 1980.
Polyvinyl, polychromed in oil; lifesize. Collection Foster Goldstrom,
Dallas and San Francisco. Courtesy O. K. Harris, New York

Perhaps we can resolve this seeming paradox once we understand what the artist means by "public." He is concerned not with *the* public as a statistical entity but with his particular public, his audience; quality rather than wide approval is what matters to him. At a minimum, this audience needs to consist of no more than one or two people whose opinions he values. Ordinarily, however, artists also need patrons among their audience who will purchase their work, thus combining moral and financial support. In contrast to a customer of applied art, for example, who knows from previous experience what he will get when he buys the products of craftsmanship, the "audience" for art merits such adjectives as critical, fickle, receptive, enthusiastic; it is uncommitted, free to accept or reject, so that anything placed before it is on trial—nobody knows in advance how it will receive the work. Hence, there is an emotional tension between artist and audience that has no counterpart in the relationship of craftsman and customer. It is this very tension, this sense of uncertainty and challenge, that the artist needs. He must feel that his work is able to overcome the resistance of the audience, otherwise he cannot be sure that what he has brought forth is a genuine creation, a work of art in fact as well as in intention. The more ambitious and original his work, the greater the tension and the more triumphant his sense of release after the response of the audience

has shown him that his leap of the imagination has been successful.

The audience whose approval looms so large in the artist's mind is a limited and special one; its members may be other artists as well as patrons, friends, critics, and interested beholders. The one quality they all have in common is an informed love of works of art—an attitude at once discriminating and enthusiastic that lends particular weight to their judgments. They are, in a word, experts, people whose authority rests on experience rather than theoretical knowledge. In reality, there is no sharp break, no difference in kind, between the expert and the layman, only a difference in degree.

Tastes

Deciding what is art and rating a work of art are two separate problems; if we had an absolute method for distinguishing art from non-art, it would not necessarily enable us to measure quality. People tend to compound the two problems into one; quite often when they ask, "Why is that art?" they mean, "Why is that *good* art?" How often have we heard this question asked—or asked it ourselves, perhaps—in front of one of the strange, disquieting works that we are likely to find nowadays in museums or art exhibitions. There usually is an undertone of exasperation, for the question implies that *we* don't think we are looking at a work of art, but that the experts—the critics, museum curators, art historians—must suppose it to be one, or why else would they put it on public display? Clearly, their standards are very different from ours; we are at a loss to understand them and we wish they'd give us a few simple, clear-cut rules to go by. Then maybe we would learn to like what we see; we would know "why it is art." But the experts do not post exact rules, and the layman is apt to fall back upon his final line of defense: "Well, I don't know anything about art, but I know what I like."

It is a formidable roadblock, this stock phrase, in the path of understanding between expert and layman. Until not so very long ago, there was no great need for the two to communicate with each other; the general public had little voice in matters of art and therefore could not challenge the judgment of the expert few. Today both sides are aware of the barrier between them (the barrier itself is nothing new, although it may be greater now than at certain times in the past) and of the need to level it. That is why books like this one are written. Let us examine the roadblock and the various unspoken assumptions that buttress it.

Our puzzled layman might be willing to grant, on the basis of our discussion so far, that art is indeed a complex and in many ways mysterious human activity about which even the experts can hope to offer only tentative and partial conclusions; but he is also likely to take this as confirming his own belief that "I don't know anything about art." Are there really people who know nothing about art? If we except small children and people with certain mental disabilities, our answer must be no, for none of us can help knowing *something* about it, just as each of us knows something about politics and economics—no matter how indifferent we may be to the issues of the day. Art is so much a part of the fabric of human living that we encounter it all the time, even if our contacts with it are limited to magazine covers, advertising posters, war memorials, television, and the buildings where we live, work, and worship. Much of this art, to be sure, is pretty shoddy—art at third- and fourth-hand, worn out by endless repetition, representing the lowest common denominator of popular taste. Still, it is art of a sort; and since it is the only art most of us ever experience, it molds our ideas on art in general. When we say, "I know what I like," we may really mean, "I like what I know (and I reject whatever fails to match the things I am familiar with)." Such likes are not in truth ours at all, for they have been imposed by habit and culture without any personal choice. To like what we know and to distrust what we do not know is an age-old human trait. We always tend to think of the past as "the good old days," while the future seems fraught with danger.

But why should so many of us cherish the illusion of having made a personal choice in art when in fact we have not? There is another unspoken assumption at work here that goes something like this: "Since art is such an 'unruly' subject that even the experts keep disagreeing with each other, my opinion is as good as theirs—it's all a matter of subjective preference. In fact, my opinion may be *better* than theirs, because as a layman I react to art in a direct, straightforward

fashion, without having my view obstructed by a lot of complicated theories. There must be something wrong with a work of art if it takes an expert to appreciate it."

But if experts appreciate art more than the uninformed, why should we not emulate them? We have seen that the road to expertness is clear and wide, and that it invites anyone with an open mind and a capacity to absorb new experiences. As our understanding grows, we find ourselves liking a great many more things than we had thought possible at the start. We gradually acquire the courage of our own convictions, until we are able to say, with some justice, that we know what we like.

LOOKING AT ART
The Visual Elements

We live in a sea of images conveying the culture and learning of modern civilization. Fostered by an unprecedented media explosion, this "visual background noise" has become so much a part of our daily lives that we take it for granted. In the process, we have become desensitized to art as well. Anyone can buy cheap paintings and reproductions to decorate a room, where they often hang virtually unnoticed, perhaps deservedly so. It is small wonder that we look at the art in museums with equal casualness. We pass rapidly from one object to another, sampling them like dishes in a smorgasbord. We may pause briefly before a famous masterpiece that we have been told we are supposed to admire, then ignore the gallery full of equally beautiful and important works around it. We will have seen the art but not really looked at it. Looking at great art is not such an easy task, for art rarely reveals its secrets readily. While the experience of a work can be immediately electrifying, we sometimes do not realize its impact until time has let it filter through the recesses of our imaginations. It even happens that something that at first repelled or confounded us emerges only many years later as one of the most important artistic events of our lives. Because so much goes into art, it makes much the same demands on our faculties as it did on the person who created it. For that reason, we must be able to respond to it on many levels. If we are going to get the most out of art, we will have to learn how to look and think for ourselves in an intelligent way, which is perhaps the hardest task of all. After all, we will not always have someone at our side to help us. In the end, the confrontation of viewer and art remains a solitary act.

Understanding a work of art begins with a sensitive appreciation of its appearance. Art may be approached and appreciated for its purely visual elements: line, color, light, composition, form, and space. These may be shared by any work of art; their effects, however, vary widely according to medium (the physical materials of which the artwork is made) and technique, which together help to determine the possibilities and limitations of what the artist can achieve. For that reason, our discussion is merged with an introduction to four major arts: graphic arts, painting, sculpture, and architecture. (The technical aspects of the major media are treated in separate sections within the main body of the text

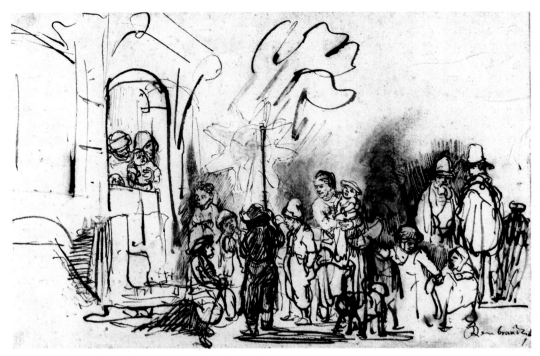

8. REMBRANDT. *THE STAR OF THE KINGS.* c. 1642.
Pen and bistre, wash, 8 × 12¾″ (20.3 × 32.4 cm). British Museum, London

and in the glossary toward the end of the book.) Just because line is discussed with drawing, however, does not mean that it is not equally important in painting and sculpture. And while form is introduced with sculpture, it is just as essential to painting, drawing, and architecture.

Visual analysis can help us to appreciate the beauty of a masterpiece, but we must be careful not to use a formulaic approach that would trivialize it. Every aesthetic "law" advanced so far has proven of dubious value, and usually gets in the way of our understanding. Even if a valid "law" were to be found—and none has yet been discovered—it would probably be so elementary as to prove useless in the face of art's complexity. We must also bear in mind that art appreciation is more than mere enjoyment of aesthetics. It is learning to understand the meaning (or iconography) of a work of art. And finally, let us remember that no work can be understood outside its historical context.

LINE. Line may be regarded as the most basic visual element. A majority of art is initially conceived in terms of contour line; its presence is often implied even when it is not actually used to describe form. And because children start out by scribbling, line is generally considered the most rudimentary component of art—although as anyone knows who has watched a youngster struggle to make a stick figure with pencil or crayon, drawing is by no means as easy as it seems. Line has traditionally been admired for its descriptive value, so that its expressive potential is easily overlooked. Yet line is capable of creating a broad range of effects.

Drawings represent line in its purest form. The appreciation of drawings as works of art dates from the Renaissance,

when the artist's creative genius first came to be valued and paper began to be made in quantity. Drawing style can be as personal as handwriting. In fact, the term "graphic art," which designates drawings and prints, comes from the Greek word for writing, *graphos.* Collectors treasure drawings because they seem to reveal the artist's inspiration with unmatched freshness. Their role as records of artistic thought also makes drawings uniquely valuable to the art historian, for they help in documenting the evolution of a work from its inception to the finished piece.

Artists themselves commonly treat drawings as a form of note-taking. Some of these notes are discarded as fruitless, while others are tucked away to form a storehouse of motifs and studies for later use. Rembrandt was a prolific draftsman who was constantly jotting down observations of daily life and other ideas for further development. His use of line was highly expressive. Many of his sketches were done in pen and ink, a medium that captured his most intimate thoughts with admirable directness. In *The Star of the Kings* (fig. 8), one of his most elaborate sheets, Rembrandt rendered the essence of each pose and expression with remarkable succinctness—the dog, for example, consists of no more than a few strokes of the pen—yet every figure emerges as an individual character. Rembrandt's draftsmanship is so forceful that it allows us to mentally trace the movements of the master's hand with astonishing vividness.

Once a basic idea is established, an artist may develop it into a more complete study. Michelangelo's study (fig. 9) of the Libyan Sibyl for the Sistine Chapel ceiling is a drawing of compelling beauty. For this sheet, he chose the softer medium of red chalk over the scratchy line of pen and ink that he used in rough sketches; his chalk approximates the tex-

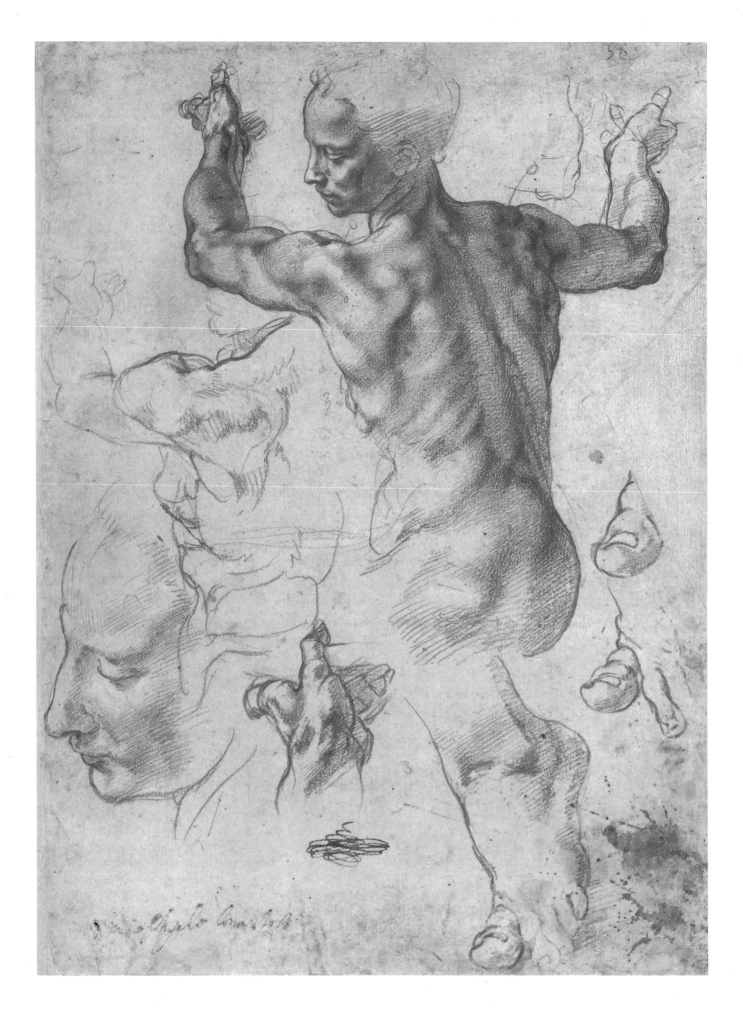

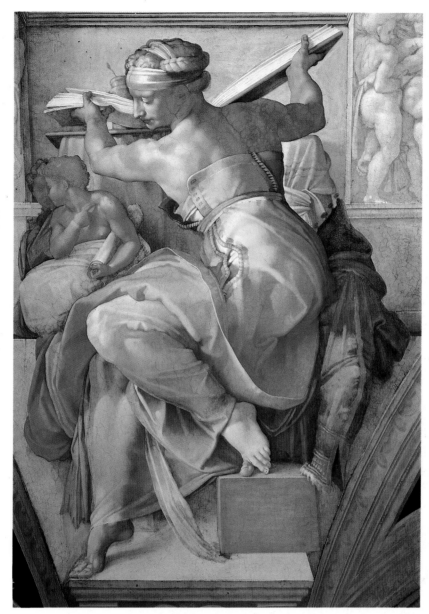

10. (*above*) MICHELANGELO. *LIBYAN SIBYL*, portion of the Sistine
Ceiling. 1508–12. Fresco. Sistine Chapel,
The Vatican, Rome

ture of flesh and captures the play of light and dark over the nude forms, giving the figure a greater sensuousness. The emphatic outline that defines each part of the form is so fundamental to the conceptual genesis and design process in all of Michelangelo's paintings and drawings that ever since his time line has been closely associated with the "intellectual" side of art.

It was Michelangelo's habit to base his female figures on male nudes drawn from life. To him, only the heroic male

9. (*opposite*) MICHELANGELO. *STUDY FOR THE LIBYAN SIBYL.*
c. 1511. Red chalk on paper, 11⅜ × 8⅜″ (28 × 21.3 cm).
The Metropolitan Museum of Art, New York.
Purchase, 1924, Joseph Pulitzer Bequest

nude possessed the physical monumentality necessary to express the awesome power of figures such as this mythical prophetess. In common with other sheets like this by him, Michelangelo's focus here is on the torso; he studied the musculature at length before turning his attention to details like the hand and toes. Since there is no sign of hesitation in the pose, we can be sure that the artist already had the conception firmly in mind; probably it had been established in a preliminary drawing. Why did he go to so much trouble when the finished sibyl is mostly clothed and must be viewed from a considerable distance below? Evidently Michelangelo believed that only by describing the anatomy completely could he be certain that the figure would be convincing. In the final painting (fig. 10) she communicates a superhuman strength, lifting her massive book of prophecies with the greatest ease.

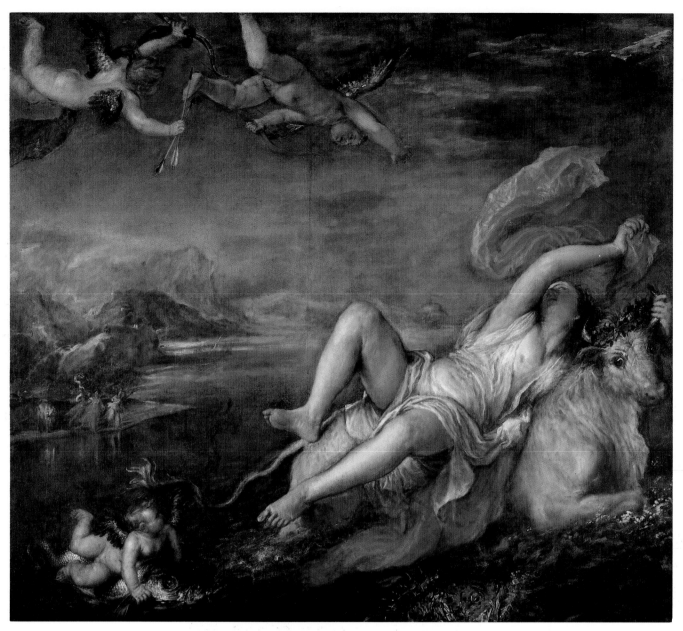

11. TITIAN. *THE RAPE OF EUROPA.*
1559–62. Oil on canvas, 70 × 80¾″ (178 × 205 cm).
Isabella Stewart Gardner Museum, Boston

COLOR. The world around us is alive with color, albeit even those of us who are not colorblind see only a relatively narrow band of the actual light spectrum. Whereas color is an adjunct element to graphics and sometimes sculpture, color is indispensable to virtually all forms of painting. This is true even of tonalism, which emphasizes dark, neutral hues like gray and brown. Of all the visual elements, color is undoubtedly the most expressive—as well as the most intractable. Perhaps for that reason, it has attracted the wide attention of researchers and theorists since the mid-nineteenth century. Along with the Post-Impressionists and, more recently, Op artists, color theorists have tried to set down their understanding of colors as perceptual and artistic laws equivalent to those of optical physics. Both Van Gogh and Seurat developed elaborate color systems, one en-

tirely personal in its meaning, the other claiming to be "scientific." We often read that red seems to advance, while blue recedes; or that the former is a violent or passionate color, the latter a sad one. Like a recalcitrant child, however, color in art refuses to be governed by any rules; they work only when the painter consciously applies them.

Notwithstanding this large body of theory, the role of color in art rests primarily on its sensuous and emotive appeal, in contrast to the more cerebral quality generally associated with line. The merits of line versus color have been the subject of a debate that first arose between partisans of Michelangelo and Titian, his great contemporary in Venice. Titian himself was a fine draftsman and absorbed the influence of Michelangelo. He nevertheless stands at the head of the coloristic tradition that descends through Rubens and Van

Gogh to the Abstract Expressionists of the twentieth century. *The Rape of Europa* (fig. 11), painted toward the end of Titian's long career, shows the painterly application of sonorous color that is characteristic of his work. Though he no doubt worked out the essential features of the composition in preliminary drawings, none have survived. Nor evidently did he transfer the design onto the canvas but worked directly on the surface, making numerous changes as he went along. By varying the consistency of his pigments, the artist was able to capture the texture of Europa's flesh with uncanny accuracy, while distinguishing it clearly from her wind-swept dress and the shaggy coat of Zeus disguised as a bull. To convey these tactile qualities, Titian built up his surface in thin coats, known as glazes. The interaction between these layers produces a richness and complexity of color that are strikingly apparent in the orange drapery where it trails off into the green seawater, which has a delicious wetness. The medium is so filmy as to become nearly translucent in parts of the landscape background, which is painted with a deft, flickering brush.

Color is so potent that it does not need a system to work its magic in art. From the heavy outlines, it is apparent that Picasso must have originally conceived *Girl Before a Mirror* (fig. 12) in terms of form; yet the picture makes no sense in black and white. He has treated his shapes much like the enclosed, flat panes of a stained-glass window to create a lively decorative pattern. The motif of a young woman contemplating her beauty goes all the way back to antiquity, but rarely has it been depicted with such disturbing overtones. Picasso's girl is anything but serene. On the contrary, her face is divided into two parts, one with a somber expression, the other with a masklike appearance whose color nevertheless betrays passionate feeling. She reaches out to touch the image in the mirror with a gesture of longing and apprehension. Now, we all feel a jolt when we unexpectedly see ourselves in a mirror, which often gives back a reflection that upsets our self-conception. Picasso here suggests this visionary truth in several ways. Much as a real mirror introduces changes of its own and does not simply give back the simple truth, so this one alters the way the girl looks, revealing a deeper reality. She is not so much examining her physical appearance as exploring her sexuality. The mirror is a sea of conflicting emotions signified above all by the color scheme of her reflection. Framed by strong blue, purple, and green hues, her features stare back at her with fiery intensity. Clearly discernible is a tear on her cheek. But it is the masterstroke of the green spot, shining like a beacon in the middle of her forehead, that conveys the anguish of the girl's confrontation with her inner self. Picasso was probably aware of the theory that red and green are complementary colors which intensify each other. However, this "law" can hardly have dictated his choice of green to stand for the girl's psyche. That was surely determined as a matter of pictorial and expressive necessity.

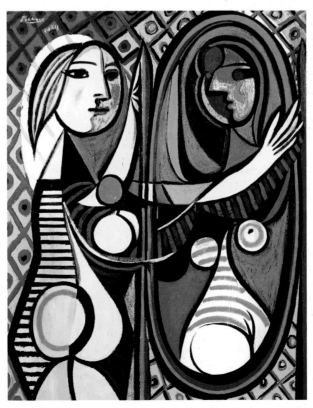

12. PABLO PICASSO. *GIRL BEFORE A MIRROR.*
March 1932. Oil on canvas, 64 × 51¼″ (162.6 × 130.2 cm).
Collection, The Museum of Modern Art, New York.
Gift of Mrs. Simon Guggenheim

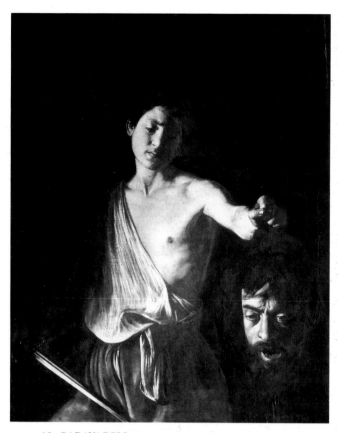

13. CARAVAGGIO. *DAVID WITH THE HEAD OF GOLIATH*.
1607 or 1609/10. Oil on canvas, 49¼ × 39⅜″ (125.1 × 100.1 cm).
Galleria Borghese, Rome

LIGHT. Except for modern light installations such as laser displays, art is concerned with reflected light effects rather than with radiant light. Artists have several ways of representing radiant light. Divine light, for example, is sometimes indicated by golden rays, at other times by a halo or aura. A candle or torch may be depicted as the source of light in a dark interior or night scene. The most common method is not to show radiant light directly but to suggest its presence through a change in the value of reflected light from dark to light. Sharp contrast (known as *chiaroscuro*, the Italian word for light-dark) is identified with the Baroque artist Caravaggio, who made it the cornerstone of his style. In *David with the Head of Goliath* (fig. 13), he employed it to heighten the drama. An intense raking light from an unseen source at the left is used to model forms and create textures. The selective highlighting endows the lifesize figure of David and the gruesome head with a startling presence. Light here serves as a device to create the convincing illusion that David is standing before us. The pictorial space, with its indeterminate depth, becomes continuous with ours, despite the fact that the frame cuts off the figure. Thus, the foreshortened arm with Goliath's head seems to extend out to the viewer from the dark background. For all its obvious theatricality, the painting is surprisingly muted: David seems to contemplate Goliath with a mixture of sadness and pity. According to contemporary sources, the severed head is a self-

portrait, but although we may doubt the identification, this disturbing image communicates a tragic vision that was soon fulfilled. Not long after the David was painted, Caravaggio killed another man in a duel, which forced him to spend the rest of his short life on the run.

Light can also be implied through color. Piet Mondrian uses white and the three primary colors—red, yellow, and blue—to signify radiant light in *Broadway Boogie Woogie* (fig. 14), a painting that immortalizes his fascination with the culture he found in America after emigrating from his native Holland during World War II. The play of color evokes with stunning success the jaunty rhythms of light and music found in New York's nightclub district during the jazz age. *Broadway Boogie Woogie* is as flat as the canvas it is painted on. Mondrian has laid out his colored "tiles" along a grid system that appropriately resembles a city map. As in a medieval manuscript decoration (fig. 387), the composition relies entirely on surface pattern.

COMPOSITION. All art requires order. Otherwise its message would emerge as visually garbled. To accomplish this, the artist must control space within the framework of a unified composition. Moreover, pictorial space must work across the picture plane, as well as behind it. Since the Early Renaissance, we have become accustomed to experiencing paintings as windows onto separate illusionistic realities. The Renaissance invention of one-point perspective—also called linear or scientific perspective—provided a geometric system for the convincing representation of architectural and open-air settings. By having the orthogonals (shown as

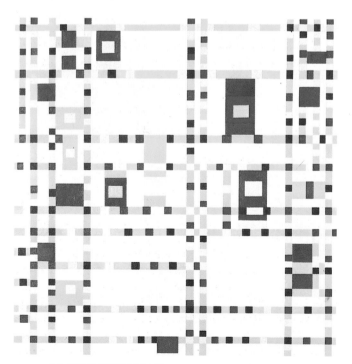

14. PIET MONDRIAN. *BROADWAY BOOGIE WOOGIE*.
1942–43. Oil on canvas, 50 × 50″ (127 × 127 cm).
Collection, The Museum of Modern Art,
New York. Given anonymously

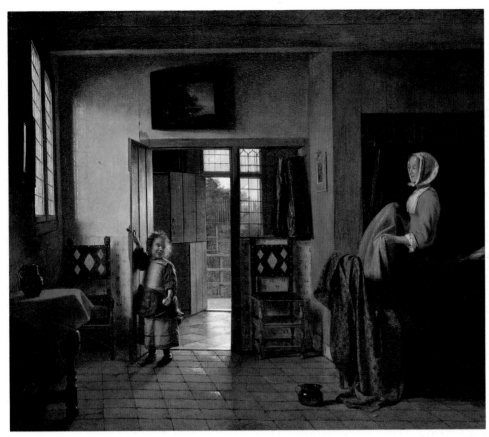

15. PIETER DE HOOCH. *THE BEDROOM.*
c. 1658–60. Oil on canvas, 20 × 23½″ (51 × 60 cm).
The National Gallery of Art, Washington, D.C. Widener Collection

diagonal lines) converge at a vanishing point on the horizon, it enabled the artist to gain command over every aspect of his composition, including the rate of recession and placement of figures. Pieter de Hooch, the Dutch Baroque artist, used one-point perspective in organizing *The Bedroom* (fig. 15). Nevertheless, the problems he faced in composing the three-dimensional space of his work were not so very different from those later confronted by Mondrian. (The surface geometry of De Hooch's painting is basically similar in design to *Broadway Boogie Woogie.*) Each part of the house is treated as a separate pocket of space and as a design element that is integrated into the scene as a whole.

The artist will usually dispense with aids like perspective and rely on his own eyes. This does not mean that he merely transcribes optical reality. *Blowing Bubbles* by the French painter Jean-Baptiste Chardin (fig. 16) depends in good measure on a satisfying composition for its success. The motif had been a popular one in earlier Dutch genre scenes, where bubbles symbolized life's brevity and, hence, the vanity of all earthly things. No such meaning can be attached to Chardin's picture, which is disarming in its simplicity. The interest lies solely in the seemingly insignificant subject and in the sense of enchantment imparted by the children's rapt attention to the moment. We know from a contemporary source that Chardin painted the youth "carefully from life and... tried hard to give him an ingenuous air." The results are anything but artless, however. The triangular shape of

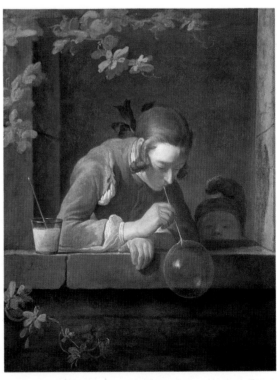

16. JEAN-BAPTISTE CHARDIN. *BLOWING BUBBLES.*
c. 1745. Oil on canvas, 36⅝ × 29⅜″ (93 × 74.6 cm).
The National Gallery of Art, Washington, D.C.
Gift of Mrs. John Simpson

the boy leaning on the ledge gives stability to the painting, which helps to suspend the fleeting instant in time. To fill out the composition, the artist includes the toddler peering intently over the ledge at the bubble, which is about the same size as his head. Chardin has carefully thought out every aspect of his arrangement. The honeysuckle in the upper left-hand corner, for example, echoes the contour of the adolescent's back, while the two straws are virtually parallel to each other. Even the crack in the stone ledge has a purpose: to draw attention to the glass of soap by setting it slightly apart.

Often the artist paints not what he sees but what he imagines. A wall painting from Thebes (fig. 17) presents a flattened view of a delightful garden in which everything is shown in profile except for the pond, which is seen from above. In order to provide the clearest, most complete idea of the scene, the Egyptian artist treated each element as an entity unto itself. Instead of using standard devices such as scale and overlapping, he treated space vertically, so that we read the trees at the bottom as being "closer" to us than those at the top, even though they are the same size. Despite the multiple vantage points and implausible bird's-eye view, the image works because it constitutes a self-contained reality. The picture, moreover, has an aesthetically satisfying decorative unity. The geometry underlying the composition reminds us once more of *Broadway Boogie Woogie*. At the same time, the presentation has such clarity that we feel as if we were seeing nature with open eyes for the first time.

Pictorial space need not conform to either conceptual or visual reality. El Greco's *Agony in the Garden* (fig. 18) uses contradictory, irrational space to help conjure up a mystical vision that instead represents a spiritual reality. Christ, isolated against a large rock that echoes His shape, is comforted by the angel bearing a golden cup, symbol of the Passion. The angel appears to kneel on a mysterious oval cloud, which envelops the sleeping disciples. In the distance to the right we see Judas and the soldiers coming to arrest the Lord. The composition is balanced by two giant clouds on either side. The entire landscape resounds with Christ's agitation, represented by the sweep of supernatural forces. The elongated forms, eerie moonlight, and expressive colors—other hallmarks of El Greco's style—help to heighten our sense of identification with Christ's suffering.

FORM. Every two-dimensional shape that we encounter in art is the counterpart to a three-dimensional form. There is nevertheless a vast difference between drawing or painting forms and sculpting them. The one transcribes, the other brings them to life, as it were. They require fundamentally different talents and attitudes toward material as well as subject matter. Although a number of artists have been competent in both painting and sculpture, only a handful managed to bridge the gap between them with complete success.

Sculpture is categorized according to whether it is carved or modeled and whether it is a relief or a free-standing

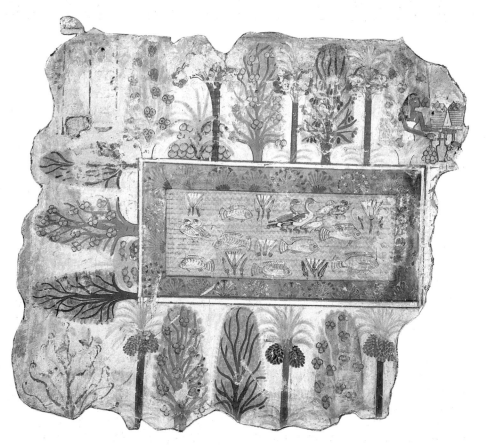

17. *A POND IN A GARDEN*. Fragment of a wall painting
from a tomb in Thebes. c. 1400 B.C. British Museum, London

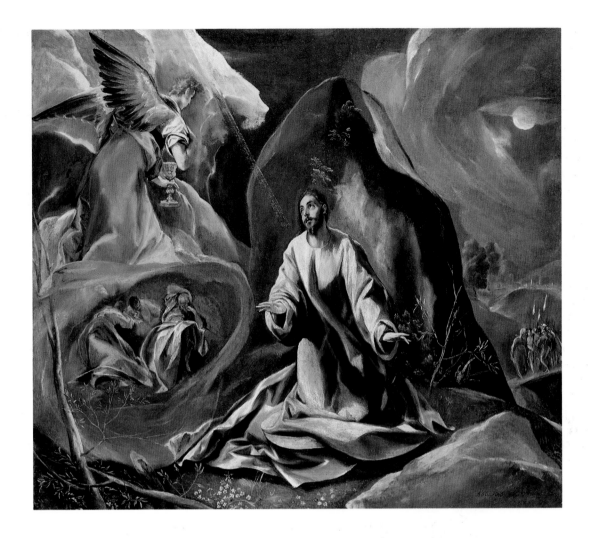

18. EL GRECO. *THE AGONY IN THE GARDEN*. 1597–1600.
Oil on canvas, 40¼ × 44¾″ (102.2 × 113.6 cm). Toledo Museum of Art,
Toledo, Ohio. Gift of Edward Drummond Libbey

19. *ALKESTIS LEAVING HADES*. Lower column drum from the Temple
of Artemis, Ephesus. c. 340 B.C. Marble, height 71″ (180.3 cm).
British Museum, London

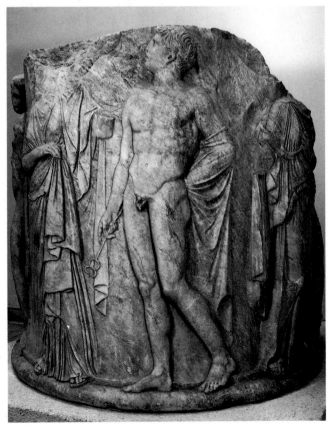

statue. Relief remains tied to the background, from which it only partially emerges, in contrast to free-standing sculpture, which is fully liberated from it. A further distinction is made between low (*bas*) relief and high (*alto*) relief, depending on how much the carving projects. However, since scale as well as depth must be taken into account, there is no single guideline, so that a third category, middle (*mezzo*) relief, is sometimes cited.

Low reliefs often share characteristics with painting. In Egypt, where low-relief carving attained unsurpassed subtlety, many reliefs were originally painted and included elaborate settings. High reliefs largely preclude this kind of pictorialism. The figures on a column drum from a Greek temple (fig. 19) have become so detached from the background that the addition of landscape or architecture elements would be both unnecessary and unconvincing. The neutral setting, moreover, is in keeping with the mythologi-

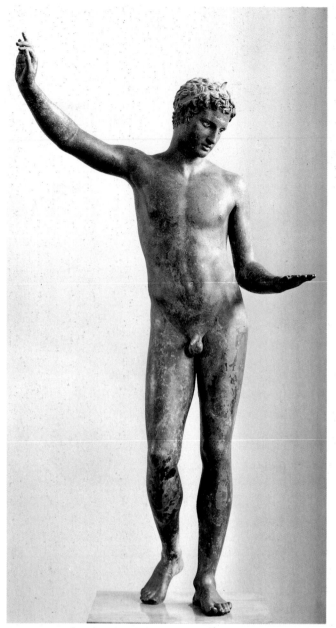

20. PRAXITELES (attr.). *STANDING YOUTH,* found in the sea off Marathon. c. 350–325 B.C. Bronze, height 51″ (129.5 cm). National Archeological Museum, Athens

cal subject, which takes place in an indeterminate time and place. In compensation, the sculptor has treated the limited free space atmospherically; yet the figures remain imprisoned in stone.

Free-standing sculpture—that is, sculpture that is carved or modeled fully in the round—is made by either of two methods. One is modeling, an additive process using soft materials such as plaster, clay, or wax. Since these materials are not very durable, they are usually cast in a more lasting medium—anything that can be poured, including molten metal, cement, even plastic. Modeling encourages "open" forms with the aid of metal armatures to support their extension into space. This in conjunction with the development of lightweight hollow-bronze casting enabled the Greeks to experiment with daring poses in monumental sculpture before

attempting them in marble. In contrast to the figure of Hades on the column drum, the bronze youth in figure 20 is free to move about, lending him a lifelike presence that is further enhanced by his dancing pose. His inlaid eyes and soft patina, accentuated by oxidation and corrosion (he was found in the Aegean Sea off the coast of Marathon), make him even more credible in a way that marble statues, with their seemingly cold and smooth finish, rarely equal, despite their more natural color (compare fig. 21).

Carving is the very opposite of modeling. It is a subtractive process that starts with a solid block, usually stone, which is highly resistant to the sculptor's chisel. The brittleness of stone and the difficulty of cutting it tend to result in the compact, "closed" forms seen in Michelangelo's *Captive* (fig. 3). One of the most daring attempts at overcoming the tyranny of mass over space is *Apollo and Daphne* by the Baroque sculptor Gianlorenzo Bernini (fig. 21). The dancelike pose of Apollo and graceful torsion of Daphne create the impression that they are moving in a carefully choreographed ballet. Time and motion have almost, but not quite, come to a standstill as the nymph begins to change into a tree rather than succumb to the god's amorous advances. The sculpture is an amazing technical achievement. Bernini is completely successful in distinguishing between the soft flesh of Daphne and the rough texture of the bark and leaves. The illusion of transformation is so convincing that we share Apollo's shock at the metamorphosis.

Like most monumental sculpture, *Apollo and Daphne* was commissioned for a specific site, which imposed severe restrictions. It was intended to be placed close to a wall and viewed across the room from a doorway slightly to the right. Bernini's ingenuity in solving this problem is confirmed by walking around the group, which is now displayed in the middle of the same room. The most characteristic view, illustrated here, corresponds to what would have been seen from the original vantage point, although the sculpture may be looked at profitably from other angles as well. The back side was never meant to be seen and provides little additional information, despite the fact that it is fully carved. As usual with this artist, however, the figures are not willing to accept these limitations and enliven the entire space around them.

SPACE. In our discussions of pictorial and sculptural space, we have repeatedly referred to architecture, for it is the principal means of organizing space. Of all the arts, it is also the most practical. Architecture's parameters are defined by utilitarian function and structural system, but there is almost always an aesthetic component as well, even when it consists of nothing more than a decorative veneer. A building proclaims the architect's concerns by the way in which it weaves these elements into a coherent program.

Architecture becomes memorable only when it expresses a transcendent vision, whether personal, social, or spiritual.

21. *(opposite)* GIANLORENZO BERNINI. *APOLLO AND DAPHNE.* 1622–24. Marble, height 96″ (243.9 cm). Galleria Borghese, Rome

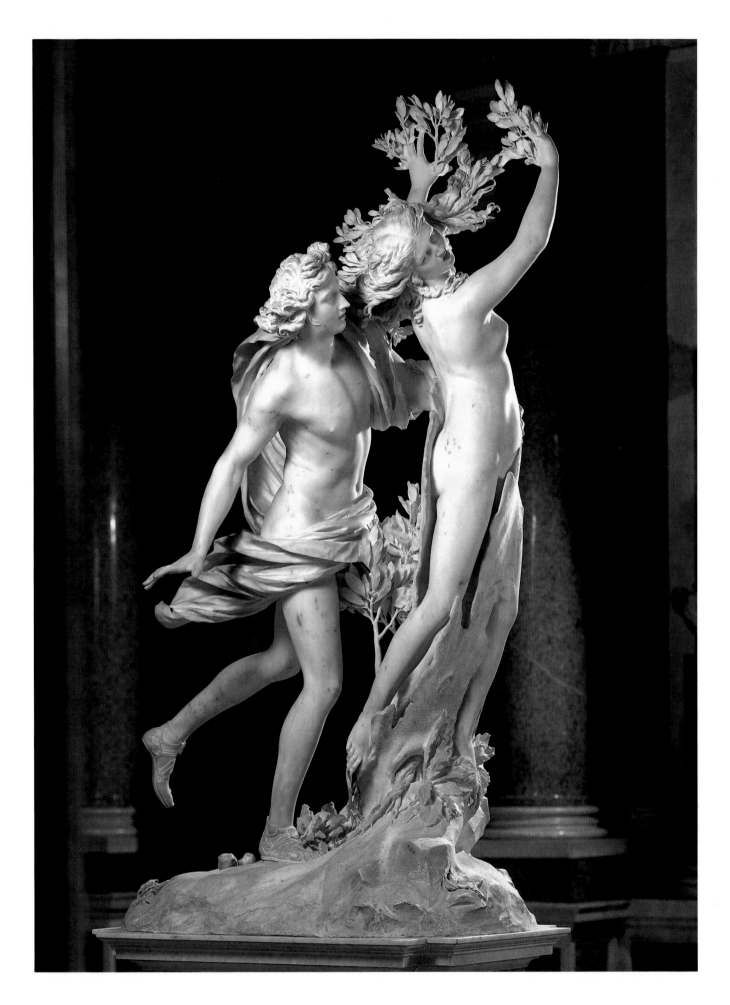

Such buildings are almost always important public places that require the marshaling of significant resources and serve the purpose of bringing people together to share common goals, pursuits, and values. Nowhere are these issues put in sharper relief than in the grandiose urban projects conceived by modern architects. They may be regarded as laboratory experiments which seek to redefine the role of architecture in shaping our lives. Limited by their very great scope, few of these ambitious proposals make it off the drawing board. Among the rare exceptions is Brasilia, the inland capital of Brazil built entirely since 1960. Presented with an unparalleled opportunity to design a major city from the ground up and with vast resources at its disposal, the design team, headed by Oscar Niemeyer, achieved undeniably spectacular results (fig. 22). Like most projects of this sort, Brasilia has a massive scale and insistent logic that make it curiously oppressive, so that despite its lavish display, Brasilia provides a chilling glimpse of the future.

Similar questions may be faced by architects of single buildings, only on a smaller scale. An extreme case is the Solomon R. Guggenheim Museum in New York by Frank Lloyd Wright. Scorned when it was first erected in the late 1950s, it is a brilliant, if idiosyncratic, creation by one of the most original architectural minds of the century. The sculptural exterior (fig. 23) announces that this can only be a museum, for it is self-consciously a work of art in its own right. As a piece of design, the Guggenheim Museum is remarkably willful. In shape it is as defiantly individual as the architect himself and refuses to conform to the boxlike apartments around it. From the outside, the structure looks like a gigantic snail, reflecting Wright's interest in organic shapes. The office area forming the "head" to the left is connected by a narrow passageway to the "shell" containing the main body of the museum.

The outside gives us some idea of what to expect inside (fig. 24), yet nothing quite prepares us for the extraordinary sensation of light and air in the main hall after being ushered through the unassuming entrance. The radical design makes it clear that Wright had completely rethought the purpose of an art museum. The exhibition area is a kind of inverted dome with a huge glass-covered eye at the top. The vast, fluid space creates an atmosphere of quiet harmony while actively shaping our experience by determining how art shall be displayed. After taking an elevator to the top of the building, one begins a leisurely descent down the gently sloping ramp. The continuous spiral provides for uninterrupted viewing, conducive to studying art. At the same time, the narrow confines of the galleries prevent us from becoming passive observers by forcing us into a direct confrontation with the works themselves. Sculpture takes on a heightened physical presence which demands that we look at it. Even paintings acquire a new prominence by protruding slightly from the curved walls, instead of receding into them. Viewing exhibitions at the Guggenheim is like being conducted through a predetermined stream of consciousness, where everything merges into a total unity. Whether one agrees with this approach or not, the building testifies to the strength of Wright's vision by precluding any other way of seeing the art.

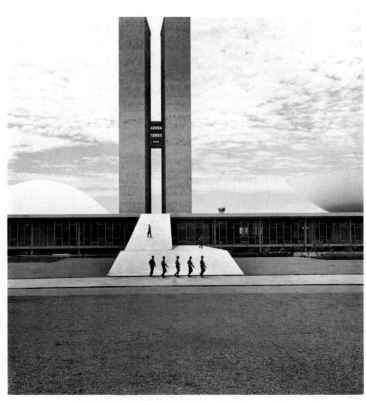

22. OSCAR NIEMEYER. Brasilia, Brazil. Completed 1960

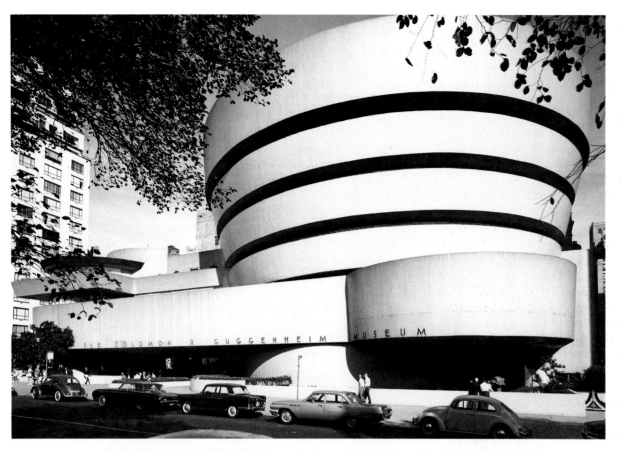

23. FRANK LLOYD WRIGHT. Solomon R. Guggenheim Museum, New York. 1956–59

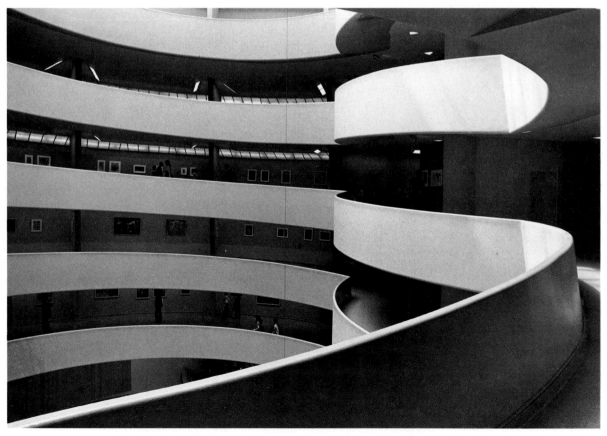

24. Interior. Solomon R. Guggenheim Museum

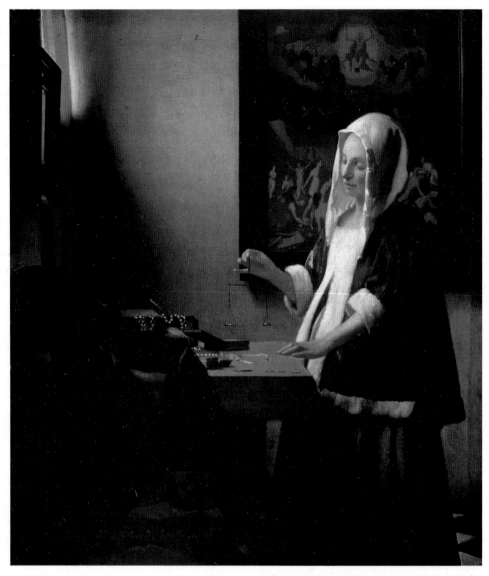

25. JAN VERMEER. *WOMAN HOLDING A BALANCE.* c. 1664. Oil on canvas, 16¾ × 15″ (42.5 × 38.1 cm).
The National Galley of Art, Washington, D.C. Widener Collection, 1942

Meaning in Context

Art has been called a visual dialogue, for though the object itself is mute, it expresses its creator's intention just as surely as if he were speaking to us. For there to be a dialogue, however, our active participation is required. If we cannot literally talk to a work of art, we can learn how to respond to it and question it in order to fathom its meaning. Finding the right answers usually involves asking the right questions. Even if we aren't sure which question to ask, we can always start with, "What would happen if the artist had done it another way?" And when we are through, we must question our explanation according to the same test of adequate proof that applies to any investigation: have we taken into account *all* the available evidence—and arranged it in a logical and coherent way? There is, alas, no step-by-step method to guide us, but this does not mean that the process is entirely mysterious. We can illustrate it by looking at some examples together; the demonstration will help us gain courage to try the same analysis the next time we enter a museum.

The great Dutch painter Jan Vermeer has been called The Sphinx of Delft, and with good reason, for all his paintings have a degree of mystery. In *Woman Holding a Balance* (fig. 25), a young woman, richly dressed in at-home wear of the day and with strings of pearls and gold coins spread out on the table before her, is contemplating a balance in her hand. The canvas is painted entirely in gradations of cool, neutral tones, except for a bit of the red dress visible beneath her jacket. The soft light from the partly open window is concentrated on her face and the cap framing it. Other beads of light reflect from the pearls and her right hand. The serene atmosphere is sustained throughout the stable composition. Vermeer places us at an intimate distance within the relatively shallow space, which has been molded around the figure. The underlying grid of horizontals and verticals is modulated by the gentle curves of the woman's form and the heap of blue drapery, as well as by the oblique angles of the mirror. The design is so perfect that we cannot move a single element without upsetting the delicate balance.

The composition is controlled in part by perspective. The vanishing point of the diagonals formed by the top of the mirror and the right side of the table lies at the juncture of the woman's little finger and the picture frame. If we look carefully at the bottom of the frame, we see that it is actually lower on the right than on the left, where it lies just below her hand. The effect is so carefully calculated that the artist must have wanted to guide our eye to the painting in the background. Though difficult to read at first, it depicts Christ at the Last Judgment, when every soul is weighed. The parallel of this subject to the woman's activity tells us that, contrary to our initial impression, this cannot be simply a scene of everyday life. The meaning is nevertheless far from clear. Because Vermeer treated forms as beads of light, it was assumed until recently that the balance holds items of jewelry and that the woman is weighing the worthlessness of earthly possessions in the face of death; hence, the painting was generally called *The Pearl Weigher* or *The Gold Weigher*. If we look closely, however, we can see that the pans contain nothing. This is confirmed by infra-red photography, which also reveals that Vermeer changed the position of the balance: to make the picture more harmonious, he placed them parallel to the picture plane instead of allowing them to recede into space. What, then, is she doing? If she is weighing temporal against spiritual values, it can be only in a symbolic sense, because nothing about the figure or the setting betrays a sense of conflict. What accounts for this inner peace? Perhaps it is self-knowledge, symbolized here by the mirror. It may also be the promise of salvation through her faith. In *Woman Holding a Balance*, as in Caravaggio's *The Calling of St. Matthew* (fig. 739), light might therefore serve not only to illuminate the scene but also to represent religious revelation. In the end, we cannot be sure, because Vermeer's approach to his subject proves as subtle as his pictorial treatment. He avoids any anecdote or symbolism that might limit us to a single interpretation. There can be no doubt, however, about his fascination with light. Vermeer's mastery of light's expressive qualities elevates his concern for the reality of appearance to the level of poetry, and subsumes its visual and symbolic possibilities. Here, then, we have found the real "meaning" of Vermeer's art.

The ambiguity in *Woman Holding a Balance* serves to heighten our interest and pleasure, while the carefully organized composition expresses the artist's underlying concept with singular clarity. But what are we to do when a work deliberately seems devoid of ostensible meaning? Modern artists can pose a gap between their intention and the viewer's understanding. The gap is, however, often more apparent than real, for the meaning is usually intelligible to the imagination at some level. Still, we feel we must comprehend intellectually what we perceive intuitively. We can partially solve the personal code in Jasper Johns' *Target with Four Faces* (fig. 26) by treating it somewhat like a rebus. Where did he begin? Surely with the target, which stands alone as an object, unlike the long box at the top, particularly when its hinged door is closed. Why a target in the first place? The size, texture, and colors inform us that this is not to be interpreted as a real target. The design is never-

theless attractive in its own right, and Johns must have chosen it for that reason. When the wooden door is up, the assemblage is transformed from a neutral into a loaded image, bringing out the nascent connotations of the target. Johns has used the same plaster cast four times, which lends the faces a curious anonymity; then he cut them off at the eyes, "the windows of the soul," rendering them even more enigmatic; finally, he crammed them into their compartments, so that they seem to press urgently out toward us. The results are disquieting, aesthetically as well as expressively.

Something so disturbing cannot be without significance—but what? We may be reminded of prisoners trying to look out from small cell windows—or perhaps "blindfolded" targets of execution. Whatever our impression, the claustrophobic image radiates an aura of menacing danger. Unlike Picasso's joining of a bicycle seat and handlebars to form a bull's head, *Target with Four Faces* combines two disparate components in an open conflict that we cannot reconcile, no matter how hard we try. The intrusion of this ominous meaning creates an extraordinary tension with the

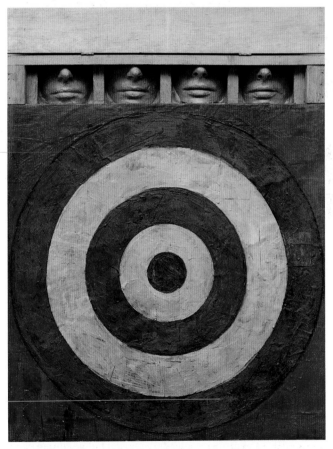

26. JASPER JOHNS. *TARGET WITH FOUR FACES*. 1955.
Assemblage: encaustic on newspaper and cloth over canvas,
26 × 26″ (66 × 66 cm) surmounted by four tinted plaster faces
in wood box with hinged front. Box, closed 3¾ × 26 × 3½″
(9.5 × 66 × 8.9 cm); overall dimensions with box open,
33⅝ × 26 × 3″ (85.3 × 66.7 × 6 cm).
Collection, The Museum of Modern Art, New York.
Gift of Mr. and Mrs. Robert C. Scull

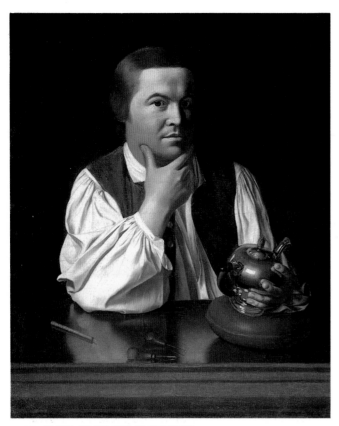

27. JOHN SINGLETON COPLEY. *PAUL REVERE.* c. 1768–70.
Oil on canvas, 38 × 28½″ (96.5 × 72.4 cm).
Museum of Fine Arts, Boston. Gift of Joseph W., William. B.,
and Edward H. R. Revere

of historical data can satisfy nearly as well. Our interest arises no doubt from the remnant of a primitive belief that an image captures not merely the likeness but also the soul of a sitter. In the age of photography, we have come to see portraits as mere likenesses and we readily forget that they call on all our skill to grasp their meaning. *Paul Revere,* painted by the American artist John Singleton Copley around 1770 (fig. 27), gives rise to questions we cannot solve with on-the-spot observations, so we must look elsewhere to answer them. The fruit of our investigation must agree with our observations; otherwise we cannot be sure that we are right.

Silversmith, printmaker, businessman, and patriot, Revere has acquired legendary status thanks to Henry Wadsworth Longfellow's long poem about his legendary midnight ride, and Copley's painting has become virtually an American icon. It has generally been treated as a workingman's portrait, so to speak. By rights, however, such a portrait ought to be much more straightforward than this and, hence, less memorable. Revere has a penetrating glance and thoughtful pose which are heightened by the sharp light, lending him an unusually forceful presence. He looks out at us with astonishing directness, as if he were reading us with the same intensity that we bring to bear on his strongly modeled features. Clearly, Revere is a thinker possessing an active intelligence, and we will recognize the pose of hand on chin as an old device used since antiquity to represent philosophers. This is certainly no ordinary craftsman here, and we may also wonder whether this is really his working outfit.

dispassionate investigation of the target's formal qualities. It is, then, this disparity between form and content that must have been Johns' goal.

How do we know we are right? After all, this is merely our "personal" interpretation, so we turn to the critics for help. We find them divided about the meaning of *Target with Four Faces,* although they agree it must have one. Johns, on the other hand, has insisted that there is none! Whom are we to believe, the critics or the artist himself? The more we think about it, the more likely it seems that both sides may be right. The artist is not always aware why he has made a work. That does not mean that there were no reasons, only that they were unconscious ones. Under these circumstances, the critic may well know the artist's mind better than he does and explain his creation more clearly. We can now understand that to Johns the leap of his imagination in *Target with Four Faces* remains as mysterious as it first seemed to us. Our account reconciles the artist's aesthetic concerns and the critics' search for meaning, and while we realize that no ultimate solution is possible, we have arrived at a satisfactory explanation by looking and thinking for ourselves.

It is all too easy to overlook the obvious, and this is especially true in looking at portraits. Those of famous people have a special appeal, for they seem to bridge a gap of time and place and to establish a personal link. In their faces we read a thousand insights about character which no amount

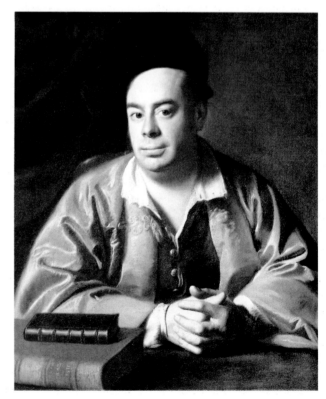

28. JOHN SINGLETON COPLEY. *NATHANIEL HURD.* c. 1765
Oil on canvas, 30 × 25½″ (76.2 × 64.8 cm).
The Cleveland Museum of Art. John Huntington Collection

Surely no silversmith would have carried out his craft in what are probably Revere's best business clothes. Simply by looking at the picture we have raised enough doubts to challenge the traditional view of this famous painting.

At this point, our questioning of the picture's surface comes to an end, for the portrait fails to yield up further clues. Once we have posed the problem of this "craftsman's" portrayal, we feel compelled to investigate it further. The more we pursue the matter, the more fascinating it becomes. Copley, we discover, had painted only a few years earlier a portrait of another Boston silversmith, Nathaniel Hurd (fig. 28). Yet this one is so different that we would never guess the sitter's trade. Hurd is wearing a casual robe and turban, and before him are two books, one of them devoted to heraldry from which he culled the coats of arms he needed for his work. Why, then, did Copley show Revere at a workbench with his engraving tools spread out before him, holding a teapot as the object of his contemplation and offering it to us for our inspection? In light of Hurd's portrait, Revere's work as a silversmith hardly explains these attributes and actions, natural as they seem. Oddly enough, the question has never been raised; yet surely the differences between the two paintings cannot be accidental.

Perhaps we can find the answer in the antecedents for each. Hurd's image can be traced back to informal portraits that originated in France in the early eighteenth century and soon became popular as well in England, where there was a rage for portraits of well-known men and women. This type of portrait was customarily reserved for artists, writers, and the like. In turn, the type gave rise to a distinctive offshoot that showed a sculptor at work in his studio with his tools prominently displayed (fig. 29). Sometimes an engraver is seen instead. There is another possible precedent: moralizing portraits, the descendants of pictures of St. Jerome, that show their subjects holding or pointing to skulls, much as Revere has the teapot in his hand. Copley was surely familiar with all of these kinds of images from the portrait engravings that we know he collected, but his exact sources for the Revere painting remain a mystery—and may never be discovered. For after 1765 Copley freely adapted and combined motifs from different prints in his paintings, often disguising their origins so completely that we cannot be certain which they were. It is likely that he conflated two or three in Revere's portrait. In any case, it is apparent that Copley has transformed Revere from a craftsman into an artist-philosopher.

Let us now look at this portrait in its larger historical and cultural context. In Europe, the craftsman's inferior position to the artist had been asserted since the Renaissance—except in England, where the newly founded Royal Academy first drew the distinction in 1768, about when Copley painted Hurd's portrait. But in the Colonies there was, as Copley himself complained, no distinction between the trades of artist and craftsman. Indeed, except for portraiture, it can be argued that the decorative arts *were* the fine arts of America.

It is significant that Copley's portrait probably dates from around the time of Revere's first efforts at making engravings, a form of art that arose, interestingly enough, out of silver- and goldsmith decorating during the late Middle

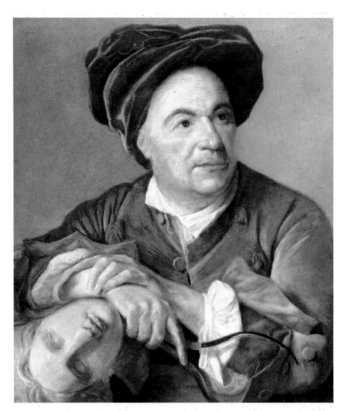

29. FRANCIS XAVIER VISPRÉ (attr.). *PORTRAIT OF LOUIS-FRANÇOIS ROUBILIAC.* c. 1750. Pastel, 24½ × 21½" (62.2 × 54.6 cm). Yale Center for British Art, New Haven, Connecticut. Paul Mellon Collection

Ages. Revere was then already involved with libertarianism, a cause which Copley himself did not share. This difference in their points of view did not prevent Copley from endowing Revere's portrait with an ingenious significance and penetrating seriousness of characterization. The painter and the silversmith must have known each other well. The portrait stands as Copley's compelling tribute to a fellow artist—and as an invaluable statement about the culture of the Colonial era.

Obviously, not everyone is in a position to undertake this kind of research—only the art historian and the occasional interested layman. But again, this does not mean that "there must be something wrong with a work of art if it takes an expert to appreciate it." On the contrary, our research serves only to affirm the portrait of Paul Revere as a masterpiece. Reacting to the portrait in "a direct, straightforward fashion," without the benefit of additional knowledge, deprives us of an understanding that is necessary for full appreciation. Critics, scholars, and curators are not our adversaries; in sharing their expertise and their knowledge of art's broader contexts with those who seek it, they expand the dimensions of our capacity for appreciating art, and they provide a model for our own find-and-seek experiences.

PROLOGUE

Gothic Painting and Sculpture

At the end of the thirteenth century, Italian painting produced an explosion of creative energy that had far-reaching impact upon the future. What were the conditions that made this possible? Medieval Italy, although strongly influenced by Northern art from Carolingian times on, had always maintained close contacts with Byzantine civilization. A new wave of Byzantine influence overwhelmed the lingering Romanesque elements in Italian painting. It is ironic that this Neo-Byzantine style (or "Greek manner," as the Italians called it) made its appearance soon after the conquest of Constantinople by the armies of the Fourth Crusade in 1204. Be that as it may, the Greek manner prevailed almost until the end of the thirteenth century, so that Italian painters were able to absorb the Byzantine tradition far more thoroughly than ever before. Eventually, toward 1300, Gothic influence spilled over into Italian painting as well, and it was the interaction of this element with the Neo-Byzantine that produced the revolutionary new style of which Giotto was the greatest exponent.

NICOLA AND GIOVANNI PISANO. During this same period, Italian architects and sculptors followed a very different course; untouched by the Greek manner, they were assimilating the Gothic style. The founder of Italian Gothic sculpture was Nicola Pisano (c. 1220/5 or before–1284?) who came to Tuscany from southern Italy around 1250. His work has been well defined as that of "the greatest—and in a sense the last—of medieval classicists." The narrative scenes, such as the *Nativity* (Vol. Two, fig. 30), on the marble pulpit he completed in 1260 for the Baptistery of Pisa Cathedral, tell us that he must have been thoroughly familiar with Roman sarcophagi. The relief is treated as a shallow box filled almost to the bursting point with solid, convex shapes. This dense crowding of figures has no counterpart in Northern Gothic

sculpture. On the other hand, it shares a striking Gothic quality of human feeling with the *Death of the Virgin* (Vol. Two, fig. 31) at Strasbourg Cathedral. The draperies, the facial types, the movements and gestures in the Strasbourg relief have a classical flavor. The pathos also has classical roots, but what marks it as Gothic is the tenderness that pervades the entire scene. We sense a bond of shared emotion among the figures, and their ability to communicate by glance and gesture with moving eloquence.

Some fifty years later Nicola's son Giovanni (1245/50–after 1314), an equally gifted sculptor, did a marble pulpit for Pisa Cathedral that also includes a *Nativity* panel (Vol. Two, fig. 32). Both Nativity scenes have much in common, as we might well expect. Yet Giovanni's slender, swaying figures, with their smoothly flowing draperies, are not derived from classical antiquity; instead, they reflect the elegant style of the royal court at Paris that had become the standard Gothic formula during the late thirteenth century. And with this change comes a new treatment of relief: to Giovanni Pisano, space is as important as sculptural form. The figures are no longer tightly packed together; they are spaced far enough apart to let us see the landscape setting that contains them, and each figure has been allotted its own pocket of space. If Nicola's *Nativity* strikes us as essentially a sequence of bulging, rounded masses, Giovanni's appears to consist mainly of cavities and shadows. Here Giovanni Pisano is following the trend toward "disembodiment" found north of the Alps around 1300.

CIMABUE. Among the Italian painters of the Greek manner, the Florentine master Cimabue (c. 1250–after 1300), who may have been Giotto's teacher, enjoyed particular fame. His impressive altar panel of the *Madonna Enthroned* (Vol. Two, fig. 33) rivals the finest Byzantine icons (Vol. Two, fig. 34) or mosaics; what distinguishes it from them is mainly its

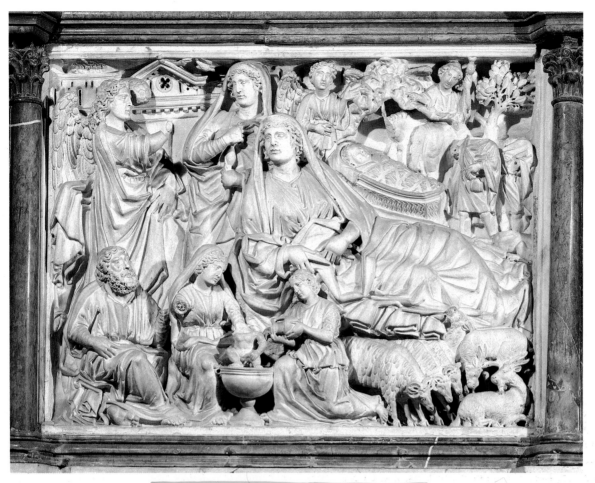

30. NICOLA PISANO. *NATIVITY*, detail of pulpit. 1259–60.
Marble. Baptistery, Pisa

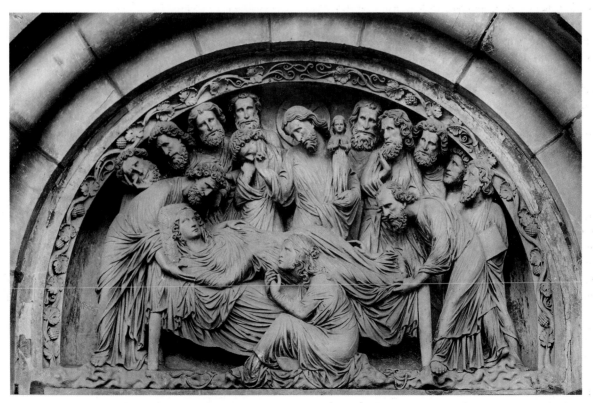

31. *DEATH OF THE VIRGIN*, tympanum of the
south transept portal, Strasbourg Cathedral. c. 1220

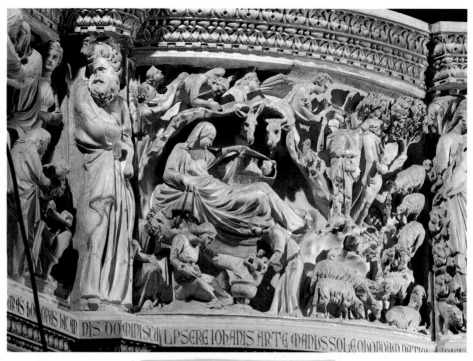

32. GIOVANNI PISANO. *THE NATIVITY*,
detail of pulpit. 1302–10. Marble. Pisa Cathedral

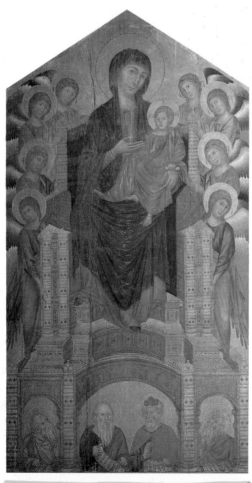

33. CIMABUE. *MADONNA ENTHRONED*. c. 1280–90.
Tempera on panel, 12'7½" × 7'4" (3.9 × 2.2 m).
Galleria degli Uffizi, Florence

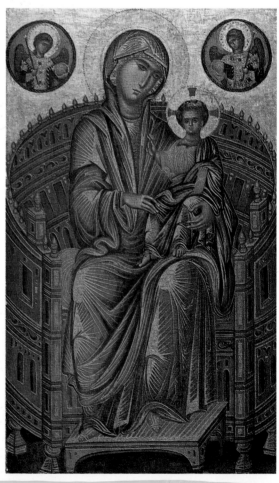

34. *MADONNA ENTHRONED*. Late 13th century. Tempera on panel,
32⅛ × 19⅜" (81.9 × 49.3 cm). The National Gallery of Art,
Washington, D.C. Andrew Mellon Collection, 1937

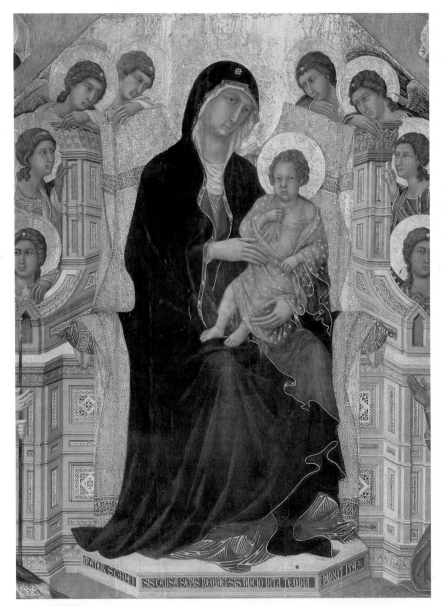

35. DUCCIO. *MADONNA ENTHRONED,* detail from center of the *Maestà Altar.*
1308–11. Tempera on panel, height 6'10½" (2.1 m). Museo dell'Opera del Duomo, Siena

greater severity of design and expression, as befits its huge size. Panels of such monumental scale had never been attempted in the East. Equally un-Byzantine is the picture's gabled shape which is echoed in the form of the throne of inlaid wood.

DUCCIO. A quarter of a century after Cimabue painted his *Madonna Enthroned,* Duccio (c. 1255–before 1319) painted the main altar of Siena Cathedral (Vol. Two, fig. 35), which the Sienese honored by calling it the *Maestà*—"majesty"—to identify the Virgin's role in the main panel as the Queen of Heaven surrounded by her celestial court of saints and angels. At first glance the two pictures may seem much alike, since both follow the same basic scheme; yet the differences are important. They reflect not only two contrasting personalities and contrasting local tastes—the gentleness of Duccio

is characteristic of Siena—but also the rapid evolution of style. In Duccio's hands the Greek manner has become unfrozen, as it were: the rigid, angular draperies give way to an undulating softness, the abstract shading-in-reverse with lines of gold is reduced to a minimum, and the bodies, faces, and hands are beginning to swell with a subtle three-dimensional life. Here the heritage of Hellenistic-Roman illusionism that had always been part of the Byzantine tradition, however dormant or submerged, is asserting itself once more. But we also sense half-hidden Gothic elements in the fluency of the drapery folds, the appealing naturalness of the Infant Christ, and the tender glances by which the figures communicate with each other. The chief source of this Gothic influence must have been Giovanni Pisano, who spent the decade 1285–95 in Siena as the sculptor-architect of the cathedral façade.

Apart from the *Madonna*, the *Maestà* includes many small compartments with scenes from the lives of Christ and the Virgin. In these panels, the most mature works of Duccio's career, the cross-fertilization of Gothic and Byzantine elements has given rise to a development of fundamental importance—a new kind of picture space. The *Annunciation of the Death of the Virgin* (Vol. Two, fig. 36) shows us something never seen before in the history of painting: two figures enclosed by an architectural interior. Ancient painters (and their Byzantine successors) were quite unable to achieve this sense of space; their architectural settings always stay *behind* the figures, so that their indoor scenes tend to look as if they were taking place in an open-air theater, on a stage without a roof. Duccio's figures, in contrast, inhabit a space that is created and defined by the architecture, as if the artist had carved a niche into his panel. This spatial framework derives from the architectural "housing" of Gothic sculpture. Northern Gothic painters, too, had tried to reproduce these architectural settings, but they could not do so without flattening them out completely. The Italian painters of Duccio's generation, on the other hand, trained as they were in the Greek manner, had acquired enough of the devices of Hellenistic-Roman illusionism to let them render such a framework without draining it of its three-dimensional qualities.

GIOTTO. As we turn from Duccio to Giotto (1267?–1336/7), we meet an artist of far bolder and more dramatic temper. Ten to fifteen years younger than Duccio, Giotto was less influenced by the Greek manner from the start, despite his probable apprenticeship under Cimabue. As a Florentine, he fell heir to Cimabue's sense of monumental scale, which made him a wall painter by instinct, rather than a panel painter. Of his surviving murals, those in the Arena Chapel, Padua, done in 1305–6, are the best preserved as well as the most characteristic. A single glance at *The Lamentation* (Vol. Two, fig. 37) will convince us that we are faced with a truly revolutionary development. It is a work of intense dramatic power. The tragic mood is brought home to us by the formal rhythm of the design as much as by the gestures and expressions of the participants. The very low center of gravity and the hunched, bending figures communicate the somber quality of the scene and arouse our compassion even before we have grasped the specific meaning of the event depicted. With extraordinary boldness, Giotto sets off the frozen forms of the human mourners against the frantic movement of the weeping angels among the clouds, as if the figures on the ground were restrained by their collective duty to maintain the stability of the composition while the angels, small and weightless as birds, do not share this burden. The impact of the drama is heightened by the severely simple setting: the descending slope of the hill acts as a unifying element and at the same time directs our glance toward the focal point of the scene, the heads of Christ and the Virgin.

Giotto presents the scene in such a way that the beholder's eye-level falls within the lower half of the picture, and thus we can imagine ourselves standing on the same ground

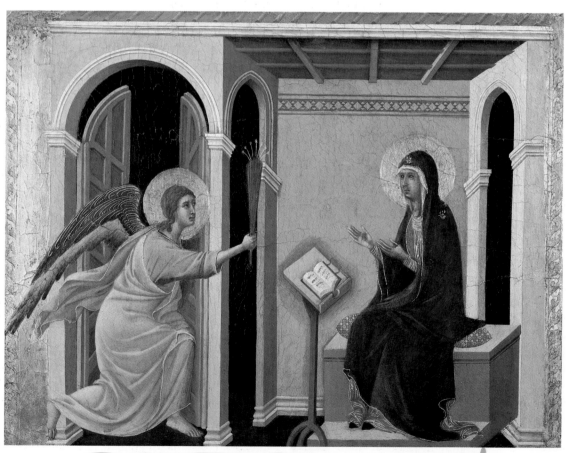

36. DUCCIO. *ANNUNCIATION OF THE DEATH OF THE VIRGIN*, from the *Maestà Altar*

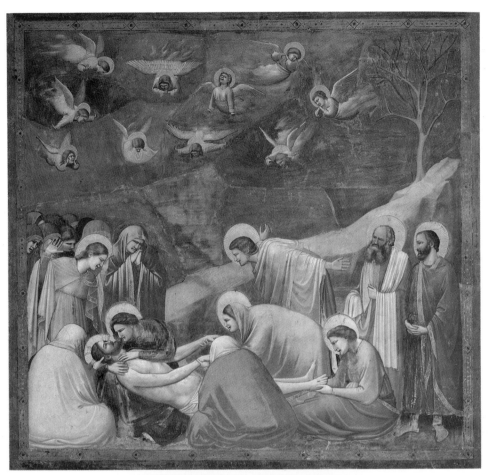

37. GIOTTO. *THE LAMENTATION*. 1305–6. Fresco.
Arena (Scrovegni) Chapel, Padua

plane as the painted figures, even though we see them from well below when standing in the chapel. He also endows his forms with a three-dimensional reality so forceful that the figures seem as solid and tangible as sculpture in the round. Yet Giotto's aim was not simply to transplant Gothic statuary into painting. By creating a radically new kind of picture space, he had also sharpened his awareness of the picture surface. His large, simple forms, the strong grouping of his figures, the limited depth of his "stage" all help to lend his scenes an inner coherence never achieved before. To his contemporaries, the tactile quality of Giotto's art must have seemed a near-miracle; it made them praise him as equal, or even superior, to the greatest of the ancient painters, because his forms looked so lifelike that they could be mistaken for reality itself. Equally significant are the stories linking Giotto with the claim that painting is superior to sculpture—not an idle boast, as it turned out, for Giotto does indeed mark the start of what might be called "the era of painting" in Western art.

The art of Giotto is so daringly original that its sources are far more difficult to trace than those of Duccio's style. Apart from his Florentine background as represented by the Greek manner of Cimabue, the young Giotto seems to have been familiar with the Neo-Byzantine painters of Rome; in that city, he probably also became acquainted with older monù-

ments—Early Christian and ancient Roman mural decoration. Classical sculpture, too, made an impression on him. More fundamental than any of these, however, was the influence of the Pisanos—Nicola, and especially Giovanni. They were the chief intermediaries through whom Giotto first came in contact with the world of Northern Gothic art. And the latter remains the most important of all the elements that entered into Giotto's style. Without the knowledge, direct or indirect, of Northern works such as the *Death of the Virgin* from Strasbourg Cathedral (see Vol. Two, fig. 31), he could never have achieved the emotional impact of his *Lamentation*.

THE LORENZETTI BROTHERS. There are few artists in the entire history of art who equal Giotto's stature as a radical innovator. He tended to dwarf the next generation of Florentine painters, which produced only followers rather than new leaders. Their contemporaries in Siena were more fortunate in this respect, since Duccio's art never had the same powerful impact. As a consequence, it was they, not the Florentines, who took the next decisive step in the development of Italian Gothic painting. The new closeness to everyday life depicted in the work of the brothers Pietro and Ambrogio Lorenzetti (both died 1348?) is coupled with Giotto's monumentality and Duccio's keen interest in problems of space.

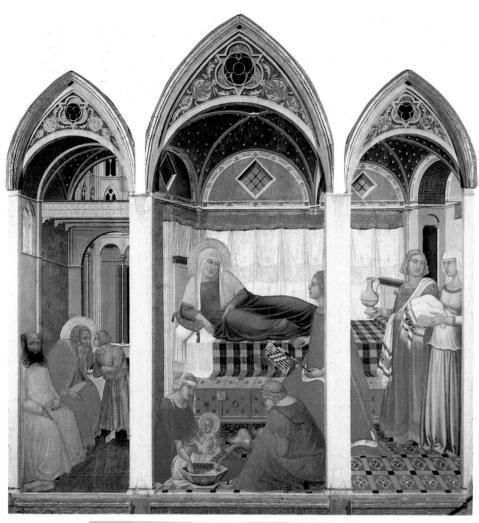

38. PIETRO LORENZETTI. *THE BIRTH OF THE VIRGIN*. 1342.
Tempera on panel, 6'1½" × 5'11½" (1.9 × 1.8 m). Museo dell'Opera del Duomo, Siena

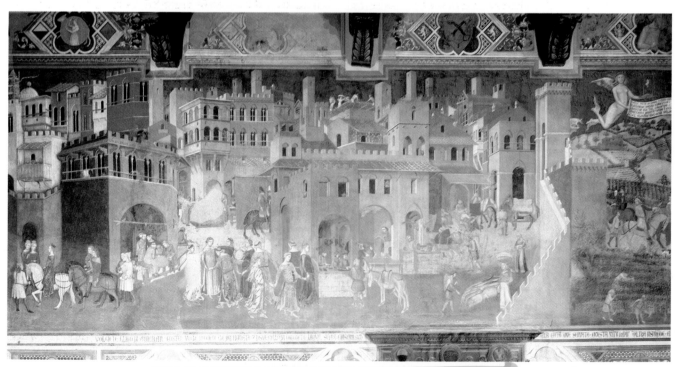

39. AMBROGIO LORENZETTI. *GOOD GOVERNMENT IN THE CITY*. 1338–40.
Fresco, width of entire wall 46' (14 m). Palazzo Pubblico, Siena

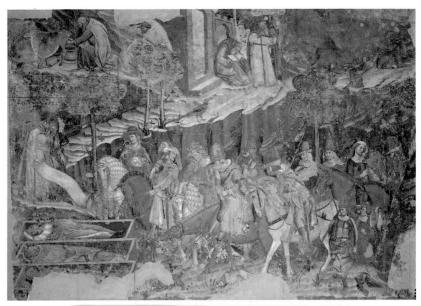

40. FRANCESCO TRAINI. *THE TRIUMPH OF DEATH* (detail).
c. 1325–50. Fresco. Camposanto, Pisa

The boldest spatial experiment is Pietro's triptych, *The Birth of the Virgin* (Vol. Two, fig. 38), where the painted architecture relates to the real architecture of the frame in such a way that the two are seen as a single unit. Moreover, the vaulted chamber in which the birth takes place occupies two panels—it continues unbroken behind the column that divides the center from the right wing. The left wing represents an anteroom that leads to a glimpse of a vast architectural space that suggests the interior of a Gothic church. What Pietro Lorenzetti achieves here is the outcome of Duccio's work three decades earlier, but only now does the picture surface assume the quality of a transparent window through which—not *on* which—we perceive the same kind of space we know from daily experience. Yet Duccio's work alone is not sufficient to explain Pietro's astonishing breakthrough; it became possible, rather, through a combination of the *architectural* picture space of Duccio and the *sculptural* picture space of Giotto.

The same procedure enabled Ambrogio Lorenzetti, in his frescoes of 1338–40 in the Siena city hall, to unfold before our eyes a comprehensive view of the entire town (Vol. Two, fig. 39). His mural forms part of an elaborate allegorical program depicting the contrast of good and bad government; hence the artist, in order to show the life of a well-ordered city-state, filled the streets and houses with teeming activity. The gay and busy crowd gives the architectural vista striking reality by introducing the human scale. On the right, the *Good Government in the Country* fresco provides a view of the Sienese countryside, fringed by mountains. It is a true landscape—the first since ancient Roman times—full of sweeping depth yet with an ingrained orderliness, a domesticated air. Here the presence of people is not accidental; they have taken full possession of nature, terracing the hillsides with vineyards and patterning the valleys with the geometry of fields and pastures.

THE BLACK DEATH. The first four decades of the fourteenth century in Florence and Siena had been a period of political stability and economic expansion as well as of great artistic achievement. In the 1340s both cities suffered a series of catastrophes, echoes of which were to be felt for many years: banks and merchants went bankrupt by the score, internal upheavals shook the government, farmers suffered repeated crop failures, and in 1348 an epidemic of bubonic plague, the Black Death, wiped out more than half the urban population. The popular reaction to these calamitous events was mixed. Many people regarded them as signs of divine wrath, warnings to a sinful humanity to forsake the pleasures of this earth; in such people the Black Death engendered a mood of otherworldly exaltation. In others, such as the gay company in Boccaccio's *Decameron*, the fear of sudden death merely intensified the desire to enjoy life while there was still time. These conflicting attitudes are reflected in a new pictorial theme, the Triumph of Death.

TRAINI. The most impressive version of this subject is an enormous fresco attributed to the Pisan master Francesco Traini (doc. c. 1321–1363). In a particularly dramatic detail (Vol. Two, fig. 40), the elegantly costumed men and women on horseback have suddenly come upon three decaying corpses in open coffins; even the animals seem terrified by the sight and smell of rotting flesh. Only the hermit, having renounced all earthly pleasures, calmly points out the lesson of the scene. But will the living accept the lesson, or will they, like the characters of Boccaccio, turn away from the shocking spectacle more determined than ever to pursue their hedonistic ways? The artist's own sympathies seem curiously divided; his style, far from being otherworldly, recalls the realism of Ambrogio Lorenzetti, although the forms are harsher and more expressive.

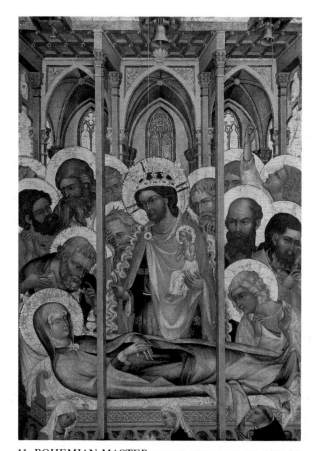

41. BOHEMIAN MASTER. *DEATH OF THE VIRGIN*. 1350–60.
Tempera on panel, 39⅜ × 28″ (100 × 71 cm).
Museum of Fine Arts, Boston.
William Francis Warden Fund: Seth K. Sweetser Fund,
The Henry C. and Martha B. Angell Coll.,
Juliana Cheney Edwards Collection, Gift of Martin Brimmer, and
Mrs. Frederick Frothingham: by exchange

Northern Gothic Painting

We are now in a position to turn to Gothic painting north of the Alps. What happened there during the latter half of the fourteenth century was determined largely by the influence of the great Italians, which was sometimes transmitted by Italian artists working on Northern soil. A major gateway of Italian influence was the city of Prague, which in 1347 became the residence of Emperor Charles IV and rapidly developed into an international cultural center second only to Paris. The *Death of the Virgin* (Vol. Two, fig. 41), by an unknown Bohemian master of about 1360, brings to mind the achievements of the great Sienese masters, although these were known to our artist only at second or third hand. The carefully articulated architectural interior betrays its descent from such works as Pietro Lorenzetti's *The Birth of the Virgin* (see Vol. Two, fig. 38), although it lacks the spaciousness of its Italian models. Italian, too, are the glowing richness of color, the vigorous modeling of the heads, and the overlapping of the figures, which reinforces the three-dimensional quality of the design but raises the awkward question of how to position the haloes (a problem faced by Italian artists as well). Still, the Bohemian master's picture is not a mere echo of Italian painting. The gestures and facial expressions convey an intensity of emotion that represents the finest heritage of Northern Gothic art. In this respect, our panel is far more akin to the *Death of the Virgin* at Strasbourg Cathedral (see Vol. Two, fig. 31) than to any Italian work.

THE INTERNATIONAL STYLE. As we approach the end of the fourteenth century, Italian influence becomes ever more important in Northern Gothic painting, until the two merge around the year 1400 to form a single dominant style throughout western Europe. This International Style was not confined to painting, but painters clearly played the main role in its development.

BROEDERLAM. Among the most important was Melchior Broederlam (fl. c. 1387–1409), a Fleming who worked for the court of the duke of Burgundy in Dijon. His shutter for an altar shrine (Vol. Two, fig. 42) which he did in 1394–99 is really two pictures within a single frame: the temple of the *Presentation* and the landscape of the *Flight into Egypt*

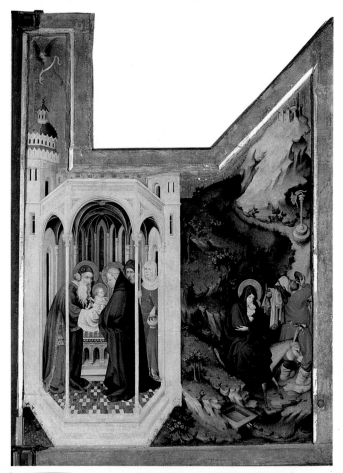

42. MELCHIOR BROEDERLAM. *PRESENTATION IN THE TEMPLE* and *FLIGHT INTO EGYPT*. 1394–99. Tempera on panel, 65¾ x 49¼″ (167 x 125 cm). Musée des Beaux-Arts, Dijon

stand abruptly side by side, even though the artist has made a half-hearted effort to persuade us that the landscape extends around the building. Compared to that of Pietro and Ambrogio Lorenzetti, Broederlam's picture space strikes us as naive in many ways—the architecture looks like a doll's house, and the details of the landscape are quite out of scale with the figures. Yet the panel conveys a strong feeling of depth. The reason for this is the subtlety of the modeling; the softly rounded shapes and the dark, velvety shadows create a sense of light and air that more than makes up for any shortcomings of scale or perspective. Our panel exemplifies a chief characteristic of the International Style: its "realism of particulars." We find it in the carefully rendered foliage and flowers, in the delightful donkey (obviously drawn from life), and in the rustic figure of St. Joseph, who looks and behaves like a simple peasant and thus helps to emphasize the delicate, aristocratic beauty of the Virgin. It is this painstaking concentration on detail that gives Broederlam's work the flavor of an enlarged miniature rather than of a large-scale painting, even though the panel is more than five feet tall.

THE LIMBOURG BROTHERS. That book illumination remained the leading form of painting in Northern Europe at the time of the International Style, despite the growing importance of panel painting, is well attested by the miniatures of the *Très Riches Heures du Duc de Berry*. Produced for the brother of the king of France, a man of far from admirable character but the most lavish art patron of his day, this luxurious book of hours represents the most advanced phase of the International Style. The artists were Pol de Limbourg and his two brothers, a group of Flemings who, like Broederlam, had settled in France. They must have visited Italy as well, for their work includes a great number of motifs and whole compositions borrowed from the great masters of Tuscany. The most remarkable pages of the *Très Riches Heures* are those of the calendar, with their elaborate depiction of human activity and nature throughout the months of the year. Such cycles, originally consisting of twelve single figures each performing an appropriate seasonal activity, had long been an established tradition in medieval art. The Limbourg brothers, however, integrated human life *in* nature, by using a continuous series of panoramas. Thus the *February* miniature (Vol. Two, fig. 43), the earliest snow landscape in the history of Western art, gives an enchantingly lyrical account of village life in the dead of winter, with the sheep huddled together in their fold, birds hungrily scratching in the barnyard, and a maid blowing on her frostbitten hands as she hurries to join her companions in the warm cottage (the front door has been omitted for our benefit), while in the middle distance we see a villager cutting branches for firewood and another driving his laden donkey toward the houses among the hills. Here the promise of the Broederlam panel has been fulfilled, as it were: landscape and architectural interiors and exteriors are harmoniously united in deep, atmospheric space. Even such intangible, evanescent things as the frozen breath of the maid, the smoke curling from the chimney, and the clouds in the sky have become "paintable."

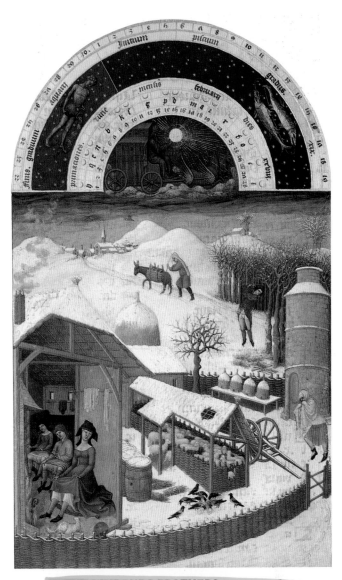

43. THE LIMBOURG BROTHERS. *FEBRUARY*, from *Les Très Riches Heures du Duc de Berry*. 1413–16. Musée Condé, Chantilly, France

GENTILE DA FABRIANO. During the later fourteenth century, it was in northern Italy, particularly hospitable to artistic influences from across the Alps, that the International Style found its greatest Italian representative in Gentile da Fabriano (c.1370–1427). He worked mainly in Venice before moving to Florence, where he painted his masterpiece, *The Adoration of the Magi* (Vol. Two, fig. 44). In his altarpiece, the costumes of the three Magi and their train are as colorful, the draperies as ample, and softly rounded, as in the North. The Holy Family on the left seems in danger of being overwhelmed by the gay and festive pageant pouring upon it from the hills in the distance. We admire the marvelously well-observed animals, which include not only the familiar ones but also hunting leopards, camels, and monkeys. (Such creatures were eagerly collected by the princes of the period, many of whom kept private zoos.) The Oriental background of the Magi is further emphasized by the Mongolian facial

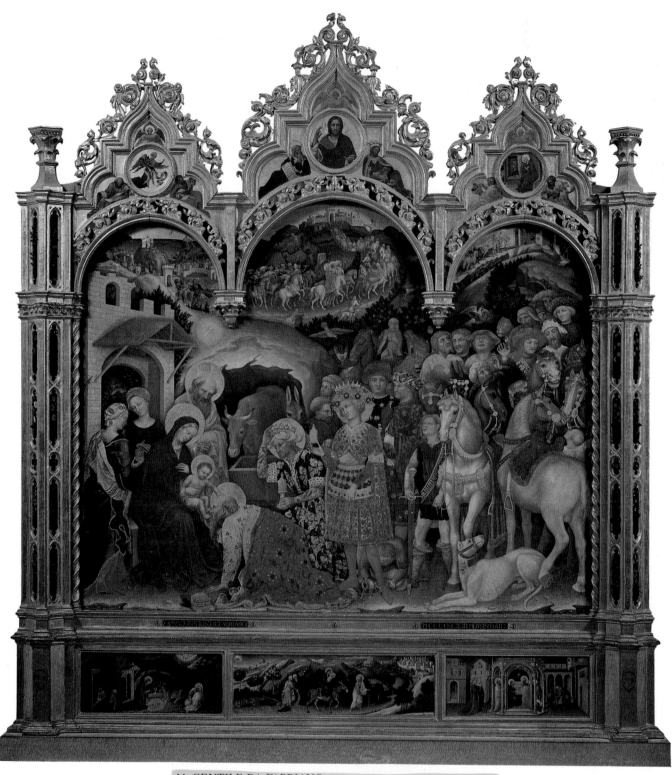

44. GENTILE DA FABRIANO. *THE ADORATION OF THE MAGI.* 1423.
Oil on panel, 9′10⅛″ × 9′3″ (3 × 2.8 m).
Galleria degli Uffizi, Florence

cast of some of their companions. It is not these exotic touches, however, that mark our picture as the work of an Italian master but something else, a greater sense of weight and physical substance than could be found in the work of the Northern representatives of the International Style. Gentile, despite his love of fine detail, is obviously a painter used to working on a monumental scale rather than as a manuscript illuminator.

PART THREE

THE RENAISSANCE, MANNERISM, AND THE BAROQUE

In discussing the transition from classical antiquity to the Middle Ages, we were able to point to a great crisis—the rise of Islam—marking the separation between the two eras. No comparable event sets off the Middle Ages from the Renaissance. The fifteenth and sixteenth centuries, to be sure, witnessed far-reaching developments: the fall of Constantinople and the Turkish conquest of southeastern Europe; the journeys of exploration that led to the founding of overseas empires in the New World, in Africa and Asia, with the subsequent rivalry of Spain and England as the foremost colonial powers; the deep spiritual crisis of Reformation and Counter Reformation.

But none of these events, however vast their effects, can be said to have produced the new era. By the time they happened, the Renaissance was well under way. Even if we disregard the minority of scholars who would deny the existence of the animal altogether, we are left with an extraordinary diversity of views on the Renaissance. Perhaps the only essential point on which most experts agree is that the Renaissance had begun when people realized they were no longer living in the Middle Ages.

This statement is not as simple-minded as it sounds; it brings out the undeniable fact that the Renaissance was the first period in history to be aware of its own existence and to coin a label for itself. Medieval people did not think they belonged to an age distinct from classical antiquity; the past, to them, consisted simply of "B.C." and "A.D.," the era "under the Law" (that is, of the Old Testament) and the era "of Grace" (that is, after the birth of Christ). From their point of view, then, history was made in Heaven rather than on earth. The Renaissance, by contrast, divided the past not according to the divine plan of salvation, but on the basis of human achievements. It saw classical antiquity as the era when civilization had reached the peak of its creative powers, an era brought to a sudden end by the barbarian invasions that destroyed the Roman Empire. During the thousand-year interval of "darkness" that followed, little was accomplished, but now, at last, this "time in-between" or "Middle Age" had been superseded by a revival of all those arts and sciences that flourished in classical antiquity. The present, the "New Age," could thus be fittingly labeled a "rebirth"— *rinascita* in Italian (from the Latin *renascere,* to be reborn), *renaissance* in French and, by adoption, in English.

The origin of this revolutionary view of history can be traced back to the 1330s in the writings of the Italian poet Francesco Petrarca, the first of the great individuals who made the Renaissance. Petrarch, as we call him, thought of the new era mainly as a "revival of the classics," limited to the restoration of Latin and Greek to their former purity and the return to the original texts of ancient authors. During the next two centuries, this concept of the rebirth of antiquity grew to embrace almost the entire range of cultural endeavor, including the visual arts. The latter, in fact, came to play a particularly important part in shaping the Renaissance, for reasons that we shall have to explore later.

That the new historic orientation—to which, let us remember, we owe our concepts of the Renaissance, the Middle Ages, and classical antiquity—should have had its start in the mind of one man is itself a telling comment on the new era. Individualism—a new self-awareness and self-assurance—enabled him to proclaim, against all established authority, his own conviction that the "age of faith" was actually an era of darkness, while the "benighted pagans" of antiquity really represented the most enlightened stage of history. Such readiness to question traditional beliefs and practices was to become profoundly characteristic of the Renaissance as a whole. Humanism, to Petrarch, meant a belief in the importance of what we still call "the humanities" or "humane letters" (rather than divine letters, or the study of Scripture); that is, the pursuit of learning in languages, literature, history, and philosophy for its own end, in a secular rather than a religious framework.

We must not assume, however, that Petrarch and his successors wanted to revive classical antiquity lock, stock, and barrel. By interposing the concept of "a thousand years of darkness" between themselves and the ancients, they acknowledged—unlike the medieval classicists—that the Graeco-Roman world was irretrievably dead. Its glories could be revived only in the mind, by nostalgic and admiring contemplation across the barrier of the "dark ages," by rediscovering the full greatness of ancient achievements in art and thought, and by endeavoring to compete with these achievements on an ideal plane.

The aim of the Renaissance was not to duplicate the works of antiquity but to equal and, if possible, to surpass them. In practice, this meant that the authority granted to the ancient models was far from unlimited. Writers strove to express themselves with Ciceronian eloquence and precision, but not necessarily in Latin. Architects continued to build the churches demanded by Christian ritual, not to duplicate pagan temples; but their churches were designed *all'antica,* "in the manner of the ancients," using an architectural vocabulary based on the study of classical structures. The humanists, however great their enthusiasm for classical philosophy, did not become neo-pagans but went to great lengths trying to reconcile the heritage of the ancient thinkers with Christianity.

The people of the Renaissance, then, found themselves in the position of the legendary sorcerer's apprentice who set out to emulate his master's achievements and in the process released far greater energies than he had bargained for. But since their master was dead, rather than merely absent, they had to cope with these unfamiliar powers as best they could, until they became masters in their own right. This process of forced growth was replete with crises and tensions. The Renaissance must have been an uncomfortable, though intensely exciting, time to live in. Yet these very tensions—or so it appears in restrospect—called forth an outpouring of creative energy such as the world had never experienced. It is a fundamental paradox that the desire to return to the classics, based on a rejection of the Middle Ages, brought to the new era not the rebirth of antiquity but the birth of modern civilization.

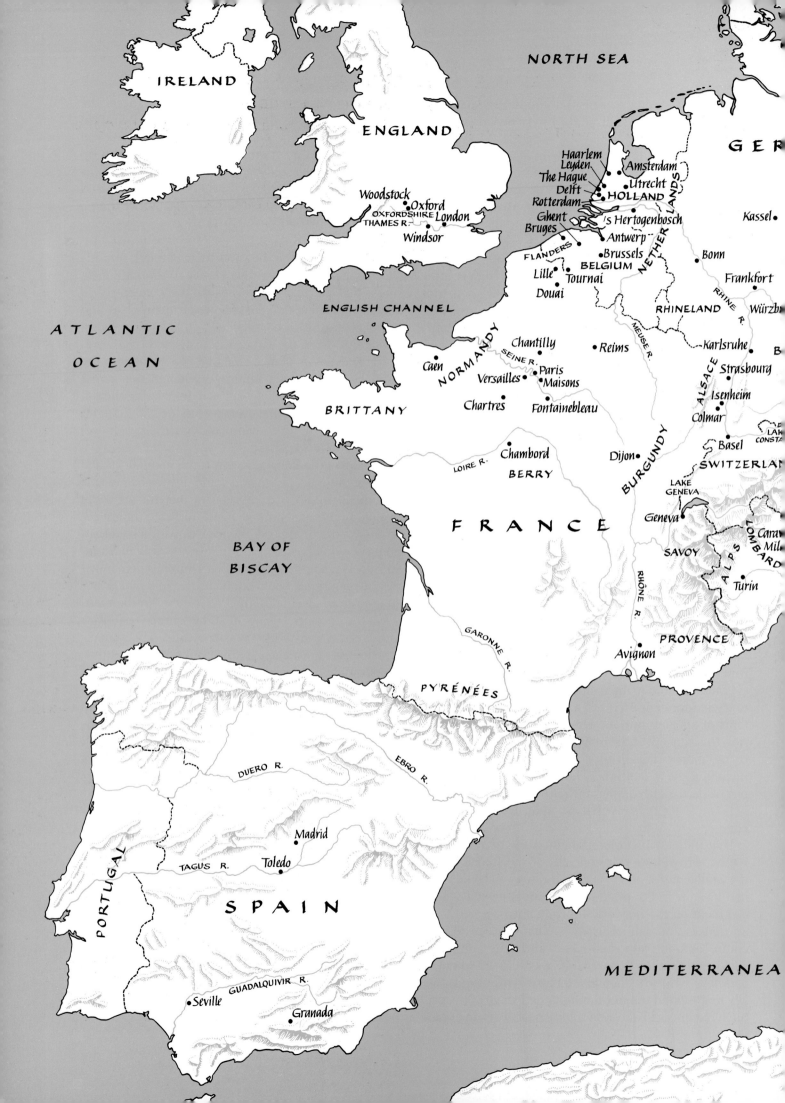

IRELAND

ENGLAND

NORTH SEA

GER

Haarlem
Leyden
The Hague
Delft
Rotterdam
Ghent
Bruges

Amsterdam
Utrecht
HOLLAND

's Hertogenbosch

Kassel

Woodstock
OXFORDSHIRE
THAMES R.
Windsor

Oxford
London

FLANDERS

Antwerp

Brussels

BELGIUM

Lille
Douai

Tournai

Bonn

Frankfort

NETHERLANDS

RHINELAND

RHINE R.

Würzb

ENGLISH CHANNEL

ATLANTIC

OCEAN

Caen

NORMANDY

SEINE R.

Chantilly

Versailles

Chartres

Paris
Maisons

Fontainebleau

Reims

MEUSE R.

Karlsruhe

ALSACE

Strasbourg

Isenheim

Colmar

B

BRITTANY

LAK
CONSTA

Basel

SWITZERLAN

Dijon

BURGUNDY

LAKE
GENEVA

Loire R.

Chambord

BERRY

FRANCE

Geneva

SAVOY

Cara
Mil
LOMBARD

BAY OF
BISCAY

RHÔNE R.

ALPS

Turin

PROVENCE

GARONNE R.

Avignon

PYRÉNÉES

EBRO R.

DUERO R.

Madrid

PORTUGAL

TAGUS R.

Toledo

SPAIN

MEDITERRANEA

Seville

GUADALQUIVIR R.

Granada

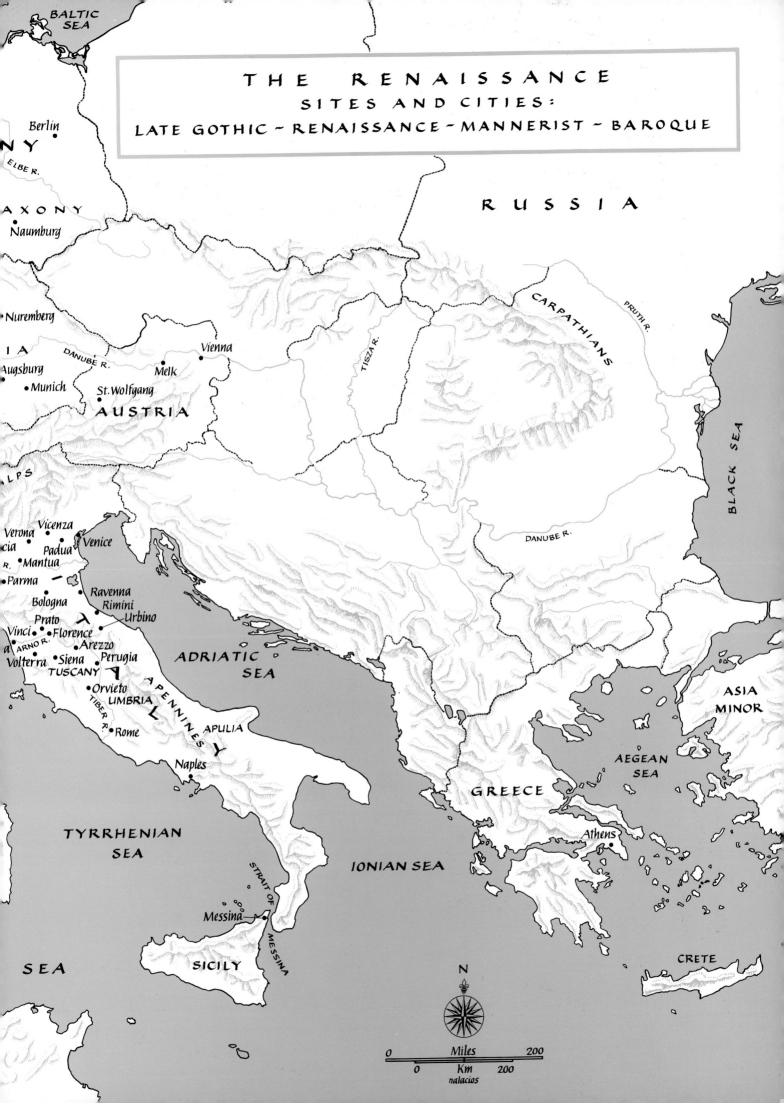

THE RENAISSANCE
SITES AND CITIES:
LATE GOTHIC ~ RENAISSANCE ~ MANNERIST ~ BAROQUE

BALTIC
SEA

Berlin

NY

ELBE R.

AXONY

Naumburg

RUSSIA

CARPATHIANS

PRUTH R.

Nuremberg

IA

Augsburg

DANUBE R.

Vienna

TISZA R.

Munich

Melk

St. Wolfgang

AUSTRIA

BLACK
SEA

LPS

DANUBE R.

Verona   Vicenza

cia   Venice

Padua

R.   Mantua

Parma

Ravenna

Bologna   Rimini

Prato   Urbino

Vinci   Florence

ARNO R.   Arezzo

a

Volterra   Siena   Perugia

TUSCANY

Orvieto

UMBRIA

TIBER R.

Rome

ADRIATIC
SEA

APENNINES

APULIA

ASIA
MINOR

AEGEAN
SEA

Naples

GREECE

TYRRHENIAN
SEA

IONIAN SEA

Athens

STRAIT OF

Messina

MESSINA

SEA

SICILY

CRETE

N

0   Miles   200

0   Km   200

nalacios

CHAPTER ONE

"LATE GOTHIC" PAINTING, SCULPTURE, AND THE GRAPHIC ARTS

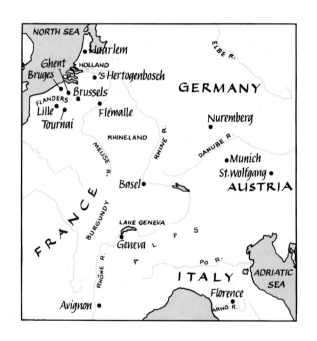

RENAISSANCE VERSUS "LATE GOTHIC" PAINTING

As we narrow our focus from the Renaissance as a whole to the Renaissance in the fine arts, we are faced with some questions that are still under debate: When did it start? Did it, like Gothic art, originate in a specific center, or in several places at the same time? Should we think of it as one new, coherent style, or as a new attitude that might be embodied in more than one style? "Renaissance-consciousness," we know, was an Italian idea, and there can be no doubt that Italy played the leading role in the development of Renaissance art, at least until the early sixteenth century.

When did this development get under way? So far as architecture and sculpture are concerned, modern scholarship agrees with the traditional view, first expressed more than five hundred years ago, that the Renaissance began soon after 1400. For painting, however, an even older tradition claims that the new era began with Giotto, who (as Boccaccio wrote about 1350) "restored to light this art which had been buried for many centuries." We cannot disregard such testimony, yet we hesitate to accept it at face value, for we must then assume that the Renaissance in painting dawned about 1300, a full generation before Petrarch. Nor did Giotto himself reject the past as an age of darkness; after all, the two chief sources of his own style were the Byzantine tradition and the influence of Northern Gothic. The artistic revolution he created from these elements does not necessarily place him in a new era, since revolutionary changes had occurred in medieval art before. It is not fair to credit this revolution to him alone, disregarding Duccio and the other great Sienese masters. Petrarch was well aware of the achievements of all these men—he wrote admiringly of both Giotto and Simone Martini—but he never claimed that they had restored to light what had been buried during the centuries of darkness.

BOCCACCIO. How, then, do we account for Boccaccio's statement about Giotto? We must understand that Boccaccio (1313–1375), an ardent disciple of Petrarch, was chiefly concerned with advancing humanism in literature. In his defense of the status of poetry, he found it useful to draw analogies with painting—had not the ancients themselves proclaimed that the two arts were alike, in Horace's famous dictum, *ut pictura poesis*?—and to cast Giotto in the role of "the Petrarch of painting," taking advantage of his already legendary fame. Boccaccio's view of Giotto as a Renaissance artist is a bit of intellectual strategy, rather than a trustworthy reflection of Giotto's own attitude. Nevertheless, what he has to say interests us because he was the first to apply Petrarch's concept of "revival after the dark ages" to one of the visual arts (even though he did it somewhat prematurely), and for his way of describing Giotto's achievement. It was he who claimed that Giotto depicted every aspect of nature so truthfully that people often mistook his paintings for reality itself. Here he implies that the revival of antiquity means for painters an uncompromising realism. And this, as we shall see, was to become a persistent theme in Renaissance thought, justifying the imitation of nature as part of the great movement "back to the classics" and tending to minimize the possible conflict between these two aims.

Boccaccio, of course, was not in a position to know how many aspects of reality Giotto and his contemporaries had failed to investigate. These aspects, we recall, were explored by the painters of the International Style, although in somewhat tentative fashion.

Netherlandish Painting

To advance beyond Gothic realism required a second revolution, which began simultaneously and independently in Florence and in the Netherlands about 1420. We have to think, therefore, of two events, both linked by a common aim—the conquest of the visible world—yet sharply separated in almost every other respect. The Florentine, or Southern, revolution was the more systematic and, in the long run, the more fundamental, since it included architecture and sculpture as well as painting; we call it the Early Renaissance. The same term is not generally applied to the new style that emerged in the North, in Flanders. We have, in fact, no satisfactory name to designate the Northern focus of the revolution, for art historians are still of two minds about its scope and significance in relation to the Renaissance movement as a whole.

"LATE GOTHIC." The customary label, "Late Gothic" (which we shall use, for the sake of convenience, with quotation marks to indicate its doubtful status), hardly does justice to the special character of Northern fifteenth-century painting. But it has some justification. It indicates, for instance, that the creators of the new style, unlike their Italian contemporaries, did not reject the International Style; rather, they took it as their point of departure, so that the break with the past was less abrupt in the North than in the South. "Late Gothic" also reminds us that fifteenth-century architecture outside Italy remained firmly rooted in the Gothic tradition.

Whatever we choose to call the style of Northern painters of this time, their artistic environment was clearly "Late Gothic" (see pages 370 and 402). How could they create a genuinely post-medieval style in such a setting, one wonders; would it not be more reasonable to regard their work, despite its great importance, as the final phase of Gothic painting? If we treat them here as the Northern counterpart of the Early Renaissance, we do so for several reasons. The great Flemish masters whose work we are about to examine had an impact that went far beyond their own region. In Italy they were as admired as the leading Italian artists of the period, and their intense realism had a conspicuous influence on Early Renaissance painting. (The Italians, we will recall, had associated the exact imitation of nature in painting with a "return to the classics.") Italian Renaissance art, in contrast, made very little impression north of the Alps during the fifteenth century.

To Italian eyes, then, "Late Gothic" painting appeared definitely post-medieval. Moreover, the situation of the Flemish painters had a close parallel in the field of music. After about 1420, the Netherlands produced a school of composers so revolutionary as to dominate the development of

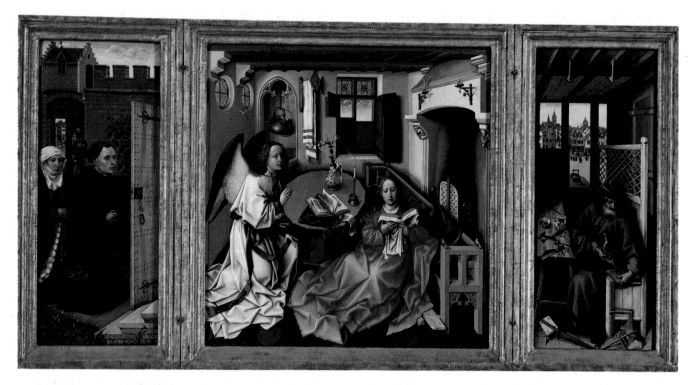

547. THE MASTER OF FLÉMALLE (ROBERT CAMPIN?). *MERODE ALTARPIECE.* c. 1425–30.
Oil on wood panels, center 25³⁄₁₆×24⅞″ (64.3×62.9 cm); each wing c. 25⅜×10⅞″ (64.5×27.4 cm).
The Metropolitan Museum of Art, New York. The Cloisters Collection, 1956

music throughout Europe for the next hundred years. How much the new style of these men was appreciated can be gathered from a contemporary source which states that "nothing worth listening to had been composed before their time." This remark, with its sweeping rejection of the "musical dark ages," links the attitude of the Flemish musicians with Italian "Renaissance-consciousness" (except for the absence of any reference to the revival of antiquity). We have no similar testimony concerning the new style of the Flemish painters, but from what we know of the impact of their work it seems likely that people felt "nothing worth looking at had been painted before their time."

THE MASTER OF FLÉMALLE. The first phase—and perhaps the decisive one—of the pictorial revolution in Flanders is represented by an artist whose name we do not know for certain. We call him the Master of Flémalle (after the fragments of a large altar from Flémalle), although he was probably identical with Robert Campin, the foremost painter of Tournai, whose career we can trace in documents from 1406 to his death in 1444. Among his finest works is the *Merode Altarpiece* (fig. 547), which he must have done soon after 1425. Comparing it with its nearest relatives, the Franco-Flemish pictures of the International Style (figs. 541–544), we see that it belongs within that tradition; yet we also recognize in it a new pictorial experience.

Here, for the first time, we have the sensation of actually looking *through* the surface of the panel into a spatial world that has all the essential qualities of everyday reality: unlimited depth, stability, continuity, and completeness. The painters of the International Style, even at their most adventurous,

had never aimed at such consistency; their commitment to reality was far from absolute. The pictures they created have the enchanting quality of fairy tales where the scale and relationship of things can be shifted at will, where fact and fancy mingle without conflict. The Master of Flémalle, in contrast, has undertaken to tell the truth, the whole truth, and nothing but the truth. He does not yet do it with ease—his objects, overly foreshortened, tend to jostle each other in space. With a determination that seems almost obsessive, he endows every last detail with its maximum concreteness by defining every aspect: its individual shape and size; its color, material, surface textures; its degree of rigidity; and its way of responding to illumination. The artist even distinguishes between the diffused light producing soft shadows and delicate gradations of brightness and the direct light entering through the two round windows; the latter accounts for the twin shadows sharply outlined in the upper part of the center panel and for the twin reflections on the brass vessel and candlestick.

The *Merode Altarpiece*, in short, transports us with shocking abruptness from the aristocratic world of the International Style to the household of a Flemish burgher. The Master of Flémalle, whether or not we believe him to have been Robert Campin, was not a court painter, but a townsman catering to the tastes of such well-to-do fellow citizens as the two donors piously kneeling outside the Virgin's chamber. Characteristically, this is the earliest Annunciation in panel painting that occurs in a fully equipped domestic interior (for contrast, see figs. 524 and 538), as well as the first to honor Joseph, the humble carpenter, by showing him at work next door.

This bold departure from tradition forced upon our artist a problem no one had faced before: how to transfer supernatural events from symbolic settings to an everyday environment, without making them look either trivial or incongruous. He has met this challenge by the method known as "disguised symbolism," which means that almost any detail within the picture, however casual, may carry a symbolic message. Thus the rosebush, and the violets and daisies in the left wing, and the lilies in the center panel, are flowers associated with the Virgin, the roses denoting her charity, the violets her humility, and the lilies her chastity; the shiny water basin and the towel on its rack are not merely ordinary household equipment but further tributes to Mary as the "vessel most clean" and the "well of living waters." Perhaps the most intriguing symbol of this sort is the candle next to the vase of lilies. It was extinguished only moments before, as we can tell from the glowing wick and the curl of smoke. But why, in broad daylight, had it been lit, and what made the flame go out? Has the divine radiance of the Lord's presence overcome the material light? Or did the flame of the candle itself represent the divine light, now extinguished to show that God has become man, that in Christ "the Word was made flesh"?

Clearly, the entire wealth of medieval symbolism survives in our picture, but it is so completely immersed in the world of everyday appearances that we are often left to doubt whether a given detail demands symbolic interpretation. Observers had long wondered, for instance, about the little box-like object on Joseph's workbench (and a similar one on the ledge outside the open window), until one scholar proposed to identify them as mousetraps intended to convey a specific theological message: according to St. Augustine, God had to appear on earth in human form so as to fool Satan—"the Cross of the Lord was the devil's mousetrap."

Since iconographic explanations of this sort require much scholarly ingenuity, we tend to think of the *Merode Altarpiece* and similar pictures as embodying a special kind of puzzle. And so they often do, to the modern beholder, although they can be enjoyed apart from knowing all their symbolic content. But what about the patrons for whom these works were painted? Did they immediately grasp the meaning of every detail? They would have had no difficulty with such well-established symbols in our picture as the flowers. Let us grant, too, that they probably understood the significance of the water basin. The message of the extinguished candle and the mousetrap could not have been common knowledge even among the well-educated, however; for these two symbols— and from their incongruity we can hardly question that they *are* symbols—make their earliest appearance in the *Merode Altarpiece*. They must be unusual ones, for St. Joseph with the mousetrap has been found in only one other picture, and the freshly extinguished candle does not recur elsewhere, so far as we know. Apparently, then, the Master of Flémalle introduced these symbols into the visual arts, yet hardly any artists adopted them despite his vast influence. But if the candle and the mousetrap were difficult to understand even in the fifteenth century, why are they in our picture at all? Did the patron (who may have been exceptionally erudite) tell the artist to put them in? Possibly, if this were the only

case of its kind. Since, however, there are countless instances of equally subtle or obscure symbolism in "Late Gothic" painting, it seems more probable that the initiative came from the artists, rather than from their various patrons.

We have reason to believe, therefore, that the Master of Flémalle was either a man of unusual learning himself, or had contact with the theologians and other scholars who could supply him with the references that suggested the symbolic meanings of things such as the extinguished candle and the mousetrap. In other words, our artist did not merely continue the symbolic tradition of medieval art within the framework of the new realistic style; he expanded and enriched it by his own efforts. But why, we wonder, did he pursue simultaneously what we are accustomed to regard as two opposite goals, realism and symbolism? To him, apparently, the two were interdependent, rather than in conflict. We might say that he needed a growing symbolic repertory because it encouraged him to explore features of the visible world never represented before (such as a candle immediately after it has been blown out, or the interior of a carpenter's shop, needed as the setting for the mousetraps). For him to paint everyday reality, he had to "sanctify" it with a maximum of spiritual significance.

This deeply reverential attitude toward the physical universe as a mirror of divine truths helps us to understand why in the Merode panels the smallest and least conspicuous details are rendered with the same concentrated attention as the sacred figures; potentially at least, everything is a symbol and thus merits an equally exacting scrutiny. The disguised symbolism of the Master of Flémalle and his successors was not an external device grafted onto the new realistic style, but ingrained in the creative process. Their Italian contemporaries must have sensed this, for they praised both the miraculous realism and the "piety" of the Flemish masters.

If we compare our illustration of the *Merode* Annunciation with those of earlier panel paintings (figs. 530, 540, 541, and 545), we see vividly that, all other differences aside, its distinctive tonality makes the Master of Flémalle's picture stand out among the rest. The jewellike brightness of the older works, their patterns of brilliant hues and lavish use of gold, have given way to a color scheme far less decorative but much more flexible and differentiated. The subdued tints— muted greens, bluish or brownish grays—show a new subtlety, and the scale of intermediate shades is smoother and has a wider range. All these effects are essential to the realistic style of the Master of Flémalle; they were made possible by the use of oil, the medium he was among the first to exploit.

TEMPERA AND OIL TECHNIQUES. The basic technique of medieval panel painting had been tempera, in which the finely ground pigments were mixed ("tempered") with diluted egg yolk. It produced a thin, tough, quick-drying coat admirably suited to the medieval taste for high-keyed, flat color surfaces. However, in tempera the different tones on the panel cannot be smoothly blended, and the continuous progression of values necessary for three-dimensional effects was difficult to achieve; also, the darks tended to look muddy and undifferentiated. For the Master of Flémalle these were serious drawbacks, which he overcame by substituting oil for the water-and-egg-yolk mixture. In a purely material sense oil was not unfamiliar to medieval artists, but it had been used only for special purposes, such as the coating of stone surfaces or painting on metal. It was the Master of Flémalle and his contemporaries who discovered its artistic possibilities. Oil, a viscous, slow-drying medium, could produce a vast variety of effects, from thin, translucent films (called "glazes") to the thickest impasto (that is, a thick layer of creamy, heavy-bodied paint); the tones could also yield a continuous scale of hues, including rich, velvety dark shades previously unknown. The medium offers a unique advantage over egg tempera, encaustic, and fresco: oils give the artist the unprecedented ability to change his mind almost at will. Without oil, the Flemish masters' conquest of visible reality would have been much more limited. Thus, from the technical point of view, too, they deserve to be called the "fathers of modern painting," for oil has been the painter's basic medium ever since.

JAN AND HUBERT VAN EYCK. Needless to say, the full range of effects made possible by oil was not discovered all at once, nor by any one man. The Master of Flémalle contributed less than Jan van Eyck, a somewhat younger and very much more famous artist, who was long credited with the actual "invention" of oil painting. About Jan's life and career we know a good deal; born about 1390, he worked in Holland from 1422 to 1424, in Lille from 1425 to 1429, and thereafter in Bruges, where he died in 1441. He was both a townsman and a court painter, highly esteemed by Duke Philip the Good of Burgundy, who occasionally sent him on confidential diplomatic errands. After 1432, we can follow Jan's career through a number of signed and dated pictures. The inscription on the frame of the great *Ghent Altarpiece* (figs. 549–51) tells us that he completed it in that year, after it had been begun by his older brother, Hubert, who had died in 1426.

Jan's earlier development, however, remains disputed; there are several "Eyckian" works, obviously older than the *Ghent Altarpiece*, that may have been painted by either of the two brothers. The most fascinating of these is a pair of panels showing the Crucifixion and the Last Judgment (fig. 548). Scholars agree that their date is between 1420 and 1425, whichever brother, Jan or Hubert, was the author.

The style of the two panels has many qualities in common with that of the *Merode Altarpiece*—the all-embracing devotion to the visible world, the unlimited depth of space, the angular drapery folds, less graceful but far more realistic than the unbroken loops of the International Style. At the same time, the individual forms are not starkly tangible, like those characteristic of the Master of Flémalle, and seem less isolated, less "sculptural"; the sweeping sense of space is the result not so much of violent foreshortening as of subtle changes of light and color. If we inspect the *Crucifixion* panel slowly, from the foreground figures to the far-off city of Jerusalem and the snow-capped peaks beyond, we see a gradual decrease in the intensity of local colors and in the contrast of light and dark. Everything tends toward a uniform tint of light bluish gray, so that the farthest mountain range merges imperceptibly with the color of the sky.

This optical phenomenon, which the Van Eycks were the first to utilize fully and systematically (the Limbourg brothers had already been aware of it, as is seen in fig. 542), is known as "atmospheric perspective," since it results from the fact that the atmosphere is never wholly transparent. Even on the clearest day, the air between us and the things we are looking at acts as a hazy screen that interferes with our ability to see distant shapes clearly; as we approach the limit of visibility, it swallows them altogether. Atmospheric perspective is more fundamental to our perception of deep space than linear perspective, which records the diminution in the apparent size of objects as their distance from the observer increases. It is effective not only in faraway vistas; in our *Crucifixion* panel, even the foreground seems enveloped in a delicate haze that softens contours, shadows, and colors, and thus the entire scene has a continuity and harmony quite beyond the pictorial range of the Master of Flémalle. How did the Van Eycks accomplish this effect? Their exact technical procedure is difficult to reconstruct, but there can be no question that they used the oil medium with extraordinary refinement. By alternating opaque and translucent layers of pigment, they were able to impart to their pictures a soft, glowing radiance of tone that has never been equaled, probably because it depends fully as much on their individual sensibilities as it does on their skillful craftsmanship.

Viewed as a whole, the *Crucifixion* seems singularly devoid of drama, as if the scene had been gently becalmed by some magic spell. Only when we concentrate on the details do we become aware of the violent emotions in the faces of the crowd beneath the cross (see page 427), and the restrained but profoundly touching grief of the Virgin Mary and her companions in the foreground. In the *Last Judgment* panel, this dual aspect of the Eyckian style takes the form of two extremes: above the horizon, all is order, symmetry, and calm, while below it—on earth and in the subterranean realm of Satan—the opposite condition prevails. The two states thus correspond to Heaven and Hell, contemplative bliss as against physical and emotional turbulence. The lower half, clearly, was the greater challenge to the artist's imaginative powers. The dead rising from their graves with frantic gestures of fear and hope, the damned being torn apart by devilish monsters more frightful than any we have seen before, all have the awesome reality of a nightmare, but a nightmare "observed" with the same infinite care as the natural world of the *Crucifixion* panel.

The *Ghent Altarpiece* (figs. 549–51), the greatest monument of early Flemish painting, presents problems so complex that our discussion must be limited to bare essentials. We have already mentioned the inscription informing us that the work, begun by Hubert, was completed by Jan in 1432. Since Hubert died in 1426, the altarpiece was presumably made in the seven-year span between 1425 and 1432. We may expect it, therefore, to introduce to us the next phase of the new style, following that of the pictures we have discussed so far. Although its basic form is a triptych—a central body with two hinged wings—each of the three units consists of four separate panels, and since, in addition, the wings are painted on both sides, the altarpiece has a total of twenty component parts of assorted shapes and sizes. The ensemble

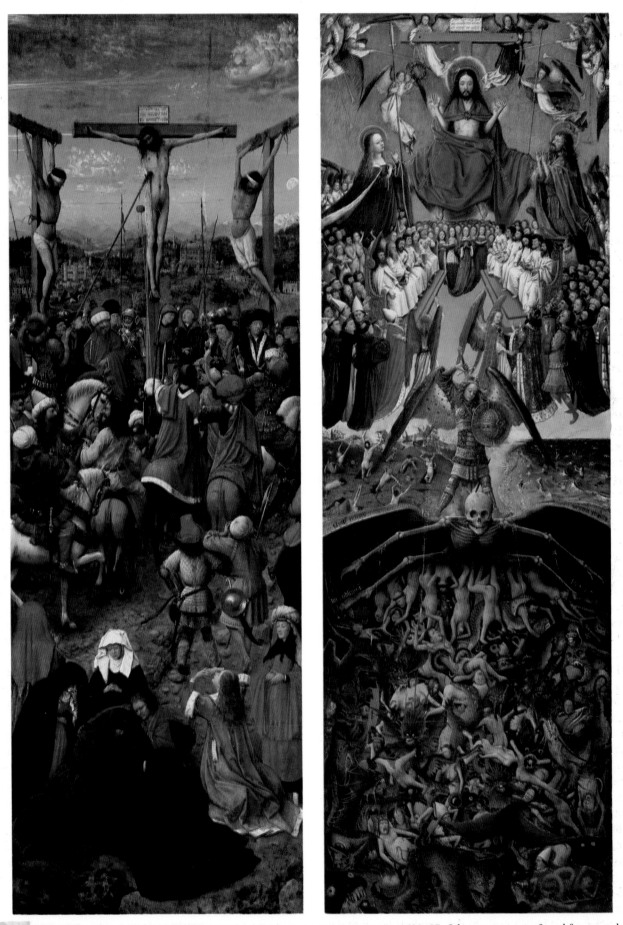

548. HUBERT and/or JAN VAN EYCK. *THE CRUCIFIXION; THE LAST JUDGMENT.* c. 1420–25. Oil on canvas, transferred from panel; each panel 22¼×7¾″ (56.5×19.4 cm). The Metropolitan Museum of Art, New York. Fletcher Fund, 1933

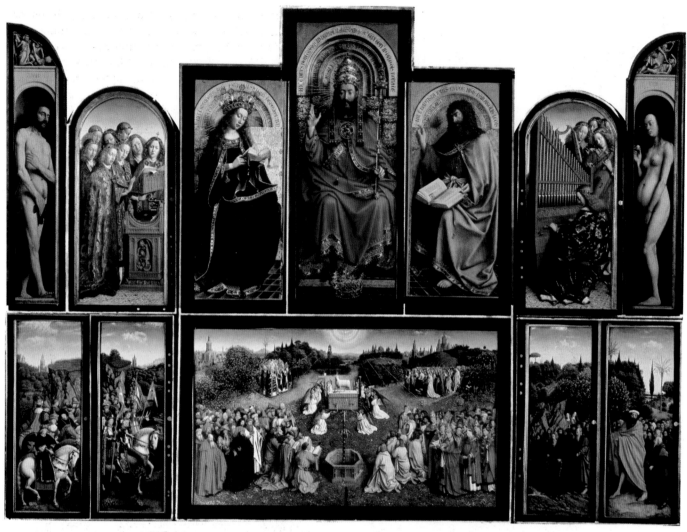

549. HUBERT and JAN VAN EYCK. *GHENT ALTARPIECE* (open). Completed 1432.
Oil on panel, 11'3"×14'5" (3.4×4.4 m). Church of St. Bavo, Ghent

makes what has rightly been called a "super-altar," overwhelming but far from harmonious, which could not have been planned this way from the start. Apparently Jan took over a number of panels left unfinished by Hubert, completed them, added some of his own, and assembled them at the behest of the wealthy donor whose portrait we see on the outside of the altar.

To reconstruct this train of events, and to determine each brother's share, is a fascinating but treacherous game. Suffice it to say that Hubert remains a somewhat shadowy figure; his style, overlaid with retouches by Jan, can probably be found in the four central panels, although these did not belong together originally. The upper three, whose huge figures in the final arrangement crush the multitude of small ones below, were intended, it seems, to form a self-contained triptych: the Lord between the Virgin Mary and St. John the Baptist. The lower panel and the four flanking it probably formed a separate altarpiece, the Adoration of the Lamb, symbolizing Christ's sacrificial death. The two panels with music-making angels may have been planned by Hubert as a pair of organ shutters.

If this set of conjectures is correct, the two tall, narrow panels showing Adam and Eve (fig. 550) are the only ones added by Jan to Hubert's stock. They certainly are the most daring of all: the earliest monumental nudes of Northern panel painting (hardly less than lifesize), magnificently observed, and caressed by the most delicate play of light and shade. Their quiet dignity—and their prominent place in the altar—suggests that they should remind us not so much of Original Sin as of our creation in God's own image. Actual evil, by contrast, is represented in the small, violently expressive scenes above, which show the story of Cain and Abel. Still more extraordinary, however, is the fact that the Adam and Eve were designed specifically for their present positions in the ensemble. Acknowledging that they would really appear this way to the spectator whose eye-level is below the bottom of the panels, Jan van Eyck has depicted them in accordance with this abnormal viewpoint and thereby established a new, direct relationship between picture space and real space.

The outer surfaces of the two wings (fig. 551) were evidently planned by Jan as one coherent unit. Here, as we would normally expect, the largest figures are not above, but in the lower tier. The two St. Johns (painted in grays to simulate sculpture, like the scenes of Cain and Abel), the donor, and his wife, each in a separate niche, are the immediate kin of the *Adam* and *Eve* panels. The upper tier has two pairs of panels of different width; the artist has made a virtue of this awkward necessity by combining all four into one interior. Such an effect, we recall, had first been created almost a century earlier (compare fig. 531), but Jan, not content with perspective devices alone, heightens the illusion by painting the shadows cast by the frames of the panels on the floor of the Virgin's chamber. Interestingly enough, this Annunciation resembles, in its homely detail, the *Merode Altarpiece*, thus providing a valuable link between the two great pioneers of Flemish realism.

Donors' portraits of splendid individuality occupy conspicuous positions in both the Merode and the Ghent altarpieces. A renewed interest in realistic portraiture had developed in the mid-fourteenth century, but until about 1420 its best achievements had been in sculpture (see fig. 506), the painters usually confining themselves to silhouettelike profile views (such as the portrait of the duke of Berry in fig. 544). Not until the Master of Flémalle, the first artist since antiquity to have real command of a close-range view of the human face from a three-quarter angle, did the portrait play a major role in Northern painting.

In addition to donors' portraits, we now begin to encounter in growing numbers small, independent likenesses whose peculiar intimacy suggests that they were treasured keep-

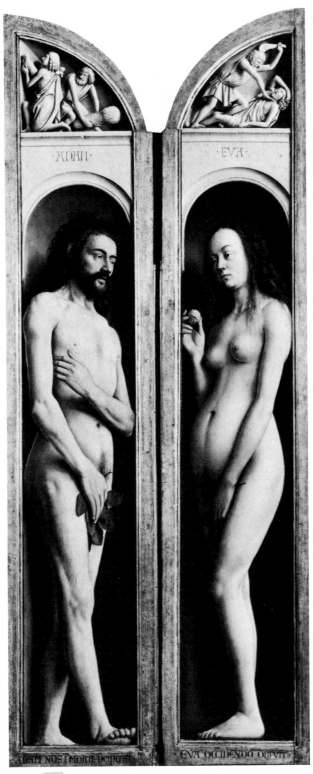

550. *ADAM* and *EVE*, details of *GHENT ALTARPIECE*, left and right wings

551. *GHENT ALTARPIECE* (closed)

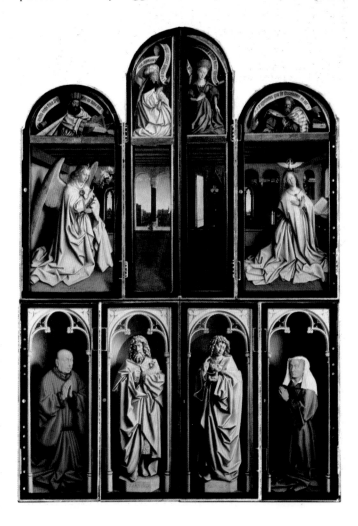

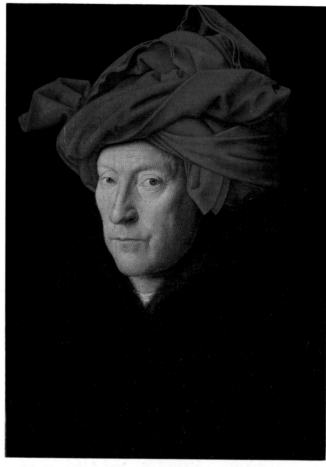

552. JAN VAN EYCK. *MAN IN A RED TURBAN (SELF- PORTRAIT?).*
1433. Oil on panel, 10¼×7½″ (26×19 cm). The National Gallery,
London. Reproduced by courtesy of the Trustees

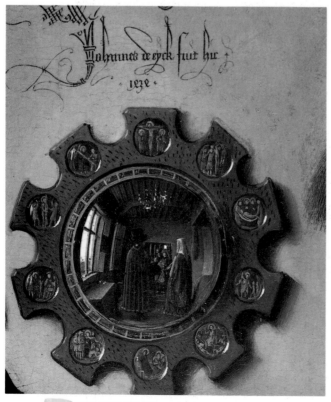

554. JAN VAN EYCK. *WEDDING PORTRAIT* (detail)

sakes, pictorial substitutes for the real presence of the sitter. One of the most fascinating is Jan van Eyck's *Man in a Red Turban* of 1433 (fig. 552), which may well be a self-portrait—the slight strain about the eyes seems to come from gazing into a mirror. The sitter is bathed in the same gentle, clear light as the Adam and Eve of the *Ghent Altarpiece;* every detail of shape and texture has been recorded with almost microscopic precision. Jan does not suppress the sitter's personality, yet this face, like all of Jan's portraits, remains a psychological puzzle. It might be described as "even-tempered" in the most exact sense of the term, its character traits balanced against each other so perfectly that none can assert itself at the expense of the rest. As Jan was fully capable of expressing emotion (we need only recall the faces of the crowd in the *Crucifixion*, or the scenes of Cain and Abel in the *Ghent Altarpiece*), the stoic calm of his portraits surely reflects his conscious ideal of human character rather than his indifference or lack of insight.

The Flemish cities where the new style of painting flourished—Tournai, Ghent, Bruges—rivaled those of Italy as centers of international banking and trade. Their foreign residents included many Italian businessmen. For one of these, perhaps a member of the Arnolfini family, Jan van Eyck painted his remarkable *Wedding Portrait*, one of the major masterpieces of the period (fig. 553). The young couple is solemnly exchanging marriage vows in the privacy of the bridal chamber. They seem to be quite alone, but as we scrutinize the mirror (fig. 554), conspicuously placed behind them, we discover in the reflection that two other persons have entered the room. One of them must be the artist, since the words above the mirror, in florid legal lettering, tell us that "Johannes de eyck fuit hic" (Jan van Eyck was here) in the year 1434.

Jan's role, then, is that of a witness; the picture purports to show exactly what he saw and has the function of a pictorial marriage certificate. Yet the domestic setting, however persuasively realistic, is replete with disguised symbolism of the most subtle kind, conveying the sacramental nature of marriage. The single candle in the chandelier, burning in broad daylight, stands for the all-seeing Christ (note the Passion scenes of the mirror frame); the shoes which the couple has taken off remind us that they are standing on "holy ground" (for the origin of the theme, see page 99); even the little dog is an emblem of marital faith, and the furnishings of the room invite similar interpretation. The natural world, as in the *Merode Altarpiece*, is made to contain the world of the spirit in such a way that the two actually become one.

ROGIER VAN DER WEYDEN. In the work of Jan van Eyck, the exploration of the reality made visible by light and color had reached a limit that was not to be surpassed for another two centuries. Rogier van der Weyden (1399/1400–1464), the third great master of early Flemish painting, set himself a different though equally important task: to recapture, within the framework of the new style created by his predecessors, the emotional drama, the pathos, of the Gothic past. We can see this immediately in his early masterpiece, *Descent from the Cross* (fig. 555), which dates from about 1435, when the artist was in his mid-thirties. Here the mod-

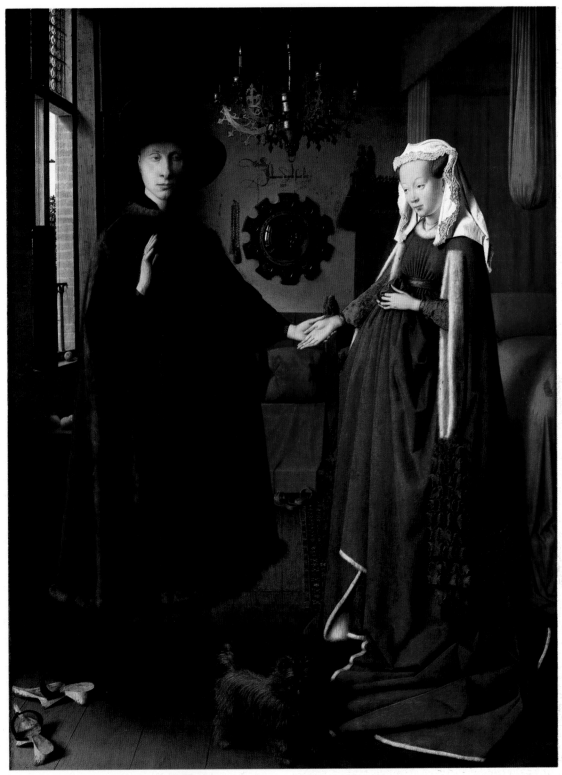

553. JAN VAN EYCK. *WEDDING PORTRAIT*. 1434.
Oil on panel, 33×22½″ (83.7×57 cm).
The National Gallery, London. Reproduced by courtesy of the Trustees

eling is sculpturally precise, with its brittle, angular drapery folds recalling the Master of Flémalle; and the soft half-shadows and rich, glowing colors show his knowledge of Jan van Eyck. Yet Rogier is far more than a mere follower of the two older men; whatever he owes to them—and it is obviously a great deal—he uses for ends that are not theirs but his. The

outward events (in this case, the lowering of Christ's body from the cross) concern him less than the world of human feeling; this *Descent*, judged for its expressive content, could well be called a *Lamentation*.

The artistic ancestry of these grief-stricken gestures and faces is in sculpture rather than in painting—from the Stras-

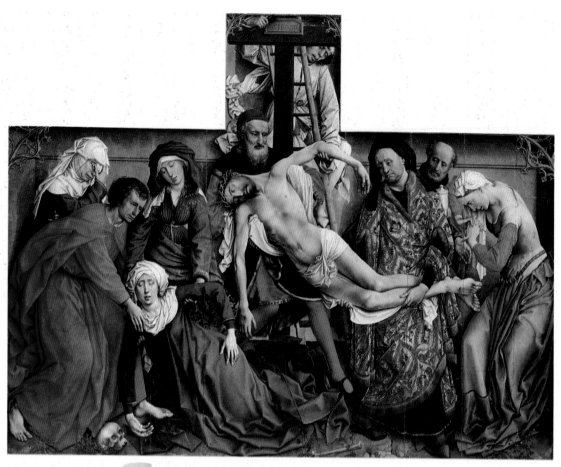

555. ROGIER VAN DER WEYDEN. *DESCENT FROM THE CROSS.*
c. 1435. Oil on panel, 7'2⅝×8'7⅛" (2.2×2.6 m).
Museo del Prado, Madrid

bourg *Death of the Virgin* (fig. 496) and the Naumburg *Crucifixion* (fig. 502) to the Bonn *Pietà* (fig. 505) and Sluter's *Moses Well* (fig. 507). It seems peculiarly fitting, therefore, that Rogier should have staged his scene in a shallow architectural niche or shrine, as if his figures were colored statues, not seen against a landscape background. This bold device gave him a double advantage in heightening the effect of this tragic event: it focused the beholder's entire attention on the foreground, and allowed him to mold the figures into a coherent, formal group. No wonder that Rogier's art, which has been well described as "at once physically barer and spiritually richer than Jan van Eyck's," set an example for countless other artists. When he died in 1464, after thirty years of unceasing activity as the foremost painter of Brussels, his influence was supreme in European painting north of the Alps. Its echoes continued to be discernible almost everywhere outside Italy until the end of the century, such was the authority of his style.

What is true of Rogier's religious works applies equally well to his portraits. The likeness of Francesco d'Este (fig. 556), an Italian nobleman resident at the Burgundian court, may strike us as less lifelike than Jan van Eyck's. Modeling is reduced to a minimum; much descriptive detail has been simplified or omitted altogether; the gracefully elongated forms of the body render an aristocratic ideal rather than the sitter's individual appearance. Yet this face, compared with

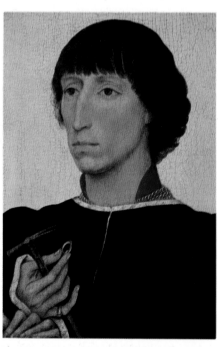

556. ROGIER VAN DER WEYDEN. *FRANCESCO D'ESTE.*
c. 1455. Tempera and oil on panel, 11¾×8" (30×20.3 cm).
The Metropolitan Museum of Art, New York.
Bequest of Michael Friedsam, 1931.
The Michael Friedsam Collection

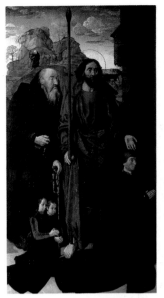
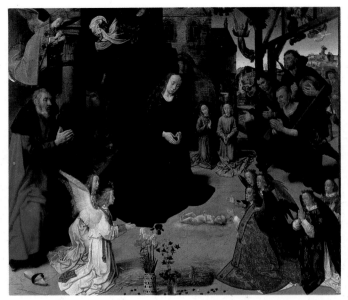
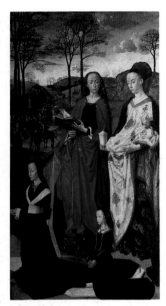

557. HUGO VAN DER GOES. *THE PORTINARI ALTARPIECE* (open). c. 1476. Tempera and oil on panel, center 8′3½″×10′ (2.5×3.1 m), wings each 8′3½″×4′7½″ (2.5×1.4 m). Galleria degli Uffizi, Florence

that of the *Man in a Red Turban* (fig. 552), conveys a more vivid sense of character. Instead of striving for the psychologically "neutral" calm of Jan's portraits, Rogier interprets the human personality by suppressing some traits and emphasizing others. In consequence, he tells us more about the inner life of his sitters, less about their outward appearance.

HUGO VAN DER GOES. Among the artists who followed Rogier van der Weyden, few succeeded in escaping from the great master's shadow. The most dynamic of these was Hugo van der Goes (c. 1440–1482), an unhappy genius whose tragic end suggests an unstable personality particularly interesting to us today. After a spectacular rise to fame in the cosmopolitan atmosphere of Bruges, he decided in 1478, when he was near forty years of age, to enter a monastery as a lay brother; for some time he continued to paint, but increasing fits of depression drove him to the verge of suicide, and four years later he was dead.

Hugo van der Goes' most ambitious work, the huge altarpiece he completed about 1476 for Tommaso Portinari, is an awesome achievement (fig. 557). While we need not search it for hints of Hugo's future mental illness, it nonetheless evokes a tense, explosive personality. Or is there no strain between the artist's devotion to the natural world (the wonderfully spacious and atmospheric landscape setting, and the wealth of precise realistic detail) and his concern with the supernatural? In the wings, for instance, the kneeling members of the Portinari family are dwarfed by their patron saints, whose gigantic size characterizes them as being of a higher order, like Joseph, the Virgin Mary, and the shepherds of the *Nativity* in the center panel, who share the same huge scale. But these latter figures are not meant to be "larger than life," for their height is normal in relation to the architecture and to the ox and ass; the angels, which are drawn to the same scale as the donors, thus appear abnormally small.

This variation of scale, although its symbolic and expressive purpose is clear, stands outside the logic of everyday ex-

perience affirmed in the environment the artist has provided for his figures. There is another striking contrast between the frantic excitement of the shepherds and the ritual solemnity of all the other figures. These field hands, gazing in breathless wonder at the newborn Child, react to the dramatic miracle of the Nativity with a wide-eyed directness never attempted before. They aroused particular admiration in the Italian painters who saw the work after it arrived in Florence in 1483.

GEERTGEN TOT SINT JANS. During the last quarter of the fifteenth century there were no painters in Flanders comparable to Hugo van der Goes, and the most original artists appeared farther north, in Holland. To one of these, Geertgen tot Sint Jans of Haarlem, who died about 1495, we owe the enchanting *Nativity* reproduced in figure 558, a picture as daring, in its quiet way, as the center panel of *The Portinari Altarpiece*. The idea of a nocturnal Nativity, illuminated mainly by radiance from the Christ Child, goes back to the International Style (see fig. 546), but Geertgen, applying the pictorial discoveries of Jan van Eyck, gives new, intense reality to the theme. The magic effect of his little panel is greatly enhanced by the smooth, simplified shapes that record the impact of light with striking clarity; the manger is a rectangular trough; the heads of the angels, the Infant, and the Virgin are all as round as objects turned on a lathe.

BOSCH. If Geertgen's uncluttered, "abstract" forms attract us specially today, another Dutch artist, Hieronymus Bosch, appeals to our interest in the world of dreams. Little is known about Bosch except that he spent his life in the provincial town of 's Hertogenbosch and that he died, an old man, in 1516. His work, full of weird and seemingly irrational imagery, has proved difficult to interpret, despite recent research, which has shown that some of it was derived from alchemy texts.

We can readily understand this problem when we study

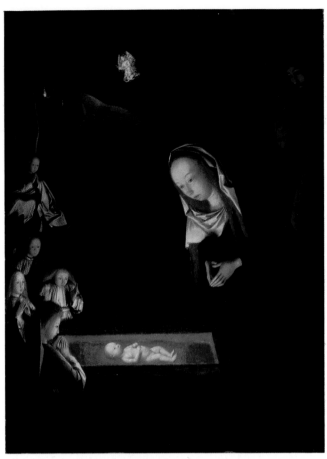

558. GEERTGEN TOT SINT JANS. *NATIVITY.* c. 1490. Oil on panel, 13½×10″ (34.3×25.7 cm). The National Gallery, London. Reproduced by courtesy of the Trustees

the triptych known as *The Garden of Delights* (fig. 559), the richest and most puzzling of Bosch's pictures. Of the three panels, only the left one has a clearly recognizable subject: the Garden of Eden, wherein the Lord introduces Adam to the newly created Eve. The landscape, almost Eyckian in its airy vastness, is filled with animals, among them such exotic creatures as an elephant and a giraffe, and also hybrid monsters of odd and sinister kinds. Behind them, the distant rock formations are equally strange. The right wing, a nightmarish scene of burning ruins and fantastic instruments of torture, surely represents Hell. But what of the center, The Garden of Delights, which is figure 560?

Here we see a landscape much like that of the Garden of Eden, populated with countless nude men and women performing a variety of peculiar actions: in the center, they parade around a circular basin on the backs of all sorts of beasts; many disport themselves in pools of water; most of them are closely linked with enormous birds, fruit, flowers, or marine animals. Only a few are openly engaged in lovemaking, yet there can be no doubt that the delights in this "garden" are those of carnal desire, however oddly disguised. The birds, fruit, and the like are symbols or metaphors which Bosch uses to depict life on earth as an unending repetition of the Original Sin of Adam and Eve, whereby we are all doomed to be the prisoners of our appetites. Nowhere does he so much as hint at the possibility of Salvation; corruption, on the animal level at least, had already asserted itself in the Garden of Eden before the Fall, and we are all destined for Hell, the Garden of Satan, with its grisly and refined instruments of torture.

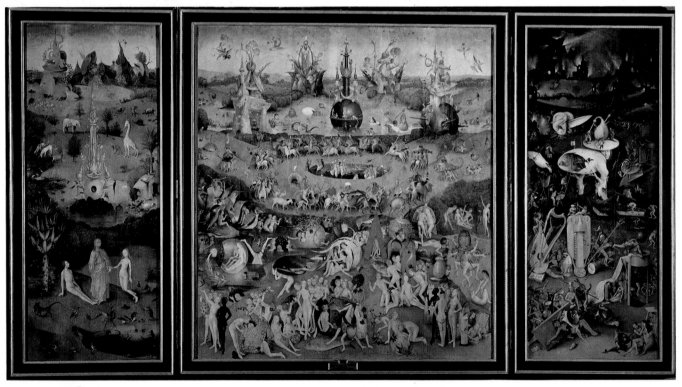

559. HIERONYMUS BOSCH. *THE GARDEN OF DELIGHTS.* c. 1510–15. Oil on panel, center 86½×76¾″ (219.7×195 cm), wings each 86½×38″ (219.7×96.6 cm). Museo del Prado, Madrid

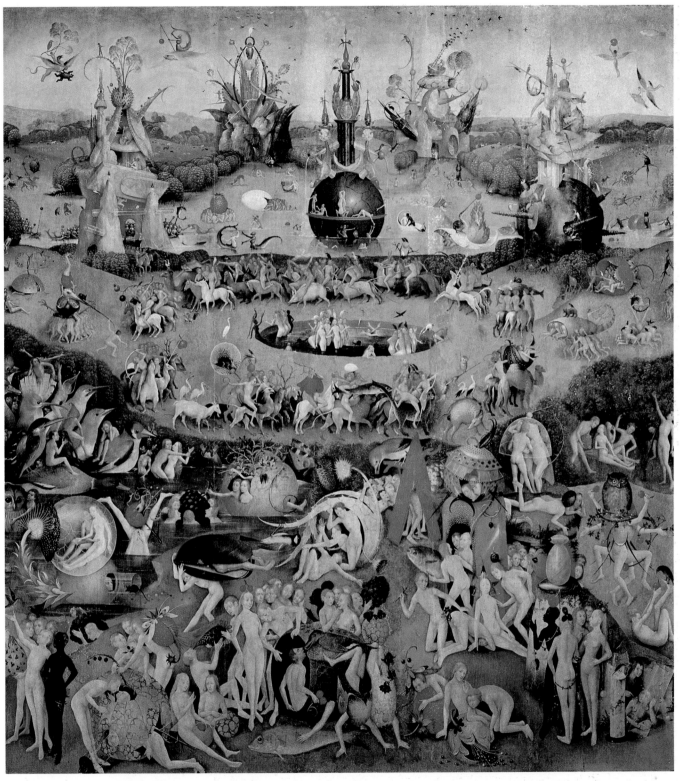

560. **HIERONYMUS BOSCH.** *GARDEN OF DELIGHTS.* Center panel, *THE GARDEN OF DELIGHTS*

So profound is Bosch's pessimism—if we read the meaning of the triptych correctly—that some scholars have refused to take it at face value; the center panel, they claim, is really an unusual vision of Paradise according to the beliefs of a secret heretical sect to which Bosch supposedly belonged. While their view has few adherents, it does point up the fundamental ambiguity of the *Garden*: there is indeed an innocence, even a haunting poetic beauty, in this panorama of human sinfulness. Consciously, Bosch was a stern moralist who intended his pictures to be visual sermons, every detail packed with didactic meaning. Unconsciously, however, he must have been so enraptured by the sensuous appeal of the world of the flesh that the images he coined with such prodigality tend to celebrate what they are meant to condemn. That, surely, is the reason why *The Garden of Delights* still evokes so strong a response today, even though we no longer understand every word of the sermon.

Swiss, German, and French Painting

We must now glance briefly at fifteenth-century art in the rest of Northern Europe. After about 1430, the new realism of the Flemish masters began to spread into France and Germany until, by the middle of the century, its influence was paramount from Spain to the Baltic. Among the countless artists (many of them still anonymous) who turned out provincial adaptations of Netherlandish painting, only a few were gifted enough to impress us today with a distinctive personality.

WITZ. One of the earliest and most original masters was Conrad Witz of Basel (1400/10–1445/46), whose altarpiece for Geneva Cathedral, painted in 1444, includes the remarkable panel shown in figure 561. To judge from the drapery, with its tubular folds and sharp, angular breaks, he must

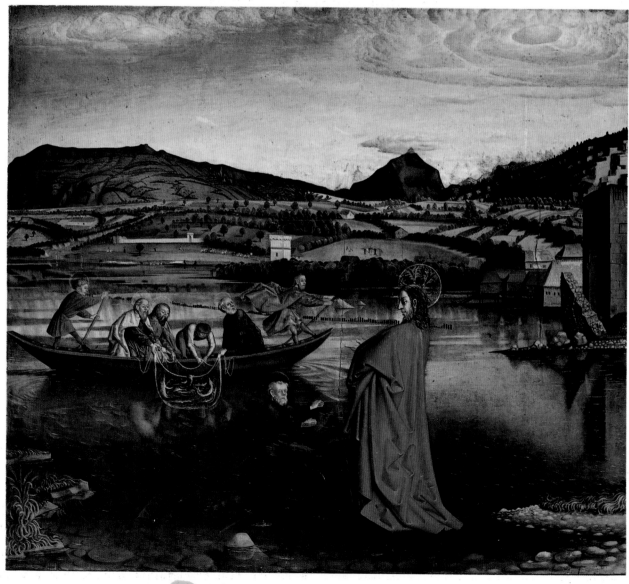

561. CONRAD WITZ. *THE MIRACULOUS DRAUGHT OF FISHES.*
1444. Oil on panel, 51×61″ (129.7×155 cm). Musée d'Art et d'Histoire, Geneva

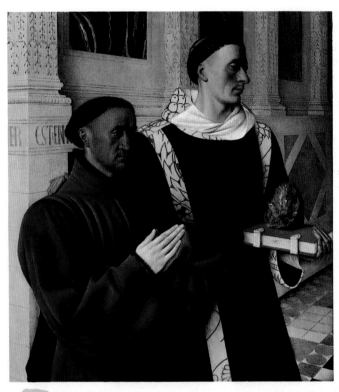

562. JEAN FOUQUET. *ETIENNE CHEVALIER AND ST. STEPHEN*,
left wing of the *MELUN DIPTYCH*. c. 1450. Oil on panel, 36½×33½″ (92.7×85 cm).
Gemäldegalerie, Staatliche Museen, Berlin

have had close contact with the Master of Flémalle. But the setting, rather than the figures, attracts our interest, and here the influence of the Van Eycks seems dominant. Witz, however, did not simply follow these great pioneers; an explorer himself, he knew more about the optical appearances of water than any other painter of his time (note especially the bottom of the lake in the foreground). The landscape, too, is an original venture, representing a specific part of the shore of the Lake of Geneva—among the earliest landscape "portraits" that have come down to us.

FOUQUET. In France, the painter Jean Fouquet (c. 1420–1481), twenty-odd years younger than Witz, had the exceptional fortune, soon after he had completed his training, of a lengthy visit to Italy, about 1445. In consequence, his work represents a unique blend of Flemish and Early Renaissance elements, although it remains basically Northern. *Etienne Chevalier and St. Stephen* (fig. 562), painted about 1450 for the left wing of a diptych, shows his mastery as a portraitist (the head of the saint seems no less individual than that of the donor); Italian influence can be seen in the style of the architecture and, less directly, in the statuesque solidity and weight of the two figures.

The artist's self-portrait from about the same time also reflects his sojourn in the South (fig. 563); it is a tiny picture executed in gold on black enamel, which must have been inspired by a late Roman miniature, such as the one reproduced in figure 313. It revives a species of "portable" portrait

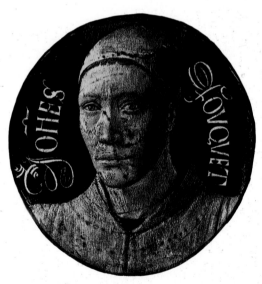

563. JEAN FOUQUET. *SELF-PORTRAIT*. c. 1450.
Gold and enamel on copper,
diameter 3″ (7.7 cm). Musée du Louvre, Paris

that was to become immensely popular, especially in England, a century later. And it has the further distinction of being the earliest clearly identified self-portrait that is a separate painting, not an incidental part of a larger work. The style of the likeness is Flemish in origin, however, rather than ancient or Renaissance. In fact, the quality of the glance recalls Jan van Eyck's *Man in a Red Turban* (fig. 552) so

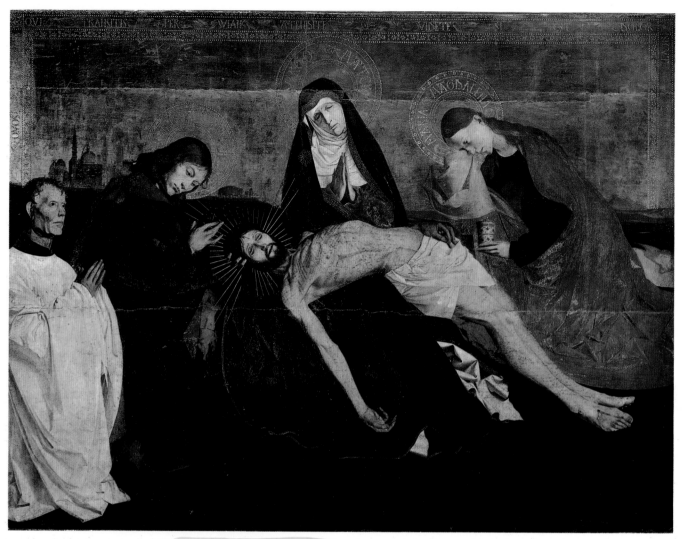

564. ENGUERRAND QUARTON. *AVIGNON PIETÀ*. c. 1470. Oil on panel,
63¾×85⅞″ (161.9×217.9 cm). Musée du Louvre, Paris

strongly that one is tempted to cite it as evidence that Jan's picture, too, must be a self-portrait.

AVIGNON PIETÀ. A Flemish style, influenced by Italian art, also characterizes the most famous of all French fifteenth-century pictures, the *Avignon Pietà* (fig. 564). As its name indicates, the panel comes from the extreme south of France. It is attributed to an artist of that region, Enguerrand Quarton. He must have been thoroughly familiar with the art of Rogier van der Weyden, for the figure types and the expressive content of the *Avignon Pietà* could be derived from no other source. At the same time, the magnificently simple and stable design is Italian rather than Northern (we first saw these qualities in the art of Giotto). Southern, too, is the bleak, featureless landscape emphasizing the monumental isolation of the figures. The distant buildings behind the donor on the left have an unmistakably Islamic flavor: did the artist mean to place the scene in an authentic Near Eastern setting? However that may be, he has created from these various features an unforgettable image of heroic pathos.

"LATE GOTHIC" SCULPTURE

If we had to describe fifteenth-century art north of the Alps in a single phrase, we might label it "the first century of panel painting," for panel painting so dominated the art of the period between 1420 and 1500 that its standards apply to manuscript illumination and stained glass and even, to a large extent, to sculpture. After the later thirteenth century, we will recall, the emphasis had shifted from architectural sculpture to the more intimate scale of devotional images, tombs, pulpits, and the like. Claus Sluter, whose art is so impressive in weight and volume, had briefly recaptured the monumental spirit of the High Gothic; but he had no real successors, although echoes of his style can be felt in French art for the next fifty years.

What ended the International Style in the sculpture of Northern Europe was the influence of the Master of Flémalle and Rogier van der Weyden. The carvers (who quite often were also painters) began to reproduce in stone or wood the style of these artists, and continued to do so, in essence, until about 1500. How completely the aims of "Late Gothic" sculpture became identified with those of painting may be seen in figures 565 and 566: the *Flying Angel* from a work of the Master of Flémalle, about 1420, anticipates all the main features of a carved angel by a fine German sculptor, Veit Stosz, almost a century later.

PACHER. The most characteristic works of the "Late Gothic" carver are wooden altar shrines, often large in size and incredibly intricate in detail. Such shrines were especially popular in the Germanic countries. One of the richest examples is the *St. Wolfgang Altarpiece* (fig. 567) by the Tyrolean sculptor and painter Michael Pacher (c. 1435–1498), in St. Wolfgang, Austria. Its lavishly gilt and colored forms make a dazzling spectacle as they emerge from the shadowy depth of the shrine under spiky Flamboyant canopies; we enjoy it—but in pictorial rather than plastic terms. We have no experience of volume, either positive or negative; the figures and setting seem to melt into a single pattern of agitated, twisting lines that permits only the heads to stand out as separate entities.

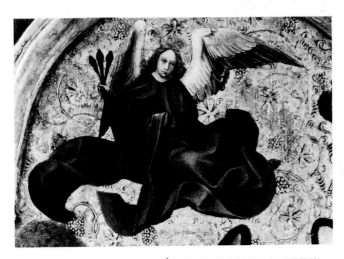

565. THE MASTER OF FLÉMALLE (ROBERT CAMPIN?).
FLYING ANGEL, detail of *ENTOMBMENT*. c. 1420.
Oil on panel. Collection Count Antoine Seilern, London

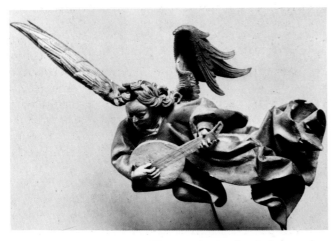

566. VEIT STOSZ. *FLYING ANGEL*, detail of
ANNUNCIATION. 1518. Wood. St. Lorenz, Nuremberg

If we compare this altarpiece with Rogier's *Descent from the Cross* (fig. 555), we realize that the latter, paradoxically, is a far more "sculptural" scene. Did Pacher, the "Late Gothic" sculptor, feel unable to compete with the painter's rendering of three-dimensional bodies and therefore choose to meet him in the pictorial realm, by extracting the maximum of drama from contrasts of light and shade? Pacher's own work seems to support this view: some years after completing the St. Wolfgang shrine he made another altarpiece, this time with a painted center (fig. 568). Again we see large figures under ornate canopies—the equivalent of a carved shrine—but now with far greater emphasis on space and volume. To say that Pacher is a painter when he sculpts, and a sculptor when he paints, is only a slight exaggeration: in this exchange, sculpture inevitably gets the short end of the bargain.

THE GRAPHIC ARTS

Printing

At this point we must take note of another important event north of the Alps—the development of printing, for pictures as well as books. Our earliest printed books in the modern sense were produced in the Rhineland soon after 1450 (we are not certain whether Gutenberg deserves the priority long claimed for him). The new technique quickly spread all over Europe and developed into an industry that had a profound effect on Western civilization, ushering in the era of general literacy.

Printed pictures, however, had hardly less importance, for without them the printed book could not have replaced the work of the medieval scribe and illuminator so quickly and completely. The pictorial and the literary aspects of printing were, indeed, closely linked from the start. But where is the start? When, and by whom, was printing invented? The beginnings of the story—which will be told here in barest outline—lie in the ancient Near East five thousand years ago. Mechanically speaking, the Sumerians were the earliest "printers," for their relief impressions on clay from stone seals were carved with both pictures and inscriptions. From Mesopotamia, the use of seals spread to India and eventually to China. The Chinese applied ink to their seals in order to impress them on wood or silk, and, in the second century A.D., they invented paper. By the ninth century, they were printing pictures and books on paper from wooden blocks carved in relief, and two hundred years later they developed movable type. Some of the products of Chinese printing surely reached the medieval West—through the Arabs, the Mongols, or travelers such as Marco Polo—although we lack direct evidence.

The technique of manufacturing paper, too, came to Europe from the East, and Chinese silk and porcelain were imported in small quantities from the fourteenth century on. Paper and printing from wood blocks were both known in the West during the later Middle Ages, but paper, as a cheap alternative to parchment, gained ground very slowly, while printing was used only for ornamental patterns on cloth. All the more astonishing is the development, beginning about 1400, that produced within the century a printing technol-

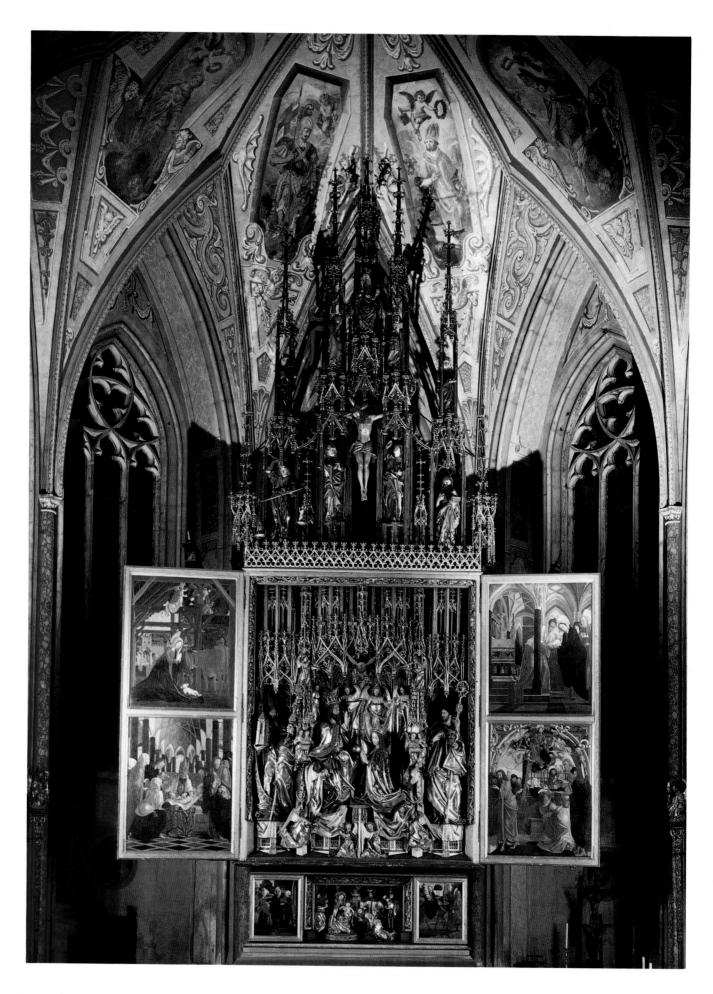

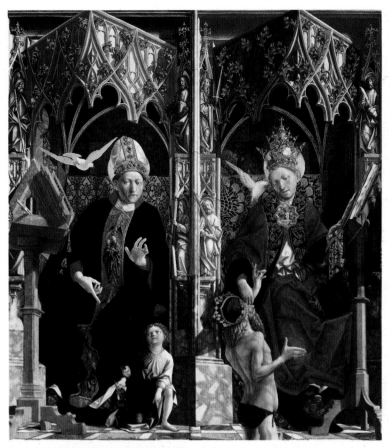

568. MICHAEL PACHER. *ST. AUGUSTINE AND ST. GREGORY*,
center panel of *ALTARPIECE OF THE FOUR LATIN FATHERS*. c. 1483.
Oil on panel, 81×77″ (205.7×195.7 cm). Pinakothek, Munich

ogy that was superior to that of the Far East and of far wider
cultural importance. After 1500, in fact, no basic changes
were made in this field until the Industrial Revolution.

Woodcut

The idea of printing pictorial designs from wood blocks onto
paper seems to have originated in Northern Europe at the
very end of the fourteenth century. Many of the oldest surviving examples of such prints, called woodcuts, are German,
others are Flemish, and some may be French; all show the
familiar qualities of the International Style. The designs were
probably furnished by painters or sculptors, but the actual
carving of the wood blocks was done by the specially trained
craftsmen who also produced wood blocks for textile prints.
As a result, early woodcuts, such as the *St. Dorothy* in figure
569, have a flat, ornamental pattern; forms are defined by
simple, heavy lines with little concern for three-dimensional
effects (there is no hatching or shading). Since the outlined
shapes were meant to be filled in with color, these prints
often recall stained glass (compare fig. 517) more than the
miniatures they replaced.

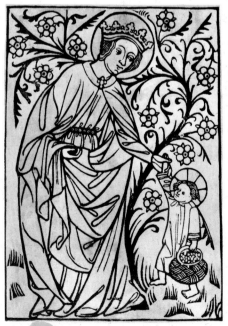

569. *ST. DOROTHY*. c. 1420. Woodcut.
Staatliche Graphische Sammlung, Munich

567. (*opposite*) MICHAEL PACHER. *ST. WOLFGANG ALTARPIECE*.
1471–81. Carved wood, figures about lifesize.
Church of St. Wolfgang, Austria

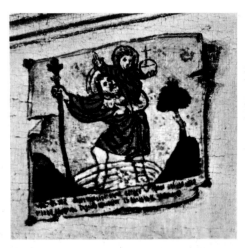

570. *WOODCUT OF ST. CHRISTOPHER*, detail from an
ANNUNCIATION by Jacques Daret (?). c. 1435.
Musée Royaux d'Art et d'Histoire, Brussels

Despite their aesthetic appeal to modern eyes, fifteenth-century woodcuts were popular art, on a level that did not attract masters of high ability until shortly before 1500. A single wood block yielded thousands of copies, to be sold for a few pennies apiece, bringing the individual ownership of pictures within everyone's reach for the first time in our history. What people did with these prints is illustrated in figure 570, a detail from a Flemish *Annunciation* panel of about 1435, where a tattered woodcut of St. Christopher is pinned up above the mantel. Perhaps it is a hint at the Virgin's journey to Bethlehem (St. Christopher was the patron of travelers), but this charmingly incongruous feature must also be understood as a disguised symbol of her humility, for only the poor would have such an object on their walls.

The St. Christopher woodcut has two lines of lettering—a short prayer, presumably—at the bottom. Inscriptions of this kind are often found among early woodcuts, the letters having been either added by hand or printed from the same block as the picture. Such woodcuts combining image and text were sometimes assembled into popular picture books, called block books.

But to carve lines of text backward in relief on a wooden block was a wearisome and particularly risky task—a single slip could ruin an entire page. Little wonder, then, that printers soon had the idea of putting each letter on its own small block. Wooden movable type carved by hand worked well for letters of large size but not for small ones; moreover, it was too expensive to use for printing long texts such as the Bible. By 1450, this problem had been solved through the introduction of metal type cast from molds, and the stage was set for book production as we know it today.

Engraving

Whoever first thought of metal type probably had the aid of goldsmiths to work out the technical production problems. This is the more plausible since many goldsmiths, as engravers, had already entered the field of printmaking. An engraving, unlike a woodcut, is printed not from a raised design but from V-shaped grooves, cut into a metal plate (usually copper) with a steel tool known as a burin. The technique of embellishing metal surfaces with engraved pictures was developed in classical antiquity (see fig. 250) and continued to be practiced throughout the Middle Ages (see fig. 449; the engraved lines are filled in with enamel). Thus, no new skill was required to engrave a plate that was to serve as the "matrix" for a paper print; the subsequent printing was done by rubbing ink into the grooves, wiping off the surface of the plate, covering it with a damp sheet of paper, and putting it through the press.

The notion of making an engraved print apparently came from the desire for an alternative, more refined and flexible, to woodcuts. (On a wood block, let us remember, lines are ridges; hence, the thinner they are, the more difficult they are to carve.) Engravings appealed from the first to a smaller and more sophisticated public. The oldest examples we know, dating from about 1430, already show the influence of the great Flemish painters; their forms are systematically modeled with fine hatched lines, and often convincingly foreshortened. Nor do engravings share the anonymity of early woodcuts: individual hands can be distinguished almost from the beginning, dates and initials shortly appear, and most of the important engravers of the last third of the fifteenth century are known to us by name. Even though the early engravers were usually goldsmiths by training, their prints are so closely linked to local painting styles that we may determine their geographic origin far more easily than for woodcuts. Especially in the Upper Rhine region, we can trace a continuous tradition of fine engravers from the time of Conrad Witz to the end of the century.

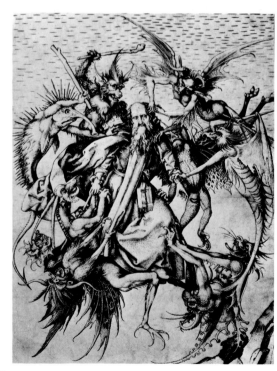

571. MARTIN SCHONGAUER. *THE TEMPTATION OF ST. ANTHONY*.
c. 1480–90. Engraving. The Metropolitan Museum of Art,
New York. Rogers Fund, 1920

SCHONGAUER. The most accomplished of these is Martin Schongauer (c. 1430–1491), the first printmaker whom we also know as a painter, and the first to gain international fame. Schongauer might be called the Rogier van der Weyden of engraving. After learning the goldsmith's craft in his father's shop, he must have spent considerable time in Flanders, for he shows a thorough knowledge of Rogier's art. His prints are replete with Rogierian motifs and expressive devices and reveal a deep temperamental affinity to the great Fleming. Yet Schongauer had his own impressive powers of invention; his finest engravings have a complexity of design, spatial depth, and richness of texture that make them fully equivalent to panel paintings, and lesser artists often found inspiration in them for large-scale pictures.

The Temptation of St. Anthony (fig. 571), one of Schongauer's most famous works, masterfully combines savage expressiveness and formal precision, violent movement and ornamental stability. The longer we look at it, the more we marvel at its range of tonal values, the rhythmic beauty of the engraved line, and the artist's ability to render every conceivable surface—spiky, scaly, leathery, furry—merely by varying the burin's attack upon the plate. He was not to be surpassed by any later engraver in this respect.

THE MASTER OF THE HAUSBUCH. For originality of conception and technique, Schongauer had only one rival among the printmakers of his time, the Master of the Hausbuch (so called after a book of drawings attributed to him). The very individual style of this artist, who was probably of Dutch origin (although he seems to have spent most of his career, from about 1475 to 1490, in the Rhineland), is the opposite of Schongauer's. His prints (such as the *Holy Family by the Rosebush*, fig. 572) are small, intimate in mood, and spontaneous, almost sketchy, in execution.

Even his tools were different from the standard engraver's equipment; instead of submitting to the somewhat impersonal discipline demanded by the burin, the Master of the Hausbuch scratched his designs into the copperplate with a fine steel needle. This technique, known as drypoint, permitted him to draw almost as freely as if he were working with

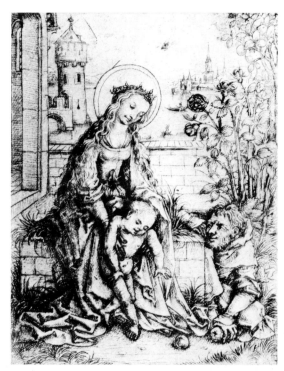

572. THE MASTER OF THE HAUSBUCH. *HOLY FAMILY BY THE ROSEBUSH*. c. 1480–90. Drypoint, 5⅝×4½″ (14.2×11.5 cm). Rijksprentenkabinet, Rijksmuseum, Amsterdam

a pen on a sheet of paper. The needle, of course, did not cut grooves as deep as those made by the burin, so that a drypoint plate was apt to wear out after yielding a mere handful of impressions, whereas an engraved plate lasted through hundreds of printings. But the drypoint technique preserved the artist's personal "handwriting" and permitted soft, atmospheric effects—velvety shadows, delicate, luminous distances—unattainable with the burin. The Master of the Hausbuch knew how to take full advantage of these possibilities. He was a pioneer in the use of a tool that was to become, a century and a half later, the supreme instrument of Rembrandt's graphic art.

CHAPTER TWO

THE EARLY RENAISSANCE IN ITALY

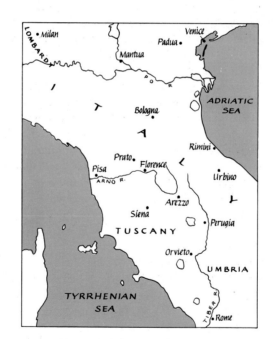

When we discussed the new style of painting that arose in Flanders about 1420, we avoided suggesting why this revolution took place at that particular time and in that particular area. This does not mean, however, that no explanation is possible. Unless we believe in sheer fate or chance, we find it difficult to place the entire burden of responsibility on the Master of Flémalle and the brothers Van Eyck; there must, we feel, be some link between their accomplishment and the social, political, and cultural setting in which they worked. But this link is as yet less apparent, and less well understood, than we might wish. Regarding the origins of Early Renaissance art, we have more insight into the special circumstances that help to explain why this style was born in Florence at the beginning of the fifteenth century, rather than elsewhere or at some other time.

In the years around 1400, Florence faced an acute threat to its independence. The powerful duke of Milan, trying to bring all of Italy under his rule, had already subjugated the Lombard plain and most of the Central Italian city-states; Florence remained the only serious obstacle to his ambition. The city put up a vigorous and successful defense on the military, diplomatic, and intellectual fronts. Of these three, the intellectual was by no means the least important; the duke had much eloquent support as a new Caesar, bringing peace and order to the country, whereas Florence, in its turn, rallied public opinion by proclaiming itself the champion of freedom against unchecked tyranny.

This propaganda war was waged on both sides by humanists, the heirs of Petrarch and Boccaccio, but the Florentines gave by far the better account of themselves. Their writings, such as *Praise of the City of Florence* (1402–3) by Leonardo Bruni (see fig. 623), give renewed focus to the Petrarchan ideal of a rebirth of the Classics: the humanist, speaking as the citizen of a free republic, asks why, among all the states of Italy, Florence alone had been able to defy the superior power of Milan; he finds the answer in her institutions, her cultural achievements, her geographical situation, the spirit of her people, and her descent from the city-states of ancient Etruria. Does not Florence today, he concludes, assume the same role of political and intellectual leadership as that of Athens at the time of the Persian Wars?

The patriotic pride, the call to greatness, implicit in this image of Florence as the "new Athens" must have aroused a deep response throughout the city, for just when the forces of Milan threatened to engulf them, the Florentines embarked upon an ambitious campaign to finish the great artistic enterprises begun a century before, at the time of Giotto. Following the competition of 1401–2 for the bronze doors of the Baptistery (see page 388), another extensive program continued the sculptural decoration of Florence Cathedral and other churches, while deliberations were resumed on how to build the dome of the Cathedral, the largest and most difficult project of all. The campaign lasted more than thirty years (it gradually petered out after the completion of the dome in 1436). Its total cost, although difficult to express in present-day financial terms, was comparable to the cost of rebuilding the Acropolis in Athens (page 172). The huge investment was itself not a guarantee of artistic quality, but, motivated by such civic enthusiasm, it provided a splendid opportunity for the emergence of creative talent and the coining of a new style worthy of the "new Athens."

From the start, the visual arts were considered essential to the resurgence of the Florentine spirit. They had been classed with the crafts, or "mechanical arts," throughout antiquity and the Middle Ages, and it cannot be chance that the first explicit statement claiming a place for them among the liberal arts occurs in the writings of the Florentine chronicler Filippo Villani, about 1400. A century later, this claim was to win general acceptance throughout the Western world. What does it imply? The liberal arts were defined by a tradition going back to Plato and comprised the intellectual disciplines necessary for a "gentleman's" education—mathematics (including musical theory), dialectics, grammar, rhetoric, and philosophy; the fine arts were excluded because they were "handiwork" lacking a theoretical basis. Thus, when the artist gained admission to this select group, the nature of his work had to be redefined: he was acknowledged as a person of ideas, rather than a mere manipulator of materials; and the work of art came to be viewed more and more as the visible record of his creative mind. This meant that works of art need not—indeed, should not—be judged by fixed standards of craftsmanship; soon everything that bore the imprint of a great master—drawings, sketches, fragments, unfinished pieces—was eagerly collected, regardless of its incompleteness.

The artist's outlook, too, underwent certain changes. Now in the company of scholars and poets, he himself often became learned and literary; he might write poems, an autobiography, or theoretical treatises. As another consequence of this new social status, artists tended to develop into one of two contrasting personality types: the man of the world, self-controlled, polished, at ease in aristocratic society; and the solitary genius, secretive, idiosyncratic, subject to fits of melancholy, and likely to be in conflict with his patrons. It is remarkable how soon this modern view of art and artists became a living reality in the Florence of the Early Renaissance.

FLORENCE: 1400–1450

Sculpture

The first half of the fifteenth century became the heroic age of the Early Renaissance. Florentine art, dominated by the original creators of the new style, retained the undisputed leadership of the movement. To trace its beginnings, we must discuss sculpture first, for the sculptors had earlier and more plentiful opportunities than the architects and painters to meet the challenge of the "new Athens." The artistic campaign had opened with the competition for the Baptistery doors, and for some time it consisted mainly of sculptural projects. Ghiberti's trial relief, we recall, does not differ significantly from the International Gothic (see fig. 516); nor do the completed Baptistery doors, even though their execution took another twenty years. In the trial panel only Ghiberti's admiration for ancient art, evidenced by the torso of Isaac, can be linked with the classicism of the Florentine humanists around 1400. Similar instances occur in other Florentine sculpture at that time. But such "quotations" of ancient sculpture, isolated and small in scale, merely recapture what Nicola Pisano had done a century before (see fig. 509).

NANNI DI BANCO. A decade after the trial relief, we find that this limited medieval classicism has been surpassed by a somewhat younger artist, Nanni di Banco (c. 1384–1421). The four saints, called the *Quattro Coronati* (fig. 573), which he made about 1410–14 for one of the niches on the exterior of the church of Or San Michele, demand to be compared not with Nicola Pisano but with the Reims *Visitation* (see fig. 497). The figures in both groups are approximately lifesize, yet Nanni's give the impression of being a good deal larger than those at Reims; their quality of mass and monumentality seems quite beyond the range of medieval sculpture, even though Nanni depended less directly on ancient models than had the sculptor of the *Visitation* or Nicola Pisano. Only the heads of the second and third of the *Coronati* recall specific examples of Roman sculpture—those memorable portrait heads of the third century A.D. (figs. 574 and 575). Nanni was obviously much impressed by their realism and their agonized expression. His ability to retain the essence of both these qualities indicates a new attitude toward ancient art, which unites classical form and content, no longer separating them as medieval classicists had done.

When Nanni carved the *Quattro Coronati*, he was still in

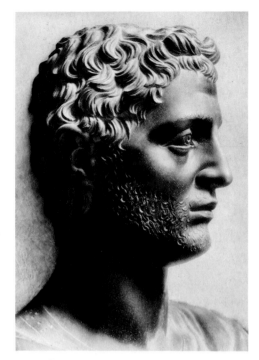

574. *FOUR SAINTS (QUATTRO CORONATI)*, head of second figure from left (figure 573)

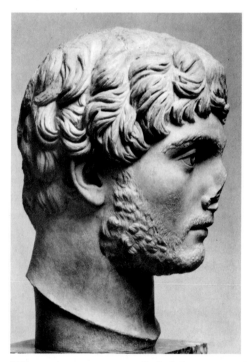

575. *PORTRAIT OF A ROMAN*. Early 3rd century A.D. Marble, lifesize. Staatliche Museen, Berlin

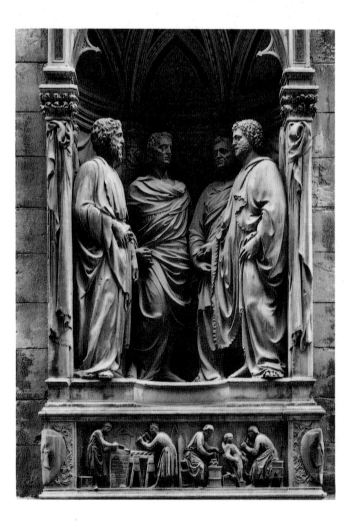

573. NANNI DI BANCO. *FOUR SAINTS (QUATTRO CORONATI)*. c. 1410–14. Marble, about lifesize. Or San Michele, Florence

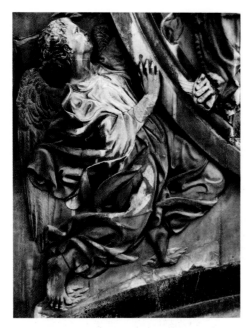

576. NANNI DI BANCO. *FLYING ANGEL*,
detail of *ASSUMPTION*. c. 1420.
Stone. Porta della Mandorla,
Florence Cathedral

Their different approaches are strikingly illustrated in Nanni's *Quattro Coronati* and Donatello's *St. Mark* (fig. 577): both are located in deep Gothic niches, but Nanni's figures cannot be divorced from the architectural setting and still seem attached, like jamb statues, to the pilasters behind them. The *St. Mark* no longer needs such shelter; perfectly balanced and self-sustaining, he would lose nothing of his immense authority if he were deprived of his present enclosure. Here is the first statue since antiquity capable of standing by itself, or, to put it another way, the first statue to recapture the full meaning of the classical *contrapposto* (see page 180). In a performance that truly marks an epoch, the young Donatello has mastered at one stroke the central achievement of ancient sculpture. He treats the human body as an articulated structure, capable of movement, and its

his early thirties. He died in 1421, leaving almost finished a huge relief of the Assumption of the Virgin for the gable above the second north portal of Florence Cathedral. In the figure of one of the flying angels that carry the Virgin heavenward (fig. 576), we see how rapidly—and surprisingly—Nanni's art evolved during the interval. The style of this figure is remote from both the classicism of the *Coronati* and the International Gothic. It recalls, instead, the flying angels of "Late Gothic" art, such as that by the Master of Flémalle (fig. 565). Both artists, at the same time and independently, had discovered how to visualize airborne figures persuasively: enveloping them in thin, loose draperies whose turbulent patterns and balloonlike bulges demonstrate the buoyant force of the wind. But the body of the Flemish angel tends to disappear among the folds, so that it seems essentially passive, whereas the body of Nanni's angel fills out the garments with its own vigorous action; this figure, we are convinced, propels itself, while its Northern counterpart merely floats.

DONATELLO'S EARLY WORKS. Comparing the two angels makes us see that Early Renaissance art, in contrast to "Late Gothic," sought an attitude toward the human body similar to that of classical antiquity. The man who did most to re-establish this attitude was Donatello, the greatest sculptor of his time. Born in 1386, several years after Nanni di Banco, he died in 1466, outliving Nanni by forty-five years. Among the "founding fathers" of the new style, he alone survived well past the middle of the century. Together with Nanni, Donatello spent the early part of his career working on commissions for Florence Cathedral and Or San Michele; they often faced the same artistic problems, yet the personalities of the two masters had little in common.

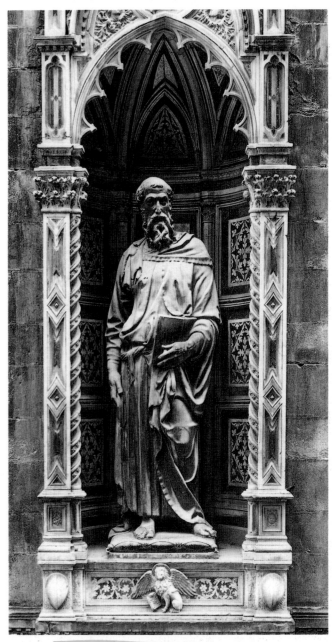

577. DONATELLO. *ST. MARK*. 1411–13. Marble,
7'9" (2.4 m). Or San Michele, Florence

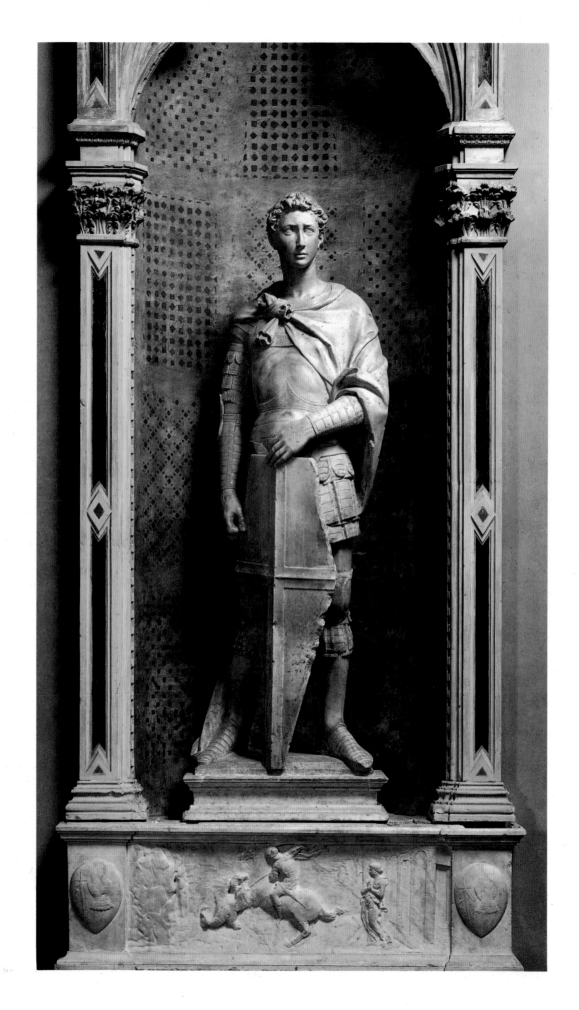

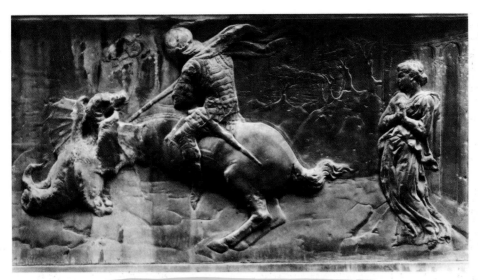

579. *ST. GEORGE AND THE DRAGON*, portion of relief below
ST. GEORGE (fig. 578). Marble, height 15¾″ (40 cm.)

drapery as a separate and secondary element, determined by the shapes underneath rather than by patterns imposed from without. Unlike the *Coronati*, the *St. Mark* looks as if he could take off his clothes. And yet he is not at all classicistic; that is, ancient motifs are not quoted as they are in Nanni's figures. Perhaps "classic" is the right word for him instead.

A few years later, about 1415–17, Donatello carved another statue for Or San Michele, the famous *St. George* (fig. 578). This niche is shallower than that of the *St. Mark*, and the young warrior saint can actually protrude from it slightly. Although encased in armor, his body and limbs are not rigid but wonderfully elastic; his stance, with the weight placed on the forward leg, conveys his readiness for combat (the right hand originally held a lance or sword). The controlled energy of his body is reflected in his eyes, which seem to scan the horizon for the approaching enemy. He is the Christian Soldier in his Early Renaissance version, spiritually akin to the *St. Theodore* at Chartres (see fig. 495), but also the proud defender of the "new Athens."

Below *St. George*'s niche is a relief panel showing the hero's best-known exploit, the slaying of a dragon (fig. 579; the maiden on the right is the captive princess whom the saint had come to liberate). Donatello has here produced another revolutionary work, devising a new kind of relief that is physically shallow (hence called *schiacciato*, "flattened-out") yet creates an illusion of infinite pictorial depth. This had already been achieved to some degree in certain Greek and Roman reliefs and by Ghiberti (compare with figs. 213, 286–91, and 516). But in all these cases, the actual carved depth is roughly proportional to the apparent depth of the space represented: the forms in the front plane are in very high relief, while those more distant become progressively lower, seemingly immersed in the background of the panel.

578. (*opposite*) DONATELLO. St. George Tabernacle, from Or San Michele, Florence. c. 1415–17. Marble, height of statue 6′10″ (2.1 m). Museo Nazionale del Bargello, Florence

Donatello discards this relationship; behind the figures, the amazing windswept landscape consists entirely of delicate surface modulations that cause the marble to catch light from varying angles. Thus every tiny ripple becomes endowed with a descriptive power infinitely greater than its real depth, and the chisel, like a painter's brush, becomes a tool for creating shades of light and dark. Yet Donatello cannot have borrowed his landscape from any painting, for no painter, at the time he did the *St. George* relief, had achieved so coherent and atmospheric a view of nature.

On the campanile of Florence Cathedral, when it was built in 1334–57, a row of tall Gothic niches had been designed for statues (barely visible above the rooftops in fig. 486). Half of these niches were still empty, and between 1416 and 1435 Donatello filled five of them. The most impressive statue of his series (fig. 580) is the unidentified prophet nicknamed *Zuccone* ("pumpkin-head"), made a dozen years after the *St. Mark*. The figure has long enjoyed special fame as a striking example of the master's realism, and there is no question that it is indeed realistic—far more so than any ancient statue or its nearest rivals, the prophets on Sluter's *Moses Well* (see fig. 507).

But, we may ask, what *kind* of realism have we here? Donatello has not followed the conventional image of a prophet (a bearded old man in Oriental-looking costume, holding a large scroll); he has invented an entirely new type, and it is difficult to account for his impulse in terms of realism. Why did he not reinterpret the old image from a realistic point of view, as Sluter had done? Donatello obviously felt that the established type was inadequate for his own conception of the subject, but how did he conceive it anew? Surely not by observing the people around him. More likely, he imagined the personalities of the prophets from what he had read about them in the Old Testament. He gained an impression, we may assume, of divinely inspired orators haranguing the multitude; and this, in turn, reminded him of the Roman orators he had seen in ancient sculpture. Hence the classical costume of the *Zuccone*, whose mantle falls

PERSPECTIVE: DONATELLO AND GHIBERTI. Donatello had learned the technique of bronze sculpture as a youth by working under Ghiberti on the first Baptistery doors. Now, in the 1420s, he began to rival his former teacher in that medium. *The Feast of Herod* (fig. 581), which he made about 1425 for the baptismal font of S. Giovanni (the Baptistery of Siena Cathedral), shows the same exquisite surface finish as Ghiberti's panels (see fig. 516), but also an expressive power that we could expect only of the master of the *Zuccone*. By classical or medieval standards, the main scene is poorly composed: the focus of the drama (the executioner presenting the head of St. John to Herod) is far to the left; the dancing Salome and most of the spectators are massed on the right; the center remains empty. Yet we see at once why Donatello created this gaping hole: it conveys, more effectively than the witnesses' gestures and expressions, the impact of the shocking sight. Moreover, the centrifugal movement of the figures helps persuade us that the picture space does not end within the panel but continues indefinitely in every direction; that the frame is merely a window through which we see this particular segment of unlimited, continuous reality. The arched openings within the panel serve to frame additional segments of the same reality, luring us farther into the depths of the palace.

This architecture, with its round arches, its fluted columns and pilasters, is not Gothic but reflects the new style launched by Filippo Brunelleschi, whose architectural achievements will occupy us soon. Brunelleschi also invented the system of linear perspective (see page 450), and *The Feast of Herod* is probably the earliest surviving example of a picture space constructed by this method. The details of the method need not concern us here, beyond saying that the system is a geometric procedure for projecting space onto a plane, analogous to the way the lens of a photographic camera now projects a perspective image on the film. Its central feature is the vanishing

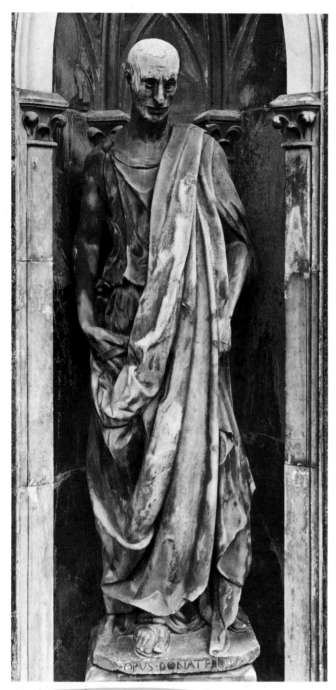

580. DONATELLO. *PROPHET (ZUCCONE),* on the campanile of Florence Cathedral. 1423–25. Marble, height 6'5" (2 m). Original now in the Museo dell'Opera del Duomo, Florence

from one shoulder like those of the toga-clad patricians in figures 283 and 286. Hence, also, the fascinating head, ugly yet noble, like Roman portraits of the third century A.D. (compare figs. 297 and 298).

To shape all these elements into a coherent whole was a revolutionary feat, an almost visible struggle. Donatello himself seems to have regarded the *Zuccone* as a particularly hard-won achievement; it is the first of his surviving works to carry his signature. He is said to have sworn "by the *Zuccone*" when he wanted to emphasize a statement and to have shouted at the statue, during his work, "Speak, speak, or the plague take you!"

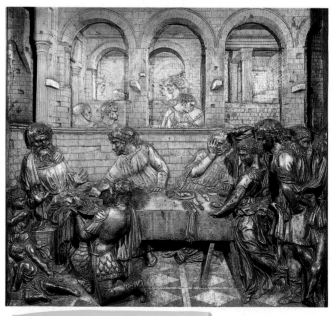

581. DONATELLO. *THE FEAST OF HEROD.* c. 1425. Gilt bronze, 23½" (59.7 cm) square. Baptismal font, Siena Cathedral

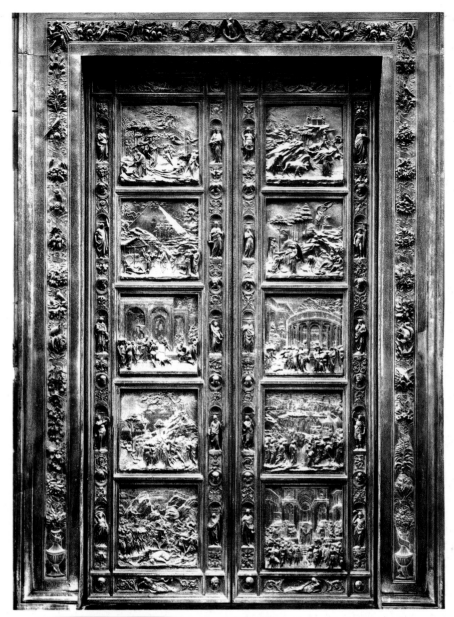

582. LORENZO GHIBERTI. *"GATES OF PARADISE,"* the east doors of Baptistery of S. Giovanni, Florence. c. 1435. Gilt bronze, height 15' (4.57 m)

point, toward which any set of parallel lines will seem to converge. If these lines are perpendicular to the picture plane, their vanishing point will be on the horizon, corresponding exactly to the position of the beholder's eye. Brunelleschi's discovery in itself was scientific rather than artistic, but it immediately became highly important to Early Renaissance artists because, unlike the perspective practices of the past, it was objective, precise, and rational (in fact, it soon became an argument for upgrading the fine arts into the liberal arts).

While empirical methods could also yield striking results, scientific perspective made it possible now to represent three-dimensional space on a flat surface in such a way that all the distances remained measurable—and this meant, in turn, that by reversing the procedure the plan could be derived from the perspective picture of a building. On the other hand, the scientific implications of the new perspective de-manded that it be consistently applied, a requirement that artists could not always live up to, for practical as well as aesthetic reasons. Since the method presupposes that the beholder's eye occupies a fixed point in space, a perspective picture automatically tells us where we must stand to see it properly. Thus the artist who knows in advance that his work will be seen from above or below, rather than at ordinary eye-level, ought to make his perspective construction correspond to these conditions; but if these are so abnormal that he must foreshorten his entire design to an extreme degree, he may disregard them and assume instead an ideal beholder, normally located. Such is the case in *The Feast of Herod*: our eye should be on a line perpendicular to the center of the panel, but in the Baptistery we must crouch low to see it correctly, as the basin to which our relief is attached is only a few feet high. (For other problems raised by the use of scientific perspective, see page 59.)

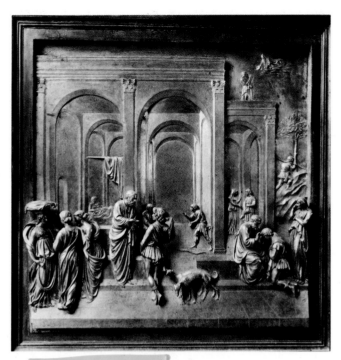

583. LORENZO GHIBERTI. *THE STORY OF JACOB AND ESAU,*
panel of the *"GATES OF PARADISE."* c. 1435. Gilt bronze,
31¼" (79.5 cm) square. Baptistery of S. Giovanni, Florence

At the same time that Donatello designed *The Feast of Herod,* Ghiberti was commissioned to do another pair of bronze doors for the Baptistery in Florence. This second set (fig. 582), so beautiful that they were soon dubbed the "Gates of Paradise," is decorated with ten large reliefs in square frames (not twenty-eight small panels in quatrefoil frames, as on the earlier doors) and shows the artist's successful conversion, under the influence of Donatello and the other pioneers of the new style, to the Early Renaissance point of view. *The Story of Jacob and Esau* (fig. 583) may be instructively contrasted with *The Feast of Herod.* It is about a decade later, and its perspective construction is more easy and assured; Brunelleschi's discovery had meanwhile been formulated in writing by Leone Battista Alberti, the author of the first Renaissance treatise on painting and, later, an important architect (see pages 469–72). The setting for Ghiberti's narrative is a spacious hall, a fine example of Early Renaissance architectural design reflecting the mature art of Brunelleschi, while the figures still remind us, by their gentle and graceful classicism, of the Gothic International Style.

THE CLASSICAL NUDE: JACOPO DELLA QUERCIA AND DONATELLO. Outside Florence, the only major sculptor at that time was Jacopo della Quercia of Siena (c. 1374–1438). Like Ghiberti, he changed his style from Gothic to Early Renaissance in mid-career, mainly through contact with Donatello. Had he grown up in Florence, he might have been one of the great leaders of the new movement from the start, but his forcefully individual art remained outside the main trend. It had no effect on Florentine art until the very end of the century, when the young Michelangelo fell under its spell. Michelangelo's admiration was aroused by the

scenes from Genesis framing the main portal of the church of S. Petronio in Bologna, among them *The Creation of Adam* (fig. 584).

The relief mode of these panels is conservative—Jacopo had little interest in pictorial depth—but the figures are daring and profoundly impressive. The figure of Adam slowly rising from the ground, as a statue brought to life might rise from its mold, recaptures the heroic beauty of a classical athlete. Here the nude body once again expresses the dignity and power of the individual as it did in classical antiquity. Yet we sense that Jacopo's Adam has not been freed from Original Sin; he contains a hint of incipient conflict as he faces the Lord; he will surely fall, but in pride of spirit rather than as a hapless victim of the Evil One.

It is instructive to compare Jacopo's *Adam* with the work that probably inspired it, an *Adam in Paradise* from an Early Christian ivory diptych (fig. 585). The latter figure represents a classicizing trend around 400 A.D. (compare fig. 331), a final attempt to preserve the Greek ideal of physical beauty within a Christian context. Adam appears as the Perfect Man, divinely appointed to "have dominion. . . over every living thing," but the classic form has already become a formula, a mere shell. And the classical nude entered the tradition of medieval art in this desiccated condition. Whenever we meet the unclothed body, from 800 to 1400, we may be sure that it is derived, directly or indirectly, from a classical source, no matter how unlikely this may seem (as in fig. 407). We may also be sure—except for a few special cases—that such nudity has a moral significance, whether negative (Adam and Eve, or sinners in Hell) or positive (the nudity of the Christ of the Passion; of saints being martyred or mortifying the flesh; of Fortitude in the guise of Hercules). Finally, medieval nudes, even the most accomplished, are devoid of that sensual appeal that we take for granted in every nude of classical antiquity. Such appeal was purposely avoided rather than unattainable, for to the medieval mind the physical beauty of the ancient "idols," especially nude statues, embodied the insidious attraction of paganism.

The fifteenth century rediscovered the sensuous beauty of the unclothed body, but by way of two separate paths. The Adam and Eve of Jan van Eyck (fig. 550), or the nudes of Bosch (fig. 559), have no precedent in either ancient or medieval art; they are, indeed, not "nude," but "naked"—people whose normal state is to be dressed and who for specific reasons appear stripped of their clothing. Jacopo's *Adam,* on the other hand, is clearly nude, in the full classical sense. So also is Donatello's bronze *David* (fig. 586), an even more revolutionary achievement, the first lifesize nude statue since antiquity that is wholly free-standing. The Middle Ages would surely have condemned it as an idol, and Donatello's contemporaries, too, must have felt uneasy about it; for many years it remained the only work of its kind. The early history of the figure is unknown, but it must have been meant for an open space where it would be visible from every side, probably standing on top of a column.

The key to its significance is the elaborate helmet of Goliath with visor and wings, a unique (and implausible) feature that can only refer to the dukes of Milan, who had threatened Florence about 1400 (see page 445) and were now warring

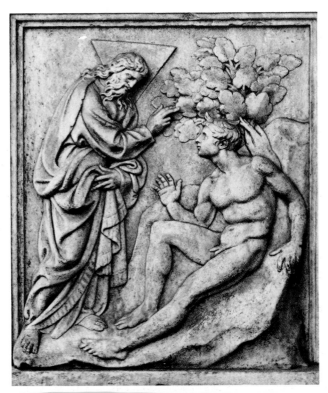

584. JACOPO DELLA QUERCIA. *THE CREATION OF ADAM.*
c. 1430. Marble, 34½×27½″ (87.7×69.8 cm).
Main portal, S. Petronio, Bologna

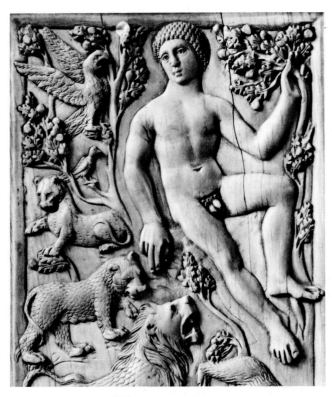

585. *ADAM IN PARADISE,*
detail of an ivory diptych. c. 400 A.D.
Museo Nazionale del Bargello, Florence

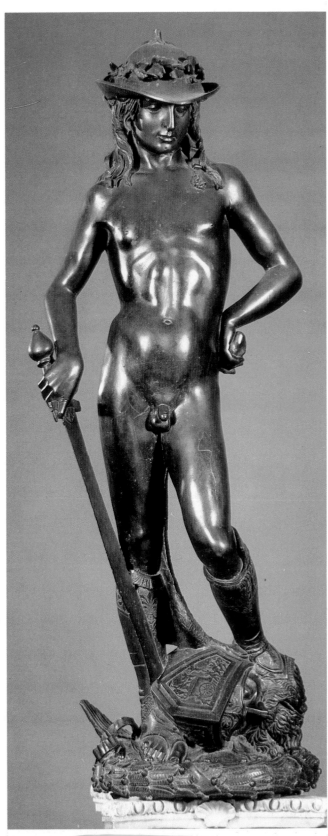

586. DONATELLO. *DAVID.* c. 1425–30.
Bronze, height 62¼″ (158 cm).
Museo Nazionale del Bargello, Florence

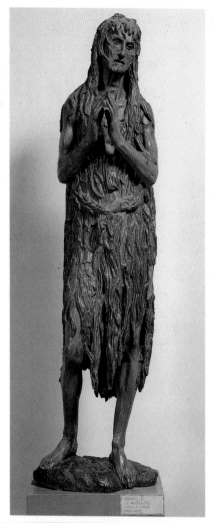

587. DONATELLO. *MARY MAGDALEN*. c. 1455.
Wood, partially gilded, height 6'2" (1.88 m).
Museo dell'Opera del Duomo, Florence

the intensity of Donatello's *Zuccone* (fig. 580), we realize that the ravaged features and wasted body of his *Mary Magdalen* betray an insight into religious experience that is not basically different from his earlier work.

DONATELLO'S LATER WORKS. Donatello was invited to Padua in 1443 to produce the *Equestrian Monument of Gattamelata,* the recently deceased commander of the Venetian armies (fig. 588). This statue, the artist's largest freestanding work in bronze, still stands in its original position on a tall pedestal near the façade of the church dedicated to St. Anthony of Padua. We already know its two chief precedents, the mounted *Marcus Aurelius* in Rome and the *Can Grande* in Verona (see figs. 296 and 514). Without directly imitating the former, the *Gattamelata* shares its material, its impressive scale, and its sense of balance and dignity; Donatello's horse, a heavy-set animal fit to carry a man in full armor, is so large that the rider must dominate it by his authority of command, rather than by physical force. The link with the Can Grande monument, though less obvious, is equally significant: both statues were made to stand next to a church façade, and both are memorials to the military prowess of the deceased. But the *Gattamelata,* in the new Renaissance fashion, is not part of a tomb; it was designed solely to immortalize the fame of a great soldier. Nor is it the self-glorifying statue of a sovereign, but a monument authorized by the Republic of Venice in special honor of distin-

against it once more in the mid-1420s. The statue, then, must be understood as a civic-patriotic public monument identifying David—weak but favored by the Lord—with Florence, and Goliath with Milan. David's nudity is most readily explained as a reference to the classical origin of Florence, and his wreathed hat as the opposite of Goliath's helmet: peace versus war. Donatello chose to model an adolescent boy, not a full-grown youth like the athletes of Greece, so that the skeletal structure here is less fully enveloped in swelling muscles; nor does he articulate the torso according to the classical pattern (compare figs. 201 and 202). In fact his *David* resembles an ancient statue only in its beautifully poised *contrapposto*. If the figure nevertheless conveys a profoundly classical air, the reason lies beyond its anatomical perfection; as in ancient statues, the body speaks to us more eloquently than the face, which by Donatello's standards is strangely devoid of individuality.

In contrast, the wood *Mary Magdalen* (fig. 587) seems so far from Renaissance ideals that at first we are tempted to see in this statue a return to such Gothic devotional images as the Bonn *Pietà* (see fig. 505). But when we look back at

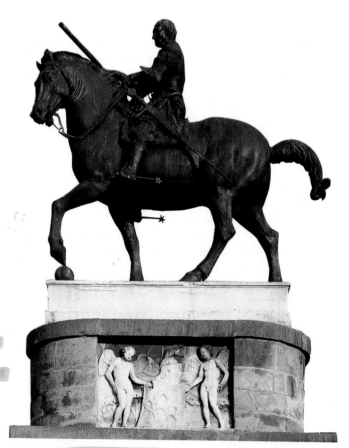

588. DONATELLO. *EQUESTRIAN MONUMENT OF GATTAMELATA*.
1445–50. Bronze, c. 11'×13' (3.35×3.96 m).
Piazza del Santo, Padua

guished and faithful service. To this purpose, Donatello has coined an image that is a complete union of ideal and reality; the general's armor combines modern construction with classical detail; the head is powerfully individual, and yet endowed with a truly Roman nobility of character.

When Donatello went home to Florence after a decade's absence, he must have felt like a stranger. The political and spiritual climate had changed, and so had the taste of artists and public (see page 455). His subsequent works, between 1453 and 1466, stand apart from the dominant trend; perhaps that is why their fierce expressiveness and personal quality exceed anything the master had revealed before. The extreme individualism of his late works confirms Donatello's reputation as the earliest "solitary genius" among the artists of the new age.

Architecture

BRUNELLESCHI. Although Donatello was its greatest and most daring master, he had not created the Early Renaissance style in sculpture all by himself. The new architecture, on the other hand, did owe its existence to one man, Filippo Brunelleschi (1377–1446). Ten years older than Donatello, Brunelleschi had begun his career as a sculptor. After failing to win the competition of 1401–2 for the first Baptistery doors, he reportedly went to Rome with Donatello. He studied the architectural monuments of the ancients, and seems to have been the first to take exact measurements of these structures. His discovery of scientific perspective may well have grown out of his search for an accurate method of recording their appearance on paper. What else he did during this long "gestation period" we do not know, but in 1417–19 we again find him competing with Ghiberti, this time for the job of building the Cathedral dome (see figs. 486 and 487). Its design had been established half a century earlier and could be altered only in details, but its vast size posed a difficult problem of construction. Brunelleschi's proposals, although contrary to all traditional practice, so impressed the authorities that this time he won out over his rival. Thus the dome deserves to be called the first work of post-medieval architecture, as an engineering feat if not for style.

The technical details need not concern us here. Brunelleschi's main achievement was to build the dome in two separate shells which are ingeniously linked to reinforce each other, rather than in one solid mass. As the total weight of the structure was thereby lightened, he could dispense with the massive and costly wooden trusswork required by the older method of construction. Instead of having building materials carried up on ramps to the required level, he designed hoisting machines; his entire scheme reflects a bold, analytical mind, always discarding conventional solutions if better ones could be devised. This fresh approach distinguishes Brunelleschi from the Gothic stonemason-architects, with their time-honored procedures.

S. Lorenzo. In 1419, while he was working out his final plans for the dome, Brunelleschi received his first opportunity to create buildings entirely of his own design. It came from the head of the Medici family, one of the leading mer-

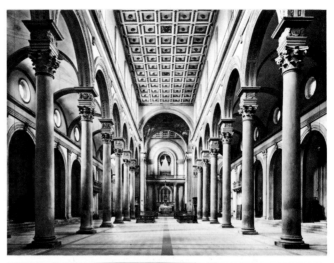

589. FILIPPO BRUNELLESCHI. S. Lorenzo, Florence. 1421–69

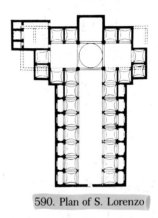

590. Plan of S. Lorenzo

chants and bankers of Florence, who commissioned him to add a sacristy to the Romanesque church of San Lorenzo. His plans for this sacristy (which was to serve also as a burial chapel for the Medici) so impressed his patron that he was immediately asked to develop a new design for the entire church. The construction, begun in 1421, was often interrupted, so that the interior was not completed until 1469, more than twenty years after the architect's death (the exterior remains unfinished to this day). Nevertheless, the building in its present form is essentially what Brunelleschi had envisioned about 1420, and thus represents the first full statement of his architectural aims (figs. 589 and 590).

The plan may not seem very novel, at first glance. Its general arrangement recalls Cistercian Gothic churches (see fig. 483); the unvaulted nave and transept link it to Sta. Croce (see fig. 484). What distinguishes it is a new emphasis on symmetry and regularity. The entire design consists of square units: four large squares form the choir, the crossing, and the arms of the transept; four more are combined into the nave; other squares, one-fourth the size of the large units, make up the aisles and the chapels attached to the transept (the oblong chapels outside the aisles were not part of the original design). We notice, however, some small deviations from this scheme—the transept arms are slightly longer than they are wide, and the length of the nave is not four but four and one-half times its width.

A few simple measurements will explain these apparent inconsistencies. Brunelleschi must have first decided to make the floor area of the choir equal to four of the small square units; the nave and transept were thus to be twice as wide as the aisles or chapels. But in fixing this system, he made no allowance for the inevitable thickness of the walls between these compartments, so that the transept arms have a width of two units, and a length of two units plus one wall-thickness; the nave is seven wall-thicknesses longer than, ideally speaking, it should be. In other words, Brunelleschi conceived S. Lorenzo as a grouping of abstract "space blocks," the larger ones being simple multiples of the standard unit. Once we understand this we realize how revolutionary he was, for his clearly defined, separate space compartments represent a radical departure from the Gothic architect's way of thinking.

The interior bears out our expectations. Cool, static order has replaced the emotional warmth, the flowing spatial movement of Gothic church interiors. S. Lorenzo does not sweep us off our feet. It does not even draw us forward after we have entered it—we are quite content to remain near the door, for our view seems to take in the entire structure almost as if, from that vantage point, we were confronted with a particularly clear and convincing demonstration of scientific perspective (compare fig. 583). The total effect recalls the "old-fashioned" Tuscan Romanesque—such as Pisa Cathedral (see fig. 430)—and Early Christian basilicas (compare fig. 318), for these monuments, to Brunelleschi, exemplified the church architecture of classical antiquity; they inspired his return to the use of the round arch and of columns, rather than piers, in the nave arcade. Yet these earlier buildings lack the transparent lightness, the wonderfully precise articulation of S. Lorenzo. Unlike Brunelleschi's, their columns are larger and more closely spaced, tending to screen off the aisles from the nave. Only the arcade of the Florentine Baptistery is as gracefully proportioned as that of S. Lorenzo, but it is a *blind* arcade, without any supporting function (see fig. 431; the Baptistery, we recall, was in Brunelleschi's day thought to have once been a classical temple).

But Brunelleschi did not revive the architectural vocabulary of the ancients out of mere antiquarian enthusiasm. The very quality that attracted him to the component parts of classical architecture must have seemed, from the medieval point of view, their chief drawback: inflexibility. A classical column, unlike a medieval column or pier, is strictly defined and self-sufficient, and its details and proportions can be varied only within narrow limits (the ancients thought of it as an organic structure comparable to the human body); the classical round arch, unlike any other arch (horseshoe, pointed, and so forth), has only one possible shape, a semicircle; the classical architrave and the classical repertory of profiles and ornaments are all subject to similarly strict rules. Not that the classical vocabulary is completely inflexible—if it were, it could not have persisted from the seventh century B.C. to the fourth century A.D. in the ancient world—but the disciplined spirit of the Greek orders, which can be felt even in the most original Roman buildings, demands regularity and consistency, and discourages sudden, arbitrary departures from the norm.

Without the aid of such a "standardized" vocabulary, Brunelleschi would have found it impossible to define the shape of his "space blocks" so convincingly. With remarkable logic, he emphasizes the edges or "seams" of the units without disrupting their rhythmic sequence. To single out a particularly noteworthy example, consider the vaulting of the aisles: the transverse arches rest on pilasters attached to the outer wall (corresponding to the columns of the nave arcade), but a continuous architrave intervenes between arch and pilaster, linking all the bays. We would expect these bays to be covered by groined vaults of the classical, unribbed type (see fig. 264); instead, we find a novel kind of vault, whose curved surface is formed from the upper part of a hemispherical dome (its radius equals half the diagonal of the square compartment). Avoiding the ribs and even the groins, Brunelleschi has created a "one-piece" vault, strikingly simple and geometrically regular, that makes of each bay a distinct unit.

Architectural Proportions. At this point we may well ask: if the new architecture consists essentially of separate elements added together, be they spaces, columns, or vaults, how did Brunelleschi relate these elements to each other? What makes the interior of S. Lorenzo seem so beautifully integrated? There is indeed a controlling principle that accounts for the harmonious, balanced character of his design. The secret of good architecture, Brunelleschi was convinced, lay in giving the "right" proportions—that is, proportional ratios expressed in simple whole numbers—to all the significant measurements of a building. The ancients had possessed this secret, he believed, and he tried to rediscover it by painstakingly surveying the remains of their monuments. What he found, and how he applied his theory to his own designs, we do not know for sure. He may have been the first, though, to think out what would be explicitly stated a few decades later in Leone Battista Alberti's *Treatise on Architecture*: that the arithmetical ratios determining musical harmony must also govern architecture, for they recur throughout the universe and are thus divine in origin.

Similar ideas, ultimately derived from the Greek philosopher Pythagoras, had been current during the Middle Ages (see page 456), but they had not before been expressed so radically, directly, and simply. When Gothic architects "borrowed" the ratios of musical theory, they did so with the aid of the theologians and far less consistently than their Renaissance successors. But even Brunelleschi's faith in the universal validity of harmonious proportions did not tell him how to allot these ratios to the parts of any given building. It left him many alternatives, and his choice among them was necessarily subjective. We may say, in fact, that the main reason S. Lorenzo strikes us as the product of a single great mind is the very individual "sense of proportion" permeating every detail.

In the revival of classical forms, Renaissance architecture found a standard vocabulary; the theory of harmonious proportions provided it with the kind of syntax that had been mostly absent in medieval architecture. Lest this comparatively inflexible order be misinterpreted as an architectural impoverishment, we might carry our linguistic analogy a bit further. It is tempting to see a parallel between the "unclassical" flexibility of medieval architecture, proliferating in regional styles, and the equally "unclassical" attitude at that time toward language, as evidenced by its barbarized Latin and the rapid growth of regional vernaculars, the ancestors of our modern Western tongues. The revival of Latin and Greek in the Renaissance did not stunt these languages; on the contrary, the classical influence made them so much more stable, precise, and articulate that Latin before long lost the dominant position it had maintained throughout the Middle Ages as the language of intellectual discourse. It is not by chance that today we can still read Renaissance literature in Italian, French, English, or German without much trouble, while texts of a century or two before can often be understood only by scholars. In a similar way, the revival of classical forms and proportions enabled Brunelleschi to transform the architectural "vernacular" of his region into a stable, precise, and articulate system. The new rationale underlying his buildings soon spread to the rest of Italy, and later to all of Northern Europe.

Pazzi Chapel. Among the surviving structures by Brunelleschi, not one exterior shows his original design unaltered by later hands, not even the façade of the Pazzi Chapel (fig. 591). The chapel was begun about 1430, but Brunelleschi (who died in 1446) could not have planned the façade in its present form. It dates from about 1460, and the top story remains incomplete. Nevertheless, it is a most original creation, totally unlike any medieval façade. A porch, reminiscent of the narthex of Early Christian churches (see

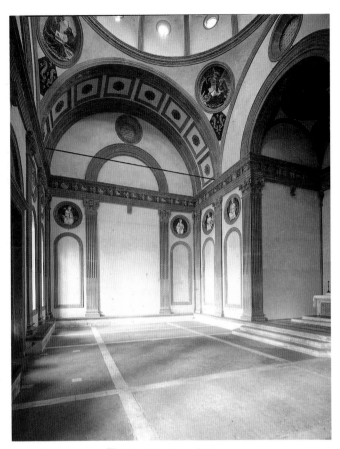

592. Interior, Pazzi Chapel

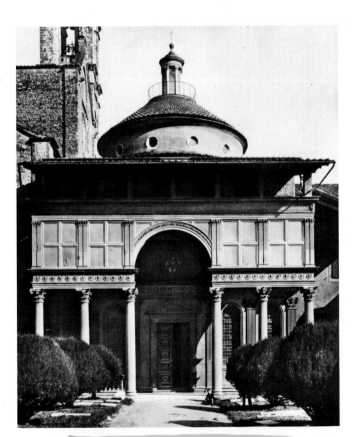

591. FILIPPO BRUNELLESCHI and others.
Pazzi Chapel, Sta. Croce, Florence. Begun 1430–33

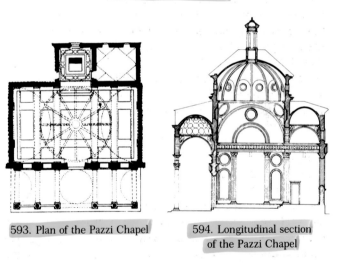

593. Plan of the Pazzi Chapel

594. Longitudinal section
of the Pazzi Chapel

fig. 317), precedes the chapel, making the façade seem to screen the main body of the structure. The central arch linking two sections of a classical colonnade is a prime innovation; it frames the portal behind, and draws attention to the dome. The plan (fig. 593) shows us that the interrupted architrave supports two barrel vaults, which in turn help to support a small dome above the central opening.

Inside the chapel, we find the same motif on a larger scale —two barrel vaults flanking the dome—and a third small dome, like that over the entrance, above the square compartment housing the altar (figs. 592 and 594). Interior surfaces are articulated much as in S. Lorenzo but their effect is richer and more festive. Here we also find some sculpture: large roundels on the four pendentives of the central dome, with reliefs of the evangelists (one of them is partly visible in fig. 592), and on the walls, twelve smaller ones of the apostles. These reliefs, however, are not essential to the design of the chapel; Brunelleschi provided the frames, but he need not have intended them to be filled with sculpture—the medallions may very well have been planned "blind," like the recessed panels below them. In any case, the medieval interdependence of architecture and sculpture (never as strong in Italy as in Northern Europe) had ceased to exist. Donatello had liberated the statue from its setting, and Brunelleschi's conception of architecture as the visual counterpart of musical harmonies did not permit sculpture to play a role more weighty than the roundels in the Pazzi Chapel.

Sto. Spirito. In the early 1430s, when the Cathedral dome was nearing completion, Brunelleschi's development as an architect entered a decisive new phase. His design for the church of Sto. Spirito (fig. 595) might be described as a perfected version of S. Lorenzo; all four arms of the cross are alike, the nave being distinguished from the others only by its greater length, and the entire structure now enveloped by an unbroken sequence of aisles and chapels. These chapels are the most surprising feature of Sto. Spirito; Brunelleschi had always shunned the apsidal shape before, but now he used it to express more dynamically the relation between interior space and its boundaries (the wall seems to bulge under the outward pressure of the space).

Sta. Maria degli Angeli. In the church of Sta. Maria degli Angeli, which Brunelleschi began about the same time as Sto. Spirito, this new tendency reaches its ultimate conclusion (fig. 596): a domed, central-plan church—the first of the Renaissance—inspired by the round and polygonal structures of Roman and Early Christian times (compare figs. 265–68, 322–24, and 334–37). Financial difficulties interfered with completing the project above the ground floor, and we cannot be sure of the design of the upper part, or even of some details in the plan. It is clear, nevertheless, that Brunelleschi here has recaptured the ancient Roman principle of the "sculptured" wall; the dome was to rest on eight heavy piers of complex shape, which belong to the same mass of masonry from which the eight chapels have been "excavated." Wall and space are both charged with energy, and the plan records the precarious balance of their pressures and counterpressures. As a conception, Sta. Maria degli Angeli was so far in advance of Brunelleschi's previous work that it must have utterly bewildered his contemporaries. It had, in fact, no echoes until the end of the century.

MICHELOZZO. The massive "Roman" style of Sta. Maria degli Angeli may explain the great disappointment of Brunelleschi's final years: the rejection by his old patrons, the Medici, of his design for their new palace. The family had risen, since the 1420s, to such power that they were in practice, if not in theory, the rulers of Florence. For that very reason they thought it prudent to avoid any ostentation that might antagonize the public. If Brunelleschi's plan for their

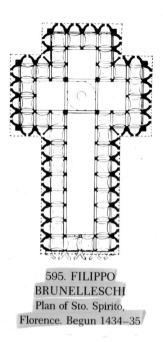

595. FILIPPO BRUNELLESCHI Plan of Sto. Spirito, Florence. Begun 1434–35

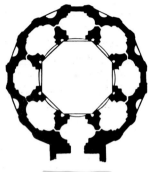

596. FILIPPO BRUNELLESCHI Plan of Sta. Maria degli Angeli, Florence. 1434–37

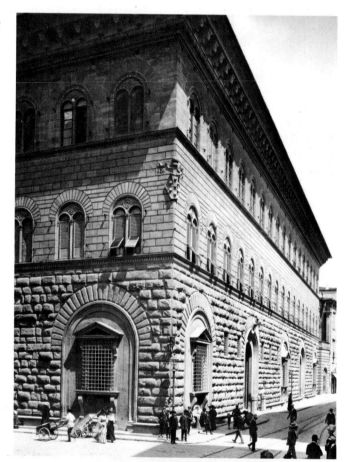

597. MICHELOZZO. Palazzo Medici-Riccardi, Florence. Begun 1444

palace followed the style of Sta. Maria degli Angeli, it probably had such imperial Roman magnificence that the Medici could not safely afford so grand an edifice. They awarded the commission to a younger and much less distinguished architect, Michelozzo (1396–1472); actual construction began in 1444, two years before Brunelleschi's death. Michelozzo's design for the Palazzo Medici-Riccardi (fig. 597) still recalls the fortresslike Florentine palaces of old (the windows on the ground floor were added by Michelangelo seventy-five years later), but the type has been transformed by Brunelleschian principles (compare fig. 491). The three stories are in a graded sequence, each complete in itself: the lowest is built of rough-hewn, "rustic" masonry like the Palazzo Vecchio; the second of smooth-surfaced blocks with "rusticated" (that is, indented) joints; the surface of the third is unbroken. On top of the structure rests, like a lid, a strongly projecting cornice inspired by those of Roman temples, emphasizing the finality of the three stories.

Painting

MASACCIO. Although Early Renaissance painting did not appear until the early 1420s, a decade later than Donatello's *St. Mark* and some years after Brunelleschi's first designs for S. Lorenzo, its inception is the most extraordinary of all; this new style was launched, single-handedly, by a young genius named Masaccio, who was only twenty-one years old at the time (he had been born in 1401) and who died at the age of twenty-seven. The Early Renaissance was already well established in sculpture and architecture by then, making Masaccio's task easier than it would have been otherwise; his achievement remains stupendous, nevertheless.

The earliest of his surviving works that can be dated fairly exactly is a fresco of 1425 in Sta. Maria Novella (fig. 598) which shows the Holy Trinity accompanied by the Virgin, St. John the Evangelist, and two donors who kneel on either side. The lowest section of the fresco, linked with a tomb below, represents a skeleton lying on a sarcophagus, with the inscription (in Italian): "What you are, I once was; what I am, you will become." Here, as in the case of the *Merode Altarpiece*, we seem to plunge into a new environment; but Masaccio's world is a realm of monumental grandeur rather than the concrete, everyday reality of the Master of Flémalle. It seems hard to believe that only two years before, in this city of Florence, Gentile da Fabriano had completed one of the masterpieces of the International Gothic (see fig. 545). What the *Trinity* fresco brings to mind is not the style of the immediate past, but Giotto's art, with its sense of the large scale, its compositional severity and sculptural volume. Yet Masaccio's renewed allegiance to Giotto was only a starting point. For Giotto, body and drapery form a single unit, as if both had the same substance; Masaccio's figures, like Donatello's, are "clothed nudes," their drapery falling like real fabric.

The setting, equally up-to-date, reveals a complete command of Brunelleschi's new architecture and of scientific perspective. This barrel-vaulted chamber is no mere niche, but a deep space wherein the figures could move freely if they wished. And—for the first time in history—we are given all the needed data to measure the depth of this painted interior. First we note that all the lines perpendicular to the picture plane converge upon a point below the foot of the cross, on the platform that supports the kneeling donors; to see the fresco properly, we must face this point, which is at normal eye-level, somewhat more than five feet above the floor of the church. The figures within the vaulted chamber

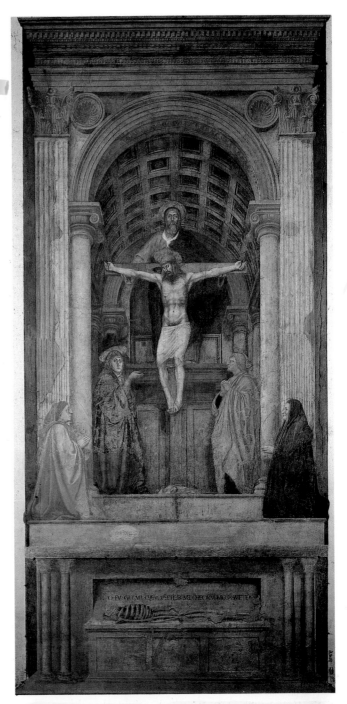

598. MASACCIO. *THE HOLY TRINITY WITH THE VIRGIN, ST. JOHN, AND TWO DONORS.* 1425. Fresco. Sta. Maria Novella, Florence

are five feet tall, slightly less than lifesize, while the donors, who are closer to us, are fully lifesize. The exterior framework is therefore "lifesize," too, since it is directly behind the donors. The distance between the pilasters corresponds to the span of the barrel vault, and both are seven feet; the circumference of the arc over this span measures eleven feet. That arc is subdivided by eight square coffers and nine ridges, the coffers being one foot wide and the ridges four inches. Applying these measurements to the length of the barrel vault (which consists of seven coffers—the nearest one is invisible behind the entrance arch) we find that the vaulted area is nine feet deep.

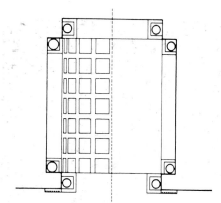

599. Ground plan of THE HOLY TRINITY

We can now draw a complete floor plan (fig. 599). A puz-zling feature may be the place of God the Father. His arms support the cross, close to the front plane, while His feet rest on a ledge attached to a wall. How far back is this surface? If it is the rear wall of the chamber, God would appear to be exempt from the laws of perspective. But in a universe ruled by reason, this cannot be so; hence Masaccio must have in-tended to locate the ledge directly behind the cross. The strong shadow that St. John casts on the wall beneath the ledge bears out our interpretation.

The largest group of Masaccio's works to come down to us are frescoes in the Brancacci Chapel in Sta. Maria del Car-mine (figs. 600–1). *The Tribute Money* (fig. 602) is the most renowned of these. It illustrates, by the age-old method known as "continuous narration" (see page 460), the story in the Gospel of Matthew (17:24–27): in the center, Christ instructs Peter to catch a fish, whose mouth will contain the tribute money for the tax collector; on the far left, in the dis-tance, Peter takes the coin from the fish's mouth; on the right, he gives it to the tax collector. Since the lower edge of

the fresco is almost fourteen feet above the floor of the chapel, Masaccio could not here co-ordinate his perspective with our actual eye-level. Instead, he expects us to imagine that we are looking directly at the central vanishing point, which is located behind the head of Christ. Oddly enough, this feat is so easy that we take note of it only if we are in an analytical frame of mind. But then, pictorial illusion of any sort is always an imaginary experience; no matter how eager we are to believe in a picture, we never mistake it for reality itself, just as we are hardly in danger of confusing a statue with a living thing.

If we could see *The Tribute Money* from the top of a suit-able ladder, the painted surface would be more visible, of course, but the illusion of reality would not be markedly im-proved. This illusion depends to only a minor degree on Brunelleschian perspective; Masaccio's weapons here are ex-actly those employed by the Master of Flémalle and the Van Eycks—he controls the flow of light (which comes from the right, where the window of the chapel is actually located), and he uses atmospheric perspective in the subtly changing tones of the landscape. (We recall Donatello's "preview" of such a setting, a decade earlier, in his small relief of St. George; compare fig. 579.)

The figures in *The Tribute Money*, even more than those in the *Trinity* fresco, display Masaccio's ability to merge the

600. (*opposite top*) Left wall of Brancacci Chapel, with frescoes by MASACCIO. Sta. Maria del Carmine, Florence

601. (*opposite bottom*) Right wall of Brancacci Chapel, with frescoes by MASOLINO and FILIPPINO LIPPI. Sta. Maria del Carmine, Florence

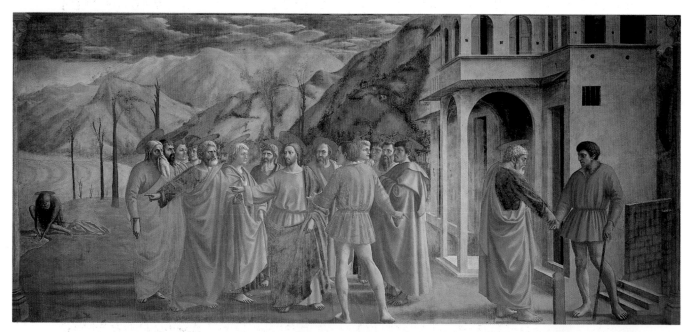

602. MASACCIO. *THE TRIBUTE MONEY.* c. 1427. Fresco. Brancacci Chapel, Sta. Maria del Carmine, Florence

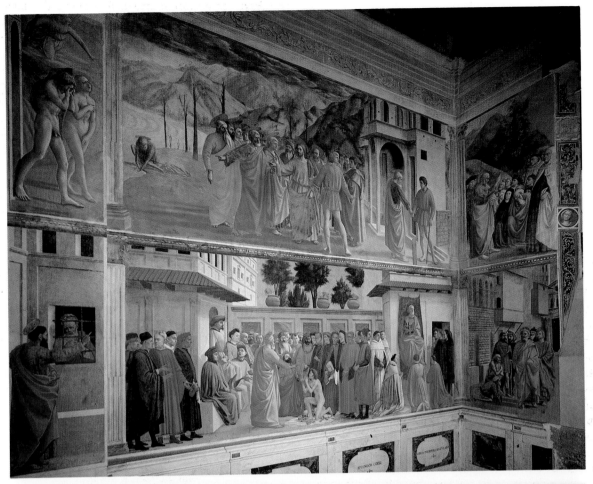

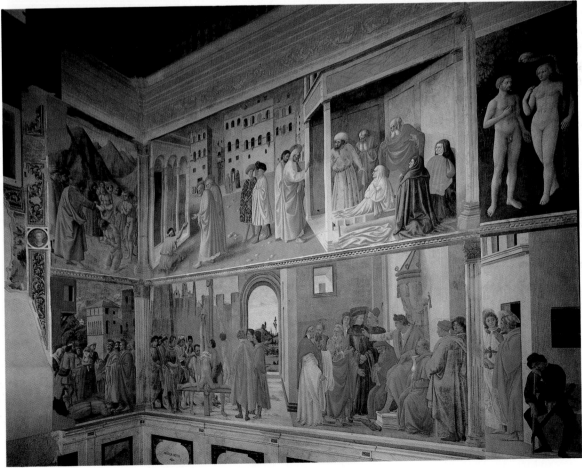

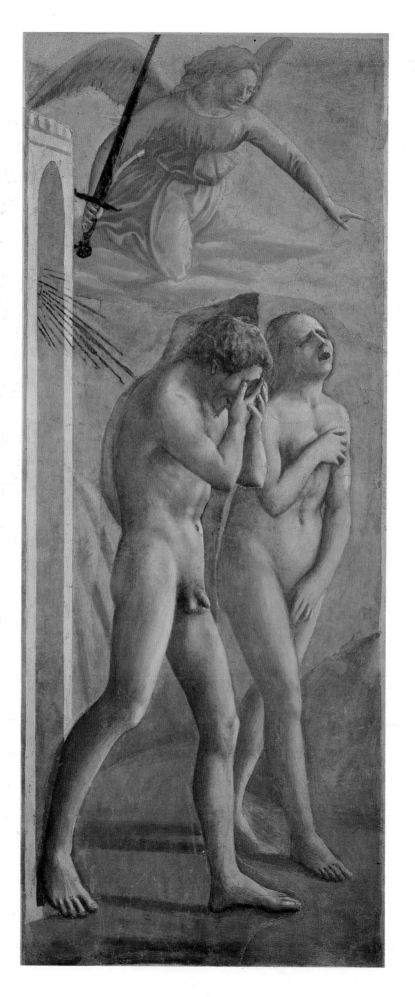

weight and volume of Giotto's figures with the new functional view of body and drapery. All stand in beautifully balanced *contrapposto*, and close inspection reveals fine vertical lines scratched in the plaster by the artist, establishing the gravitational axis of each figure from the head to the heel of the engaged leg. This makes the figures rather static, however; the narrative is conveyed to us by intense glances and a few emphatic gestures, rather than by physical movement. But in another fresco of the Brancacci Chapel, *The Expulsion from Paradise* (fig. 603), Masaccio proves decisively his ability to display the human body in motion. The tall, narrow format leaves little room for a spatial setting; the gate of Paradise is only indicated, and in the background are a few shadowy, barren slopes. Yet the soft, atmospheric modeling, and especially the forward-moving angel, boldly foreshortened, suffice to convey a free, unlimited space. In conception this scene is clearly akin to Jacopo della Quercia's Bolognese reliefs (see fig. 584). Masaccio's grief-stricken Adam and Eve, though less dependent on ancient models, are equally striking exemplars of the beauty and power of the nude human form.

While he had a mural painter's temperament, Masaccio was equally skilled in panel painting. His large polyptych, made in 1426 for the Carmelite church in Pisa, has since been dispersed among various collections. Its center panel shows a *Madonna Enthroned* (fig. 604), of the monumental Florentine type introduced by Cimabue and reshaped by Giotto (see figs. 522 and 529), and may be instructively compared with these. The traditional elements—including the gold ground—are still present: a large, high-backed throne dominates the composition and on either side are adoring angels (here only two). The kneeling angels in Giotto's *Madonna* have become lute players, seated on the lowest step of the throne, and the Christ Child is no longer blessing us but eating a bunch of grapes (a symbolic act alluding to the Passion and the Eucharist, the grapes referring to wine, which represents the Saviour's blood).

It is no surprise, after the *Trinity* fresco, that Masaccio replaces Giotto's ornate but frail Gothic throne with a solid and austere stone seat in the style of Brunelleschi, or that he uses perspective expertly (note especially the two lutes). We are perhaps less prepared by the murals to find such delicacy and precision in painting the light on the surfaces. Within the picture, sunlight enters from the left—not the brilliant glare of noontime but the softer glow of the setting sun (some of the shadows on the throne permit us to determine its exact angle). There are consequently no harsh contrasts between light and shade; subtle half-shadows intervene, producing a rich scale of transitional hues. The light retains its full descriptive function, while acting as an independent force that imposes a common tonality—and a common mood—upon all the forms it touches. Clearly, Masaccio's awareness of natural light as a pictorial factor matches that of his Flemish contemporaries, but he lacked their technical means to explore it so fully.

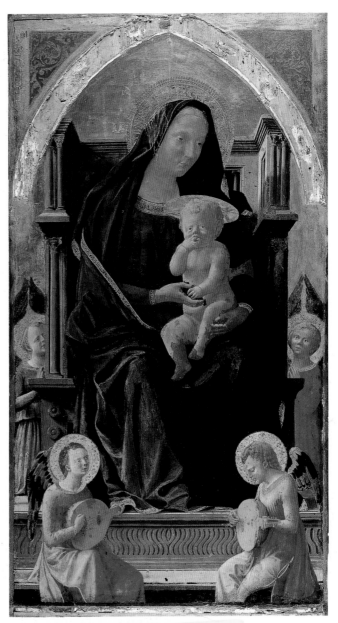

604. MASACCIO. *MADONNA ENTHRONED*. 1426. Oil on panel, 56 × 29″ (142 × 73.6 cm). The National Gallery, London.
Reproduction by courtesy of the Trustees

FRA FILIPPO LIPPI. Masaccio's early death left a gap that was not filled for some time. Among his younger contemporaries only Fra Filippo Lippi (c. 1406–1469) seems to have had close contact with him. Fra Filippo's earliest dated work, the *Madonna Enthroned* of 1437 (fig. 605), evokes Masaccio's earlier *Madonna* in several important ways—the lighting, the heavy throne, the massive three-dimensional figures, the drapery folds over the Virgin's legs. Nevertheless, the picture lacks Masaccio's monumentality and severity; in fact, it seems downright cluttered by comparison. The background is a domestic interior (note the Virgin's bed on the right), and the vividly patterned marble throne displays a prayer book and a scroll inscribed with the date. Such a quantity of realistic detail, as well as the rather undisciplined perspective, indicates an artistic temperament very different from Masaccio's; it also suggests that Fra Filippo must have seen

603. (*opposite*) MASACCIO. *THE EXPULSION FROM PARADISE*. c. 1427.
Fresco. Brancacci Chapel, Sta. Maria del Carmine, Florence

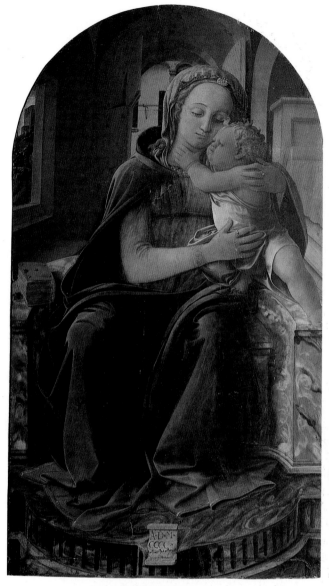

605. FRA FILIPPO LIPPI. *MADONNA ENTHRONED.*
1437. Panel, 45×25½″ (114.7×64.8 cm).
Galleria Nazionale d'Arte Antica, Rome

early Masacciesque outlook in a particularly significant way, for Fra Filippo lived until 1469 and played a decisive role in setting the course of Florentine painting during the second half of the century.

FRA ANGELICO. If Fra Filippo depended more on Donatello than on Ghiberti, the opposite is true of his slightly older contemporary, Fra Angelico (c. 1400–1455). He, too, was a friar ("fra" means "brother"), but, unlike Fra Filippo, he took his vows seriously and rose to a responsible position within his order. When, during the years 1437–52, the monastery of S. Marco in Florence was rebuilt, Fra Angelico embellished it with numerous frescoes. The large *Annunciation* (fig. 606) from this cycle has been dated about 1440 by some scholars, about 1450 by others—either date is plausible, for this artist, like Ghiberti, developed slowly, and his style underwent no decisive changes during the 1440s. Fra Angelico preserves the very aspects of Masaccio—his dignity, directness, and spatial order—that Fra Filippo had rejected. But his figures, much as we may admire their lyrical tenderness, never achieve the physical and psychological self-assurance that characterizes the Early Renaissance.

DOMENICO VENEZIANO. In 1439 a gifted painter from Venice, Domenico Veneziano, settled in Florence. We can only guess at his age (he was probably born about 1410 and he died in 1461), training, and previous work. He must, however, have been in sympathy with the spirit of Early Renaissance art, for he quickly became a thoroughgoing Florentine-by-choice, and a master of great importance in his new home. His *Madonna and Child with Saints*, shown in figure 607, is one of the earliest examples of a new type of altar panel that was to prove popular from the mid-fifteenth century on, the so-called *Sacra Conversazione* ("sacred conversation"). The scheme includes an enthroned Madonna, framed by architecture, and flanked by saints who may converse with her, with the beholder, or among themselves.

Looking at Domenico's panel, we can understand the wide appeal of the *Sacra Conversazione*. The architecture and the space it defines are supremely clear and tangible, yet elevated above the everyday world; and the figures, while echoing the formal solemnity of their setting, are linked with each other and with us by a thoroughly human awareness. We are admitted to their presence, but they do not invite us to join them; like spectators in a theater, we are not allowed "on stage." (In Flemish painting, by contrast, the picture space seems a direct extension of the beholder's everyday environment; compare fig. 547.)

The basic elements of our panel were already present in Masaccio's *Holy Trinity* fresco; Domenico must have studied it carefully, for his St. John looks at us while pointing toward the Madonna, repeating the glance and gesture of Masaccio's Virgin. Domenico's perspective setting is worthy of the older master, although the slender proportions and colored inlays of his architecture are less severely Brunelleschian. His figures, too, are balanced and dignified like Masaccio's, but without the same weight and bulk. The slim, sinewy bodies of the male saints, with their highly individualized, expressive faces, show Donatello's influence (fig. 580).

Flemish paintings (perhaps during his visit to northeastern Italy in the mid-1430s).

Finally, we must note another novel aspect of this *Madonna*: the painter's interest in movement, which is evident in the figures and, even more strikingly, in parts of the drapery (such as the curly, fluid edge of the Virgin's headdress and the curved folds of her mantle streaming to the left, accentuating her own turn to the right). These effects are found earlier in the relief sculpture of Donatello and Ghiberti—compare the dancing Salome in *The Feast of Herod* (fig. 581) and the maidens in the lower left-hand corner of *The Story of Jacob and Esau* (fig. 583). It is not surprising that these two artists should have so strongly affected Florentine painting in the decade after Masaccio's death. Age, experience, and prestige gave them authority unmatched by any painter then active in the city. Their influence, and that of the Flemish masters, modified Fra Filippo's

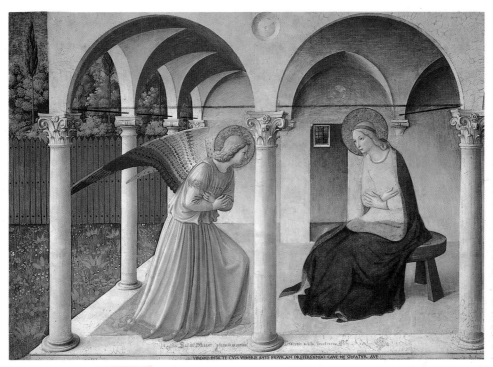

606. FRA ANGELICO. *THE ANNUNCIATION*. c. 1440–50. Fresco. S. Marco, Florence

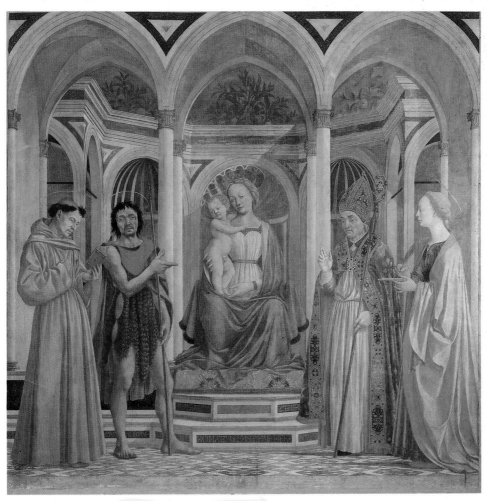

607. DOMENICO VENEZIANO. *MADONNA AND CHILD WITH SAINTS.*
c. 1455. Oil on panel, 6′7½×6′11⅞″ (2×2.1 m).
Galleria degli Uffizi, Florence

In his use of color, however, Domenico owes nothing to Masaccio; unlike the great Florentine master, he treats color as an integral part of his work, and the *Sacra Conversazione* is quite as remarkable for its color scheme as for its composition. The blond tonality, its harmony of pink, light green, and white set off by strategically placed spots of red, blue, and yellow, reconciles the decorative brightness of Gothic panel painting with the demands of perspective space and natural light. Ordinarily, a *Sacra Conversazione* is an indoor scene, but this one takes place in a kind of loggia flooded with sunlight streaming in from the right (note the cast shadow behind the Madonna). The surfaces of the architecture reflect the light so strongly that even the shadowed areas glow with color. Masaccio had achieved a similar quality of light in his *Madonna* of 1426 (which Domenico surely knew). In this *Sacra Conversazione*, the older master's discovery is applied to a far more complex set of forms, and integrated with Domenico's exquisite color sense. The influence of its distinctive tonality can be felt throughout Florentine painting of the second half of the century.

PIERO DELLA FRANCESCA. When Domenico Veneziano settled in Florence, he had as an assistant a young man from southeastern Tuscany named Piero della Francesca (c. 1420–1492), who became his most important disciple and one of the truly great artists of the Early Renaissance. Surprisingly enough, Piero left Florence after a few years, never to return. The Florentines seem to have regarded his work as somewhat provincial, and from their point of view they were right. Piero's style, even more strongly than Domenico's, reflected the aims of Masaccio; he retained this allegiance to the founding father of Italian Renaissance painting throughout his long career, whereas Florentine taste developed after 1450 in a different direction.

Piero's most impressive achievement is the fresco cycle in the choir of S. Francesco in Arezzo, which he painted from about 1452 to 1459 (fig. 608). Its many scenes represent the legend of the True Cross (that is, the origin and history of the cross used for Christ's crucifixion). The section seen in figure 609 shows the Empress Helena, the mother of Constantine the Great, discovering the True Cross and the two crosses of the thieves who died beside Christ (all three had been hidden by enemies of the Faith). On the left, they are being lifted out of the ground, and on the right, the True Cross is identified by its power to bring a dead youth back from the dead.

Piero's link with Domenico Veneziano is readily apparent from his colors. The tonality of this fresco, although less luminous than in Domenico's *Sacra Conversazione*, is similarly blond, evoking early morning sunlight in much the same way. Since the light enters the scene at a low angle, in a direction almost parallel to the picture plane, it serves both to define the three-dimensional character of every shape and to lend drama to the narrative. But Piero's figures have a harsh grandeur that recalls Masaccio, or even Giotto, more than Domenico. These men and women seem to belong to a lost heroic race, beautiful and strong—and silent. Their inner life is conveyed by glances and gestures, not by facial expressions. Above all, they have a gravity, both physical and

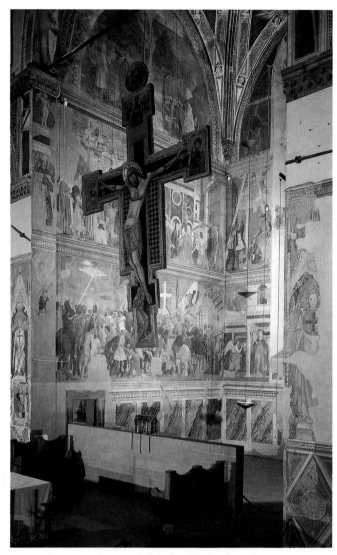

608. View into main chapel, with frescos by PIERO DELLA FRANCESCA. S. Francesco, Arezzo

emotional, that makes them seem kin to Greek sculpture of the Severe Style (see figs. 204 and 205).

How did Piero arrive at these memorable images? Using his own testimony, we may say that they were born of his passion for perspective. More than any artist of his day, Piero believed in scientific perspective as the basis of painting; in a rigorously mathematical treatise—the first of its kind—he demonstrated how it applied to stereometric bodies and architectural shapes, and to the human form. This mathematical outlook permeates all his work. When he drew a head, an arm, or a piece of drapery, he saw them as variations or compounds of spheres, cylinders, cones, cubes, and pyramids, endowing the visible world with some of the impersonal clarity and permanence of stereometric bodies. We may call him the earliest ancestor of the abstract artists of our own time, for they, too, work with systematic simplifications of natural forms. (The medieval artist, in contrast, had used the opposite procedure, building natural forms on geometric scaffoldings; see fig. 518.) It is not surprising that Piero's fame is greater today than ever before.

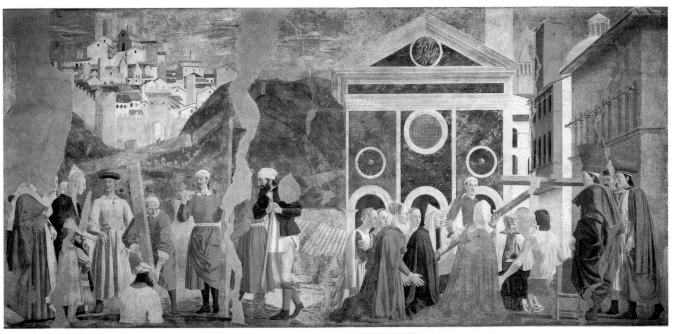

609. PIERO DELLA FRANCESCA. *THE DISCOVERY AND PROVING OF THE TRUE CROSS.* c. 1460.
Fresco, 11'8⅜"×6'4" (356×193 cm). S. Francesco, Arezzo

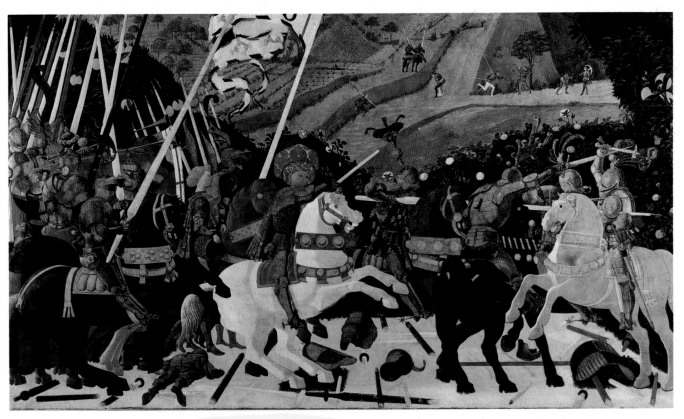

610. PAOLO UCCELLO. *BATTLE OF SAN ROMANO.* c. 1455. Tempera and silver foil on wood panel,
6'×10'5¾" (1.8×3.2 m). The National Gallery, London. Reproduced by courtesy of the Trustees

UCCELLO. In mid-fifteenth-century Florence there was only one painter who shared—and may have helped to inspire—Piero's devotion to perspective: Paolo Uccello (1397–1475). His *Battle of San Romano* (fig. 610), painted about the same time as Piero's frescoes in Arezzo, shows an extreme preoccupation with stereometric shapes. The ground is covered with a gridlike design of discarded weapons and pieces of armor—a display of perspective studies neatly arranged to include one fallen soldier. The landscape, too, has been subjected to a process of stereometric abstraction, matching the foreground. Despite these strenuous efforts, however, the panel has none of the crystalline order and clar-

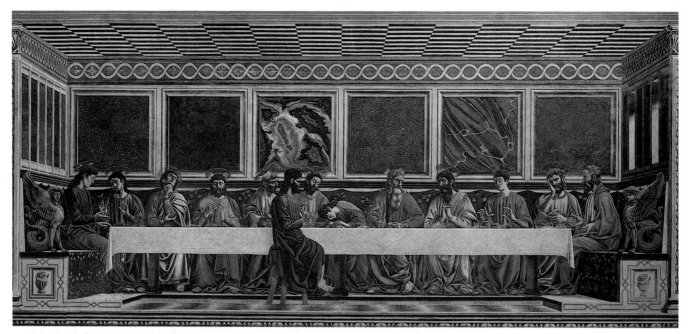

611. ANDREA DEL CASTAGNO. *THE LAST SUPPER*. c. 1445–50. Fresco. S. Apollonia, Florence

ity of Piero della Francesca's work. In the hands of Uccello, perspective produces strangely disquieting, fantastic effects; what unites his picture is not its spatial construction but its surface pattern, decoratively reinforced by spots of brilliant color and the lavish use of gold.

Uccello had been trained in the Gothic International Style of painting; it was only in the 1430s that he was "converted" to the Early Renaissance outlook by the new science of perspective. This he superimposed on his earlier style like a straitjacket. The result is a fascinating and highly unstable mixture. As we study this panel we realize that surface and space are more at war than the mounted soldiers, who get entangled with each other in all sorts of implausible ways.

CASTAGNO. The third dimension held no difficulties, however, for Andrea del Castagno (c. 1423–1457), the most gifted Florentine painter of Piero della Francesca's own generation. Less subtle but more forceful than Domenico Veneziano, Castagno recaptures something of Masaccio's monumentality in his *The Last Supper* (fig. 611), one of the frescoes he painted in the refectory of the convent of S. Apollonia. The event is set in a richly paneled alcove designed as an extension of the real space of the refectory. As in medieval representations of the subject, Judas sits in isolation on the near side of the table, opposite Christ. The rigid symmetry of the architecture, emphasized by the colorful inlays, enforces a similar order among the figures and threatens to imprison them; there is so little communication among the apostles— only a glance here, a gesture there—that a brooding silence hovers over the scene.

Castagno, too, must have felt confined by a scheme imposed on him by the rigid demands of both tradition and perspective, for he used a daringly original device to break the symmetry and focus the drama of the scene. Five of the six panels on the wall behind the table are filled with subdued

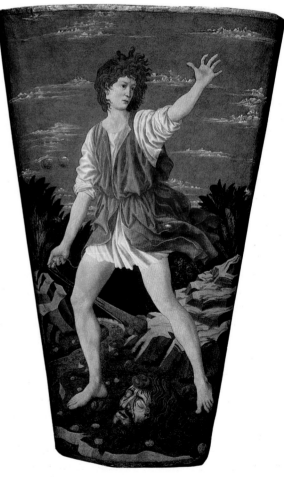

612. ANDREA DEL CASTAGNO. *DAVID*.
c. 1450–57. Leather, surface curved,
height 45½″ (115.8 cm).
The National Gallery of Art,
Washington, D.C. Widener Collection

varieties of colored marble, but above the heads of St. Peter, Judas, and Christ, the marble panel has a veining so garish and explosive that a bolt of lightning seems to descend on Judas' head. When Giotto revived the ancient technique of illusionistic marble textures, he hardly anticipated that it could hold such expressive significance.

Some five years after *The Last Supper,* between 1450 and 1457 (the year of his death), Castagno produced the remarkable *David* in figure 612. It is painted on a leather shield—to be used for display, not protection—and its owner probably wanted to convey an analogy between himself and the biblical hero, since David is here defiant as well as victorious. This figure differs fundamentally from the apostles of *The Last Supper.* Solid volume and statuesque immobility have given way to graceful movement, conveyed by both the pose and the windblown hair and drapery; the modeling of the earlier figures has been minimized, so that the David seems to be in relief rather than in the round, the forms now defined mainly by their outlines. This dynamic linear style has important virtues, but they are far from those of Masaccio. During the 1450s, the artistic climate of Florence changed greatly; Castagno's *David* is early evidence of the outlook that was to dominate the second half of the century.

CENTRAL AND NORTHERN ITALY: 1450–1500

As the founding fathers of Early Renaissance art and their immediate heirs disappeared one by one in the middle years of the century, a younger generation began to assert itself. At the same time, the seeds planted by Florentine masters in other regions of Italy—we recall Donatello's stay in Padua—were burgeoning; when some of these regions, notably the northeast, produced distinctive versions of the new style, Tuscany ceased to have the privileged position it had enjoyed before.

Architecture

ALBERTI. In architecture, the death of Brunelleschi in 1446 brought to the fore Leone Battista Alberti (1404–1472), whose career as a practicing architect had been long delayed, like Brunelleschi's own. Until he was forty, Alberti seems to have been interested in the fine arts only as an antiquarian and theorist; he studied the monuments of ancient Rome, composed the earliest Renaissance treatises on sculpture and painting, and began a third treatise, far more exhaustive than the other two, on architecture. After about 1430, he was close to the leading artists of his day (the treatise *On Painting* is dedicated to Brunelleschi and refers to "our dear friend" Donatello) and began to practice art as a dilettante; eventually he became a professional architect of outstanding ability. Highly educated in classical literature and philosophy, as an artist he exemplifies both the humanist and the person of the world.

Palazzo Rucellai, Florence. The design for the Palazzo Rucellai (fig. 613) may be Alberti's critique of the slightly earlier Medici Palace (see fig. 597). Again we meet the heavy cornice and the three-story scheme, but the articulation of the façade is more strict and more self-consciously classical. It consists of three superimposed orders of pilasters, separated by wide architraves, in imitation of the Colosseum (see fig. 263). Yet Alberti's pilasters are so flat that they remain part of the wall, and the entire façade seems to be one surface on which the artist projects a linear diagram of the Colosseum exterior. If we are to grasp the logic of this curiously abstract and theoretical design, we must understand that Alberti has met here—perhaps for the first time—an issue that became fundamental to Renaissance architecture: how to apply a classical system of articulation to the exterior of a nonclassical structure. Whether Brunelleschi ever coped with the same problem is difficult to say; only his exterior design for the Pazzi Chapel survives, but not unaltered, and it is too special a case to permit general conclusions. Alberti's solution acknowledges the primacy of the wall, reducing the classical system to a network of incised lines.

S. Francesco, Rimini. For his first church exterior, Alberti tried a radically different alternative. Sigismondo Malatesta, lord of the town of Rimini, engaged him toward 1450 to turn the Gothic church of S. Francesco into a "temple of fame" and a burial site for himself, his wife, and the humanists of his court. Alberti encased the older building in a Renaissance

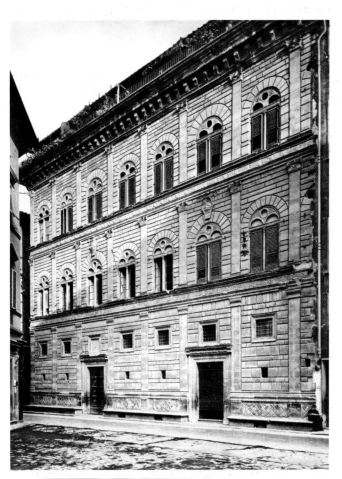

613. LEONE BATTISTA ALBERTI. Palazzo Rucellai, Florence. 1446–51

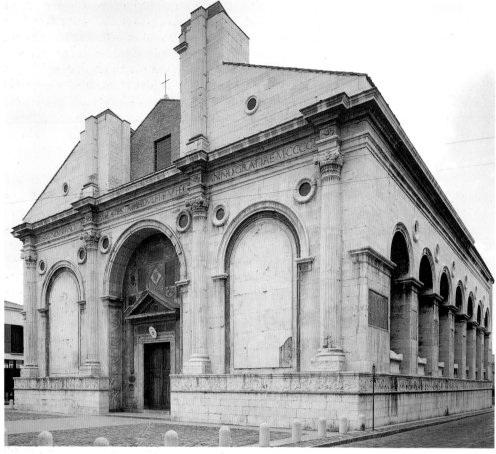

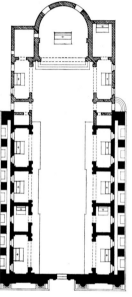

615. Plan of S. Francesco

shell, the sides consisting of austere, deeply recessed niches, arched above and containing stone sarcophagi (figs. 614 and 615). The façade has three similar niches, the large one framing the central portal, the other two (now filled in) intended to receive the sarcophagi of Sigismondo and his wife.

But the façade niches are flanked by columns, in a scheme clearly derived from the triumphal arches of ancient Rome (see fig. 300). Unlike the pilasters of the Palazzo Rucellai, these columns are not part of the wall; although partly embedded in it, they project so strongly that we see them as separate entities. We notice, too, that they are set on separate blocks, rather than on the platform supporting the walls, and that they would have nothing to support if the entablature had not been made to project above each capital. These projections make the vertical divisions of the façade more conspicuous than the horizontal ones, and we expect each column to support some important feature of the upper story. Yet Alberti planned such a feature (an arched niche with a window, and framed by pilasters) only above the portal; the second story fails to fulfill the promise of the first. Perhaps our artist would have modified this aspect of his design in the end, but the whole enterprise was never finished, and the great dome, projected as its crowning feature, was never built. If the classical system of the Palazzo Rucellai is in danger of being devoured by the wall, that of S. Francesco retains too much of its ancient Roman character to fit the shape of a basilican façade. (See, for contrast, the medieval approach to this task in fig. 428.)

S. Andrea, Mantua. Only toward the end of his career did Alberti find a fully satisfactory answer to his problem. In the majestic façade of S. Andrea at Mantua (fig. 616), designed in 1470, he has superimposed the triumphal-arch motif—now with a huge center niche—upon a classical temple front, and projected this combination onto the wall. Significantly enough, he again uses flat pilasters that acknowledge the primacy of the wall surface, but these pilasters, unlike those of the Palazzo Rucellai, are clearly differentiated from their surroundings. They are of two sizes; the larger ones are linked with the unbroken architrave and the strongly outlined pediment, and form what is known as a "colossal" order for all three stories of the façade wall, balancing exactly the horizontal and vertical impulses within the design. So intent was Alberti on stressing the inner cohesion of the façade that he made its height equal to its width, even though this height is appreciably lower than that of the nave of the church. Thus, the upper portion of the west wall protrudes above the pediment. Since this part is behind the façade, it is relatively invisible from the street; Alberti's compromise is more disturbing in photographs, which must be taken from a point high above street level to avoid distortion. While the façade is thus physically distinct from the main body of the structure, artistically there is complete continuity with the interior of the church, where the same colossal order, the same proportions, and the same triumphal-arch motif reappear on the nave walls (see the plan, fig. 617): the façade offers an exact "preview" of the interior.

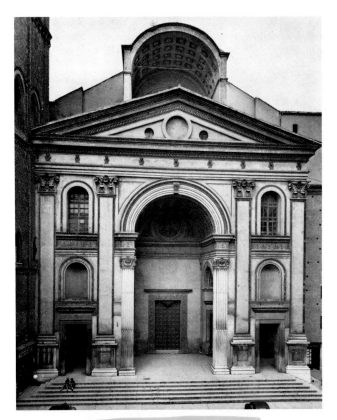

616. LEONE BATTISTA ALBERTI
S. Andrea, Mantua. Designed 1470

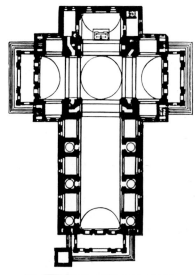

617. Plan of S. Andrea, Mantua
(transept, dome, and choir are later additions)

Comparing the plan with Brunelleschi's Sto. Spirito (fig. 595), we are struck by its revolutionary compactness. Had the church been completed as planned, the difference would be even stronger, for Alberti's design had no transept, dome, or choir, only a nave terminating in an apse. The aisles are replaced by chapels alternately large and small, and there is no clerestory; the colossal pilasters and the arches of the large chapels support a barrel vault of impressive span (the nave is as wide as the façade). Alberti has here drawn upon his memories of the massive vaulted halls in ancient Roman baths and basilicas (compare fig. 270), yet he interprets his classical models as freely as in his façade design. They no longer embody an absolute authority that must be quoted literally, but serve as a valuable store of motifs to be utilized at will. With this sovereign attitude toward his sources, he was able to create a structure that truly deserves to be called a "Christian temple."

CENTRAL-PLAN CHURCHES. Nevertheless, S. Andrea, which occupies the site of an older church (note the Gothic campanile next to the façade) with consequent limitations on the designer's freedom, does not conform to the ideal shape of sacred buildings defined in Alberti's *Treatise on Architecture*. There he explains that the plan of such structures should be either circular, or of a shape derived from the circle (square, hexagon, octagon, and so forth), because the circle is the perfect as well as the most natural figure and therefore a direct image of Divine reason.

This argument rests, of course, on Alberti's faith in the God-given validity of mathematically determined proportions (discussed on page 456); but how could he reconcile it with the historical evidence? After all, the standard form of both ancient temples and Christian churches was longitudinal. But, he reasoned, the basilican church plan became traditional only because the early Christians worshiped in private Roman basilicas. Since pagan basilicas were associated with the dispensing of justice (which originates from God), he admitted that their shape has some relationship to sacred architecture, but since they cannot rival the sublime beauty of the temple, their purpose is human rather than divine.

In speaking of temples, Alberti arbitrarily disregarded the standard form and relied instead on the Pantheon (see figs. 265–68), the round temple at Tivoli (see figs. 255 and 256), and the domed mausoleums (which he mistook for temples). Moreover, he asked, had not the early Christians themselves acknowledged the sacred character of these structures by converting them to their own use? Here he could point to such monuments as Sta. Costanza (see figs. 322–24), the Pantheon (which had been used as a church ever since the early Middle Ages), and the Baptistery in Florence (supposedly a former temple of Mars).

Alberti's ideal church, then, demands a design so harmonious that it would be a revelation of divinity, and would arouse pious contemplation in the worshiper. It should stand alone, elevated above the surrounding everyday life, and light should enter through openings placed high, for only the sky should be seen through them. That such an isolated, central-plan structure was ill-adapted to the requirements of Catholic ritual made no difference to Alberti; a church, he believed, must be a visible embodiment of "divine proportion," and the central plan alone permitted attainment of this.

When Alberti formulated these ideas in his treatise, about 1450, he could have cited only Brunelleschi's revolutionary—and unfinished—Sta. Maria degli Angeli as a modern example of a central-plan church (fig. 596). Toward the end of the century, after his treatise became widely known, the central-plan church gained general acceptance; between 1500 and 1525 it became a vogue reigning supreme in High Renaissance architecture.

GIULIANO DA SANGALLO. It is no mere coincidence that Sta. Maria delle Carceri in Prato (figs. 618–20), an early and distinguished example of this trend, was begun in 1485, the date of the first printed edition of Alberti's treatise. Its architect, Giuliano da Sangallo (c. 1443–1516), must have been an admirer of Brunelleschi—many features of the design recall the Pazzi Chapel—but the basic shape of his structure conforms closely to Alberti's ideal. Except for the dome, the entire church would fit neatly inside a cube, since its height (up to the drum) equals its length and width. By cutting into the corners of this cube, as it were, Giuliano has formed a Greek cross (a plan he preferred for its symbolic value). The dimensions of the four arms stand in the simplest possible ratio to those of the cube: their length is one-half their width, their width one-half their height. The arms are barrel-vaulted, and the dome rests on these vaults, yet the dark ring of the drum does not quite touch the supporting arches, making the dome seem to hover, weightless, like the pendentive domes of Byzantine architecture (compare fig. 351). There can be no doubt that Giuliano wanted his dome to accord with the age-old tradition of the Dome of Heaven; the single round opening in the center and the twelve on the perimeter clearly refer to Christ and the apostles. Brunelleschi had anticipated this feature in the Pazzi Chapel, but Giuliano's dome, crowning a perfectly symmetrical structure, conveys its symbolic value far more strikingly.

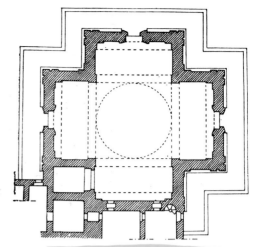

619. Plan of Sta. Maria delle Carceri

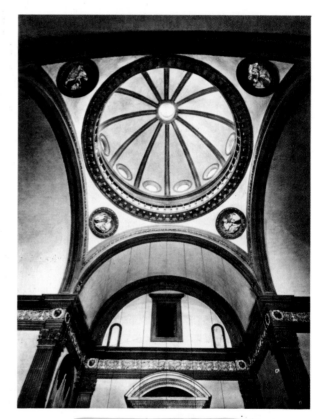

620. Interior, Sta. Maria delle Carceri

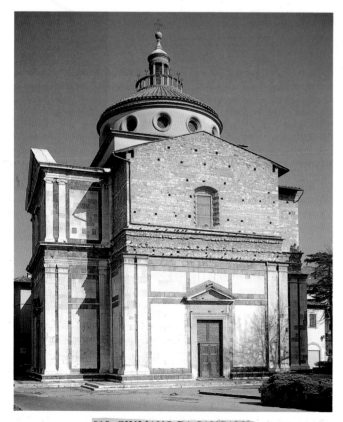

618. GIULIANO DA SANGALLO
Sta. Maria delle Carceri, Prato. 1485

Sculpture

Donatello left Florence for Padua in 1443; his ten-year absence had an effect similar to that of Brunelleschi's death. But whereas Alberti took Brunelleschi's place in architecture, there was no young sculptor of comparable stature to take Donatello's. The consequence of his absence was to bring into greater prominence the other sculptors remaining in the city. The new talents who appeared on the scene between 1443 and 1453 grew up under the influence of these men; it was the younger sculptors who brought about the

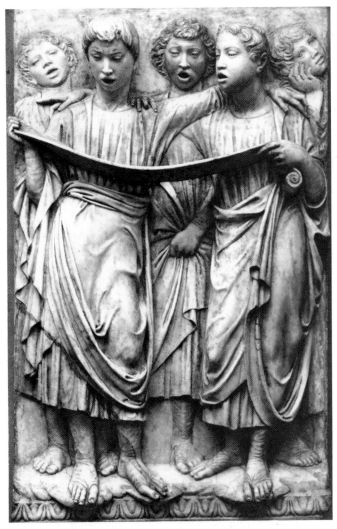

621. LUCA DELLA ROBBIA. *SINGING ANGELS,* from the
CANTORIA. c. 1435. Marble, c. 38×24″ (96.7×61 cm).
Museo dell'Opera del Duomo, Florence

changes Donatello must have seen with dismay when he returned to Florence.

LUCA DELLA ROBBIA. Ghiberti aside, the only significant sculptor in Florence after Donatello left was Luca della Robbia (1400–1482). He had made his reputation in the 1430s with the marble reliefs of his *Cantoria,* or singers' pulpit, in the Cathedral. The *Singing Angels* panel reproduced here (fig. 621) shows the beguiling mixture of sweetness and gravity characteristic of all of Luca's work. Its style, we realize, has very little to do with Donatello; instead, it recalls the classicism of Nanni di Banco (see fig. 573), with whom Luca may have worked as a youth. We also sense a touch of Ghiberti here and there, as well as the powerful influence of classicistic Roman reliefs (such as fig. 286). But Luca, despite his great gifts, lacked a capacity for growth. He never, so far as we know, did a free-standing statue, and the *Cantoria* remained his most ambitious achievement.

For the rest of his long career, he devoted himself almost exclusively to sculpture in terracotta—a cheaper and less demanding medium than marble—which he covered with enamellike glazes to mask its surface and make it impervious to weather. His finest works in this technique, such as *The Resurrection* in figure 622, have the dignity and charm of the *Cantoria* panels. The white glaze creates the impression of marble, with a deep blue for the background of the lunette. Other colors were confined almost entirely to the decorative framework of Luca's reliefs. This restraint, however, lasted only while he was in active charge of his workshop. Later, the quality of the modeling deteriorated and the simple harmony of white and blue often gave way to an assortment of more vivid hues. At the end of the century, the della Robbia shop had become a factory, turning out small Madonna panels and garish altarpieces for village churches by the score.

Because of Luca's almost complete withdrawal from the domain of marble carving, there was a real shortage of capable marble sculptors in the Florence of the 1440s. By the time Donatello returned, this gap had been filled by a group of men, most of them still in their twenties, from the little hill towns to the north and east of Florence. That region had long supplied the city with stonemasons and carvers; now, because the exceptional circumstances gave them special

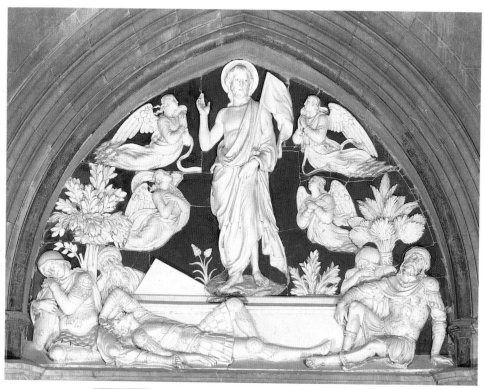

622. LUCA DELLA ROBBIA. *THE RESURRECTION.* 1442–45.
Glazed terracotta, 63×87½" (160×222.2 cm).
Museo Nazionale del Bargello, Florence

opportunities, the most gifted of them developed into artists of considerable importance.

BERNARDO ROSSELLINO. Oldest of these, Bernardo Rossellino (1409–1464) seems to have begun as a sculptor and architect in Arezzo. He established himself in Florence about 1436, but received no commissions of real consequence until some eight years later, when he was entrusted with the tomb of Leonardo Bruni (fig. 623). This great humanist and statesman had played a vital part in the city's affairs ever since the beginning of the century (see page 445). When he died in 1444, he received a grand funeral "in the manner of the ancients," and his monument, too, was probably ordered by the government. Since he had been born in Arezzo, however, his native town also wished to honor him, and its representatives may have helped to secure the commission for Bernardo, whom they knew from his earlier activity there. One wonders what chance Bernardo would have had if Donatello had been available.

Although the Bruni monument is not the earliest Renaissance tomb, nor even the earliest large-scale tomb of a humanist, it can claim to be the first memorial that fully expresses the spirit of the new era. Echoes of Bruni's funeral *all'antica* are everywhere: the deceased reclines on a bier supported by Roman eagles, his head wreathed in laurel and his hands enfolding a volume, presumably his own *History of Florence,* rather than a prayer book—a fitting tribute to the man who, more than any other, had helped to establish the new historical perspective of the Florentine Early Renaissance. On the classically severe sarcophagus, two winged genii display an inscription very different from those on medieval tombs; instead of recording the name, rank, and age of the deceased and the date of his death, it refers only to his timeless accomplishments: "At Leonardo's passing, history grieves, eloquence is mute, and it is said that the Muses, Greek and Latin alike, cannot hold back their tears." The religious aspect of the tomb is confined to the lunette, where the Madonna is adored by angels.

The entire monument may thus be viewed as an attempt to reconcile two contrasting attitudes toward death—the retrospective, commemorative outlook of the ancients (see page 191), and the Christian concern with afterlife and salvation. Bernardo's design is admirably suited to such a program, balancing architecture and sculpture within a compact, self-contained framework. Its dominant motif, the two pilasters supporting a round arch resting on a strongly accented architrave, suggests Alberti, who employed it repeatedly. It is derived from the entrance to the Pantheon (see fig. 266), which accounts for its use in church portals such as that of S. Andrea in Mantua (fig. 616). While Bernardo may have adopted it for the Bruni tomb on purely aesthetic grounds, it is possible that he also meant to convey a symbolic meaning—the deceased on his bier, pausing at the gateway between one life and the next. Perhaps he even wanted us to associate the motif with the Pantheon, the "temple of the immortals" for pagans and Christians alike; once dedicated to all the gods of the Roman world, it had been rededicated to all the martyrs when it became a church, and in the High Renaissance it was to receive the remains of yet another breed of immortals—such famous artists as Raphael.

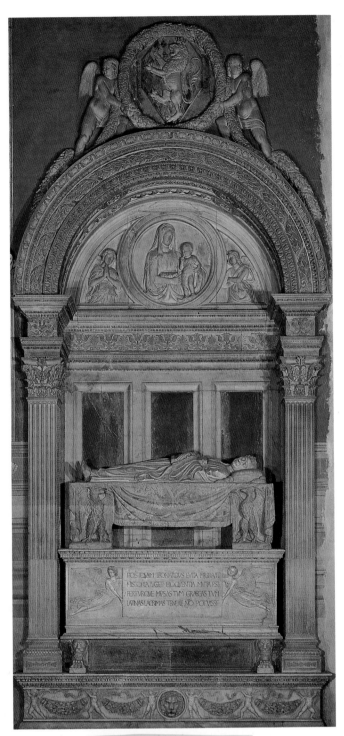

623. BERNARDO ROSSELLINO
Tomb of Leonardo Bruni, c.1445–50.
Marble, height 20' (6.1 m to top of arch).
Sta. Croce, Florence

such as his very gifted younger brother Antonio and other members of the same generation. Their share in Bernardo's sculptural projects is hard to identify, however, for their personalities were not distinct until they began to work independently. Nor have we yet a clear conception of Bernardo's own style as a sculptor. In any event, all the tombs, tabernacles, and the reliefs of the Madonna produced by the younger men between 1450 and 1480 have a common ancestor in the Bruni monument, whatever other elements we may discern in them.

THE PORTRAIT BUST.   Since Bernardo Rossellino and his artistic descendants concentrated their efforts on sculptural ensembles of the kind we have labeled church furniture, free-standing statues are—with one or two possible exceptions—absent from their works. They produced only one form of large-scale sculpture in the round that was not intended for an architectural context—the marble portrait bust. The great Roman tradition of realistic portrait sculpture, we recall, had died out in late antiquity; its revival was long credited to Donatello (who certainly knew and admired Roman portraits, as we saw in the *Zuccone*), but the earliest examples we know all date from the 1450s, and none is by Donatello. It seems far more likely, therefore, that the Renaissance portrait bust originated among the younger marble sculptors from the circle of Bernardo Rossellino.

The attractive example shown in figure 624 was carved in 1456 by Antonio Rossellino (1427–1479). It represents a highly esteemed Florentine physician, Giovanni Chellini, whose personality—at once sardonic and kindly—has been

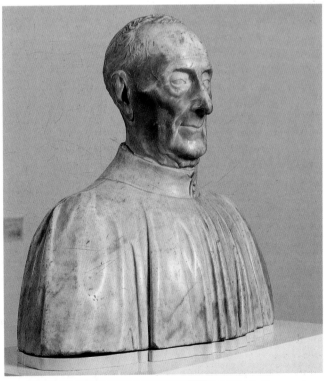

624. ANTONIO ROSSELLINO. *GIOVANNI CHELLINI.* 1456.
Marble, height 20" (50.7 cm). Victoria & Albert Museum, London
(Crown copyright reserved)

The sculptural style of the Bruni tomb is not easy to define, since its component parts vary a good deal in quality. Broadly speaking, it reflects the classicism of Ghiberti and Luca della Robbia; echoes of Donatello are few and indirect. Bernardo surely employed assistants here, as he did in his subsequent commissions. During the later 1440s, his workshop was the only training ground for ambitious young marble sculptors, observed with extraordinary precision. Comparing it with Roman heads (such as figs. 282 and 283, and 293–99), we cannot say the resemblance to them is striking. In fact, these Roman busts, however realistic they may seem at first, all look idealized in some respect (not always physically) beside our Florentine doctor, who radiates an individuality far beyond any attained in ancient times. He is linked to his Roman predecessors only by the idea of portrait sculpture in the round as an effective—and enduring—substitute for the sitter's real presence. Stylistically, the ancestry of Antonio's bust is to be found among the heads of effigies, such as that of Leonardo Bruni, for it was in tomb sculpture that realistic portraiture had first been revived, often with the aid of death masks. Although our piece was carved during the sitter's lifetime, its insistence on documenting every wrinkle makes it look like a death-mask portrait suddenly brought to life. Fortunately, Antonio Rossellino did not permit this preoccupation with the details of facial topography to diminish his concern with the sitter's qualities as a human being.

POLLAIUOLO. The popularity of portrait busts after about 1450 suggests a demand for works to be shown in the homes of individual art patrons. The collecting of sculpture, widely practiced in ancient times, apparently ceased during the Middle Ages; the taste of kings and feudal lords—those who could afford to collect for personal pleasure—ran to gems, jewelry, goldsmith's work, illuminated manuscripts, and precious fabrics. The habit was re-established in fifteenth-century Italy as an aspect of the "revival of antiquity." Humanists and artists first collected ancient sculpture, especially small bronzes (such as fig. 232), which were numerous and of convenient size; before long, contemporary artists began to cater to the spreading vogue, with portrait busts and with small bronzes of their own "in the manner of the ancients."

A particularly fine piece of this kind (fig. 625) is by Antonio del Pollaiuolo (1431–1498), who represents a sculptural style very different from that of the marble carvers we discussed above. Trained as a goldsmith and metalworker, probably in the Ghiberti workshop, he was deeply impressed by the late styles of both Donatello and Castagno, as well as by ancient art. From these sources, he evolved the distinctive manner that appears in our *Hercules and Antaeus*. To create a freestanding group of two figures in violent struggle, even on a small scale, was a daring idea in itself; even more astonishing is the way Pollaiuolo has endowed his composition with a centrifugal impulse: limbs seem to radiate in every direction from a common center, and we see the full complexity of their movements only when we turn the statuette before our eyes. Despite its strenuous action, the group is in perfect balance. To stress the central axis, Pollaiuolo, as it were, grafted the upper part of Antaeus onto the lower part of his adversary.

There is no precedent for this design among earlier statuary groups of any size, ancient or Renaissance; our artist has simply given a third dimension to a composition from the field of drawing or painting. He himself was a painter and engraver as well as a bronze sculptor, and we know that about 1465 he did a large picture of Hercules and Antaeus, now lost, for the Medici Palace (our statuette also belonged to the Medici).

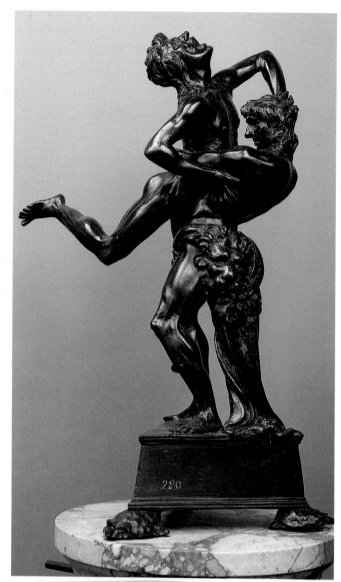

625. ANTONIO DEL POLLAIUOLO. *HERCULES AND ANTAEUS.* c. 1475. Bronze, height 18″ (45.8 cm, with base). Museo Nazionale del Bargello, Florence

Few of his paintings have survived, and only a single engraving, the *Battle of the Ten Naked Men* (fig. 626). This print, however, is of great importance, since it represents Pollaiuolo's most elaborate pictorial design. Its subject—undoubtedly a classical one—has not yet been convincingly identified, but that matter is not so significant; the primary purpose of the engraving, obviously, was to display Pollaiuolo's mastery of the nude body in action. About 1465–70, when the print must have been produced, this was still a novel problem, and Pollaiuolo contributed more than any other master to its solution. An interest in movement, coupled with slender proportions and an emphasis on outline rather than on modeling, had been seen in Castagno's *David*, for example (fig. 612), which in these respects is clearly the progenitor of the *Ten Naked Men*. Pollaiuolo also drew upon the action poses he found in certain types of ancient painted vases (compare fig. 215). But he realized that a full under-

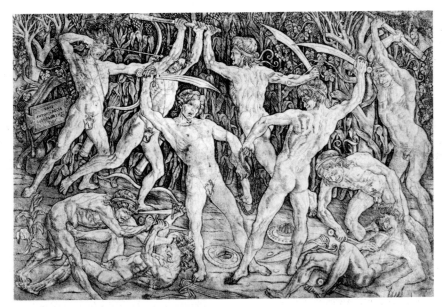

626. ANTONIO DEL POLLAIUOLO. *BATTLE OF THE TEN NAKED MEN.* c. 1465–70.
Engraving. 15⅛×23¼″ (38.3×59 cm). The Metropolitan Museum of Art, New York.
Joseph Pulitzer Bequest, 1917

standing of bodily movement demands a detailed knowledge of anatomy, down to the last muscle and sinew.

All of these ten naked men do indeed have an oddly "flayed" appearance, as if their skin had been stripped off to reveal the play of muscles underneath, and so, to a somewhat lesser degree, do the two figures of our statuette. Equally novel are their facial expressions, as strained as the bodily movements. We have already encountered contorted features in the work of Donatello and Masaccio (see figs. 581, 587, and 603), but the anguish they convey does not arise from, or accompany, the extreme physical action of Pollaiuolo's struggling nudes.

NICCOLÒ DELL'ARCA. The importance of this integration of motion and emotion is strikingly evident in figure 627, which shows one of the mourners from a lifesize group of the *Lamentation* by Niccolò dell'Arca, about 1485–90. We know of no direct link between that work and Pollaiuolo—Niccolò (c. 1435–1494) came from Apulia and lived mostly in Bologna—yet it could not have been created without Pollaiuolo's influence. The facial expression itself is not unprecedented, but coupled with the vehement forward rush, the movement of the entire figure overpowers us, as it does in the *Nike of Samothrace* (see fig. 229).

VERROCCHIO. Although Pollaiuolo, during the late years of his career, did two monumental bronze tombs for St. Peter's in Rome, he never had an opportunity to execute a large-scale free-standing statue. For such works we must turn to his slightly younger contemporary Andrea del Verrocchio (1435–1488), the greatest sculptor of his day and the only one to share some of Donatello's range and ambition. A modeler as well as a carver—we have works of his in marble, terracotta, silver, and bronze—he combined elements from Antonio Rossellino and Antonio del Pollaiuolo into a unique

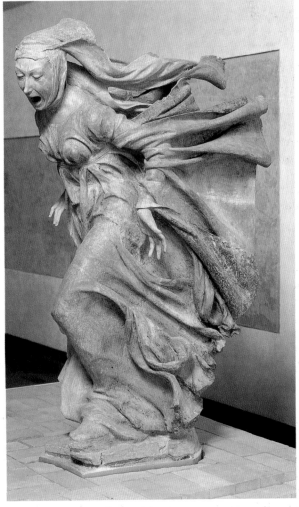

627. NICCOLÒ DELL'ARCA. *THE LAMENTATION*
(detail). c. 1485–90. Terracotta, lifesize.
Sta. Maria della Vita, Bologna

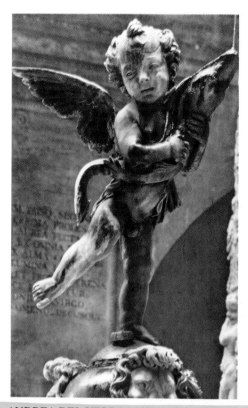

628. ANDREA DEL VERROCCHIO. *PUTTO WITH DOLPHIN.*
c. 1470. Bronze, height 27″ (68.8 cm, without base).
Palazzo Vecchio, Florence

synthesis. He was also a respected painter and the teacher of Leonardo da Vinci (something of a misfortune, for ever since, he has been the object of slighting comparisons).

His most popular work in Florence, because of its location in the courtyard of the Palazzo Vecchio as well as its perennial charm, is the *Putto with Dolphin* (fig. 628). It was designed as the center of a fountain—the dolphin is spouting a jet of water, as if responding to the hug it has to endure—for one of the Medici villas near Florence. The term "putto" (plural, "putti") designates one of the nude, often winged children that accompany more weighty subjects in ancient art; they personify spirits of various kinds (such as the spirit of love, in which case we call them cupids), usually in a merry and playful way. They were reintroduced during the Early Renaissance, both in their original identity and as child angels. The dolphin associates Verrocchio's *Putto* with the classical kind (note the small putto and dolphin in fig. 284). Artistically, however, he is closer to Pollaiuolo's *Hercules and Antaeus* than to ancient art, despite his larger size and greater sense of volume. Again the forms fly out in every direction from a central axis, but here the movement is graceful and continuous rather than jagged and broken; the stretched-out leg, the dolphin, and the arms and wings fit into an upward spiral, making the figure seem to revolve before our eyes.

By a strange coincidence, the crowning achievement of Verrocchio's career, as of Donatello's, was the bronze equestrian monument of a Venetian army commander: Bartolommeo Colleoni (fig. 629). In his will, Colleoni had re-

quested such a statue and, by way of encouragement, had left a sizable fortune to the Republic of Venice. He obviously knew the Gattamelata monument and wanted to ensure the same honor for himself. Verrocchio, too, must have regarded Donatello's work as the prototype of his own statue. Yet he did not simply imitate his illustrious model; he reinterpreted the theme less subtly, perhaps, but no less impressively. The horse, graceful and spirited rather than robust and placid, is modeled with the same sense of anatomy-in-action that we saw in the nudes of Pollaiuolo; its thin hide reveals every vein, muscle, and sinew, in strong contrast with the rigid surfaces of the armored figure bestriding it. Since the horse is also smaller in relation to the rider than Gattamelata's, Colleoni looms in the saddle like the very embodiment of forceful dominance. Legs rigidly straight, one shoulder thrust forward, he surveys the scene before him with the utter concentration of Donatello's *St. George* (fig. 578), but his lip is now contemptuously curled.

Neither *Gattamelata* nor *Colleoni* is a portrait in the specific sense of the term; both project an idealization of the personality that each artist associated with successful leadership in war. If *Gattamelata* conveys steadfast purpose and nobility of character, *Colleoni* radiates an almost frightening sense of power. As an image of awesome self-assurance, it recalls the *Can*

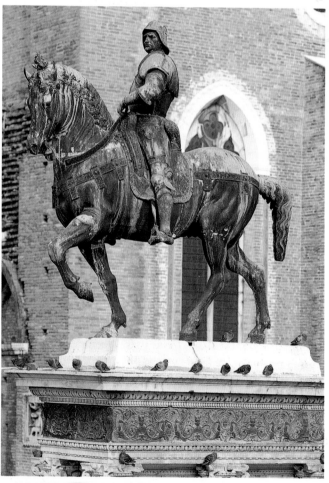

629. ANDREA DEL VERROCCHIO. *EQUESTRIAN MONUMENT OF COLLEONI.* c. 1483–88. Bronze, height 13′ (3.9 m).
Campo SS. Giovanni e Paolo, Venice

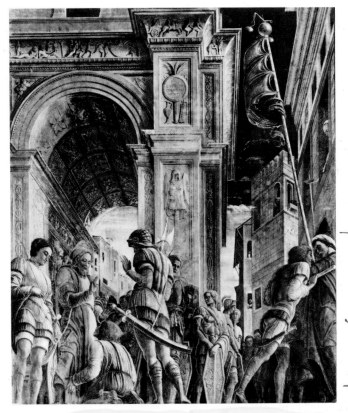

630. **ANDREA MANTEGNA.** *ST. JAMES LED TO HIS EXECUTION.*
c. 1455. Fresco. Ovetari Chapel,
Church of the Eremitani, Padua (destroyed 1944)

Grande (see fig. 514) rather than the *Gattamelata* monument. Perhaps Verrocchio visited the tomb of the Can Grande (who was well remembered in Florence as the patron of Dante) and decided to translate the wonderful arrogance of the statue into the style of his own day. In any case, Colleoni got a great deal more than he had bargained for in his will.

Painting

Before we resume our discussion of Florentine painting, we must consider the growth of Early Renaissance art in northern Italy. The International Style in painting and sculpture lingered there until the mid-century, and architecture retained a strongly Gothic flavor long after the adoption of a classical vocabulary. We shall disregard North Italian architecture and sculpture between 1450 and 1500, as there are hardly any achievements of major consequence in either field. Instead, we shall focus upon painting in Venice and its dependent territories, for during these same years a great tradition was born here that was to flourish for the next three centuries. The Republic of Venice, although more oligarchic, and unique in its eastward orientation, had many ties with Florence; it is not surprising, therefore, that she, rather than the duchy of Milan, should have become the leading center of Early Renaissance art in northern Italy.

MANTEGNA. Florentine masters had been carrying the new style to Venice and to the neighboring city of Padua since the 1420s. Fra Filippo Lippi, Uccello, and Castagno had all worked there at one time or another. Still more important was Donatello's ten-year sojourn. Their presence, however, evoked only rather timid local responses until, shortly before 1450, the young Andrea Mantegna (1431–1506) emerged as an independent master. He was first trained by a minor Paduan painter, but his early development was decisively shaped by the impressions he received from locally available Florentine works and—we may assume—by personal contact with Donatello. Next to Masaccio, Mantegna was the most important painter of the Early Renaissance. And he, too, was a precocious genius, fully capable at seventeen of executing commissions of his own. Within the next decade, he reached artistic maturity, and during the next half-century—he died at the age of seventy-five—he broadened the range of his art but never departed, in essence, from the style he had formulated in the 1450s.

His greatest achievement of that time, the frescoes in the Church of the Eremitani in Padua, was almost entirely destroyed by an accidental bomb explosion in 1944—a more grievous loss than the murals of Camposanto of Pisa (see fig. 535). The scene we reproduce in figure 630, *St. James Led to His Execution* is the most dramatic of the cycle because of its daring "worm's-eye view" perspective, which is based on the beholder's actual eye-level (the central vanishing point is below the bottom of the picture, somewhat to the right of center). The architectural setting consequently looms large, as in Masaccio's *Trinity* fresco (see fig. 598). Its main feature, a huge triumphal arch, although not a copy of any

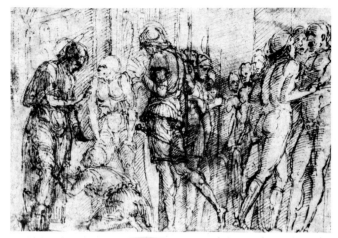

631. ANDREA MANTEGNA. *ST. JAMES LED TO HIS EXECUTION.*
c. 1455. Pen drawing, 6⅛×9¼″ (15.7×23.5 cm).
Collection G. M. Gathorne-Hardy, Donnington Priory,
Newbury, Berkshire, England

known Roman monument, looks so authentic in every detail
that it might as well be.

Here Mantegna's devotion to the visible remains of antiquity, almost like that of an archaeologist, shows his close association with the learned humanists at the University of
Padua (who had the same reverence for every word of ancient literature). No Florentine painter or sculptor of the time
could have transmitted such an attitude to him. The same
desire for authenticity can be seen in the costumes of the
Roman soldiers (compare fig. 284); it even extends to the
use of "wet" drapery patterns, an invention of Classical Greek
sculpture inherited by the Romans (see fig. 286). But the
tense figures, lean and firmly constructed, and especially
their dramatic interaction, clearly derive from Donatello.
Mantegna's subject hardly demands this agitated staging:
the saint, on the way to his execution, blesses a paralytic and
commands him to walk. But the large crowd of bystanders,
many of them expressing by glance and gesture how deeply
the miracle has stirred them, generates an extraordinary
emotional tension that erupts into real physical violence on
the far right. The great spiral curl of the banner merely echoes the turbulence below.

By rare good luck, a sketch for this fresco has survived
(fig. 631), the earliest instance we know of a drawing that
permits us to compare the preliminary and final versions of
such a design. (Among the drawings by earlier masters,
none, it seems, is related to a known picture in the same
way.) This sketch differs from the *sinopie*—full-scale drawings on the wall (see fig. 536)—in its tentative, unsettled
quality; the composition has not yet taken full shape; still
growing, as it were, the image in our drawing is "unfinished"
both in conception and in the sense that the forms are set
down in a quick, shorthand style. We note, for example, that
here the perspective is closer to normal, indicating that the
artist worked out the exact scheme only on the wall. Our
drawing also offers proof of what we suspected in the case
of Masaccio: that Early Renaissance artists actually conceived their compositions in terms of nude figures. The
group on the right is still in that first stage, and in the others

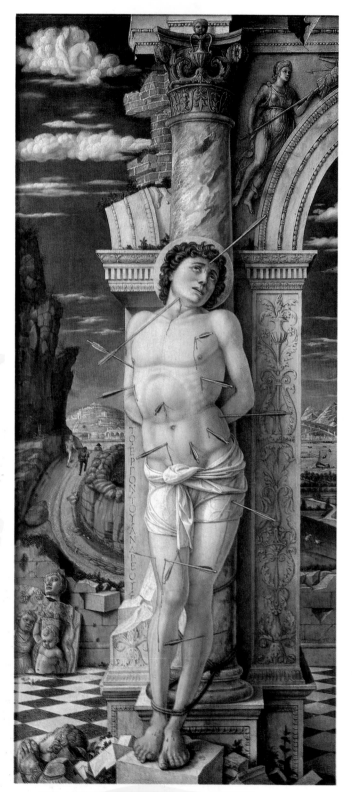

632. ANDREA MANTEGNA. *ST. SEBASTIAN.* c. 1455–60.
Tempera on panel, 26¾×11⅞″ (68×30.6 cm).
Kunsthistorisches Museum, Vienna

the outlines of the body show clearly beneath the costume. But the drawing is more than only a document; it is a work of art in its own right. The very quickness of its "handwriting" gives it an immediacy and rhythmic force that are necessarily lost in the fresco.

On the evidence of these works, we would hardly expect Mantegna to be much concerned with light and color. The *St. Sebastian* panel reproduced in figure 632, painted only a few years after the Paduan frescoes, proves that he was. In the foreground, to be sure, we find the familiar array of classical remains (including, this time, the artist's signature in Greek). The saint, too, looks more like a statue than a living body. But beyond we see a wonderfully atmospheric landscape and a deep blue sky dotted with the softest of white clouds. The entire scene is bathed in the warm radiance of late afternoon sunlight, which creates a gently melancholy mood, making the pathos of the dying saint doubly poignant. The background of our panel would hardly be conceivable without the influence, direct or indirect, of the Van Eycks (compare fig. 548, left).

Some works of the great Flemish masters had surely reached Florence as well as Venice between 1430 and 1450, and must have been equally admired in both cities; but in Venice they had more immediate effect, evoking the interest in lyrical, light-filled landscapes that became an ingrained part of Venetian Renaissance painting.

BELLINI. In the painting of Giovanni Bellini (c. 1431–1516), Mantegna's brother-in-law, we trace the further growth of the Flemish tradition. Bellini was slow to mature; his finest pictures, such as *St. Francis in the Desert* (fig. 633), date from the last decades of the century or later. The saint is here so small in comparison to the setting that he seems almost incidental, yet his mystic rapture before the beauty of the visible world sets our own response to the view that is spread out before us, ample and intimate at the same time. He has left his wooden pattens behind and stands barefoot on holy ground, like Moses in the Lord's presence (see page 99). Bellini's contours are less brittle than those of Mantegna, the colors are softer and the light more glowing, and he shares the tender regard of the great Flemings for every detail of nature. Unlike the Northerners, however, he can define the beholder's spatial relationship to the landscape—the rock formations of the foreground are structurally clear and firm, like architecture rendered by the rules of scientific perspective.

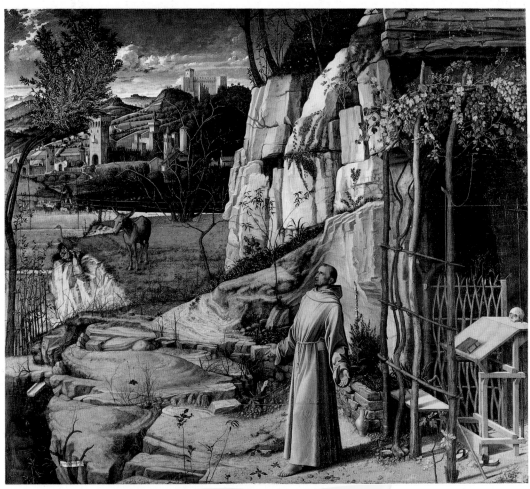

633. GIOVANNI BELLINI. *ST. FRANCIS IN THE DESERT.* c. 1485.
Oil and tempera on panel, 49 × 55⅞" (124 × 141.7 cm).
The Frick Collection, New York (Copyright)

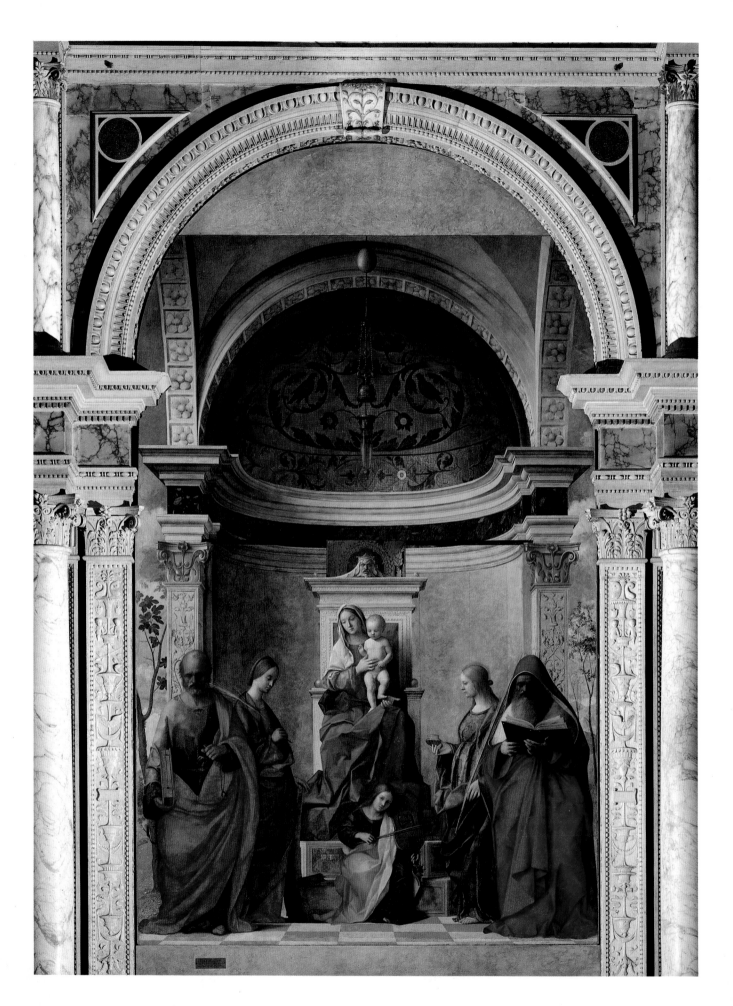

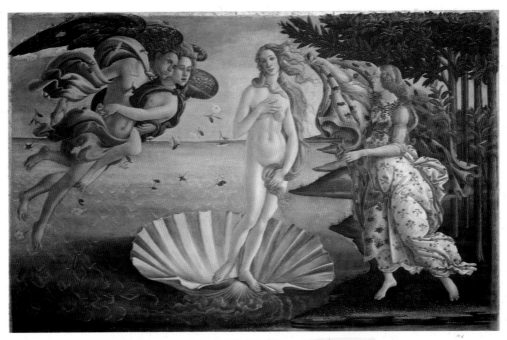

635. SANDRO BOTTICELLI. *THE BIRTH OF VENUS.* c. 1480.
Tempera on canvas, 5'8⅞"×9'1⅞" (1.8×2.8 m). Galleria degli Uffizi, Florence

As the foremost painter of the city of Venice, Bellini produced a number of formal altar panels of the *Sacra Conversazione* type. His compositional pattern is well exemplified by the latest—and most monumental—member of the series, the *Madonna and Saints* of 1505 in S. Zaccaria (fig. 634). Compared to Domenico Veneziano's *Sacra Conversazione* (fig. 607), the architectural setting is a good deal simpler but no less impressive: we stand in the nave of a church, near the crossing (which is partly visible), with the apse filling almost the entire panel. The figures appear in front of the apse, however, under the great vaulted canopy of the crossing. The structure is not a real church, for its sides are open and the entire scene is flooded with gentle sunlight, just as Domenico Veneziano had placed his figures in a semi-outdoors setting. The Madonna's solid, high-backed throne and the music-making angel on its lowest step are derived (through many intermediaries, no doubt) from Masaccio's *Madonna* of 1426 (fig. 604).

What differentiates this altar immediately from its Florentine ancestors is not merely the ample spaciousness of the design but its wonderfully calm, meditative mood; instead of "conversation," we sense the figures' deep communion, which makes all rhetorical gestures unnecessary. We shall encounter this quality again and again in Venetian painting; here, from the way the aged master has bathed the entire scene in a delicate aerial haze, we see it as through a diffusing filter of atmosphere. All harsh contrasts are eliminated, light and shadow blend in almost imperceptible gradations, and colors glow with a new richness and depth. In this magical moment, Bellini becomes the true heir of the two great-

est painters of the fifteenth century, uniting the Florentine grandeur of Masaccio with the Northern poetic intimacy of Jan van Eyck.

BOTTICELLI. We return once more to Florence. The trend forecast by Castagno's *David* substitutes energetic, graceful movement and agitated linear contours for the stable monumentality of the Masaccio style; its climax comes in the final quarter of the century, in the art of Sandro Botticelli (1444/5–1510). Trained by Fra Filippo Lippi—whose *Madonna* (fig. 605) already had undercurrents of linear movement—and strongly influenced by Pollaiuolo, Botticelli soon became the favorite painter of the so-called Medici circle, those patricians, literati, scholars, and poets surrounding Lorenzo the Magnificent, the head of the Medici family and, for all practical purposes, the real ruler of the city.

For one member of this group, Botticelli did *The Birth of Venus* (fig. 635), probably his most famous picture. Its kinship with Pollaiuolo's *Battle of the Ten Naked Men* (fig. 626) is unmistakable, the shallow modeling and the emphasis on outline producing an effect of low relief rather than of solid, three-dimensional shapes; in both we note a lack of concern with deep space—the ornamentalized thicket forms a screen behind the naked men much like the grove on the right-hand side of the Venus. But the differences are just as striking. Botticelli evidently does not share Pollaiuolo's passion for anatomy; his bodies are more attenuated and drained of all weight and muscular power; they seem to float even when they touch the ground. All this seems to deny the basic values of the founding fathers of Early Renaissance art, yet the picture does not look medieval: the bodies, ethereal though they be, retain their voluptuousness; they are genuine nudes (see our discussion, pages 452–54) enjoying full freedom of movement.

634. (*opposite*) GIOVANNI BELLINI. *MADONNA AND SAINTS.* 1505. Panel, 16'5⅛"×7'9" (5×2.4 m). S. Zaccaria, Venice

NEO-PLATONISM. To understand this paradox, we must consider the meaning of our picture, and the general use of classical subjects in Early Renaissance art. During the Middle Ages, classical form had become divorced from classical subject matter. Artists could only draw upon the ancient repertory of poses, gestures, expressions, and so forth by changing the identity of their sources: philosophers became apostles, Orpheus turned into Adam, Hercules into Samson. When medieval artists had occasion to represent the pagan gods, they based their pictures on literary descriptions rather than visual models. This was the situation, by and large, until the mid-fifteenth century. Only with Pollaiuolo—and Mantegna in northern Italy—does classical form begin to rejoin classical content. Pollaiuolo's lost paintings of the Labors of Hercules (about 1465) mark the earliest instance—so far as we know—of large-scale subjects from classical mythology depicted in a style inspired by ancient monuments; and *The Birth of Venus* contains the first monumental image since Roman times of the nude goddess in a pose derived from classical statues of Venus (see fig. 220). Moreover, the subject of the picture is clearly meant to be serious, even solemn.

How could such images be justified in a Christian civilization, without subjecting both artist and patron to the accusation of neo-paganism? In the Middle Ages, classical myths had at times been interpreted didactically, however remote the analogy, as allegories of Christian precepts. Europa abducted by the bull, for instance, could be declared to signify the soul redeemed by Christ. But such pallid constructions were hardly an adequate excuse for reinvesting the pagan gods with their ancient beauty and strength. To fuse the Christian faith with ancient mythology, rather than merely relate them, required a more sophisticated argument. This was provided by the Neo-Platonic philosophers, whose fore-

most representative, Marsilio Ficino, enjoyed tremendous prestige during the later years of the fifteenth century and after. Ficino's thought was based as much on the mysticism of Plotinus (see page 241) as on the authentic works of Plato. He believed that the life of the universe, including human life, was linked to God by a spiritual circuit continuously ascending and descending, so that all revelation, whether from the Bible, Plato, or classical myths, was one. Similarly, he proclaimed that beauty, love, and beatitude, being phases of this same circuit, were one. Thus Neo-Platonists could invoke the "celestial Venus" (that is, the nude Venus born of the sea, as in our picture) interchangeably with the Virgin Mary, as the source of "divine love" (meaning the cognition of divine beauty). This celestial Venus, according to Ficino, dwells purely in the sphere of Mind, while her twin, the ordinary Venus, engenders "human love."

Once we understand that Botticelli's picture has this quasi-religious meaning, it seems less astonishing that the two wind gods on the left look so much like angels and that the personification of Spring on the right, who welcomes Venus ashore, recalls the traditional relation of St. John to the Saviour in the Baptism of Christ (compare fig. 441). As baptism is a "rebirth in God," the birth of Venus evokes the hope for "rebirth" from which the Renaissance takes its name. Thanks to the fluidity of Neo-Platonic doctrine, the number of possible associations to be linked with our painting is almost limitless. All of them, however, like the celestial Venus herself, "dwell in the sphere of Mind," and Botticelli's deity would hardly be a fit vessel for them if she were less ethereal.

Neo-Platonic philosophy and its expression in art were obviously too complex to become popular outside the select and highly educated circle of its devotees. In 1494, the suspicions

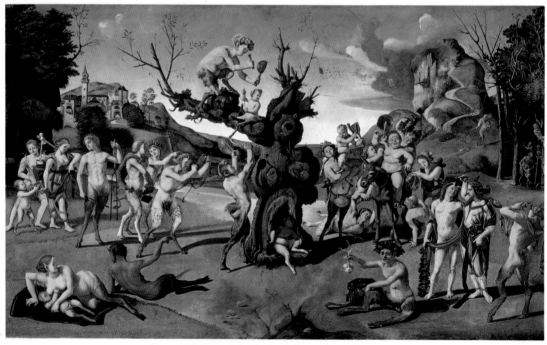

636. PIERO DI COSIMO. *THE DISCOVERY OF HONEY.* c. 1499. Tempera on wood panel, 31¼×50⅝" (79.2×128.5 cm). Worcester Art Museum, Worcester, Massachusetts

of ordinary people were confirmed by the friar Girolamo Savonarola, an ardent advocate of religious reform, who gained a huge following with his sermons attacking the "cult of paganism" in the city's ruling circle. Botticelli himself was perhaps a follower of Savonarola and reportedly burned a number of his "pagan" pictures. In his last works—he seems to have stopped painting entirely after 1500—he returns to traditional religious themes but with no essential change in style.

PIERO DI COSIMO. Figure 636, a panel by Botticelli's younger contemporary Piero di Cosimo (1462–1521), illustrates a view of pagan mythology diametrically opposed to that of the Neo-Platonists. Instead of "spiritualizing" the pagan gods, it brings them down to earth as beings of flesh and blood. In this alternate theory, humanity had slowly risen from a barbaric state through the discoveries and inventions of a few exceptionally gifted individuals; gratefully remembered by posterity, these were finally accorded the status of gods. St. Augustine subscribed to such a view (which can be traced back to Hellenistic times) without facing all of the implications expressed by ancient authors. The complete theory was not revived until the late fifteenth century: it postulates a gradual evolution from the animal level, which thus conflicts with the scriptural account of Creation. This could be glossed over, however, by making a happy idyl out of the achievements of these pagan "culture heroes" to avoid the impression of complete seriousness—exactly what Piero di Cosimo did in our picture.

Its title, *The Discovery of Honey*, refers to the central episode, a group of satyrs busying themselves about an old willow tree. They have discovered a swarm of bees, and are making as much noise as possible with their pots and pans to induce the bees to cluster on one of the branches. The satyrs will then collect the honey, from which they will produce mead. Behind them, to the right, some of their companions are about to discover the source of another fermented beverage; they are climbing trees to collect wild grapes. Beyond is a barren rock, while on the left are gentle hills and a town. This contrast does not imply that the satyrs are city dwellers; it merely juxtaposes civilization, the goal of the future, with untamed nature. Here the "culture hero" is, of course, Bacchus, who appears in the lower right-hand corner, a tipsy grin on his face, next to his ladylove, Ariadne. Despite their classical appearance, Bacchus and his companions do not in the least resemble the frenzied revelers of ancient mythology. They have an oddly domestic air, suggesting a fun-loving family clan on a picnic. The brilliant sunlight, the rich colors, and the far-ranging landscape make the scene a still more plausible extension of everyday reality. We can well believe that Piero di Cosimo, in contrast to Botticelli, admired the great Flemish realists, and this landscape would be inconceivable without the strong influence of *The Portinari Altarpiece* (compare fig. 557).

GHIRLANDAIO. Not only Piero was receptive to the realism of the Flemings. Domenico Ghirlandaio (1449–1494), another contemporary of Botticelli, shared this attitude. Ghirlandaio's fresco cycles are so replete with portraits that

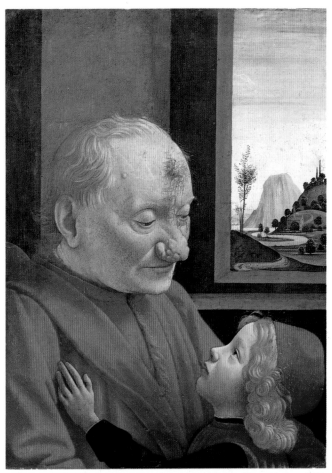

637. DOMENICO GHIRLANDAIO. *AN OLD MAN AND HIS GRANDSON.*
c. 1480. Tempera and oil on wood panel,
24⅛×18″ (61.2×45.5 cm). Musée du Louvre, Paris

they almost serve as family chronicles of the wealthy patricians who sponsored them. Among his most affecting individual portraits is the panel *An Old Man and His Grandson* (fig. 637). Lacking the pictorial delicacy of Flemish portraits, it nevertheless reflects their precise attention to surface texture and facial detail. But no Northern painter could have rendered like Ghirlandaio the tender human relationship between the little boy and his grandfather. Psychologically, our panel plainly bespeaks its Italian origin.

PERUGINO. Rome, long neglected during the papal exile in Avignon, became once more, in the later fifteenth century, an important center of art patronage. As the papacy regained its political power on Italian soil, the occupants of the Chair of St. Peter began to beautify both the Vatican and the city, in the conviction that the monuments of Christian Rome must outshine those of the pagan past. The most ambitious pictorial project of those years was the decoration of the walls of the Sistine Chapel about 1482. Among the artists who carried out this large cycle of Old and New Testament scenes we encounter most of the important painters of Central Italy, including Botticelli and Ghirlandaio, although the frescoes do not, on the whole, represent their most distinguished work.

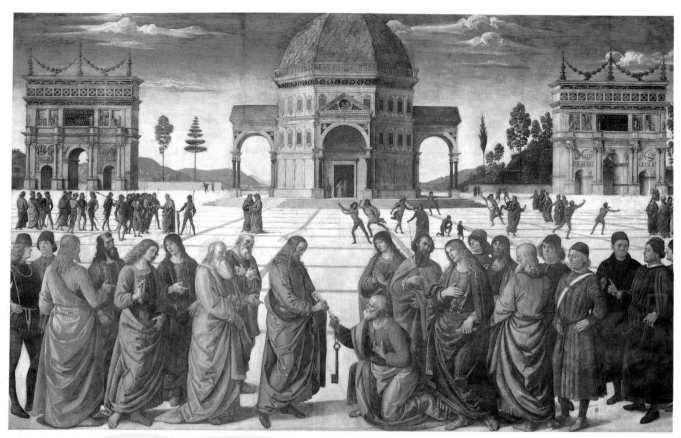

638. PIETRO PERUGINO. *THE DELIVERY OF THE KEYS.* 1482. Fresco. Sistine Chapel, The Vatican, Rome

There is, however, one exception to this: *The Delivery of the Keys* (fig. 638) by Pietro Perugino (c. 1450–1523) must rank as his finest achievement. Born near Perugia in Umbria (the region southeast of Tuscany), Perugino maintained close ties with Florence. His early development had been decisively influenced by Verrocchio, as the statuesque balance and solidity of the figures in *The Delivery of the Keys* still suggest. The gravely symmetrical design conveys the special importance of the subject in this particular setting (the authority of St. Peter as the first pope—and that of all his successors—rests on his having received the keys to the Kingdom of Heaven from Christ Himself). A number of contemporaries, with powerfully individualized features, witness the solemn event. Equally striking is the vast expanse of the background, its two Roman triumphal arches (both modeled on the Arch of Constantine) flanking a domed structure in which we recognize the ideal church of Alberti's *Treatise on Architecture.* The spatial clarity, achieved by the mathematically exact perspective of this view, is the heritage of Piero della Francesca, who spent much of his later life working for Umbrian clients, notably the duke of Urbino. And also from Urbino, shortly before 1500, Perugino received a pupil whose fame would soon obscure his own—Raphael, the most classic master of the High Renaissance.

SIGNORELLI. Luca Signorelli (1445/50–1523) is linked to Perugino by a similar background, although his personality is infinitely more dramatic. Of provincial Tuscan origin, he had been a disciple of Piero della Francesca before coming to Florence in the 1470s. Like Perugino, Signorelli was strongly impressed by Verrocchio, but he also admired the energy, expressiveness, and anatomic precision of Pollaiuolo's nudes. Combining these influences with Piero's cubic solidity of form and mastery of perspective foreshortening, Signorelli achieved a style of epic grandeur that later made a lasting imprint upon the mind of Michelangelo. He reached the climax of his career just before 1500 with the four monumental frescoes, representing the end of the world, on the walls of the S. Brizio Chapel in Orvieto Cathedral—especially the most dynamic of these, *The Damned Cast into Hell* (fig. 639). What most strikes us is not Signorelli's use of the nude body as an expressive instrument—even though he far surpasses his predecessors in this respect—but the deep sense of tragedy that pervades the scene. Signorelli's Hell, the exact opposite of Bosch's (compare fig. 559), is illuminated by the full light of day, without nightmarish machines of torture or grotesque monsters. The damned retain their human dignity, and the devils, too, are humanized; even in Hell, the Renaissance faith in humanity does not lose its force.

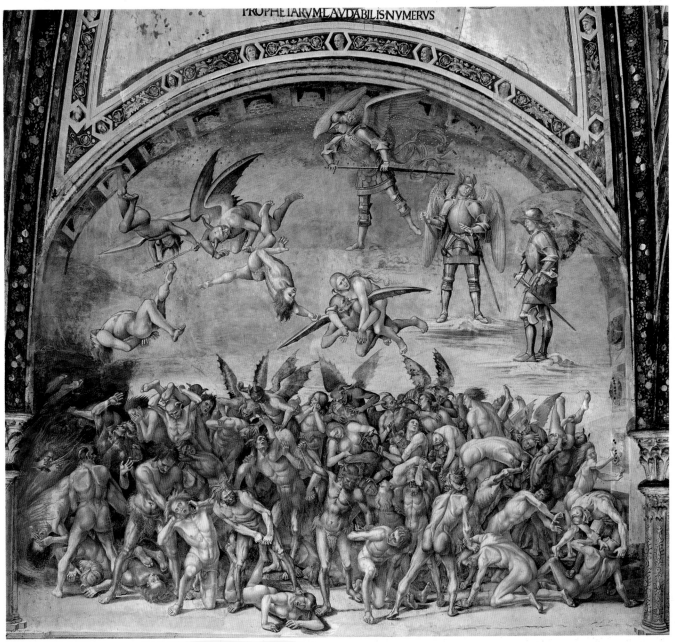

639. LUCA SIGNORELLI. *THE DAMNED CAST INTO HELL.* 1499–1500. Fresco. S. Brizio Chapel, Orvieto Cathedral

CHAPTER THREE
THE HIGH RENAISSANCE IN ITALY

It used to be taken for granted that the High Renaissance followed upon the Early Renaissance as naturally and inevitably as noon follows morning. The great masters of the sixteenth century—Leonardo, Bramante, Michelangelo, Raphael, Giorgione, Titian—were thought to have shared the ideals of their predecessors, but to have expressed them so completely that their names became synonyms for perfection. They represented the climax, the classic phase, of Renaissance art, just as Phidias seemed to have brought the art of ancient Greece to its highest point. This view could also explain why these two classic phases were so short; if art is assumed to develop along the pattern of a ballistic curve, its highest point cannot be expected to last more than a moment.

Since the 1920s, art historians have come to realize the shortcomings of this scheme. When we apply it literally, the High Renaissance becomes so absurdly brief, for example, that we wonder whether it happened at all. Moreover, we hardly increase our understanding of the Early Renaissance if we regard it as a "not-yet-perfect High Renaissance," any more than an Archaic Greek statue can be satisfactorily viewed from a Phidian standpoint. Nor is it very useful to insist that the subsequent post-Classical phase, whether Hellenistic or "Late Renaissance," must be decadent. The image of the ballistic curve has now been abandoned, and we have gained a less assured, but also less arbitrary, estimate of what, for lack of another term, we still call the High Renaissance.

In some fundamental respects, we shall find that the High Renaissance was indeed the culmination of the Early Renaissance, while in other respects it represented a departure. Certainly the tendency to view the artist as a sovereign genius, rather than as a devoted craftsman, was never stronger than during the first half of the sixteenth century. Plato's concept of genius—the spirit entering into the poet that causes him to compose in a "divine frenzy"—had been broadened by Marsilio Ficino and his fellow Neo-Platonists to include the architect, the sculptor, and the painter. Individuals of genius were thought to be set apart from ordinary mortals by the divine inspiration guiding their efforts, and worthy of being called "divine," "immortal," and "creative" (before 1500, *creating*, as distinct from *making*, was the privilege of God alone).

This cult of genius had a profound effect on the artists of the High Renaissance. It spurred them to vast and ambitious goals, and prompted their awed patrons to support such enterprises. But since these ambitions often went beyond the humanly possible, they were apt to be frustrated by external as well as internal difficulties, leaving the artist with a sense of having been defeated by a malevolent fate. At the same time, the artist's faith in the divine origin of inspiration led him to rely on subjective, rather than objective, standards of truth and beauty. If Early Renaissance artists felt bound by what they believed to be universally valid rules, such as the numerical ratios of musical harmony and the laws of scientific perspective, their High Renaissance successors were less concerned with rational order than with visual effectiveness. They evolved a new drama and a new rhetoric to engage the emotions of the beholder, whether sanctioned or not by classical precedent. In fact, the works of the great High Renaissance masters immediately became classics in their own right, their authority equal to that of the most renowned monuments of antiquity.

But here we encounter a contradiction: if the creations of genius are viewed as unique by definition, they cannot be successfully imitated by lesser artists, however worthy they may seem of such imitation. Unlike the founders of the Early Renaissance, the leading artists of the High Renaissance did not set the pace for a broadly based "period style" that could be practiced on every level of quality. The High Renaissance produced astonishingly few minor masters; it died with those who had created it, or even before. Of the six great personalities mentioned above, only Michelangelo and Titian lived beyond 1520.

External conditions after that date were undoubtedly less favorable to the High Renaissance style than those of the first two decades of the century. Yet the High Renaissance might well have ended soon even without the pressure of circumstances; its harmonious grandeur was inherently unstable, a balance of divergent qualities. Only these qualities, not the balance itself, could be transmitted to the artists who reached maturity after 1520. In pointing out the limited and precarious nature of the High Renaissance we do not mean to deny its tremendous impact upon later art. For most of the next three hundred years, the great personalities of the early six-teenth century loomed so large that the achievements of their predecessors seemed to belong to a forgotten era. Even when the art of the fourteenth and fifteenth centuries was finally rediscovered, people still acknowledged the High Renaissance as the turning point, referring to all painters before Raphael as "the Primitives."

Leonardo da Vinci

One of the strangest aspects of the High Renaissance—and one important reason why, within the limitations set forth above, it rightfully deserves to be called a period—is the fact that its key monuments were all produced between 1495 and 1520, despite the great differences in age of the men creating them. Bramante, the oldest, was born in 1444, Raphael in 1483, and Titian about 1488–90. Yet the distinction of being the earliest High Renaissance master belongs to Leonardo da Vinci, not to Bramante.

Born in 1452 in the little Tuscan town of Vinci, Leonardo was trained in Florence by Verrocchio. Conditions there must not have suited him; at the age of thirty he went to work for the duke of Milan as a military engineer, and only secondarily as an architect, sculptor, and painter.

ADORATION OF THE MAGI. He left behind, unfinished, the most ambitious work he had then begun, a large *Adoration of the Magi*, for which he had made many preliminary studies. Its design shows a geometric order and a precisely constructed perspective space that recall Florentine painting in the wake of Masaccio, rather than the style prevailing about 1480. The most striking—and indeed revolutionary—

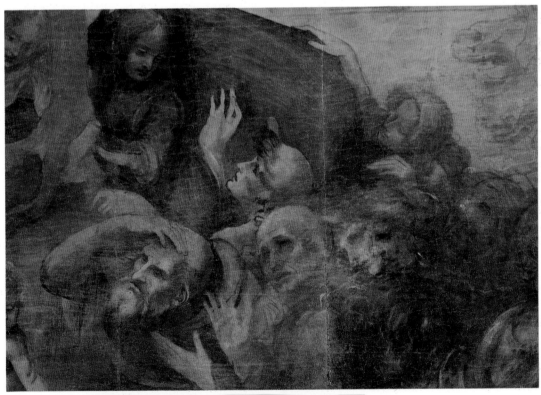

640. LEONARDO DA VINCI. *ADORATION OF THE MAGI* (detail). 1481–82.
Monochrome on panel. Galleria degli Uffizi, Florence

aspect of the panel is the way it is painted, although Leonardo had not even completed the underpainting.

Our detail (fig. 640) is taken from the area to the right of center, which is more nearly finished than the rest; the forms seem to materialize softly and gradually, never quite detaching themselves from a dusky realm. Leonardo, unlike Pollaiuolo or Botticelli, thinks not of outlines, but of three-dimensional bodies made visible, in varying degrees, by the incidence of light. In the shadows, these shapes remain incomplete; their contours are merely implied. In this method of modeling (called *chiaroscuro*, "light-and-dark"), the forms no longer stand abruptly side by side but partake of a new pictorial unity, the barriers between them having been partially broken down. And there is a comparable emotional continuity as well: the gestures and faces of the crowd convey with touching eloquence the reality of the miracle they have come to behold. We will recognize the influence of both Pollaiuolo and Verrocchio in the mobile expressiveness of these figures, but Leonardo may also have been impressed by the breathless shepherds in the *The Portinari Altarpiece*, then newly installed in Florence (see fig. 557).

VIRGIN OF THE ROCKS. Soon after arriving in Milan, Leonardo did *The Virgin of the Rocks* (fig. 641), another altar panel, which suggests what the *Adoration* would have looked like if it had been completed. Here the figures emerge from the semidarkness of the grotto, enveloped in a moisture-laden atmosphere that delicately veils their forms. This fine haze (called *sfumato*), more pronounced than similar effects in Flemish and Venetian painting, lends a peculiar warmth and intimacy to the scene. It also creates a remote, dreamlike quality, and makes the picture seem a poetic vision rather than an image of reality pure and simple. The subject—the infant St. John adoring the Infant Christ in the presence of the Virgin and an angel—is mysterious in many ways, without immediate precedent: the secluded, rocky setting, the pool in front, and the plant life, carefully chosen and exquisitely rendered, all hint at symbolic meanings that are somehow hard to define. And on what level, or levels, of significance are we to interpret the relationships among the four figures? Perhaps the key is the conjunction of gestures—protective, pointing, and blessing—toward the center of the group. However puzzling its content, few pictures cast a more enduring spell.

LAST SUPPER. Despite their originality, the *Adoration* and the *Virgin of the Rocks* do not yet differ clearly, in conception, from the aims of the Early Renaissance. But Leonardo's *The Last Supper*, later by a dozen years, has always been recognized as the first classic statement of the ideals of High Renaissance painting (fig. 642). Unhappily, the famous mural began to deteriorate a few years after its completion; the artist, dissatisfied with the limitations of the traditional fresco technique, experimented in an oil-tempera medium that did not adhere well to the wall. We thus need some effort to imagine its original splendor. Yet what remains is more than sufficient to account for its tremendous impact. Viewing the composition as a whole, we are struck at once by its balanced stability; only afterward do we discover that this balance has

been achieved by the reconciliation of competing, even conflicting, claims such as no previous artist had attempted.

A comparison with Castagno's *The Last Supper* (fig. 611), painted half a century before, is particularly instructive here: the spatial setting in both cases seems like an annex to the real interior of the refectory, but Castagno's architecture has a strangely oppressive effect on the figures while Leonardo's, despite its far greater depth, does not. The reason for this becomes clear when we realize that in the earlier work the perspective space has been conceived autonomously—it was there before the figures entered, and would equally suit another group of diners. Leonardo, in contrast, began with the figure composition, and the architecture had merely a supporting role from the start. The central vanishing point, which governs our view of the interior, is located behind the head of Christ in the exact middle of the picture, and thus becomes charged with symbolic significance. Equally plain is the symbolic function of the main opening in the back wall; its projecting pediment acts as the architectural equiv-

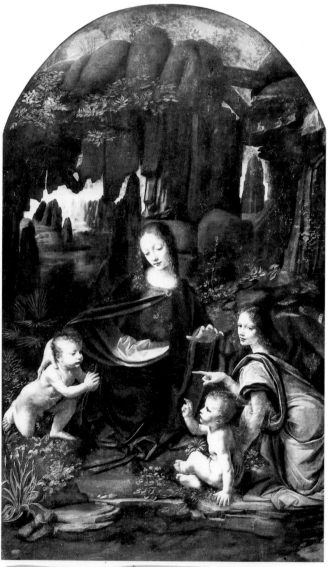

641. LEONARDO DA VINCI. *THE VIRGIN OF THE ROCKS*. c. 1485. Oil on panel, 75×43½″ (190.5×110.5 cm). Musée du Louvre, Paris

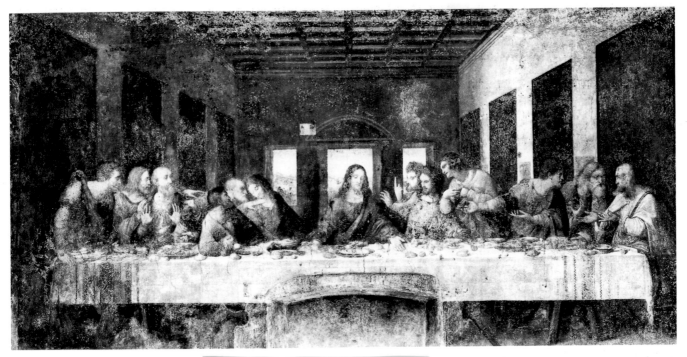

642. LEONARDO DA VINCI. *THE LAST SUPPER.* c. 1495–98.
Tempera wall mural, 15′2″×28′10″ (4.6×8.8 m). Sta. Maria delle Grazie, Milan

alent of a halo. We thus tend to see the perspective frame-work of the scene almost entirely in relation to the figures, rather than as a pre-existing entity. How vital this relation-ship is we can easily test by covering the upper third of the picture: the composition then takes on the character of a frieze, the grouping of the apostles is less clear, and the calm triangular shape of Christ becomes merely passive, instead of acting as a physical and spiritual force.

The Saviour, presumably, has just spoken the fateful words, "One of you shall betray me," and the disciples are asking, "Lord, is it I?" We actually see nothing that contra-dicts this interpretation, but to view the scene as one partic-ular moment in a psychological drama hardly does justice to Leonardo's intentions. These went well beyond a literal ren-dering of the biblical narrative, for he crowded together all the disciples on the far side of the table, in a space quite inadequate for so many people. He clearly wanted to con-dense his subject physically by the compact, monumental grouping of the figures, and spiritually by presenting many levels of meaning at one time. Thus the gesture of Christ is one of submission to the divine will, and of offering. It is a hint at Christ's main act at the Last Supper, the institution of the Eucharist ("And as they were eating, Jesus took bread . . . and gave it to the disciples, and said, Take and eat; this is my body. And he took the cup. . . saying, Drink ye all of it; for this is my blood. . ."). And the apostles do not merely react to these words; each of them reveals his own person-ality, his own relationship to the Saviour. (Note that Judas is no longer segregated from the rest; his dark, defiant profile sets him apart well enough.) They exemplify what the artist wrote in one of his notebooks, that the highest and most difficult aim of painting is to depict "the intention of man's soul" through gestures and movements of the limbs—a dic-tum to be interpreted as referring not to momentary emo-tional states but to the inner life as a whole.

BATTLE OF ANGHIARI. In 1499, the duchy of Milan fell to the French, and Leonardo, after brief trips to Mantua and Venice, returned to Florence. He must have found the cul-tural climate very different from his recollections of it; the Medici had been expelled, and the city was briefly a republic again, until their return. For a while, Leonardo seems to have been active mainly as an engineer and surveyor, but in 1503 the city commissioned him to do a mural for the council chamber of the Palazzo Vecchio, with some famous event from the history of Florence as its subject. Leonardo chose

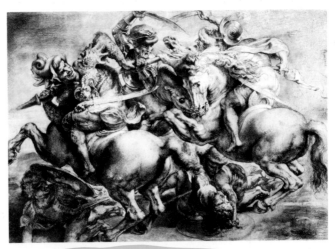

643. PETER PAUL RUBENS. Drawing after Leonardo's cartoon for *THE BATTLE OF ANGHIARI.* c. 1600. Cabinet des Dessins, Musée du Louvre, Paris

the Battle of Anghiari, where the Florentine forces had once defeated the Milanese army. He completed the cartoon (a full-scale drawing) and had just begun the mural itself when, in 1506, he returned once more to Milan at the request of the French, abandoning the commission. The cartoon for *The Battle of Anghiari* survived for more than a century, and enjoyed enormous fame.

Today we know it only through Leonardo's preliminary sketches and through copies of the cartoon by later artists, notably a splendid drawing by Peter Paul Rubens (fig. 643; see page 568). Leonardo had started with the historical accounts of the engagement; as his plans crystallized, however, he abandoned factual accuracy and created a monumental group of soldiers on horseback that represents a condensed, timeless image of the spirit of battle, rather than any specific event. His concern with "the intention of man's soul"—in this case, a savage fury that has seized not only the combatants but the animals as well—is even more evident here than in *The Last Supper*. *The Battle of Anghiari* stands at the opposite end of the scale from Uccello's *Battle of San Romano* (fig. 610), where nothing has been omitted except the fighting itself. Yet Leonardo's battle scene is not one of uncontrolled action; its dynamism is held in check by the hexagonal outline that stabilizes this seething mass. Once again, balance has been achieved by the reconciliation of competing claims.

MONA LISA. While working on *The Battle of Anghiari*, Leonardo painted his most famous portrait, the *Mona Lisa* (fig. 644). The delicate *sfumato* of *The Virgin of the Rocks* is here so perfected that it seemed miraculous to the artist's contemporaries. The forms are built from layers of glazes so gossamer-thin that the entire panel seems to glow with a gentle light from within. But the fame of the *Mona Lisa* comes not from this pictorial subtlety alone; even more intriguing is the psychological fascination of the sitter's personality. Why, among all the smiling faces ever painted, has this particular one been singled out as "mysterious"? Perhaps the reason is that, as a portrait, the picture does not fit our expectations. The features are too individual for Leonardo to have simply depicted an ideal type, yet the element of idealization is so strong that it blurs the sitter's character. Once

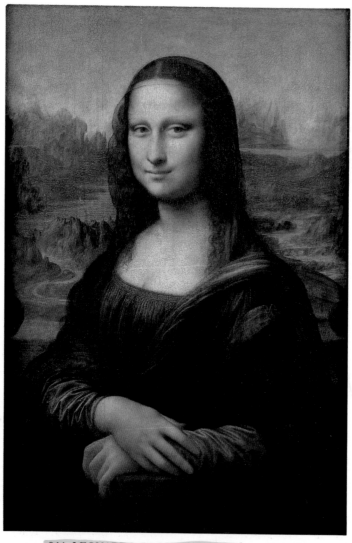

644. LEONARDO DA VINCI. *MONA LISA*. c. 1503–5.
Oil on panel, 30¼×21″ (77×53.5 cm). Musée du Louvre, Paris

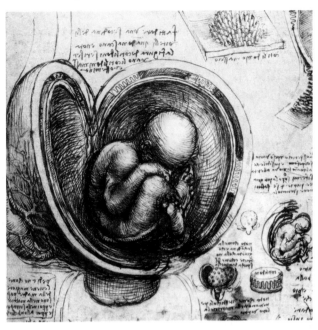

645. LEONARDO DA VINCI. *EMBRYO IN THE WOMB*.
c. 1510. Detail of pen drawing, 11⅞ × 8⅜″ (30.4 × 21.5 cm).
Windsor Castle, Royal Library. © 1991. Her Majesty Queen Elizabeth II

again the artist has brought two opposites into harmonious balance. The smile, also, may be read in two ways: as the echo of a momentary mood, and as a timeless, symbolic expression (somewhat like the "Archaic smile" of the Greeks; see figures 168, 169, and 171). Clearly, the Mona Lisa embodies a quality of maternal tenderness which was to Leonardo the essence of womanhood. Even the landscape in the background, composed mainly of rocks and water, suggests elemental generative forces.

DRAWINGS. In his later years (he died in France in 1519), Leonardo devoted himself more and more to his scientific interests. Art and science, we recall, were first united in Brunelleschi's discovery of systematic perspective; Leonardo's work is the climax of this trend. The artist, he believed, must know not only the rules of perspective but all the laws of nature, and the eye was to him the perfect instrument for gaining such knowledge. The extraordinary scope of his own inquiries is attested in the hundreds of drawings and notes that he hoped to incorporate into an encyclopedic set of treatises. How original he was as a scientist is still a matter of debate, but in one field his importance remains undisputed: he created the modern scientific illustration, an essential tool for anatomists and biologists. A drawing such as the *Embryo in the Womb* (fig. 645) combines his own vivid observation with the analytic clarity of a diagram, or—to paraphrase Leonardo's own words—sight and insight.

Contemporary sources show that Leonardo was esteemed as an architect. Actual building seems to have concerned him less, however, than problems of structure and design. The numerous architectural projects in his drawings were intended, for the most part, to remain on paper. Yet these sketches, especially those of his Milanese period, have great historic importance, for only in them can we trace the tran-

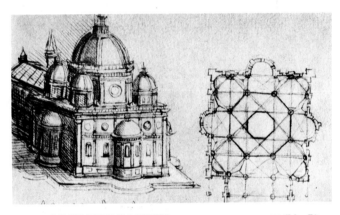

646. LEONARDO DA VINCI. *PROJECT FOR A CHURCH* (Ms. B).
c. 1490. Pen drawing. Bibliothèque de l'Arsenal, Paris

sition from the Early to the High Renaissance in architecture.

The domed, centrally planned churches of the type illustrated in figure 646 hold particular interest for us; the plan recalls Brunelleschi's Sta. Maria degli Angeli (see fig. 596), but the new relationship of the spatial units is more complex, while the exterior, with its cluster of domes, is more monumental than any Early Renaissance structure. In conception, this design stands halfway between the dome of Florence Cathedral and the most ambitious structure of the sixteenth century, the new basilica of St. Peter's in Rome (compare figs. 486, 649, and 650). It gives evidence, too, of Leonardo's close contact, during the 1490s, with the architect Donato Bramante (1444–1514), who was then also working for the duke of Milan. Bramante went to Rome after Milan fell to the French; it was in Rome, during the last fifteen years of his life, that he became the creator of High Renaissance architecture.

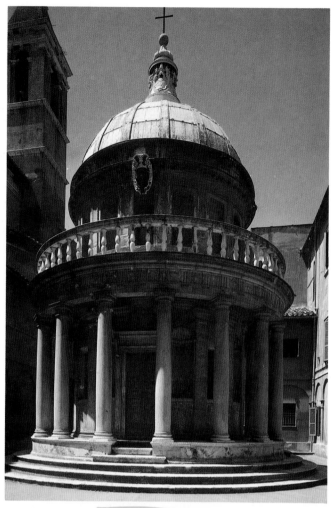

647. DONATO BRAMANTE
The Tempietto, S. Pietro in Montorio, Rome. 1502

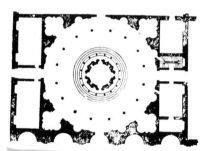

648. Plan of the Tempietto (after Serlio, in
Regole generali di Architettura)

Bramante

THE TEMPIETTO. The new style is shown fully formed in Bramante's Tempietto at S. Pietro in Montorio (figs. 647 and 648), designed soon after 1500. This chapel, which marks the site of St. Peter's crucifixion, was planned to be surrounded by a circular, colonnaded courtyard. The Tempietto would then have appeared less isolated from its environment than it does today, for Bramante intended it to be set within a "molded" exterior space—a conception as bold and novel as the design of the chapel itself. Its nickname, "little tem-

ple," seems well deserved: in the three-step platform and the severe Doric order of the colonnade, Classical temple architecture is more directly recalled than in any fifteenth-century structure. Equally striking is Bramante's application of the "sculptured wall" principle, in the Tempietto itself and in the courtyard; not since Brunelleschi's Sta. Maria degli Angeli have we seen such deeply recessed niches, "excavated" from heavy masses of masonry. These cavities are counterbalanced by the convex shape of the dome and by strongly projecting moldings and cornices. As a result, the Tempietto has a monumental weight that belies its modest size.

ST. PETER'S, ROME. The Tempietto is the earliest of the great achievements that made Rome the center of Italian art during the first quarter of the sixteenth century. Most of them belong to the decade 1503–13, the papacy of Julius II. It was he who decided to replace the old basilica of St. Peter's, which had long been in precarious condition, with a church so magnificent as to overshadow all the monuments of ancient imperial Rome. The task naturally fell to Bramante, the foremost architect in the city. His original design, of 1506, is known to us only from a plan (fig. 649) and from the medal commemorating the start of the building campaign (fig.

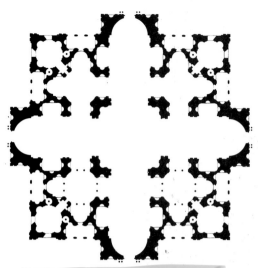

649. DONATO BRAMANTE. Original plan for St. Peter's, Rome. 1506 (after Geymüller)

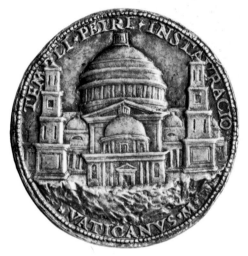

650. CARADOSSO. Bronze medal. showing Bramante's design for St. Peter's. 1506. British Museum, London

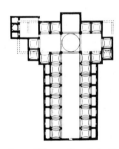

651. Plan of Brunelleschi's S. Lorenzo, Florence, reproduced at the same scale as figure 649

ambition, who wanted to unite all Italy under his command and thus to gain a temporal power matching the spiritual authority of his office. Bramante's design is indeed of truly imperial magnificence: a huge dome, hemispherical like that of the Tempietto, crowns the crossing of the barrel-vaulted arms of a Greek cross, with four lesser domes and tall corner towers filling the angles. This plan fulfills all the demands laid down by Alberti for sacred architecture (see page 471); based entirely on the circle and the square, it is so rigidly symmetrical that we cannot tell which apse was to hold the high altar. Bramante envisioned four identical façades like that on the medal of 1506, dominated by the same repertory of severely classical forms we saw in the Tempietto: domes, half-domes, colonnades, pediments.

These simple geometric shapes, however, do not prevail inside the church. Here the "sculptured wall" reigns supreme: the plan shows no continuous surfaces, only great, oddly shaped "islands" of masonry that have been well described by one critic as giant pieces of toast half-eaten by a voracious space. The actual size of these "islands" can be visualized only if we compare the measurements of Bramante's church with those of earlier buildings. S. Lorenzo in Florence, for instance, has a length of 268 feet, less than half that of the new St. Peter's (550 feet). Figure 651, which reproduces the plan of S. Lorenzo on the same scale as Bramante's plan (fig. 649), proves that Bramante's reference to the Pantheon and the Basilica of Constantine was no idle boast; his plan dwarfs these monuments, as well as every Early Renaissance church (each arm of the Greek cross has about the dimensions of the Basilica of Constantine).

How did he propose to build a structure of such overwhelming size? Cut stone and brick, the materials favored by medieval architects, would not do, for technical and economic reasons; only construction in concrete, as used by the Romans but largely forgotten during the Middle Ages, was strong and cheap enough to fill Bramante's needs (see page 218). By reviving this ancient technique, he opened a new era in the history of architecture, for concrete permitted designs of far greater flexibility than the building methods of the medieval masons. The possibilities of the material, however, were not fully exploited for some time to come. The construction of St. Peter's progressed at so slow a pace that in 1514, when Bramante died, only the four crossing piers had actually been built. For the next three decades the campaign was carried on hesitantly by architects trained under Bramante, who modified his design in a number of ways. A new and decisive phase in the history of St. Peter's began only in 1546, when Michelangelo took charge; the present appearance of the church (fig. 666) is largely shaped by his ideas. But this must be considered in the context of Michelangelo's career as a whole.

Michelangelo

The concept of genius as divine inspiration, a superhuman power granted to a few rare individuals and acting through them, is nowhere exemplified more fully than in the life and work of Michelangelo (1475–1564). Not only his admirers viewed him in this light; he himself, steeped in the tradition of Neo-Platonism (see page 484), accepted the idea of his

650), which shows the exterior in rather imprecise perspective. These are sufficient, however, to bear out the words Bramante reportedly used to define his aim: "I shall place the Pantheon on top of the Basilica of Constantine."

To surpass the two most famous structures of Roman antiquity by a Christian edifice of unexampled grandeur— nothing less would have satisfied Julius II, a pontiff of vast

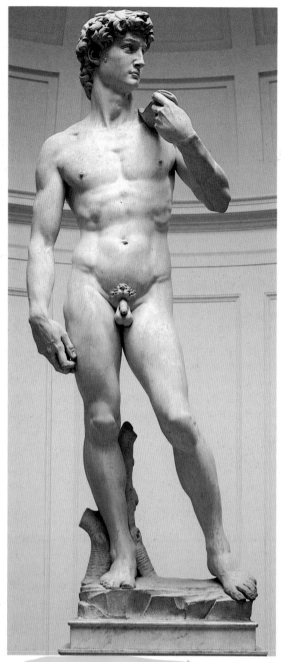

652. MICHELANGELO. *DAVID.* 1501–4. Marble,
height of figure 13′5″ (4.08 m). Galleria dell'Accademia, Florence

eyes. Only the "liberation" of real, three-dimensional bodies from recalcitrant matter could satisfy his urge (for his procedure, see comment on the *Captive*, pages 45–47). Painting, for him, should imitate the roundness of sculptured forms, and architecture, too, must partake of the organic qualities of the human figure.

Michelangelo's faith in the human image as the supreme vehicle of expression gave him a sense of kinship with Classical sculpture closer than that of any Renaissance artist. Among recent masters he admired Giotto, Masaccio, Donatello, and Jacopo della Quercia more than the men he knew as a youth in Florence. Yet his mind was decisively shaped by the cultural climate of Florence during the 1480s and 1490s; both the Neo-Platonism of Marsilio Ficino and the religious reforms of Savonarola profoundly affected him. These conflicting influences reinforced the tensions within Michelangelo's personality, his violent changes of mood, his sense of being at odds with himself and with the world. As he conceived his statues to be human bodies released from their marble prison, so the body was the earthly prison of the soul—noble, surely, but a prison nevertheless. This dualism of body and spirit endows his figures with their extraordinary pathos; outwardly calm, they seem stirred by an overwhelming psychic energy that has no release in physical action.

DAVID. The unique qualities of Michelangelo's art are fully present in his *David* (fig. 652), the earliest monumental statue of the High Renaissance. Commissioned of the artist in 1501, when he was twenty-six, the huge figure was designed to be placed high above the ground, on one of the buttresses of Florence Cathedral. The city fathers chose instead to put it in front of the Palazzo Vecchio, as the civic-patriotic symbol of the Florentine republic (see fig. 491; it has since been replaced by a modern copy).

We can well understand their decision. The head of Goliath being omitted, Michelangelo's *David* looks challenging—not a victorious hero but the champion of a just cause. Vibrant with pent-up energy, he faces the world like Donatello's *St. George* (see fig. 578), although his nudity links him to the older master's bronze *David* as well. But the style of the figure proclaims an ideal very different from the wiry slenderness of Donatello's youths. Michelangelo had just spent several years in Rome, where he had been deeply impressed with the emotion-charged, muscular bodies of Hellenistic sculpture. Although the *Laocoön* (see fig. 230), shortly to become the most famous work in this style, had not then been discovered, other Hellenistic statues were accessible to him. Their heroic scale, their superhuman beauty and power, and the swelling volume of their forms became part of Michelangelo's own style and, through him, of Renaissance art in general. Yet the *David* could never be taken for an ancient statue. In the *Laocoön* and similar works (compare fig. 228) the body "acts out" the spirit's agony, while the *David*, at once calm and tense, shows the action-in-repose so characteristic of Michelangelo.

TOMB OF JULIUS II. This trait persists in the *Moses* (fig. 653) and the two "slaves" (figs. 654 and 655), carved about a decade later. They were part of the vast sculptural program

genius as a living reality, although it seemed to him at times a curse rather than a blessing. The element that brings continuity to his long and stormy career is the sovereign power of his personality, his faith in the subjective rightness of everything he created. Conventions, standards, and traditions might be observed by lesser spirits; he could acknowledge no authority higher than the dictates of his genius.

Unlike Leonardo, for whom painting was the noblest of the arts because it embraced every visible aspect of the world, Michelangelo was a sculptor—more specifically, a carver of marble statues—to the core. Art, for him, was not a science but "the making of men," analogous (however imperfectly) to divine creation; hence the limitations of sculpture that Leonardo decried were essential virtues in Michelangelo's for the Tomb of Julius II, which would have been Michelangelo's greatest achievement had he carried it out as originally planned. The majestic *Moses*, meant to be seen from below, has the awesome force which the artist's contemporaries called *terribilità*—a concept akin to the sublime. His pose, both watchful and meditative, suggests a man capable of wise leadership as well as towering wrath. The "slaves" are more difficult to interpret: they seem to have belonged to a series representing the arts, now shackled by the death of their greatest patron; later, apparently, they came to signify the territories conquered by Julius II. Be that as it may, Michelangelo has conceived the two figures as a contrasting pair, the so-called *Dying Slave* (fig. 654) yielding to his bonds, the *Rebellious Slave* (fig. 655) struggling to free himself. Perhaps their allegorical meaning mattered less to him than their expressive content, so evocative of the Neo-Platonic image of the body as the earthly prison of the soul.

THE SISTINE CEILING. The Tomb of Julius II remained unfinished when the pope interrupted Michelangelo's labors on the project at an early stage, half-forcing, half-cajoling the reluctant artist to fresco the ceiling of the Sistine Chapel in the Vatican (fig. 656). Driven by his desire to resume work

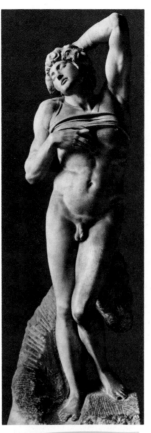

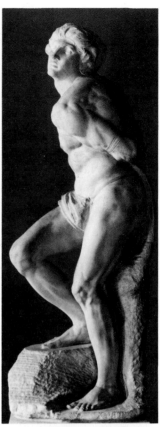

654. MICHELANGELO
"THE DYING SLAVE." 1513–16.
Marble, height 7'6" (2.28 m).
Musée du Louvre, Paris

655. MICHELANGELO
"THE REBELLIOUS SLAVE." 1513–16.
Marble, height 7' (2.13 m).
Musée du Louvre, Paris

on the tomb, Michelangelo completed the entire ceiling in four years, 1508–12. He produced a masterpiece of truly epochal importance. The ceiling is a huge organism with hundreds of figures rhythmically distributed within the painted architectural framework, dwarfing the earlier murals (fig. 638) by its size, and still more by its compelling inner unity. In the central area, subdivided by five pairs of girders, are nine scenes from Genesis, from the Creation of the World (at the far end of the chapel) to the Drunkenness of Noah.

The theological scheme of these scenes and the rich program accompanying them—the nude youths, the medallions, the prophets and sibyls, the scenes in the spandrels—has not been fully explained, but we know that it links early history and the coming of Christ, the beginning of time and its end (*The Last Judgment* on the end wall above the altar, although it was painted a quarter of a century later and is not visible in figure 656, must have been intended from the start). We do not know how much responsibility Michelangelo had for the program; he was not a man to submit to dictation, and the subject matter of the ceiling fits his cast of mind so perfectly that his own desires cannot have conflicted strongly with those of his patron. What greater theme could he wish than the Creation of the World, the Fall of Man, and our ultimate reconciliation with the Lord?

A detailed survey of the Sistine Ceiling would fill a book; we shall have to be content with two of the four major scenes

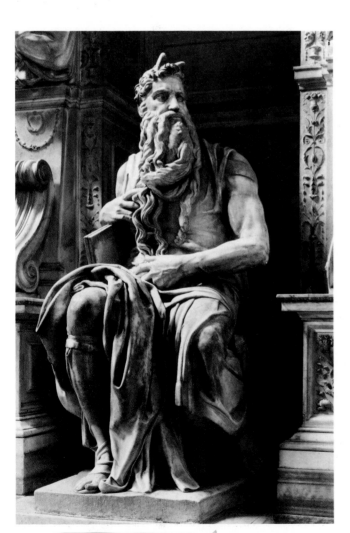

653. MICHELANGELO. *MOSES.* c. 1513–15. Marble, height 7'8½" (2.35 m). S. Pietro in Vincoli, Rome

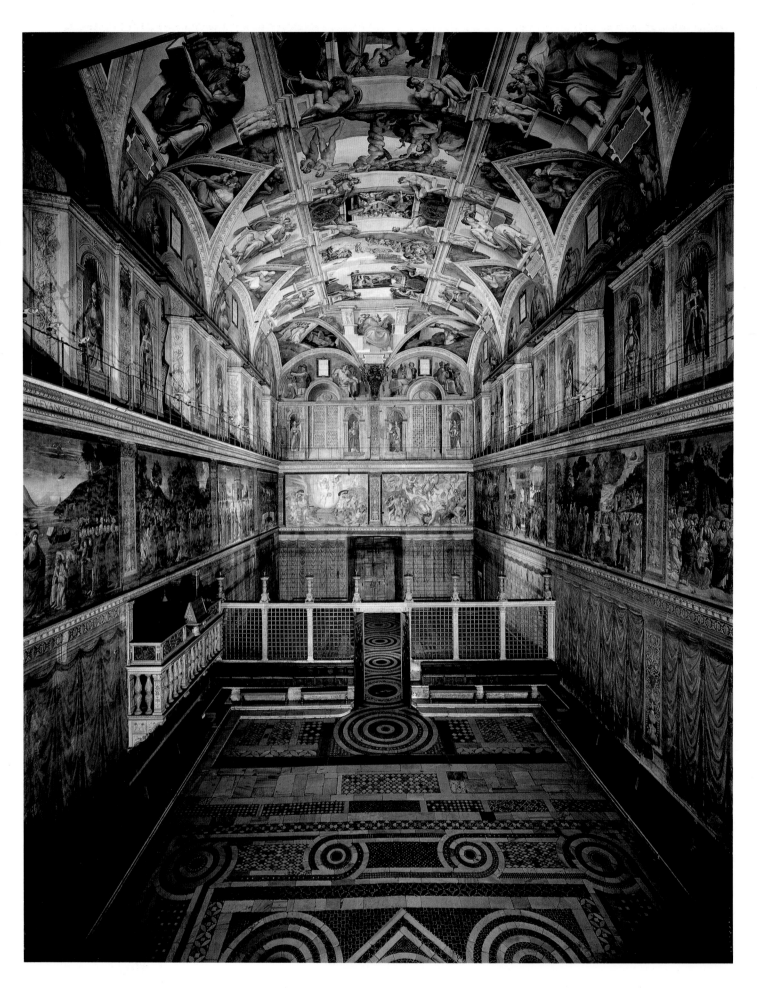

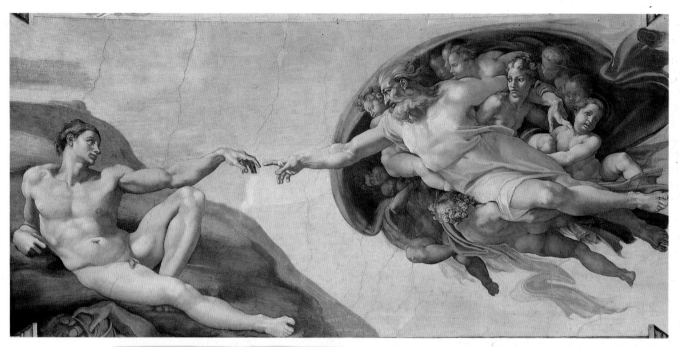

657. MICHELANGELO. *THE CREATION OF ADAM*, portion of the Sistine Ceiling. 1508–12. Fresco

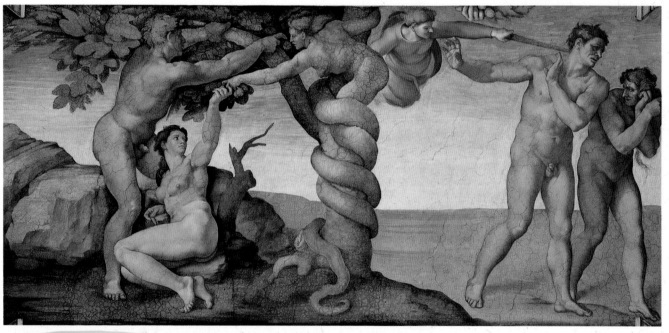

658. MICHELANGELO. *THE FALL OF MAN* and *THE EXPULSION FROM THE GARDEN OF EDEN*, portion of the Sistine Ceiling. 1508–12. Fresco

in the center portion. Of these, the *Creation of Adam* (fig. 657) must have stirred Michelangelo's imagination most deeply; it shows not the physical molding of Adam's body but the passage of the divine spark—the soul—and thus achieves a dramatic juxtaposition of Man and God unrivaled by any other artist. Jacopo della Quercia approximated it (see fig. 584), but without the dynamism of Michelangelo's design that contrasts the earth-bound Adam and the figure of

656. (*opposite*) Interior of the Sistine Chapel showing Michelangelo's ceiling fresco. The Vatican, Rome

God rushing through the sky. This relationship becomes even more meaningful when we realize that Adam strains not only toward his Creator but toward Eve, whom he sees, yet unborn, in the shelter of the Lord's left arm.

Michelangelo has been called a poor colorist—unjustly, as the recently undertaken cleaning of the frescoes has revealed. *The Fall of Man* and *The Expulsion from the Garden of Eden* (fig. 658) show the bold, intense hues typical of the whole ceiling. The range of his palette is astonishing. Contrary to what had been thought, the heroic figures have anything but the quality of painted sculpture. Full of life, they act out their epic roles in illusionistic "windows" that punc-

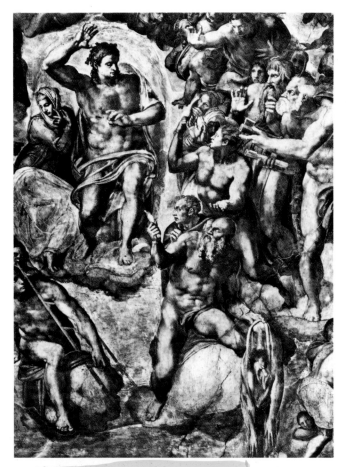

659. MICHELANGELO. *THE LAST JUDGMENT* (detail, with self-portrait). 1534–41. Fresco. Sistine Chapel, The Vatican, Rome

Lord is the Apostle Bartholomew, holding a human skin to represent his martyrdom (he had been flayed). The face on that skin, however, is not the saint's but Michelangelo's own. In this grimly sardonic self-portrait (so well hidden that it was recognized only in modern times) the artist has left his personal confession of guilt and unworthiness.

THE MEDICI CHAPEL. The interval between the Sistine Ceiling and *The Last Judgment* coincides with the papacies of Leo X (1513–21) and Clement VII (1523–34); both were members of the Medici family, and preferred to employ Michelangelo in Florence. His activities centered on S. Lorenzo, the Medici church. A century after Brunelleschi's revolutionary design for the sacristy (see page 455), Leo X decided to build a matching structure—the New Sacristy—to house the tombs of Lorenzo the Magnificent, Lorenzo's brother Giuliano, and two younger members of the family, also named Lorenzo and Giuliano. Michelangelo took early charge of this project and worked on it for fourteen years, completing the architecture and two of the tombs, those for the lesser Lorenzo and Giuliano (fig. 660). The New Sacristy was thus conceived as an architectural-sculptural ensemble; it is the only work of the artist where his statues remain in the setting planned specifically for them.

ture the architectural setting. Michelangelo does not simply color the areas within the contours but builds up his forms from broad and vigorous brushstrokes in the tradition of Giotto and Masaccio. *The Expulsion* is particularly close to Masaccio's (see fig. 603)

The panels in the center of the ceiling are interrupted by garland-bearing youths that recur at regular intervals (see fig. 656). These wonderfully animated figures play an important role in Michelangelo's design; they form a kind of chain linking the Genesis scenes, yet their significance remains uncertain. Are they images of human souls? Do they represent the world of pagan antiquity? Whatever the answer, they seem to belong to the same category of being as the "slaves" from the Tomb of Julius II; again the symbolic intent is overpowered by the wealth of expression Michelangelo has poured into these figures.

THE LAST JUDGMENT. When Michelangelo returned to the Sistine Chapel in 1534, over twenty years later, the Western world was enduring the spiritual and political crisis of the Reformation (see page 542). We perceive with shocking directness how the mood has changed as we turn from the radiant vitality of Michelangelo's ceiling fresco to the somber vision of his *Last Judgment*. The Blessed and Damned alike huddle together in tight clumps, pleading for mercy before a wrathful God (fig. 659). Straddling a cloud just below the

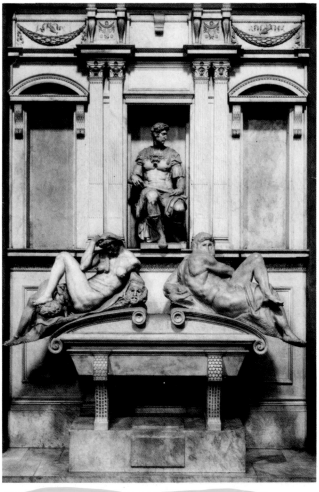

660. MICHELANGELO. Tomb of Giuliano de'Medici. 1524–34. Marble, height of central figure 71″ (180.5 cm). New Sacristy, S. Lorenzo, Florence

The design of the two tombs still shows some kinship with such Early Renaissance tombs as that of Leonardo Bruni (see fig. 623), but the differences weigh more heavily: there is no inscription, the effigy has been replaced by two allegorical figures (*Day* on the right, *Night* on the left), and the statue of Giuliano, in classical military garb, bears no resemblance to the deceased Medici. ("A thousand years from now, nobody will know what he looked like," Michelangelo is said to have remarked.) What is the meaning of this triad? The question, put countless times, has never found a satisfactory answer. Michelangelo's plans for the Medici tombs underwent so many changes of form and program while the work was underway that the present state of the monuments can hardly be the final solution; rather, the dynamic process of design was arbitrarily halted by the artist's departure for Rome in 1534. *Day* and *Night* were certainly designed to rest on horizontal surfaces, not the curved, sloping lid of the present sarcophagus.

Perhaps they were not even intended for this particular tomb. Giuliano's niche is too narrow and too shallow to accommodate him comfortably. Other figures and reliefs were planned, but never executed. Was their omission intentional or accidental? Despite all this, the tomb of Giuliano remains a compelling visual unit. The great triangle of the statues is held in place by a network of verticals and horizontals whose slender, sharp-edged forms heighten the roundness and weight of the sculpture. *Giuliano*, the ideal image of the prince, is a younger and more pensive counterpart of the *Moses*; the reclining figures contrast in mood, like the "slaves." Derived from ancient river gods (compare fig. 6), they embody the quality of action-in-repose more dramatically than any other works by Michelangelo: in the brooding menace of *Day*, and in the disturbed slumber of *Night*, the dualism of body and soul is expressed with unforgettable grandeur.

LAURENTIAN LIBRARY. Concurrently with the New Sacristy, Michelangelo built the Laurentian Library, adjoining S. Lorenzo, to house for the public the vast collection of books and manuscripts belonging to the Medici family. In the vestibule (fig. 661) his full powers as a creator of new architectural forms are displayed for the first time. By the standards of the 1520s, based on the classical ideal of Bramante, everything here is wrong: the pediment above the door is broken; the pilasters of the niches taper downward; the columns belong to no recognizable order; the scroll brackets sustain nothing. Most paradoxical, however, from the point of view of established practice, are the recessed columns: though structurally logical—the columns support heavy piers, which in turn support the roof beams (fig. 662)—this feature upsets a hallowed rule of architectural propriety: that in the classical post-and-lintel system the columns (or pilasters) and entablature must project from the wall on which they have been superimposed, to stress their separate identities. The system could be reduced to a linear pattern (as in the Palazzo Rucellai, fig. 613), but no one before Michelangelo had dared to defy it by incorporating columns into the wall.

The entire design demonstrates what Vasari, the artist's biographer, had in mind when he wrote that Michelangelo's architecture "broke the bonds and chains of . . . common

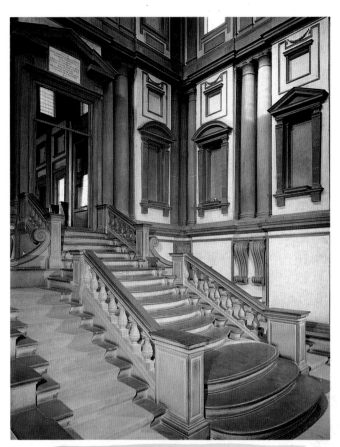

661. MICHELANGELO. Vestibule of the Laurentian Library, Florence. Begun 1524; stairway designed 1558–59

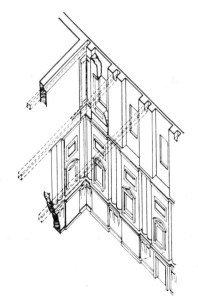

662. Axonometric diagram of structural system, Vestibule of the Laurentian Library (after Ackerman)

usage." The purpose of these innovations is, of course, expressive rather than functional; the walls push inward between the columns to make of the vestibule a kind of "compression chamber" where the beholder experiences an almost physical stress. Our unease is heightened by the blank stare of the empty niches and by the nightmarish stairway, which flows downward and outward so relentlessly that we wonder if we dare brave the current by mounting the steps.

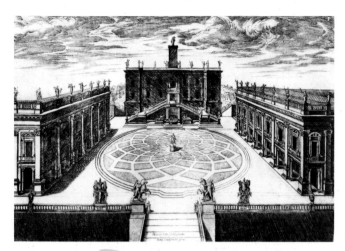

663. MICHELANGELO. *THE CAMPIDOGLIO*
(engraving by Étienne Dupérac, 1569)

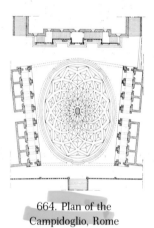

664. Plan of the
Campidoglio, Rome

CAMPIDOGLIO. During the last thirty years of his life, architecture became Michelangelo's main preoccupation. In 1537–39, he received the most ambitious commission of his career: to reshape the Campidoglio, the top of Rome's Capitoline Hill, into a square with a monumental frame worthy of this venerable site, once the symbolic center of ancient Rome. At last he could plan on a grand scale, and he took full advantage of the opportunity. Although not completed until long after his death, the project was carried out essentially as he had designed it—the most imposing civic center ever built, and a model for countless others. Pope Paul III took the initiative by transferring the equestrian monument of Marcus Aurelius (see fig. 296) to the Campidoglio, and Michelangelo designed its base; the statue became the focal point of his entire scheme, placed at the apex of a gently rising oval mound.

Three sides of the piazza are defined by palace facades, so that the visitor, after ascending the flight of steps on the fourth side, finds himself enclosed in a huge "outdoor room." The effect of the ensemble cannot be rendered by photographs. Even the best view, an engraving based on Michelangelo's design (fig. 663), conveys it very imperfectly: it shows the complete bilateral symmetry of the scheme, and the energetic sense of progression along the main axis toward the Senators' Palace, but it distorts the shape of the piazza, which is not a rectangle but a trapezoid (the flanking facades are divergent, fig. 664). This peculiarity was imposed on Michelangelo by the existing site; the Senators' Palace, and the Conservators' Palace on the right, were older buildings that had to be preserved behind newly designed exteriors, and they were placed at an angle of 80 instead of 90 degrees. But he turned into an asset what would have hin-

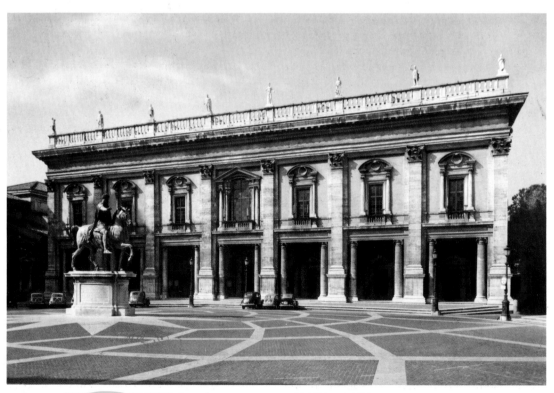

665. MICHELANGELO. Palazzo dei Conservatori, Campidoglio, Rome. Designed c. 1545

dered a less imaginative architect: the divergence of the flanks makes the Senators' Palace look larger than it is, dramatically dominating the piazza.

The whole conception has the visual effectiveness of a stage set—note that in the engraving the "New Palace" on the left is a mere show front with nothing behind it. Yet this façade and its twin on the opposite side are not shallow screens but vigorously three-dimensional structures (fig. 665) with the most "muscular" juxtaposition of voids and solids, of horizontals and verticals, of any piece of architecture since Roman antiquity. They share the striking feature of an open portico, which links the piazza and façades as a courtyard is related to the arcades of a cloister.

The columns and stone beams of the porticoes are inscribed within a colossal order of pilasters that supports a heavy cornice topped by a balustrade; the entire design is based on the classic post-and-lintel principle. We have encountered these elements on the façades of the Pazzi Chapel and Alberti's S. Andrea, and in the Tempietto of Bramante (see figs. 591, 616, and 647), but it was Michelangelo who welded them into a coherent system. For the Senators' Palace he employed the colossal order and balustrade above a tall basement, which emphasizes the massive quality of the building. The single entrance at the top of the huge double-ramped stairway seems to gather all the spatial forces set in motion by the oval mound and the divergent flanks, and thus provides a dramatic climax for the visitor traversing the piazza.

ST. PETER'S. With the Campidoglio, the colossal order became firmly established in the repertory of monumental architecture. Michelangelo himself used it again on the exterior of St. Peter's (fig. 666), with equally impressive results. The system of the Conservators' Palace, with windows now replacing the open loggias, and an attic instead of the balustrade, could here be adapted perfectly to the jagged contour of the plan; unlike Bramante's many-layered elevation (see fig. 650) the colossal order emphasized the compact body of the structure, thus setting off the dome more dramatically. The same desire for compactness and organic unity led Michelangelo to simplify the interior, without changing its centralized character (figs. 667 and 668). He brought the complex spatial sequences of Bramante's plan (see fig. 649) into one cross-and-square, and defined its main axis by modifying the exterior of the eastern apse and projecting a portico for it. This part of his design was never carried out. The dome, however, although largely built after his death, reflects his ideas in every important respect.

Bramante had planned his dome as a stepped hemisphere above a narrow drum, which would have seemed to press down on the church below; Michelangelo's conveys the opposite sensation, a powerful thrust that draws energy upward from the main body of the structure. The high drum, the strongly projecting buttresses accented by double columns, the ribs, the raised curve of the cupola, the tall lantern—all contribute verticality at the expense of the horizontals. We may recall the Florence Cathedral dome (see fig. 486), from which Michelangelo borrowed not only the double-shell construction but the Gothic profile. Yet the effects are immensely different: the smooth planes of Brunelleschi's dome

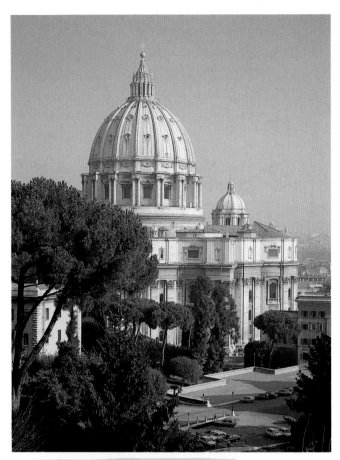

666. MICHELANGELO. St. Peter's, Rome, seen from the west. 1546–64 (dome completed by GIACOMO DELLA PORTA, 1590)

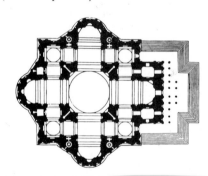

667. MICHELANGELO. Plan for St. Peter's

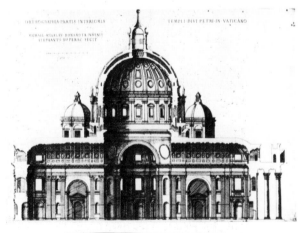

668. Longitudinal section of St. Peter's (engraving by Étienne Dupérac, 1569)

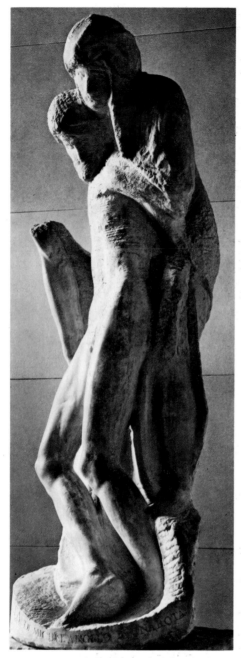

669. MICHELANGELO. *MILAN PIETÀ*
(*RONDANINI PIETÀ*). c. 1555–64.
Marble, height 6'5" (1.96 m).
Castello Sforzesco, Milan

give no hint of the internal stresses, while Michelangelo finds a sculptured shape for these contending forces, and relates them to those in the rest of the building (the impulse of the paired colossal pilasters below is taken up by the double columns of the drum, continues in the ribs, and culminates in the lantern). The logic of this design is so persuasive that few domes built between 1600 and 1900 fail to acknowledge it in some way.

MILAN PIETÀ. Michelangelo's magnificent assurance in handling such projects as the Campidoglio and St. Peter's seems to belie his portrayal of himself as a limp skin in *The*

Last Judgment. It is indeed difficult to reconcile these contrasting aspects of his personality. Did he, perhaps, toward the end of his life, find greater fulfillment in architecture than in shaping human bodies? In his last piece of sculpture, the *Milan Pietà* (fig. 669), he is groping for new forms, as if his earlier work had become meaningless to him. Also known as the *Rondanini Pietà*, the group is a fragment, destroyed partly by his own hand; he was still struggling with it a few days before he died. The theme—especially its emotional content—suggests that he intended it for his own tomb. These two figures have no trace of High Renaissance rhetoric; silently hovering, they evoke the devotional images of medieval art. Like the master's self-portrait (see fig. 659), the *Milan Pietà* occupies an intensely private realm. Its plea for redemption is addressed to no human audience, but to God.

Raphael

If Michelangelo exemplifies the solitary genius, Raphael belongs just as surely to the opposite type: the artist as a person of the world. The contrast between the two was as clear to their contemporaries as it is to us. Although each had his partisans, both enjoyed equal fame. Today our sympathies are less evenly divided:

> In the room the women come and go
> Talking of Michelangelo.
>
> (T. S. Eliot)

So do a lot of us, including the authors of historical novels and fictionalized biographies, while Raphael (1483–1520) is usually discussed only by historians of art. The younger master's career is too much a success story, his work too replete with seemingly effortless grace, to match the tragic heroism of Michelangelo. As an innovator, Raphael seems to contribute less than Leonardo, Bramante, and Michelangelo, the three artists whose achievements were basic to his. Yet he is the central painter of the High Renaissance; our conception of the entire style rests more on his work than on any other master's.

The genius of Raphael was a unique power of synthesis that enabled him to merge the qualities of Leonardo and Michelangelo, creating an art at once lyric and dramatic, pictorially rich and sculpturally solid. This power is already present in the first works he made in Florence (1504–8), after he completed his apprenticeship with Perugino. The meditative calm of the *Madonna del Granduca* (fig. 670) still reflects the style of his teacher (compare fig. 638). But the forms are ampler and enveloped in Leonardesque *sfumato*; the Virgin, grave and tender, makes us think of the *Mona Lisa* without engendering any of her mystery.

THE SCHOOL OF ATHENS. Michelangelo's influence on Raphael asserted itself somewhat later. Its full force can be felt only in Raphael's Roman works. At the time Michelangelo began to paint the Sistine Ceiling, Julius II summoned the younger artist from Florence and commissioned him to decorate a series of rooms in the Vatican Palace. The first room, the Stanza della Segnatura (fig. 671), may have

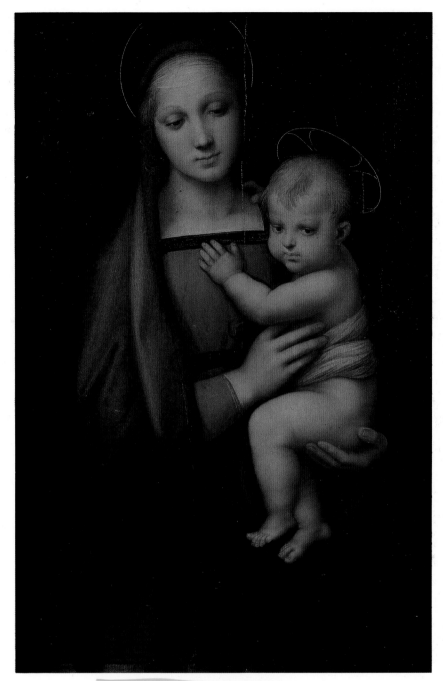

670. RAPHAEL. *MADONNA DEL GRANDUCA*. c. 1505.
Oil on panel, 33×21½″ (83.5×54.7 cm).
Palazzo Pitti, Florence

housed the pope's library, and Raphael's cycle of frescoes on its walls and ceiling refers to the four domains of learning—theology, philosophy, law, and the arts.

Of these frescoes, *The School of Athens* (fig. 672) has long been acknowledged as Raphael's masterpiece and the perfect embodiment of the classical spirit of the High Renaissance. Its subject is "the Athenian school of thought," a group of famous Greek philosophers gathered around Plato and Aristotle, each in a characteristic pose or activity. Raphael must have already seen the Sistine Ceiling, then nearing completion. He evidently owes to Michelangelo the expressive en-

ergy, the physical power, and the dramatic grouping of his figures. Yet Raphael has not simply borrowed Michelangelo's repertory of gestures and poses; he has absorbed it into his own style, and thereby given it different meaning.

Body and spirit, action and emotion, are now balanced harmoniously, and every member of this great assembly plays his role with magnificent, purposeful clarity. The total conception of *The School of Athens* suggests the spirit of Leonardo's *The Last Supper* (fig. 642) rather than the Sistine Ceiling. This holds true of the way Raphael makes each philosopher reveal "the intention of his soul," distinguishes the

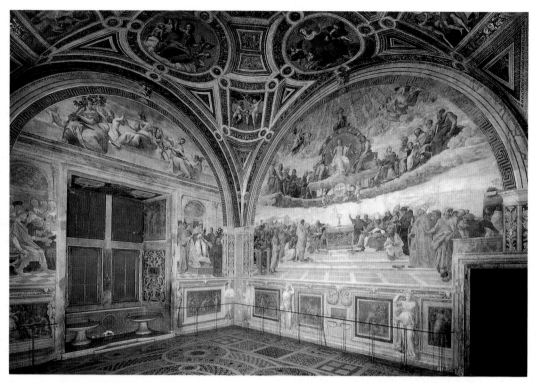

671. Stanza della Segnatura, with frescos by RAPHAEL. Vatican Palace, Rome

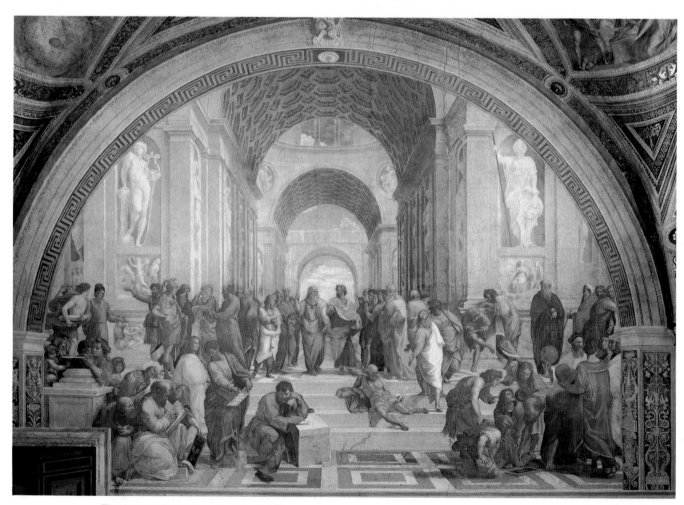

672. RAPHAEL. *THE SCHOOL OF ATHENS.* 1510–11. Fresco. Stanza della Segnatura, Vatican Palace, Rome

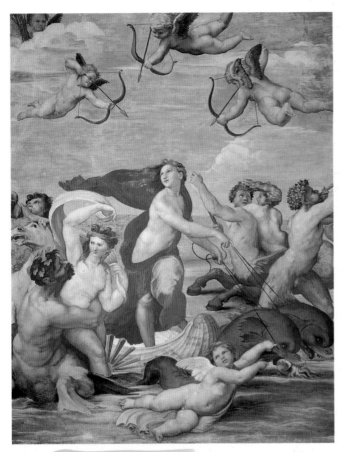

673. RAPHAEL. *GALATEA*. 1513. Fresco, 9'8⅛"×7'4"
(3×2.2 m). Villa Farnesina, Rome

movement is not generated by the figures but imposed on them from without, so that it never detaches itself from the surface of the canvas.

PORTRAITS. Early in his career Raphael had already shown a special talent for portraiture. It is another tribute to his genius for synthesis that he combined the realism of fifteenth-century portraits (such as fig. 637) with the human ideal of the High Renaissance (which, in the *Mona Lisa*, nearly overpowers the sitter's individuality). Raphael did not flatter or conventionalize his subjects; surely Pope Leo X (fig. 674) looks here no handsomer than he did in reality. His sullen, heavy-jowled features have been recorded in concrete, almost Flemish detail. Nevertheless, the pontiff has a commanding presence, his aura of power and dignity emanating more from his inner being than from his exalted office. Raphael, we feel, has not falsified the sitter's personality but ennobled and focused it, as if he had been fortunate enough to observe Leo X in his finest hour. The two cardinals, who lack this balanced strength although they are studied with equal care, enhance by contrast the sovereign quality of the main figure. Even the pictorial treatment shows a similar gradation: Leo X has been set off from his companions, his reality heightened by intensified light, color, and texture.

relations among individuals and groups, and links them in formal rhythm. Also Leonardesque is the centralized, symmetrical design, and the interdependence of the figures and their architectural setting. But compared with the hall of the *Last Supper*, Raphael's classical edifice—its lofty dome, barrel vault, and colossal statuary—shares far more of the compositional burden. Inspired by Bramante, it seems like an advance view of the new St. Peter's. Its geometric precision and spatial grandeur bring to a climax the tradition begun by Masaccio (see fig. 598), continued by Domenico Veneziano and Piero della Francesca, and transmitted to Raphael by his teacher Perugino.

GALATEA. Raphael never again set so splendid an architectural stage. To create pictorial space, he relied increasingly on the movement of human figures, rather than perspective vistas. In the *Galatea* of 1513 (fig. 673), the subject is again classical—the beautiful nymph Galatea, vainly pursued by Polyphemus, belongs to Greek mythology—but here the cheerful and sensuous aspect of antiquity is celebrated, in contrast to the austere idealism of *The School of Athens*. Its composition recalls *The Birth of Venus* (fig. 635), a picture Raphael knew from his Florentine days, yet their very resemblance emphasizes their profound dissimilarity. Raphael's full-bodied, dynamic figures take on their expansive spiral movement from the vigorous *contrapposto* of Galatea; in Botticelli's picture, the

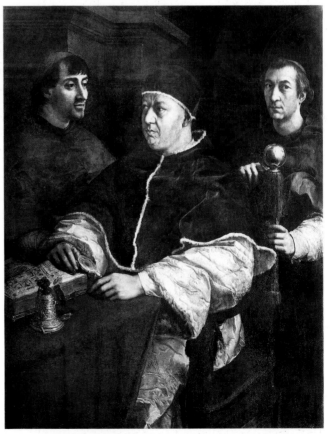

674. RAPHAEL. *POPE LEO X WITH GIULIO DE'MEDICI AND LUIGI DE'ROSSI*. c. 1518. Oil on panel,
60⅝×46⅞" (154×119 cm).
Galleria degli Uffizi, Florence

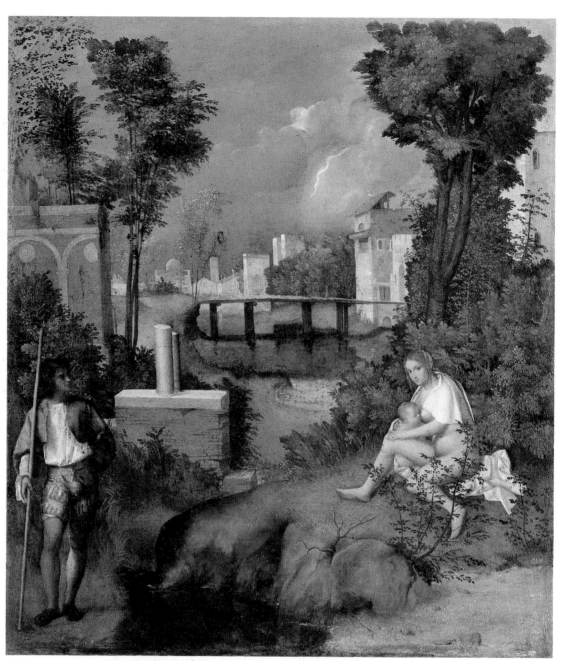

675. GIORGIONE. *THE TEMPEST.* c. 1505. Oil on canvas,
31¼×28¾″ (79.5×73 cm). Galleria dell'Accademia, Venice

Giorgione

The distinction between Early and High Renaissance art, so marked in Florence and Rome, is far less sharp in Venice. Giorgione (1478–1510), the first Venetian painter to belong to the new sixteenth century, left the orbit of Giovanni Bellini only during the final years of his short career.

THE TEMPEST. Among his very few mature works, *The Tempest* (fig. 675) is both the most individual and the most enigmatic. Our first glance may show us little more than a particularly charming reflection of Bellinesque qualities, familiar from the *St. Francis in Ecstasy* (fig. 633) and the S. Zaccaria altarpiece (fig. 634). The difference is one of mood—and this mood, in *The Tempest*, is subtly, pervasively

pagan. Bellini's landscape is meant to be seen through the eyes of St. Francis, as a piece of God's creation. Giorgione's figures, by contrast, do not interpret the scene for us; belonging themselves to nature, they are passive witnesses—victims, almost—of the thunderstorm about to engulf them. Who are they? So far, the young soldier and the nude mother with her baby have refused to disclose their identity, and the subject of the picture remains unknown. The present title is a confession of embarrassment, yet it is not inappropriate, for the only "action" is that of the tempest. Whatever its intended meaning, the scene is like an enchanted idyl, a dream of pastoral beauty soon to be swept away. Only poets had hitherto captured this air of nostalgic reverie; now, it entered the repertory of the painter. *The Tempest* initiates what was to become an important new tradition.

Titian

Giorgione died before he could explore in full the sensuous, lyrical world he had created in *The Tempest*. He bequeathed this task to Titian (1488/90–1576), an artist of comparable gifts who was decisively influenced by Giorgione, and who dominated Venetian painting for the next half-century.

BACCHANAL. Titian's *Bacchanal* of about 1518 (fig. 676) is frankly pagan, inspired by an ancient author's description of such a revel. The landscape, rich in contrasts of cool and warm tones, has all the poetry of Giorgione, but the figures are of another breed: active and muscular, they move with a joyous freedom that recalls Raphael's *Galatea* (fig. 673). By this time, many of Raphael's compositions had been engraved (see fig. 5), and from these reproductions Titian became familiar with the Roman High Renaissance. A number of the celebrants in his *Bacchanal* also reflect the influence of classical art. Titian's approach to antiquity, however, is very different from Raphael's; he visualizes the realm of classical myths as part of the natural world, inhabited not by animated statues but by beings of flesh and blood. The figures of the *Bacchanal* are idealized beyond everyday reality just enough to persuade us that they belong to a long-lost golden age. They invite us to share their blissful state in a way that makes Raphael's *Galatea* seem cold and remote by comparison.

THE PESARO MADONNA. This quality of festive animation reappears in many of Titian's religious paintings, such as the *Madonna with Members of the Pesaro Family* (fig. 677). Although we recognize the composition as a variant of the *Sacra Conversazione* (compare figs. 607 and 634), Titian has thoroughly transformed it by replacing the familiar frontal view with an oblique one. The Virgin is now enthroned in a great barrel-vaulted hall open on either side, a High Renaissance counterpart of the architectural setting in Bellini's *Madonna and Saints* in S. Zaccaria; because the view is diagonal, open sky and clouds now fill most of the background. Except for the kneeling donors, every figure is in motion—turning, leaning, gesturing; the officer with the flag seems almost to lead a charge up the steps. Yet the design remains harmoniously self-contained despite the strong element of drama. Brilliant sunlight makes every color and texture sparkle, in keeping with the joyous spirit of the altar. The only hint of tragedy is the cross of the Passion held by two angel-putti, hidden by clouds from the participants in the *Sacra Conversazione* but not from us—a tiny note adding poignancy to the scene.

PORTRAITS. After Raphael's death, Titian became the most sought-after portraitist of the age. His prodigious gifts, evident in the donors' portraits in the altar just discussed, are even more striking in the *Man with the Glove* (fig. 678). The dreamy intimacy of this portrait, with its soft outline and deep shadows, still reflects the style of Giorgione. Lost in thought, the young man seems quite unaware of us; this slight melancholy in his features conjures up the poetic appeal of *The*

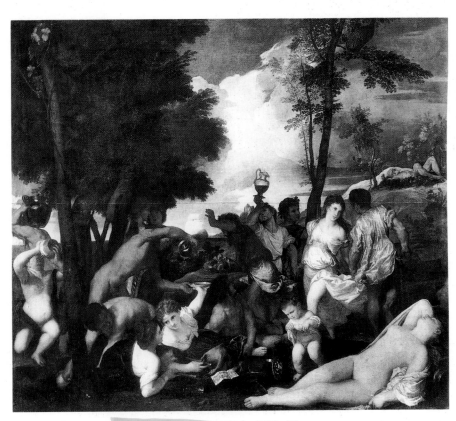

676. TITIAN. *BACCHANAL.* c. 1518. Oil on canvas,
5'8⅞" × 6'4" (1.7 × 1.9 m). Museo del Prado, Madrid

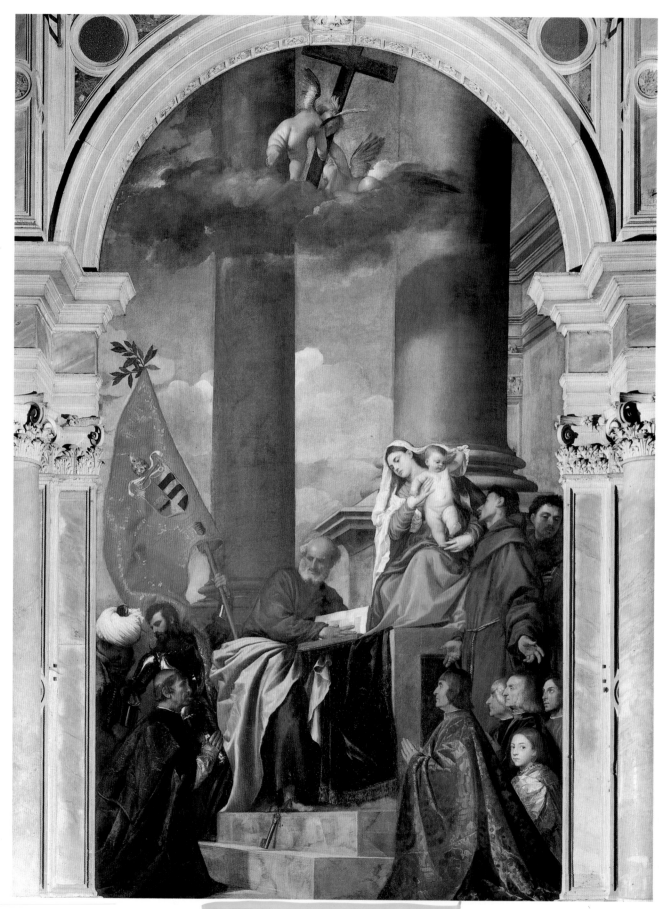

677. TITIAN. *MADONNA WITH MEMBERS OF THE PESARO
FAMILY.* 1526. Oil on canvas, 16′×8′10″ (4.9×2.7 m).
Sta. Maria del Gloriosa dei Frari, Venice

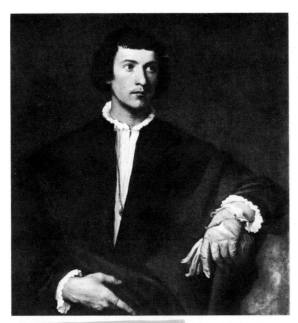

678. TITIAN. *MAN WITH THE GLOVE.* c. 1520. Oil on canvas,
39½×35″ (100.3×89 cm). Musée du Louvre, Paris

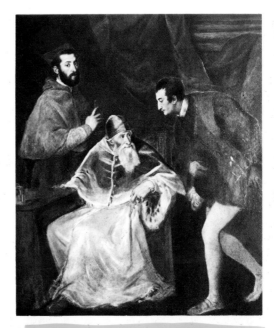

679. TITIAN. *POPE PAUL III AND HIS GRANDSONS.*
1546. Oil on canvas, 6′10″×5′8″ (2.1×1.7 m).
Museo di Capodimonte, Naples

Tempest. The breadth and power of form, however, goes far beyond Giorgione's. In Titian's hands, the possibilities of oil technique—rich, creamy highlights, deep dark tones that are transparent and delicately modulated—now are fully realized; the separate brushstrokes, hardly visible before, become increasingly free. We can see the rapid pace of his development by turning from the *Man with the Glove* to the papal group portrait *Pope Paul III and His Grandsons* (fig. 679), painted a quarter-century later. The quick, slashing strokes here endow the entire canvas with the spontaneity of a first sketch—some parts of it are, in fact, unfinished—even though the formal composition is derived from Raphael's *Pope Leo X* (fig. 674). In the freer technique Titian's uncanny grasp of human character also comes out: the tiny figure of the pope, shriveled with age, dominates his tall attendants with awesome authority. Comparing these two portraits by Titian, we see that a change of pictorial technique is no mere surface phenomenon. It reflects a change of the artist's aim.

LATE WORKS. This correspondence of form and technique is even clearer in *Christ Crowned with Thorns* (fig. 680), a masterpiece of Titian's old age. The shapes emerging from the semidarkness now consist wholly of light and color; despite the heavy impasto, the shimmering surfaces have lost every trace of material solidity and seem translucent, aglow from within. In consequence, the violent physical action has been miraculously suspended. What lingers in our minds is not the drama but the strange mood of serenity—engendered by deep religious feeling.

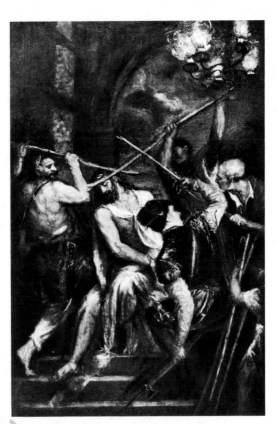

680. TITIAN. *CHRIST CROWNED WITH THORNS.* c. 1570.
Oil on canvas, 9′2″×6′ (2.8×1.8 m).
Pinakothek, Munich

CHAPTER FOUR
MANNERISM AND OTHER TRENDS

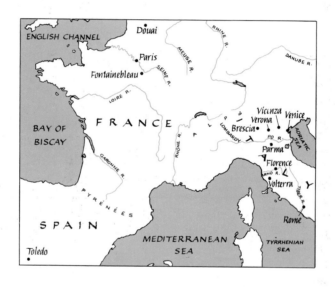

What happened after the High Renaissance? Eighty years ago the question would simply have been answered thus. After the High Renaissance came the Late Renaissance, which was dominated by shallow imitators of the great masters of the previous generation and lasted until the Baroque style emerged at the end of the century. Although today we take a far more positive view of the artists who reached maturity after 1520, and generally discard the term "Late Renaissance" as misleading, we have still to agree on a name for the seventy-five years separating the High Renaissance from the Baroque. Any one label implies that the period has one style, and nobody has succeeded in defining such a style. But if there is no single style in the years 1525–1600, why should this span be regarded as a period at all, except in the negative sense of an interval between two high points, as the Renaissance viewed the Middle Ages? Perhaps this difficulty can be resolved by thinking of this period as a time of crisis that gave rise to several competing tendencies rather than one dominant ideal—or as a time full of inner contradictions, not unlike the present, and thus peculiarly fascinating to us.

PAINTING

Mannerism in Florence and Rome

Among the various trends in art after the High Renaissance, that of Mannerism is one of the most discussed today. But in scope and significance the term remains problematic: its original meaning was narrow and derogatory, designating a group of mid-sixteenth-century painters in Rome and Florence whose self-consciously "artificial," mannered style was derived from certain aspects of Raphael and Michelangelo. More recently, the cold and rather barren formalism of their work has been recognized as a special form of a wider movement that placed "inner vision," however subjective or fantastic, above the twin authority of nature and the ancients; some scholars have broadened the definition of Mannerism to include even the later style of Michelangelo himself—which is rather like calling Phidias a classicist.

ROSSO. The first indications of disquiet in the High Renaissance appear shortly before 1520, in the work of some young painters in Florence. By 1521, Rosso Fiorentino (1495–1540), the most eccentric member of this group, expressed the new attitude with full conviction in *The Descent from the Cross* (fig. 681). Nothing has prepared us for the shocking impact of this latticework of spidery forms spread out against the dark sky. The figures are agitated yet rigid, as if congealed by a sudden, icy blast; even the draperies have brittle, sharp-edged planes; the acid colors and the light, brilliant but unreal, reinforce the nightmarish effect of the scene. Here is what amounts to a revolt against the classical balance of High Renaissance art; a profoundly disquieting, willful, visionary style that indicates a deep inner anxiety. Vasari's statement that Rosso committed suicide is probably untrue, yet seems plausible enough as we look at this picture.

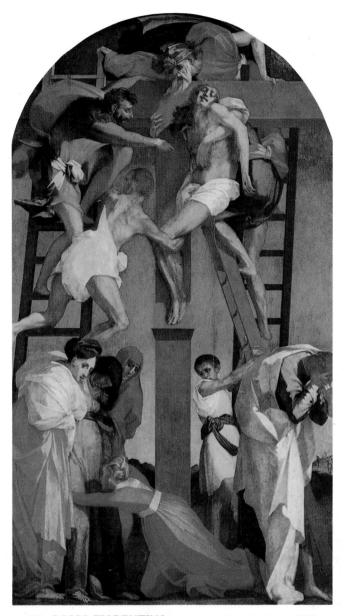

681. ROSSO FIORENTINO. *DESCENT FROM THE CROSS.* 1521. Panel, 11′×6′5½″ (3.4×2 m). Pinacoteca Communale, Volterra

PONTORMO. Pontormo (1494–1556/7), a friend of Rosso's, had an equally strange personality. Introspective and shy, he shut himself up in his quarters for weeks on end, inaccessible even to his friends. His wonderfully sensitive drawings, such as the *Study of a Young Girl* (fig. 682), well reflect these facets of his character; the sitter, moodily gazing into space, seems to shrink from the outer world, as if scarred by the trauma of some half-remembered experience.

PARMIGIANINO. This "anticlassical" style of Rosso and Pontormo, the first phase of Mannerism, was soon replaced by another aspect of the movement. This was less overtly anticlassical, less laden with subjective emotion, but equally far removed from the confident, stable world of the High Renaissance. The *Self-Portrait* (fig. 683) by Parmigianino

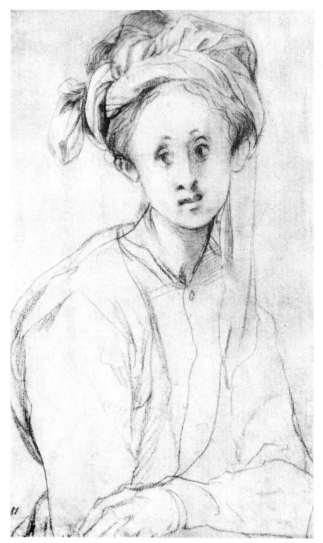

682. PONTORMO. *STUDY OF A YOUNG GIRL.* c. 1526.
Sanguine drawing. 9¾×5⅝″ (24.7×14.8 cm).
Gabinetto Disegni e Stampe degli Uffizi, Florence

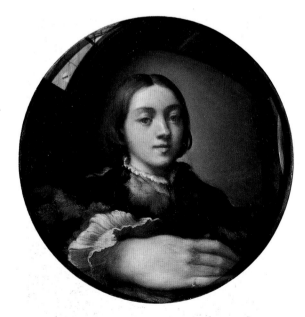

683. PARMIGIANINO. *SELF-PORTRAIT.* 1524. Oil on panel,
diameter 9⅝″ (24.7 cm). Kunsthistorisches Museum, Vienna

(1503–1540) suggests no psychological turmoil; the artist's appearance is bland and well groomed, veiled by a delicate Leonardesque *sfumato*. The distortions, too, are objective, not arbitrary, for the picture records what Parmigianino saw as he gazed at his reflection in a convex mirror. Yet why was he so fascinated by this view "through the looking glass"? Earlier painters who used the same device as an aid to observation had "filtered out" the distortions (as in figs. 552 and 563), except when the mirror image was contrasted with a direct view of the same scene (fig. 553). But Parmigianino substitutes his painting for the mirror itself, even employing a specially prepared convex panel. Did he perhaps want to demonstrate that there is no single "correct" reality, that distortion is as natural as the normal appearance of things?

Characteristically, his scientific detachment soon changed into its very opposite. Vasari tells us that Parmigianino, as he neared the end of his brief career (he died at thirty-seven), was obsessed with alchemy and became "a bearded, long-haired, neglected, and almost savage or wild man." Certainly his strange imagination is evident in his most famous work, *The Madonna with the Long Neck* (fig. 684), painted after he had returned to his native Parma from several years' sojourn in Rome. He had been deeply impressed with the rhythmic grace of Raphael's art (compare fig. 673), but he has transformed the older master's figures into a remarkable new breed: their limbs, elongated and ivory-smooth, move with effortless languor, embodying an ideal of beauty as remote from nature as any Byzantine figure. Their setting is equally arbitrary, with a gigantic—and apparently purposeless—row of columns looming behind the tiny figure of a prophet; Parmigianino seems determined to prevent us from measuring anything in this picture by the standards of ordinary experience. Here we have approached that "artificial" style for which the term "Mannerism" was originally coined. *The Madonna with the Long Neck* is a vision of unearthly perfection, its cold elegance no less compelling than the violence in Rosso's *Descent*.

ETCHINGS. We must say a word about etching as a new medium. By the early sixteenth century, the techniques of woodcut and engraving were employed mainly to reproduce other works. The creative printmakers of the day, however, preferred etching, often combined with drypoint (see fig. 572). Although etching was introduced in the North, the first artists to explore its possibilities seriously were the Italian Mannerists. Parmigianino's *The Entombment* (fig. 685) looks very much like his ink drawings in retaining a sketchlike immediacy that conveys the agitation of the scene and captures his nervous temperament.

An etching is made by coating a copperplate with resin to make an acid-resistant "ground," through which the design is scratched with a needle, laying bare the metal surface underneath. The plate is then bathed in an acid that etches (or "bites") the lines into the copper. The depth of these grooves varies with the strength and duration of the bath, and the biting is usually by stages. After a brief immersion in the acid bath the etcher will apply a protective coating to the plate in those areas where the lines should be faint. He then immerses the plate until it is time to protect the less delicate

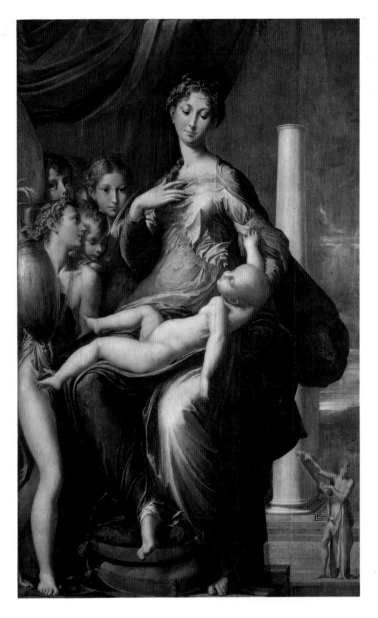

684. PARMIGIANINO. *THE MADONNA WITH THE LONG NECK.*
c. 1535. Oil on panel, 7'1"×4'4" (2.2×1.3 m).
Galleria degli Uffizi, Florence

685. PARMIGIANINO. *THE ENTOMBMENT.* Etching printed
in brown ink, 12¼×9⅜" (31.3×23.8 cm).
Los Angeles County Museum of Art.
Collection of Mary Stansburg Ruiz

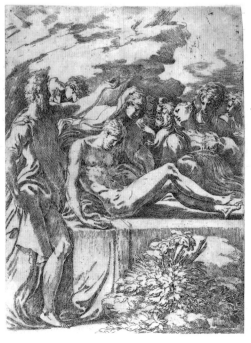

lines, and so on. To scratch a design into the resinous ground is, of course, an easier task than to scratch it into the copperplate itself; hence, an etched line is smoother and more flexible than a drypoint line. An etched plate is also more durable; like an engraved one, it yields a far greater number of prints than a drypoint plate. Its chief virtue is its wide tonal range, including velvety dark shades not possible in engraving or woodcut.

BRONZINO. Keyed to a sophisticated, even rarefied taste, the elegant phase of Italian Mannerism appealed particularly to such aristocratic patrons as the grand duke of Tuscany and the king of France, and soon became international (see fig. 724). The style produced splendid portraits, like that of Eleanora of Toledo (fig. 686), the wife of Cosimo I de'Medici, by Cosimo's court painter Agnolo Bronzino (1503–1572). The sitter here appears as the member of an exalted social caste, not as an individual personality; congealed into immobility behind the barrier of her lavishly ornate costume, Eleanora seems more akin to Parmigianino's *Madonna*—compare the hands—than to ordinary flesh and blood.

ANGUISSOLA. We have not encountered a woman artist since ancient Greece (see fig. 160), although this does not mean that there were none in the meantime. Pliny, for example, mentions in his *Natural History* (bk. XXXV) the names and describes the work of women artists in Greece and Rome, and there are records of women manuscript illuminators during the Middle Ages. We must remember, however, that the vast majority of all artists remained anonymous until the "Late Gothic" period, so that all but a few works specifically by women have proved impossible to identify. Women began to emerge as distinct artistic personalities about 1550. The first of these to be widely recognized in her own lifetime was Sofonisba Anguissola (c. 1535–1625). The oldest of six artistic daughters from a prominent family in Cremona, she showed a precocious talent and at an early age

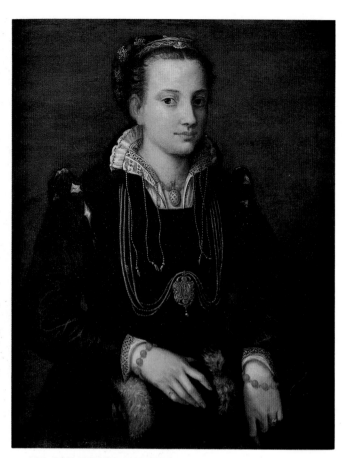

687. SOFONISBA ANGUISSOLA. *PORTRAIT OF THE ARTIST'S SISTER MINERVA.* c. 1559. Oil on canvas, 33½ × 26″ (85 × 66 cm). Milwaukee Art Museum, Layton Art Collection. Gift of the Family of Mrs. Fred Vogel, Jr.

exchanged drawings with Michelangelo. After establishing her reputation as a portraitist while still a young woman, she was called to Madrid, where she spent twenty years as a court painter until marriage brought her back to Italy. She became such a celebrity that her self-portraits, often showing her playing a spinet, were in considerable demand. Anguissola was highly regarded throughout her lifetime—Van Dyck drew her likeness shortly before her death—and her success was an important inspiration to other women artists. While her commissioned portraits follow the formal conventions of the day, she was at her best in more intimate paintings of her family, like the charming portrait she made of her sister Minerva shortly before leaving for Spain (fig. 687).

Mannerism in Venice

TINTORETTO. Mannerism did not appear in Venice until the middle of the century. Its leading exponent, Jacopo Tintoretto (1518–1594), an artist of prodigious energy and inventiveness, combined qualities of both its anticlassical and elegant phases in his work. He reportedly wanted "to paint like Titian and to design like Michelangelo," but his relationship to these two masters, though real enough, was as peculiar as Parmigianino's was to Raphael. *Christ Before Pilate* (fig. 688), one of his many huge canvases for the

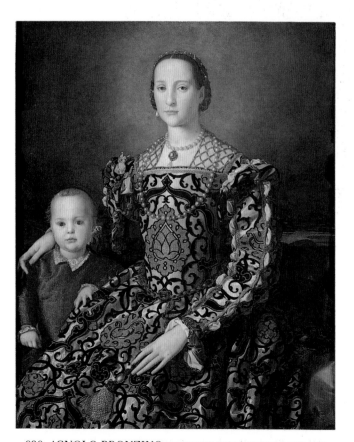

686. AGNOLO BRONZINO. *ELEANORA OF TOLEDO AND HER SON GIOVANNI DE'MEDICI.* c. 1550. Oil on panel, 45¼×37¾″ (115×96 cm). Galleria degli Uffizi, Florence

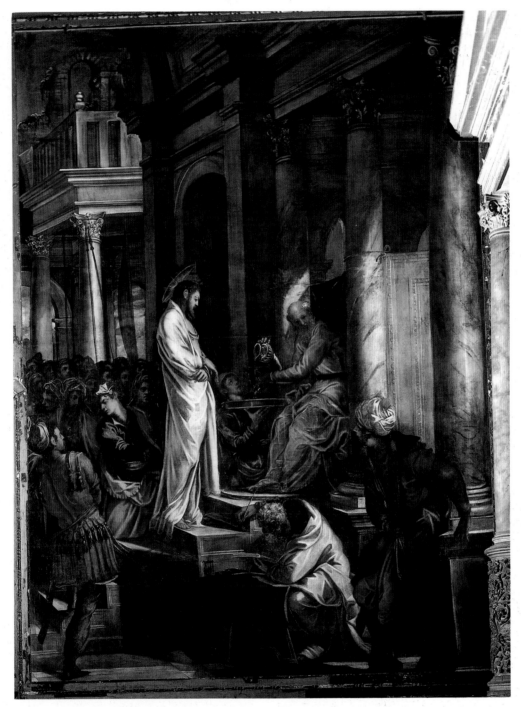

688. JACOPO TINTORETTO. *CHRIST BEFORE PILATE.* 1566–67.
c. 18'1"×13'3½" (5.5×4.1 m). Scuola di San Rocco, Venice

Scuola di San Rocco, the home of the Confraternity of St. Roch, contrasts tellingly with Titian's *Christ Crowned with Thorns* (see fig. 680); the bold brushwork, the glowing colors, and the sudden lights and shadows show what Tintoretto owed to the older artist, and indeed the entire composition recalls the *Madonna with Members of the Pesaro Family* (see fig. 677). Yet the total effect is unmistakably Mannerist: the feverish emotionalism of the flickering, unreal light, and the ghostly Christ, pencil-slim and motionless among the agitated Michelangelesque figures, remind us of Rosso's Descent.

Even more spectacular is Tintoretto's last major work, *The Last Supper* (fig. 689). This canvas denies in every possible way the classic values of Leonardo's version (see fig. 642), painted almost exactly a century before. Christ, to be sure, still occupies the center of the composition, but now the table is placed at a sharp angle to the picture plane in exaggerated perspective; His small figure in the middle distance is distinguishable mainly by the brilliant halo. Tintoretto has gone to great lengths to give the event an everyday setting, cluttering the scene with attendants, containers of food and drink, and domestic animals. But this serves only to contrast dramati-

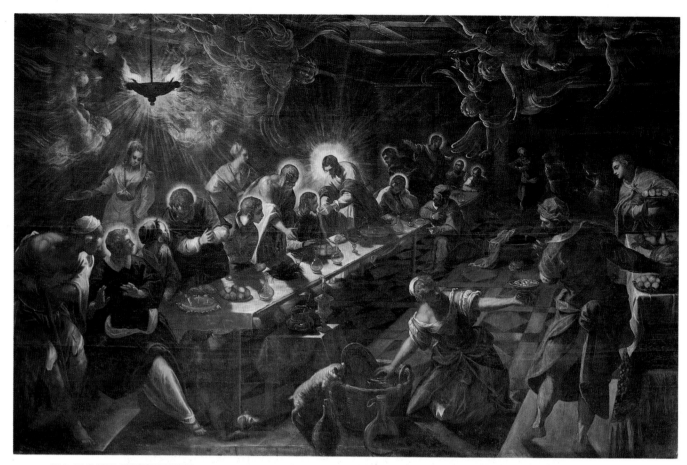

689. JACOPO TINTORETTO. *THE LAST SUPPER*. 1592–94. Oil on canvas, 12′×18′8″ (3.7×5.7 m). S. Giorgio Maggiore, Venice

cally the natural with the supernatural, for there are also celestial attendants—the smoke from the blazing oil lamp miraculously turns into clouds of angels that converge upon Christ just as He offers His body and blood, in the form of bread and wine, to the disciples. Tintoretto's main concern has been to make visible the institution of the Eucharist, the transubstantiation of earthly into divine food; he barely hints at the human drama of Judas' betrayal, so important to Leonardo (Judas can be seen isolated on the near side of the table, but his role is so insignificant that he could almost be mistaken for an attendant).

EL GRECO. The last—and perhaps the greatest—Mannerist painter was also trained in the Venetian School. Domenikos Theotocopoulos (1541–1614), nicknamed El Greco, came from Crete, which was then under Venetian rule. His earliest training must have been from a Cretan artist still working in the Byzantine tradition. Soon after 1560 El Greco arrived in Venice and quickly absorbed the lessons of Titian, Tintoretto, and other masters. A decade later, in Rome, he came to know the art of Raphael, Michelangelo, and the Central Italian Mannerists. In 1576/77 he went to Spain, settling in Toledo for the rest of his life. Yet he re-

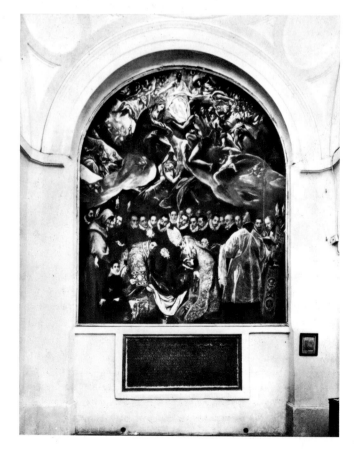

690. Chapel with *THE BURIAL OF COUNT ORGAZ*. 1586.
S. Tomé, Toledo, Spain

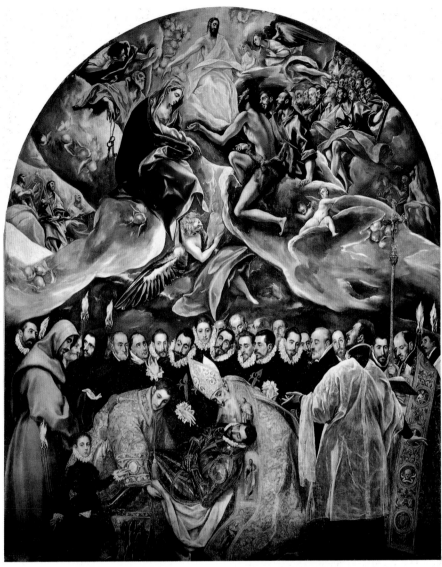

691. EL GRECO. *THE BURIAL OF COUNT ORGAZ*. 1586. Oil on canvas,
16′×11′10″ (4.9×3.6 m). S. Tomé, Toledo, Spain

mained an alien in his new homeland; although the spiritual climate of the Counter Reformation, which was especially intense in Spain, may account for the exalted emotionalism of his mature work, contemporary Spanish painting was too provincial to impress him. His style had already been formed before he arrived in Toledo. He never forgot his Byzantine background—until the very end of his career, he signed his pictures in Greek.

The largest and most resplendent of El Greco's major commissions is *The Burial of Count Orgaz* (figs. 690 and 691); the huge canvas in the church of Santo Tomé honors a medieval benefactor so pious that St. Stephen and St. Augustine miraculously appeared at his funeral and themselves lowered the body into its grave. The burial took place in 1323, but El Greco represents it as a contemporary event, portraying among the attendants many of the local nobility and clergy; the dazzling display of color and texture in the armor and vestments could hardly be surpassed by Titian himself. Directly above, the count's soul (a small, cloudlike figure like

the angels in Tintoretto's *The Last Supper*) is carried to Heaven by an angel. The celestial assembly filling the upper half of the picture is painted very differently from the lower half: every form—clouds, limbs, draperies—takes part in the sweeping, flamelike movement toward the distant figure of Christ. Here, even more than in Tintoretto's art, the various aspects of Mannerism fuse into a single ecstatic vision.

The full import of the work, however, becomes clear only when we see it in its original setting. Like an enormous window, it fills one entire wall of its chapel. The bottom of the canvas is 6 feet above the floor, and as the chapel is only about 18 feet deep, we must look sharply upward to see the upper half of the picture. El Greco's violent foreshortening is calculated to achieve an illusion of boundless space above, while the lower foreground figures appear as on a stage (their feet cut off by the molding just below the picture). The large stone plaque also belongs to the ensemble, representing the front of the sarcophagus into which the two saints lower the body of the count; it thus explains the action within the picture. The beholder, then, perceives three levels of reality: the grave itself, supposedly set into the wall at eye-level and closed by an actual stone slab; the contemporary re-enactment of the miraculous burial; and the vision of celestial glory witnessed by some of the participants. By chance, El Greco's task here was analogous to Masaccio's in his *Trinity* mural (see fig. 598); the contrast measures the dynamic evolution of Western art since the Early Renaissance.

From El Greco's Venetian training came his mastery of portraiture. We generally know little of his relationship to his sitters, but in his memorable portrait of Fray Felix Hortensio Paravicino (fig. 692), the sitter, an important scholar and poet, was also a friend who praised El Greco's genius in several sonnets. This portrait is an artistic descendant of Titian's *Man with the Glove* and the portraits of Pontormo (see figs. 678 and 682), yet the mood is not one of either reverie or withdrawal. Paravicino's frail, expressive hands and the pallid face, with its sensitive mouth and burning eyes, convey a spiritual ardor of compelling intensity. Such, we like to think, were the saints of the Counter Reformation—mystics and intellectuals at the same time.

Proto-Baroque

If Mannerism produced the personalities that today seem most "modern"—El Greco's fame is greater now than it ever was before—its dominance was not uncontested in the sixteenth century. Another trend that also emerged about 1520

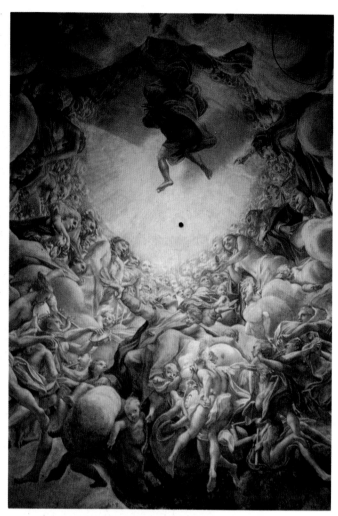

693. CORREGGIO. *THE ASSUMPTION OF THE VIRGIN* (portion). c. 1525. Fresco. Dome, Parma Cathedral

694. (*opposite*) CORREGGIO. *JUPITER AND IO*. c. 1532. Oil on canvas, 64½×27¾" (163.8×70.5 cm). Kunsthistorisches Museum, Vienna

anticipated so many features of the Baroque style that it might be labeled Proto-Baroque.

CORREGGIO. Correggio (1489/94–1534), the most important representative of this trend, was a phenomenally gifted North Italian painter who spent most of his brief career in Parma. He absorbed the influence of Leonardo and the Venetians as a youth, then of Michelangelo and Raphael, but their ideal of classical balance did not attract him. His largest work, the fresco of *The Assumption of the Virgin* in the dome of Parma Cathedral (fig. 693), is a masterpiece of illusionistic perspective, a vast, luminous space filled with soaring figures. Although they move with such exhilarating ease that the force of gravity seems not to exist for them, they are healthy, energetic beings of flesh and blood, not disembodied spirits, and they frankly delight in their weightless condition.

For Correggio, there was little difference between spiritual and physical ecstasy, as we see by comparing *The Assumption of the Virgin* with his *Jupiter and Io* (fig. 694), one

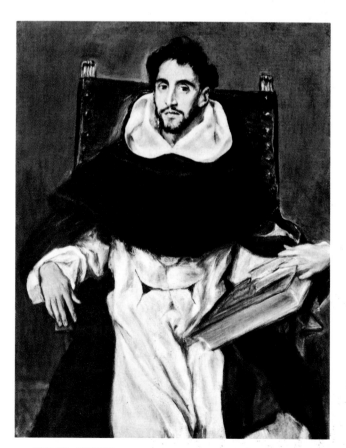

692. EL GRECO. *FRAY FELIX HORTENSIO PARAVICINO*. c. 1605. Oil on canvas, 44½×33¾" (112.5×85.5 cm). Museum of Fine Arts, Boston

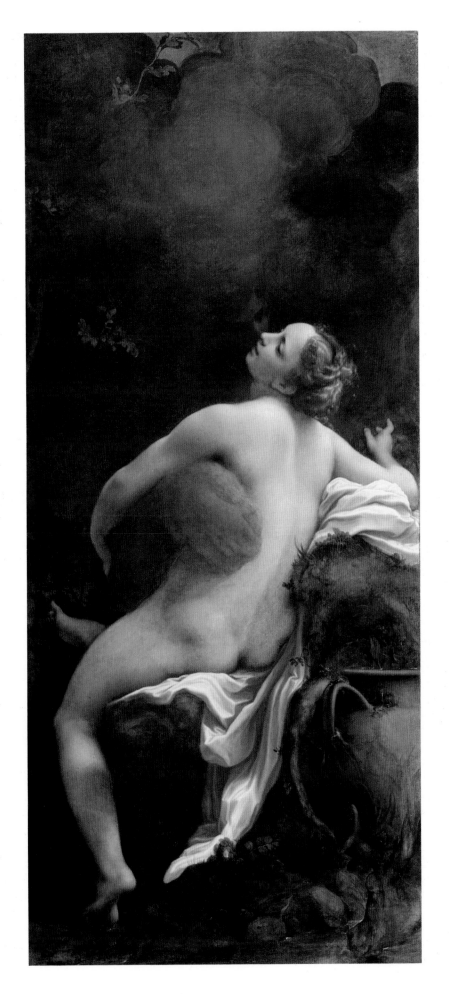

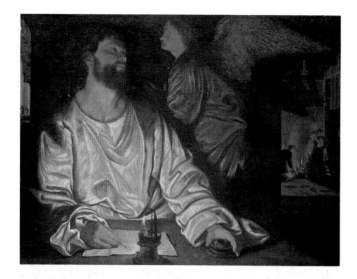

canvas in a series illustrating the loves of the classical gods. The nymph, swooning in the embrace of a cloudlike Jupiter, is the direct kin of the jubilant angels in the fresco. Leonardesque *sfumato*, combined with a Venetian sense of color and texture, produces an effect of exquisite voluptuousness that far exceeds Titian's in his *Bacchanal* (see fig. 676). Correggio had no immediate successors or any lasting influence on the art of his century, but toward 1600 his work began to be widely appreciated. For the next century and a half he was admired as the equal of Raphael and Michelangelo—while the Mannerists, so important before, were largely forgotten.

Realism

A third trend in sixteenth-century painting in Italy is to be associated with the towns along the northern edge of the Lombard plain, such as Brescia and Verona. A number of artists in that region worked in a style based on Giorgione and Titian, but with a stronger interest in everyday reality.

SAVOLDO. One of the earliest and most attractive of these North Italian realists was Girolamo Savoldo (c. 1480–1550), from Brescia, whose *St. Matthew and the Angel* (fig. 695) must be contemporary with Parmigianino's *Madonna with the Long Neck.* The broad, fluid manner of painting reflects the dominant influence of Titian, yet the great Venetian master would never have placed the Evangelist in so thoroughly domestic an environment. The humble scene in the background shows the saint's milieu to be lowly indeed, and makes the presence of the angel doubly miraculous. This tendency to visualize sacred events among ramshackle buildings and simple people had been characteristic of "Late Gothic" painting; Savoldo must have acquired it from that source. The nocturnal lighting, too, recalls such Northern pictures as the *Nativity* by Geertgen tot Sint Jans (see fig. 558). But the main source of illumination in Geertgen's panel is the Divine radiance of the Child, and Savoldo uses an ordinary oil lamp for his similarly magic and intimate effect.

VERONESE. In the work of Paolo Veronese (1528–1588), North Italian realism takes on the splendor of a pageant. Born

695. (*above*) GIROLAMO SAVOLDO. *ST. MATTHEW AND THE ANGEL.* c. 1535. Oil on canvas, 36¾×49″ (93.3×124.5 cm). The Metropolitan Museum of Art, New York. Marquand Fund, 1912

696. PAOLO VERONESE. *CHRIST IN THE HOUSE OF LEVI.* 1573. Oil on canvas, 18′ 2″×42′ (5.5×12.8 m). Galleria dell'Accademia, Venice

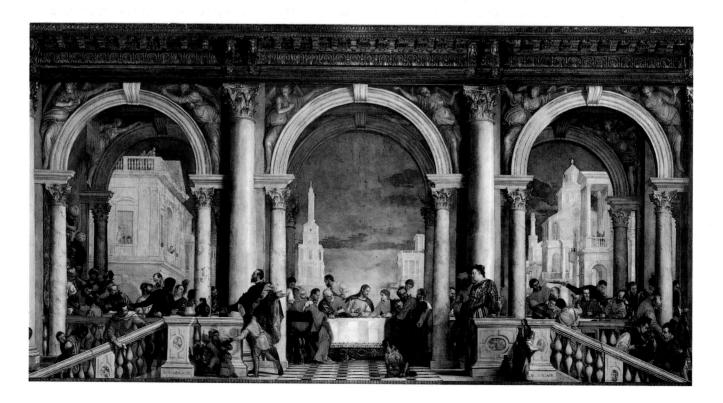

and trained in Verona, Veronese became, after Tintoretto, the most important painter in Venice; although utterly unlike each other in style, both found favor with the public. The contrast is strikingly evident if we compare Tintoretto's *The Last Supper* and Veronese's *Christ in the House of Levi* (fig. 696), both with similar subjects. Veronese avoids all reference to the supernatural. His symmetrical composition harks back to Leonardo and Raphael, the festive mood of the scene reflects Titian's work of the 1520s (compare fig. 677), and at first the picture looks like a High Renaissance work born fifty years too late. Yet we miss one essential: the elevated, ideal conception of humanity underlying the work of High Renaissance masters. Veronese paints a sumptuous banquet, a true feast for the eyes, but not "the intention of man's soul."

Significantly, we are not even sure which event from the life of Christ he originally meant to depict, for he gave the canvas its present title only after he had been summoned by the religious tribunal of the Inquisition, on the charge of filling his picture with "buffoons, drunkards, Germans, dwarfs, and similar vulgarities" unsuited to its sacred character. The account of this trial shows that the tribunal thought the painting represented the Last Supper; Veronese's testimony never made clear whether it was the Last Supper, or the Supper in the House of Simon. To him, apparently, this distinction made little difference; in the end, he settled on a convenient third title, the Supper in the House of Levi, which permitted him to leave the offending incidents in place. He argued that they were no more objectionable than the nudity of Christ and the Heavenly Host in Michelangelo's *Last Judgment*, but the tribunal failed to see the analogy: ". . . in the Last Judgment it was not necessary to paint garments, and there is nothing in those figures that is not spiritual."

The Inquisition, of course, considered only the impropriety of Veronese's art, not its unconcern with spiritual depth. His dogged refusal to admit the justice of the charge, his insistence on his right to introduce directly observed details, however "improper," and his indifference to the subject of the picture spring from an attitude so startlingly "extroverted" that it was not generally accepted until the nineteenth century. The painter's domain, Veronese seems to say, is the entire visible world, and here he acknowledges no authority other than his senses.

SCULPTURE

Italian sculptors of the later sixteenth century fail to match the achievements of the painters. Perhaps Michelangelo's overpowering personality discouraged new talent in this field, but the dearth of challenging new tasks is a more plausible reason. In any case, the most interesting sculpture of this period was produced outside of Italy, and in Florence—after the death of Michelangelo in 1564—the leading sculptor was a Northerner.

Mannerism, First and Second Phases

BERRUGUETE. If the anticlassical phase of Mannerism, represented by the style of Rosso and Pontormo, has no

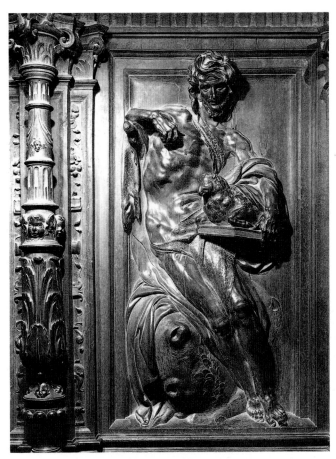

697. ALONSO BERRUGUETE. *ST. JOHN THE BAPTIST.*
c. 1540. Wood, 31½×19¼″ (80×49 cm).
Toledo Cathedral, Spain

sculptural counterpart, the work of the Spaniard Alonso Berruguete (c. 1489–1561) most closely approaches it. Berruguete had been associated with the founders of the anticlassical trend in Florence about 1520; his *St. John the Baptist* (fig. 697), one of the reliefs carved twenty years later for the wood choir stalls of Toledo Cathedral, still reflects this experience. The angular, emaciated body, clawlike hands, and fixed, wide-eyed stare recall the otherworldly expressiveness of Rosso's *Descent from the Cross* (see fig. 681).

CELLINI. The second, elegant phase of Mannerism appears in countless sculptural examples in Italy and abroad. The best-known representative of the style is Benvenuto Cellini (1500–1571), the Florentine goldsmith and sculptor who owes much of his fame to his picaresque autobiography. The gold saltcellar for King Francis I of France (fig. 698), Cellini's major work in precious metal to escape destruction, well displays the virtues and limitations of his art. To hold condiments is obviously the lesser function of this lavish conversation piece. Because salt comes from the sea and pepper from the land, Cellini placed the boat-shaped salt container under the guardianship of Neptune, while the pepper, in a tiny triumphal arch, is watched over by a personification of Earth. On the base are figures representing the four seasons and the four parts of the day.

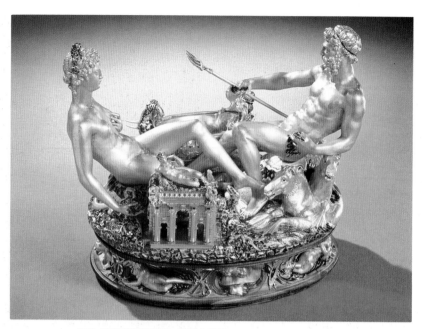

698. BENVENUTO CELLINI. *SALTCELLAR OF FRANCIS I.*
1539–43. Gold with enamel, 10¼×13⅛" (26×33.3 cm).
Kunsthistorisches Museum, Vienna

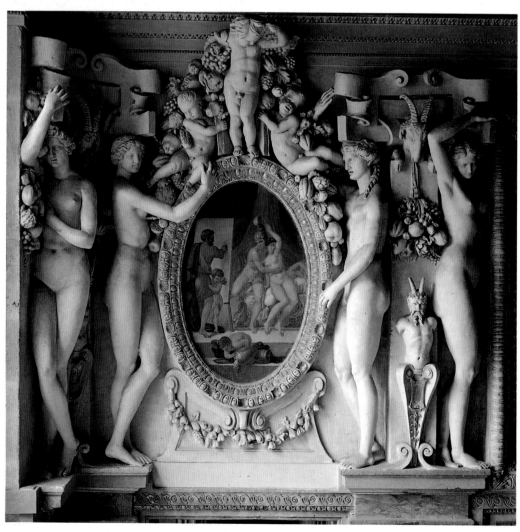

699. FRANCESCO PRIMATICCIO. STUCCO FIGURES. c. 1541–45.
Room of the Duchesse d'Estampes, Château of Fontainebleau, France

The entire object thus reflects the cosmic significance of the Medici tombs (compare fig. 660), but on this miniature scale Cellini's program turns into playful fancy; he wants to impress us with his ingenuity and skill, and to charm us with the grace of his figures. The allegorical significance of the design is simply a pretext for this display of virtuosity. When he tells us, for instance, that Neptune and Earth each have a bent and a straight leg to signify mountains and plains, we can only marvel at the divorce of form from content. Despite his boundless admiration for Michelangelo, Cellini's elegant figures on the saltcellar are as elongated, smooth, and languid as Parmigianino's (see fig. 684).

PRIMATICCIO. Parmigianino also strongly influenced Francesco Primaticcio (1504–1570), Cellini's rival at the court of Francis I. A man of many talents, Primaticcio designed the interior decoration of some of the main rooms in the royal château of Fontainebleau, combining painted scenes and a richly sculptured stucco framework. The section shown in figure 699 caters to the same aristocratic taste that admired Cellini's saltcellar. The four maidens are not burdened with any specific allegorical significance—their role recalls the nudes of the Sistine Ceiling—but perform a task for which they seem equally ill-fitted: they reinforce the piers that sustain the ceiling. These willowy caryatids epitomize the studied nonchalance of second-phase Mannerism.

GIOVANNI BOLOGNA. Cellini, Primaticcio, and the other Italians employed by Francis I made Mannerism the dominant style in mid-sixteenth-century France, and their influence went far beyond the royal court. It must have reached a gifted young sculptor from Douai in northern France, Jean de Bologne (1529–1608), who went to Italy about 1555 for further training and stayed to become, under the Italianized name of Giovanni Bologna, the most important sculptor in Florence during the last third of the century. His over-lifesize marble group, *The Rape of the Sabine Woman* (fig. 700), won particular acclaim, and still has its place of honor near the Palazzo Vecchio.

The subject, drawn from the legends of ancient Rome, seems an odd choice for statuary; the city's founders, an adventurous band of men from across the sea, so the story goes, tried vainly to find wives among their neighbors, the Sabines, and resorted at last to a trick: having invited the entire Sabine tribe into Rome for a peaceful festival, they fell upon them with arms, took the women away by force, and thus ensured the future of their race. Actually, the artist designed the group with no specific subject in mind, to silence those critics who doubted his ability as a monumental sculptor in marble. He selected what seemed to him the most difficult feat, three figures of contrasting character united in a common action. Their identities were disputed among the learned connoisseurs of the day, who finally settled on the *Rape of the Sabine Woman* as the most suitable title.

Here, then, is another artist who is noncommittal about subject matter, although his unconcern had a different motive from Veronese's. Giovanni Bologna's self-imposed task

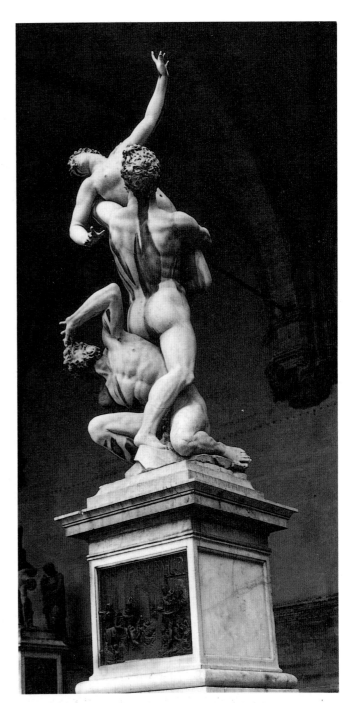

700. GIOVANNI BOLOGNA. *THE RAPE OF THE SABINE WOMAN.* Completed 1583. Marble, height 13′6″ (4.1 m). Loggia dei Lanzi, Florence

was to carve in marble, on a massive scale, a sculptural composition that was to be seen not from one but from all sides; this had hitherto been attempted only in bronze and on a much smaller scale (see fig. 625). He has solved this purely formal problem, but only by insulating his group from the world of human experience. These figures, spiraling upward as if confined inside a tall, narrow cylinder, perform a well-rehearsed choreographic exercise the emotional meaning of which remains obscure. We admire their discipline but we find no trace of genuine pathos.

ARCHITECTURE

Mannerism

The concept of Mannerism as a period style, we recall, had been coined for painting. We have not encountered any difficulty in applying it to sculpture. Can it usefully be extended to architecture as well? And if so, what qualities must we look for? These questions have proved surprisingly difficult to answer very precisely. Some buildings, to be sure, would be called Mannerist by almost everyone today; but this does not give us a viable definition of Mannerism as an architectural period style.

VASARI. Such a structure is the Palazzo degli Uffizi in Florence, by Giorgio Vasari (1511–1574). It consists of two long wings—originally intended, as the name Uffizi suggests, for offices—facing each other across a narrow court, linked at one end by a loggia (fig. 701). Vasari's inspiration is not far to seek: the "tired" scroll brackets and the peculiar combination of column and wall have their source in the vestibule of the Laurentian Library (on page 501 we cited Vasari's praise for Michelangelo's unorthodox use of the classical vocabulary). Yet his design lacks the sculptural power and expressiveness of its model; rather, the Uffizi loggia forms a screen as weightless as the façade of the Pazzi Chapel (see fig. 591). What is tense in Michelangelo's design becomes merely ambiguous—the architectural members seem as devoid of energy as the human figures of second-phase Mannerism, and their relationships as studiedly "artificial."

AMMANATI. The same is true of the courtyard of the Palazzo Pitti (fig. 702) by Bartolommeo Ammanati (1511–1592), despite its display of muscularity. Here the three-story scheme of superimposed orders, derived from the Colos-

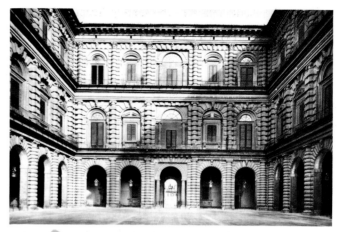

702. BARTOLOMMEO AMMANATI. Courtyard of the Palazzo Pitti, Florence. 1558–70

seum, has been overlaid with an extravagant pattern of rustication that "imprisons" the columns, reducing them to an oddly passive role. These welts disguise rather than enhance the massiveness of the masonry, the overall corrugated texture making us think of the fancies of a pastry cook.

PALLADIO. If these qualities are Mannerism in architecture, can we find it in the work of Andrea Palladio (1518–1580), the greatest architect of the later sixteenth century, second in importance only to Michelangelo? Unlike Vasari, who was a painter and historian as well as an architect (his artists' *Lives* provides the first coherent account of Italian Renaissance art), or Ammanati, who was a sculptor-architect, Palladio stands in the tradition of the humanist and theoretician Leone Battista Alberti.

Although his career centered on his native town of Vicenza, his buildings and theoretical writings soon brought him international status. Palladio insisted that architecture must be governed both by reason and by certain universal rules that were perfectly exemplified by the buildings of the ancients. He thus shared Alberti's basic outlook and his firm faith in the cosmic significance of numerical ratios (see page 456). But the two differed in how each related theory and practice. With Alberti, this relationship had been loose and flexible, whereas Palladio believed quite literally in practicing what he preached. His architectural treatise is consequently more practical than Alberti's—this helps to explain its huge success—while his buildings are linked more directly with his theories. It has even been said that Palladio designed only what was, in his view, sanctioned by ancient precedent. If the results are not necessarily classic in style, we may call them "classicistic" (to denote a conscious striving for classic qualities); this is indeed the usual term for both Palladio's work and theoretical attitude.

The Villa Rotonda (figs. 703 and 704), one of Palladio's finest buildings, perfectly illustrates the meaning of classicism. An aristocratic country residence near Vicenza, it consists of a square block surmounted by a dome and is faced on all four sides with identical porches in the shape of temple fronts. Alberti had defined the ideal church as such a completely symmetrical, centralized design (page 471), and it is

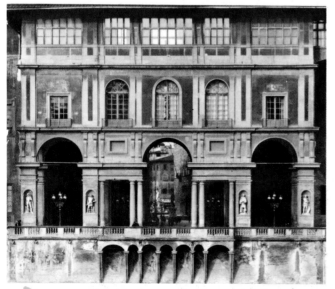

701. GIORGIO VASARI. LOGGIA OF THE PALAZZO DEGLI UFFIZI, Florence (view from the Arno River). Begun 1560

evident that Palladio found in the same principles the ideal country house. But how could he justify a context so purely secular for the solemn motif of the temple front? Surprisingly enough, he was convinced, on the basis of ancient literary sources, that Roman private houses had porticoes like these (excavations have since disproved him; see page 229). Yet Palladio's use of the temple front here is not mere antiquarianism; he probably persuaded himself that it was legitimate because he regarded this feature as desirable for both beauty and utility. In any case, the porches of the Villa Rotonda, beautifully correlated with the walls behind, are an organic part of his design. They lend the structure an air of serene dignity and festive grace that still appeals to us today.

The façade of S. Giorgio Maggiore in Venice (fig. 705), of about the same date as the Villa Rotonda, adds to the same effect a new sumptuousness and complexity. Palladio's problem here was how to create a classically integrated façade for a basilican church, He surely knew Alberti's solution (S. Andrea in Mantua; see fig. 616), a temple front enclosing

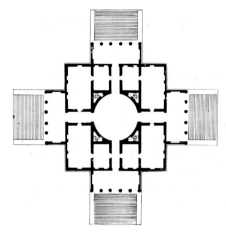

703. Plan of the Villa Rotonda

704. ANDREA PALLADIO. Villa Rotonda, Vicenza. c. 1567–70

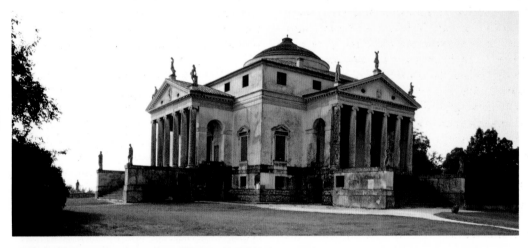

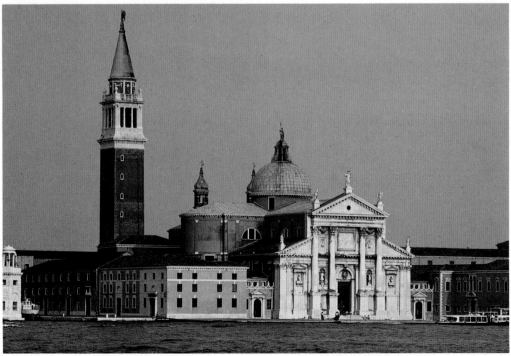

705. ANDREA PALLADIO. S. Giorgio Maggiore, Venice. Designed 1565

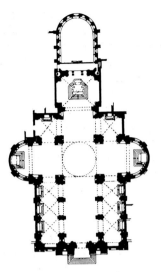

706. Plan of S. Giorgio Maggiore

a triumphal-arch motif; but this design, although impressively logical and compact, did not fit the cross section of a basilica and really circumvented the problem. Palladio—again following what he believed to be ancient precedent—found a different answer: he superimposed a tall, narrow temple front on another low and wide one to reflect the different heights of nave and aisles. Theoretically, it was a perfect solution. In practice, however, he found that he could not keep the two systems as separate as his classicistic conscience demanded and still integrate them into a harmonious whole. This conflict makes ambiguous those parts of the design that have, as it were, a dual allegiance; this might be interpreted as a Mannerist quality. The plan (fig. 706), too, suggests a duality: the main body of the church is strongly centralized—the transept is as long as the nave—but the longitudinal axis reasserts itself in the separate compartments for the main altar and the chapel beyond.

Proto-Baroque

VIGNOLA AND DELLA PORTA. Palladio's immense authority as a designer keeps the conflicting elements in the façade and plan of S. Giorgio from actually clashing. In less

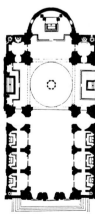

707. GIACOMO VIGNOLA
Plan of Il Gesù, Rome. 1568

assured hands, such a precarious union would break apart. A more generally applicable solution was evolved just at that time in Rome by Giacomo Vignola (1507–1573) and Giacomo della Porta (c. 1540–1602), architects who had assisted Michelangelo at St. Peter's and were still using his architectural vocabulary. The church of Il Gesù (Jesus), a building whose importance for subsequent church architecture can hardly be exaggerated, is the mother church of the Jesuits; its design must have been closely supervised so as to conform to the aims of the militant new order, founded in 1540. We may thus view it as the architectural embodiment of the spirit of the Counter Reformation.

The planning stage of the structure began in 1550 (Michelangelo himself once promised a design, but apparently never furnished it); the present ground plan, by Vignola, was adopted in 1568 (fig. 707). It contrasts in almost every possible respect with Palladio's S. Giorgio: a basilica, strikingly compact, dominated by its mighty nave. The aisles have been replaced by chapels, thus "herding" the congregation quite literally into one large, hall-like space directly in view of the altar; the attention of this "audience" is positively directed toward altar and pulpit, as our view of the interior (fig. 708) confirms. (The painting shows how the church would look from the street if the center part of the façade were removed; for the later, High Baroque decoration of the nave vault, see fig. 753.) We also see here an unexpected feature that the ground plan cannot show: the dramatic contrast between the dim illumination in the nave and the abundant light beyond,

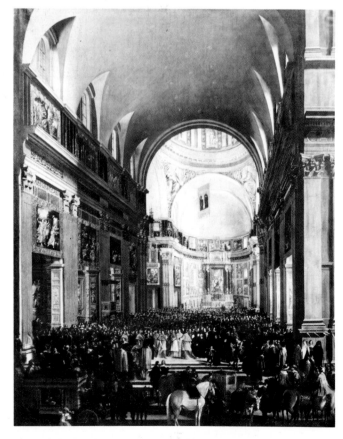

708. ANDREA SACCHI and JAN MIEL. *URBAN VIII VISITING IL GESÙ*. 1639–41. Oil on canvas. Galleria Nazionale d'Arte Antica, Rome

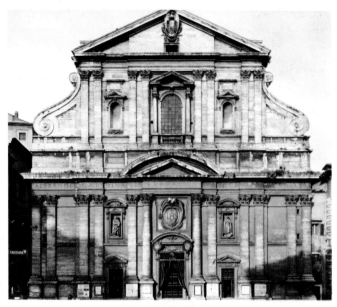

709. GIACOMO DELLA PORTA
Façade of Il Gesù, Rome. c. 1575–84

in the eastern part of the church, supplied by the large windows in the drum of the dome. Light has been consciously exploited for its expressive possibilities—a novel device, "theatrical" in the best sense—to give Il Gesù a stronger emotional focus than we have yet found in a church interior.

Despite its great originality, the plan of Il Gesù is not entirely without precedent (see fig. 617). The façade, by Giacomo della Porta, is as bold as the plan (fig. 709), although it, too, has its earlier sources. The paired pilasters and broken architrave of the lower story are clearly derived from Michelangelo's design for the exterior of St. Peter's (compare fig. 666). In the upper story the same pattern recurs on a somewhat smaller scale, with four instead of six pairs of supports; the difference in width is bridged by two scroll-shaped buttresses. A large pediment crowns the façade, which retains the classic proportions of Renaissance architecture (the height equals the width).

What is fundamentally new here is the very element that was missing in the façade of S. Giorgio: the integration of all the parts into one whole. Giacomo della Porta, freed from classicistic scruples by his allegiance to Michelangelo, gave the same vertical rhythm to both stories of the façade; this rhythm is obeyed by all the horizontal members (note the broken entablature), but the horizontal divisions in turn determine the size of the vertical members (hence no colossal order). Equally important is the emphasis on the main portal: its double frame—two pediments resting on coupled pilasters and columns—projects beyond the rest of the façade and gives strong focus to the entire design. Not since Gothic architecture has the entrance to a church received such a dramatic concentration of features, attracting the attention of the beholder outside the building much as the concentrated light beneath the dome channels that of the worshiper inside.

What are we to call the style of Il Gesù? Obviously, it has little in common with Palladio, and it shares with Florentine architecture of the time only the influence of Michelangelo. But this influence reflects two very different phases of the great master's career: the contrast between the Uffizi and Il Gesù is hardly less great than that between the vestibule of the Laurentian Library and the exterior of St. Peter's. If we label the Uffizi Mannerist, the same term will not serve us for Il Gesù. As we shall see, the design of Il Gesù will become basic to Baroque architecture; by calling it Proto-Baroque, we suggest both its seminal importance for the future and its special place in relation to the past.

CHAPTER FIVE

THE RENAISSANCE
IN THE NORTH

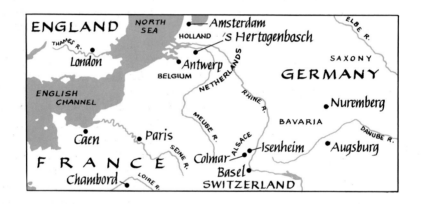

North of the Alps, most fifteenth-century artists had remained indifferent to Italian forms and ideas. Since the time of the Master of Flémalle and the Van Eycks they had looked to Flanders, rather than to Tuscany, for leadership. This relative isolation ended suddenly, toward the year 1500; as if a dam had burst, Italian influence flowed northward in an ever wider stream, and Northern Renaissance art began to replace "Late Gothic." That term, however, has a far less well-defined meaning than "Late Gothic," which refers to a single, clearly recognizable stylistic tradition. The diversity of trends north of the Alps is even greater than in Italy during the sixteenth century. Nor does Italian influence provide a common denominator, for this influence is itself diverse: Early Renaissance, High Renaissance, and Mannerist, all in regional variants from Lombardy, Venice, Florence, and Rome. Its effects, too, may vary greatly; they may be superficial or profound, direct or indirect, specific or general.

The "Late Gothic" tradition remained much alive, if no longer dominant, and its encounter with Italian art resulted in a kind of Hundred Years' War among styles that ended only when, in the early seventeenth century, the Baroque emerged as an international movement. The full history of this "war" is yet to be written; its major issues are hard to trace through all the battles, truces, and shifting alliances. Its course, moreover, was decisively affected by the Reformation, which had a far more immediate impact on art north of the Alps than in Italy. Our account, then, must be oversimplified, emphasizing the heroic phases of the struggle at the expense of the lesser (but, in the long run, equally significant) skirmishes.

GERMANY

Painting and the Graphic Arts

Let us begin with Germany, the home of the Reformation, where the main battles of the "war of styles" took place during the first quarter of the century. Between 1475 and 1500, it had produced such important masters as Michael Pacher and Martin Schongauer (see figs. 567, 568, and 571), but these hardly prepare us for the astonishing burst of creative energy that was to follow. The range of achievements of this period—comparable, in its brevity and brilliance, to the Italian High Renaissance—is measured by the contrasting personalities of its greatest artists: Matthias Grünewald and Albrecht Dürer. Both died in 1528, probably at about the same age, although we know only Dürer's birth date (1471). Dürer quickly became internationally famous, while Grünewald, who was born about 1470–1480, remained so obscure that his real name, Mathis Gothart Nithart, was discovered only at the end of the nineteenth century.

GRÜNEWALD. Grünewald's fame, like that of El Greco, has developed almost entirely within our own century. In the Northern art of his time, he alone, in his main work, the *Isenheim Altarpiece*, overwhelms us with something like the power of the Sistine Ceiling. (Characteristically enough, this extraordinary work was long believed to be by Dürer.) The altarpiece, painted between 1509/10 and 1515 for the mon-astery church of the Order of St. Anthony at Isenheim, in Alsace, is now in the museum of the nearby town of Colmar; a carved shrine with two sets of movable wings, it has three stages, or "views."

The first and outermost, when all the wings are closed, shows *The Crucifixion* (fig. 710)—probably the most impressive ever painted. In one respect it is very medieval: Christ's terrible agony and the desperate grief of the Virgin, St. John, and Mary Magdalen recall the older German *Andachtsbild* (see fig. 505). But the pitiful body on the cross with its twisted limbs, its countless lacerations, its rivulets of blood, is on a heroic scale that raises it beyond the merely human, and thus reveals the two natures of Christ. The same message is conveyed by the flanking figures: the three historic witnesses on the left mourn Christ's death as a man, while John the Baptist, on the right, points with calm emphasis to Him as the Saviour. Even the background suggests this duality: this Golgotha is not a hill outside Jerusalem, but a mountain towering above lesser peaks. The Crucifixion, lifted from its familiar setting, thus becomes a lonely event silhouetted against a deserted, ghostly landscape and a blue-black sky. Darkness is over the land, in accordance with the Gospel, yet brilliant light bathes the foreground with the force of sudden revelation. This union of time and eternity, of reality and symbolism, gives Grünewald's *Crucifixion* its awesome grandeur.

When the outer wings are opened, the mood of the *Isenheim Altarpiece* changes dramatically (fig. 711). All three scenes in this second "view"—the Annunciation, the Angel Concert for the Madonna and Child, and the Resurrection (fig. 712)—celebrate events as jubilant in spirit as the Crucifixion is austere. Most striking in comparison with "Late Gothic" painting is the sense of the movement pervading these panels—everything twists and turns as though it had a life of its own. The angel of the Annunciation enters the room like a gust of wind that blows the Virgin backward; the Risen Christ shoots from His grave with explosive force; the canopy over the Angel Concert seems to writhe in response to the heavenly music. This vibrant energy has thoroughly reshaped the brittle, spiky contours and angular drapery patterns of "Late Gothic" art. Grünewald's forms are soft, elastic, fleshy. His light and color show a corresponding change: commanding all the resources of the great Flemish masters, he employs them with unexampled boldness and flexibility. His color scale is richly iridescent, its range matched only by the Venetians. And his exploitation of colored light is altogether without parallel at that time. In the luminescent angels of the Concert, the apparition of God the Father and the Heavenly Host above the Madonna, and, most spectacularly, the rainbow-hued radiance of the Risen Christ, Grünewald's genius has achieved miracles through light that remain unsurpassed to this day.

How much did Grünewald owe to Italian art? Nothing at all, we are first tempted to reply. Yet he must have learned from the Renaissance in more ways than one: his knowledge of perspective (note the low horizons) and the physical vigor of some of his figures cannot be explained by the "Late Gothic" tradition alone, and occasionally his pictures show architectural details of Southern origin. Perhaps the most im-

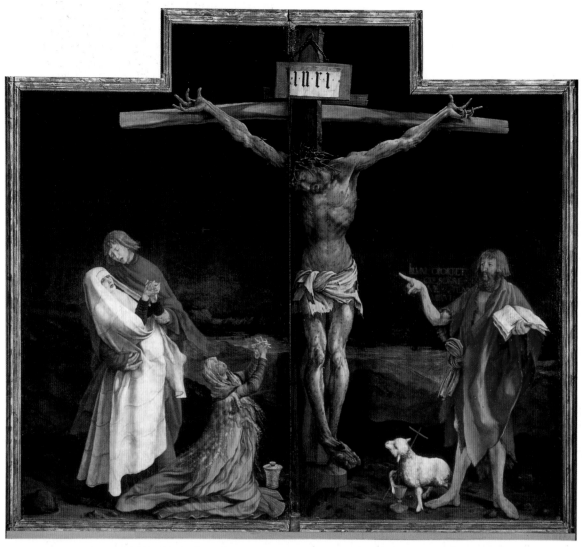

710. MATTHIAS GRÜNEWALD. *THE CRUCIFIXION*, from the *ISENHEIM ALTARPIECE* (closed).
c. 1510–15. Oil on panel, 8'10"×10'1" (2.7×3.1 m). Musée Unterlinden, Colmar, France

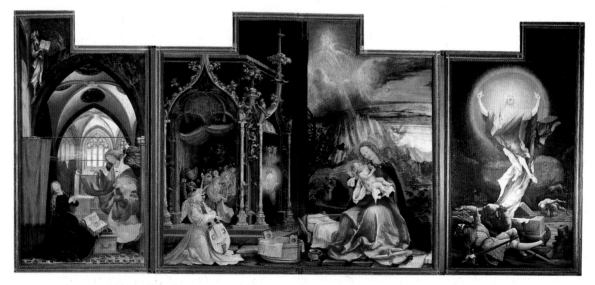

711. MATTHIAS GRÜNEWALD. *THE ANNUNCIATION; VIRGIN AND CHILD WITH ANGELS; THE RESURRECTION.*
Second view of the *ISENHEIM ALTARPIECE.* c. 1510–15. Oil on wood panel, each wing 8'10"×4'8" (2.69×1.42 m);
center panel 8'10"×11'2½" (2.69×3.41 m). Musée Unterlinden, Colmar, France

712. (*opposite*) MATTHIAS GRÜNEWALD. *THE RESURRECTION*, from second view of the *ISENHEIM ALTARPIECE*

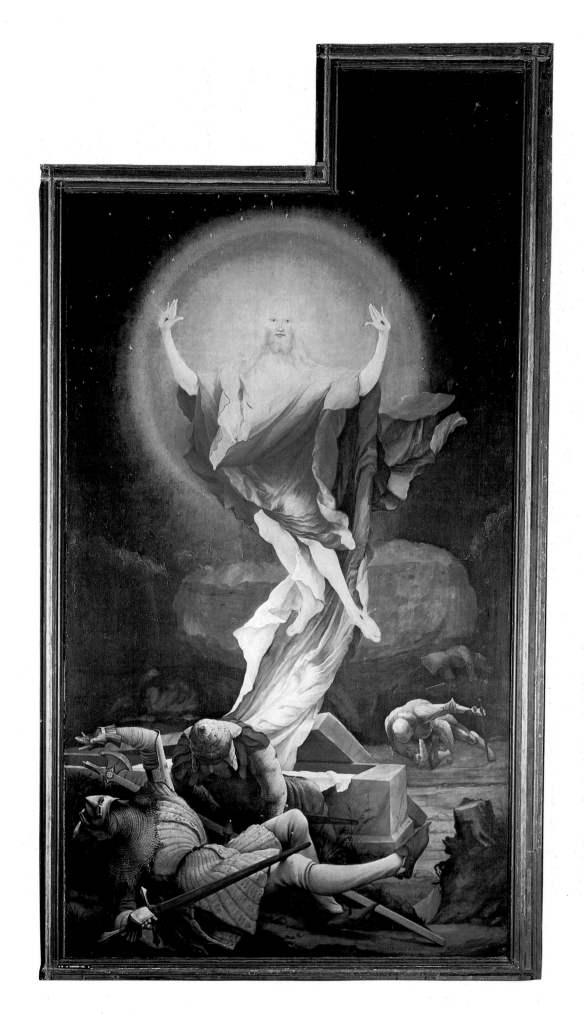

portant effect of the Renaissance on him, however, was psychological. We know little about his career, but he apparently did not lead the settled life of a craftsman-painter controlled by the rules of his guild; he was also an architect, an engineer, something of a courtier, and an entrepreneur; and he worked for many different patrons and stayed nowhere for very long. He was in sympathy with Martin Luther (who frowned upon religious images as "idolatrous"), even though, as a painter, he depended on Catholic patronage.

In a word, Grünewald seems to have shared the free, individualistic spirit of Italian Renaissance artists; the daring of his pictorial vision likewise suggests a reliance on his own resources. The Renaissance, then, had a liberating influence on him but did not change the basic cast of his imagination. Instead, it helped him to epitomize the expressive aspects of the "Late Gothic" in a style of unique intensity and individuality.

DÜRER.   For Dürer (1471–1528), the Renaissance held a richer meaning. Attracted to Italian art while still a young journeyman, he visited Venice in 1494/5 and returned to his native Nuremberg with a new conception of the world and the artist's place in it. The unbridled fantasy of Grünewald's art was to him "a wild, unpruned tree" (he used this phrase for painters who worked by rules of thumb, without theoretical foundations) that needed the discipline of the objective, rational standards of the Renaissance. Taking the Italian view that the fine arts belong among the liberal arts, he also adopted the ideal of the artist as a gentleman and humanistic scholar. By steadily cultivating his intellectual interests he came to encompass in his lifetime a vast variety of techniques and subjects. And since he was the greatest printmaker of the time, he had a wide influence on sixteenth-century art through his woodcuts and engravings, which circulated everywhere in Europe.

Dürer's youthful copies after Mantegna and other Early Renaissance masters display his eager and intuitive grasp of the essentials of their alien style. Even more astonishing are his watercolors made on the way back from Venice, such as

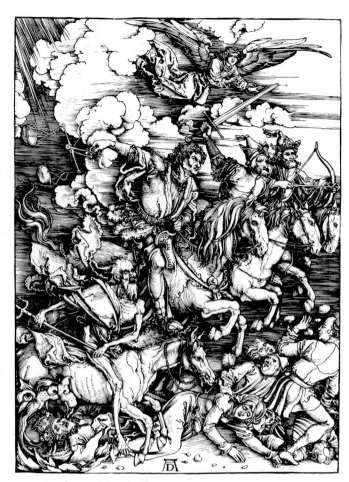

714. ALBRECHT DÜRER. *THE FOUR HORSEMEN OF THE APOCALYPSE.* c. 1497–98. Woodcut, 15½×11⅛″ (39.3×28. 3 cm)

the one inscribed "Italian Mountains" (fig. 713). Significantly, Dürer did not record the name of the spot; the specific location had no interest for him. The title he jotted down seems exactly right, for this is not a "portrait," but a "study from the model" perceived in timeless freshness. The calm rhythm of this panorama of softly rounded slopes conveys a view of nature in its organic wholeness that was, in those years, matched only by Leonardo.

After the breadth and lyricism of the *Italian Mountains*, the expressive violence of the woodcuts illustrating the Apocalypse, Dürer's most ambitious graphic work of the years following his return from Venice, is doubly shocking. The gruesome vision of *The Four Horsemen* (fig. 714) seems at first to return completely to the "Late Gothic" world of Martin Schongauer (compare fig. 571). Yet the physical energy and solid, full-bodied volume of these figures would have been impossible without Dürer's earlier experience in copying the works of such artists as Mantegna. At this stage, Dürer's style has much in common with Grünewald's. The comparison with Schongauer's *The Temptation of St. Anthony*, however, is instructive from another point of view; it shows how thoroughly Dürer has redefined his medium—the woodcut—by enriching it with the linear subtleties of engraving. In his hands, woodcuts lose their former charm as popular art, but gain the precise articulation of a fully matured graphic style.

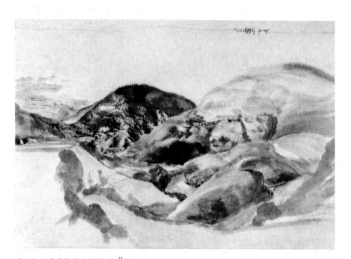

713. ALBRECHT DÜRER. *ITALIAN MOUNTAINS.* c. 1495 or 1505–6. Brush drawing in watercolor, 8¼×12¼″ (21×31.2 cm). The Ashmolean Museum, Oxford

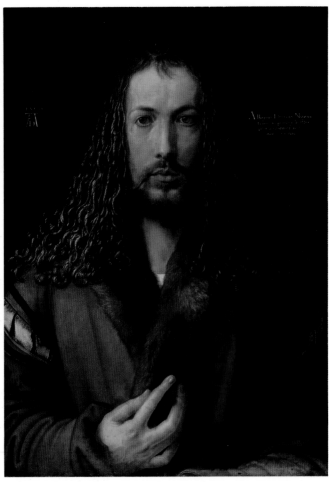

715. ALBRECHT DÜRER. *SELF-PORTRAIT.* 1500.
Oil on panel, 26¼×19¼″ (66.3×49 cm).
Pinakothek, Munich

He set a standard that soon transformed the technique of woodcuts all over Europe.

The first artist to be fascinated by his own image, Dürer was in this respect more of a Renaissance personality than any Italian artist. His earliest known work, a drawing made at thirteen, is a self-portrait, and he continued to produce self-portraits throughout his career. Most impressive, and peculiarly revealing, is the panel of 1500 (fig. 715): pictorially, it belongs to the Flemish tradition (compare Jan van Eyck's *Man in a Red Turban,* fig. 552), but the solemn, frontal pose and the Christ-like idealization of the features assert an authority quite beyond the range of ordinary portraits. The picture looks, in fact, like a secularized icon (see fig. 345), reflecting not so much Dürer's vanity as the seriousness with which he regarded his mission as an artistic reformer. (One thinks of Martin Luther's "Here I stand; I cannot do otherwise.")

The didactic aspect of Dürer's art is clearest perhaps in the engraving *Adam and Eve* of 1504 (fig. 716), where the biblical subject serves as a pretext for the display of two ideal nudes: Apollo and Venus in a Northern forest (compare figs. 220 and 222). No wonder they look somewhat incongruous; unlike the picturesque setting and its animal inhabitants, Adam and Eve are constructed figures—not the male and female observed from life, but exemplars of what Dürer believed to be perfect proportions.

The same approach, now applied to the body of a horse, is evident in *Knight, Death, and Devil* (fig. 717), one of the artist's finest prints. But this time there is no incongruity: the knight on his beautiful mount, poised and confident as an equestrian statue, embodies an ideal both aesthetic and moral. He is the Christian Soldier steadfast on the road of faith toward the Heavenly Jerusalem, undeterred by the hideous horseman threatening to cut him off, or the grotesque devil behind him. The dog, another symbol of virtue, loyally follows his master despite the lizards and skulls in his path. Italian Renaissance form, united with the heritage of "Late Gothic" symbolism (whether open or disguised), here takes on a new, characteristically Northern significance.

The subject of *Knight, Death, and Devil* seems to have been derived from the *Manual of the Christian Soldier* by Erasmus of Rotterdam, the greatest of Northern humanists. Dürer's own convictions were essentially those of Christian humanism; they made him an early and enthusiastic follower of Martin Luther, although, like Grünewald, he continued to work for Catholic patrons. Nevertheless, his new faith can be sensed in the growing austerity of style and sub-

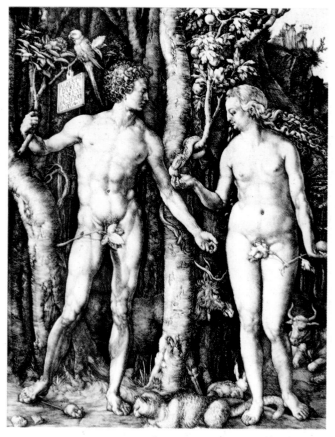

716. ALBRECHT DÜRER. *ADAM AND EVE*. 1504.
Engraving, 9⅞×7⅝″ (25.2×19.4 cm).
Museum of Fine Arts, Boston

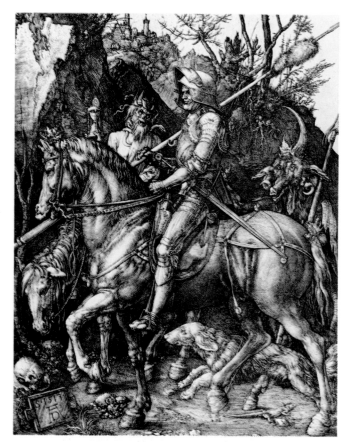

717. ALBRECHT DÜRER. *KNIGHT, DEATH, AND DEVIL*.
1513. Engraving, 9⅞×7½″ (25×19 cm).
Museum of Fine Arts, Boston

ject in his religious works after 1520. The climax of this trend is represented by *The Four Apostles* (fig. 718), paired panels containing what has rightly been termed Dürer's artistic testament.

Dürer presented the panels in 1526 to the city of Nuremberg, which had joined the Lutheran camp the year before. The chosen Apostles are basic to Protestant doctrine (John and Paul face one another in the foreground, with Peter and Mark behind). Quotations from their writings, inscribed below in Luther's translation, warn the city government not to mistake human error and pretense for the will of God; they plead against Catholics and ultrazealous Protestant radicals alike. But in another, more universal sense, the four figures represent the Four Temperaments (and, by implication, the other cosmic quartets—the seasons, the elements, the times of day, and the ages of man) encircling, like the cardinal points of the compass, the Deity who is at the invisible center of this "triptych." In keeping with their role, the Apostles have a cubic severity and grandeur such as we have not encountered since Masaccio and Piero della Francesca.

That the style of *The Four Apostles* has evoked the names of these great Italians is no coincidence, for Dürer devoted a good part of his last years to the theory of art, including a treatise on geometry based on a thorough study of Piero della Francesca's discourse on perspective. Often he went beyond his Italian sources; he invented, for instance, a device for producing an image by purely mechanical means to demon-

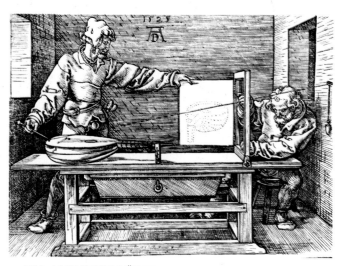

719. ALBRECHT DÜRER. *DEMONSTRATION OF PERSPECTIVE*,
from the artist's treatise on geometry. 1525. Woodcut

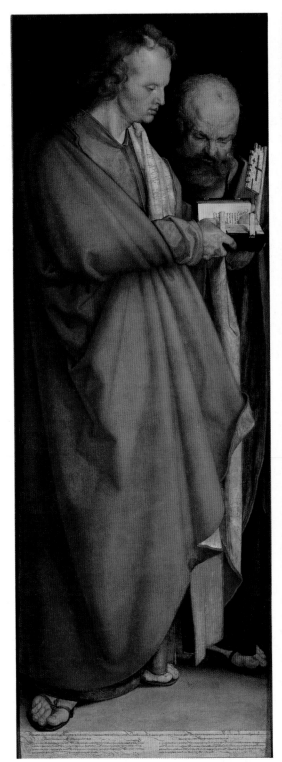
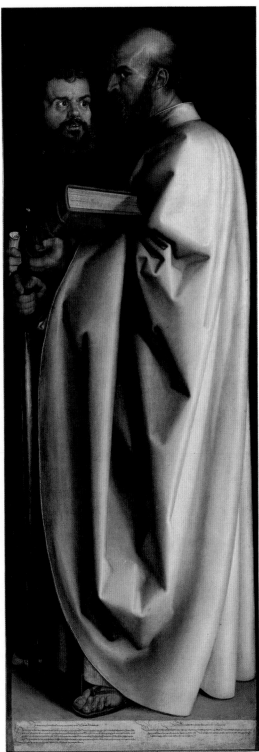

718. ALBRECHT DÜRER. *THE FOUR APOSTLES.* 1523–26.
Oil on panel, each 85×30″ (216×76.5 cm).
Pinakothek, Munich

strate the objective validity of perspective (fig. 719). Two men "draw" the lute as it would appear to us if we looked at it from the spot on the wall marked by a little hook; the string passing through the hook substitutes for the visual rays. The man on the left attaches it to successive points on the contour of the lute; the other man marks where the string passes through the vertical frame (the picture plane) and makes corresponding dots on the drawing board hinged to the frame. Dürer, of course, knew that such an image was the record of a scientific experiment, not a work of art; neither was he really interested in a method for making pictures without human skill or judgment. Nevertheless, his device, however clumsy, is the first step toward the principle of the photographic camera (see page 902).

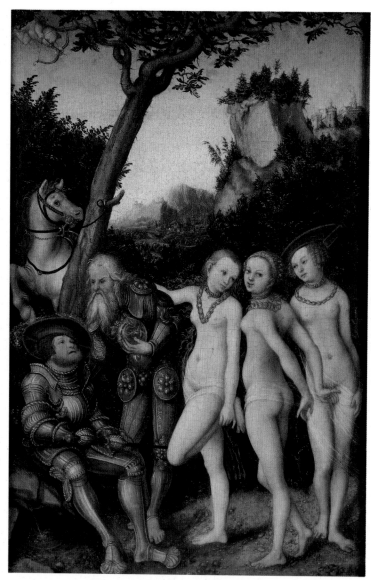

720. LUCAS CRANACH THE ELDER. *THE JUDGMENT OF PARIS.*
1530. Oil on panel, 13½×8¾″ (34.3×22.3 cm).
Staatliche Kunsthalle, Karlsruhe

CRANACH THE ELDER. Dürer's hope for a monumental art embodying the Protestant faith remained unfulfilled. Other German painters, notably Lucas Cranach the Elder (1472–1553), also tried to cast Luther's doctrines into visual form, but created no viable tradition. Such efforts were doomed, since the spiritual leaders of the Reformation looked upon them with indifference or, more often, outright hostility. Cranach the Elder is best remembered today for his portraits and his delightfully incongruous mythological scenes. In *The Judgment of Paris* (fig. 720) nothing, could be less classical than the three coquettish damsels, whose wriggly nakedness fits the Northern background better than does the nudity of Dürer's *Adam and Eve*. Paris is a German knight clad in fashionable armor, indistinguishable from the nobles at the court of Saxony who were the artist's patrons. The playful eroticism, small size, and precise, miniaturelike detail of the picture make it plainly a collector's item, attuned to the tastes of a provincial aristocracy.

ALTDORFER. As remote from the classic ideal, but far more impressive, is *The Battle of Issus* by Albrecht Altdorfer (c. 1480–1538), a Bavarian painter somewhat younger than Cranach (fig. 721). Without the text on the tablet suspended in the sky, and the other inscriptions, we could not possibly identify the subject, Alexander's victory over Darius. The artist has tried to follow ancient descriptions of the actual number and kind of combatants in the battle, but this required him to adopt a bird's-eye view whereby the two protagonists are lost in the antlike mass of their own armies (contrast the Hellenistic representation of the same subject in fig. 302). Moreover, the soldiers' armor and the fortified town in the distance are unmistakably of the sixteenth century.

The picture might well show some contemporary battle, except for one feature: the spectacular sky, with the sun triumphantly breaking through the clouds and "defeating" the moon. The celestial drama above a vast Alpine landscape, obviously correlated with the human contest below, raises the scene to the cosmic level. This is strikingly similar to the vision of heavenly glory above the Virgin and Child in the *Isenheim Altarpiece* (see fig. 711). Altdorfer may indeed be viewed as a later, and lesser, Grünewald. Although Altdorfer, too, was an architect, well acquainted with perspective and the Italian stylistic vocabulary, his paintings show the unruly imagination already familiar from the work of the older mas-

ter. But Altdorfer is also unlike Grünewald: he makes the human figure incidental to its spatial setting, whether natural or architectural. The tiny soldiers of *The Battle of Issus* have their counterpart in his other pictures, and he painted at least one landscape with no figures at all—the earliest "pure" landscape (Dürer's sketch, *Italian Mountains*, figure 713, not being a finished work of art).

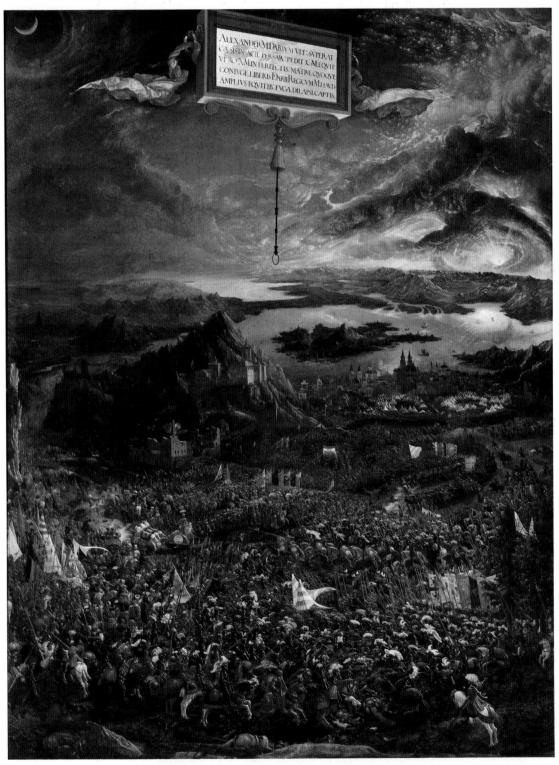

721. ALBRECHT ALTDORFER. *THE BATTLE OF ISSUS*. 1529.
Oil on panel, 62×47″ (157.5×119.5 cm). Pinakothek, Munich

Portraiture

HOLBEIN. Gifted though they were, Cranach and Altdorfer both evaded the main challenge of the Renaissance so bravely faced—if not always mastered—by Dürer: the human image. Their style, antimonumental and miniaturelike, set the pace for dozens of lesser masters; perhaps the rapid decline of German art after Dürer's death was due to a failure of ambition, among artists and patrons alike. The career of Hans Holbein the Younger (1497–1543)—the one painter of whom this is not true—confirms the general rule. Born and raised in Augsburg, a center of international commerce in South Germany particularly open to Renaissance ideas, he left at the age of eighteen for Switzerland. By 1520, he was firmly established in Basel as a designer of woodcuts, a splendid decorator, and an incisive portraitist. His likeness of Erasmus of Rotterdam (fig. 722), painted soon after the famous author had settled in Basel, gives us a truly memorable image of Renaissance man: intimate yet monumental, this doctor of humane letters has an intellectual authority formerly reserved for the doctors of the Church. Yet Holbein must have felt confined in Basel, for in 1523–24 he traveled to France, apparently intending to offer his services to Francis I; two years later, Basel was in the throes of the Reformation crisis, and he went to England, hoping for commissions at the court of Henry VIII (Erasmus, recommending him to Thomas More, wrote: "Here [in Basel] the arts are out in the cold"). On his return in 1528, he used

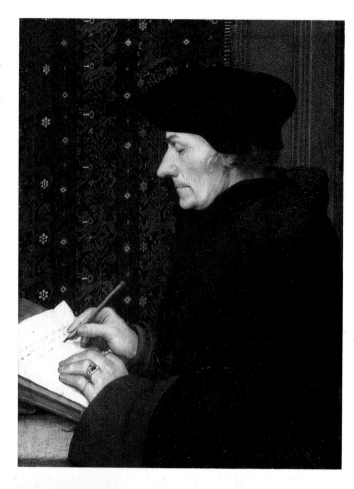

722. HANS HOLBEIN THE YOUNGER
ERAMUS OF ROTTERDAM.
c. 1523. Oil on panel,
16½×12½" (42×31.4 cm).
Musée du Louvre, Paris

723. HANS HOLBEIN THE YOUNGER
HENRY VIII. 1540.
Oil on panel,
32½×29" (82.6×74.5 cm).
Galleria Nazionale
d'Arte Antica, Rome

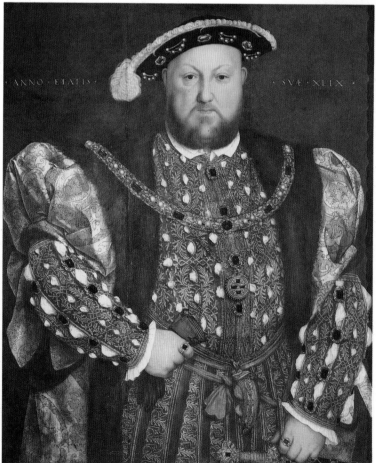

his English earnings to buy a house for his family. But Basel, becoming meanwhile fanatically Protestant, had iconoclastic riots; despite the entreaties of the city council, Holbein departed for London in 1532. He went back to Basel only once, in 1538, while traveling on the Continent as court painter to Henry VIII. The council made a last attempt to keep him at home, but Holbein had become an artist of international fame to whom Basel now seemed provincial indeed. His style, too, had gained an international flavor: the portrait of Henry VIII (fig. 723) shares with Bronzino's *Eleanora of Toledo* (see fig. 686) the immobile pose, the air of unapproachability, and the precisely rendered costume and jewels. While Holbein's picture, unlike Bronzino's, does not yet reflect the Mannerist ideal of elegance—the rigid frontality and physical bulk of Henry VIII create an overpowering sensation of the king's ruthless, commanding presence—both clearly belong to the same species of court portrait.

The link between the two may lie in such French works as Jean Clouet's *Francis I* (fig. 724), which Holbein could have seen on his travels. (For Francis I as a patron of Italian Mannerists, see page 523.) The type evidently was coined at the royal court of France, where its ancestry can be traced back as far as Jean Fouquet (see fig. 562). It gained international currency between 1525 and 1550.

Although Holbein's pictures molded British taste in aristocratic portraiture for decades, he had no English disciples of real talent. The Elizabethan genius was more literary and

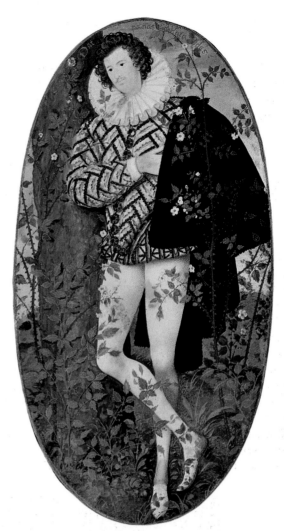

725. NICHOLAS HILLIARD. *A YOUNG MAN AMONG ROSES.* c.1588. Oil on parchment, shown at actual size: 5⅜×2¾" (13.7×7 cm). Victoria & Albert Museum, London (Crown copyright reserved)

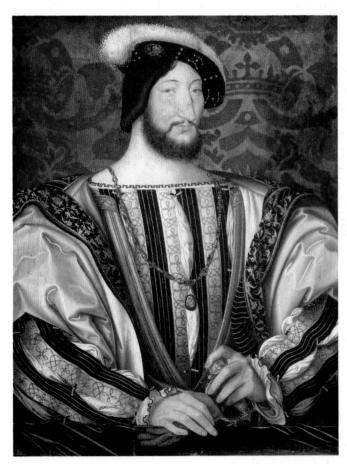

724. JEAN CLOUET. *FRANCIS I.* c. 1525–30. Tempera and oil on panel, 37¾×29" (96×74.5 cm). Musée du Louvre, Paris

musical than visual, and the demand for portraits in the later sixteenth century continued to be filled largely by visiting foreign artists.

HILLIARD. The most notable English painter of the period was Nicholas Hilliard (1547–1619), a goldsmith who also specialized in miniature portraits on parchment, tiny keepsakes often worn by their owners as jewelry. These "portable portraits" had been invented in antiquity (see fig. 313) and were revived in the fifteenth century (see fig. 563). Holbein, too, produced miniature portraits, which Hilliard acknowledged to be his model. We see this link with the older master in the even lighting and meticulous detail of *A Young Man Among Roses* (fig. 725), but the elongated proportions and the pose of languorous grace come from Italian Mannerism, probably via Fontainebleau (compare fig. 699). Our lovesick youth also strikes us as the descendant of the fashionable attendants at the court of the duke of Berry (see fig. 544). We can imagine him besieging his lady with sonnets and madrigals before presenting her with this exquisite token of devotion.

THE NETHERLANDS

Painting

The Netherlands in the sixteenth century had the most turbulent and painful history of any country north of the Alps. When the Reformation began, they were part of the far-flung empire of the Hapsburgs under Charles V, who was also king of Spain. Protestantism quickly became powerful in the Netherlands, and the attempts of the crown to suppress it led to open revolt against foreign rule. After a bloody struggle, the northern provinces (today's Holland) emerged at the end of the century as an independent state, while the southern ones (roughly corresponding to modern Belgium) remained in Spanish hands.

The religious and political strife might have had catastrophic effects on the arts, yet this, astonishingly, did not happen. Sixteenth-century Netherlandish painting, to be sure, does not equal that of the fifteenth in brilliance, nor did it produce any pioneers of the Northern Renaissance comparable to Dürer and Holbein. This region absorbed Italian elements more slowly than Germany, but more steadily and systematically, so that instead of a few isolated peaks of achievement we find a continuous range. Between 1550 and 1600, their most troubled time, the Netherlands produced the major painters of Northern Europe, who paved the way for the great Dutch and Flemish masters of the next century.

Two main concerns, sometimes separate, sometimes interwoven, characterize Netherlandish sixteenth-century painting: to assimilate Italian art, from Raphael to Tintoretto (in an often dry and didactic manner), and to develop a repertory supplementing, and eventually replacing, the traditional religious subjects. All the secular themes that loom so large in Dutch and Flemish painting of the Baroque era—landscape, still life, genre (scenes of everyday life)—were first defined between 1500 and 1600. The process was gradual, shaped less by the genius of individual artists than by the need to cater to popular taste as church commissions became steadily scarcer (Protestant iconoclastic zeal was particularly widespread in the Netherlands). Still life, landscape, and genre had been part of the Flemish tradition since the Master of Flémalle and the brothers Van Eyck—we remember the objects grouped on the Virgin's table in the *Merode Altarpiece*, and Joseph in his workshop (fig. 547); or the setting of the Van Eyck *Crucifixion* (fig. 548). But these had remained ancillary elements, governed by the principle of disguised symbolism and subordinated to the devotional purpose of the whole. Now they became independent, or so dominant that the religious subject could be relegated to the background.

AERTSEN. *The Meat Stall* (fig. 726) by Pieter Aertsen (1508/9–1575) is such an essentially secular picture: the tiny, distant figures, representing the Flight into Egypt, are

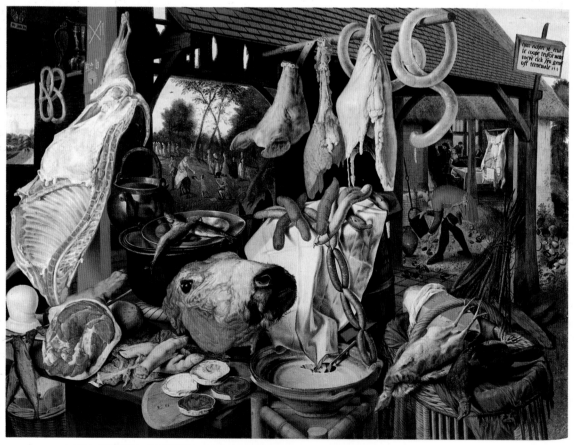

726. PIETER AERTSEN. *THE MEAT STALL.* 1551. Oil on panel, 48½×59″ (123.3×150 cm).
University Art Collections, Uppsala University, Sweden

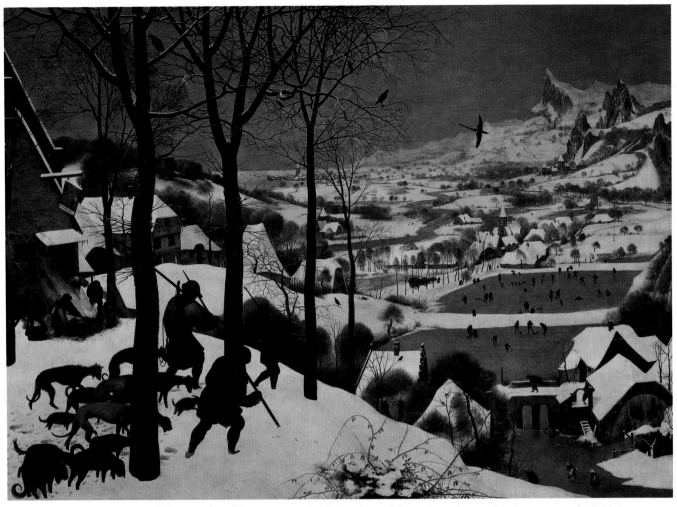

727. PIETER BRUEGEL THE ELDER. *THE RETURN OF THE HUNTERS*. 1565.
Oil on panel, 46½×63¾″ (117×162 cm). Kunsthistorisches Museum, Vienna

a mere pretext, almost blotted out by the avalanche of edibles in the foreground. We see little interest here in selection or formal arrangement; the objects, piled in heaps or strung from poles, are meant to overwhelm us with their sensuous reality (note the large size of the panel). Aertsen is remembered today mainly as a pioneer of the independent still life, but he seems to have first painted such pictures as a sideline, until he saw many of his altarpieces destroyed by iconoclasts. Perhaps still life assumed a new importance for him when he moved, about 1555, from Antwerp to Amsterdam.

BRUEGEL THE ELDER. Pieter Bruegel the Elder (1525/30–1569), the only genius among these Netherlandish painters, explored landscape and peasant life. Although his career was spent in Antwerp and Brussels, he may have been born near 's Hertogenbosch; certainly the work of Hieronymus Bosch deeply impressed him, and he is in many ways as puzzling to us as the older master. What were his religious convictions, his political sympathies? We know little about him, but his preoccupation with folk customs and the daily life of humble people seems to have sprung from a complex philosophical attitude. Bruegel was highly educated, the friend of

humanists, and patronized by the Hapsburg court. Yet he apparently never worked for the Church, and when he dealt with religious subjects he did so in an oddly ambiguous way.

His attitude toward Italian art is also hard to define: a trip to the South in 1552–53 took him to Rome, Naples, and the Strait of Messina, but the famous monuments admired by other Northerners seem not to have interested him; he returned instead with a sheaf of magnificent landscape drawings, especially Alpine views. He was probably much impressed by the landscape painting in Venice—its integration of figures and scenery and the progression in space from foreground to background (see figs. 675 and 676).

Out of these memories came such sweeping landscapes in Bruegel's mature style as *The Return of the Hunters* (fig. 727), one of a set depicting the months. Such series, we recall, had begun with medieval calendar illustrations, and Bruegel's winter scene still shows its descent from the February page in the *Très Riches Heures du Duc de Berry* (see fig. 542). Now, however, nature is more than a setting for human activities; it is the main subject of the picture. Men and women in their seasonal occupations are incidental to the majestic annual cycle of death and rebirth that is the breathing rhythm of the cosmos.

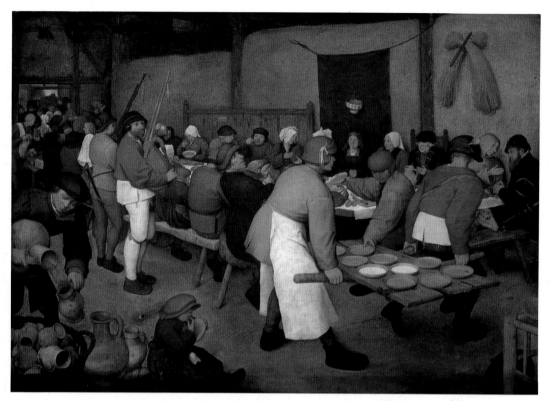

728. PIETER BRUEGEL THE ELDER. *PEASANT WEDDING.*
c. 1565. Oil on panel, 44⅞×64″ (114×162.5 cm). Kunsthistorisches Museum, Vienna

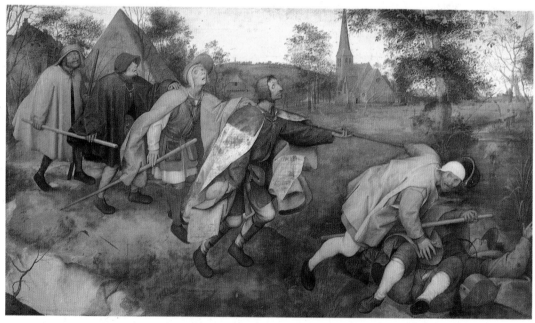

729. PIETER BRUEGEL THE ELDER. *THE BLIND LEADING THE BLIND.* c. 1568.
Oil on panel, 34½×60⅝″ (85×154 cm). Museo di Capodimonte, Naples

The *Peasant Wedding* (fig. 728) is Bruegel's most memorable scene of peasant life. These are stolid, crude folk, heavy-bodied and slow, yet their very clumsiness gives them a strange gravity that commands our respect. Painted in flat colors with minimal modeling and no cast shadows, the figures nevertheless have a weight and solidity that remind us of Giotto; space is created in assured perspective, and the entire composition is as monumental and balanced as that of any Italian master. Why, we wonder, did Bruegel endow this commonplace ceremony with the solemnity of a biblical event? Was it because he saw in the life of the peasant, free of the ambitions and vanities of city dwellers, the natural, hence the ideal, condition of humanity? Bruegel's philosophical detachment from religious and political fanaticism also informs one of his last pictures, *The Blind Leading the Blind* (fig. 729). Its source is the Gospels (Matt. 15:12–19): Christ says, speaking of the Pharisees, "And if the blind lead the blind, both shall fall into the ditch." This parable of human folly recurs in humanistic literature, and we know it in at least one earlier representation, but the tragic depth of Bruegel's forceful image gives new urgency to the theme. Perhaps he found the biblical context of the parable specially relevant to his time: the Pharisees had asked why Christ's disciples, violating religious traditions, did not wash their hands before meals; He answered, "Not that which goeth into the mouth defileth a man; but that which cometh out of the mouth." When this offended the Pharisees, He called them the blind leading the blind, explaining that "whatsoever entereth in at the mouth goeth into the belly, and is cast out. . . . But those things which proceed out of the mouth come forth from the heart; and they defile the man. For out of the heart proceed evil thoughts, murders . . . blasphemies." Could Bruegel have thought that this applied to the controversies then raging over details of religious ritual?

FRANCE

Architecture and Sculpture

We have deferred our discussion of sixteenth-century architecture and sculpture north of the Alps because in these fields Italy had no significant influence before the 1520s. France began to assimilate Italian art somewhat earlier than the other countries and was the first to achieve an integrated Renaissance style; we shall therefore confine our discussion to French monuments. As we might expect, architects still trained in the Gothic tradition could not adopt the Italian style all at once; they readily used its classical vocabulary, but its syntax gave them trouble for many years.

SOHIER.   One glance at the choir of St.-Pierre at Caen (fig. 730), built by Hector Sohier, shows that he followed the basic pattern of French Gothic church choirs (compare fig. 457), simply translating flamboyant decoration into the vocabulary

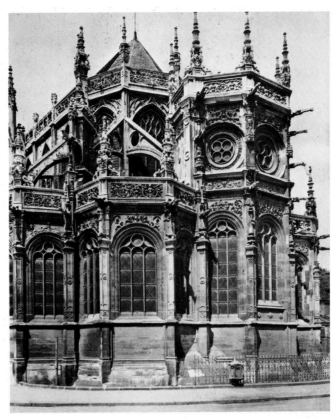

730. HECTOR SOHIER. Choir of St.-Pierre, Caen. 1528–45

of the new language: finials become candelabra, pier buttresses are shaped like pilasters, and the round-arched windows of the ambulatory chapels have geometric tracery.

CHÂTEAU OF CHAMBORD.   The Château of Chambord (fig. 731) is stylistically more complicated. Its plan, and the turrets, high-pitched roofs, and tall chimneys, recall the Gothic Louvre (see fig. 543); yet the design—greatly modified by later French builders—was originally by an Ital-

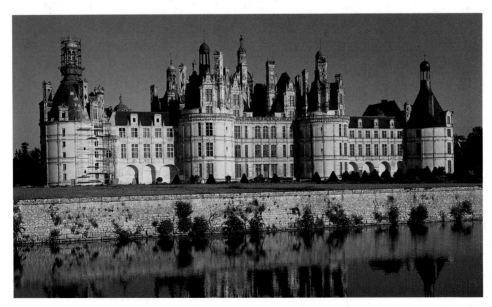

731. The Château of Chambord (north front). Begun 1519

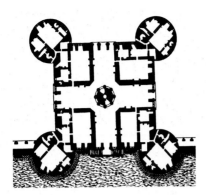

732. Plan of center portion, Château of Chambord (after Du Cerceau)

ian pupil of Giuliano da Sangallo. And his was surely the plan of the center portion (fig. 732), which is quite unlike its French predecessors. This square block, developed from the keep of medieval castles (see page 367), has a central staircase fed by four corridors; these form a Greek cross dividing the interior into four square sections. Each section is further subdivided into one large and two smaller rooms, and a closet—in modern parlance, a suite or apartment. The functional grouping of these rooms, originally imported from Italy, was to become a standard pattern in France. It represents the starting point of all modern "designs for living."

LESCOT. Francis I, who built Chambord, decided in 1546 to replace the Louvre with a new palace on the old site. He died before the project was more than begun, but his architect, Pierre Lescot (c. 1515–1578), continued it under Henry II, quadrupling the size of the court. This enlarged scheme was not completed for more than a century; Lescot built only the southern half of the court's west side (fig. 733), its "classic" phase, so called to distinguish it from the style of such buildings as Chambord. This distinction is well warrranted: the Italian vocabulary of Chambord, and St.-Pierre at Caen,

is based on the Early Renaissance, while Lescot drew on the work of Bramante and his successors.

The details of Lescot's façade have an astonishing classical purity, yet we would not mistake it for an Italian structure. Its distinctive quality comes not from Italian forms superficially applied, but from a genuine synthesis of the traditional château with the Renaissance palazzo. Italian, of course, are the superimposed classical orders (see figs. 613 and 702), the pedimented window frames, and the arcade on the ground floor. But the continuity of the façade is interrupted by three projecting pavilions that have supplanted the château turrets, and the high-pitched roof is also traditionally French. The vertical accents thus overcome the horizonal ones (note the broken architraves), their effect reinforced by the tall, narrow windows.

GOUJON. Equally un-Italian is the rich sculptural decoration covering almost the entire wall surface of the third story. These reliefs, admirably adapted to the architecture, are by Jean Goujon (c. 1510–1565?), the finest French sculptor of the mid-century. Unfortunately, they have been much restored. To get a more precise idea of Goujon's style we must turn to the relief panels from the *Fontaine des Innocents* (two are shown in figs. 734 and 735), which have survived intact, although their architectural framework is lost. These graceful figures recall the Mannerism of Cellini (see fig. 698) and, even more, Primaticcio's decorations at Fontainebleau (see fig. 699). Like Lescot's architecture, their design combines classical details of remarkable purity with a delicate slenderness that gives them a uniquely French air.

PILON. A more powerful sculptor—indeed, the greatest of the later sixteenth century—was Germain Pilon (c. 1535–1590). In his early years he, too, learned a good deal from Primaticcio, but he soon developed his own idiom by merging the Mannerism of Fontainebleau with elements taken from ancient sculpture, Michelangelo, and the Gothic tradi-

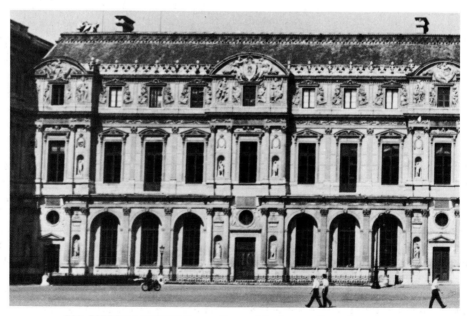

733. PIERRE LESCOT. Square Court of the Louvre, Paris. Begun 1546

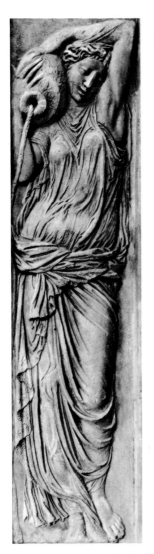
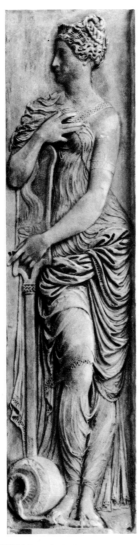

734, 735. JEAN GOUJON. Reliefs from
the *FONTAINE DES INNOCENTS*. 1548–49. Paris

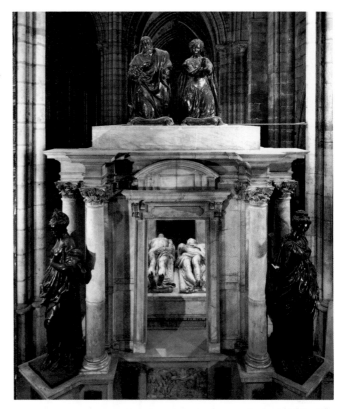

736. FRANCESCO PRIMATICCIO and GERMAIN PILON.
Tomb of Henry II. 1563–70. Abbey Church of St.-Denis, Paris

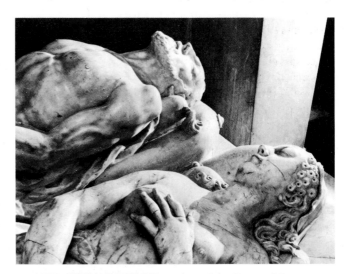

737. GERMAIN PILON. *GISANTS* of the King and Queen,
detail of the Tomb of Henry II

tion. His main works are monumental tombs, of which the earliest and largest was for Henry II and Catherine de' Medici (fig. 736). Primaticcio built the architectural framework, an oblong, free-standing chapel on a platform decorated with bronze and marble reliefs. Four large bronze statues of Virtues, their style reminiscent of Fontainebleau, mark the corners. On the top of the tomb are bronze figures of the king and queen kneeling in prayer; inside the chapel, the couple reappear recumbent as marble *gisants*, or nude corpses (fig. 737).

This contrast of effigies had been a characteristic feature of Gothic tombs since the fourteenth century: the *gisant* expressed the transient nature of the flesh, usually showing the body in an advanced stage of decomposition, with vermin sometimes crawling through its open cavities. How could this gruesome image take on Renaissance form without losing its emotional significance? Pilon's solution is brilliant: by idealizing the *gisants* he reverses their former meaning. These figures—the recumbent queen in the pose of a classical Venus, the king in that of the dead Christ—evoke neither horror nor pity but, rather, the pathos of a beauty that

persists even in death. The shock effect of their predecessors has given way to a poignancy that is no less intense. Remembering our earlier distinction between the classical and medieval attitudes toward death (see page 474), this poignancy may be defined: the Gothic *gisant*, which emphasizes physical decay, represents the future state of the body, in keeping with the whole "prospective" character of the medieval tomb; Pilon's *gisants*, however, are "retrospective," yet do not deny the reality of death. In this union of opposites—never to be achieved again, even by Pilon himself—lies the greatness of these figures.

CHAPTER SIX

THE BAROQUE IN ITALY AND GERMANY

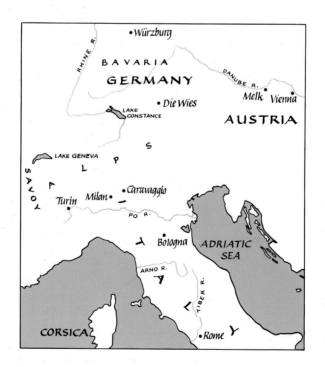

Baroque has been the term used by art historians for more than a century to designate the dominant style of the period 1600–1750. Its original meaning—"irregular, contorted, grotesque"—is now largely superseded. It is generally agreed that the new style was born in Rome during the final years of the sixteenth century. What remains under dispute is whether the Baroque is the final phase of the Renaissance, or an era distinct from both Renaissance and modern. We have chosen the first alternative, while admitting that a good case can be made for the second. Which of the two we adopt is perhaps less important than an understanding of the factors that must enter into our decision.

And here we run into a series of paradoxes. It has been claimed that the Baroque style expresses the spirit of the Counter Reformation; yet the Counter Reformation, a dynamic movement of self-renewal within the Catholic Church, had already done its work by 1600—Protestantism was on the defensive, some important territories had been recaptured for the old faith, and neither side any longer had the power to upset the new balance. The princes of the Church who supported the growth of Baroque art were known for worldly splendor rather than piety. Besides, elements of the new style penetrated the Protestant North so quickly that we should guard against overstressing its Counter Reformation aspect.

Equally problematic is the assertion that Baroque is "the style of absolutism," reflecting the centralized state ruled by an autocrat of unlimited powers. Although absolutism reached its climax during the reign of Louis XIV in the later seventeenth century, it had been in the making since the 1520s (under Francis I in France, and the Medici dukes in Tuscany). Moreover, Baroque art flourished in bourgeois Holland no less than in the absolutist monarchies; and the style officially sponsored under Louis XIV was a notably subdued, classicistic kind of Baroque.

We encounter similar difficulties when we try to relate Baroque art to the science and philosophy of the period. Such a link did exist in the Early and High Renaissance: an artist then could also be a humanist and a scientist. But during the seventeenth century, scientific and philosophical thought became too complex, abstract, and systematic for the artist to share; gravitation, calculus, and Descartes' *Cogito, ergo sum* (I think, therefore I am) could not stir the artist's imagination. Thus Baroque art is not simply the result of religious, political, or intellectual developments. Interconnections surely existed, but we do not yet understand them very well. Until we do, let us think of the Baroque style as one among other basic features—the newly fortified Catholic faith, the absolutist state, and the new role of science—that distinguish the period 1600–1750 from what had gone before.

PAINTING IN ITALY

Around 1600 Rome became the fountainhead of the Baroque, as it had of the High Renaissance a century before, by gathering artists from other regions to perform challenging new tasks. The papacy patronized art on a large scale, with the aim of making Rome the most beautiful city of the Christian world "for the greater glory of God and the Church." This campaign had begun as early as 1585; the artists then on hand were late Mannerists of feeble distinction, but it soon attracted ambitious young masters, especially from northern Italy. These talented men created the new style.

CARAVAGGIO. Foremost among these northerners was a painter of genius, called Caravaggio after his birthplace near Milan (1571–1610), whose several monumental canvases for a chapel in the church of S. Luigi dei Francesi (fig. 738), from 1599 to 1602, include *The Calling of St. Matthew* (fig. 739). This extraordinary picture is remote from both Mannerism and the High Renaissance; its only antecedent is the "North Italian realism" of artists like Savoldo (see fig. 695). But Caravaggio's realism is such that a new term, "naturalism," is needed to distinguish it from the earlier kind.

Never have we seen a sacred subject depicted so entirely in terms of contemporary low life. Matthew, the tax-gatherer, sits with some armed men—evidently his agents—in what is a common Roman tavern; he points questioningly at himself as two figures approach from the right. The arrivals are poor people, their bare feet and simple garments contrasting strongly with the colorful costumes of Matthew and his companions. Why do we sense a religious quality in this scene? Why do we not mistake it for an everyday event? What identifies one of the figures as Christ? Surely it is not the Saviour's halo (the only supernatural feature in the picture), an inconspicuous gold band that we might well overlook. Our eyes fasten instead upon His commanding gesture, borrowed from Michelangelo's *Creation of Adam* (fig. 657), which "bridges" the gap between the two groups.

Most decisive, however, is the strong beam of sunlight above Christ that illuminates His face and hand in the gloomy interior, thus carrying His call across to Matthew. Without this light—so natural yet so charged with symbolic meaning—the picture would lose its magic, its power to make us aware of the divine presence. Caravaggio here gives moving, direct form to an attitude shared by certain great saints of the Counter Reformation: that the mysteries of faith are revealed not by intellectual speculation but spontaneously, through an inward experience open to all men. His paintings have a "lay Christianity," untouched by theological dogma, that appealed to Protestants no less than Catholics. This quality made possible his profound—though indirect—influence on Rembrandt, the greatest religious artist of the Protestant North.

In Italy, Caravaggio fared less well. His work was acclaimed by artists and connoisseurs, but ordinary people, for whom it was intended, regarded it as lacking propriety and reverence. They resented meeting their own kind in these paintings, preferring religious imagery of a more idealized and rhetorical sort.

GENTILESCHI. Until the middle of the nineteenth century, women artists were largely restricted to painting portraits, genre scenes, and still lifes; the obstacles they met in getting instruction in figure drawing and anatomy effectively barred them from painting narrative subjects. Many carved

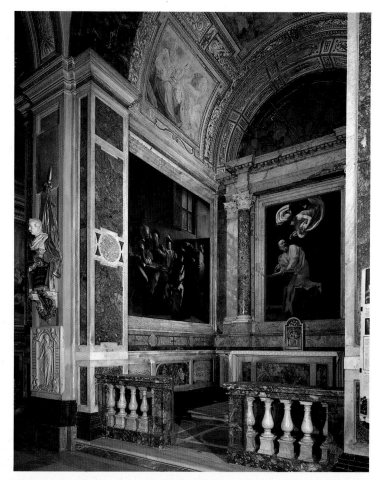

738. Contarelli Chapel,
S. Luigi dei Francesi,
Rome

739. CARAVAGGIO
THE CALLING OF ST. MATTHEW.
c. 1599–1602.
Oil on canvas.
11′1″×11′5″
(3.4×3.5 m).
Contarelli Chapel,
S. Luigi dei Francesi, Rome

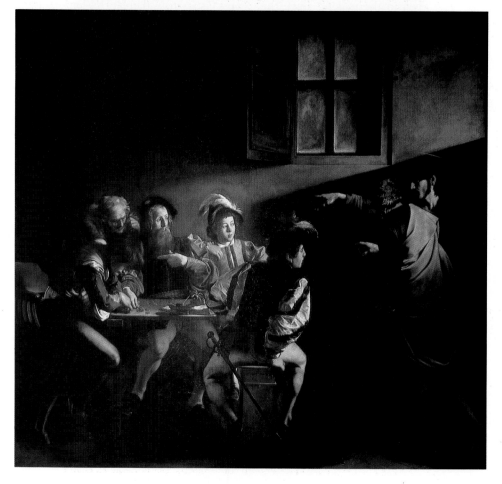

out successful careers, however, often emerging as the equals or superiors of the men in whose styles they were trained (see page 516). The exceptions to this generalization were certain Italian women born into artistic families, for whom painting came naturally. Their major role began in the seventeenth century with Artemisia Gentileschi (1593–c.1653).

The daughter of painter Orazio Gentileschi, she was born in Rome and became one of the leading painters and personalities of her day. Her characteristic subjects are Bathsheba, the unfortunate object of King David's obsessive passion, and Judith, who saved her people by beheading the Assyrian general Holofernes. Both subjects were popular during the Ba-

roque era, which delighted in erotic and violent scenes. While Gentileschi's early paintings of Judith take her father's and Caravaggio's work as their points of departure, our example (fig. 740) is a fully mature, independent work. The inner drama is uniquely hers, and no less powerful for its restraint in immortalizing Judith's courage. Rather than the decapitation itself, the artist shows the instant after. Momentarily distracted, Judith gestures theatrically as her servant stuffs Holofernes' head into a sack. The object of their attention remains hidden from view, heightening the air of intrigue. The hushed, candlelit atmosphere in turn establishes a mood of exotic mystery that conveys Judith's complex emotions with unsurpassed understanding.

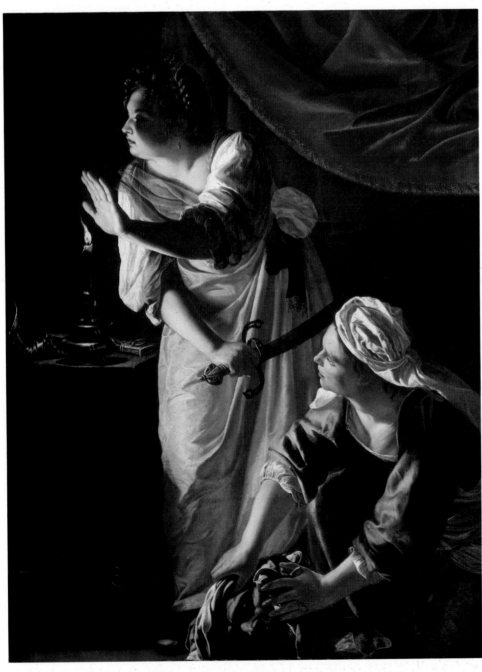

740. ARTEMISIA GENTILESCHI. *JUDITH AND MAIDSERVANT WITH THE HEAD OF HOLOFERNES.* c. 1625. Oil on canvas, 72½×55¾″ (184.1×141.6 cm). The Detroit Institute of Arts. Gift of Leslie H. Green

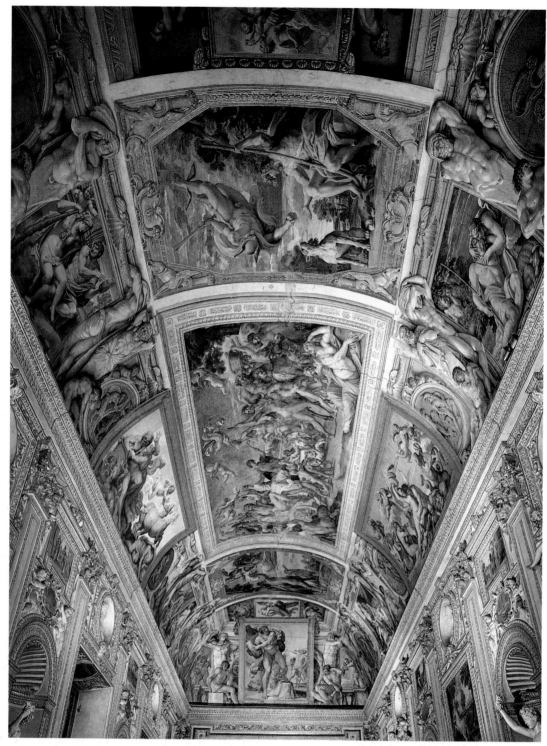

741. ANNIBALE CARRACCI. Ceiling fresco. 1597–1601. Gallery, Palazzo Farnese, Rome

ANNIBALE CARRACCI. The conservative wishes of the simpler people in Italy were met by artists less radical—and less talented—than Caravaggio, who took their lead from another newcomer among Roman painters, Annibale Carracci (1560–1609). Annibale came from Bologna, where he and two other members of his family had evolved an anti-Mannerist style since the 1580s. In 1597–1604 he produced his most ambitious work, the ceiling fresco in the gallery of the Farnese Palace (fig. 741), which soon became so famous

that it was thought second only to the murals of Michelangelo and Raphael.

The historical significance of the Farnese Gallery is indeed great, though our enthusiasm for it as a work of art may no longer be undivided. Our detail (fig. 742) shows Annibale's rich and intricate design: the narrative scenes, like those of the Sistine Ceiling, are surrounded by painted architecture, simulated sculpture, and nude, garland-holding youths. Yet the Farnese Gallery does not merely imitate Michelangelo's

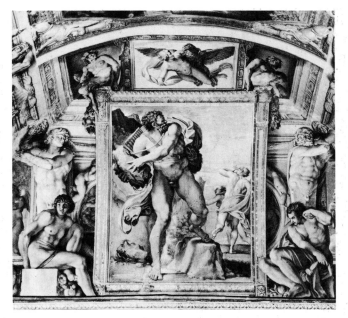

742. ANNIBALE CARRACCI. Ceiling fresco (detail). 1597–1601.
Gallery, Palazzo Farnese, Rome

masterpiece. The style of the main subjects, the Loves of the Classical Gods, is reminiscent of Raphael's *Galatea* (see fig. 673), and the whole is held together by an illusionistic scheme that reflects Annibale's knowledge of Correggio and the great Venetians. Carefully foreshortened and illuminated from below (note the shadows), the nude youths and the simulated sculpture and architecture appear real; against this background the mythologies are presented as simulated easel pictures. Each of these levels of reality is handled with consummate skill, and the entire ceiling has an exuberance that sets it apart from both Mannerism and High Renaissance art. Annibale Carracci was a reformer rather than a revolutionary; like Caravaggio, who apparently admired him, he felt that art must return to nature, but his approach was less sin-

gle-minded, balancing studies from life with a revival of the classics (which to him meant the art of antiquity, and of Raphael, Michelangelo, Titian, and Correggio). At his best, he succeeded in fusing these diverse elements, although their union always remained somewhat precarious.

RENI. To artists who were inspired by it, the Farnese Gallery seemed to offer two alternatives. Pursuing the Raphael-esque style of the mythological panels, they could arrive at a deliberate, "official" classicism; or they could take their cue from the sensuous illusionism present in the framework. The first choice is exemplified by Guido Reni (1575–1642) in his *Aurora* (fig. 743), a ceiling fresco showing Apollo in his chariot—the Sun—led by Aurora (Dawn). Despite its rhythmic

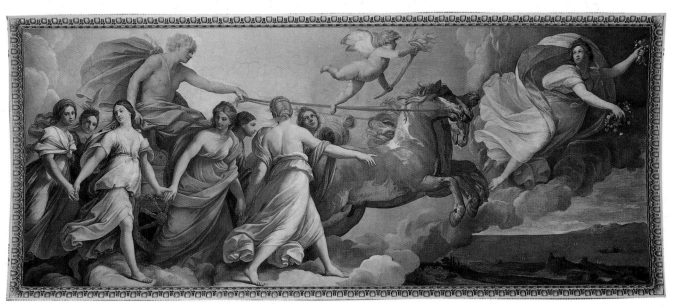

743. GUIDO RENI. *AURORA*. Ceiling fresco. 1613. Casino Rospigliosi, Rome

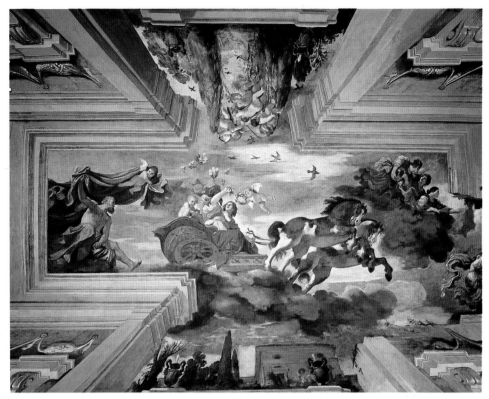

744. GUERCINO. *AURORA*. Ceiling fresco. 1621–23. Villa Ludovisi, Rome

grace, this relieflike design would seem like more than a pallid reflection of High Renaissance art were it not for the glowing and dramatic light that gives it an emotional impetus that the figures alone could never achieve.

GUERCINO. Its very opposite is the *Aurora* ceiling by Guercino (fig. 744). Here architectural perspective, combined with the pictorial illusionism of Correggio and the intense light and color of Titian, converts the entire surface into one limitless space; the figures sweep past as if propelled by stratospheric winds. With this work, Guercino (1591–1666) started what soon became a veritable flood of similar visions (see figs. 753 and 769).

DA CORTONA. The most overpowering of these is the ceiling fresco by Pietro da Cortona (1596–1669) in the great hall of the Barberini Palace in Rome, a glorification of the reign of the Barberini pope, Urban VIII (fig. 745). As in the Farnese Gallery, the ceiling area is subdivided by a painted framework simulating architecture and sculpture, but beyond it we now see the unbounded space of the sky, as in Guercino's *Aurora*. Clusters of figures, perched on clouds or soaring freely, swirl above as well as below this framework, creating a dual illusion: some figures appear to hover well inside the hall, perilously close to our heads, while others recede into a light-filled, infinite distance. Their dynamism almost literally sweeps us off our feet. Here the Baroque style reaches a resounding climax.

LANDSCAPES. The sculptured precision of the Farnese Gallery does not do justice to the important Venetian element in Annibale Carracci's style. This is most striking in his landscapes, such as the monumental *Landscape with the Flight into Egypt* (fig. 746). Its pastoral mood and the soft light and atmosphere hark back to Giorgione and Titian (see figs. 675 and 676). The figures, however, play a far less conspicuous role here; they are, indeed, as small and incidental as in any Northern landscape (compare fig. 727). Nor does the character of the panorama at all suggest the Flight into Egypt—it would be equally suitable for almost any story, sacred or profane. Still, we feel that the figures could not be removed altogether (though we can imagine them replaced by others). This is not the untamed nature of Northern landscapes. The old castle, the roads and fields, the flock of sheep, the ferryman with his boat, all show that this "civilized," hospitable countryside has been inhabited for a long time. Hence the figures, however tiny, do not appear lost or dwarfed into insignificance, because their presence is implicit in the orderly, domesticated quality of the setting. This firmly constructed "ideal landscape" evokes a vision of nature that is gentle yet austere, grand but not awesome. We shall meet its descendants again and again in the next two centuries.

745. (*opposite top*) PIETRO DA CORTONA
GLORIFICATION OF THE REIGN OF URBAN VIII.
Portion of ceiling fresco. 1633–39. Palazzo Barberini, Rome

746. (*opposite bottom*) ANNIBALE CARRACCI
LANDSCAPE WITH THE FLIGHT INTO EGYPT. c. 1603.
Oil on canvas, 48¼×98½″ (122.7×250.3 cm).
Galleria Doria Pamphili, Rome

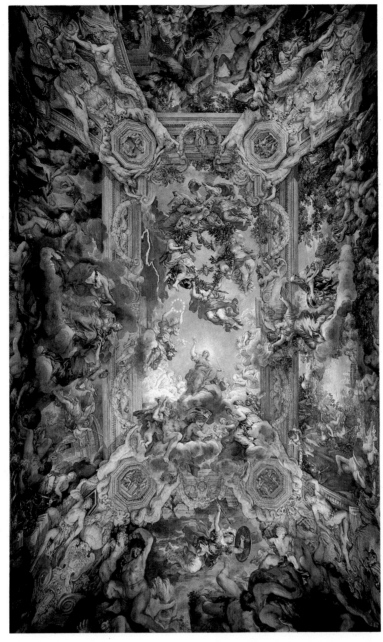

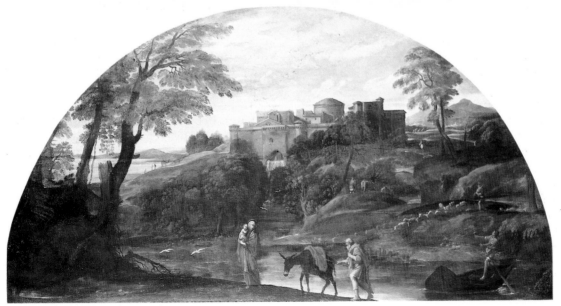

ARCHITECTURE AND SCULPTURE IN ITALY

ST. PETER'S. In architecture, the beginnings of the Baroque style cannot be defined as precisely as in painting. In the vast ecclesiastical building program that got under way in Rome toward the end of the sixteenth century, the most talented young architect to emerge was Carlo Maderno (1556–1629); in 1603 he was given the task of completing, at long last, the church of St. Peter's. The pope had decided to add a nave to Michelangelo's building (fig. 667), converting it into a basilica. The change of plan, which may have been prompted by the example of Il Gesù (see figs. 707 and 709), made it possible to link St. Peter's with the Vatican Palace (fig. 747, right). Maderno's design for the façade follows the pattern established by Michelangelo for the exterior of the church—a colossal order supporting an attic—but with a dramatic emphasis on the portals. There is what can only be described as a crescendo effect from the corners toward the center: the spacing of the supports becomes closer, pilasters turn into columns, and the façade wall projects step by step.

This quickened rhythm, we recall, had been hinted at a generation earlier, in Giacomo della Porta's façade of Il Gesù (see fig. 709). Maderno made it the dominant principle of his façade designs, not only for St. Peter's but for smaller churches as well; in so doing, he replaced the traditional notion of the church façade as one continuous wall surface—a concept not yet challenged by the façade of Il Gesù—with the "façade-in-depth," dynamically related to the open space before it. The possibilities implicit in this new concept were not to be exhausted until a hundred and fifty years later.

BERNINI. The enormous size of St. Peter's made the decoration of its interior a uniquely difficult task—how to relate

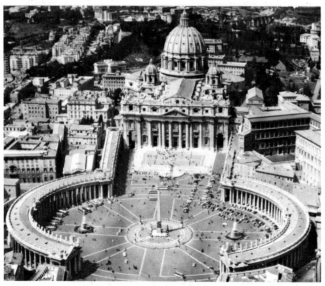

747. Aerial view of St. Peter's, Rome.
Nave and façade by CARLO MADERNO, 1607–15;
colonnade by GIANLORENZO BERNINI, designed 1657

its chill vastness to the human scale and imbue it with a measure of emotional warmth. That the problem was solved is very largely to the merit of Gianlorenzo Bernini (1598–1680), the greatest sculptor-architect of the century. St. Peter's occupied him at intervals during most of his long and prolific career; he began by designing the huge bronze canopy for the main altar under the dome (fig. 748).

The tabernacle is a splendid fusion of architecture and sculpture. Four ornate, spiral-shaped columns support an upper platform; at its corners are statues of angels and vigorously curved scrolls which raise high the symbol of the victory of Christianity over the pagan world, a cross above a golden orb. The entire structure is so alive with expressive energy that it strikes us as the very epitome of Baroque style. Yet its most astonishing feature, the corkscrew columns, had been invented in late antiquity, and even employed, on a much smaller scale, in the old basilica of St. Peter's; Bernini could claim the best possible precedent for his own use of the motif. Nor is this the only instance of an affinity between Baroque and ancient art: several monuments of Roman architecture of the second and third centuries A.D. seem to anticipate the style of the seventeenth (see figs. 277–80).

A similar relationship can be discovered between Hellenistic and Baroque sculpture. If we compare Bernini's *David* (fig. 749) with Michelangelo's (see fig. 652) and ask which is closer to the Pergamum frieze or the *Laocoön Group* (see figs. 228 and 230), our vote must go to Bernini. His figure shares with the Hellenistic works that unison of body and spirit, of motion and emotion, which Michelangelo so conspicuously avoids. This does not mean that Bernini is more classical than Michelangelo; it indicates, rather, that both the Baroque and the High Renaissance acknowledged the authority of ancient art, but each period drew inspiration from a different aspect of antiquity.

But Bernini's *David*, obviously, is in no sense an echo of the *Laocoön Group*. If we ask what makes it Baroque, the simplest answer would be the implied presence of Goliath. Unlike earlier statues of David, Bernini's is conceived not as one self-contained figure but as "half of a pair," his entire action focused on his adversary. Did Bernini, we wonder, plan a statue of Goliath to complete the group? He never did, for his *David* tells us clearly enough where *he* sees the enemy. Consequently, the space between David and his invisible opponent is charged with energy: it "belongs" to the statue. If we stand directly in front of this formidable fighter, our first impulse is to get out of the line of fire.

Bernini's *David* shows us what distinguishes Baroque sculpture from the sculpture of the two preceding centuries: its new, active relationship with the space it inhabits. It eschews self-sufficiency for an illusion—the illusion of presences or forces that are implied by the behavior of the statue. Because it so often presents an "invisible complement" (like the Goliath of Bernini's *David*), Baroque sculpture has been denounced as a tour de force, attempting essentially pictorial effects that are outside its province. The accusation is pointless, for illusion is the basis of every artistic experience, and we cannot very well regard some kinds or degrees of illusion as less legitimate than others. It is true, however, that Baroque art acknowl-

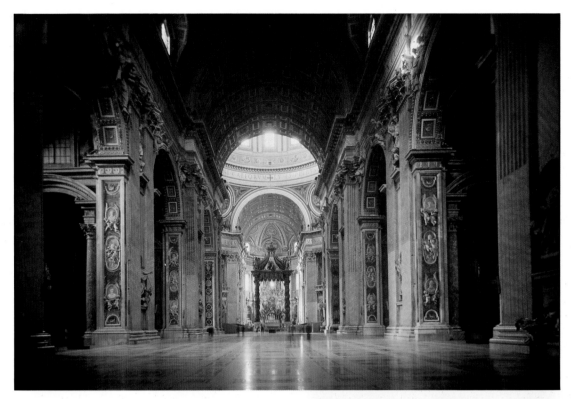

748. CARLO MADERNO. Nave, with Bernini's
Tabernacle (1624–33) at crossing, St. Peter's, Rome

edges no sharp distinction between sculpture and painting. The two may enter into a symbiosis previously unknown or, more precisely, both may be combined with architecture to form a compound illusion, like that of the stage. Bernini, who had a passionate interest in the theater, was at his best when he could merge architecture, sculpture, and painting in this fashion.

His masterpiece is the Cornaro Chapel, containing the famous group called *The Ecstasy of St. Theresa* (fig. 750), in the church of Sta. Maria della Vittoria. Theresa of Avila, one of the great saints of the Counter Reformation, had described how an angel pierced her heart with a flaming golden arrow: "The pain was so great that I screamed aloud; but at the same time I felt such infinite sweetness that I wished the pain to last forever. It was not physical but psychic pain, although it affected the body as well to some degree. It was the sweetest caressing of the soul by God."

Bernini has made this visionary experience as sensuously real as Correggio's *Jupiter and Io* (see fig. 694); the angel, in a different context, would be indistinguishable from Cupid, and the saint's ecstasy is palpably physical. Yet the two figures, on their floating cloud, are illuminated (from a hidden window above) in such a way as to seem almost dematerialized in their gleaming whiteness. The beholder experiences them as visionary. The "invisible complement" here, less specific than David's but equally important, is the force that carries the figures heavenward, causing the turbulence of their drapery. Its nature is suggested by the golden rays, which come from a source high above the altar: in an illusionistic fresco on the vault of the chapel, the glory of the

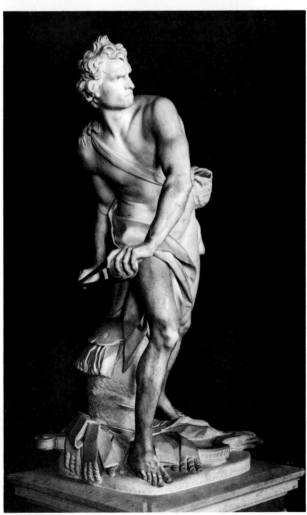

749. GIANLORENZO BERNINI. *DAVID.* 1623. Marble,
lifesize. Galleria Borghese, Rome

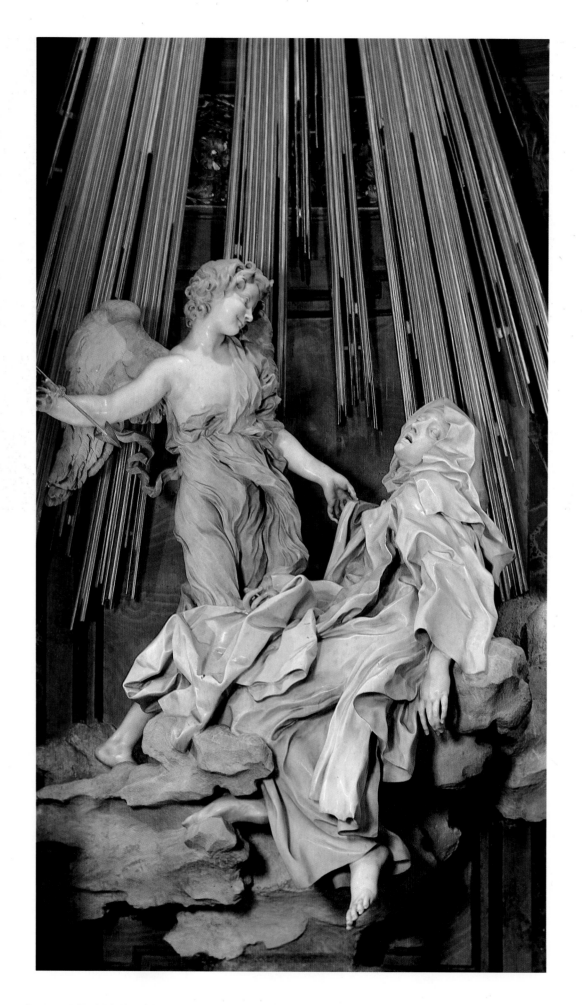

heavens is revealed as a dazzling burst of light from which tumble clouds of jubilant angels (fig. 751). It is this celestial "explosion" that gives force to the thrusts of the angel's arrow and makes the ecstasy of the saint believable.

To complete the illusion, Bernini even provides a built-in audience for his "stage": on the sides of the chapel are balconies resembling theater boxes, where we see marble figures—members of the Cornaro family—who also witness the ecstasy. Their space and ours are the same, and thus part of everyday reality, while the ecstasy, housed in a strongly framed niche, occupies a space that is real but beyond our reach. The ceiling fresco, finally, represents the infinite, unfathomable space of Heaven. We may recall that *The Burial of Count Orgaz* and its setting also form a whole embracing three levels of reality (see page 520); we are able to analyze for ourselves the profound difference between Baroque and Mannerism by contrasting these two chapels.

Some years later Bernini created another compound display, on an even grander scale, in the choir of St. Peter's (fig. 748, far background, and fig. 752)—a climax for the visitor

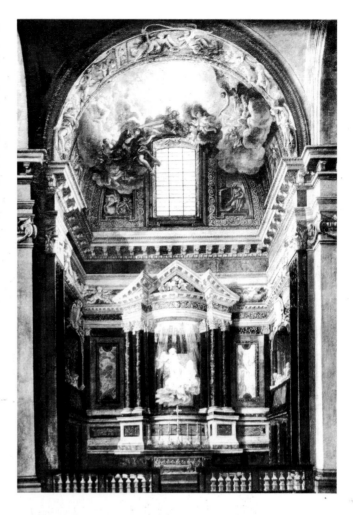

750. (*opposite*) GIANLORENZO BERNINI. *THE ECSTASY OF ST. THERESA.* 1645–52. Marble, lifesize. Cornaro Chapel, Sta. Maria della Vittoria, Rome

751. (*right*) *THE CORNARO CHAPEL.* 18th-century painting. Staatliches Museum, Schwerin, Germany

752. (*below*) GIANLORENZO BERNINI. *THRONE OF ST. PETER.* 1657–66. Gilt bronze, marble, and stucco. Apse, St. Peter's, Rome

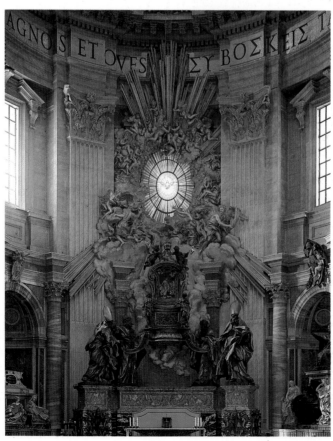

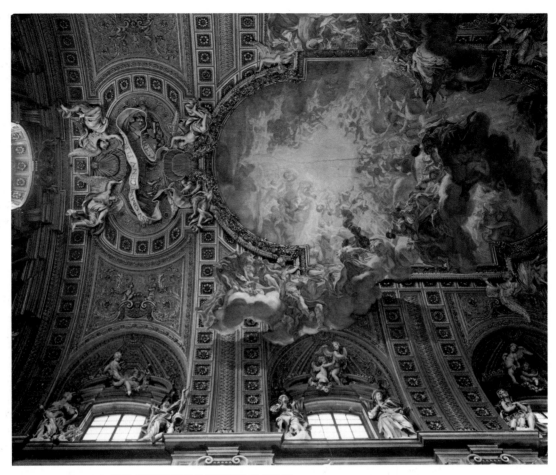

753. GIOVANNI BATTISTA GAULLI. *TRIUMPH OF THE NAME OF JESUS.*
Ceiling fresco. 1672–85. Il Gesù, Rome

at the very end of the church. Again the focus is a burst of heavenly light (through a real window of stained glass) that propels a mass of clouds and angels toward us. These clouds envelop the bronze *Throne of St. Peter,* which hovers weightless in mid-air, anchored to the hands of the Four Fathers of the Church.

The interior decoration of Il Gesù is further evidence of Bernini's imaginative daring (fig. 753), although his role in this case was only advisory. The commission for the ceiling frescoes went to Giovanni Battista Gaulli, his young protégé; a talented assistant, Antonio Raggi, did the stucco sculpture. As we see the nave fresco spilling so dramatically over its frame, then turning into sculptured figures, it is clear that the plan must be Bernini's; here again we sense the spirit of the Cornaro Chapel.

While designing the *Throne of St. Peter,* Bernini also conceived as "exterior decoration" the magnificent oval piazza in front of St. Peter's (see fig. 747). It acts as an immense atrium, framed by colonnades which the artist himself likened to the motherly, all-embracing arms of the Church. The basilica integrated with so grandiose a setting of "molded" open space can be compared, for sheer impressiveness, only with the ancient Roman sanctuary at Palestrina (see figs. 257–59).

BORROMINI. As a personality, Bernini represents a type we first met among the artists of the Early Renaissance, a self-assured, expansive person of the world. His great rival in architecture, Francesco Borromini (1599–1667), was the opposite type: a secretive and emotionally unstable genius, he died by suicide. The temperamental contrast between the two would be evident from their works alone, even without the testimony of contemporary witnesses. Both exemplify the climax of Baroque architecture in Rome, yet Bernini's design for the colonnade of St. Peter's is dramatically simple and unified, while Borromini's structures are extravagantly complex. Bernini himself agreed with those who denounced Borromini for flagrantly disregarding the classical tradition, enshrined in Renaissance theory and practice, that architecture must reflect the proportions of the human body.

We understand this accusation when we look at Borromini's first major project, the church of S. Carlo alle Quattro Fontane (figs. 754–56). The vocabulary is not unfamiliar, but the syntax is new and disquieting; the ceaseless play of concave and convex surfaces makes the entire structure seem elastic, "pulled out of shape" by pressures that no previous building could have withstood. The plan is a pinched oval suggesting a distended and half-melted Greek cross, as if it had been drawn on rubber; the inside of the dome, too, looks

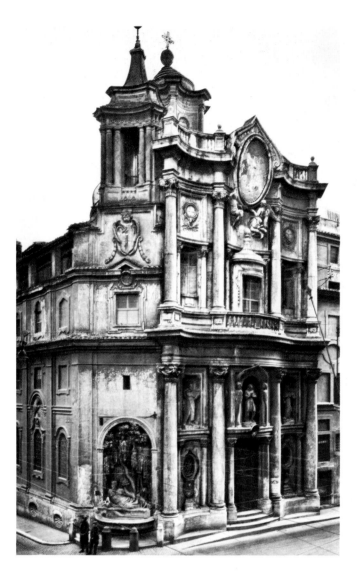

"stretched"—if the tension were relaxed, it would snap back to normal. The façade was designed almost thirty years later, and the pressures and counterpressures here reach their maximum intensity. Borromini merges architecture and sculpture in a way that must have shocked Bernini; no such fusion had been ventured since Gothic art.

S. Carlo alle Quattro Fontane established Borromini's local and international fame. "Nothing similar," wrote the head of the religious order for which the church was built, "can be found anywhere in the world. This is attested by the foreigners who . . . try to procure copies of the plan. We have been asked for them by Germans, Flemings, Frenchmen, Italians, Spaniards, and even Indians. . . ." The design of Borromini's next church, S. Ivo (figs. 757 and 758), is more compact and equally daring. Its plan, a star-hexagon, belongs unequivocally to the central type; Borromini may have been thinking of octagonal structures, such as S. Vitale, Ravenna (compare figs. 334–37). But he did not subdivide the space into a tall, domed "nave" ringed by an ambulatory or chapels; he covered all of it with one great dome, continuing the star-hexagon pattern up to the circular base of the lantern. Again the concave-convex rhythm dominates the entire design—the structure might almost be described as a larger version of the Temple of Venus at Baalbek, turned inside out (see figs. 278 and 279).

A third project by Borromini is of special interest as a High Baroque critique of St. Peter's. Maderno had found one problem insoluble: although his new façade forms an impressive unit with Michelangelo's dome when seen from a distance, the dome is gradually hidden by the façade as we approach

754. (*above*) FRANCESCO BORROMINI. Façade, S. Carlo alle Quattro Fontane,. Rome. 1665–67

755. (*right*) Plan of S. Carlo alle Quattro Fontane. Begun 1638

756. (*far right*) Dome, S. Carlo alle Quattro Fontane

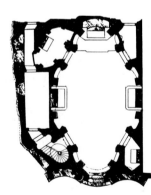

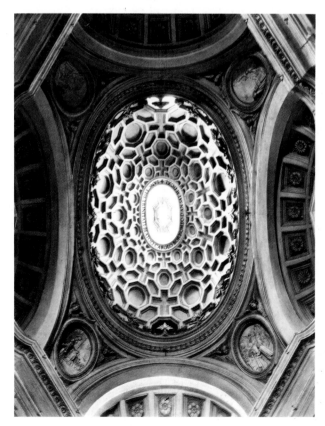

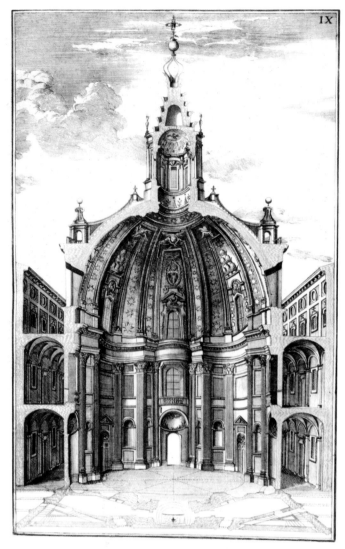

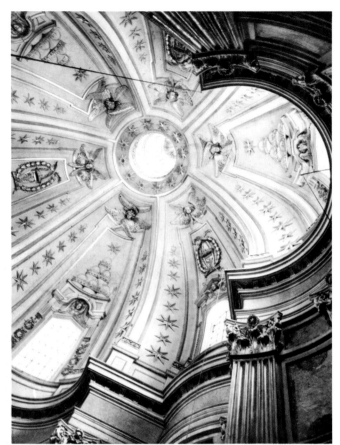

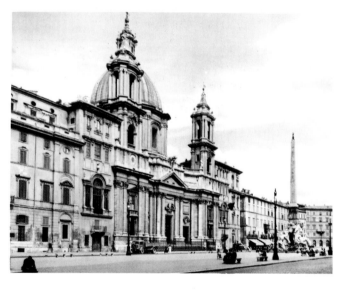

757. (*above*) FRANCESCO BORROMINI.
Section, S. Ivo, Rome. Begun 1642

758. (*upper right*) Dome, S. Ivo

759. (*right*) FRANCESCO BORROMINI.
S. Agnese in Piazza Navona, Rome. 1653–63

the church. Borromini designed the façade of S. Agnese in Piazza Navona (fig. 759) with this conflict in mind. Its lower part is adapted from the façade of St. Peter's, but curves inward, so that the dome—a tall, slender version of Michelangelo's—functions as the upper part of the façade. The dramatic juxtaposition of concave and convex, always characteristic of Borromini, is further emphasized by the two towers (such towers were also once planned for St. Peter's), which form a monumental triad with the dome. Once again Borromini joins Gothic and Renaissance features—the two-tower façade and the dome—into a remarkably "elastic" compound.

GUARINI. The wealth of new ideas that Borromini introduced was to be exploited not in Rome but in Turin, the capital of Savoy, which became the creative center of Ba-

roque architecture in Italy toward the end of the seventeenth century. In 1666, that city attracted Borromini's most brilliant successor, Guarino Guarini (1624–1683), a Theatine monk whose architectural genius was deeply grounded in philosophy and mathematics. His design for the façade of Palazzo Carignano (figs. 760 and 761) repeats on a larger scale the undulating movement of S. Carlo alle Quattro Fontane (see fig. 754), using a highly individual vocabulary. Incredibly, the exterior of the building is entirely of brick, down to the last ornamental detail.

Still more extraordinary is Guarini's dome of the Chapel of the Holy Shroud—a round structure attached to Turin Cath-

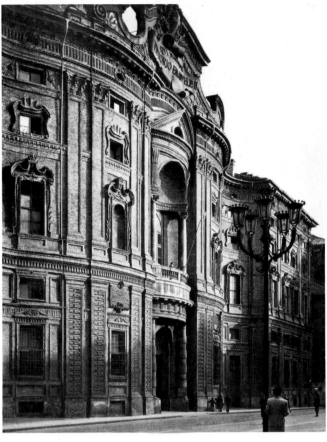

760. GUARINO GUARINI. Façade of Palazzo
Carignano, Turin. Begun 1679

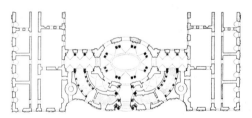

761. Plan of Palazzo Carignano

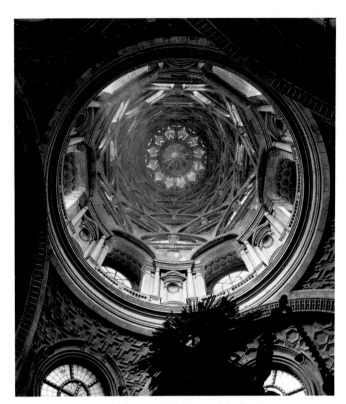

762. GUARINO GUARINI. Dome, Chapel of
the Holy Shroud, Turin Cathedral. 1668–94

763. (*right*) Plan of the Chapel of the Holy
Shroud, and (below) of the dome

764. (*below*) Wooden dome of the Ulu Mosque,
Erzurum, Seljuk. c. 1150

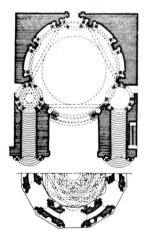

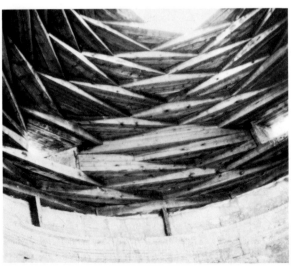

edral (figs. 762 and 763). The tall drum, with alternating
windows and tabernacles, consists of familiar Borrominesque
motifs, but beyond it we enter a realm of pure illusion. The
interior surface of the dome of S. Carlo alle Quattro Fontane,
though dematerialized by light and the honeycomb of fanciful coffers, was still recognizable (see fig. 756); but here the
surface has disappeared completely in a maze of segmental
ribs, and we find ourselves staring into a huge kaleidoscope.
Above this seemingly endless funnel of space hovers the dove
of the Holy Spirit within a bright, twelve-pointed star.

So far as we know, there is only one similar dome anywhere in the history of art: that of the Ulu Mosque at
Erzurum in Turkish Armenia, built about 1150 (fig. 764).

How could Guarini have known about it? Or did he recapture its effect entirely by coincidence? Guarini's dome retains the old symbolic meaning of the Dome of Heaven (see page 472, figs. 618–20). But the objective harmony of the Renaissance has here become subjective, a compelling experience of the infinite. If Borromini's style at times suggested a synthesis of Gothic and Renaissance, Guarini takes the next, decisive step; in his theoretical writings, he contrasts the "muscular" architecture of the ancients with the opposite effect of Gothic churches—which appear to stand only by means of some kind of miracle—and he expresses equal admiration for both. This attitude corresponds exactly to his own practice; by using the most advanced mathematical techniques of his day, he achieved architectural miracles even greater than those of the seemingly weightless Gothic structures.

GERMANY AND AUSTRIA

It is not surprising that the style invented by Borromini and furthered by Guarini should achieve its climax north of the Alps, in Austria and southern Germany, where such a synthesis of Gothic and Renaissance was sure of a particularly warm response. In these countries, ravaged by the Thirty Years' War, the number of buildings remained small until near the end of the seventeenth century; Baroque was an imported style, practiced mainly by visiting Italians. Not until the 1690s did native designers come to the fore. There followed a period of intense activity that lasted more than fifty years and gave rise to some of the most imaginative creations in the history of architecture. We must be content with a small sampling of these monuments, erected for the glorification of princes and prelates who, generally speaking, deserve to be remembered only as lavish patrons of the arts.

FISCHER VON ERLACH. Johann Fischer von Erlach (1656–1723), the first great architect of the Late Baroque in Central Europe, is linked most directly to the Italian tradition. His design for the church of St. Charles Borromaeus in Vienna (figs. 765 and 766) combines the façade of Borromini's S. Agnese and the Pantheon portico (figs. 759 and 265), with a pair of huge columns derived from the Column of Trajan (see fig. 292), which here substitute for façade towers. (The actual façade towers have become corner pavilions, reminiscent of the Louvre court; compare fig. 733.) With these inflexible elements of Roman Imperial art embedded into the elastic curvatures of his church, Fischer von Erlach expresses, more boldly than any Italian Baroque architect, the power of the Christian faith to absorb and transfigure the splendors of antiquity.

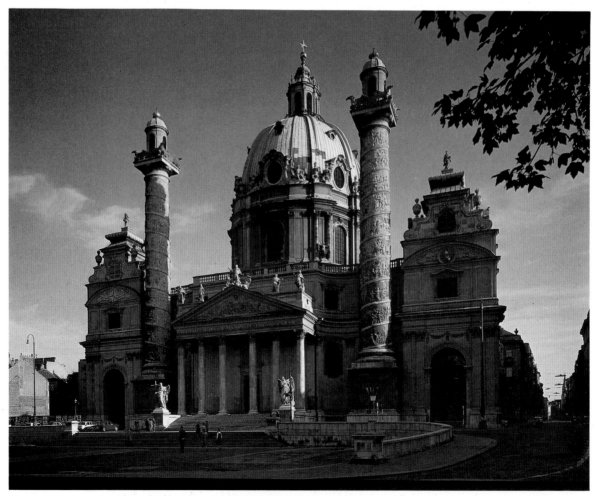

765. JOHANN FISCHER VON ERLACH. Façade of St. Charles Borromaeus (Karlskirche), Vienna. 1716–37

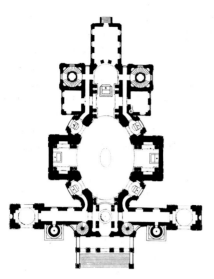

766. Plan of St. Charles Borromaeus

PRANDTAUER. Even more monumental, thanks to its superb site, is the Monastery of Melk (fig. 767) by Jakob Prandtauer (1660–1726). The buildings form a tightly knit unit that centers on the church: it occupies the crest of a promontory above the Danube, rising from the rock, not like a fortress but like a vision of heavenly glory. The interior of the church (fig. 768) still reflects the plan of Il Gesù, but the abundant illumination, the play of curves and countercurves, and the weightless grace of the stucco sculpture give it an airy lightness far removed from the Roman Baroque. The vaults and wall surfaces seem thin and pliable, like membranes easily punctured by the expansive power of space.

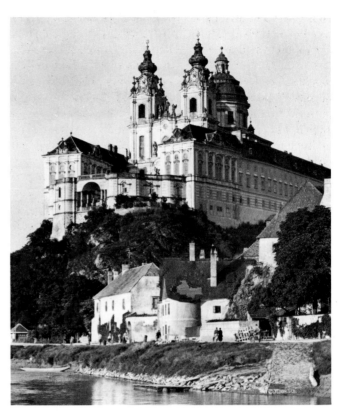

767. JAKOB PRANDTAUER. Monastery Church, Melk, Austria. Begun 1702

768. PRANDTAUER, BEDUZZI, and MUNGGENAST. Interior, Monastery Church, Melk. Completed c. 1738

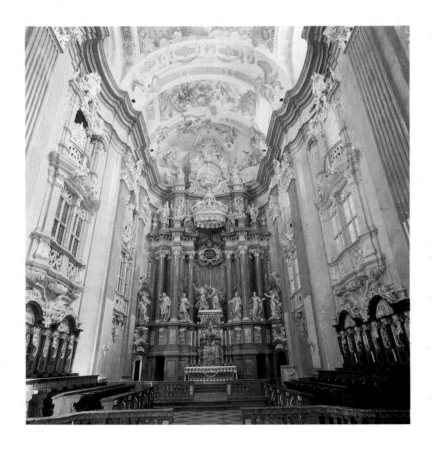

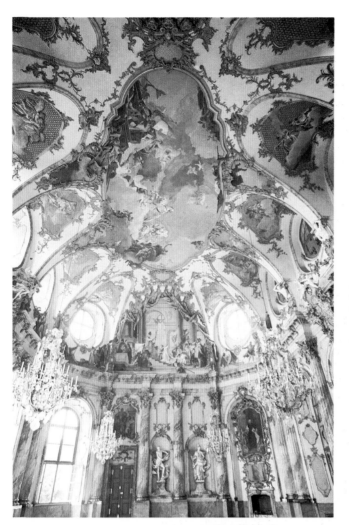

NEUMANN. This tendency is carried further by the architects of the next generation, among whom Balthasar Neumann (1687–1753) was the most prominent. His largest project, the Episcopal Palace in Würzburg, includes the breathtaking Kaisersaal (fig. 769), a great oval hall decorated in white, gold, and pastel shades — the favorite color scheme of the mid-eighteenth century. Structural members such as columns, pilasters, and architraves are now minimized; windows and vault segments are framed by continuous, ribbon-like moldings, and the white surfaces are spun over with irregular ornamental designs. This repertory of lacy, curling motifs, invented in France about 1700, is the hallmark of the Rococo style (see page 598), which is here happily combined with German Late Baroque architecture.

TIEPOLO. The membranelike ceiling so often gives way to illusionistic openings of every sort that we no longer feel it to be a spatial boundary. These openings do not, however, reveal avalanches of figures propelled by dramatic bursts of light, like those of Roman ceilings (compare fig. 753), but blue sky and sunlit clouds, and an occasional winged creature soaring in this limitless expanse. Only along the edges are there solid clusters of figures (fig. 770). Here the last,

769. BALTHASAR NEUMANN.
The Kaisersaal, Residenz, Würzburg. 1719–44.
Frescoes by GIOVANNI BATTISTA TIEPOLO, 1751

770. GIOVANNI BATTISTA TIEPOLO. Ceiling fresco (detail),
1751. The Kaisersaal, Residenz, Würzburg

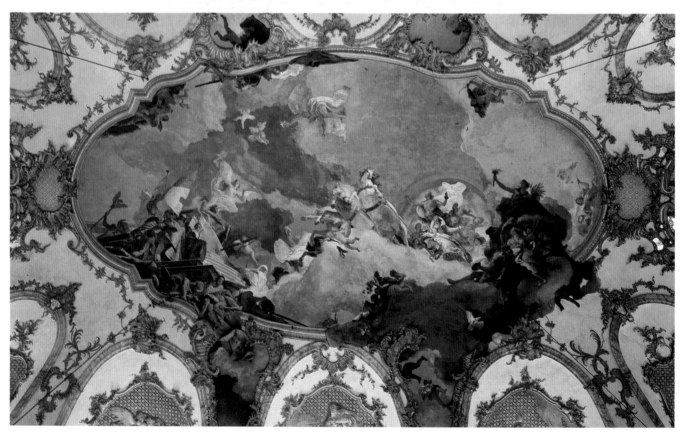

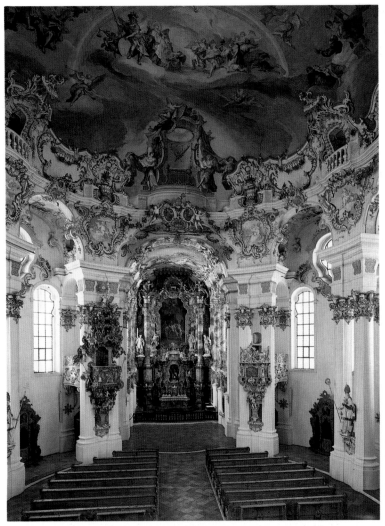

771. DOMINIKUS ZIMMERMANN. Interior, Die Wies,
Upper Bavaria. 1745–54

and most refined, stage of illusionistic ceiling decoration is represented by its greatest master, Giovanni Battista Tiepolo (1696–1770). Venetian by birth and training, Tiepolo blended the tradition of High Baroque illusionism with the pageantry of Veronese. His mastery of light and color, the grace and felicity of his touch, made him famous far beyond his home territory. In the Würzburg frescoes his powers are at their height. He was afterward invited to decorate the Royal Palace in Madrid, where he spent his final years.

ZIMMERMANN. A contemporary of Balthasar Neumann, Dominikus Zimmermann (1685–1766), created what may be the finest spatial design of the mid-eighteenth century, the Bavarian pilgrimage church nicknamed "Die Wies" (figs. 771 and 772). The exterior is so plain that its interior richness seems truly overwhelming. Like the Kaisersaal, its shape is oval, but since the ceiling rests on paired, free-standing supports, the spatial configuration is more complex and fluid; despite the playful Rococo decor, we are reminded of a German Gothic *Hallenkirche* (see fig. 481). Guarini's prophetic revaluation of Gothic architecture has here become reality.

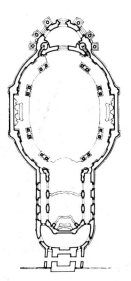

772. Plan of Die Wies

CHAPTER SEVEN
THE BAROQUE IN FLANDERS, HOLLAND, AND SPAIN

FLANDERS

Painting

RUBENS. Although Rome was its birthplace, the Baroque style soon became international. Among the artists who helped bring this about, the great Flemish painter Peter Paul Rubens (1577–1640) holds a place of unique importance. It might be said that he finished what Dürer had started a hundred years earlier—the breakdown of the artistic barriers between North and South. Rubens' father was a prominent Antwerp Protestant who fled to Germany to escape Spanish persecution during the war of independence (see page 568); the family returned to Antwerp after his death, when Peter Paul was ten years old, and the boy grew up a devout Catholic. Trained by local painters, Rubens became a master in 1598, but developed a personal style only when, two years later, he went to Italy.

During his eight years in the South, he eagerly studied ancient sculpture, the masterpieces of the High Renaissance (see his splendid drawing after Leonardo's *Battle of Anghiari*, fig. 643), and the work of Caravaggio and Annibale Carracci, absorbing the Italian tradition far more thoroughly than had any Northerner before him. He competed, in fact,

with the best Italians of his day on even terms, and could well have made his career in Italy. When his mother's illness in 1608 brought him back to Flanders, he meant the visit to be brief. But he received a special appointment as court painter to the Spanish regent, which permitted him to establish a workshop in Antwerp, exempt from local taxes and guild regulations. Rubens thus had the best of both worlds, for he was valued at court not only as an artist, but as a confidential adviser and emissary. Diplomatic errands gave him entrée to the royal households of the major powers, where he procured sales and commissions, while he was also free to carry out, aided by a growing number of assistants, a vast volume of work for the city of Antwerp, for the Church, and for private patrons.

The Raising of the Cross (fig. 773), the first major altarpiece Rubens produced after his return, shows strikingly how much he owed to Italian art. The muscular figures, modeled to display their physical power and passionate feeling, recall the Sistine Ceiling and the Farnese Gallery; the lighting suggests Caravaggio's. The panel is more heroic in scale and conception than any previous Northern work, yet Rubens is also a meticulous Flemish realist in such details as the foliage, the armor of the soldier, and the

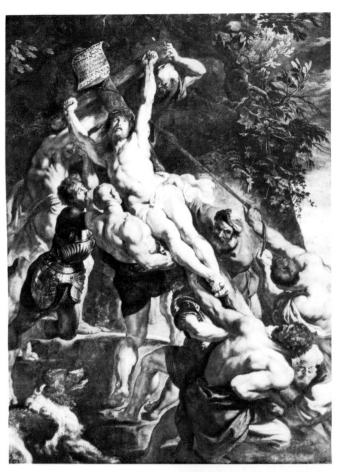

curly-haired dog in the foreground. These varied elements, integrated with sovereign mastery, form a composition of tremendous dramatic force. The unstable pyramid of bodies, swaying precariously, bursts the limits of the frame in a characteristically Baroque way, making the beholder feel like a participant in the action.

In the decade of the 1620s, Rubens' dynamic style reached its climax in his huge decorative schemes for churches and palaces. The most famous, probably, is the cycle in the Luxembourg Palace in Paris, glorifying the career of Marie de'Medici, the widow of Henri IV and mother of Louis XIII. Our illustration shows the artist's oil sketch for one episode, the young queen landing in Marseilles (fig. 774). Hardly an exciting subject—yet Rubens has turned it into a spectacle of unprecedented splendor. As Marie de'Medici walks down the gangplank, Fame flies overhead sounding a triumphant blast on two trumpets, and Neptune rises from the sea with his fish-tailed crew; having guarded the queen's journey, they rejoice at her arrival. Everything flows together here in swirling movement: heaven and earth, history and allegory—

773. PETER PAUL RUBENS. *THE RAISING OF THE CROSS.* 1609–10. Center panel of a triptych, 15′×11′2″ (4.6×3.4 m). Antwerp Cathedral

774. PETER PAUL RUBENS. *MARIE DE'MEDICI, QUEEN OF FRANCE, LANDING IN MARSEILLES.* 1622–23. Oil on panel, 25×19¾″ (63.5×50.3 cm). Pinakothek, Munich

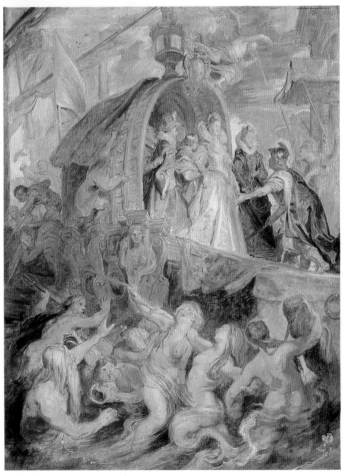

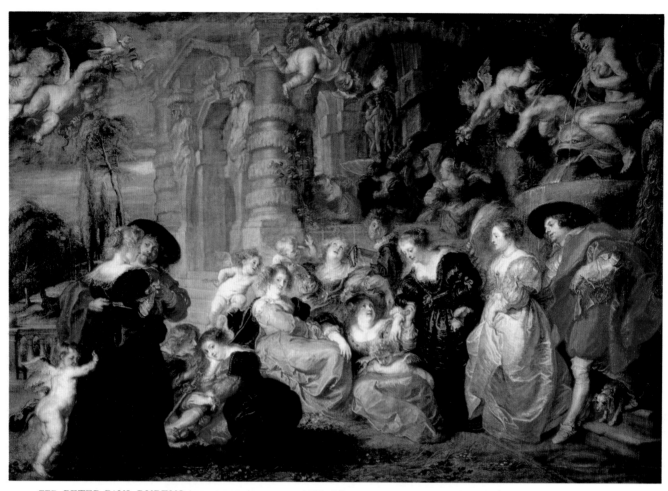

775. PETER PAUL RUBENS. *THE GARDEN OF LOVE.* c. 1638. Oil on canvas, 6'6"×9'3½" (2×2.8 m). Museo del Prado, Madrid

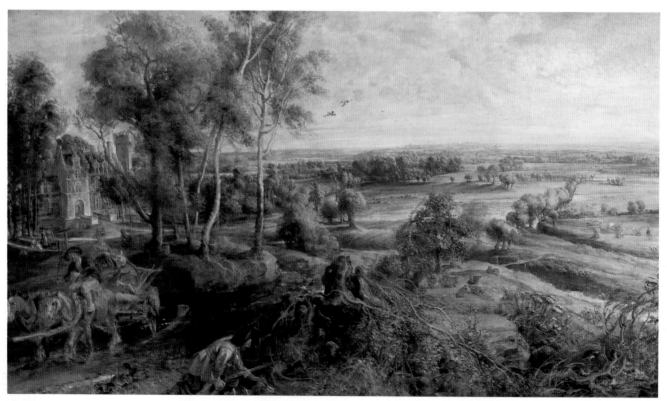

776. PETER PAUL RUBENS. *LANDSCAPE WITH THE CHÂTEAU OF STEEN.* 1636.
Oil on panel, 53×93" (134.5×236.7 cm). The National Gallery, London. Reproduced by courtesy of the Trustees

even drawing and painting, for Rubens used oil sketches like this one to prepare his compositions. Unlike earlier artists, he preferred to design his pictures in terms of light and color from the very start (most of his drawings are figure studies or portrait sketches). This unified vision, adumbrated but never fully achieved by the great Venetians, was Rubens' most precious legacy to subsequent painters.

Around 1630, the turbulent drama of Rubens' preceding work changes to a late style of lyrical tenderness inspired by Titian, whom Rubens rediscovered, as it were, in the royal palace while he visited Madrid. *The Garden of Love* (fig. 775) is one result of this encounter, as glowing a tribute to life's pleasures as Titian's *Bacchanal* (see fig. 676). But these celebrants belong to the present, not to a golden age of the past, though they are playfully assaulted by swarms of cupids. To understand the artist's purpose, we must first realize that this subject, the Garden of Love, had been a feature of Northern painting ever since the courtly style of the International Gothic. The early versions, however, merely showed groups of fashionable young lovers in a garden—they were genre scenes pure and simple. By combining this tradition with Titian's classical mythologies, Rubens has created an enchanted realm where myth and reality become one.

The picture must have had special meaning for him, since he had just married a beautiful girl of sixteen (his first wife died in 1626). He also bought a country house, the Château of Steen, and led the leisurely life of a squire. This change induced a renewed interest in landscape painting, which he had practiced only intermittenly before. Here, too, the power of his genius is undiminished. In *Landscape with the Château of Steen* (fig. 776), a magnificent open space sweeps from the hunter and his prey in the foreground to the mist-veiled hills along the horizon. As a landscapist, Rubens is the heir of both Pieter Bruegel and Annibale Carracci (compare figs. 727 and 746), again creating a synthesis from his Northern and Southern sources.

VAN DYCK. Besides Rubens, only one Flemish Baroque artist won international stature. Anthony van Dyck (1599–1641) was that rarity among painters, a child prodigy. Before he was twenty, he had become Rubens' most valued assistant. But he lacked the older master's vitality and inventiveness, and his fame is based mainly on his portraits, especially those he painted in England as court painter to Charles I, during 1632–41. Among the most attractive is *Charles I Hunting* (fig. 777); the king stands near a horse and two grooms against a landscape backdrop. Representing the sovereign at ease, it might be called a "dismounted equestrian portrait"—less rigid than a formal state portrait, but hardly less grand. The fluid Baroque movement of the setting contrasts oddly with the self-conscious elegance of the king's pose, which still suggests the stylized grace of Elizabethan portraits (compare fig. 725). Van Dyck has brought the Mannerist court portrait up to date, rephrasing it in the pictorial language of Rubens and Titian. He created a new aristocratic portrait tradition that continued in England until the late eighteenth century, and had considerable influence on the Continent as well.

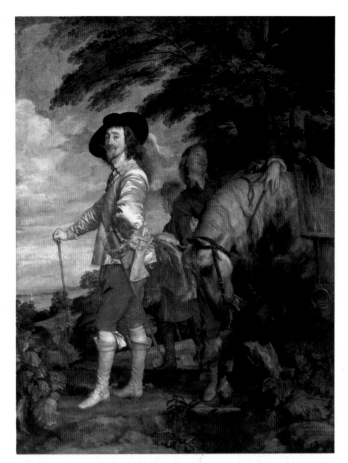

777. ANTHONY VAN DYCK. *PORTRAIT OF CHARLES I HUNTING.*
c. 1635. Oil on canvas, 8'11"×6'11½"
(2.7×2.1 m). Musée du Louvre, Paris

HOLLAND

Painting

In contrast to Flanders, where all of art was overshadowed by the majestic personality of Rubens, Holland produced a bewildering variety of masters and styles. The new nation was proud of its hard-won freedom. Though the cultural links with Flanders remained strong, several factors encouraged the quick development of Dutch artistic traditions. Unlike Flanders, where all artistic activity radiated from Antwerp, Holland had a number of flourishing local schools; besides Amsterdam, the commercial capital, we find important groups of painters in Haarlem, Utrecht, Leyden, Delft, and other towns. Holland was a nation of merchants, farmers, and seafarers, and its religion was Reformed Protestant; Dutch artists had not the large-scale commissions sponsored by State and Church that were available throughout the Catholic world. While municipal authorities and civic bodies provided a certain amount of art patronage, their demands were limited, so that the private collector now became the painter's chief source of support.

This condition had already existed to some extent before (see page 542), but its full effect can be seen only after 1600. There was no shrinkage of output; on the contrary, the general public developed so insatiable an appetite for pictures that the

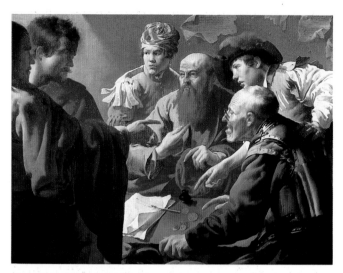

778. HENDRICK TERBRUGGHEN. *THE CALLING OF ST. MATTHEW.*
1621. Oil on canvas, 40×54″ (101.5×137.2 cm).
Centraal Museum, Utrecht

whole country became gripped by a kind of collector's mania. John Evelyn, during a visit to Holland in 1641, noted in his diary that "it is an ordinary thing to find a common farmer lay out two or three thousand pounds in this commodity. Their houses are full of them, and they vend them at their fairs to very great gain." Pictures had indeed become a commodity, and their trade followed the law of supply and demand. Many artists produced "for the market" rather than for individual patrons.

The mechanism of the market has been said to raise a barrier between artist and public, and to degrade or falsify the "true worth" of the work of art. But such charges are unrealistic: the true worth of a work of art is always unstable, and dependent on time and circumstance; even those who believe in timeless values in art will concede that these values cannot be expressed in money. The art market reflects the dominant, rather than the most discerning, taste of the moment; works by artists now regarded as mediocre may once have been overpriced; others, highly valued today, seem once to have sold too cheaply. Yet the system in antiquity and the Middle Ages, when artists were paid on standards of craftsmanship, was hardly fairer in rewarding aesthetic merit. The market does form a barrier between artist and patron, but there are advantages in this as well as drawbacks.

To subject artists to the impersonal pressure of supply and demand in an egalitarian society is not necessarily worse than to make them depend on the favor of princes. The lesser ones will tend to become specialists, steadily producing their marketable pictures, while artists of independent spirit, perhaps braving public indifference and economic hardship, will paint as they please and rely for support on the discerning minority. The collectors' mania in seventeenth-century Holland caused an outpouring of artistic talent comparable only to Early Renaissance Florence, although many Dutch were lured into becoming painters by hopes of success that failed to come true. Even the greatest masters were sometimes hard-pressed (it was not unusual for an artist to keep an inn, or run a small business on the side). Yet they survived—less secure, but freer.

UTRECHT SCHOOL. The Baroque style came to Holland from Antwerp, through the work of Rubens, and from Rome, through direct contact with Caravaggio and his followers. Although most Dutch painters did not go to Italy, in the early years of the century there were some who did, principally from Utrecht, a town with strong Catholic traditions. It is not surprising that these artists were more attracted by Caravaggio's realism and "lay Christianity" than by Annibale Carracci's classicism. *The Calling of St. Matthew* by Hendrick Terbrugghen (1588–1629), the oldest of this group (fig. 778), directly reflects Caravaggio's earlier version (fig. 739): the sharp light, the dramatic timing, and the everyday detail. While the Utrecht School produced no great artists, its members were important for transmitting the style of Caravaggio to other Dutch masters who then made better use of these new Italian ideas.

HALS. One of the first to profit from this experience was Frans Hals (1580/85–1666), the great portrait painter of Haarlem. He was born in Antwerp, and what little is known of his early work suggests the influence of Rubens. His developed style, however, seen in such pictures as *The Jolly Toper* (fig. 779), combines Rubens' robustness and breadth with a concentration on the "dramatic moment" that must be derived, via Utrecht, from Caravaggio. Everything here conveys complete spontaneity: the twinkling eyes and half-open mouth, the raised hand, the teetering wineglass, and—most important of all—the quick way of setting down the forms. Hals works in dashing brushstrokes, each so clearly

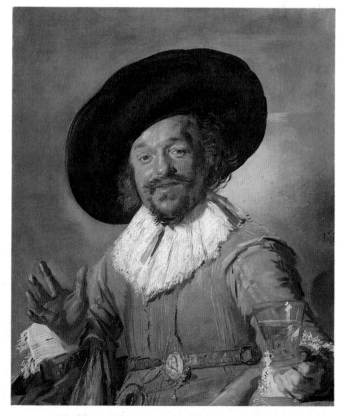

779. FRANS HALS. *THE JOLLY TOPER.* c. 1628–30.
Oil on canvas, 31⅞×26¼″ (81×66.6 cm).
Rijksmuseum, Amsterdam

visible as a separate entity that we can almost count the total number of "touches." With this open, split-second technique, the completed picture has the immediacy of a sketch (compare that by Rubens, fig. 774). The impression of a race against time is, of course, deceptive; Frans Hals spent hours, not minutes, on this lifesize canvas, but he maintains the illusion of having done it all in the wink of an eye.

These qualities are even more forceful in the *Malle Babbe* (fig. 780), one of the artist's genre pictures. A lower-class counterpart of *The Jolly Toper*, this folk character, half witch (note the owl), half village idiot, screams invectives at other guests in a tavern. Hals seems to share their attitude toward this benighted creature—one of cruel amusement rather than sympathy—but his characterization is masterfully sharp and his lightninglike brushwork has the bravura of incredible skill.

In the artist's last canvases these pictorial fireworks are transmuted into an austere style of great emotional depth. His group portrait, *The Women Regents of the Old Men's Home at Haarlem* (fig. 781), the institution where he spent his final years, has an insight into human character matched only in Rembrandt's late style (compare figs. 786 and 787).

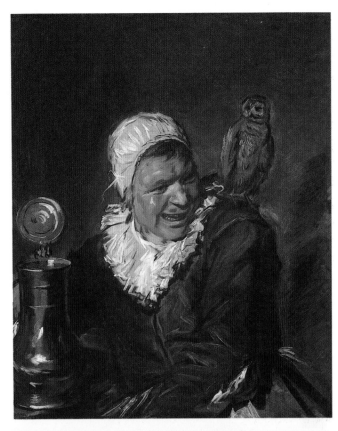

780. FRANS HALS. *MALLE BABBE*. c. 1650. Oil on canvas, 29½×25″ (75×63.5 cm). Gemäldegalerie, Berlin

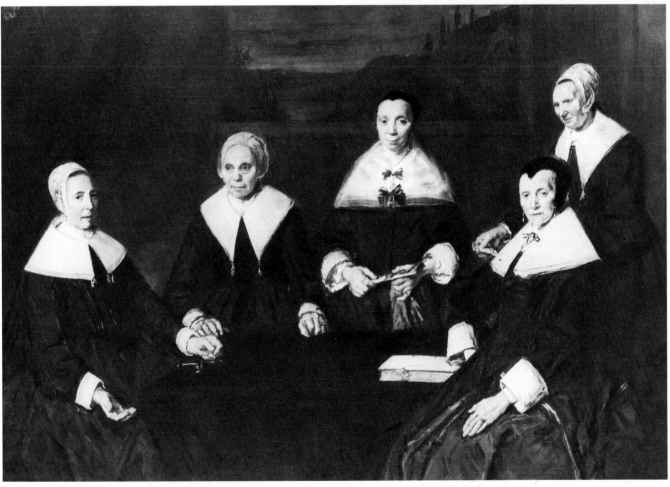

781. FRANS HALS. *THE WOMEN REGENTS OF THE OLD MEN'S HOME AT HAARLEM*. 1664. Oil on canvas, 67×98″ (170.3×249 cm). Frans Halsmuseum, Haarlem

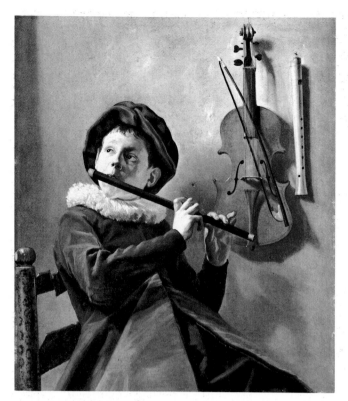

782. JUDITH LEYSTER. *BOY PLAYING A FLUTE*. 1630–35.
Oil on canvas, 28⅛ × 24⅛" (73 × 62 cm).
Nationalmuseum, Stockholm

The daily experience of suffering and death has so etched the faces of these women that they seem themselves to have become images of death—gentle, inexorable, and timeless.

LEYSTER. Hals' virtuosity was such that it could not be imitated readily, and his followers were necessarily few. The only one of importance was Judith Leyster (1609–1660). Like many women artists before modern times, her career was partially curtailed by motherhood. Leyster's enchanting *Boy Playing a Flute* (fig. 782) is her masterpiece. Its style is closer to Terbrugghen's than to Hals'. The rapt musician is a memorable expression of a gentle activity. To convey this spirit, Leyster investigated the poetic quality of light with a quiet intensity that anticipates the work of Jan Vermeer a generation later (see pages 580–81).

REMBRANDT. Like Hals, Rembrandt (1606–1669), the greatest genius of Dutch art, was stimulated at the beginning of his career by indirect contact with Caravaggio; his earliest pictures are small, sharply lit, and intensely realistic. Many deal with Old Testament subjects—a lifelong preference. They show both his greater realism and his new emotional attitude. Since the beginning of Christian art, episodes from the Old Testament had often been represented for the light they shed on Christian doctrine (the Sacrifice of Isaac, for example, "prefigured" the sacrificial death of Christ), rather than for their own sake. This perspective not only limited the choice of subjects, it also colored their interpretation. Rem-

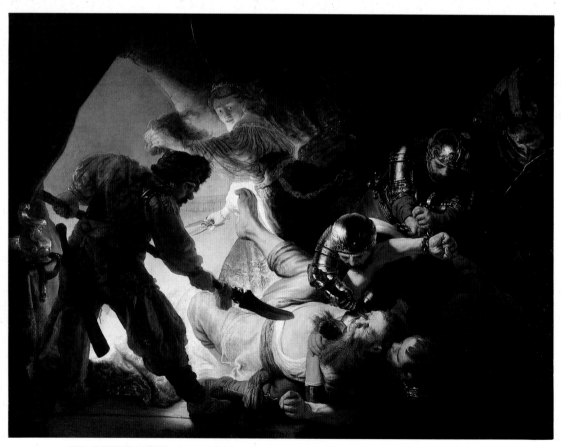

783. REMBRANDT. *THE BLINDING OF SAMSON*. 1636. Oil on canvas, 7'9"×9'11" (2.4×3 m).
Städelsches Kunstinstitut, Frankfurt

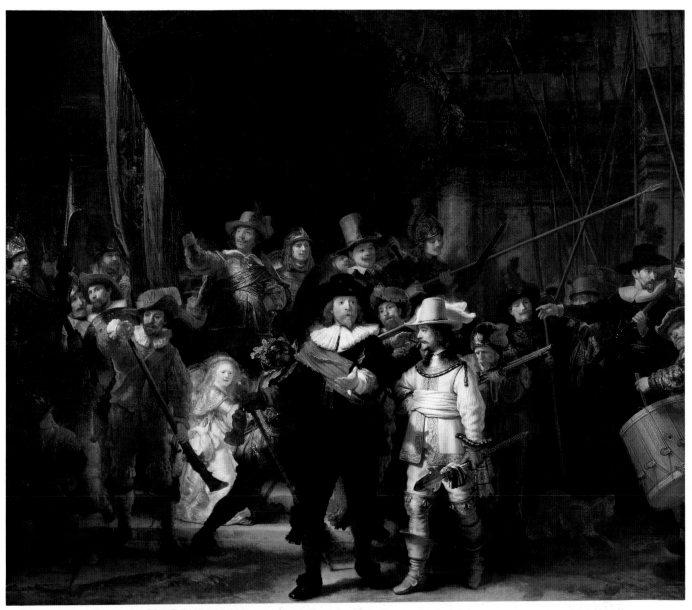

784. REMBRANDT. *THE NIGHT WATCH (THE COMPANY OF CAPTAIN FRANS BANNING COCQ).*
1642. Oil on canvas, 12′2″×14′7″ (3.8×4.4 m). Rijksmuseum, Amsterdam

brandt, by contrast, viewed the stories of the Old Testament in the same lay Christian spirit that governed Caravaggio's approach to the New Testament: as direct accounts of God's ways with His human creations. How strongly these stories affected him is evident from *The Blinding of Samson* (fig. 783). Painted in the full-blown High Baroque style he developed in the 1630s, it shows us the Old Testament world in Oriental splendor and violence, cruel yet seductive. The flood of brilliant light pouring into the dark tent is unabashedly theatrical, heightening the drama to the pitch of *The Raising of the Cross* (fig. 773) by Rubens, whose work Rembrandt sought to rival.

Rembrandt was at this time an avid collector of Near Eastern paraphernalia, which serve as props in these pictures. He was now Amsterdam's most sought-after portrait painter, as well as a man of considerable wealth. This prosperity petered out in the 1640s; the turning point may have been his famous group portrait known as *The Night Watch* (fig. 784). The huge canvas—originally it was even larger—shows a military company, whose members had each contributed toward the cost. But Rembrandt did not do them equal justice. Anxious to avoid a mechanically regular design, he made the picture a virtuoso performance of Baroque movement and lighting; in the process some of the figures were plunged into shadow, and some were hidden by overlapping. Legend has it that the people whose portraits he had thus obscured were dissatisfied. There is no evidence that they were; we do know, however, that the painting was admired in its time.

Like Michelangelo, Rembrandt has been the subject (one might say, the victim) of many fictionalized biographies. In these, the artist's fall from public favor is usually explained by the "catastrophe" of *The Night Watch*. Actually, his fortunes declined after 1642 less suddenly and completely than his romantic admirers would have us believe. Certain impor-

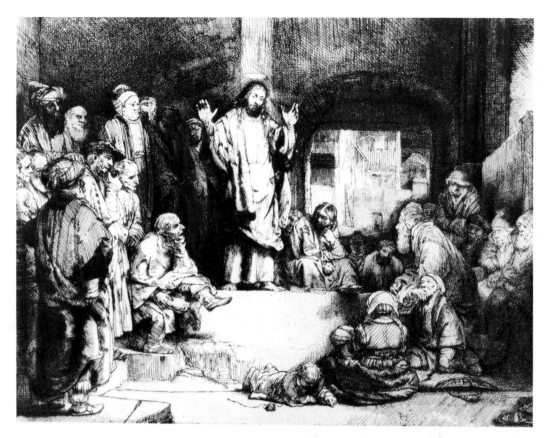

785. REMBRANDT. *CHRIST PREACHING.* c. 1652. Etching, 6⅛×8⅛″ (15.6×20.6 cm).
The Metropolitan Museum of Art, New York. Bequest of Mrs. H. O. Havemeyer, 1929

786. REMBRANDT. *SELF-PORTRAIT.* 1658.
Oil on canvas, 52⅝×40⅞ (133.6×103.8 cm).
The Frick Collection, New York (Copyright)

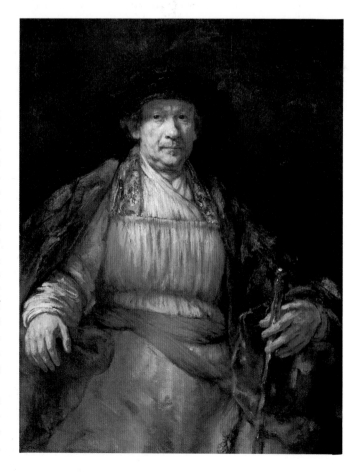

tant people in Amsterdam continued to be his steadfast friends and supporters, and he received some major public commissions in the 1650s and 1660s; his financial difficulties resulted largely from poor management. Still, the 1640s were a period of crisis, of inner uncertainty and external troubles. Rembrandt's outlook changed profoundly: after about 1650, his style eschews the rhetoric of the High Baroque for lyric subtlety and pictorial breadth. Some exotic trappings from the earlier years remain, but they no longer create an alien, barbarous world. Rembrandt's etchings from these years, such as *Christ Preaching* (fig. 785), show this new depth of feeling. The sensuous beauty seen in *The Blinding of Samson* has now yielded to a humble world of bare feet and ragged clothes. The scene is full of the artist's deep feeling of compassion for the poor and outcast who make up Christ's audience. Rembrandt had a special sympathy for the Jews, as the heirs of the biblical past and as the patient victims of persecution; they were often his models. This print, like the sketch in figure 8, strongly suggests some corner in the Amsterdam ghetto, and surely incorporates observations of life from the drawings he habitually made throughout his career. Here it is the magic of light that en-

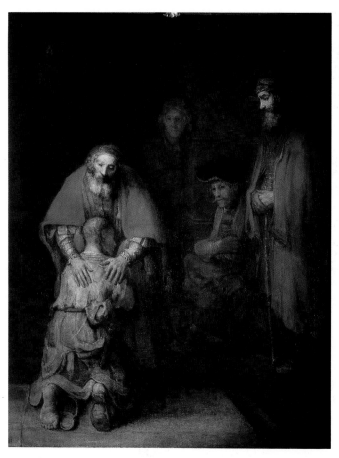

787. REMBRANDT. *THE RETURN OF THE PRODIGAL SON.*
c. 1665. Oil on canvas, 8'8"×6'7¾" (2.6×2.1 m).
Hermitage Museum, Leningrad

788. JAN VAN GOYEN. *FORT ON A RIVER.* 1644.
Panel, 16¾×29¾" (42.6×75.6 cm).
Museum of Fine Arts, Boston

dows *Christ Preaching* with spiritual significance. Rembrandt's importance as a graphic artist is second only to Dürer's, although we get no more than a hint from this single example.

In the many self-portraits Rembrandt painted over his long career, his view of himself reflects every stage of his inner development—experimental in the early Leyden years; theatrically disguised in the 1630s; frank toward the end of his life, as in our example (fig. 786). While partially indebted to Titian's sumptuous portraits (compare fig. 678), Rembrandt scrutinizes himself with the same typically Northern candor found in Jan van Eyck's *Man in a Red Turban* (see fig. 552).

This self-analytical approach helps to account for the simple dignity we see in the religious scenes that play so large a part in Rembrandt's work toward the end of his life. *The Return of the Prodigal Son* (fig. 787), painted a few years before his death, is perhaps Rembrandt's most moving picture. It is also his quietest—a moment stretching into eternity. So pervasive is the mood of tender silence that the beholder senses a spontaneous kinship with this group—our bond of shared experience is perhaps stronger and more intimate here than in any earlier work of art..

LANDSCAPE AND STILL LIFE PAINTERS. Rembrandt's religious pictures demand an insight that was beyond the capacity of all but a few collectors. Most art buyers in Holland preferred subjects within their own experience—landscapes, architectural views, still lifes, everyday scenes. These various types, we recall, originated in the latter half of the sixteenth century (see page 542); as they became fully defined, an unheard-of specialization began. The trend was not confined to Holland. We find it everywhere to some degree, but Dutch painting was its fountainhead, in both volume and variety. There were, in fact, so many subtypes within each major division mentioned above that we can illustrate only a small sampling. *Fort on a River* (fig. 788) by Jan van Goyen (1596–1656) is a new kind of landscape that enjoyed great popularity because its elements were so familiar; the distant town

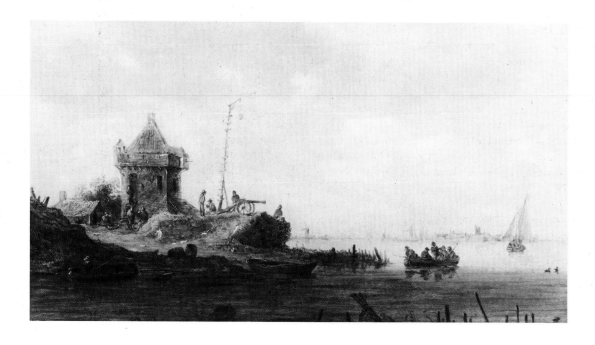

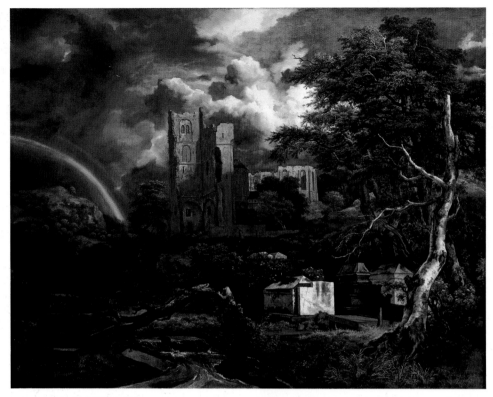

789. JACOB VAN RUISDAEL. *THE JEWISH CEMETERY.* 1655–60. Oil on canvas, 4'6"×6'2½" (1.42×1.89 m).
© The Detroit Institute of Arts, Detroit. Gift of Julius H. Haass in memory of his brother Dr. Ernest W. Haass

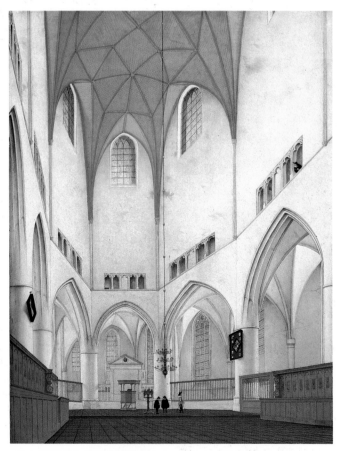

790. PIETER SAENREDAM. *INTERIOR OF THE CHOIR OF ST. BAVO'S*
CHURCH AT HAARLEM. 1660. Oil on panel, 27⅞×21⅝" (70.4×54.8 cm).
Worcester Art Museum, Worcester, Massachusetts.
Charlotte E. W. Buffington Fund

under a looming gray sky, seen through a moisture-laden atmosphere across an expanse of water—this view is still characteristic of the Dutch countryside today. No one knew better than Van Goyen how to evoke the special mood of these "nether lands," ever threatened by the sea.

Natural forces also dominate in *The Jewish Cemetery* (fig. 789) by Jacob van Ruisdael (1628/29–1682), the greatest Dutch landscape painter. The scene is frankly imaginary: the thunderclouds passing over a wild, deserted mountain valley, the medieval ruin, the torrent that has forced its way between ancient graves, all create a mood of deep melancholy. Nothing endures on this earth, the artist tells us—time, wind, and water grind all to dust, the feeble works of human hands as well as the trees and rocks. Ruisdael's vision of nature in relation to civilization is thus the exact opposite of Annibale Carracci's (compare fig. 746): it inspires that awe on which the Romantics, a century later, were to base their concept of the Sublime.

Nothing at first seems further removed from *The Jewish Cemetery* than the painstakingly precise *Interior of the Choir of St. Bavo's Church at Haarlem* (fig. 790), painted by Pieter Saenredam at exactly the same time. Yet it, too, is meant to invite meditation, rather than serve merely as a topographic record (these views were often freely invented). The medieval structure, stripped of all furnishings and whitewashed under Protestant auspices, is no longer a house of worship. It has become a place for the dead (note the tomb slabs in the floor), and in its crystalline spaciousness we feel the silence of a graveyard. Again we are reminded that all is Vanity.

Even still life can be tinged with this melancholy sense of the passing of all earthly pleasures; the message may lie in such established symbols as death's-heads and extinguished candles, or be conveyed by means less direct. Willem Claesz. Heda's *Still Life* (fig. 791) belongs to a widespread type, the "breakfast piece," showing the remnants of a meal. Food and drink are less emphasized than luxury objects—

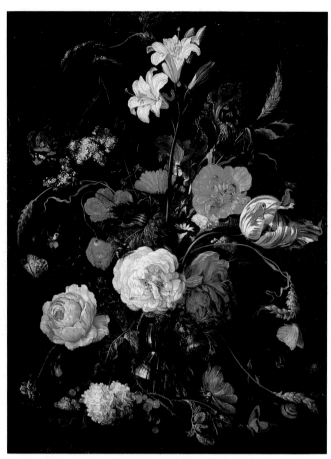

792. JAN DAVIDSZ. DE HEEM. *FLOWER STILL LIFE.*
c. 1665. Oil on canvas, 21¼×16½" (54×42 cm).
The Ashmolean Museum, Oxford.
Bequeathed by Daisy Linda Ward

crystal goblets and silver dishes—carefully juxtaposed for their contrasting shape, color, and texture.

How different this seems from the piled-up edibles of Aertsen's *The Meat Stall* (see fig. 726)! But virtuosity was not Heda's only aim: his "story," the human context of these grouped objects, is suggested by the broken glass, the half-peeled lemon, the overturned silver dish; whoever sat at this table has been suddenly forced to abandon the meal. The curtain that time has lowered on the scene, as it were, invests the objects with a strange pathos. The disguised symbolism of "Late Gothic" painting lives on here in a new form.

Other types of still life, such as flower pieces, can be traced directly to their symbolic origins. How much of the older meaning survives in these examples is still being debated. Was Jan Davidsz. de Heem, the artist of the beautiful flower piece in figure 792, aware of the significance of each blossom, and of the butterflies, moths, and snails he put into the picture, and did he assemble his bouquet to this end? Or was he content to make it a feast for the eyes? Whatever the impulses were, these flowers have such Baroque vitality that they fairly leap from their vase.

STEEN. The vast class of pictures termed genre is as varied as that of landscapes and still lifes: it ranges from tavern

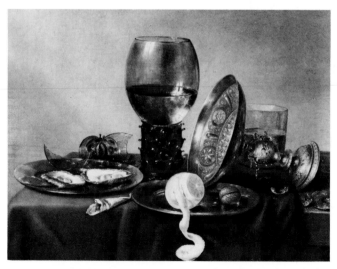

791. WILLEM CLAESZ. HEDA. *STILL LIFE.* 1634.
Oil on panel, 16⅞×22⅞" (43×57 cm).
Boymans-van Beuningen Museum, Rotterdam

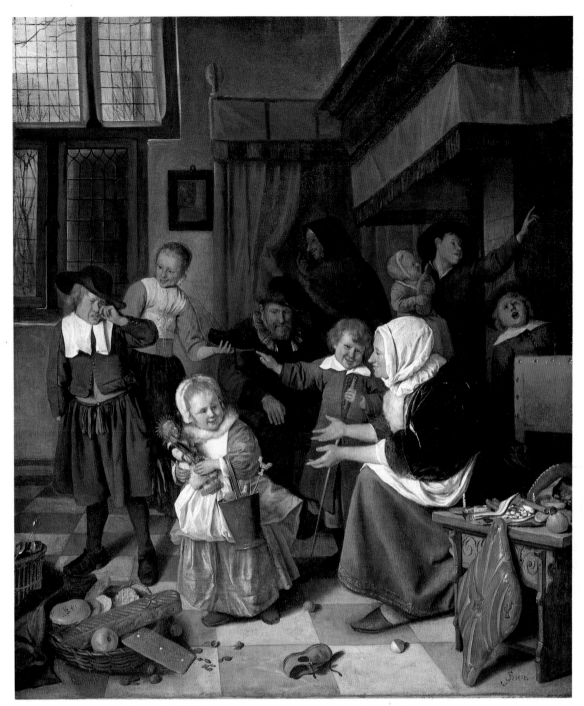

793. JAN STEEN. *THE FEAST OF ST. NICHOLAS.* c. 1660–65. Oil on canvas,
32¼×27¾″ (82×70.5 cm). Rijksmuseum, Amsterdam

brawls to refined domestic interiors. *The Feast of St. Nicholas* (fig. 793) by Jan Steen (1625/26–1679) is midway between: St. Nicholas has just paid his pre-Christmas visit to the household, leaving toys, candy, and cake for the children. Everybody is jolly except the bad boy on the left, who has received only a birch rod. Steen tells this story with relish, embroidering it with many delightful details. Of all the Dutch painters of daily life, he was the sharpest, and the most good-humored, observer. To supplement his earnings he kept an inn, which perhaps explains his keen insight into human behavior. His sense of timing and his characterization often

remind us of Frans Hals (compare fig. 780), while his story-telling stems from the tradition of Pieter Bruegel the Elder (compare fig. 728).

VERMEER. In the genre scenes of Jan Vermeer, by contrast, there is hardly any narrative. Single figures, usually women, engage in simple, everyday tasks (see fig. 25); when there are two, as in *The Letter* (fig. 794), they do no more than exchange glances. They exist in a timeless "still life" world, seemingly calmed by some magic spell. The cool, clear light that filters in from the left is the only active element, working

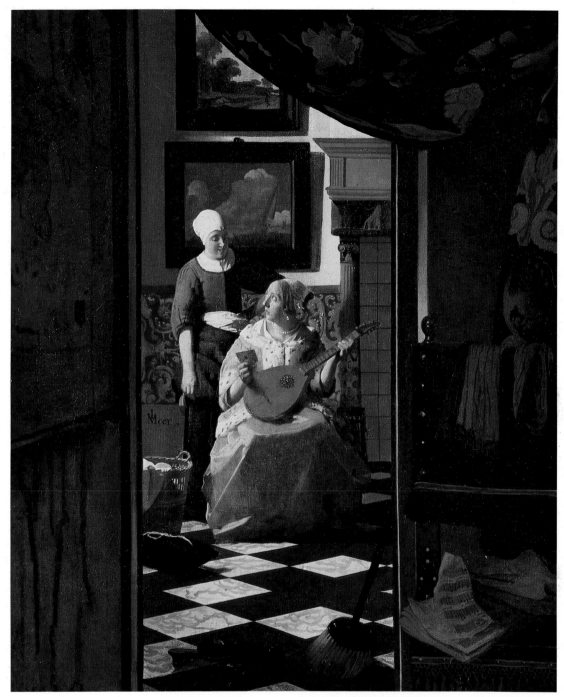

794. JAN VERMEER. *THE LETTER*. 1666. Oil on canvas,
17¼×15¼″ (43.3×38.3 cm). Rijksmuseum, Amsterdam

its miracles upon all the objects in its path. As we look at *The Letter*, we feel as if a veil had been pulled from our eyes; the everyday world shines with jewellike freshness, beautiful as we have never seen it before. No painter since Jan Van Eyck *saw* as intensely as this.

But Vermeer, unlike his predecessors, perceives reality as a mosaic of colored surfaces—or perhaps more accurately, he translates reality into a mosaic as he puts it on canvas. We see *The Letter* as a perspective "window," but also as a plane, a "field" composed of smaller fields. Rectangles predominate, carefully aligned with the picture surface, and there are no "holes," no undefined empty spaces. These interlocking shapes give to Vermeer's work a uniquely modern quality within seventeenth-century art. How did he acquire it? We know very little about him except that he was born in Delft in 1632 and lived and worked there until his death at forty-three, in 1675. Some of his works show the influence of Carel Fabritius, the most brilliant of Rembrandt's pupils; other pictures suggest his contact with the Utrecht School. But none of this really explains the genesis of his style, so daringly original that his genius was not recognized until about a century ago.

SPAIN

Painting

Spain is the last country to be surveyed in this chapter, for Spanish Baroque painting cannot be fully understood without some knowledge of artistic events in Italy and the Netherlands. During the sixteenth century, at the height of its political and economic power, Spain had produced great saints and writers, but no artists of the first rank. Nor did El Greco's presence prove a stimulus to native talent. The stimulus came, rather, from Caravaggio (though we do not know exactly how it was transmitted) and Flemish painting. Soon after Aertsen and his contemporaries in the Netherlands established the field of still life, Spanish masters began to develop their own versions.

SANCHEZ COTÁN. In the example by Juan Sanchez Cotán (1561–1627), who was an early and remarkable Spanish painter of still lifes (fig. 795), we see the distinctive character of this tradition. In contrast to the lavish display of food or luxury objects in Northern pictures, we here find an order and an austere simplicity that give a new context to these vegetables. They are so deliberately arranged that we cannot help wondering what symbolic significance the artist meant to convey. In any case, the juxtaposition of bright sunlight and impenetrable darkness, of painstaking realism and abstract form, creates a memorable image.

ZURBARÁN. Sanchez Cotán's still lifes make one think of the style of Caravaggio, whose influence was certainly felt by the second decade of the century, especially in Seville, the home of the most important Spanish Baroque painters. Among them, Francisco de Zurbarán (1598–1664) stands out for the quiet intensity of his devotional pictures, such as

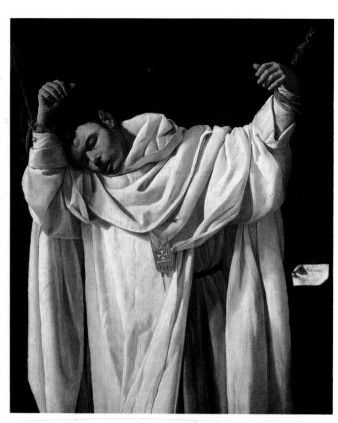

796. FRANCISCO DE ZURBARÁN. *ST. SERAPION.* 1628.
Oil on canvas, 47½×41″ (120.7×104.1 cm).
Wadsworth Atheneum, Hartford, Connecticut.
Ella Gallup Sumner and Mary Catlin Sumner Collection

St. Serapion (fig. 796). Although Caravaggesque in style, it is filled with an ascetic piety that is uniquely Spanish, and the very absence of rhetorical pathos makes this image of a martyred monk profoundly moving.

VELÁZQUEZ. Likewise, Diego Velázquez (1599–1660) painted in a Caravaggesque vein during his early years, but his interests centered on genre and still life rather than religious themes. *The Water Carrier of Seville* (fig. 797), which he did at the age of twenty, already shows his genius: his powerful grasp of individual character and dignity invests this everyday scene with the solemn spirit of a ritual. A few years later, Velázquez was appointed court painter and moved to Madrid, where he spent the rest of his life, doing mainly portraits of the royal family. The earlier of these still show the precise division of light and shade and the clear outlines of his Seville period, but after the late 1620s his work acquired a new fluency and richness.

Meanwhile he had become a friend of Rubens, who probably helped him to discover the beauty of the many Titians in the king's collection, but did not influence him directly. He also traveled in Italy, where in 1650 he painted the magnificent portrait of Pope Innocent X (fig. 798). The picture is meant to evoke the great tradition of the papal portraits of Raphael (compare fig. 674), but its fluid brushwork and glowing color derive from Titian. And the sitter's gaze, sharply focused on the beholder, conveys a passionate and powerful personality.

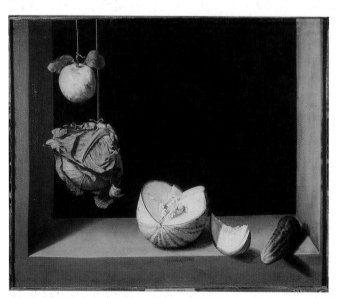

795. JUAN SANCHEZ COTÁN. *QUINCE, CABBAGE,*
MELON, AND CUCUMBER. c. 1602. Oil on canvas,
27⅛×33¼″ (68.8×84.4 cm). San Diego Museum of Art.
Gift of Misses Anne R. and Amy Putnam

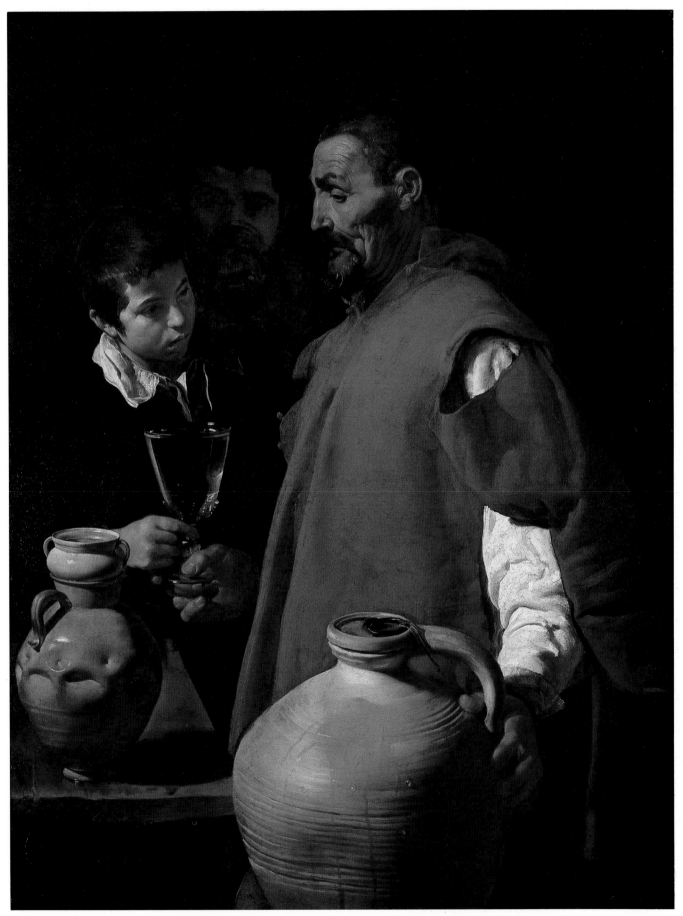

797. DIEGO VELÁZQUEZ. *THE WATER CARRIER OF SEVILLE*. c. 1619. Oil on canvas,
41½×31½″ (105.3×80 cm). Wellington Museum, London (Crown copyright reserved)

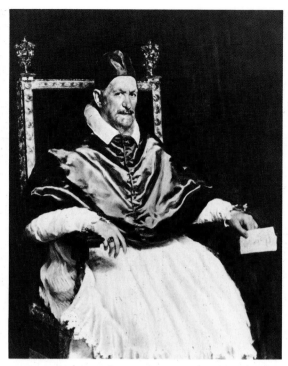

798. DIEGO VELÁZQUEZ. *POPE INNOCENT X.* 1650.
Oil on canvas, 55×45¼″ (139.7×115 cm).
Galleria Doria Pamphili, Rome

The Maids of Honor (fig. 799) displays Velázquez' mature style at its fullest, at once a group portrait and a genre scene. It might be subtitled "the artist in his studio," for Velázquez shows himself at work on a huge canvas; in the center is the little Princess Margarita, who has just posed for him, among her playmates and maids of honor. The faces of her parents, the king and queen, appear in the mirror on the back wall. Have they just stepped into the room, to see the scene exactly as we do, or does the mirror reflect part of the canvas—presumably a full-length portrait of the royal family—on which the artist has been working? This ambiguity is characteristic of Velázquez' fascination with light. Unlike Rembrandt, he was concerned with its optical rather than its metaphysical mysteries, but these he penetrated more completely than any painter of his time except Vermeer.

The varieties of direct and reflected light in *The Maids of Honor* are almost limitless, and the artist challenges us to find them: we are expected to match the mirror image against the paintings on that wall, and against the "picture" of the man in the open doorway. Velázquez could not have known Vermeer's work, for the latter was then only twenty-four, but he may have known scenes of domestic genre by older Dutch painters. Looking at the open, sketchy brushwork in figure 799, we wonder if he could also have known Frans Hals (compare fig. 779). Yet Velázquez' technique is far more varied and subtle, with delicate glazes setting off the impasto of the highlights. The colors, too, have a Venetian richness unmatched by Hals. Nor does Velázquez seem interested in catching time on the wing; his aim is not to show figures in motion, but the movement of light itself and the infinite range of its effects on form and color. For Velázquez, light *creates* the visible world. Not until two centuries later shall we meet painters capable of realizing the implications of this discovery.

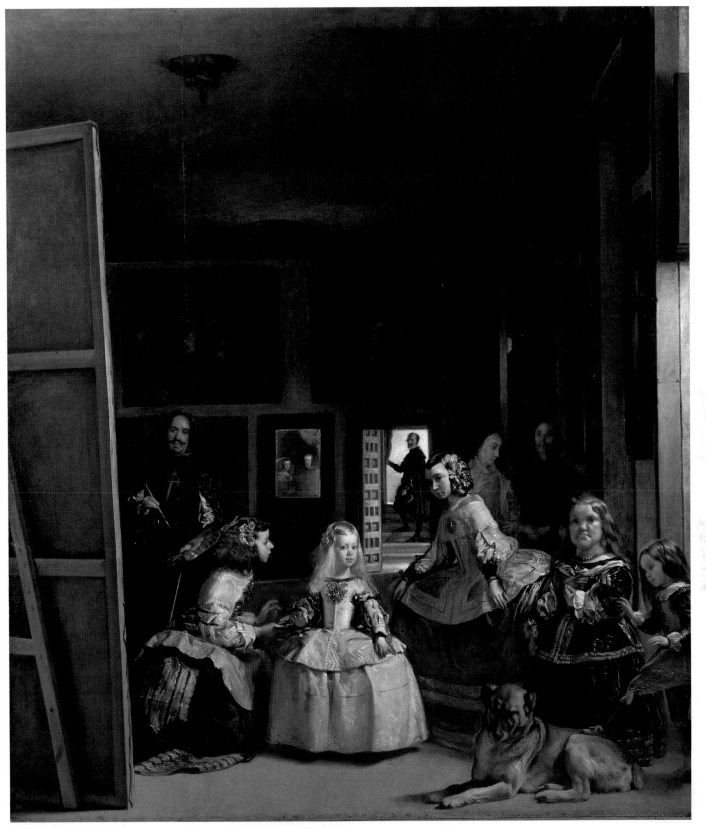

799. DIEGO VELÁZQUEZ. *THE MAIDS OF HONOR*. 1656.
Oil on canvas, 10'5"×9' (3.2×2.7 m). Museo del Prado, Madrid

CHAPTER EIGHT

THE BAROQUE AND ROCOCO IN FRANCE AND ENGLAND

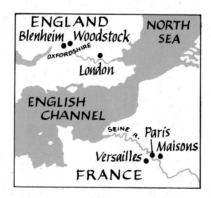

FRANCE

Painting

Under Louis XIV, France became the most powerful nation of Europe, militarily and culturally; by the late seventeenth century, Paris was vying with Rome as the world capital of the major and minor arts—a position it had held for centuries. How did this amazing change come about? Because of the Palace of Versailles and other vast projects glorifying the king of France, we are tempted to think of French art in the age of Louis XIV as the expression—and one of the products—of absolutism. This is true of the climactic phase of Louis' reign, 1660–85, but by that time French seventeenth-century art already had its distinctive style. The French are reluctant to call this style Baroque; to them, it is the Style of Louis XIV; often they also describe the art and literature of the period as "classic."

The term "classic," so used, has three meanings: as a synonym for "highest achievement," it implies that the Style of Louis XIV corresponds to the High Renaissance in Italy, or the age of Pericles in ancient Greece; the term also refers to the emulation of the form and subject matter of classical antiquity; finally, "classic" suggests qualities of balance and restraint, like those of the classic styles of the High Renaissance and of ancient art. The second and third of these meanings describe what could be called, more accurately, "classicism." And since the Style of Louis XIV reflects Italian Baroque art, however modified, we must label it "classicistic Baroque" or "Baroque classicism."

This classicism was the official court style by 1660–85, but its origin was not political. It sprang, rather, from the persistent tradition of sixteenth-century art, which in France was more intimately linked with the Italian Renaissance than in any other northern country (page 525). Classicism was also nourished by French humanism, with its intellectual heritage of reason and Stoic virtue. These factors retarded the spread of the Baroque in France, and modified its interpretation. Rubens' Medici Cycle, for example, had no effect on French art until the very end of the century (see fig. 774); in the 1620s, the young painters in France were still assimilating the Early Baroque.

DE LA TOUR. Some of these painters were oriented toward Caravaggio, and they developed astonishingly original styles; the importance of one of these artists, Georges de La Tour (1593–1652), was recognized comparatively late. His *Joseph the Carpenter* (fig. 800) might be mistaken for a genre scene, yet its devotional spirit has the power of Caravaggio's *The Calling of St. Matthew* (see fig. 739). The boy Jesus holds a candle—a favorite device with La Tour—which lights the scene with an intimacy and tenderness reminiscent of

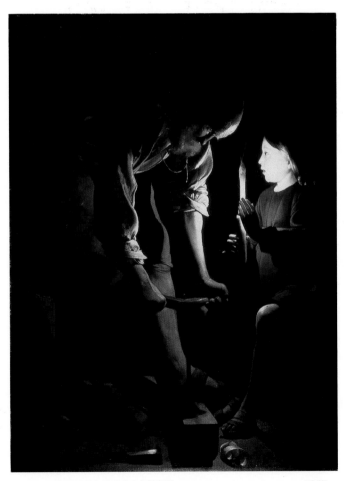

800. GEORGES DE LA TOUR. *JOSEPH THE CARPENTER*. c. 1645.
Oil on canvas, 51⅛×39¾″ (130×100 cm). Musée du Louvre, Paris

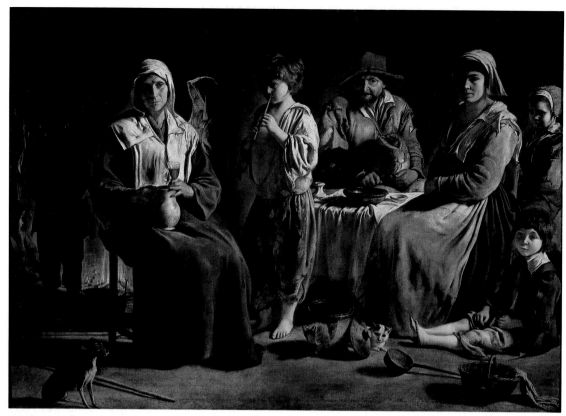

801. LOUIS LE NAIN. *PEASANT FAMILY.* c. 1640. Oil on canvas, 44½×62½″ (113×158.7 cm). Musée du Louvre, Paris

Geertgen tot Sint Jans (compare fig. 558). Strangely enough, La Tour also shares Geertgen's tendency to reduce his forms to geometric simplicity.

LE NAIN. The *Peasant Family* (fig. 801) by Louis Le Nain (1593–1648) is equally impressive. Like the peasant pictures of seventeenth-century Holland and Flanders, it stems from a tradition going back to Pieter Bruegel the Elder (see fig. 728). But the Netherlandish scenes of low life are humorous or satirical (see fig. 780), whereas Le Nain endows them with a human dignity and monumental weight that recall Velázquez' *The Water Carrier of Seville* (see fig. 797). Like Georges de La Tour, Louis Le Nain was also rediscovered in modern times, but he did not have to wait quite so long.

POUSSIN. Why were these important painters so quickly forgotten? The reason is simple: the clarity, balance, and restraint of their art, when measured against other Caravagesque painters, might be termed "classical," but neither was a "classicist"—and after the 1640s, classicism was supreme in France. The artist who did most to bring this about was Nicolas Poussin (1593/94–1665). The greatest French painter of the century, and the earliest French painter in history to win international fame, Poussin nevertheless spent almost his entire career in Rome. His development also was somewhat paradoxical, as we see in figures 802 and 803: both works show his profound allegiance to antiquity, but in style and attitude they are much farther apart than the seven years' difference in date would suggest.

Cephalus and Aurora is inspired by Titian's warm, rich color and by his approach to classical mythology (compare fig. 676). Poussin, too, visualizes antiquity here as a poetic dream world, although the unalloyed bliss of Titian's *Bacchanal* is now overcast with melancholy (his favorite subjects are tales of frustrated love). By contrast, *The Rape of the Sabine Women* must be seen altogether differently. The strongly modeled figures are "frozen in action," like statues, and many are in fact derived from Hellenistic sculpture; behind them Poussin has set reconstructions of Roman architecture that he believed to be archaeologically correct. Emotion is abundantly displayed, yet it so lacks spontaneity that it fails to touch us. Clearly, the attitude here reflected is not Titian's but Raphael's—more precisely, that of Raphael as filtered through Annibale Carracci and his school (compare figs. 741 and 743). Venetian qualities have been consciously suppressed for the severe discipline of an intellectual style.

Poussin now strikes us as a man who knew his own mind only too well, an impression confirmed by the numerous letters in which he expounded his views to friends and patrons. The highest aim of painting, he believed, is to represent noble and serious human actions. These must be shown in a logical and orderly way—not as they really happened, but as they would have happened if nature were perfect. To this end, the artist must strive for the general and typical; appealing to the mind rather than the senses, he should suppress such trivialities as glowing color, and stress form and composition. In a good picture, the beholder must be able to "read" the exact emotions of each figure, and relate them to

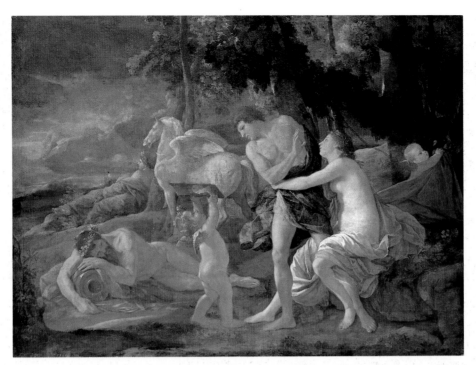

802. NICOLAS POUSSIN. *CEPHALUS AND AURORA*. c. 1630. Oil on canvas, 38×51″ (96.7×129.7 cm).
The National Gallery, London. Reproduced by courtesy of the Trustees

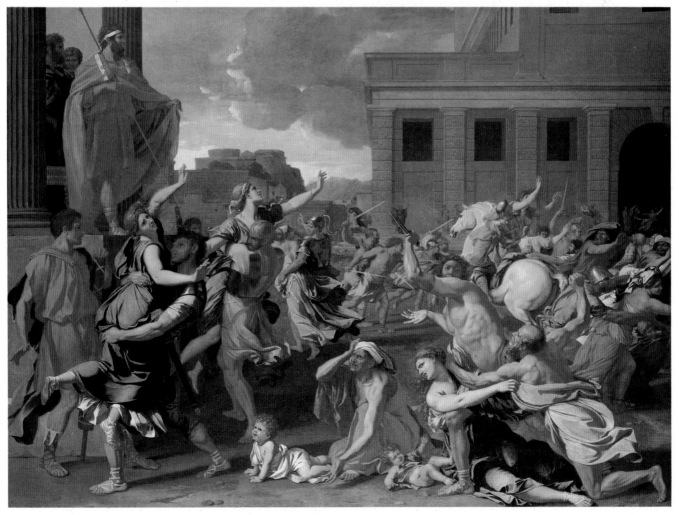

803. NICOLAS POUSSIN. *THE RAPE OF THE SABINE WOMEN*. c. 1636–37. Oil on canvas, 60⅞×82⅝″ (154.4×209.8 cm).
The Metropolitan Museum of Art, New York. Harris Brisbane Dick Fund, 1946

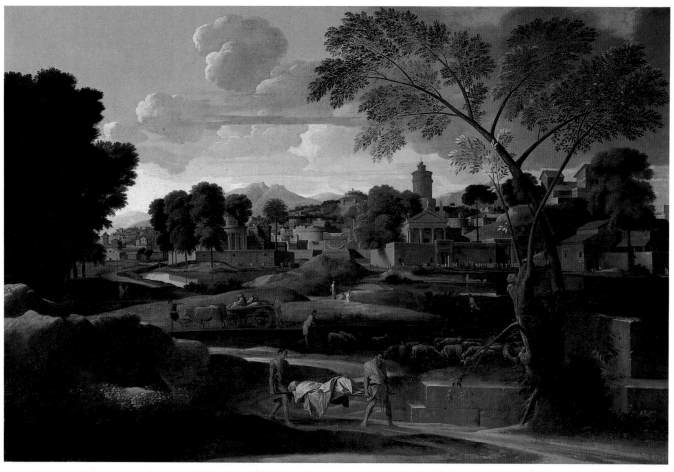

804. NICOLAS POUSSIN. *LANDSCAPE WITH THE BURIAL OF PHOCION.* 1648.
Oil on canvas, 47×70½″ (119.7×179 cm). Musée du Louvre, Paris.

the given event. These ideas were not new—we recall Leonardo's statement that the highest aim of painting is to depict "the intention of man's soul" and the ancient dictum *ut pictura poesis* (see pages 423 and 491)—but before Poussin, no one made the analogy between painting and literature so close, nor put it into practice so single-mindedly. His method accounts for the cold and over-explicit rhetoric in *The Rape of the Sabine Women* that makes the picture so much less accessible to us than his earlier *Cephalus and Aurora.*

Poussin even painted landscapes according to this theoretical view, with surprisingly impressive results. The *Landscape with the Burial of Phocion* (fig. 804) follows the tradition of Annibale Carracci's "ideal landscapes" (see fig. 746), but the careful order of its spaces is almost mathematically precise. Yet the effect of rational clarity has a somber calm as pervasive as the lyricism of Annibale's countryside. This mood is attuned to Poussin's theme, the burial of a Greek hero who died because he refused to conceal the truth: the landscape becomes itself a memorial to Stoic virtue. Although we may no longer read the scene so specifically, we still respond to its austere beauty.

CLAUDE LORRAINE. If Poussin developed the heroic qualities of the "ideal landscape," the great French landscapist

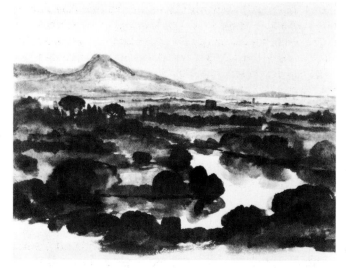

805. CLAUDE LORRAINE. *TIBER FROM MONTE MARIO.* c. 1650.
Brown wash drawing on paper, 7⅜×10½″ (18.5×26.8 cm).
British Museum, London. Bequested by Richard Payne Knight, 1824

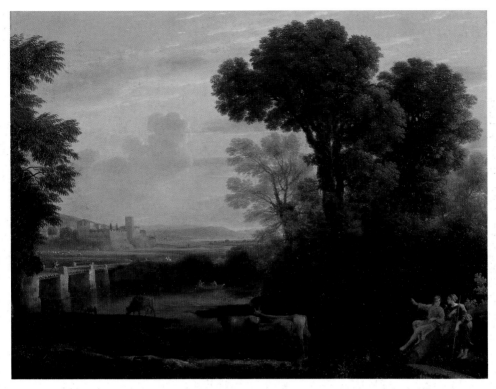

806. CLAUDE LORRAINE. *A PASTORAL LANDSCAPE*. c. 1650.
Oil on copper, 15½×21″ (39.3×53.3 cm).
Yale University Art Gallery, New Haven, Connecticut. Leo C. Hanna, Jr., Fund

Claude Lorraine (1600–1682) brought out its idyllic aspects. He, too, spent almost his entire career in Rome and explored the country nearby—the Campagna—more thoroughly and affectionately than any Italian. Countless drawings made on the spot, such as the miraculously fresh and sensitive example in figure 805, bear witness to his extraordinary powers of observation. These sketches, however, were only the raw material for his paintings, which do not aim at topographic exactitude but evoke the poetic essence of a countryside filled with echoes of antiquity. Often, as in *A Pastoral Landscape* (fig. 806), the compositions are suffused with the hazy, luminous atmosphere of early morning or late afternoon; the space expands serenely, rather than receding step-by-step as in Poussin's landscapes. An air of nostalgia hangs over such vistas, of past experience gilded by memory; hence they appealed especially to Northerners who had seen Italy only briefly—or, perhaps, not at all.

Architecture

MANSART. In France itself, meanwhile, the foundations of Baroque classicism in architecture were laid by a group of designers whose most distinguished member was François Mansart (1598–1666). Apparently he never visited Italy, but other French architects had already imported and acclimatized some aspects of the Roman Early Baroque, especially in church design, so that Mansart was not unfamiliar with the new Italian style. What he owed to it, however, is hard to determine; his most important buildings are châteaux, and in this field the French Renaissance tradition outweighed

any direct Italian Baroque influences. The Château of Maisons near Paris, built for a newly risen administrative official, shows Mansart's mature style at its best. The vestibule leading to the grand staircase (fig. 807) has a particularly beautiful effect, severe yet festive. On seeing the classically pure articulation of the walls, one first thinks of Palladio, whose treatise Mansart certainly knew and admired. But sculpture is used here in the characteristically French way, as an integral part of architectural design; and the complex curves of the vaulting tell us that this structure, for all its classicism, belongs to the Baroque.

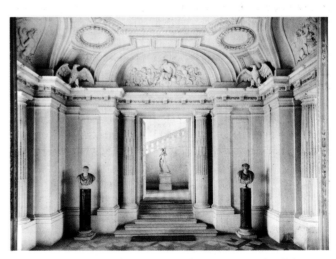

807. FRANÇOIS MANSART.
Vestibule, Château of Maisons. 1642–50

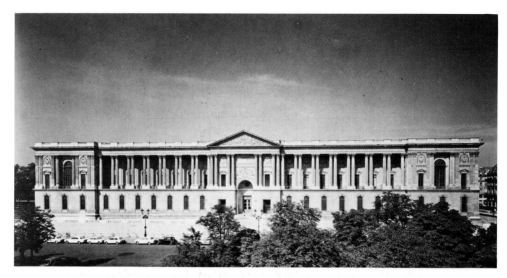

808. CLAUDE PERRAULT. East Front of the Louvre, Paris. 1667–70

LOUIS XIV, COLBERT, AND THE LOUVRE. Mansart died too soon to have a share in the climactic phase of Baroque classicism, which began not long after young Louis XIV took over the reins of government in 1661. Jean-Baptiste Colbert, the king's chief adviser, built the administrative apparatus supporting the power of the absolute monarch. In this system, aimed at subjecting the thoughts and actions of the entire nation to strict control from above, the visual arts had the task of glorifying the king, and the official "royal style," in both theory and practice, was classicism. That this choice was deliberate we know from the history of the first great project Colbert directed, the completion of the Louvre. Work on the palace had proceeded intermittently for over a century, along the lines of Lescot's design (see fig. 733); what remained to be done was to close the square court on the east side with an impressive façade.

Colbert, dissatisfied with the proposals of French architects, invited Bernini to Paris, hoping the most famous master of the Roman Baroque would do for the French king what he had already done so magnificently for the Church. Bernini spent several months in Paris in 1665 and submitted three designs, all on a scale that would completely engulf the extant palace. After much argument and intrigue, Louis XIV rejected these plans, and turned over the problem of a final solution to a committee of three: Louis Le Vau, his court architect, who had worked on the project before; Charles Lebrun, his court painter; and Claude Perrault, who was a student of ancient architecture, not a professional architect. All three were responsible for the structure that was actually built (fig. 808), although Perrault is usually credited with the major share.

The design in some ways suggests the mind of an archaeologist, but one who knew how to select those features of classical architecture that would link Louis XIV with the glory of the Caesars and yet be compatible with the older parts of the palace. The center pavilion is a Roman temple front, and the wings look like the flanks of that temple folded outward. The temple theme demanded a single order of freestanding columns, yet the Louvre had three stories—a dif-

ficulty skillfully resolved by treating the ground story as the podium of the temple, and recessing the upper two behind the screen of the colonnade. The entire design combines grandeur and elegance in a way that fully justifies its fame.

The East Front of the Louvre signaled the victory of French classicism over Italian Baroque as the "royal style." Ironically, this great exemplar proved too pure, and Perrault soon faded from the architectural scene.

PALACE OF VERSAILLES. Baroque features, although not officially acknowledged, reappeared in the king's vastest enterprise, the Palace of Versailles. This shift corresponded to the king's own taste. Louis XIV was interested less in architectural theory and monumental exteriors than in the lavish interiors that would make suitable settings for himself and his court. Thus the man to whom he really listened was not an architect, but the painter Lebrun (1619–1690), who became supervisor of all the king's artistic projects. As chief dispenser of royal art patronage, he commanded so much power that for all practical purposes he was the dictator of the arts in France. Lebrun had spent several years studying under Poussin in Rome. But the great decorative schemes of the Roman Baroque must also have impressed him, for they stood him in good stead twenty years later, both in the Louvre and at Versailles. He became a superb decorator, utilizing the combined labors of architects, sculptors, painters, and craftsmen for ensembles of unheard-of splendor, such as the Salon de la Guerre at Versailles (fig. 809).

To subordinate all the arts to a single goal—here, the glorification of Louis XIV—was in itself Baroque; if he went less far than Bernini, Lebrun nevertheless drew freely on his memories of Rome. The Salon de la Guerre seems in many ways closer to the Cornaro Chapel than to the vestibule at Maisons (compare figs. 751 and 807). And, as in so many Italian Baroque interiors, the separate ingredients are less impressive than the effect of the whole.

The Palace of Versailles, just over eleven miles from the center of Paris, was begun in 1669 by Le Vau, who designed the elevation of the Garden Front (fig. 810). He died within

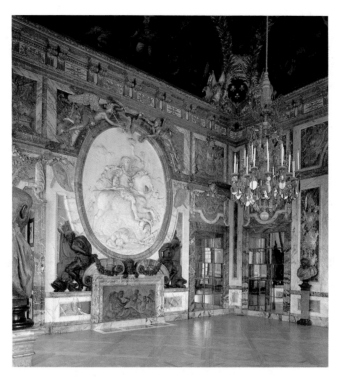

809. HARDOUIN-MANSART, LEBRUN, and COYSEVOX.
Salon de la Guerre, Palace of Versailles. Begun 1678

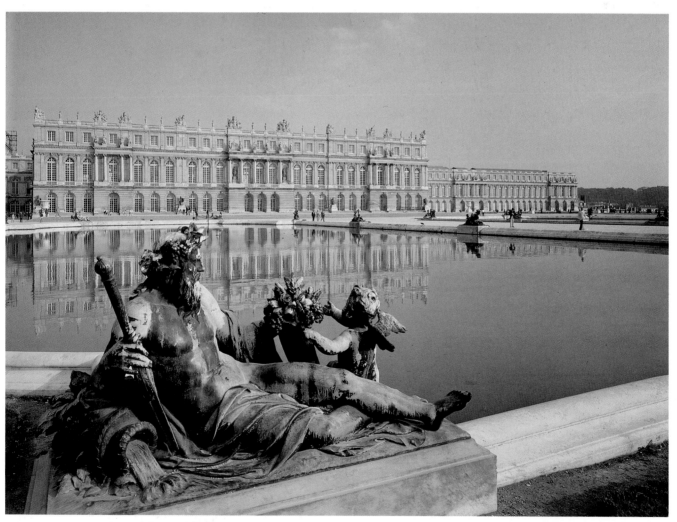

810. LOUIS LE VAU and JULES HARDOUIN-MANSART. Garden Front, center block, Palace of Versailles. 1669–85

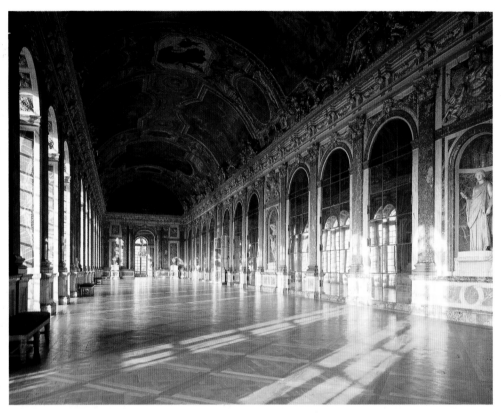

811. HARDOUIN-MANSART, LEBRUN, and COYSEVOX. Galerie des Glaces (Hall of Mirrors), Palace of Versailles

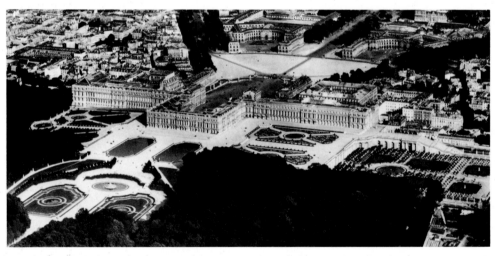

812. Aerial view, Palace of Versailles

a year, and the entire project, under Jules Hardouin-Mansart (1646–1708), a great-nephew of François Mansart (see page 591), was vastly expanded to accommodate the ever-growing royal household. The Garden Front, intended by Le Vau to be the principal view of the palace, was stretched to an enormous length with no modification of the architectural membering; the original façade design, a less severe variant of the East Front of the Louvre, now looks repetitious and out of scale. The whole center block contains a single room, the famous Galerie des Glaces (Hall of Mirrors, fig. 811), with the Salon de la Guerre (War) and its counterpart, the Salon de la Paix (Peace), at either end.

GARDENS OF VERSAILLES. Apart from the magnificent interior, the most impressive aspect of Versailles is the park extending west of the Garden Front for several miles (the aerial view in figure 812 shows only a small part of it). Its design, by André Le Nôtre (1613–1700), is so strictly correlated with the plan of the palace that it becomes a continuation of the architectural space. Like the interiors, these formal gardens, with their terraces, basins, clipped hedges, and statuary, were meant to provide an appropriate setting for the king's appearances in public. They form a series of "outdoor rooms" for the splendid fetes and spectacles that Louis XIV so enjoyed. The spirit of absolutism is even more

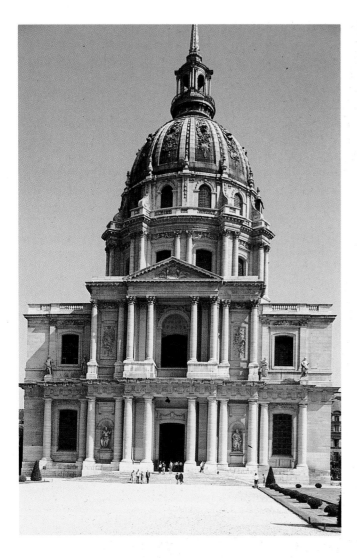

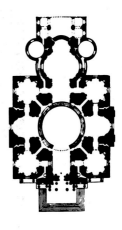

813. JULES HARDOUIN-MANSART
Church of the Invalides,
Paris. 1680–91

814. (*right*) Plan of the
Church of the Invalides

"pseudo-shell" with a large opening at the top, so that the heavenly glory seems mysteriously illuminated and suspended in space; "theatrical" lighting so boldly directed would do honor to any Italian Baroque architect.

Sculpture

The official "royal style" was attained in sculpture by a process much like that in architecture. Bernini, while in Paris, had carved a marble bust of Louis XIV, and had also been commissioned to do an equestrian statue of the king. This project, for which he made a splendid terracotta model (fig. 815), shared the fate of his Louvre designs. Although he portrayed the king in classical military garb, the statue was rejected; apparently it was too dynamic to safeguard the dignity of Louis XIV. This decision was far-reaching, for equestrian statues of the king were later erected throughout France as symbols of royal authority, and Bernini's design, had it succeeded, might have set the pattern for these monuments.

striking in this geometric regularity imposed upon an entire countryside than it is in the palace itself.

HARDOUIN-MANSART. At Versailles, Jules Hardouin-Mansart worked as a member of a team, constrained by the design of Le Vau. His own architectural style can be better seen in the Church of the Invalides (figs. 813 and 814), named after the institution for disabled soldiers of which it formed one part. The plan, consisting of a Greek cross with four corner chapels, is based ultimately—with various French intermediaries—on Michelangelo's plan for St. Peter's (see fig. 667); its only Baroque element is the oval choir. The dome, too, reflects the influence of Michelangelo (figs. 666 and 668), and the classicistic vocabulary of the façade is reminiscent of the East Front of the Louvre. Yet the exterior as a whole is unmistakably Baroque: the façade breaks forward repeatedly in the crescendo effect introduced by Maderno (see fig. 747); and façade and dome are closely correlated (see fig. 759). The dome itself is the most original, and the most Baroque, feature of Hardouin-Mansart's design; tall and slender, it rises in one continuous curve from the base of the drum to the spire atop the lantern. On the first drum rests, surprisingly, a second, narrower drum; its windows provide light for the painted vision of heavenly glory inside the dome, but they themselves are hidden behind a

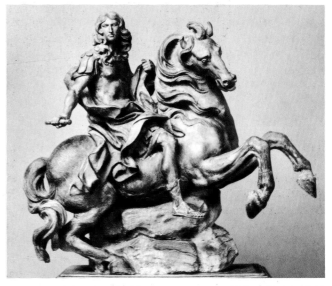

815. GIANLORENZO BERNINI. *MODEL FOR EQUESTRIAN STATUE OF LOUIS XIV.* 1670. Terracotta, height 30" (76.3 cm).
Galleria Borghese, Rome

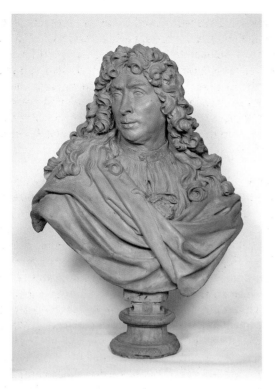

816. ANTOINE COYSEVOX. *CHARLES LEBRUN.* 1676.
Terracotta, height 26″ (66 cm). The Wallace Collection, London.
Reproduced by permission of the Trustees

COYSEVOX. Antoine Coysevox (1640–1720) was another sculptor employed by Lebrun at Versailles. In his large stucco relief in the Salon de la Guerre (see fig. 809), the victorious Louis XIV retains the pose of Bernini's equestrian statue. Coysevox's bust of Lebrun (fig. 816) repeats—again with a certain restraint—the general outlines of Bernini's bust of Louis XIV. The face, however, shows a realism and a subtlety of characterization that are Coysevox' own. He is the first of a long line of distinguished French portrait sculptors.

PUGET. Coysevox approached the Baroque in sculpture as closely as Lebrun would permit. Pierre-Paul Puget (1620–1694), the greatest and the most Baroque of French seventeenth-century sculptors, had no success at court until after Colbert's death, when the power of Lebrun was on the decline. *Milo of Crotona* (fig. 817), Puget's finest statue, may safely be compared to one by Bernini. Its composition is more contained than that of Bernini's *David* (see fig. 749), yet the agony of the hero has such force that its impact on the beholder is almost physical; the internal tension fills every particle of marble with intense life. The figure also recalls the *Laocoön Group* (see fig. 230). That, one suspects, is what made it acceptable to Louis XIV.

The Royal Academy

Centralized control over the visual arts was exerted by Colbert and Lebrun not only through the power of the purse; it also included a new system of educating artists in the officially approved style. Throughout antiquity and the Middle Ages, artists had been trained by apprenticeship, and this time-honored practice still prevailed in the Renaissance. But as painting, sculpture, and architecture gained the status of liberal arts, artists wished to supplement their "mechanical" training with theoretical knowledge. For this purpose, "art academies" were founded, patterned on the academies of the humanists (the name is derived from the Athenian grove where Plato met with his disciples). Art academies appeared first in Italy, in the later sixteenth century; they seem to have been private associations of artists who met periodically to draw from the model and discuss questions of art theory. These academies later became formal institutions that took over some functions from the guilds, but their teaching was limited and far from systematic.

Such was the Royal Academy of Painting and Sculpture in Paris, founded in 1648; when Lebrun became its director, in 1663, he established a rigid curriculum of compulsory instruction in practice and theory, based on a system of "rules"; this set the pattern for all later academies, including their modern successors, the art schools of today. Much of this body of doctrine was derived from Poussin's views (see pages

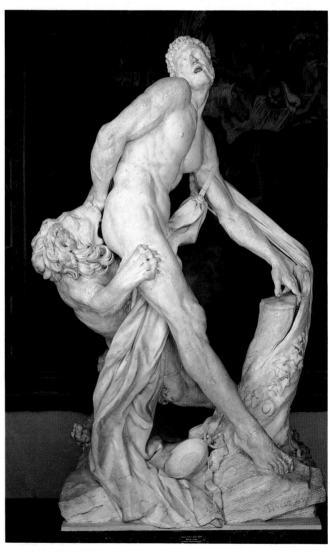

817. PIERRE PAUL PUGET. *MILO OF CROTONA.* 1671–83.
Marble, height 8′10½″ (2.7 m). Musée du Louvre, Paris

588–90) but carried to rationalistic extremes. The Academy even devised a method for tabulating, in numerical grades, the merits of artists past and present in such categories as drawing, expression, and proportion. The ancients received the highest marks, needless to say, then came Raphael and his school, and Poussin; the Venetians, who "overemphasized" color, ranked low, and the Flemish and Dutch lower still. Subjects were similarly classified, from history (classical or biblical) at the top to still life at the bottom.

"POUSSINISTES" VS. "RUBÉNISTES." It is hardly surprising that this straight-jacket system produced no significant artists. Even Lebrun, as we have seen, was far more Baroque in his practice than we would expect from his classicistic theory. The absurd rigidity of the official doctrine generated, moreover, a counterpressure that vented itself as soon as Lebrun's authority began to decline. Toward the end of the century, the members of the Academy formed two warring factions over the issue of drawing versus color: the conservatives (or "Poussinistes") against the "Rubénistes." The conservatives defended Poussin's view that drawing, which appealed to the mind, was superior to color, which appealed to the senses; the "Rubénistes" advocated color, rather than drawing, as being more true to nature. They also pointed out

that drawing, admittedly based on reason, appeals only to the expert few, whereas color appeals to everyone. This argument had revolutionary implications, for it proclaimed the layman to be the ultimate judge of artistic values, and challenged the Renaissance notion that painting, as a liberal art, could be appreciated only by the educated mind. By the time Louis XIV died, in 1715, the dictatorial powers of the Academy had been overcome, and the influence of Rubens and the great Venetians was everywhere.

WATTEAU. In 1717 the "Rubénistes" scored their final triumph when the painter Jean-Antoine Watteau (1684–1721) was admitted to the Academy with *A Pilgrimage to Cythera* (fig. 818). This picture violated all academic canons, and its subject did not conform to any established category. But the Academy, now very accommodating, invented for Watteau the new category of *fêtes galantes* (elegant fetes or entertainments). The term refers less to this one canvas than to the artist's work in general, which mainly shows scenes of elegant society, or comedy actors, in parklike settings. He characteristically interweaves theater and real life so that no clear distinction can be made between the two. *A Pilgrimage to Cythera* includes yet another element—classical mythology: these young couples have come to Cythera, the island of love,

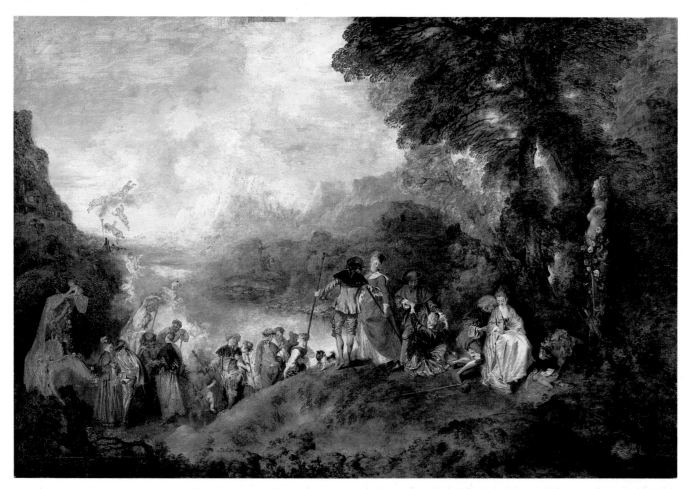

818. JEAN-ANTOINE WATTEAU. *A PILGRIMAGE TO CYTHERA*. 1717.
Oil on canvas, 4'3"×6'4½" (1.3×1.9 m). Musée du Louvre, Paris

forms Pierrot into Everyman, with whom he evidently identified himself. The face and pose have a poignancy that suggests a subtle sense of alienation. Like the rest of the actors, except the doctor on the donkey who looks mischievously at us, he seems lost in his own thoughts. Still, it is difficult to define his mood. Through the refined treatment of the features, the artist builds up an expression of elusive eloquence.

Rococo

The work of Watteau gives the signal for a shift in French art and society. After the death of Louis XIV, the centralized administrative machine that Colbert had created ground to a stop. The nobility, hitherto attached to the court at Versailles, were now freer of royal surveillance. Many of them chose not to return to their ancestral châteaux in the provinces, but to live instead in Paris, where they built elegant town houses, known as *hôtels*. Because these city sites were usually cramped and irregular, they offered scant opportunity for impressive exteriors; the layout and decor of the rooms became the architects' main concern. As state-sponsored building activity was declining, the field of "design for private living" took on a new importance. The *hôtels* demanded a style of interior decoration less grandiloquent and cumbersome than Lebrun's—an intimate, flexible style that would give greater scope to individual fancy uninhibited by classicistic dogma. French designers created the Rococo (or "the Style of Louis XV," as it is often called in France) in response to this need. The name fits well, although it was

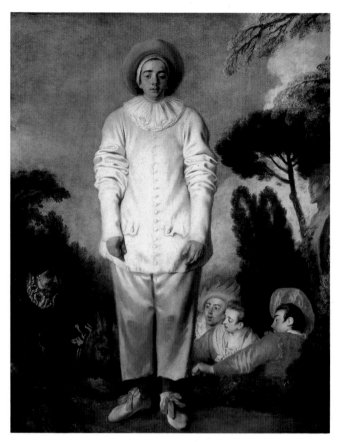

819. JEAN-ANTOINE WATTEAU. *GILLES AND FOUR OTHER CHARACTERS FROM THE COMMEDIA DELL'ARTE (PIERROT)*. c. 1719. Oil on canvas, 72½×58⅛″ (184×149 cm). Musée du Louvre, Paris

to pay homage to Venus (whose garlanded image appears on the far right). They are about to board the boat, accompanied by swarms of cupids.

The scene at once recalls Rubens' *The Garden of Love* (compare fig. 775), but Watteau has added a touch of poignancy, lending them a poetic subtlety reminiscent of Giorgione (see fig. 675). His figures, too, have not the robust vitality of Rubens'; slim and graceful, they move with the studied assurance of actors who play their roles so superbly that they touch us more than reality ever could. They recapture in Baroque form an earlier ideal of "mannered" elegance (compare figs. 544 and 725).

Watteau was separated from even his most faithful followers by an unbridgeable gulf in human understanding and artistic ability. Shortly before his death, Watteau painted perhaps his most moving work: *Pierrot* (fig. 819), known traditionally as *Gilles* after a similar character in the Italian *commedia dell' arte*. It was probably done as a sign for a café owned by a friend of the artist who retired from the stage after achieving fame in the racy role of the clown. The troupe's performance having ended, the actor has stepped forward to face the audience. The other characters all bear highly individualized likenesses, no doubt belonging to friends from the same circle. Yet the painting transcends portraiture and its purpose as an advertisement. Pierrot is lifesize, so that he confronts us as a full human being, not simply as a stock character. In the process, Watteau trans-

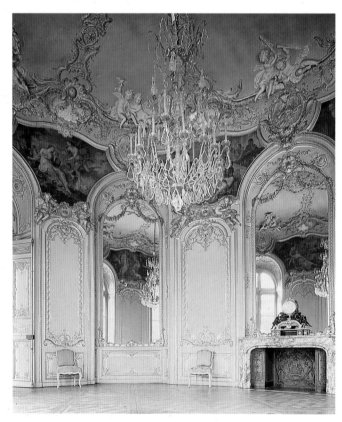

820. GERMAIN BOFFRAND. Salon de la Princesse, Hôtel de Soubise, Paris. Begun 1732

coined as a caricature of *rocaille* (echoing the Italian *barocco*), which meant the playful decoration of grottoes with irregular shells and stones. Rococo was a refinement in miniature of the curvilinear, "elastic" Baroque of Borromini and Guarini, and thus could be happily united with Austrian and German Late Baroque architecture (figs. 769 and 771).

BOFFRAND. Most French examples of the style, such as the Salon de la Princesse in the Hôtel de Soubise, by Germain Boffrand (fig. 820), are smaller in scale and less exuberant than those in Central Europe; the ceiling frescoes and decorative sculpture in palaces and churches are unsuited to domestic interiors, however lavish. We must therefore remember that in France, Rococo painting and sculpture were less closely linked with their architectural settings than in Italy, Austria, and Germany, although they reflect the same taste that produced the Hôtel de Soubise.

CLODION. Characteristic of Rococo sculpture are small groups like Clodion's *Satyr and Bacchante* (fig. 821), designed to be viewed at close range. Their coquettish eroticism is another form of "miniature Baroque," a playful echo of the ecstasies of Bernini and Puget (compare fig. 750).

FRAGONARD. Much Rococo painting is the counterpart of Clodion's sculpture: intimate in scale and deliciously sensual in style and subject, it lacks the emotional depth that distinguishes Watteau's art. The finest painter in this vein was Jean-Honoré Fragonard (1732–1806); his *Bathers* (fig. 822) must here suffice to represent its class. A franker "Rubéniste" than Watteau, Fragonard paints with a fluid breadth and spontaneity reminiscent of Rubens' oil sketches (see fig. 774). His figures move with a floating grace that

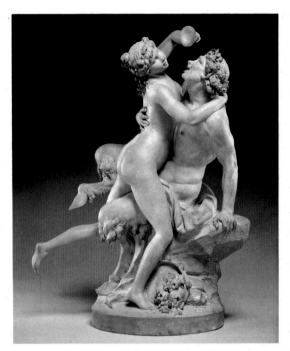

821. CLAUDE-MICHEL CLODION. *SATYR AND BACCHANTE*.
c. 1775. Terracotta, height 23¼" (59 cm).
The Metropolitan Museum of Art, New York.
Bequest of Benjamin Altman, 1913

also links him with Tiepolo, whose work he had admired in Italy (compare fig. 769). Fragonard had the misfortune to outlive his era; his pictures became outmoded as the French Revolution approached. After 1789 he was reduced to poverty, and he died, forgotten, in the heyday of Napoleon. However, the style he practiced with such mastery had not

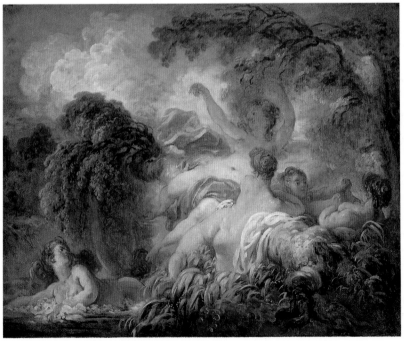

822. JEAN-HONORÉ FRAGONARD. *BATHERS*. c. 1765. Oil on canvas,
25¼×31½" (64×80 cm). Musée du Louvre, Paris

been the only alternative open to him and the other French painters of his generation.

CHARDIN. Fragonard's art might have been different had he followed that of his first teacher, Jean-Baptiste Siméon Chardin (1699–1779), whose style can be called Rococo only with reservations. The "Rubénistes" had cleared the way for a new interest in the Dutch masters as well, and Chardin is the finest painter of still life and genre in this trend. His genre scenes, such as *Back from the Market* (fig. 823), show life in a Parisian middle-class household with such feeling for the beauty hidden in the commonplace, and so clear a sense of spatial order, that we can compare him only to Vermeer. But his remarkable technique is quite unlike any Dutch artist's. Devoid of bravura, his brushwork renders the light on colored surfaces with a creamy touch that is both analytical and subtly poetic. His still lifes usually reflect the same modest environment, eschewing the "object appeal" of their Dutch predecessors. In *Kitchen Still Life* (figure 824), we see only the common objects that belong in any kitchen: earthenware jugs, a casserole, a copper pot, a piece of raw meat, smoked herring, two eggs. But how important they seem, each so firmly placed in relation to the rest, each so worthy of the artist's—and our—scrutiny! Despite his concern with formal problems, evident in the beautifully balanced design, Chardin treats these objects with a respect close to reverence. Beyond their shapes, colors, and textures,

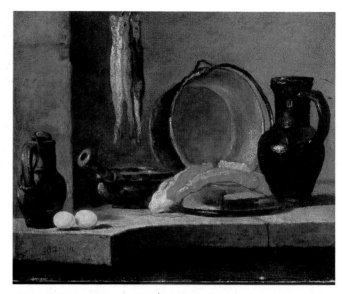

824. JEAN-BAPTISTE SIMÉON CHARDIN. *KITCHEN STILL LIFE.* c. 1731. Oil on canvas, 12½×15⅜″ (32×39 cm). The Ashmolean Museum, Oxford. Bequeathed by Mrs. W. F. R. Weldon

they are to him symbols of the life of common people. In spirit, if not in subject matter, Chardin is more akin to Le Nain and Sanchez Cotán (see pages 588 and 582) than to any Dutch painter.

VIGÉE-LEBRUN. It is from portraits that we can gain the clearest understanding of the French Rococo, for the transformation of the human image lies at the heart of the era. In portraits of the aristocracy, people were endowed with the illusion of character as a natural attribute of their station in life, stemming from their noble birth. But the finest achievements of Rococo portraiture were reserved for the depiction of women, hardly a surprising fact in a society that idolized the cult of love and feminine beauty. One of the finest practitioners in this vein was Marie-Louise-Elisabeth Vigée-Lebrun (1755–1842).

Throughout Vigée's long life she enjoyed great fame, which took her to every corner of Europe—even Russia when she fled the French Revolution. *The Duchesse de Polignac* (fig. 825) was painted a few years after Vigée had become the portraitist for Queen Marie Antoinette, and it amply demonstrates her ability. The duchess has the eternally youthful loveliness of Fragonard's *Bathers* (fig. 822), made all the more persuasive by the artist's ravishing treatment of her clothing. At the same time, there is a sense of transience in the engaging mood that exemplifies the Rococo's whimsical theatricality. Interrupted in her singing, the lyrical duchess becomes a real-life counterpart to the poetic creatures in Watteau's *Pilgrimage to Cythera* (fig. 818), by way of the delicate sentiment she shares with the girl in Chardin's *Back from the Market* (fig. 823).

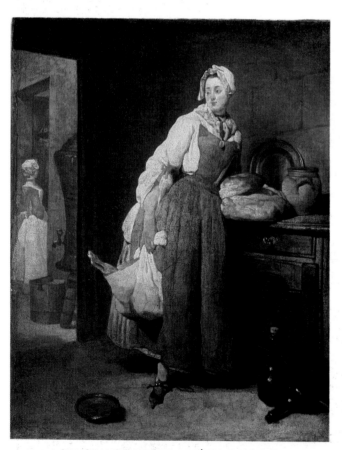

823. JEAN-BAPTISTE SIMÉON CHARDIN. *BACK FROM THE MARKET.* 1739. Oil on canvas, 18½×14¾″ (47×37.5 cm). Musée du Louvre, Paris

825. (*opposite*) MARIE-LOUISE-ELISABETH VIGÉE-LEBRUN. *THE DUCHESSE DE POLIGNAC.* 1783. Oil on canvas, 38¾×28″ (98.3×71 cm). © The National Trust Waddesdon Manor

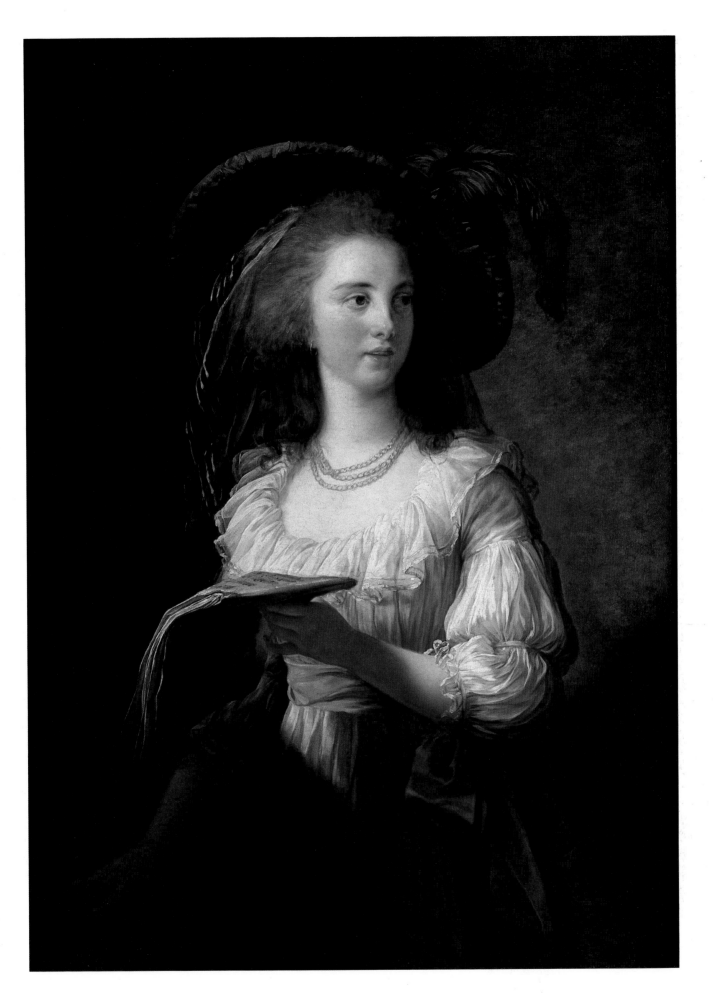

ENGLAND

Architecture

We have not mentioned English architecture since our discussion of the Perpendicular style (see fig. 478). This insular form of "Late Gothic" proved extraordinarily persistent; it absorbed the stylistic vocabulary of the Italian Renaissance during the sixteenth century, but as late as 1600, English buildings still retained a "Perpendicular syntax"—that is to say, their stage of development corresponded to Chambord, or the choir of St.-Pierre at Caen (see figs. 730 and 731).

JONES. The first architect of the English Renaissance was Inigo Jones (1573–1652). Although he went to Italy about 1600, and again in 1613, he did not bring back the Early Baroque but returned a thoroughgoing Palladian. The Banqueting House he built at Whitehall in London (fig. 826) conforms in every respect to the principles in Palladio's treatise, yet does not copy any specific building by Palladio. Symmetrical and self-sufficient, it is, for its date, more like a Renaissance palazzo than any other building north of the Alps. Jones' style, supported by Palladio's authority as a theorist, stood as a beacon of classicist orthodoxy in England for two hundred years.

WREN. This classicism can be seen in some parts of St. Paul's Cathedral (figs. 827–29) by Sir Christopher Wren (1632–1723), the great English architect of the late seventeenth century: note the second-story windows and, especially, the dome, which looks like Bramante's Tempietto (see fig. 647), much enlarged. St. Paul's is otherwise an up-to-date Baroque design reflecting a thorough acquaintance with contemporary architecture in Italy and France. Sir Christopher came close to being a Baroque counterpart of the Renaissance artist-scientist. An intellectual prodigy, he first

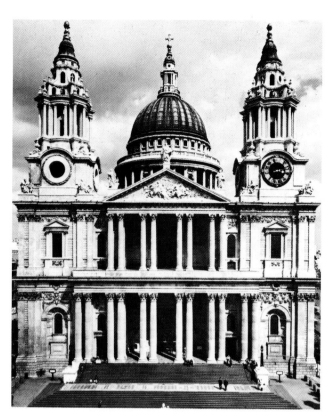

827. SIR CHRISTOPHER WREN. Façade of St. Paul's Cathedral, London. 1675–1710

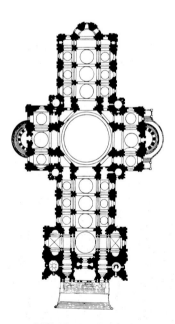

828. Plan of St. Paul's

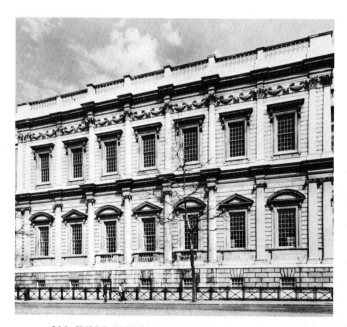

826. INIGO JONES. West front, Banqueting House, Whitehall Palace, London

studied anatomy, then physics, mathematics, and astronomy, and was highly esteemed by Sir Isaac Newton. His serious interest in architecture did not begin until he was about thirty. However—and this seems to be characteristic of the Baroque as opposed to the Renaissance—there is apparently no direct link between his scientific and artistic ideas. (It is hard to determine whether his technological knowledge significantly affected the shape of his buildings.)

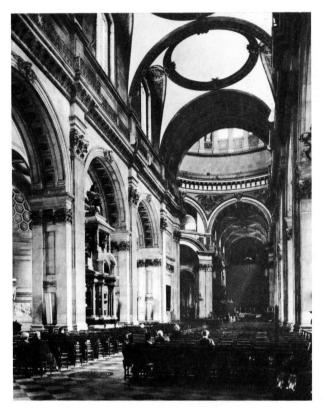

829. Interior, St. Paul's

830. SIR JOHN VANBRUGH.
Blenheim Palace, Woodstock. Begun 1705

Had not the great London fire of 1666 destroyed the Gothic cathedral of St. Paul, and many lesser churches, Sir Christopher might have remained an amateur architect. But following that catastrophe, he was named to the royal commission for rebuilding the city, and a few years later he began his designs for St. Paul's. The tradition of Inigo Jones did not suffice for this task, beyond providing a starting point. On his only trip abroad, Sir Christopher had visited Paris at the time of the dispute over the completion of the Louvre, and he must have sided with Perrault, whose design for the East Front is clearly reflected in the façade of St. Paul's. Yet, despite his belief that Paris provided "the best school of architecture in Europe," Sir Christopher was not indifferent to the achievements of the Roman Baroque. He must have wanted the new St. Paul's to be the St. Peter's of the Church of England—soberer and not so large, but equally impressive. His dome, like that of St. Peter's, has a diameter as wide as nave and aisles combined, but it rises high above the rest of the structure and dominates even our close view of the façade. The lantern and the upper part of the clock towers also suggest that he knew S. Agnese in Piazza Navona (see fig. 759), probably from drawings or engravings.

VANBRUGH. Italian Baroque elements are still more conspicuous in Blenheim Palace (fig. 830), designed by Sir John Vanbrugh (1664–1726); the grandiose structure was presented by a grateful nation to the victorious duke of Marlborough. Vanbrugh, like Bernini, had a strong interest in the theater (he was a popular playwright). Their kinship seems even closer when we compare the façade of Blenheim, its colossal order and framing colonnade, with the piazza of St. Peter's (see fig. 747).

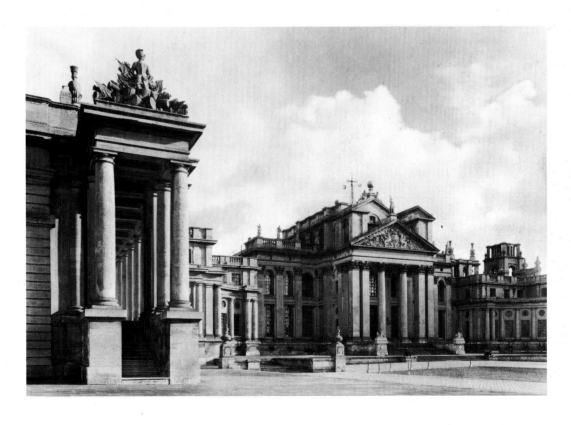

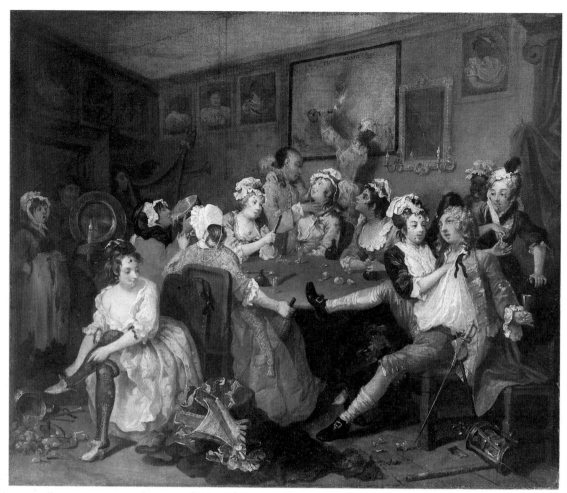

831. WILLIAM HOGARTH. *THE ORGY,* Scene III of *THE RAKE'S PROGRESS.*
c. 1734. Oil on canvas, 24½ × 29½″ (62.2 × 74.9 cm). Sir John Soane's Museum, London

Painting

The development of English seventeenth-century architecture follows the French pattern: toward 1700, the High Baroque wins out over a classicistic tradition. Yet England never accepted the subsequent Rococo. The pomp of Blenheim soon became the object of satire, and the second quarter of the eighteenth century produced a Palladianism more rationalistic than Inigo Jones' and, at that time, unique in all Europe (see fig. 847). But French Rococo painting, from Watteau to Fragonard, had a decisive—though unacknowledged—effect across the Channel and helped, in fact, to bring about the first school of English painting since the Middle Ages that had more than local importance.

HOGARTH. The earliest of these painters, William Hogarth (1697–1764), made his mark in the 1730s with a new kind of picture, which he described as "modern moral subjects . . . similar to representations on the stage." He wished to be judged as a dramatist, he said, even though his "actors" could only "exhibit a dumb show." These pictures, and the engravings he made from them for popular sale, came in sets, with details recurring in each scene to unify the sequence. Hogarth's "morality plays" teach, by horrid example, the solid

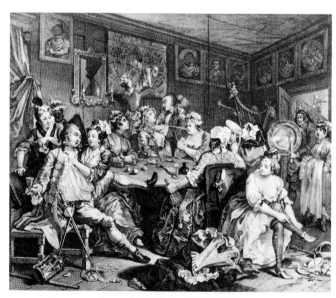

832. WILLIAM HOGARTH. *HE REVELS (THE ORGY),*
Scene III of *THE RAKE'S PROGRESS.* 1735. Engraving.
The Metropolitan Museum of Art, New York.
Harris Brisbane Dick Fund, 1932

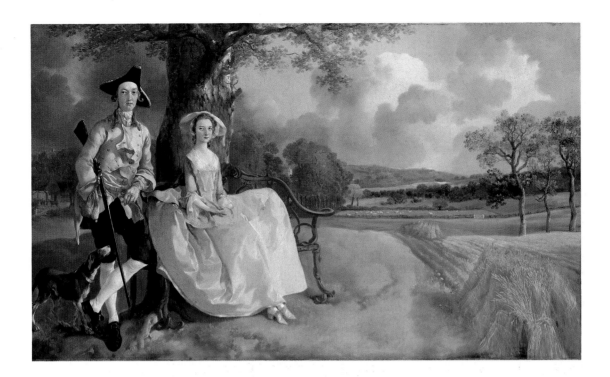

middle-class virtues: they show a country girl who succumbs to the temptations of fashionable London; the evils of corrupt elections; aristocratic rakes who live only for ruinous pleasure, marrying wealthy women of lower status for their fortunes (which they soon dissipate).

In *The Orgy* (figs. 831 and 832), from *The Rake's Progress*, the young wastrel is overindulging in wine and women. The scene is so full of visual clues that a full account would take pages, plus constant references to the adjoining episodes. Yet, however literal-minded, the picture has great appeal. Hogarth combines some of Watteau's sparkle with Jan Steen's narrative gusto (compare figs. 818 and 793), and so entertains us that we enjoy his sermon without being overwhelmed by its message. He is probably the first artist in history to become a social critic in his own right.

GAINSBOROUGH. Portraiture remained the only constant source of income for English painters. Here too, the eighteenth century produced a style that differed from the continental traditions that had dominated this field. Its greatest master, Thomas Gainsborough (1727–1788), began by painting landscapes, but ended as the favorite portraitist of British high society. His early portraits, such as *Robert Andrews and His Wife* (fig. 833), have a lyrical charm that is not always found in his later pictures. Compared to Van Dyck's artifice in *Charles I Hunting* (see fig. 777), this country squire and his wife are unpretentiously at home in their setting. The landscape, although derived from Ruisdael and his school, has a sunlit, hospitable air never achieved (or desired) by the Dutch masters; and the casual grace of the two figures indirectly recalls Watteau's style. Later portraits by Gainsborough, such as the very fine one of the great actress Mrs. Siddons (fig. 834), have other virtues: a cool elegance that translates Van Dyck's aristocratic poses into late–eighteenth-century terms, and a fluid, translucent technique reminiscent of Rubens.

833. THOMAS GAINSBOROUGH. *ROBERT ANDREWS AND HIS WIFE*. c. 1748–50. Oil on canvas, 27½×47″ (69.7×119.3 cm). The National Gallery, London. Reproduced by courtesy of the Trustees

834. THOMAS GAINSBOROUGH. *MRS. SIDDONS*. 1785 Oil on canvas, 49½×39″ (125.7×99.1 cm). The National Gallery, London. Reproduced by courtesy of the Trustees

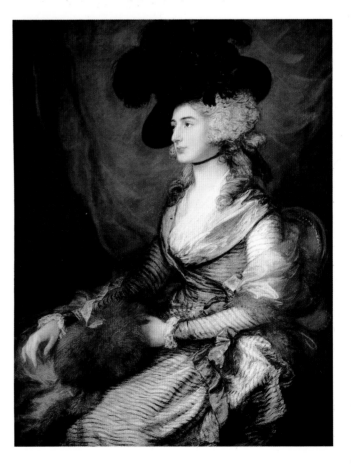

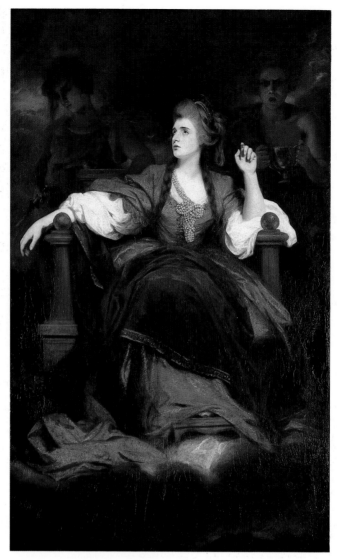

835. SIR JOSHUA REYNOLDS. *MRS. SIDDONS AS THE*
TRAGIC MUSE. 1784, Oil on canvas, 93×57½″ (236.5×146 cm).
Henry E. Huntington Library and Art Gallery,
San Marino, California

REYNOLDS. Gainsborough painted *Mrs. Siddons* in conscious opposition to his great rival on the London scene, Sir
Joshua Reynolds (1723–1792), who just before had portrayed the same sitter as the Tragic Muse (fig. 835). Reynolds, the President of the Royal Academy since its founding
in 1768, was the protagonist of the academic approach to art,
which he had acquired during two years in Rome. Like his
French predecessors, he formulated in his famous *Discourses* what he felt were necessary rules and theories. His
views were essentially those of Lebrun, tempered by British
common sense. Again like Lebrun, he found it difficult to
live up to his theories in actual practice. Although he preferred history painting in the grand style, the vast majority
of his works are portraits "enabled," whenever possible, by
allegorical additions or disguises like those in his picture of
Mrs. Siddons. His style owed a good deal more to the Venetians, the Flemish Baroque, and even to Rembrandt (note

the lighting in his *Mrs. Siddons*) than he conceded in theory,
though he often recommended following the example of earlier masters.

Reynolds was generous enough to give praise to
Gainsborough, whom he outlived by a few years, and whose
instinctive talent he must have envied: he eulogized him as
one who saw with the eye of a painter rather than a poet.
There is more truth to this statement than it might seem.
Gainsborough's paintings epitomized the Enlightenment
philosopher David Hume's idea that painting must incorporate both nature and art. Gainsborough himself was a simple
and unpretentious man who exemplified Hume's "natural
man," free of excessive pride or humility. Reynolds' approach, on the other hand, as enunciated in his *Discourses*,
was based on the Roman poet Horace's dictum that art must
conform to the example of poetry, be it epic or tragic. His
frequent borrowing of poses from the antique was intended

to ennoble the sitter by elevating him or her from an individual to a universal type through association with the great art of the past and the ideals it embodied. This heroic model was closely related to the writings of the playwright Samuel Johnson and the practices of the actor David Garrick, both of whom were Reynolds' close friends.

In this, Gainsborough was the very opposite of Reynolds. Yet, for all of the differences between them, the two artists had more in common than they cared to admit, artistically and also philosophically. Reynolds and Gainsborough looked back to Van Dyck, drawing different lessons from his example. Both emphasized, albeit in varying degrees, the visual appeal and technical proficiency of their paintings. Moreover, their portraits of Mrs. Siddons bear an unmistakable relationship to the Rococo style of France—note their resemblance to Vigée's *Duchesse* (fig. 825)—yet remain distinctly English in character. Hume and Johnson were similarly linked by an abiding skepticism. If anything, Johnson's writings, which inspired Reynolds, were more bitterly pessimistic than Hume's, which generally advocated a tolerant and humane ethical system.

Sculpture

English sculpture has not been discussed in these pages since that of the thirteenth century (see fig. 501). During the Reformation, it will be recalled, there was a wholesale destruction of sculpture in England. This had so chilling an effect that for two hundred years the demand for statuary of any kind was too low to sustain more than the most modest local production. With the rise of a vigorous English school of painting, however, sculptural patronage grew as well, and during the eighteenth century England set an example for the rest of Europe in creating the "monument to genius"—statues in public places honoring culture heroes such as Shakespeare, a privilege hitherto reserved for heads of state.

ROUBILIAC. One of the earliest and most ingratiating of these statues is that of the great composer George Frederick Handel (fig. 836), by the French-born Louis-François Roubiliac (1702–1762). It was also the first to be made of a culture hero within his lifetime (the next to achieve this distinction would be Voltaire in France, a full generation later; see fig. 845). Roubiliac—who is portrayed in figure 29—carved the figure in 1738 for the owner of Vauxhall Gardens in London, a pleasure park with dining facilities and an orchestra stand where Handel's music was often performed, so that the statue served two purposes: homage and advertising. Handel is in the guise of Apollo, the god of music,

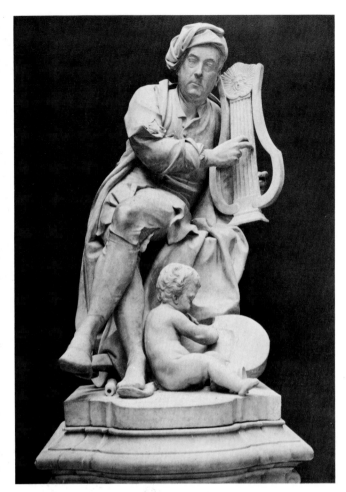

836. LOUIS-FRANÇOIS ROUBILIAC. *GEORGE FREDERICK HANDEL.* 1738. Marble, lifesize. Victoria & Albert Museum, London (Crown copyright reserved)

playing a classical lyre; a putto at his feet writes down the divine music. But Handel is a most domestic Apollo, in slippers and a worn dressing gown, a soft beret on his head instead of the then customary wig. Although Roubiliac shows himself in full command of the Baroque sculptural tradition, the studied informality of his deified *Handel* seems peculiarly English: touches such as the right foot resting upon rather than inside the slipper (a hint at the composer's gouty big toe?) suggest that he sought advice from Hogarth, with whom he was on excellent terms. Be that as it may, *Handel* was Roubiliac's first big success in his adopted homeland, and it became the forebear of countless monuments to culture heroes everywhere (see fig. 934).

ILLUSTRATED TIME CHART III

1300

Papacy in Avignon 1309–76
Hundred Years War, France and England 1337–1453
Black Death throughout Europe 1347–50

Petrarch, first humanist (1304–74)
Boccaccio (1313–75)

1400

Death of Giangaleazzo Visconti of Milan (1402) removes threat to political independence of Florence
Joan of Arc burned at stake for heresy and sorcery 1431
Cosimo de'Medici, leading citizen of Florence 1434–64
Council of Florence attempts to reunite Catholic and Orthodox faiths 1439

Leonardo Bruni (c. 1374–1444); *History of Florence*
Prince Henry the Navigator of Portugal (1394–1460) promotes geographic exploration
Leon Battista Alberti (1404–72), *On Architecture; On Painting*
Earliest record of suction pump c. 1440

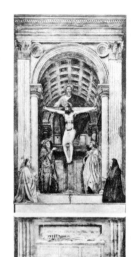

Masaccio, *Trinity* fresco

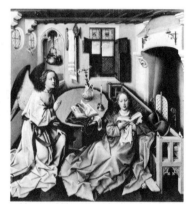

Master of Flémalle, *Merode Altarpiece*

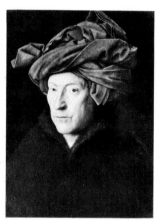

Jan van Eyck, *Man in Red Turban*

1450

Hapsburg rule of Holy Roman Empire begins 1452
Constantinople falls to Turks 1453
Pico della Mirandola, Neo-Platonist (1463–94)
Lorenzo de'Medici, "the Magnificent," virtual ruler of Florence 1469–92
Pius II, humanist pope (r. 1458–64)
Ferdinand and Isabella unite Spain 1469
Granada, last Moslem stronghold in Spain, falls 1492
Spain and Portugal divide southern New World 1493–94
Cabot claims eastern North America for England 1497
Charles VIII of France invades Italy 1494–99
Henry VII (r. 1485–1509), first Tudor king of England
Savonarola virtual ruler of Florence 1494; burned at stake for heresy 1498

François Villon, French poet (born c. 1431)
Marsilio Ficino, Italian Neo-Platonic philosopher (1433–99)
Refugees from Constantinople bring Greek manuscripts to Italy after 1453
Diaz rounds Cape of Good Hope 1486
Columbus discovers America 1492
Sebastian Brant, *Ship of Fools* 1494
Vasco da Gama reaches India, returns to Lisbon 1497–99

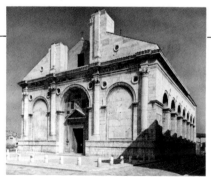

Alberti, S. Francesco, Rimini

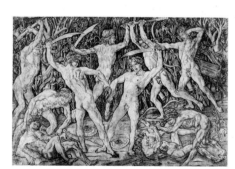

Pollaiuolo, *Battle of Ten Naked Men*

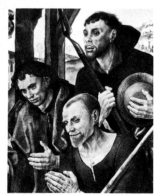

Hugo van der Goes, *Portinari Altar*

1500

Nanni di Banco, *Four Saints*
Donatello, *St. Mark; St. George*
Brunelleschi begins career as architect 1419,
   Florence Cathedral dome. Subsequently, all
   in Florence: S. Lorenzo; Pazzi Chapel;
   Sto. Spirito; Sta. Maria degli Angeli
Donatello, *Zuccone; Feast of Herod*
Masaccio, *Trinity* fresco; Brancacci
   Chapel frescoes
Master of Flémalle, *Merode Altarpiece*
Jacopo della Quercia, portal of S. Petronio, Bologna
Donatello, *David*
Jan van Eyck, *Ghent Altarpiece; Man
   in a Red Turban*
Rogier van der Weyden, *Descent from
   the Cross*
Ghiberti, *"Gates of Paradise,"*
   Baptistery, Florence
Luca della Robbia, *Cantoria*
Filippo Lippi, *Madonna*
Fra Angelico, S. Marco frescoes, Florence
Conrad Witz, *Geneva Altar*
Michelozzo, Palazzo Medici-Riccardi,
   Florence
Domenico Veneziano, *Madonna and Saints*
Donatello, *Gattamelata*, Padua
Bernardo Rossellino, Tomb of Leonardo
   Bruni, Sta. Croce, Florence
Castagno, *The Last Supper*
Alberti, Palazzo Rucellai, Florence

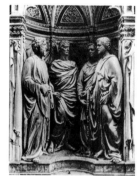

Nanni di Banco, *Four Crowned Saints*

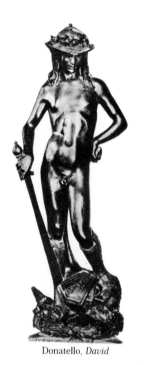

Donatello, *David*

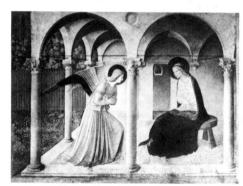

Fra Angelico, S. Marco frescoes

Alberti, S. Francesco, Rimini; S. Andrea,
   Mantua
Donatello, *Magdalen*
Mantegna, Ovetari Chapel frescoes,
   Padua
Antonio Rossellino, *Giovanni Chellini*
Piero della Francesca, Arezzo frescoes
Pollaiuolo, *Battle of Ten Naked Men*, en-
   graving
Pacher, *St. Wolfgang Altar*
Pollaiuolo, *Hercules and Antaeus*
Hugo van der Goes, *Portinari Altar*
Schongauer, *Temptation of St. Anthony*,
   engraving
Botticelli, *Birth of Venus*
Leonardo, *Adoration of the Magi*
Perugino, *Delivery of the Keys*, Sistine
   Chapel, Rome
Verrocchio, *Colleoni*, Venice
Giuliano da Sangallo, Sta. Maria delle
   Carceri, Prato
Giovanni Bellini, *St. Francis*
Leonardo, *Virgin of the Rocks*
Dürer, *Four Horsemen of the Apocalypse*,
   woodcut

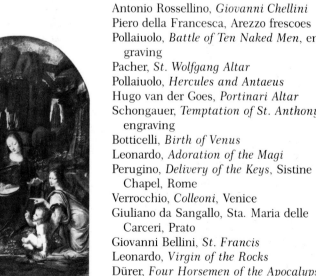

Leonardo, *Virgin of the Rocks*

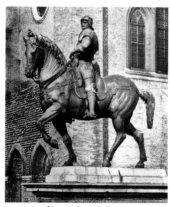

Verrocchio, *Colleoni*

1500

Erasmus of Rotterdam, *In Praise of Folly* 1511

Martin Luther (1483–1546) posts 95 theses 1517; excommunicated 1521

Charles V elected Holy Roman Emperor 1519; Sack of Rome 1527

Cortés wins Aztec empire in Mexico for Spain 1519; Pizarro conquers Peru 1532

Suleiman the Magnificent ascends Turkish throne 1520; threatens Vienna 1525

Machiavelli, *The Prince* 1532

Henry VIII of England (r. 1509–47) founds Anglican Church 1534

Peasants' Revolt in Germany 1524–25

Ignatius of Loyola founds Jesuit order 1534

John Calvin, *Institutes of the Christian Religion* 1536

Wars of Lutheran vs. Catholic princes in Germany; Peace of Augsburg (1555) lets each sovereign decide religion of his subjects

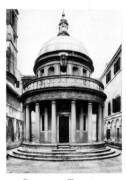

Bramante, Tempietto

Balboa sights Pacific Ocean 1513

Thomas More, *Utopia* 1516

Portuguese reach China 1516; Japan 1543

First circumnavigation of the globe by Magellan and crew 1520–22

Castiglione, *The Courtier* 1528

François Rabelais, French writer, *Gargantua* 1532

Paracelsus, Swiss alchemist (1493–1541)

Copernicus refutes geocentric view of universe 1543

Vesalius, *De Humani Corporis Fabrica* 1543

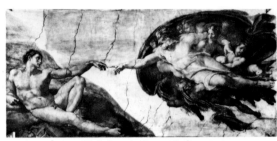

Michelangelo, Sistine Ceiling

1550

Council of Trent for Catholic reform 1545–63

St. Francis Xavier, Jesuit missionary, dies in Goa, India 1552

Alexander Knox founds Presbyterian Church 1560

St. Theresa of Avila, Spanish saint (1515–82)

Giordano Bruno (1548–1600) burned at the stake for heresy in Venice

Ivan the Terrible of Russia (r. 1547–84)

Charles V retires 1556; son Philip II king of Spain, Netherlands, New World

Elizabeth I of England (r. 1558–1603)

Turkish sea power crushed at Lepanto 1571

Netherlands revolt against Spain 1568; northern provinces declare independence 1581

Spanish Armada defeated by English 1588

Henry IV of France (r. 1589–1610) Edict of Nantes (1598) establishes religious toleration

Lutheranism state religion in Denmark 1560

Montaigne, French essayist (1533–92)

Agricola, *De re metallica* 1556

Vasari, *Lives* 1564

Tycho Brahe, Danish astronomer (1546–1601)

Sir Philip Sidney, English poet (1554–86)

Francis Bacon, English writer (1561–1626)

Christopher Marlowe, English dramatist (1564–93)

William Shakespeare (1564–1616)

Hilliard, *Young Man Among Roses*, miniature

1600

English East India Company founded 1600; Dutch East India Company 1602

Jamestown, Virginia, founded 1607

King James Bible 1611

Romanov dynasty founded in Russia 1613

Thirty Years' War 1618–48

William Bradford (1590–1657), governor of Plymouth Colony (founded 1620)

Cardinal Richelieu, adviser to Louis XIII, consolidates power of king 1624–42

Japanese isolation against all Europeans except token Dutch begins 1639

Cardinal Mazarin governs France during minority of Louis XIV 1643–61

Charles I of England beheaded 1649; Commonwealth 1649–53

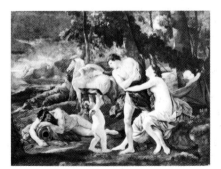

Poussin, *Cephalus and Aurora*

Cervantes, *Don Quixote* 1605–1615

Johannes Kepler establishes planetary system 1609–1619

Napier's treatise on logarithms 1614

Harvey describes circulation of blood 1628

Galileo (1564–1642) invents telescope 1609; establishes scientific method

John Donne, English poet (1572–1631)

René Descartes (1596–1650), *Discourse on Method*

Pierre Corneille, French dramatist (1606–84)

Harvard College founded 1636

Torricelli measures pressure of atmosphere 1644

Royal Academy of Paris founded 1648

1650

1500

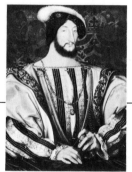

Bellini, *Madonna and Saints*

Bosch, *Garden of Delights*
Michelangelo, *David*
Bramante, Tempietto, new St. Peter's, Rome
Leonardo, *Mona Lisa*
Giorgione, *Tempest*
Michelangelo, Sistine Ceiling, Rome
Raphael, *School of Athens*, Rome
Grünewald, *Isenheim Altar*
Michelangelo, *Moses* and two *"Slaves"*
Titian, *Bacchanal*
Château of Chambord, France
Rosso, *Descent from the Cross*
Michelangelo, Medici tombs;
    Laurentian Library, Florence
Dürer, *Four Apostles*
Correggio, *Assumption of the Virgin*
Altdorfer, *Battle of Issus*
Parmigianino, *Madonna with Long Neck*
Clouet, *Francis I*
Holbein, *Henry VIII*
Titian, *Pope Paul III*
Michelangelo begins Campidoglio, Rome
    1537–39; architect of St. Peter's 1546
Lescot, Square Court, Louvre, Paris
Goujon, *Fontaine des Innocents*, Paris

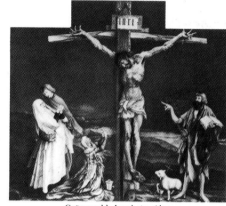

Grünewald, *Isenheim Altar*

1550

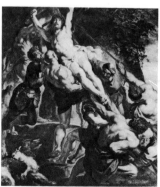

Clouet, *Francis I*

Michelangelo, *Milan Pietà* (last work)
Ammanati, Palazzo Pitti courtyard, Florence
Hilliard, *Young Man Among Roses*, miniature
Vasari, Uffizi, Florence
Pilon, Tomb of Henry II, Paris
Bruegel, *Peasant Wedding*
Palladio, S. Giorgio Maggiore, Venice;
    Villa Rotonda, Vicenza
Vignola and Della Porta, Il Gesù, Rome
Veronese, *Christ in the House of Levi*
El Greco, *Burial of Count Orgaz*
Tintoretto, *Last Supper*
Giovanni Bologna, *Rape of Sabine
    Woman*
Caravaggio, *Calling of St. Matthew*
Annibale Carracci, Farnese Gallery
    ceiling, Rome

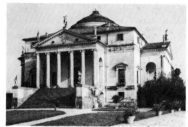

Palladio, Villa Rotonda

1600

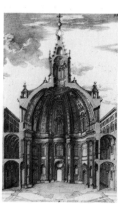

Maderno, nave and façade of St. Peter's,
    Rome; Bernini's colonnade
Rubens, *Raising of the Cross*
Reni, *Aurora*
Jones, Banqueting House, London
Guercino, *Aurora*
Bernini, *David*
Hals, *Jolly Toper*
Pietro da Cortona, Palazzo Barberini ceiling, Rome
Van Dyck, *Charles I Hunting*
Borromini, S. Carlo alle Quattro Fontane, Rome
Borromini, S. Ivo, Rome
Rembrandt, *Night Watch*
F. Mansart, Château of Maisons, France
Bernini, Cornaro Chapel, Rome
Poussin, *Cephalus and Aurora*

Rubens, *Raising of the Cross*

Borromini, S. Ivo, Rome

1650

1650

Charles II restores English monarchy
    1660
Jacques Bossuet, French orator (1627–
    1704)
Spinoza, Dutch philosopher (1632–77)
Society of Friends (Quakers) founded 1668
English Parliament passes Habeas Cor-
    pus Act 1679
Frederick William, the Great Elector
    (r. 1640–88), founds power of Prussia
Louis XIV absolute ruler of France (r. 1661–
    1715); revokes Edict of Nantes 1685
Glorious Revolution against James II of
    England 1688; Bill of Rights

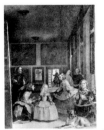

Velázquez, *Maids of Honor*

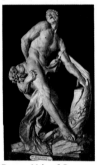

Puget, *Milo of Crotona*

Thomas Hobbs, *Leviathan* 1651
Molière, French dramatist (1622–73)
Pascal, French scientist and philosopher
    (1623–62)
Boyle's Law of gas pressure 1662
Royal Society, London, founded 1662
Great Fire and Plague of London 1665–66
Milton, *Paradise Lost* 1667
Isaac Newton, theory of gravity 1687
John Locke, *Essay Concerning Human
    Understanding*, 1690
Racine, *Phèdre* 1677
Bunyan, *Pilgrim's Progress* 1678
Leibniz, German philosopher (1646–1716)

1700

Peter the Great (r. 1682–1725) western-
    izes Russia, defeats Sweden
English and allies defeat French at Blen-
    heim 1704
Robert Walpole first prime minister
    1721–42
Wesley brothers found Methodism 1738
Frederick the Great of Prussia defeats
    Austria 1740–45

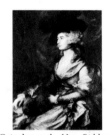

Gainsborough, *Mrs. Siddons*

Alexander Pope, *Rape of the Lock* 1714
Defoe, *Robinson Crusoe* 1719
Swift, *Gulliver's Travels* 1726
John Gay, *The Beggar's Opera* 1728
Linnaeus, *Systema Naturae* 1737
Giovanni Battista Vico, Italian historian
    (1668–1744)
Pompeii and Herculaneum discovered 1745
Montesquieu, *Spirit of Laws* 1748

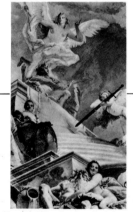

1750

Seven Years' War (1756–63): England
    and Prussia vs. Austria and France,
    called French and Indian War in
    America; French defeated in battle of
    Quebec 1769
Catherine the Great (r. 1762–96) ex-
    tends Russian power to Black Sea
Partition of Poland among Russia, Prus-
    sia, Austria 1772–95
American Revolution begins 1775
French Revolution begins 1789

Tiepolo, *Würzburg ceiling fresco*

Voltaire, *Candide* 1759
James Watt patents steam engine 1769
Edward Jenner demonstrates smallpox
    vaccine 1796

1800

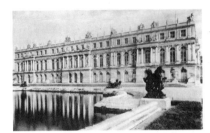

Le Vau and Hardouin-Mansart, Versailles

Ruisdael, *Jewish Cemetery*
Velázquez, *Maids of Honor*
Bernini, *Throne of St. Peter*
Rembrandt, *Self-Portrait*
Steen, *The Feast of St. Nicholas*
Vermeer, *The Letter*
Perrault, East front of Louvre, Paris
Bernini, Model for equestrian statue
    of Louis XIV
Guarini, Chapel of Holy Shroud, Turin
Puget, *Milo of Crotona*
Coysevox, *Charles Lebrun*
Wren, St. Paul's, London
Le Vau and Hardouin-Mansart,
    Versailles, begun 1669
Guarini, Palazzo Carignano, Turin

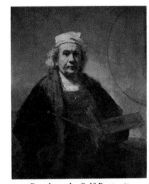

Rembrandt, *Self-Portrait*

———— 1700

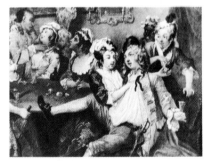

Hogarth, *Rake's Progress*

Prandtauer, Monastery at Melk
Vanbrugh, Blenheim Palace
Fischer von Erlach, St. Charles,
    Vienna
Neumann, Episcopal Palace,
    Würzburg
Boffrand, Hôtel de Soubise
Hogarth, *Rake's Progress*
Chardin, *Kitchen Still Life*

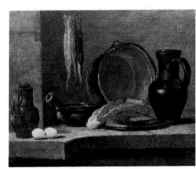

Chardin, *Kitchen Still Life*

———— 1750

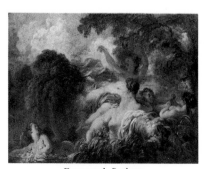

Fragonard, *Bathers*

Tiepolo, Würzburg ceiling fresco
Fragonard, *Bathers*
Vigée-Lebrun, *Duchesse de Polignac*
Zimmerman, "Die Wies," Bavaria
Gainsborough, *Mrs. Siddons*

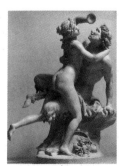

Clodion, *Satyr and Bacchante*

———— 1800

PART FOUR

THE MODERN WORLD

The era to which we ourselves belong has not yet acquired a name of its own. Perhaps this does not strike us as peculiar at first—we are, after all, still in midstream—but considering how promptly the Renaissance coined a name for itself, we may well ponder the fact that no key concept comparable to the "rebirth of antiquity" has emerged in the two hundred years since our era began. It is tempting to make "revolution" such a concept, because rapid and violent change has indeed characterized the modern world. Yet we cannot discern a common impulse behind these developments, for the modern era began with revolutions of two kinds: the Industrial Revolution, symbolized by the invention of the steam engine, and the political revolution, under the banner of democracy, in America and France.

Both of these revolutions are still going on; industrialization and democracy, as goals, are sought over most of the world. Western science and Western political thought (and, in their wake, all the other products of modern Western civilization—food, dress, art, music, literature) will soon belong to all, although they have been challenged by nationalism, religion, and other ideologies that command allegiance. These two movements are so closely linked today that we tend to think of them as different aspects of one process—with effects more far-reaching than any since the Neolithic Revolution ten thousand years ago. Still, the twin revolutions of modern times are not the same; the more we try to define their relationship, and to trace their historic roots, the more paradoxical they seem. Both are founded on the idea of progress; but whereas progress in science during the past two centuries has been continuous and measurable, we can hardly make this claim for our pursuit of happiness, however we choose to define it.

Here, then, is the conflict fundamental to our era. Today, having cast off the framework of traditional authority which confined and sustained us before, we can act with a latitude both frightening and exhilarating. In a world where all values may be questioned, we search constantly for our own identity and for the meaning of human existence, individual and collective. Our knowledge about ourselves is now vastly greater, but this has not reassured us as we had hoped. Modern civilization lacks the cohesiveness of the past; it no longer proceeds by readily identifiable periods, nor are there clear period styles to be discerned in art or in any form of endeavor.

Instead, we find a continuity of another kind, that of movements and countermovements. Spreading like waves, these "isms" defy national, ethnic, and chronological boundaries; never dominant anywhere for long, they compete or merge with each other in endlessly shifting patterns. Hence our account of modern art is guided more by movements than by countries. Only in this way can we hope to do justice to the fact that modern art, all regional differences notwithstanding, is as international as modern science.

615

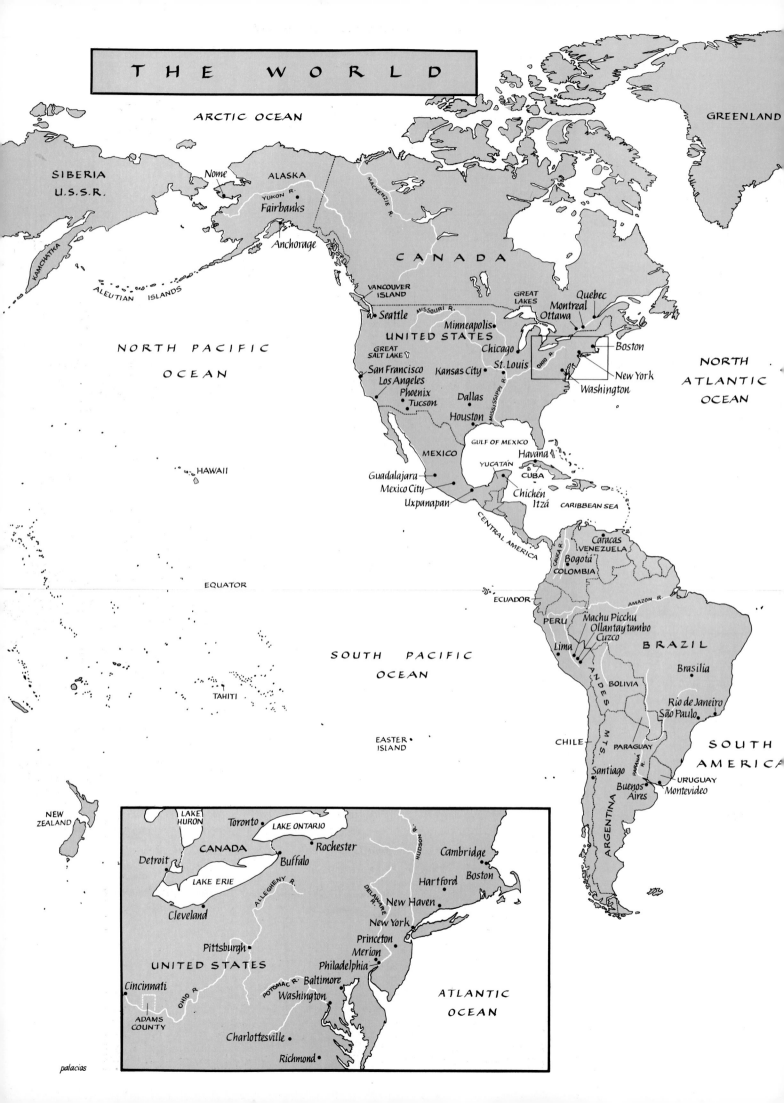

THE WORLD

ARCTIC OCEAN

GREENLAND

SIBERIA
U.S.S.R.

Nome

ALASKA

YUKON R.
Fairbanks

Anchorage

KAMCHATKA

ALEUTIAN ISLANDS

CANADA

NORTH PACIFIC
OCEAN

VANCOUVER
ISLAND

Seattle

MACKENZIE R.

GREAT
LAKES

Quebec
Montreal
Ottawa

Boston

MISSOURI R.

Minneapolis

UNITED STATES

GREAT
SALT LAKE

Chicago

NORTH
ATLANTIC
OCEAN

San Francisco
Los Angeles

Kansas City

St. Louis

OHIO R.

New York
Washington

Phoenix
Tucson

HAWAII

Dallas

Houston

MISSISSIPPI

GULF OF MEXICO

Havana

MEXICO

YUCATÁN

CUBA

Guadalajara
Mexico City

Chichén
Itzá

CARIBBEAN SEA

Uxpanapan

CENTRAL AMERICA

EQUATOR

Caracas
VENEZUELA

CAUCA R.
Bogotá
COLOMBIA

ECUADOR

AMAZON R.

PERU

Machu Picchu
Ollantaytambo
Cuzco

BRAZIL

SOUTH PACIFIC
OCEAN

Lima

ANDES

Brasília

TAHITI

BOLIVIA

Rio de Janeiro
São Paulo

EASTER
ISLAND

CHILE

MTS.

PARAGUAY

SOUTH
AMERICA

PARANÁ R.

NEW
ZEALAND

Santiago

ARGENTINA

Buenos
Aires

URUGUAY
Montevideo

LAKE
HURON

Toronto

LAKE ONTARIO

CANADA

Rochester

Detroit

Buffalo

Cambridge

LAKE ERIE

ALLEGHENY R.

HUDSON

Hartford

Boston

Cleveland

DELAWARE R.

New Haven

New York

Pittsburgh

Princeton

UNITED STATES

Merion

Philadelphia

Cincinnati

OHIO R.

POTOMAC R.

Baltimore

Washington

ATLANTIC
OCEAN

ADAMS
COUNTY

Charlottesville

Richmond

palacios

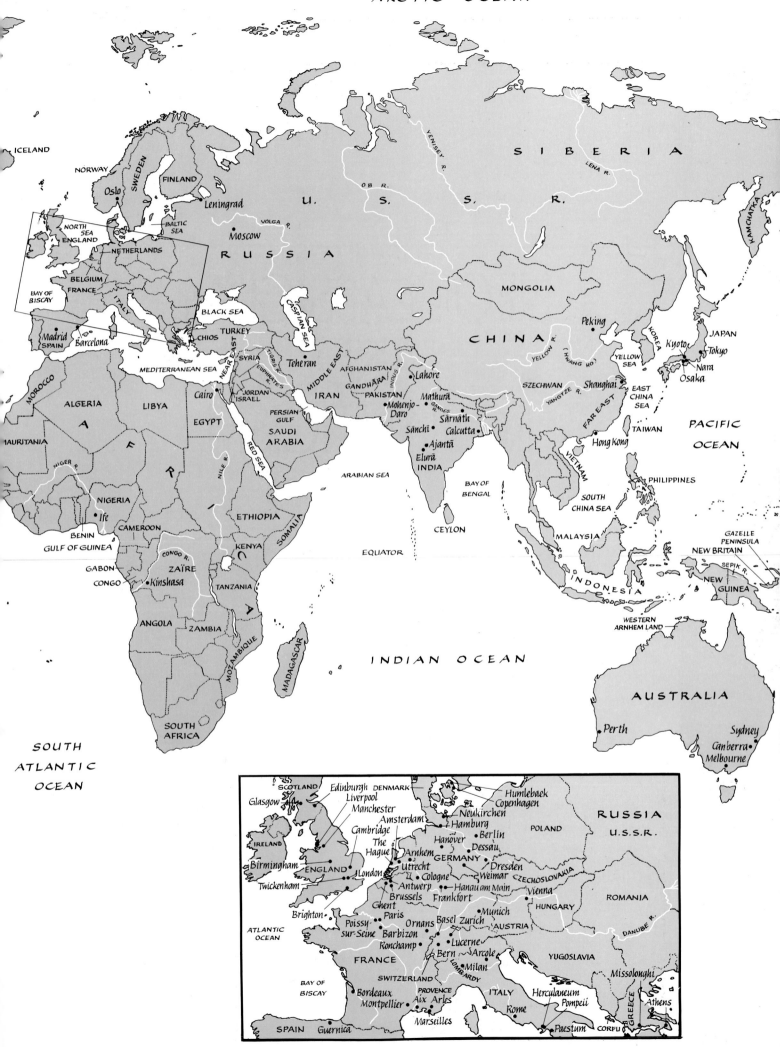

CHAPTER ONE
NEOCLASSICISM AND ROMANTICISM

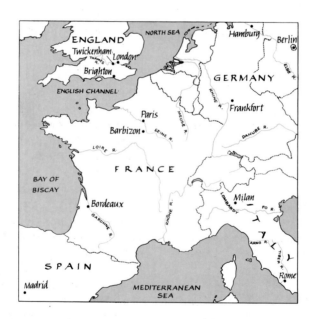

The history of the two movements to be dealt with in this chapter covers roughly a century, from about 1750 to 1850. Paradoxically, Neoclassicism has been seen as the opposite of Romanticism on the one hand and as no more than one aspect of it on the other. The difficulty is that the two terms are not evenly matched—any more than are "quadruped" and "carnivore." Neoclassicism is a new revival of classical antiquity, more consistent than earlier classicisms, and one that was linked, at least initially, to Enlightenment thought. Romanticism, by contrast, refers not to a specific style but to an attitude of mind that may reveal itself in any number of ways—including classicism. Romanticism, therefore, is a far broader concept and is correspondingly hard to define. To compound the difficulty, the Neoclassicists and early Romantics were exact contemporaries who in turn overlapped the preceding generation of Rococo artists. David and Goya, for example, were born within a few years of each other. And in England the leading representatives of the Rococo, Neoclassicism, and Romanticism—Reynolds, West, and Fuseli—shared many of the same ideas, although they were otherwise separated by clear differences in style and approach.

Neoclassicism

If the modern era was born during the American Revolution of 1776 and the French Revolution of 1789, these cataclysmic events were preceded by a revolution of the mind that had begun half a century earlier. Its standard-bearers were those thinkers of the Enlightenment in England and France—Hume, Voltaire, Rousseau, and others—who proclaimed that all human affairs ought to be ruled by reason and the common good, rather than by tradition and established authority. In the arts, as in economics, politics, and religion, this rationalist movement turned against the prevailing practice: the ornate and aristocratic Rococo. In the mid-eighteenth century, the call for a return to reason, nature, and morality in art meant a return to the ancients—after all, had not the classical philosophers been the original "apostles of reason"? The first to formulate this view was Johann Joachim Winckelmann, the German art historian and theorist who popularized the famous phrase about the "noble simplicity and calm grandeur" of Greek art (in his *Thoughts on the Imitation of Greek Works . . .*, published in 1755). His ideas deeply impressed two painters then living in Rome, the German Anton Raphael Mengs and the Scotsman Gavin Hamilton, as well as the French painter Joseph-Marie Vien. All three had strong antiquarian leanings but otherwise limited artistic powers—which may be why they accepted Winckelmann's doctrine so readily; their work is less important than their effect as teachers and propagators of the "Winckelmann program" during the 1760s and 1770s. To these artists, a return to the classics meant the style and "academic" theory of Poussin, combined with a maximum of archaeological detail newly gleaned from ancient sculpture and the excavations of Pompeii.

PAINTING
France

GREUZE. In France, the thinkers of the Enlightenment, who were the intellectual forerunners of the Revolution, strongly fostered the anti-Rococo trend in painting. This reform, at first a matter of content rather than style, accounts for the sudden fame, about 1760, of Jean-Baptiste Greuze (1725–1805). *The Village Bride* (fig. 837), like his other pictures of those years, is a scene of lower-class family life. What distinguishes it from earlier genre paintings (compare fig. 793) is its contrived, stagelike character, borrowed from Hogarth's "dumb show" narratives (see figs. 831 and 832). But Greuze had neither wit nor satire. His pictorial sermon illustrates the social gospel of Jean-Jacques Rousseau: that the poor, in contrast to the immoral aristocracy, are full of "natural" virtue and honest sentiment. Everything is intended to remind us of this, from the declamatory gestures and expressions of the actors to the smallest detail, such as the hen with her chicks in the foreground: one chick has left the brood and sits alone on a saucer, like the bride who is about to leave her "brood."

Strangely enough, *The Village Bride* was acclaimed a masterpiece, and the loudest praise came from Diderot, that apostle of Reason and Nature. Here at last was a painter with a social mission who appealed to the beholder's moral sense instead of merely giving pleasure, like the frivolous artists of the Rococo! Diderot, in the first flush of enthusiasm, accepted the narrative of Greuze's pictures as "noble and serious human action" in Poussin's sense.

DAVID. Diderot modified his views later, when a far more gifted and rigorous "Neo-Poussinist" appeared on the scene—Jacques Louis David (1748–1825). A disciple of Vien, David had developed his Neoclassic style in Rome during the years 1775–81. In his *The Death of Socrates* (fig. 838), of 1787, he seems more "Poussiniste" than Poussin himself (see fig. 803); the composition unfolds like a relief, parallel to the picture plane, and the figures are as solid—and as immobile—as statues. Yet David has added one unexpected element: the lighting, sharply focused and casting precise shadows, is derived from Caravaggio, and so is the firmly realistic detail (note the hands and feet, the furniture, the texture of the stone surfaces). In consequence, the picture has a quality of life rather astonishing in so doctrinaire a statement of the new ideal style. The very harshness of the design suggests that its creator was passionately engaged in the issues of his age, artistic as well as political. Socrates, about to drain the poison cup, is shown here not only as an example of Ancient Virtue, but also as the founder of the "religion of Reason," a Christ-like figure (there are twelve disciples in the scene).

David took an active part in the French Revolution, and for some years he had a power over the artistic affairs of the nation comparable only to Lebrun's a century before. During this time he painted his greatest picture, *The Death of Marat* (fig. 839). David's deep emotion has made a masterpiece from a subject that would have embarrassed any lesser artist, for Marat, one of the political leaders of the Revolution, had

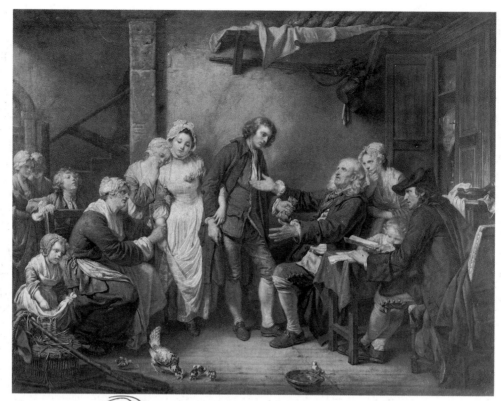

837. JEAN-BAPTISTE GREUZE. *THE VILLAGE BRIDE.* 1761.
Oil on canvas, 36×46½″ (91.3×118 cm). Musée du Louvre, Paris

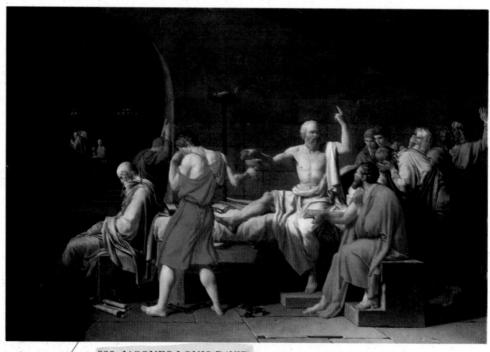

838. JACQUES-LOUIS DAVID. *THE DEATH OF SOCRATES.* 1787.
Oil on canvas, 51×77¼″ (129.5×196.2 cm).
The Metropolitan Museum of Art, New York. Wolfe Fund, 1931.
Catherine Lorillard Wolfe Collection

839. (*opposite*) JACQUES-LOUIS DAVID. *THE DEATH OF MARAT.* 1793.
Oil on canvas, 65×50½″ (165×128.3 cm).
Musées Royaux des Beaux-Arts de Belgique, Brussels

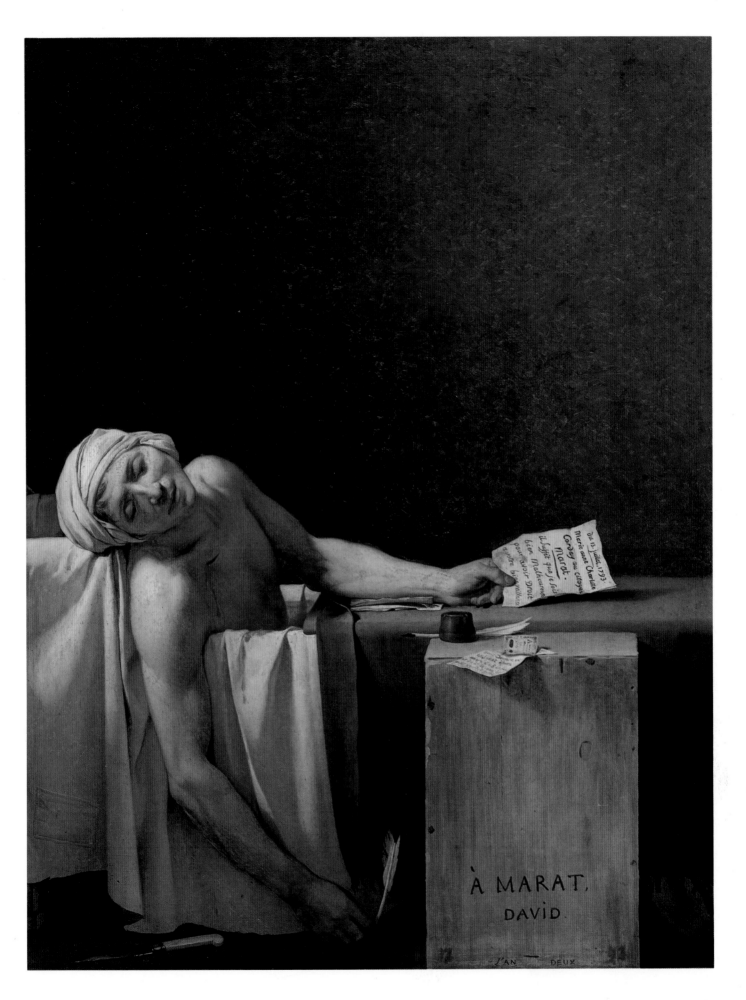

been murdered in his bathtub. A painful skin condition required immersion, and he did his work there, with a wooden board serving as his desk. One day a young woman named Charlotte Corday burst in with a personal petition, and plunged a knife into his chest while he read it.

David has composed the scene with a stark directness that is awe-inspiring. In this canvas, which was planned as a public memorial to the martyred hero, classical art coincides with devotional image and historical account. Because classical art could offer little specific guidance here, the artist—far more than in *The Death of Socrates*—has drawn on the Caravaggesque tradition of religious art. It is no accident that his *Marat* reminds us so strongly of Zurbarán's *St. Serapion* (see fig. 796).

England

WEST. The martydom of another hero was immortalized by Benjamin West (1738–1820) in *The Death of General Wolfe* (fig. 840). West traveled to Rome from Pennsylvania in 1760 and caused something of a sensation, since no American painter had appeared in Europe before. He relished his role of frontiersman—on being shown the *Apollo Belvedere* (see fig. 222) he reportedly exclaimed, "How like a Mohawk warrior!" He also quickly absorbed the lessons of Mengs and Hamilton; when he went to London a few years later, he was in command of the most up-to-date style, and became first a founder-member of the Royal Academy, then, after the death of Reynolds, its president. His career was thus European rather than American. Yet he always took pride in his New World background.

We can sense this in *The Death of General Wolfe*, his most famous work. Wolfe's death in 1759, occurring in the siege of Quebec during the French and Indian War, had aroused

considerable feeling in London. When West, among others, decided to represent this event, two methods were open to him: he could give a factual account with the maximum of historic accuracy, or he could use "the grand manner," Poussin's ideal conception of history painting (see page 588), with figures in classical costume. Had West been a European follower of Mengs and Hamilton, he would surely have chosen the latter course; however, he knew the American scene too well for that. He merged the two approaches: his figures wear contemporary dress, and the conspicuous figure of the Indian places the event in the New World for those unfamiliar with the subject; yet all the attitudes and expressions are "heroic." The composition, in fact, recalls an old and hallowed theme, the lamentation over the dead Christ (see fig. 528), dramatized by Baroque lighting.

West thus endowed the death of a modern military hero both with the rhetorical pathos of "noble and serious human actions," as defined by academic theory, and with the trappings of a real event. He created an image that expresses a phenomenon basic to modern times: the shift of emotional allegiance from religion to nationalism. No wonder his picture had countless successors during the nineteenth century.

COPLEY. West's gifted compatriot, John Singleton Copley of Boston (1738–1815), moved to London just two years before the American Revolution. As New England's outstanding portrait painter, he had adapted the formulas of the British portrait tradition to the cultural climate of his home town (see page 69).

In Europe, Copley turned to history painting in the manner of West, thus losing his provincial virtues. Most memorable as a work of art is his *Watson and the Shark* (fig. 841). Watson, attacked by a shark while swimming in Havana har-

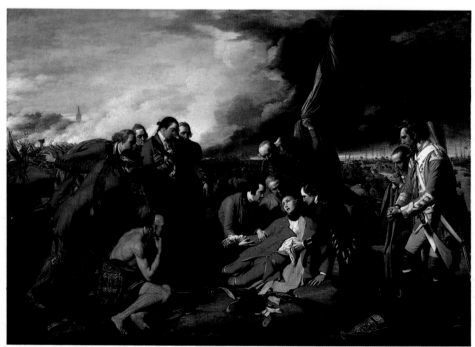

840. BENJAMIN WEST. *THE DEATH OF GENERAL WOLFE.* 1770. Oil on canvas, 59½×84″ (151×213.7 cm). National Gallery of Canada, Ottawa. Gift of the Duke of Westminster

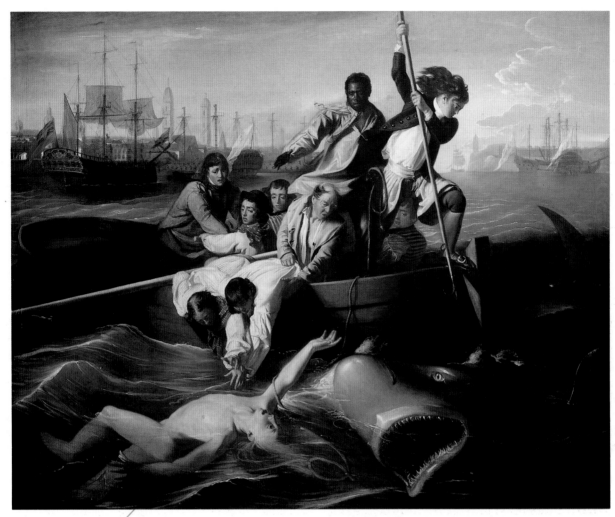

841. JOHN SINGLETON COPLEY. *WATSON AND THE SHARK*. 1778.
Oil on canvas, 72½×90¼″ (184×229.5 cm). Museum of Fine Arts, Boston.
Gift of Mrs. George von Lengerke Meyer. Courtesy, Museum of Fine Arts, Boston

bor, had been dramatically rescued; much later he commissioned Copley to depict this gruesome experience. Perhaps he thought that only a painter newly arrived from America would do full justice to the exotic flavor of the incident; Copley, in turn, must have been fascinated by the task of translating the story into pictorial terms. Following West's example, he made every detail as authentic as possible (here the black man has the purpose of the Indian in *The Death of General Wolfe*) and utilized all the emotional resources of Baroque painting to invite the beholder's participation. The shark becomes a monstrous embodiment of evil, the man with the boat hook resembles an Archangel Michael fighting Satan, and the nude youth, recalling a fallen gladiator, flounders helplessly between the forces of doom and salvation. Copley may also have remembered representations of Jonah and the Whale: these include the elements of his scene, although the action is reversed (the prophet is thrown overboard into the jaws of the sea monster). This kind of moral allegory is exemplary of Neoclassicism as a whole, and despite its charged emotion, the picture has the same logic and clarity found in David's *The Death of Socrates*.

KAUFFMAN. One of the leading Neoclassicists in England was Swiss-born Angelica Kauffman (1741–1807). A founding member of the Royal Academy, she spent fifteen years in London among the circle of Reynolds and West, whom she had met in Winckelmann's circle in Rome (see page 619). From the antique this disciple of Mengs developed a delicate style admirably suited to the interiors of Robert Adam (see page 629), which she was often commissioned to adorn. Nevertheless, Kauffman's most ambitious works are narrative paintings, of which the artist John Henry Fuseli (see page 642) observed, "Her heroines are herself." *The Artist in the Character of Design Listening to the Inspiration of Poetry* (fig. 842) combines both aspects of her art. One of her most appealing paintings, it must have held particular meaning for her. The prototype of the allegorical "friendship" pictures showing two female figures that remained popular into the Romantic era, it is eloquent testimony to women's struggle to gain recognition in the arts. That the artist has assumed the guise of Design, who bears her features, suggests her strong sense of identification with the muse.

STUBBS. George Stubbs (1724–1806), who painted portraits of racehorses—and sometimes their owners—for a living, developed a new type of animal picture full of feeling for the grandeur and violence of nature. On a visit to North Africa, he is said to have seen a horse killed by a lion; certainly this image haunted his imagination. *Lion Attacking a Horse* (fig. 843) can be seen as an animal counterpart to Copley's *Watson and the Shark*, and it has similar allegorical overtones as well. People have no place in this realm, "red in tooth and claw," and the artist identified himself emotionally with the horse, whose pure whiteness contrasts so dramatically—and symbolically—with the sinister rocks of the lion's domain. Thunderclouds racing across the sky reinforce the mood of doom; the poor horse, frightened also by the approaching storm, seems doubly defenseless against these forces of destruction. We respond to the horse as to the unfortunate Watson—with mixed fascination and horror.

Although it looks forward to Romanticism, Stubbs' effort at endowing his animals with nearly human action and emotion was the beginning of a larger investigation that was typical of the Enlightenment. He later made a series of drawings for a book of comparative anatomy—including one which could well be used to illustrate Plato's dictum that human beings are featherless bipeds—which emphasize the similarities in physiology and psychology between people and animals. His scientific curiosity and comprehensive approach relate him to the attempt by Diderot in his massive *Encyclopédie* to unite knowledge and philosophy into a single, coherent system.

COZENS. Picturesque landscape painting was as characteristic of the Enlightenment as the English garden (see page 626), to which it was closely related. As the term implies, the picturesque was a way of looking at nature through the eyes of landscape painters. The scenery of Italy and the idyllic landscapes of Claude first taught the English to appreciate

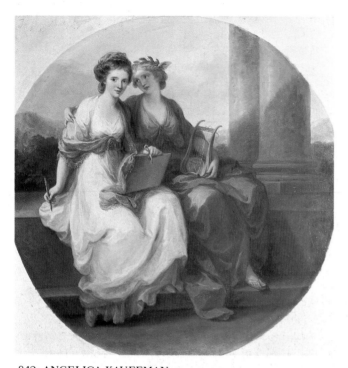

842. ANGELICA KAUFFMAN. *THE ARTIST IN THE CHARACTER OF DESIGN LISTENING TO THE INSPIRATION OF POETRY.* 1782. Oil on canvas, circular 24″ diameter (61 cm). The Iveagh Bequest, Kenwood, London [English Heritage]

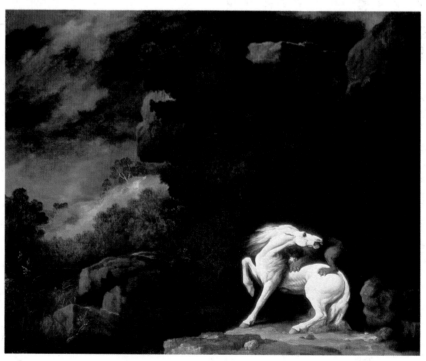

843. GEORGE STUBBS. *LION ATTACKING A HORSE.* 1770. Oil on canvas, 40⅛×50¼″ (102×127.6 cm). Yale University Art Gallery, New Haven, Connecticut. Gift of the Yale University Art Gallery Associates

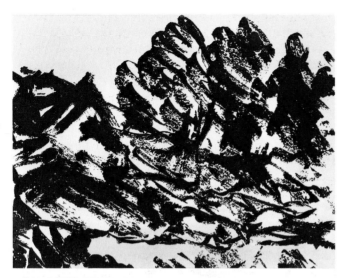

844. ALEXANDER COZENS. *LANDSCAPE*, from *A NEW METHOD OF ASSISTING THE INVENTION IN DRAWING ORIGINAL COMPOSITIONS OF LANDSCAPE.* 1784–86. Aquatint. The Metropolitan Museum of Art, New York. Rogers Fund, 1906

born, they show, if nothing else, a highly individual graphic rhythm.

Because it relies on art, the Cozens method still falls within the picturesque, while the sweeping nature of his attempt places it within the Enlightenment, with its love of systems. Needless to say, however, it has far-reaching implications, theoretical as well as practical. But these could hardly have been understood by his contemporaries; they regarded the "blot-master" as ridiculous. Nevertheless, the "method" was not forgotten, its memory kept alive partly by its very notoriety. The two great masters of Romantic landscape in England, John Constable and William Turner, both profited from it, although they differed in almost every other way.

SCULPTURE

Unlike painters, Neoclassical sculptors were overwhelmed by the authority accorded (since Winckelmann) to ancient statues such as the *Apollo Belvedere* (see fig. 222), praised as being supreme manifestations of the Greek genius while in fact most of them were mechanical Roman copies after

nature. In articulating sentiments inspired by these examples, English nature poets further validated the aesthetic response to nature, often through references to mythology. The picturesque was soon joined by wilder scenes reflecting a taste for the sublime—that delicious sense of awe experienced before grandiose nature defined by Edmund Burke in *Inquiry into the Origin of Our Ideas of the Sublime and the Beautiful* of 1756. After touring the rugged lake region of England, William Gilpin (1780) claimed, however, that the picturesque lay somewhere between Burke's extremes, since it is neither vast nor smooth but finite and rough. It later came to include a topographical mode and a rustic mode, but remained fundamentally a way of manipulating nature to conform to artistic examples.

Alexander Cozens (c. 1717–1786), who helped to originate the picturesque, soon tired of these models which, he felt, could produce only stereotyped variations on an established theme. The direct study of nature (important though it was) could not be the new starting point, for it did not supply the imaginative, poetic quality that for him constituted the essence of landscape painting. As a teacher, Cozens developed what he called "a new method of assisting the invention in drawing original compositions of landscapes" which he published, with illustrations such as figure 844, shortly before his death. What was this method? Leonardo da Vinci, Cozens noted, had observed that an artist could stimulate his imagination by trying to find recognizable shapes in the stains on old walls: why not produce such chance effects on purpose, to be used in the same way? Crumple a sheet of paper, smooth it; then, while thinking generally of landscape, blot it with ink, using as little conscious control as possible (our illustration is such an "ink-blot landscape"). With this as the point of departure, representational elements may be picked out in the configuration of blots, and then elaborated into a finished picture. The important difference between the two methods is that Cozens' blots are not a work of nature but a work of art—even though only half-

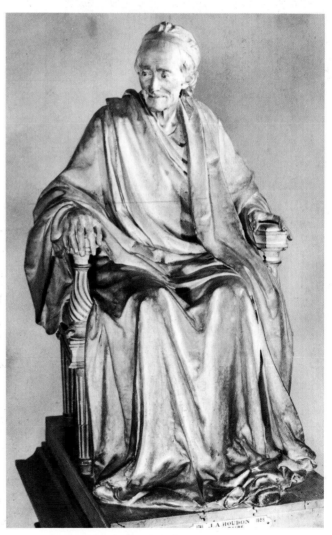

845. JEAN-ANTOINE HOUDON. *VOLTAIRE.* 1781. Terracotta model for marble, height 47" (119.3 cm). Musée Fabre, Montpellier, France

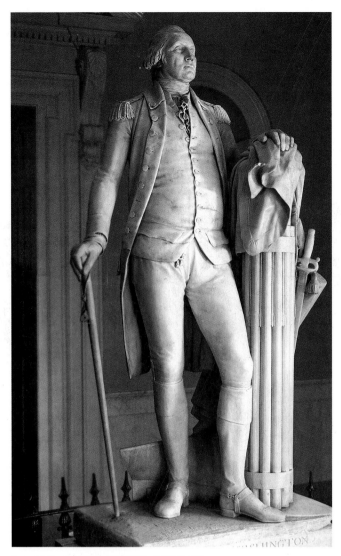

846. JEAN-ANTOINE HOUDON. *GEORGE WASHINGTON.*
1788–92. Marble, height 74" (1.9 m).
State Capitol, Richmond, Virginia

Hellenistic pieces of no great distinction. (When Goethe saw the newly discovered Late Archaic sculpture from Aegina, see figs. 179 and 180, he pronounced it clumsy and inferior.) How could a modern artist rise above the quality of these works, if he was everywhere assured that they were the acme of sculptural achievement?

HOUDON. As we might deduce from what has just been said, portraiture proved the most viable field for Neoclassic sculpture. Its most distinguished practitioner, Jean Antoine Houdon (1741–1828), still retains the acute sense of individual character introduced by Coysevox (see fig. 816). His fine statue of Voltaire (fig. 845) does full justice to the sitter's skeptical wit and wisdom, and the classical drapery enveloping the famous sage—to stress his equivalence to ancient philosophers—is not disturbing, for he wears it as casually as a dressing gown.

Houdon was subsequently invited to America to portray George Washington; he made two versions, one in classical and one in modern costume. Even the latter (fig. 846),

though meticulously up-to-date in detail, has a classical pose and displays the fasces, a bundle of rods that symbolizes union. We can feel the chill breath of the *Apollo Belvedere* (fig. 222), as it were, on the becalmed, smooth surfaces.

ARCHITECTURE

England

THE PALLADIAN REVIVAL. England was the birthplace of Neoclassicism. The earliest sign of this attitude was the Palladian revival in the 1720s, sponsored by a wealthy amateur, Lord Burlington. Chiswick House (figs. 847 and 848), adapted from the Villa Rotonda (see figs. 703 and 704), is compact, simple, and geometric—the antithesis of the Baroque pomp of Blenheim Palace. What distinguishes this style from earlier classicisms is less its external appearance than its motivation: instead of merely reasserting the superior authority of the ancients, it claimed to satisfy the demands of reason, and thus to be more "natural" then the Baroque. This rationalism explains the abstract, segmented look of Chiswick House—the surfaces are flat and unbroken, the ornament is meager, the temple portico juts out abruptly from the blocklike body of the structure.

THE ENGLISH GARDEN. Should such a villa be set in a geometric, formal garden, like Le Nôtre's at Versailles (see fig. 810)? Indeed not, Lord Burlington and his circle maintained; that would be unnatural, hence contrary to reason. So they invented what became known all over Europe as "the English landscape garden." Carefully planned to look unplanned, with winding paths, irregularly spaced clumps of trees, and little lakes and rivers instead of symmetrical basins and canals, the "reasonable" garden must seem as unbounded, as full of surprise and variety, as nature itself. It must, in a word, be "picturesque," like the landscapes of Claude Lorraine (figs. 805 and 806)—which English landscape architects now took as their source of inspiration—and include little temples half concealed by the shrubbery, or artificial ruins, "to draw sorrowful reflections from the soul."

Such sentiments were not new; they had often been expressed before in poetry and painting. But to project them onto nature itself, through planned irregularity, was a new idea. The landscape garden, a work of art intended *not* to look like a work of art, blurred the long-established demarcation between artifice and reality, and thus set an important precedent for the revival styles to come. After all, the landscape garden stands in the same relation to nature as a synthetic ruin to an authentic one, an imitation to a genuine folk song, or a Neoclassic or Neo-Gothic building to its ancient or medieval model. When the fashion spread to the other side of the Channel, it was welcomed not merely as a new way to lay out gardens, but as a vehicle of Romantic emotion.

Of all the landscape gardens laid out in England in the mid-eighteenth century, that at Stourhead most nearly retains its original appearance. Its creators, the banker Henry Hoare and the designer Henry Flitcroft, were both enthusiastic followers of Lord Burlington and William Kent; Stourhead is unique not only for its fine preservation but also for the owner's active role in planning every detail of its de-

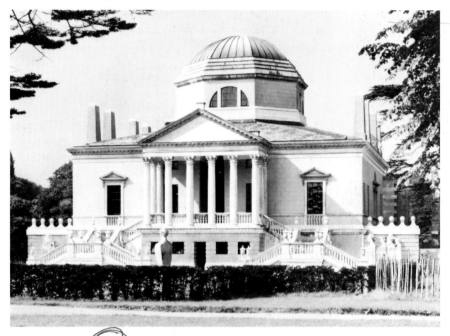

847. LORD BURLINGTON and WILLIAM KENT.
Chiswick House, near London. Begun 1725

848. Plan of Chiswick House

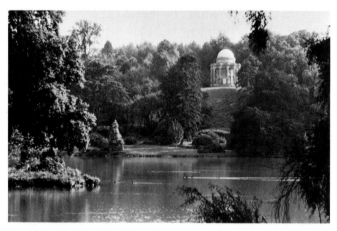

849. HENRY FLITCROFT and HENRY HOARE. Landscape garden with Temple of Apollo. Stourhead, England. 1744–65

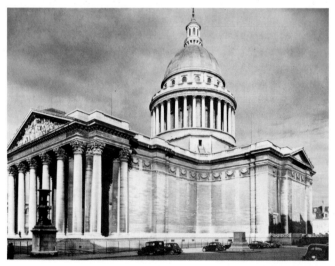

850. JACQUES-GERMAIN SOUFFLOT. The Panthéon (Ste.-Geneviève), Paris. 1755–92

velopment. Our view (fig. 849) is across a small lake made by damming the river Stour; high on the far shore is the Temple of Apollo modeled on the Temple of Venus at Baalbek (see fig. 278), which became known in the West only after 1757. Occupying other focal points at Stourhead are a grotto, a Temple of Venus, a Pantheon, a genuine Gothic cross, and a neo-medieval tower built to commemorate King Alfred the Great, "the Father of His People."

France

SOUFFLOT. The rationalist movement against the Baroque (or, rather, against the Rococo) came somewhat later in France. Its first great monument, the Panthéon in Paris, by Jacques-Germain Soufflot (1713–1780), was built as the church of Ste.-Geneviève, but secularized during the Revolution (fig. 850). Its dome, interestingly enough, is derived from St. Paul's Cathedral in London (see fig. 827), indicating England's new importance for continental architects. The smooth, sparsely decorated surfaces are abstractly severe, akin to those of Chiswick House, while the huge portico is modeled directly on ancient Roman temples. From this coolly precise exterior we would never suspect that Soufflot also had a strong interest in Gothic churches. He admired them, not for the seeming miracles they perform but for their structural elegance—a rationalist version of Guarini's point of view (see fig. 762). His ideal, in fact, was "to combine the classic orders with the lightness so admirably displayed by certain Gothic buildings." Soufflot, however, did not study Gothic architecture in detail, as later generations of architects would.

BOULLÉE. Étienne-Louis Boullée (1728–1799) was half a generation younger than Soufflot and far more daring. He built little, but his teaching at the Royal Academy helped to create a tradition of visionary architecture that flourished

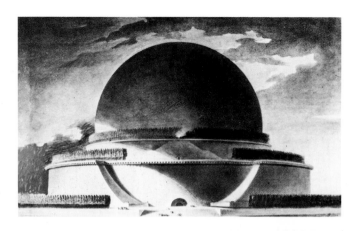

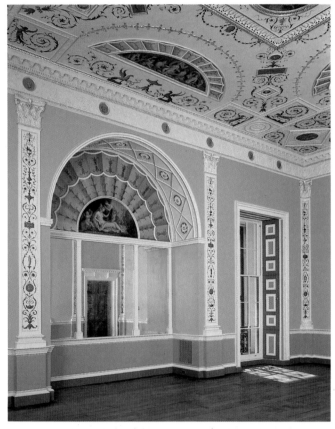

during the last third of the century and the early years of the next. Boullée's ideal was an architecture of "majestic nobility," an effect he sought to achieve by combining huge, simple masses. Most of his designs were for structures on a scale so enormous that they could hardly be built even today.

He hailed the sphere as the perfect form, since no trick of perspective can alter its appearance (except, of course, its apparent size). Thus he projected a memorial to Isaac Newton as a gigantic hollow sphere, mirroring the universe (fig. 851). "O Newton!" he exclaimed, "I conceived the idea of surrounding you with your discovery, and thus, somehow, of surrounding you with yourself." The interior was to be bare, apart from an empty sarcophagus symbolizing the mortal remains of the great man, but the surface of its upper half was pierced by countless small holes, points of light meant to give the illusion of stars. Plans such as this have a utopian grandeur that dwarfs the boldest ambitions of earlier architects. Largely forgotten during most of the nineteenth century, Boullée and his successors were rediscovered in the early twentieth, when architects again dared to "think the unthinkable."

Neoclassicism and the Antique

The mid-eighteenth century was greatly stirred by two experiences: the rediscovery of Greek art as the original source of classic style, and the excavations at Herculaneum and Pompeii, which for the first time revealed the daily life of the

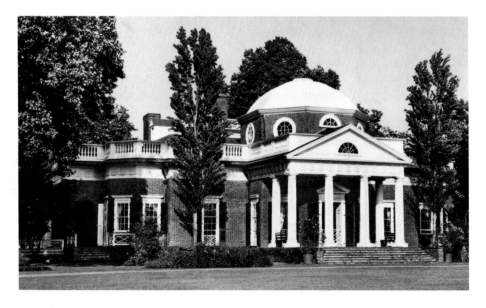

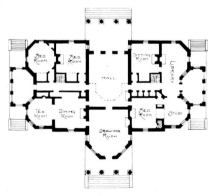

853. (*left*) THOMAS JEFFERSON. Monticello, Charlottesville, Virginia. 1770–84; 1796–1806

854. (*above*) Plan of Monticello

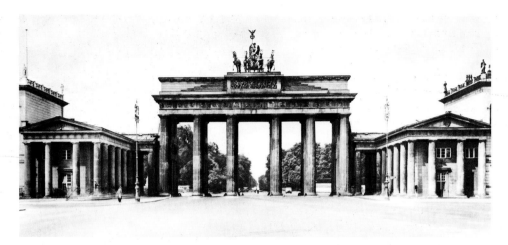

855. KARL LANGHANS. The Brandenburg Gate, Berlin. 1788–91

ancients and the full range of their arts and crafts. Richly illustrated books about the Acropolis at Athens, the temples at Paestum, and the finds at Herculaneum and Pompeii were published in England and France; archaeology caught everyone's imagination.

ADAM. From this came a new style of interior decoration, seen at its finest in the works of the Englishman Robert Adam (1728–1792), such as the room from Lansdowne House (fig. 852). Adapted from Roman stucco ornament (compare fig. 289), it echoes the delicacy of Rococo interiors but with a characteristically Neoclassic insistence on planar surfaces, symmetry, and geometric precision.

JEFFERSON. Meanwhile, the Palladianism launched by Lord Burlington had spread overseas to the American Colonies, where it became known as the Georgian style; a specimen of great distinction is Thomas Jefferson's house, Monticello (figs. 853 and 854). Built of brick with wooden trim, in design it is not so doctrinaire as Chiswick House (note the less compact plan and the numerous windows). Instead of using the Corinthian order, Jefferson (1743–1826) preferred the Roman Doric, although the late eighteenth century came to favor the heavier and more austere Greek Doric.

This "Greek revival" phase of Neoclassicism had been pioneered in England, on a small scale; it was quickly taken up everywhere, since it was believed to embody more of the "noble simplicity and calm grandeur" of classical Greece than did the later, less "masculine" orders. Greek Doric was also the least flexible order, hence particularly difficult to adapt to modern tasks even when combined with Roman or Renaissance elements. Only rarely could Greek Doric architecture furnish a direct model for Neoclassic structures: such a case is the Brandenburg Gate in Berlin (fig. 855), derived from the Propylaea on the Acropolis in Athens (see fig. 191).

The Romantic Movement

The Enlightenment, paradoxically, liberated not only reason but also its opposite: it helped to create a new wave of emotionalism that was to last for the better part of a century, and came to be known as Romanticism. The word derives from the late–eighteenth-century vogue for medieval tales of adventure (such as the legends of King Arthur or the Holy Grail), called "romances" because they were written in a Romance language, not in Latin. This interest in the long-neglected "Gothick" past was·symptomatic of a general trend. Those who, in the mid-eighteenth century, shared a revulsion against the established social order and religion—against established values of any sort—could either try to found a new order based upon their faith in the power of reason, or they could seek release in a craving for emotional experience. Their common denominator was a desire to "return to Nature." The rationalist acclaimed Nature as the ultimate source of reason, while the Romantic worshiped her as unbounded, wild, and ever-changing. If people were only to behave "naturally," the Romantic believed, giving their impulses free rein, evil would disappear. In the name of nature, the Romantics exalted liberty, power, love, violence, the Greeks, the Middle Ages, or anything else that aroused them, although actually they exalted emotion as an end in itself. In its most extreme form, this attitude could be expressed only through direct action, not through works of art. (It has motivated some of the noblest—and vilest—acts of our era.) No artist, then, can be a wholehearted Romantic, for the creation of a work of art demands some detachment, self-awareness, and discipline. What Wordsworth, the great Romantic poet, said of poetry in 1798—that it is "emotion recollected in tranquility"—applies also to the visual arts.

To cast fleeting experience into permanent form, the Romantic artist needs a style. But since he is in revolt against the old order, this cannot be the established style of his time;

it must come from some phase of the past to which he feels linked by "elective affinity" (another Romantic concept). Romanticism thus favors the revival not of one style, but of a potentially unlimited number of styles. In fact, revivals—the rediscovery and utilization of forms hitherto neglected or disliked—became a stylistic principle: the "style" of Romanticism in art (and, to a degree, in literature and music).

Seen in this context, Neoclassicism was simply the first phase of Romanticism, a revival that continued all the way through the nineteenth century, although it came to represent conservative taste. Indeed, the two seem so interdependent that we should prefer a single name for both, especially after 1800, if we could find a suitable one. ("Romantic Classicism" has not won wide acceptance.) Perhaps it is best, then, to think of them as two sides of the same modern coin. If we maintain the distinction between them, it is because, until about 1800, Neoclassicism loomed larger than the other Romantic revivals, and because of the Enlightenment's dedication to the cause of liberty as against the cult of the individual represented by the Romantic hero.

PAINTING

It is one of the many apparent contradictions of Romanticism that it became, despite the untrammeled freedom of individual creativity, art for the rising professional and commercial class which effectively dominated nineteenth-century society and which replaced state commissions and aristocratic patronage as the most important source of support for artists. Painting remains the greatest creative achievement of Romanticism in the visual arts precisely because it was less de-

pendent than architecture or sculpture on public approval. It held a correspondingly greater appeal for the individualism of the Romantic artist; moreover, it could better accommodate the themes and ideas of Romantic literature. Romantic painting was not essentially illustrative. But literature, past and present, now became a more important source of inspiration for painters than ever before and provided them with a new range of subjects, emotions, and attitudes. Romantic poets, in turn, often saw nature with a painter's eye. Many had a strong interest in art criticism and theory; some, notably Goethe and Victor Hugo, were capable draftsmen; and William Blake cast his visions in both pictorial and literary form (see page 643). Within the Romantic movement, art and literature have a complex, subtle, and by no means one-sided relationship.

Spain

GOYA. Before pursuing Romantic painting in France and England, we must take account of the great Spanish painter Francisco Goya (1746–1828), David's contemporary and the only artist of the age who may be called, unreservedly, a genius. When Goya first arrived in Madrid in 1766, he found both Mengs and Tiepolo working there. He was much impressed with Tiepolo (see page 566), whom he must have recognized immediately as the greater of the two; he did not respond to the growing Neoclassic trend during his brief visit to Rome five years later. His early works, in a delightful late Rococo vein, reflect the influence of Tiepolo and the French masters (Spain had produced no painters of significance for over a century).

But during the 1780s, Goya became more of a libertarian;

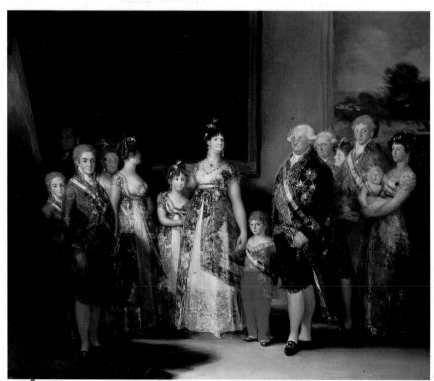

856. FRANCISCO GOYA. *THE FAMILY OF CHARLES IV.* 1800. Oil on canvas, 9'2"×11' (2.8×3.4 m). Museo del Prado, Madrid

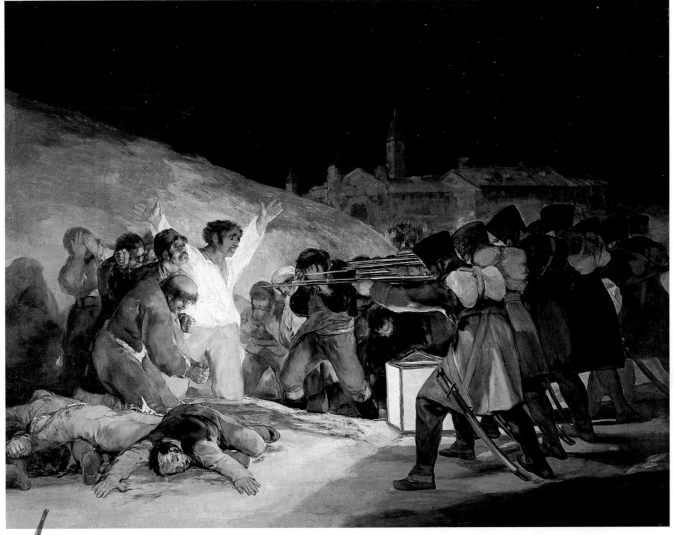

857. FRANCISCO GOYA. *THE THIRD OF MAY, 1808.* 1814–15. Oil on canvas, 8'9"×13'4" (2.7×4.1 m). Museo del Prado, Madrid

he surely sympathized with the Enlightenment and the Revolution, and not with the king of Spain, who had joined other monarchs in war against the young French Republic. Yet Goya was much esteemed at court, especially as a portrait painter. He abandoned the Rococo for a Neo-Baroque style based on Velázquez and Rembrandt, the masters he had come to admire most. It is this Neo-Baroque style that announces the arrival of Romanticism.

The Family of Charles IV (fig. 856), Goya's largest royal portrait, deliberately echoes Velázquez' *The Maids of Honor* (see fig. 799): the entire clan has come to visit the artist, who is painting in one of the picture galleries of the palace. As in the earlier work, shadowy canvases hang behind the group and the light pours in from the side, although its subtle gradations owe as much to Rembrandt as to Velázquez. The brushwork, too, has an incandescent sparkle rivaling that of *The Maids of Honor.* Although Goya does not utilize the Caravaggesque Neoclassicism of David, his painting has more in common with David's work than we might think. Like David, he practices a revival style and, in his way, is equally devoted to the unvarnished truth: he uses the Neo-Baroque of Romanticism to unmask the royal family.

Psychologically, *The Family of Charles IV* is almost shockingly modern. No longer shielded by the polite conventions of Baroque court portraiture, the inner being of these individuals has been laid bare with pitiless candor. They are like a collection of ghosts: the frightened children, the bloated king, and—in a master stroke of sardonic humor—the grotesquely vulgar queen, posed like Velázquez' Princess Margarita (note the left arm and the turn of the head). How could Goya get away with this? Did the royal family fail to realize what he had done to them? Goya, we realize, must have painted them as they saw themselves, while unveiling the truth for all the world to see.

When Napoleon's armies occupied Spain in 1808, Goya and many of his countrymen hoped that the conquerors would bring the liberal reforms so badly needed. The savage behavior of the French troops crushed these hopes and generated a popular resistance of equal savagery. Many of Goya's works from 1810–15 reflect this bitter experience. The greatest is *The Third of May, 1808* (fig. 857), commemorating the execution of a group of Madrid citizens. Here the blazing color, broad, fluid brushwork, and dramatic nocturnal light are more emphatically Neo-Baroque than ever. The picture

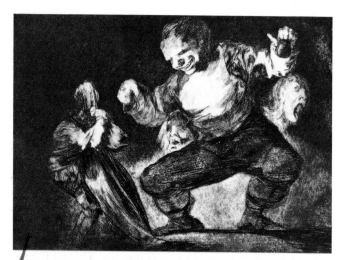

858. FRANCISCO GOYA. *BOBABILICON (LOS PROVERBIOS, NO. 4)*. c. 1818. Etching. The Metropolitan Museum of Art, New York. Dick Fund, 1931

has all the emotional intensity of religious art, but these martyrs are dying for Liberty, not the Kingdom of Heaven; and their executioners are not the agents of Satan but of political tyranny—a formation of faceless automatons, impervious to their victims' despair and defiance. The same scene was to be re-enacted countless times in modern history. With the clairvoyance of genius, Goya created an image that has become a terrifying symbol of our era.

After the defeat of Napoleon, the restored Spanish monarchy brought a new wave of repression, and Goya withdrew more and more into a private world of nightmarish visions such as *Bobabilicon* (Big Booby), an etching from the series *Los Proverbios* (fig. 858). Although suggested by proverbs and popular superstitions, many of these scenes defy exact analysis. They belong to that realm of subjectively experienced horror which we will meet in Fuseli's *The Nightmare* (see fig. 876), but are infinitely more compelling. Finally, in 1824, Goya went into voluntary exile; after a brief stay in Paris, he settled in Bordeaux, where he died. His importance for the Neo-Baroque Romantic painters of France is well attested by the greatest of them, Eugène Delacroix (see pages 635–36), who said that the ideal style would be a combination of Michelangelo's and Goya's art.

France

GROS. The reign of Napoleon, with its glamour and its adventurous conquests in remote parts of the world, gave rise to French Romantic painting. It emerged from the studio of Jacques-Louis David, who became an ardent admirer of Napoleon and executed several large pictures glorifying the emperor. As a portrayer of the Napoleonic myth, however, he was partially eclipsed by artists who had been his students. They felt the style of David too confining and fostered a Baroque revival to capture the excitement of the age. David's favorite pupil, Antoine-Jean Gros (1771–1835), shows us Napoleon as a twenty-seven-year-old general leading his troops at the Battle of Arcole in northern Italy (fig. 859). Painted in

Milan, soon after the series of victories that gave the French the Lombard plain, it conveys Napoleon's magic as an irresistible "man of destiny," with a Romantic enthusiasm David could never match.

After Napoleon's empire collapsed, David spent his last years in exile in Brussels, where his major works were playfully amorous subjects drawn from ancient myths or legends and painted in a coolly sensuous style he had initiated in Paris. He turned his pupils over to Gros, urging him to return to Neoclassic orthodoxy. Much as Gros respected his teacher's doctrines, his emotional nature impelled him toward the color and drama of the Baroque. He remained torn between his pictorial instincts and these academic principles; he never achieved David's authority and ended his life by suicide.

GÉRICAULT. The Neo-Baroque trend initiated in France by Gros aroused the imagination of many talented younger men. *Mounted Officer of the Imperial Guard* (fig. 860), painted by Théodore Géricault (1791–1824) at the astonishing age of twenty-one, offers the same conception of the Romantic hero as Gros' *Napoleon at Arcole* (see fig. 859), but on a large scale and with a Rubens-like energy.

For Géricault, politics no longer had the force of a faith. All he saw in Napoleon's campaigns was the thrill—irresistible to the Romantic—of violent action. Ultimately, the ancestors of this splendid figure are the equestrian soldiers

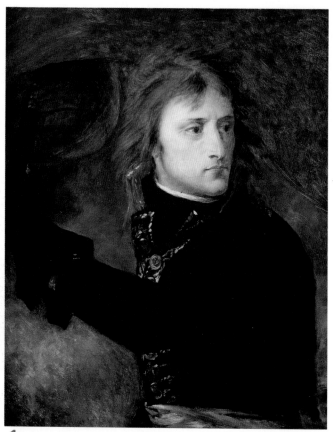

859. ANTOINE-JEAN GROS. *NAPOLEON AT ARCOLE*. 1796. Oil on canvas, 29½×23″ (74.9×58.2 cm). Musée du Louvre, Paris

in Leonardo's *Battle of Anghiari* (see fig. 643). Géricault, himself an enthusiastic horseman, later became interested in the British animal painters such as George Stubbs (see page 624). But his chief heroes, apart from Gros and the great Baroque masters, were David and Michelangelo.

A year's study in Italy deepened his understanding of the nude as an image of expressive power; he was then ready to begin his most ambitious work, *The Raft of the "Medusa"* (fig. 861). The *Medusa*, a government vessel, had foundered off the West African coast with hundreds of men on board; only a handful were rescued, after many days on a makeshift raft which had been set adrift by the ship's cowardly captain and officers. The event attracted Géricault's attention because it was a political scandal—like many French liberals, he opposed the monarchy that was restored after Napoleon— and a modern tragedy of epic proportions. He went to extraordinary lengths in trying to achieve a maximum of authenticity: he interviewed survivors, had a model of the raft built, even studied corpses in the morgue. This search for uncompromising truth is like David's, and *The Raft* is indeed remarkable for its powerfully realistic detail.

Yet these preparations were subordinate in the end to the spirit of heroic drama that dominates the canvas. Géricault depicts the exciting moment when the men on the raft first glimpse the rescue ship. From the prostrate bodies of the dead and dying in the foreground, the composition is built up to a climax in the group that supports the frantically waving black man, so that the forward surge of the survivors par-

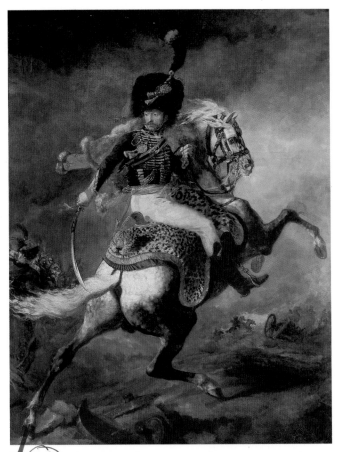

860. THÉODORE GÉRICAULT. *MOUNTED OFFICER OF THE IMPERIAL GUARD.* 1812. Oil on canvas, 9'7"×6'4½" (2.9×1.9 m). Musée du Louvre, Paris

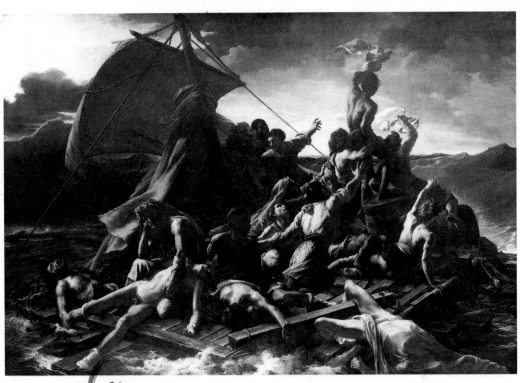

861. THÉODORE GÉRICAULT. *THE RAFT OF THE "MEDUSA."* 1818–19. Oil on canvas, 16'1"×23'6" (4.9×7.2 m). Musée du Louvre, Paris

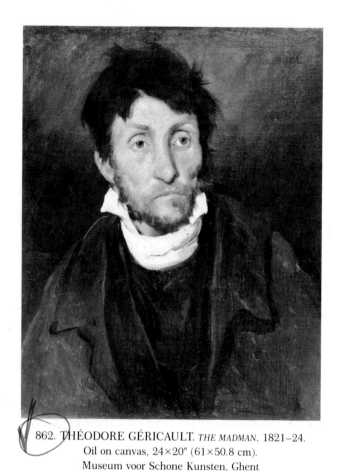

862. THÉODORE GÉRICAULT. *THE MADMAN*. 1821–24.
Oil on canvas, 24×20″ (61×50.8 cm).
Museum voor Schone Kunsten, Ghent

allels the movement of the raft itself. Sensing, perhaps, that this theme of "man against the elements" would have strong appeal across the Channel (where Copley had painted *Watson and the Shark* forty years before; fig. 841), Géricault took the monumental canvas to England on a traveling exhibit in 1820.

His numerous studies for it had taught him how to explore extremes of the human condition scarcely touched by earlier artists. He went now not only to the morgue, but to the insane asylum of Paris. There he became a friend of Dr. Georget, a pioneer in modern psychiatry, and painted for him a series of portraits of individual patients to illustrate various types of derangement, such as that in figure 862. The conception and execution of this oil sketch has an immediacy that recalls Frans Hals, but Géricault's sympathy toward his subject makes his work contrast tellingly with *Malle Babbe* (see fig. 780); this ability to see the victims of mental disease as fellow human beings, not as accursed or bewitched outcasts, is one of the noblest fruits of the Romantic movement.

INGRES. The mantle of David finally descended upon his pupil Jean-Auguste-Dominique Ingres (1780–1867). Too young to share in the political passions of the Revolution, Ingres never was an enthusiastic Bonapartist; in 1806 he went to Italy and remained for eighteen years. Only after his return did he become the high priest of the Davidian tradition, defending it from the onslaughts of younger artists.

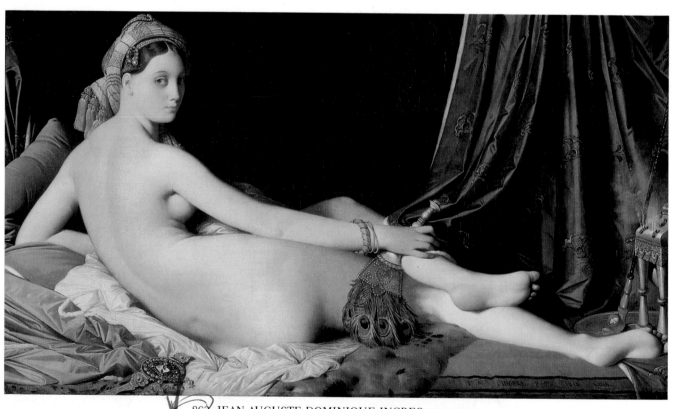

863. JEAN-AUGUSTE-DOMINIQUE INGRES. *ODALISQUE*.
1814. Oil on canvas, 35¼×63¾″ (89.7×162 cm).
Musée du Louvre, Paris

What had been a revolutionary style only half a century before now congealed into rigid dogma, endorsed by the government and backed by the weight of conservative opinion.

Ingres is usually called a Neoclassicist, and his opponents Romantics. Actually, both factions stood for aspects of Romanticism: the Neoclassic phase, with Ingres as the last important survivor, and the Neo-Baroque, first adumbrated in Gros' *Napoleon at Arcole* in France. These two camps seemed to revive the old quarrel between "Poussinistes" and "Rubénistes" (see page 597). The original "Poussinistes" had never quite practiced what they preached, and Ingres' views, too, were far more doctrinaire than his pictures. He always held that drawing was superior to painting, yet a canvas such as his *Odalisque* (fig. 863) reveals an exquisite sense of color; instead of merely tinting his design, he sets off the petal-smooth limbs of this Oriental Venus ("odalisque" is a Turkish word for a harem slave girl) with a dazzling array of rich tones and textures. The exotic subject, redolent with the enchantment of the *Thousand and One Nights*, is itself characteristic of the Romantic movement; it would be perfectly at home in the Royal Pavilion at Brighton (see fig. 894). Despite Ingres' professed worship of Raphael, this nude embodies no classical ideal of beauty. Her proportions, her languid grace, and the strange mixture of coolness and voluptuousness remind us, rather, of Parmigianino (compare fig. 684).

History painting as defined by Poussin remained Ingres' lifelong ambition, but he had great difficulty with it, while portraiture, which he pretended to dislike, was his strongest gift and his steadiest source of income. He was, in fact, the last great professional in a field soon to be dominated by the camera.

Ingres' *Louis Bertin* (fig. 864) at first glance looks like a kind of "super-photograph." But this impression is deceptive; comparing it with the preliminary pencil drawing (fig. 865), we realize how much interpretation the portrait contains. The drawing, quick, sure, and precise, is a masterpiece of detached observation, but the painting endows the sitter with a massive force of personality. Bertin's pose is shifted slightly to the left, opening his jacket to lend the figure greater weight, while the position of his powerful hands, which are barely indicated in the drawing, has been adjusted to convey an almost leonine strength. Ingres further applies the Caravaggesque Neoclassicism he had inherited from David to introduce slight changes of light and emphasis in the face, subtly altering its expression, which now manifests an almost frightening intensity.

Among the Romantics, only Ingres could so unify psychological depth and physical accuracy. His followers concentrated on physical accuracy alone, competing vainly with the camera; the Neo-Baroque Romantics, in contrast, emphasized the psychological aspect to such a degree that their portraits tended to become records of the artist's private emotional relationship with the sitter (see fig. 868). Often these are interesting and moving, but they are no longer portraits in the full sense of the term.

DELACROIX. The year 1824 was crucial for French painting. Géricault died (after a riding accident); Ingres returned to France from Italy, and had his first public success; the

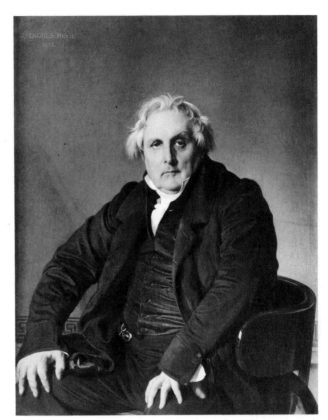

864. JEAN-AUGUSTE-DOMINIQUE INGRES. *LOUIS BERTIN*.
1832. Oil on canvas, 46×37½" (116.7×95.3 cm).
Musée du Louvre, Paris

noble

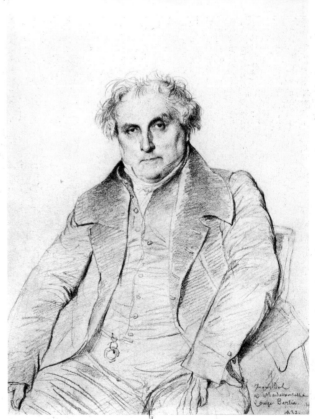

865. JEAN-AUGUSTE-DOMINIQUE INGRES. *LOUIS BERTIN*.
1832. Pencil drawing. Musée du Louvre, Paris

first showing in Paris of works by the English Romantic painter John Constable was a revelation to many French artists (see pages 643–44); and *The Massacre at Chios* (fig. 866) established Eugène Delacroix as the foremost Neo-Baroque Romantic painter. An admirer of both Gros and Géricault, Delacroix (1798–1863) had been exhibiting for some years, but the *Massacre*—conservatives called it "the massacre of painting," others acclaimed it enthusiastically—made his reputation. For the next quarter century, he and Ingres were acknowledged rivals, and their polarity, fostered by partisan critics, dominated the artistic scene in Paris.

Like *The Raft of "The Medusa," The Massacre* was inspired by a contemporary event: the Greek war of independence against the Turks, which stirred a sympathetic response throughout Western Europe (the full title is *Scenes of the Massacre at Chios: Greek Families Awaiting Death or Slavery*). Delacroix, however, aimed at "poetic truth" rather than at recapturing a specific, actual event. He shows us an intoxicating mixture of sensuousness and cruelty, but he does not succeed in forcing us to suspend our disbelief. While we revel in the sheer splendor of the painting, we do not quite accept the human experience as authentic; we react, in other words, much as we do to J. M. W. Turner's *Slave Ship* (see fig. 881).

One reason may be the discontinuity of the foreground, with its dramatic contrasts of light and shade, and the luminous sweep of the landscape behind (Delacroix is said to have hastily repainted part of the latter after seeing Constable's work). Originally, the background of *The Massacre* was probably like that in Géricault's *Mounted Officer* (fig. 860; the Turkish horseman directly recalls Géricault's earlier picture).

Delacroix's sympathy with the Greeks did not prevent his sharing the enthusiasm of fellow Romantics for the Near East. He was enchanted by a visit to North Africa in 1832, finding there a living counterpart of the violent, chivalric, and picturesque past evoked in Romantic literature. His sketches from this trip supplied him with a large repertory of subjects for the rest of his life—harem interiors, street scenes, lion hunts. It is fascinating to compare his *Odalisque* (fig. 867) with Ingres' version (fig. 863): reclining in ecstatic repose, she exudes passionate abandon and animal vitality—the exact opposite of Ingres' ideal.

This contrast persists in the portraiture of these perennial antagonists. Delacroix rarely painted portraits on commission; his finest examples are of his personal friends and fellow victims of the "Romantic agony," such as the famous Polish composer Frédéric Chopin (fig. 868). Here we see the

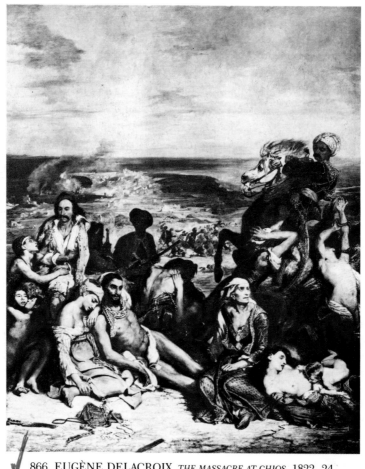

866. EUGÈNE DELACROIX. *THE MASSACRE AT CHIOS*. 1822–24. Oil on canvas, 13'10"×11'7" (4.2×3.5 m). Musée du Louvre, Paris

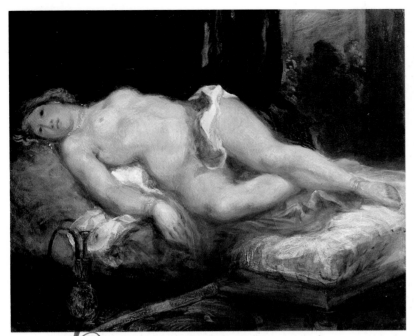

867. EUGÈNE DELACROIX. *ODALISQUE*. 1845–50.
Oil on canvas, 14⅞×18¼″ (37.3×46.5 cm).
Fitzwilliam Museum, Cambridge, England. Reproduction by
permission of the Syndics of the Fitzwilliam Museum

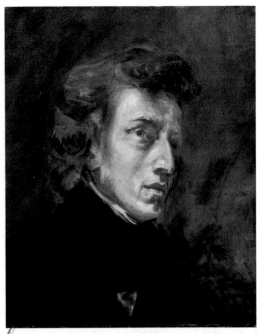

868. EUGÈNE DELACROIX. *FRÉDÉRIC CHOPIN*.
1838. Oil on canvas, 18×15″ (45.5×38 cm).
Musée du Louvre, Paris

image of the Romantic hero at its purest: a blend of Gros'
Napoleon at Arcole and Géricault's *The Madman*, the composer is consumed by the fire of his genius.

DAUMIER. The later work of Delacroix reflects the attitude
that eventually doomed the Romantic movement: its growing
detachment from contemporary life. History, literature, the
Near East—these were the domains of the imagination
where he sought refuge from the turmoil of the Industrial
Revolution. It is ironic that Honoré Daumier (1808–1879),
one of the few Romantic artists who did not shrink from reality, remained in his day practically unknown as a painter;
his pictures had little impact until after his death. A biting
political cartoonist, Daumier contributed satirical drawings
to various Paris weeklies for most of his life. He turned to
painting in the 1840s but found no public for his work. Only
a few friends encouraged him and, a year before his death,
arranged his first one-man show.

Although Daumier is sometimes called a realist, his work
falls entirely within the range of Romanticism. The neat outlines and systematic crosshatching in Daumier's early cartoons (figure 869 is a sample) show his conservative training.
He quickly developed a bolder and more personal style of
draftsmanship, however, and his paintings of the 1850s and
1860s have the full pictorial range of the Neo-Baroque. Their
subjects vary widely; many show aspects of everyday urban
life that also occur in his cartoons, now viewed from a

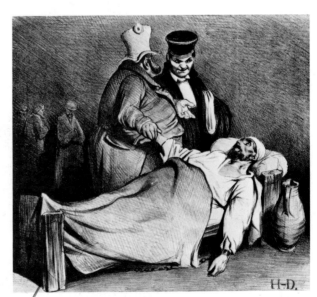

869. HONORÉ DAUMIER. *IT'S SAFE TO RELEASE THIS ONE!*
1834. Lithograph

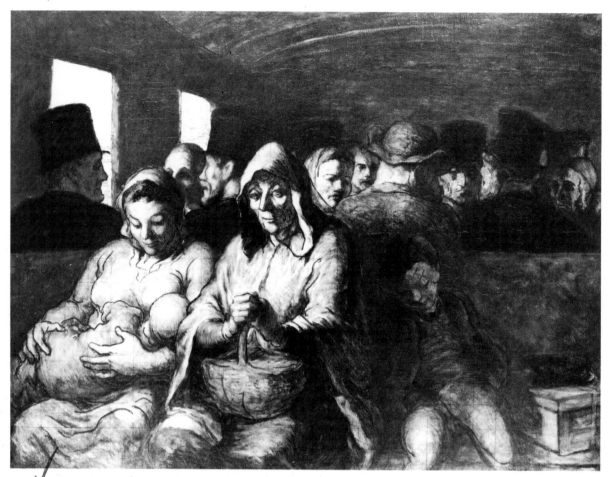

870. HONORÉ DAUMIER. *THE THIRD-CLASS CARRIAGE.* c. 1862. Oil on canvas, 26×35½″ (66×90.3 cm).
The Metropolitan Museum of Art, New York. Bequest of Mrs. H. O. Havemeyer, 1929. The H. O. Havemeyer Collection

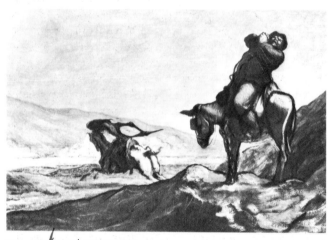

871. HONORÉ DAUMIER. *DON QUIXOTE ATTACKING THE WINDMILLS.*
c. 1866. Oil on canvas, 22¼×33″ (56.5×83.7 cm).
Collection Mr. Charles S. Payson, New York

painter's rather than a satirist's angle. *The Third-Class Carriage* (fig. 870) is such a work. Daumier's forms reflect the compactness of François Millet's (see page 640), but are painted so freely that they must have seemed raw and "unfinished" even by Delacroix's standards. Yet its power is derived from this very freedom; his concern is not for the tangible surface of reality but for the emotional meaning behind it.

In *The Third-Class Carriage*, he has captured a peculiarly modern human condition, "the lonely crowd": these people have in common only that they are traveling together in one railway car. Though they are physically crowded, they take no notice of one another—each is alone with his or her own thoughts. Daumier explores this state with an insight into character and a breadth of human sympathy worthy of Rembrandt, whose work he revered. His feeling for the dignity of the poor also suggests Louis Le Nain, who had recently been rediscovered by French critics (compare fig. 801; the old woman on the left seems the direct ancestor of the central figure in *The Third-Class Carriage*).

Other paintings by Daumier have subjects more characteristic of Romanticism. The numerous canvases and drawings of the adventures of Don Quixote, from Cervantes' sixteenth-century novel, show the perennial fascination this theme had for him. The lanky knight-errant, vainly trying to

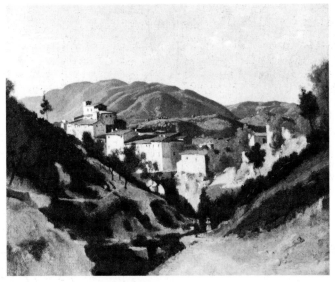

872. CAMILLE COROT. *PAPIGNO.* 1826.
13×15¾″ (33×40 cm). Private collection

live his dream of noble deeds, and Sancho Panza, the dumpy materialist, seemed to embody for Daumier a tragic conflict within human nature that forever pits the soul against the body, ideal aspirations against harsh reality. In *Don Quixote Attacking the Windmills* (fig. 871), this polarity is forcefully realized: the mock hero dashes off in the noonday heat toward an invisible, distant goal, while Panza helplessly wrings his hands, a monument of despair. Again we marvel at the strength, the sculptured simplicity, of Daumier's shapes, and the expressive freedom of his brushwork, which make Delacroix's art seem almost tame and conventional by comparison.

LITHOGRAPHS. Nearly all of Daumier's cartoons were done with lithography. Invented in Germany shortly before 1800 by Alois Senefelder, it is the most important of the planographic processes, meaning that the print is made on a flat surface. Using a greasy crayon or ink, called tusche, the artist draws or brushes the design onto a special lithographic stone; alternatively, it can be transferred from paper. (Metals such as zinc and aluminum have also been used as plates.) Once the design is fixed by an acid wash, the surface is dampened, then rolled with oily ink which adheres to the greasy design but is repelled by water. The print is made by rubbing moistened paper under light pressure against the stone. Because a limitless number of prints can be pulled relatively cheaply, lithography has been closely associated from the beginning with commercial printing and the popular press.

French Landscape Painting

Owing to the cult of nature, landscape painting became the most characteristic form of Romantic art. The Romantics believed that God's laws could be seen written in nature. While it arose out of the Enlightenment, their faith, known as pantheism, was based not on rational thought but on subjective experience, and the appeal to the emotions rather than the intellect made those lessons all the more compelling. In order to express the feelings inspired by nature, the Romantics sought to transcribe landscape as faithfully as possible. Whereas the Neoclassicists subjected landscape to prescribed ideas of beauty and linked it to historical subjects, the Romantics modified the appearance of nature to evoke heightened states of mind in accordance with dictates of the imagination, the only standard they ultimately recognized.

COROT. The first and surely the greatest French Romantic landscape painter was Camille Corot (1796–1875). Today his finest work seems not to be his late landscapes, misty and poetic; it is the early ones that establish his importance for the development of modern landscape painting. In 1825 he went to Italy for two years and explored the countryside around Rome, like a latter-day Claude Lorraine. But Corot did not transform his sketches into idealized pastoral visions; what Claude recorded only in his drawings—the quality of a particular place at a particular time (see fig. 805)—Corot made into paintings, small canvases done on the spot in an hour or two.

Such a work is his view of Papigno, an obscure little hill town (fig. 872). In size and immediacy, these quickly executed pictures are analogous to Constable's oil sketches (see fig. 879), yet they stem from different traditions. If Constable's view of nature, which emphasizes the sky as "the chief organ of sentiment," is derived from Dutch seventeenth-century landscapes, Corot's instinct for architectural clarity and stability recalls Poussin and Claude. But he, too, insists on "the truth of the moment"; his exact observation and his readiness to seize upon any view that attracted him during his excursions show the same commitment to direct visual experience. The Neoclassicists had also painted oil sketches out-of-doors; Corot's willingness, however, to accept them as independent works of art marks him unmistakably as a Romantic.

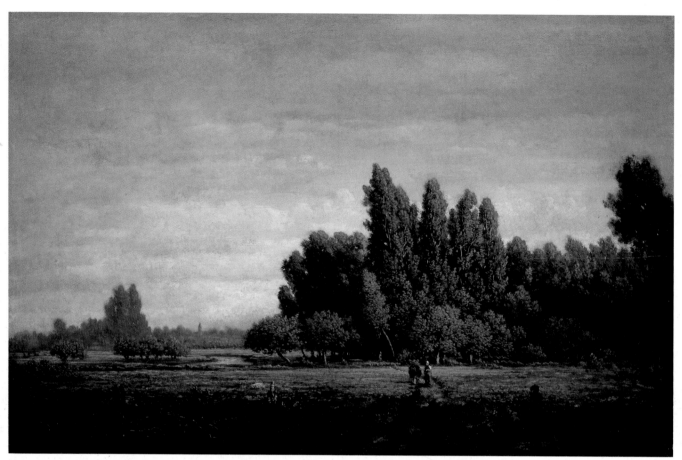

873. THÉODORE ROUSSEAU. *A MEADOW BORDERED BY TREES*,
c. 1840–45. Oil on panel, 16⅜×24⅜″ (41.6×61.9 cm).
The Metropolitan Museum of Art, New York. Bequest Robert Graham Dun, 1911

ROUSSEAU. Corot's fidelity to nature was an important model for the Barbizon School, though he was not actually a member. This group of younger painters centering on Théodore Rousseau (1812–1867) settled in the village of Barbizon, near Paris, to paint landscapes and scenes of rural life. Enthused, however, by Constable, whose work had been exhibited in Paris in 1824, they turned to the Northern Baroque landscape as an alternative to the Neoclassical tradition. From Ruisdael's example (fig. 789), Rousseau learned how to imbue his encrusted forms and gnarled trees with a sense of inner life, but it was the hours of solitary contemplation in the forest of Fontainebleau that enabled him to penetrate nature's secrets. *A Meadow Bordered by Trees* (fig. 873) is typical of his landscapes, which are filled with a simple veneration that admirably reflects the rallying cry of the French Romantics—sincerity.

MILLET. *The Sower* (fig. 874) by François Millet (1814–1875), another of the artists of the Barbizon School, has a somewhat self-conscious flavor. Blurred in the hazy atmosphere, this "hero of the soil" is nevertheless a timeless image. (Could Millet have known the pathetic sower from the October page of the *Très Riches Heures du Duc de Berry*? Compare fig. 543.) Ironically, the painting monumentalizes a rural way of life that was rapidly disappearing under the pressure of the Industrial Revolution.

BONHEUR. Millet and the Barbizon School advocated a return to nature as a way of fleeing the ills attendant to industrialization and urbanization. Despite their conservative outlook, the popular revolution of 1848 elevated them to a new prominence in French art. That same year Rosa Bonheur (1822–1899), also an artist of the out-of-doors, received a French government commission that led to her first great success and helped to establish her as a leading painter of animals—and eventually as the most famous woman artist of her time. Her painting *Plowing in the Nivernais* (fig. 875) was exhibited the following year, after a winter spent in making studies from life. The theme of humanity's union with nature had already been popularized in, among other works, the country romances of George Sand. Bonheur's picture shares Millet's reverence for peasant life, but the real subject here, as in all her work, is the animals within the landscape; these she depicts with compelling accuracy, a quality which later placed her among the most original Realists.

874. (*opposite*) FRANÇOIS MILLET. *THE SOWER.* c. 1850.
Oil on canvas, 40×32½″ (101.6×83.3 cm).
Museum of Fine Arts, Boston.
Gift of Quincy Adams Shaw through Quincy A. Shaw, Jr.,
and Mrs. Marion Shaw Haughton

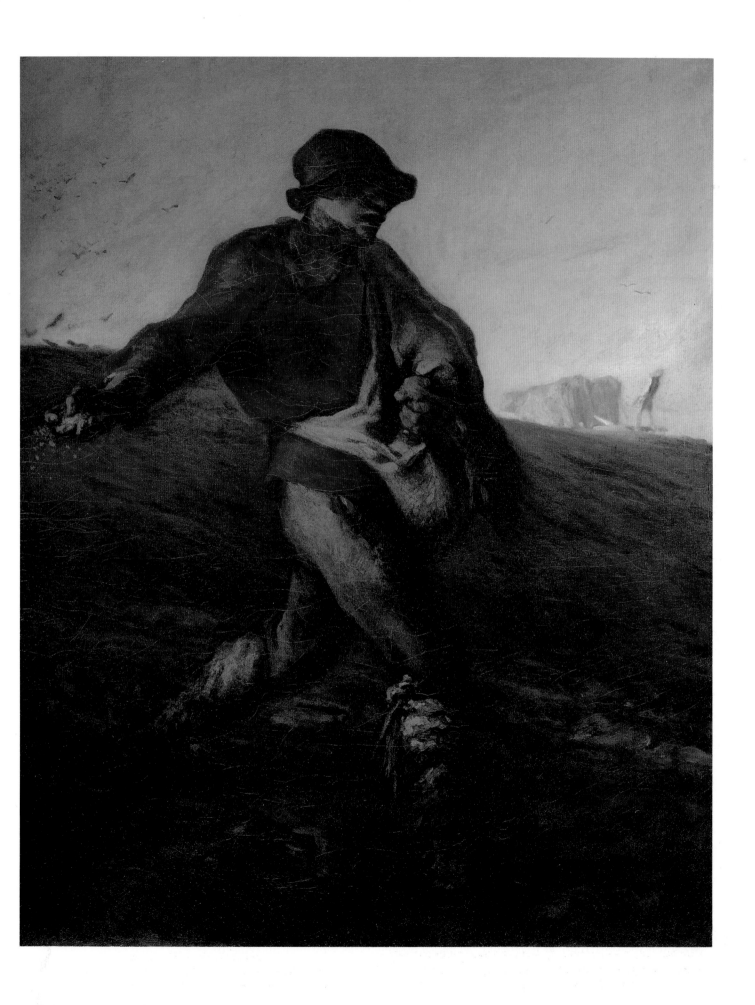

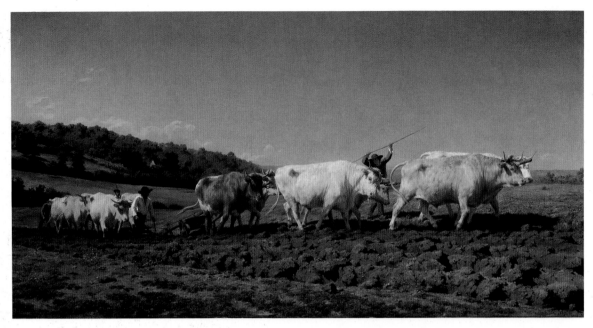

875. ROSA BONHEUR. *PLOWING IN THE NIVERNAIS.* 1849. Oil on canvas, 5′9″×8′8″ (1.8×2.6 m). Musée d'Orsay, Paris

England

FUSELI. England was as precocious in nurturing Romanticism as it had been in promoting Neoclassicism. In fact, one of its first representatives, John Henry Fuseli (1741–1825), was the contemporary of West and Copley. This Swiss-born painter—originally named Füssli—had an extraordinary impact on his time, more perhaps because of his adventurous and forceful personality than the merits of his work. Ordained a minister at twenty, he had left the Church by 1764 and gone to London in search of freedom. Encouraged by Reynolds, he spent the 1770s in Rome. There he encountered Gavin Hamilton, but Fuseli based his style on Michelangelo and the Mannerists, not on Poussin and the antique. A German acquaintance of those years described him as "extreme in everything, Shakespeare's painter." Shakespeare and Michelangelo were indeed his twin gods; he even visualized a Sistine Chapel with Michelangelo's figures transformed into Shakespearean characters where the sublime would be the common denominator for "classic" and "Gothic" Romanticism. Such fusion marks Fuseli as a transitional figure. He espoused many of the same Neoclassical theories as Reynolds, West, and Kauffman, but bent their rules almost to the breaking point. We see this in *The Nightmare* (fig. 876): the sleeping woman—more Mannerist than Michelangelesque—is Neoclassic. The grinning devil and the luminescent horse, on the other hand, come from the demon-ridden world of medieval folklore, while the Rembrandtesque lighting reminds us of Reynolds (compare fig. 835).

Here the Romantic quest for terrifying experiences leads not to physical violence but to the dark recesses of the mind. What was the genesis of *The Nightmare*? Nightmares often have a strongly sexual connotation, sometimes quite openly expressed, at other times concealed behind a variety of dis-

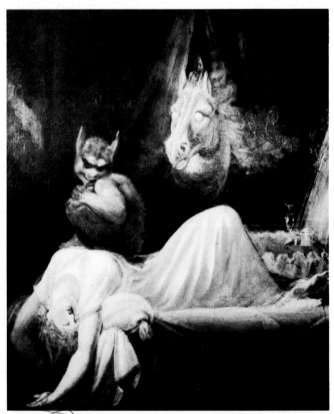

876. JOHN HENRY FUSELI. *THE NIGHTMARE.* c. 1790. Oil on canvas, 29½×25¼″ (75.5×64 cm). Frankfurter Goethe-Museum, Frankfurt

guises. We know that Fuseli originally conceived the subject not long after his return from Italy, when he had fallen violently in love with a friend's niece who soon married a merchant, much to the artist's distress. We can see in the picture a projection of his "dream girl," with the demon taking the artist's place while the horse, a well-known erotic symbol, looks on.

BLAKE. Later, in London, Fuseli befriended the poet-painter William Blake (1757–1827), who possessed an even greater creativity and stranger personality than his own. A recluse and visionary, Blake produced and published his own books of poems with engraved text and hand-colored illustrations. Though he never left England, he acquired a large repertory of Michelangelesque and Mannerist motifs from engravings and through the influence of Fuseli. He also conceived a tremendous admiration for the Middle Ages, and came closer than any other Romantic artist to reviving pre-Renaissance forms (his books were meant to be the successors of illuminated manuscripts).

These elements are all present in Blake's memorable image *The Ancient of Days* (fig. 877). The muscular figure, radically foreshortened and fitted into a circle of light, is derived from Mannerist sources (see fig. 878), while the symbolic compasses come from medieval representations of the Lord as Architect of the Universe. With these precedents, we would expect the Ancient of Days to signify Almighty God, but in Blake's esoteric mythology, he stands rather for the power of reason, which the poet regarded as ultimately destructive, since it stifles vision and inspiration. To Blake, the "inner eye" was all-important; he felt no need to observe the visible world around him.

English Landscape Painting

It was, however, in landscape rather than in narrative painting that English painting reached its fullest expression. Landscape inspired the Romantics with passions so exalted that only in the hands of the greatest history painters could humans equal nature in power as protagonists. Hence, the Romantic landscape lies outside the descriptive and emotional range of the eighteenth century. It superseded the beautiful, the sublime, and the picturesque by subsuming all three.

CONSTABLE. During the eighteenth century, landscape paintings had been, for the most part, imaginative exercises conforming to Northern and Italian examples. John Constable (1776–1837) admired both Ruisdael and Claude Lorraine, yet he strenuously opposed all flights of fancy. Landscape painting, he believed, must be based on observable facts; it should aim at "embodying a pure apprehension of natural effect." Toward that end, he painted countless oil sketches out-of-doors. These were not the first such studies, but, more than his predecessors, he was concerned with the intangible qualities—conditions of sky, light, and atmosphere—rather than with the concrete details of the scene. Often, as in *Hampstead Heath* (fig. 879), the land serves as no more than a foil for the ever-changing drama overhead, which he studied with a meteorologist's accuracy, the better to grasp its infinite variety. In endeavoring to record these fleeting effects, he arrived at a painting technique as broad, free, and personal as that of Cozens' "ink-blot landscapes," even though his point of departure was the exact opposite.

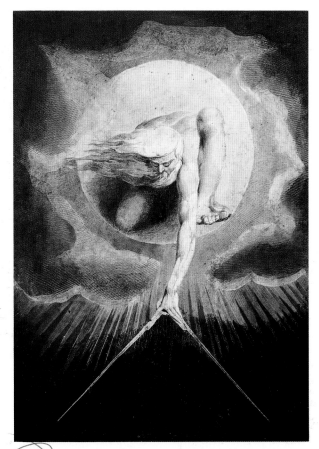

877. WILLIAM BLAKE. *THE ANCIENT OF DAYS*, frontispiece of *EUROPE, A PROPHESY*. 1794. Metal relief etching, hand-colored. Library of Congress, Washington, D.C. Lessing J. Rosenwald Collection

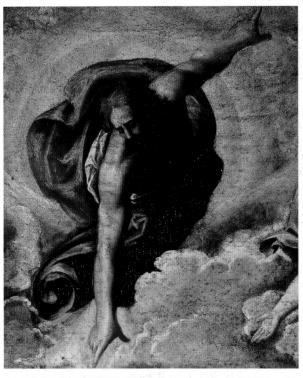

878. TADDEO ZUCCARI. *THE CONVERSION OF ST. PAUL* (detail). c. 1555. Palazzo Doria Pamphili, Rome

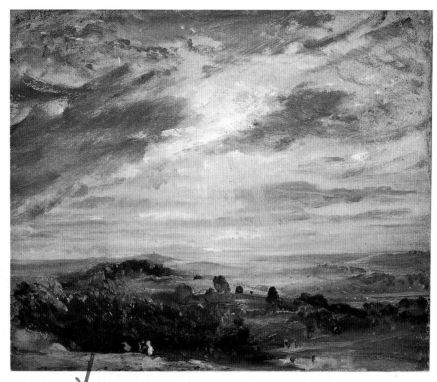

879. JOHN CONSTABLE. *HAMPSTEAD HEATH*. 1821.
Oil sketch, 10×12″ (25.3×30.5 cm). City Art Galleries, Manchester, England

All of Constable's pictures show familiar views of the English countryside. It was, he later claimed, the scenery around his native Stour Valley that made him a painter. Although he painted the final versions in his studio, he prepared them by making oil studies based on sketches from nature. The sky, to him, remained "the key note, standard scale, and the chief organ of sentiment," as a mirror of those sweeping forces so dear to the Romantic view of nature. In *The Haywain* (fig. 880), painted the same year as *Hampstead Heath*, he has caught a particularly splendid moment—a great sweep of wind, sunlight, and clouds playing over the spacious landscape. The earth and sky seem both to have become organs of sentiment informed with the artist's poetic sensibility. At the same time, there is an intimacy in this monumental composition that reveals Constable's deep love of the countryside. This new, personal note is characteristically Romantic. Since Constable has painted the landscape with such conviction, we see the scene through his eyes and believe him, even though it perhaps did not look quite this way in reality.

TURNER. Joseph Mallord William Turner (1775–1851) arrived at a style that Constable deprecatingly but acutely described as "airy visions, painted with tinted steam." Turner began as a watercolorist; the use of translucent tints on white paper may help to explain his preoccupation with colored light. Like Constable, he made copious studies from nature (though not in oils), but the scenery he selected satisfied the Romantic taste for the Picturesque and the Sublime—mountains, the sea, or sites linked with historic events; in his full-scale pictures he often changed these views so freely that they became quite unrecognizable.

Many of Turner's landscapes are linked with literary themes and bear such titles as *The Destruction of Sodom*, or *Snowstorm: Hannibal Crossing the Alps*, or *Childe Harold's Pilgrimage: Italy*. When they were exhibited, he would add appropriate quotations from ancient or modern authors to the catalogue, or he would make up some lines himself and claim to be "citing" his own unpublished poem, "Fallacies of Hope." Yet these canvases are the opposite of history painting as defined by Poussin: the titles indeed indicate "noble and serious human actions," but the tiny figures, lost in the seething violence of nature, suggest the ultimate defeat of all endeavor—"the fallacies of hope."

The Slave Ship (fig. 881) is one of Turner's most spectacular visions, and illustrates how he transmuted his literary sources into "tinted steam." First entitled *Slavers Throwing Overboard the Dead and Dying—Typhoon Coming On*, the painting compounds several levels of meaning. Like Gericault's *The Raft of the "Medusa"* (see fig. 861), which had been exhibited in England in 1820, it has to do, in part, with a specific incident that Turner had recently read about: when an epidemic broke out on a slave ship, the captain jettisoned his human cargo because he was insured against the loss of slaves at sea, but not by disease. Turner also thought of a relevant passage from *The Seasons*, by the eighteenth-century poet James Thompson, that describes how sharks follow a slave ship during a typhoon, "lured by the scent of steaming crowds, or rank disease, and death." The title of the picture conjoins the slaver's action and the typhoon—but in what relation? Are the dead and dying slaves being cast into the sea against the threat of the storm (perhaps to lighten the ship)? Is the typhoon nature's retribution for the captain's greed and cruelty? Of the many storms at sea that

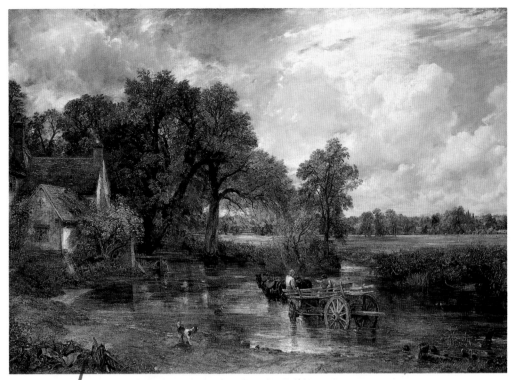

880. JOHN CONSTABLE. *THE HAYWAIN.* 1821. Oil on canvas, 51¼×73″
(130.1×185.4 cm). The National Gallery, London.
Reproduced by courtesy of the Trustees

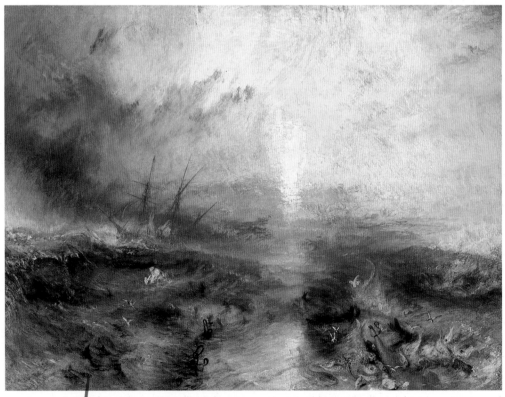

881. JOSEPH MALLORD WILLIAM TURNER. *THE SLAVE SHIP.*
1840. Oil on canvas, 35¾×48″ (90.5×122 cm).
Museum of Fine Arts, Boston.
Henry Lillie Pierce Fund (Purchase)

Turner painted, none has quite this apocalyptic quality. A cosmic catastrophe seems about to engulf everything, not merely the "guilty" slaver but the sea itself with its crowds of fantastic and oddly harmless-looking fish.

While we still feel the force of Turner's imagination, most of us today, perhaps with a twinge of guilt, enjoy the tinted steam for its own sake rather than as a vehicle of the awesome emotions the artist meant to evoke. Even in terms of the values he himself acknowledged, Turner strikes us as "a virtuoso of the Sublime," led astray by his very exuberance. He must have been pleased by praise from the theorist John Ruskin, that protagonist of the moral superiority of Gothic style, who saw in *The Slave Ship*, which he owned, "the true, the beautiful, and the intellectual"—all qualities that raised Turner above older landscape painters. Still, Turner may have come to wonder if his tinted steam had its intended effect on all beholders. Soon after finishing *The Slave Ship*, he could have read in his copy of Goethe's *Color Theory*, recently translated into English, that yellow has a "gay, softly exciting character," while orange-red suggests "warmth and gladness." Would these be the emotions aroused by *The Slave Ship* in a viewer who did not know its title?

Germany

FRIEDRICH. In Germany, as in England, landscape was the finest achievement of Romantic painting, and the underlying ideas, too, were often strikingly similar. When Caspar David Friedrich (1774–1840), the most important German Romantic artist, painted *The Polar Sea* (fig. 882), he may have known of Turner's "Fallacies of Hope," for in an earlier picture on the same theme, now lost, he had inscribed the name "Hope" on the crushed vessel. In any case, he shared Turner's attitude toward human fate. The painting, as so often before, was inspired by a specific event which the artist endowed with symbolic significance: a dangerous moment in William Parry's Arctic expedition of 1819–20.

One wonders how Turner might have depicted this scene—perhaps it would have been too static for him. But Friedrich was attracted by this immobility; he has visualized the piled-up slabs of ice as a kind of megalithic monument to human defeat built by nature herself. Infinitely lonely, it is a haunting reflection of the artist's own melancholy. There is no hint of tinted steam—the very air seems frozen—nor any subjective handwriting; we look right through the pigment-covered surface at a reality that seems created without the painter's intervention.

This technique, impersonal and meticulous, is peculiar to German Romantic painting. It stems from the early Neoclassicists—Mengs, Hamilton, and Vien—but the Germans, whose tradition of Baroque painting was weak, adopted it more wholeheartedly than the English or the French. About 1800, German painters, calling themselves the Nazarenes, rediscovered what they regarded as their native pictorial heritage: the "medieval" painters of the fifteenth and early six-

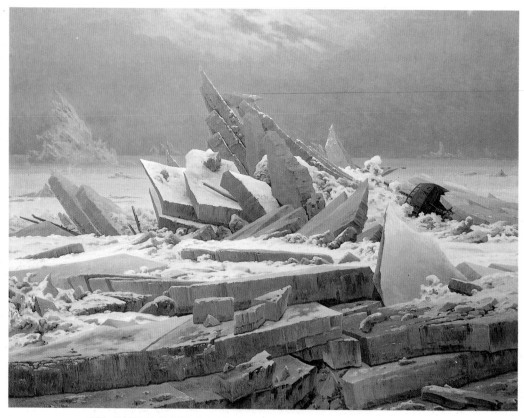

882. CASPAR DAVID FRIEDRICH. *THE POLAR SEA*. 1824. Oil on canvas,
38½ × 50½" (97.7 × 128.2 cm). Kunsthalle, Hamburg

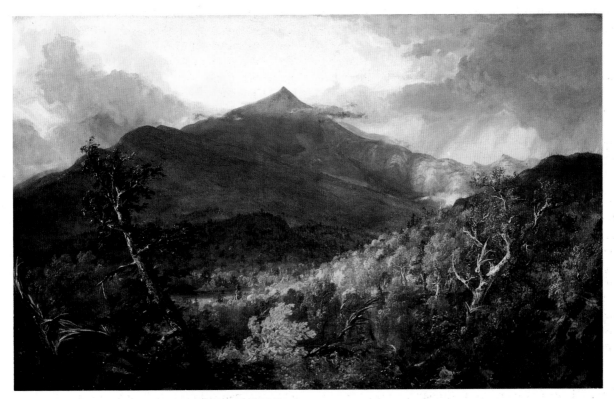

883. THOMAS COLE. *SCHROON MOUNTAIN, ADIRONDACKS.*
1838. Oil on canvas, 39⅜×63″ (100×160 cm).
The Cleveland Museum of Art. The Hinman B. Hurlbut Collection

teenth centuries. This "Gothic Revival," however, remained limited to subject matter and technique; the painstaking precision of the old German masters merely reinforced the Neoclassic emphasis on form at the expense of color. Although in Friedrich's hands this technique yielded extraordinary effects, it was a handicap for most German artists who lacked his compelling imagination.

United States

Painting following the American Revolution was dominated by protégés of Benjamin West, who took every young artist arriving from the New World under his wing. Strangely enough, the only ones to enjoy much success were portraitists such as Gilbert Stuart. Using the fashionable conventions of Joshua Reynolds, they conferred the aura of established aristocracy on the Federalists, who were only too eager to forget the recent revolutionary past enshrined by the history painters. What the United States wanted was an art based not on the past but on the present. During the 1820s, Americans found their history painting in genre scenes descended from Dutch and English examples. At the same time, they discovered landscape painting. (Before then, settlers were far too busy carving out homesteads to pay much attention to the poetry of nature's moods.)

The attitude toward landscape began to change only as the surrounding wilderness was gradually tamed, allowing Americans for the first time to see nature as the escape from

civilization that inspired European painters. As in England, the contribution of the poets proved essential to shaping American ideas about nature. By 1825, they were calling on artists to depict the wilderness as the most conspicuous feature of the New World and its emerging civilization. Pantheism virtually became a national religion during the Romantic era. While it could be frightening, nature was everywhere, and was believed to play a special role in determining the American character. Led by Thomas Cole (1801–1848), the founder of the Hudson River School—which flourished from 1825 until the Centennial celebration in 1876—American painters elevated the forests and mountains to symbols of the United States.

COLE. Like many early American landscape painters, Cole came from England, where he was trained as an engraver, and learned the rudiments of painting from an itinerant artist in the Midwest. It was his genius to invent the means of expressing the elemental power of the country's primitive landscape by transforming the formulas of the English picturesque, following a summer sketching tour up the Hudson River. Because he also wrote poetry, Cole was able to create a visual counterpart to the literary rhetoric of the day. *Schroon Mountain, Adirondacks* (fig. 883) shows the peak rising majestically, like a pyramid, from the forest below. It is treated as a symbol of permanence surrounded by death and decay, signified by the autumnal foliage, passing storm, and lightning-blasted trees. Stirred by sublime emotion, the artist heightened the dramatic lighting, so that the broad landscape becomes a revelation of God's eternal laws.

BINGHAM. *Fur Traders Descending the Missouri* (fig. 884) by George Caleb Bingham (1811–1879) shows this close identification with the land in a different way. The picture is both a landscape and a genre scene, and it is full of the vastness and silence of the wide-open spaces. The two trappers in their dugout canoe, gliding downstream in the misty sunlight, are entirely at home in this idyllic setting. The assertion of human presence in this hospitable setting portrays the United States as a benevolent Eden in which settlers assume their rightful place. Rather than being dwarfed by a vast and often hostile continent, these hardy pioneers live in an ideal state of harmony with nature, symbolized by the waning daylight. The picture carries us back to the river life of Mark Twain's childhood. At the same time, it reminds us of how much Romantic adventurousness went into the westward expansion of the United States. The scene owes much of its haunting charm to the silhouette of the black cub chained to the prow and its reflection in the water. This masterstroke adds a note of primitive mystery that we shall not meet again until the work of Henri Rousseau (see page 696).

SCULPTURE

The development of sculpture follows the pattern of painting. However, we shall find it a good deal less venturesome than either painting or architecture. The unique virtue of sculpture—its solid, space-filling reality (or, if you will, its "idol" quality)—was not congenial to the Romantic temperament. The rebellious and individualistic urges of Romanticism could find expression in rough, small-scale sketches but rarely survived the laborious process of translating the sketch into a permanent, finished monument. The new standard of uncompromising, realistic "truth" was embarrassing to the sculptor. When a painter renders clothing, anatomical detail, or furniture with photographic precision he does not produce a duplicate of reality, but a representation of it; while to do so in sculpture comes dangerously close to mechanical reproduction—a handmade equivalent of the plaster cast. Sculpture thus underwent a crisis that was resolved only toward the end of the century.

CANOVA. At the beginning of the Romantic era, we find at first an adaptation of the Neoclassical style to new ends by sculptors, especially older ones. The most famous of them,

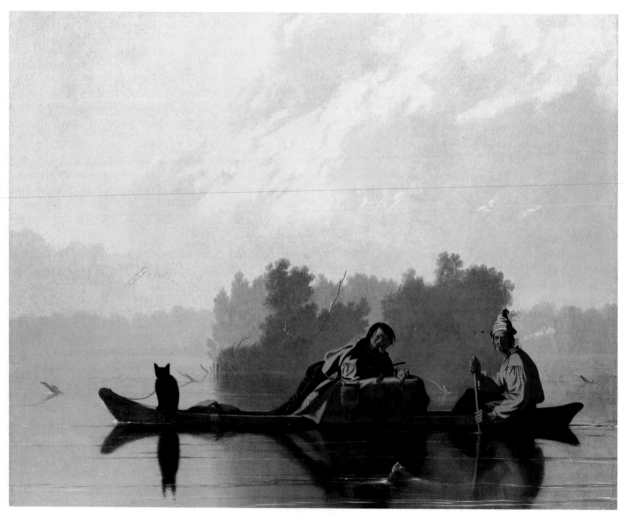

884. GEORGE CALEB BINGHAM. *FUR TRADERS DESCENDING THE MISSOURI*. c. 1845. Oil on canvas, 29×36″ (73.7×91.3 cm). The Metropolitan Museum of Art, New York. Morris K. Jesup Fund, 1933

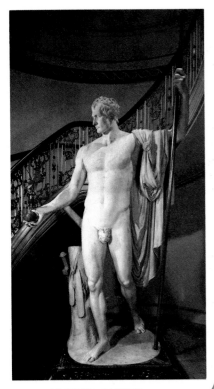

885. ANTONIO CANOVA. *NAPOLEON.*
1806. Marble, over lifesize.
Apsley House, London

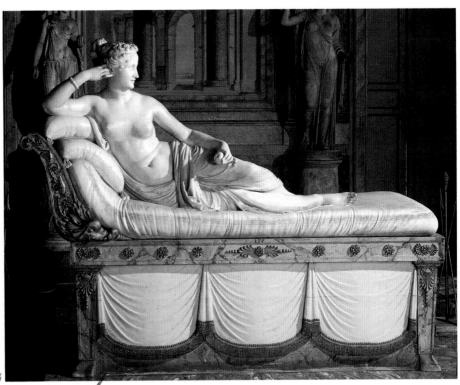

886. ANTONIO CANOVA. *PAULINE BORGHESE AS VENUS.* 1808.
Marble, lifesize. Galleria Borghese, Rome

Antonio Canova (1757–1822), produced a colossal nude statue of Napoleon (fig. 885) inspired by portraits of ancient rulers whose nudity indicates their status as divinities. The elevation of the emperor to a god marks a shift away from the noble ideals of the Enlightenment that had given rise to Neoclassicism. The glorification of the hero as a noble example, seen in Houdon's statue of George Washington (fig. 846), is abandoned in favor of the Romantic cult of the individual. There is no longer any higher authority—neither religion, nor reason is invoked—only the imperative of Greek art remains unquestioned as a style divorced from content. Not to be outdone, Napoleon's sister Pauline Borghese permitted Canova to sculpt her as a reclining Venus (fig. 886). The statue is so obviously idealized as to still any gossip; we recognize it as a precursor, more classically proportioned, of Ingres' *Odalisque* (see fig. 863). She is equally typical of early Romanticism, which incorporated Rococo eroticism but in a less sensuous form. Strangely enough, *Pauline Borghese* seems less three-dimensional than the painting. She is designed like a "relief in the round," for front and back view only, and her very considerable charm radiates almost entirely from the fluid grace of her contours.

Here we also encounter the problem of representation versus duplication, not in the figure itself but in the pillows, mattress, and couch. The question recurs on a larger scale in Canova's most ambitious work, the Tomb of the Archduchess Maria Christina (fig. 887). Its design, again essentially linear and relieflike though the statues are carved in the round, has no precedents in earlier tombs: the deceased ap-

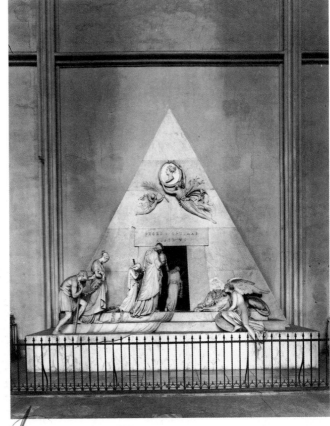

887. ANTONIO CANOVA. Tomb of the Archduchess Maria Christina. 1798–1805. Marble, lifesize. Augustinerkirche, Vienna

pears only in a portrait medallion framed by a snake biting its own tail, a symbol of eternity. Presumably, but not actually, the urn carried by the woman in the center contains her ashes. This is an ideal burial service performed by classical figures, mostly allegorical (the group on the left represents the Three Ages of Man), who are about to enter the pyramid-shaped tomb.

What troubles us is that this ensemble, in contrast to the tombs of earlier times (such as fig. 623), does not include the real burial place—the pyramid is a sham, a shallow façade built against the wall of the church. But if we must view the monument as a sort of theatrical performance in marble, we expect the artist to characterize it as such by creating a "stage space" that will set it apart from its surroundings (like Bernini's *The Ecstasy of St. Theresa*; see fig. 751). Since Canova has not done this, the performance becomes confusingly realistic. Should we join the "actors" on their perfectly real marble steps? No, for we cannot follow them into a mock pyramid. What distinguishes the real from the mock architecture? To what level of reality does the cloth on the steps belong?

PRÉAULT. This dilemma could be resolved in two ways: by reviving a pre-classical style sufficiently abstract to restore the autonomous reality of sculpture, or by a return to the frankly theatrical Baroque. Only the latter alternative proved generally feasible at the time, although there were isolated attempts to explore the former. Auguste Préault (1809–1879), who was the boldest sculptor of his day and whose personality closely approached the Romantic ideal, experimented in both directions. His relief, *Slaughter* (fig. 888), is brimming with a physical and emotional violence far beyond anything found in Baroque art, yet its expressive distortions, its irrational space filled to the bursting point with writhing shapes, evoke memories of Gothic sculpture (compare fig. 513). In fact, the helmeted knight's face next to that of the screaming mother hints that the subject itself is medieval: some dread apocalyptic event beyond one's control. But in true Romantic fashion Préault does not define this event. He proclaimed, "Je ne suis pas pour le fini. Je suis pour l'infini" (I am not for the finite. I am for the infinite), a play on words conveying his preference for the unfinished over the finished as well as for the infinite over the finite.

RUDE. When *Slaughter* was shown to the public in 1834 it found few admirers. One of these must have been the somewhat older sculptor François Rude (1784–1855), as suggested by his own masterpiece, the splendidly rhetorical *La Marseillaise* (fig. 889) on one pier of the Arc de Triomphe in Paris. The soldiers, volunteers of 1792 rallying to defend the Republic, are still in classical guise, but the Genius of Liberty above them imparts her great forward-rushing movement to the entire group. She would not be unworthy of Puget (see fig. 817).

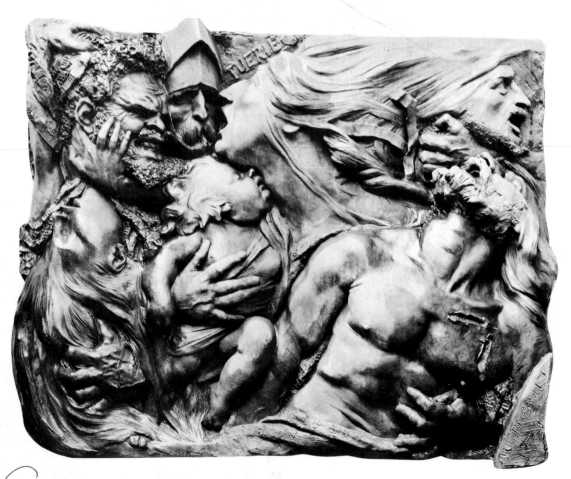

888. AUGUSTE PRÉAULT. *SLAUGHTER.* 1834. Bronze, 43×55″ (109.2×139.7 cm). Musée des Beaux-Arts, Chartres

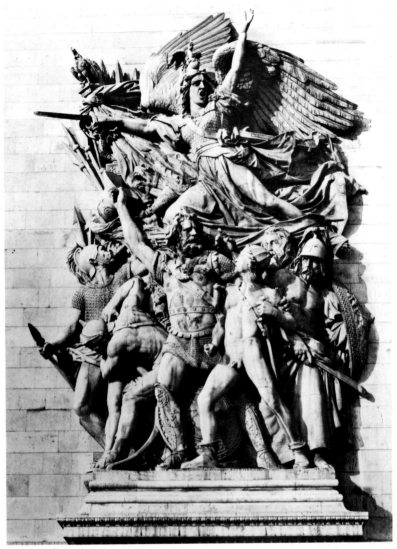

889. FRANÇOIS RUDE. *LA MARSEILLAISE.* 1833–36. Stone,
c. 42×26′ (12.8×7.9 m). Arc de Triomphe, Paris

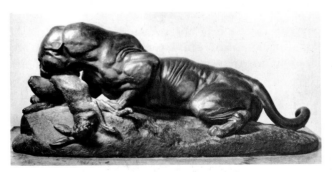

890. ANTOINE-LOUIS BARYE.
JAGUAR DEVOURING A HARE.
1850–51. Bronze, 16½×37½″ (42×95.3 cm).
Musée du Louvre, Paris

BARYE. The ultimate source of *La Marseillaise* is pictorial.
In a similar way, Stubbs' *Lion Attacking a Horse* (see fig.
843) is the sire of animal groups by Antoine-Louis Barye
(1795–1875), the Romantic sculptor closest to Delacroix.
The forms of his *Jaguar Devouring a Hare* (fig. 890) have
energy and volume; their simplicity, for all the anatomical
detail, is rare indeed in mid–nineteenth-century sculpture.
However, these qualities can be found only in Barye's smaller
pieces; as an architectural sculptor he is disappointingly academic.

CARPEAUX. Rude's real successor in the field of architectural sculpture was Jean-Baptiste Carpeaux (1827–1875),
whose famous group for the façade of the Paris Opéra, *The
Dance* (fig. 891), perfectly matches Charles Garnier's Neo-
Baroque architecture (see page 655). The plaster model in
our illustration is both livelier and more precise than the final
stone group (visible in fig. 899, lower right). Its coquettish
gaiety derives from small Rococo groups such as Clodion's

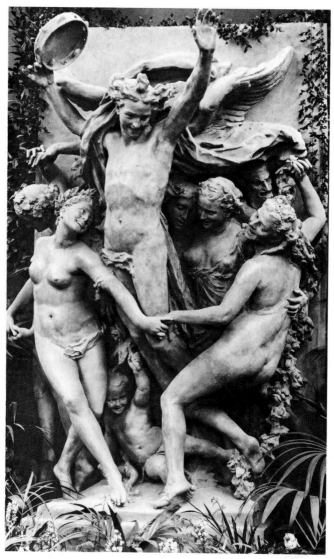

891. JEAN-BAPTISTE CARPEAUX. *THE DANCE.* 1867–69.
Plaster model, c. 15'×8'6" (4.6×2.6 m). Musée de l'Opéra, Paris

(see fig. 821), and its sense of scale, too, seems at odds with its size—although the figures look smaller than life, the group is actually fifteen feet tall. Nor is this the only discrepancy; Carpeaux's figures, unlike Clodion's, look undressed rather than nude. We do not accept them as legitimate denizens of the realm of mythology, and they slightly embarrass us, as if "real people" were acting out a Rococo scene. A single leg, detached from this group, might well be mistaken for a cast from nature. "Truth" here has destroyed the ideal reality that was still intact for Clodion a century before.

ARCHITECTURE

Given the individualistic nature of Romanticism, we might expect the range of revival styles to be widest in painting, the most personal and private of the visual arts, and least wide in architecture, the most communal and public. Yet the opposite is true. Painters and sculptors were unable to aban-

don Rennaissance habits of representation, and never really revived medieval art, or ancient art before the Classical Greek era. Architects were not subject to this limitation, and the revival styles persisted longer in architecture than in the other arts.

Classic and Gothic Revivals

Characteristically, at the time architects launched the Classic revival, they also started a Gothic revival. England was far in advance here, as it was in the development of Romantic literature and painting. Gothic architecture had never wholly disappeared in England—for special purposes, Gothic forms were used on occasion even by Sir Christopher Wren and Sir John Vanbrugh (see pages 602–3), but these were survivals of an authentic, if outmoded, tradition. The conscious revival, by contrast, was linked with the cult of the picturesque, and with the vogue for medieval (and pseudo-medieval romances.

WALPOLE. In this spirit Horace Walpole (1717–1797), midway in the century, enlarged and "gothicized" his country house, Strawberry Hill (figs. 892 and 893). Despite its studied irregularity, the rambling structure has dainty, flat surfaces that remind us strongly of Robert Adam (compare fig. 852); the interior looks almost as if decorated with lace-paper doilies. This playfulness, so free of dogma, gives Strawberry Hill its special charm. Gothic here is still an "exotic" style; it appeals because it is strange, but for that very reason it must be "translated," like a medieval romance, or the Chinese motifs that crop up in Rococo decoration.

NASH. The Romantic imagination saw Gothic and the mysterious East in much the same light, as John Nash's (1752–1835) Royal Pavilion at Brighton (fig. 894) well demonstrates half a century later. The style of this "stately pleasure dome," a cream-puff version of the Taj Mahal (see fig. 373), was then known as Indian Gothic. It is equally characteristic of Romanticism, however, that by 1800 the Gothic was a fully acceptable alternative to the Greek revival as a style for major churches.

LATROBE. Benjamin Latrobe (1764–1820), an Anglo-American who became, under Jefferson, the most influential architect of "Federal" Neoclassicism, submitted a design in each style for the Cathedral in Baltimore; the Neoclassic one was chosen, but it might well have been the Neo-Gothic. The exterior of the present building (fig. 895) has walls that resemble Soufflot's Panthéon, a dome of more severe design,

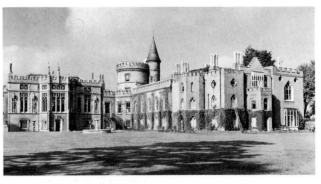

892. HORACE WALPOLE, with WILLIAM ROBINSON and others. Strawberry Hill, Twickenham. 1749–77

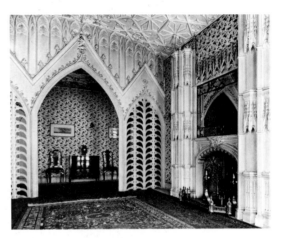

893. Interior, Strawberry Hill

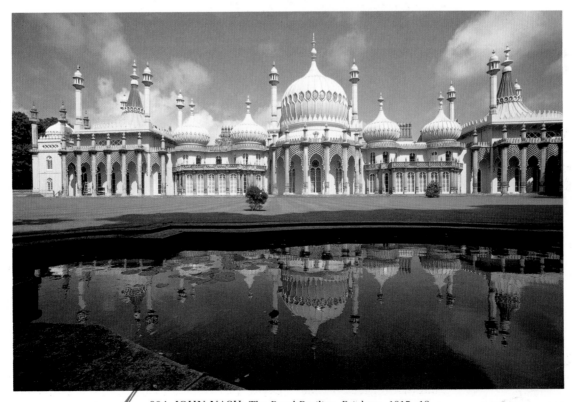

894. JOHN NASH. The Royal Pavilion, Brighton. 1815–18

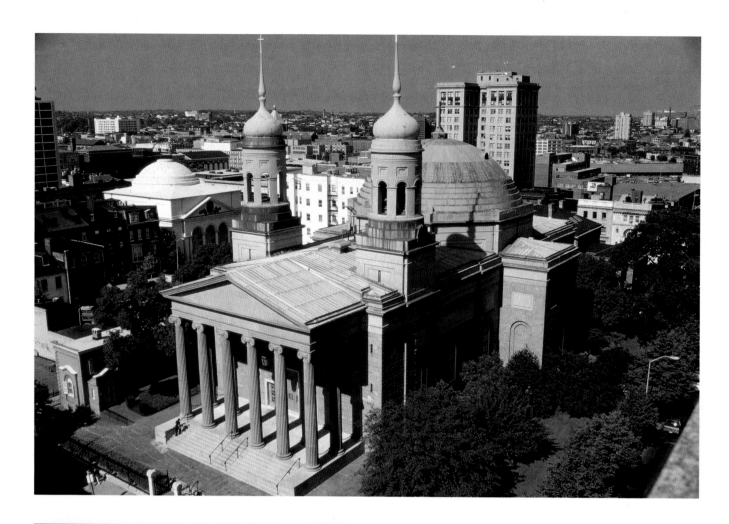

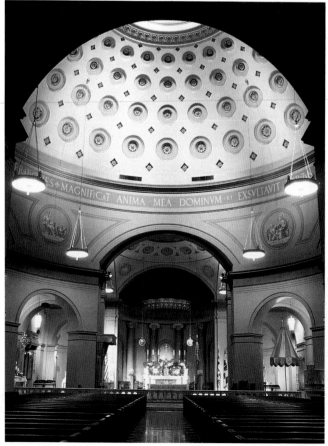

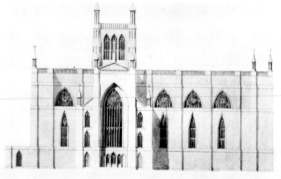

895. (*top*) BENJAMIN LATROBE. Baltimore Cathedral
(Basilica of the Assumption),
Baltimore, Maryland. Begun 1805

896. (*left*) Interior, Baltimore Cathedral

897. (*above*) BENJAMIN LATROBE. Alternative design
for Baltimore Cathedral

a temple front, and bell towers of disguised Gothic-Baroque ancestry (the bulbous crowns are not his work).

Far more distinguished is the interior (fig. 896). Although inspired by the domed and vaulted spaces of ancient Rome, especially the Pantheon (see fig. 266), Latrobe was not interested in archaeological correctness. The "muscularity" of Roman structures has been suppressed; moldings, profiles, and coffers are no more than linear accents that do not disturb the continuous, abstract surfaces. In this Romantic interpretation, the spatial qualities of ancient architecture become vast, pure, Sublime. The strangely weightless interior presents almost that combination of classic form and Gothic lightness first postulated by Soufflot; it also shows the free and imaginative look of the mature Neoclassic style, when handled by a gifted architect. Had the Gothic design (fig. 897) been chosen, the exterior might have been more striking, but the interior probably less impressive. Like most Romantic architects seeking the Sublime, Latrobe viewed Gothic churches "from the outside in"—as mysterious, looming structures silhouetted against the sky—but nourished his spatial fantasy on Roman monuments.

After 1800, the choice between the classic and Gothic modes was more often resolved in favor of Gothic. Nationalist sentiments, strengthened in the Napoleonic wars, became important factors, for England, France, and Germany each tended to think that Gothic expressed its particular national genius. Certain theorists, notably John Ruskin, also regarded Gothic as superior for ethical or religious reasons (it was "honest" and "Christian").

BARRY AND PUGIN. All these considerations were conjoined in the design, by Sir Charles Barry (1785–1860) and A. N. Welby Pugin (1812–1852), for the Houses of Parliament in London, the largest monument of the Gothic revival (fig. 898). As the seat of a vast and complex governmental apparatus, but at the same time as a focus of patriotic feeling, it presents a curious mixture—repetitious symmetry governs the main body of the structure and "picturesque" irregularity its silhouette. Meanwhile, the stylistic alternatives were continually increased for architects by other revivals.

Neo-Baroque and Neo-Renaissance

GARNIER. When, by mid-century, the Renaissance, and then the Baroque, returned to favor, the revival movement had come full circle: Neo-Renaissance and Neo-Baroque replaced the Neoclassic. This final phase of Romantic architecture, which dominated the years 1850–75 and lingered through 1900, is epitomized in the Paris Opéra (figs. 899–901), designed by Charles Garnier (1825–1898). Its Neo-Baroque quality derives more from the profusion of sculpture—including Carpeaux's *The Dance* (fig. 891)—and ornament than from its architectural vocabulary: the paired columns of the façade, "quoted" from the East Front of the Louvre (see fig. 808), are combined with a smaller order, in a fashion suggested by Michelangelo (see fig. 665). Only the fluid curves of the Grand Staircase recall the High Baroque. The whole building looks "overdressed," its luxurious vulgarity so naïve as to be disarming. It reflects the taste of the

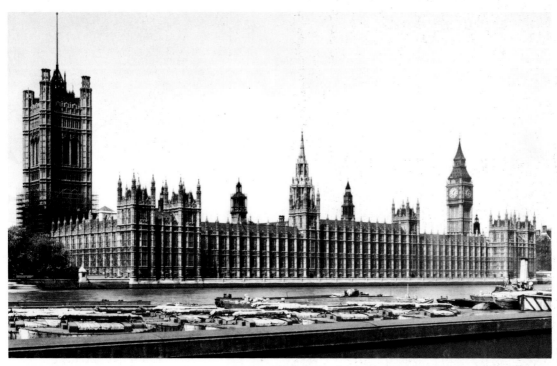

898. SIR CHARLES BARRY and A. N. WELBY PUGIN. The Houses of Parliament, London. Begun 1836

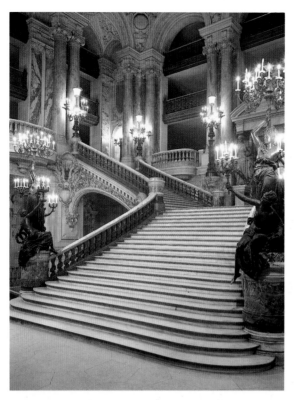

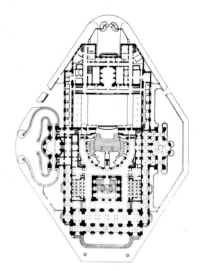

899. (*left*) Grand Staircase, the Opéra,

900. (*below*) Plan of the Opéra

901. (*bottom*) CHARLES GARNIER. The Opéra Paris. 1861–74

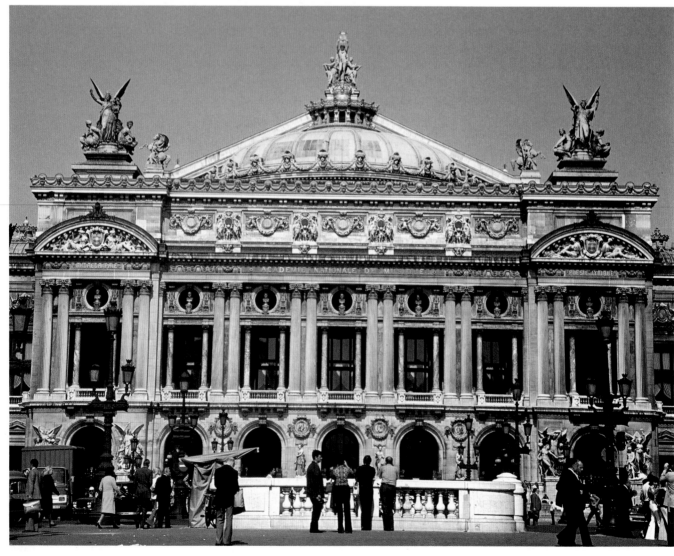

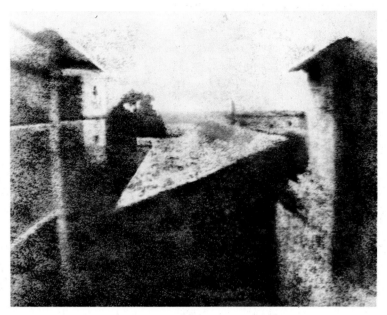

902. JOSEPH NICÉPHORE NIÉPCE. *VIEW FROM HIS WINDOW AT LE GRAS.*
1826. Heliograph, 6½×7⅞″ (16.5×20 cm).
Gernsheim Collection, University of Texas at Austin

beneficiaries of the Industrial Revolution, newly rich and powerful, who saw themselves as the heirs of the old aristocracy and thus found the styles predating the French Revolution more appealing than classical or Gothic.

PHOTOGRAPHY

Is photography art? The fact that we still pose the question testifies to the continuing debate. The answers have varied with the changing definition and understanding of art. In itself, of course, photography is simply a medium, like oil paint or pastel, used to make art but having no inherent claim to being art. After all, what distinguishes an art from a craft is why, not how, it is done. But photography shares creativity with art because, by its very nature, its performance necessarily involves the imagination. Any photograph, even a casual snapshot, represents both an organization of experience and the record of a mental image. The subject and style of a photograph thus tell us about the photographer's inner and outer worlds. Furthermore, like painting and sculpture, photography participates in aspects of the same process of seek-and-find. Photographers may not realize what they respond to until after they see the image that has been printed.

Like woodcut, etching, engraving, and lithography, photography is a form of printmaking that is dependent on mechanical processes. But in contrast to the other graphic media, photography has always been tainted as the product of a new technology—apart from pushing a button or lever, or setting up special effects, no active intervention is required of the artist's hand to guide an idea. For this reason, the camera has usually been considered to be little more than a recording device.

Photography, however, is by no means a neutral medium; its reproduction of reality is never completely faithful.

Whether we realize it or not, the camera alters appearances; photographs reinterpret the world around us, making us literally see it in new terms.

Photography and painting are in parallel response to their times and have generally expressed the same world view. Sometimes the camera's power to extend our way of seeing has been realized first by the painter's creative vision. The two nevertheless differ fundamentally in their approach and temperament: painters communicate their understanding through techniques that represent their cumulative response over time; photographers recognize the moment when the subject before them corresponds to the mental image they have formed of it.

It is hardly surprising that photography and art have enjoyed an uneasy relationship from the start. Artists have generally treated the photograph something like a preliminary sketch, as a convenient source of ideas or record of motifs to be fleshed out and incorporated into a finished work. Academic painters found the detail provided by photographs to be in keeping with their own precise naturalism; many other kinds of artists resorted to photographs, though not always admitting it. Photography has in turn been heavily influenced throughout its history by the painter's media, and photographs may still be judged according to how well they imitate paintings and drawings. To understand photography's place in the history of art, however, we must learn to recognize its particular strengths and inherent limitations.

The Founders of Photography

In 1822 a French inventor named Joseph Nicéphore Niépce (1765–1833) succeeded, at the age of fifty-seven, in making the first permanent photographic image, although his earliest surviving example (fig. 902) dates from four years later. He then joined forces with a younger man, Louis-Jacques-

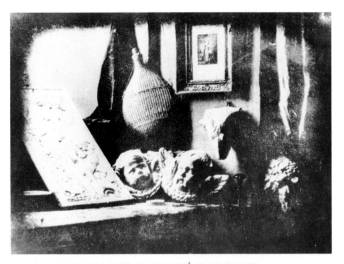

903. LOUIS-JACQUES-MANDÉ DAGUERRE. *STILL LIFE.*
1837. Daguerreotype, 6½×8½″ (16.5×21.7 cm).
Société Française de Photographie, Paris

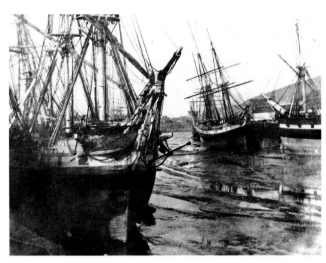

904. WILLIAM HENRY FOX TALBOT. *SAILING CRAFT.*
c. 1845. Science Museum, London

Mandé Daguerre (1789–1851), who had devised an improved camera. After ten more years of chemical and mechanical research, the daguerreotype, using positive exposures, was unveiled publicly in 1839 and the age of photography was born. The announcement spurred the Englishman William Henry Fox Talbot (1800–1877) to complete his own photographic process, involving a paper negative from which positives could be made, that he had been pursuing independently since 1833.

What motivated the earliest photographers? They were searching for an artistic medium, not for a device of practical utility. Though Niépce was a research chemist rather than an artist, his achievement was an outgrowth of his efforts to improve the lithographic process. Daguerre was a skilled painter, and he probably turned to the camera to heighten the illusionism in his huge painted dioramas, which were the sensation of Paris during the 1820s and 1830s. Fox Talbot saw in photography a substitute for drawing, as well as a means of reproduction, after using a camera obscura as a tool to sketch landscapes while on a vacation. The interest that all of the founders had in the artistic potential of the medium they had created is reflected in their photographs. Daguerre's first picture (fig. 903) imitates a type of still life originated by Chardin; Fox Talbot's *Sailing Craft* (fig. 904) looks like the English marine paintings of his day.

That the new medium should have a mechanical aspect was particularly appropriate. It was as if the Industrial Revolution, having forever altered civilization's way of life, had now to invent its own method for recording itself—although the transience of modern existence was not captured by "stopping the action" until the 1870s. Photography underwent a rapid series of improvements, including inventions for better lenses, glass plate negatives, and new chemical processes, which provided faster emulsions and more stable images; since many of its initial limitations were overcome around midcentury, it would be misleading to tell the early history of the medium in terms of technological developments, important though they were.

The basic mechanics and chemistry of photography, moreover, had been known for a long time. The camera obscura, a box with a small hole in one end, dates back to antiquity; in the sixteenth century it was widely used for visual demonstrations. The camera was fitted with a mirror and then a lens in the Baroque period, which saw major advances in optical science culminating in Newtonian physics. By the 1720s it had become an aid in drawing architectural scenes; and at the same time, silver salts were discovered to be light-sensitive.

Why, then, did it take another hundred years for someone to put this knowledge together? Much of the answer lies in the nature of scientific revolutions, which as a rule involve combining old technologies and concepts with new ones. (They do this in response to changing world views that they, in turn, influence.) Photography was neither inevitable in the history of technology, nor necessary to the history of art; yet it was an idea whose time had clearly come. If we try for a moment to imagine that photography was invented a hundred years earlier, we will find this to be impossible simply on artistic, apart from technological, grounds: the eighteenth century was too devoted to fantasy to be interested in the literalness of photography. Rococo portraiture, for example, was more concerned with providing a flattering image than an accurate likeness, and the camera's straightforward record would have been totally out of place. Even in architectural painting, extreme liberties were willingly taken with topographical truth.

The invention of photography was a response to the artistic urges and historical forces that underlie Romanticism. Much of the impulse came from a quest for the True and the Natural. The desire for "images made by Nature" can already be seen, on the one hand, in Cozens' ink-blot compositions (see fig. 844; "natural" because they were made by chance), and, on the other, in the late–eighteenth-century vogue for silhouette portraits (traced from the shadow of the sitter's profile), which led to attempts to record such shadows on light-sensitive materials. David's harsh realism in *The Death of Marat* (see fig. 839) had already proclaimed the cause of unvarnished truth; so did Ingres' *Louis Bertin* (fig. 864), which established the standards of physical reality and character portrayal that photographers would follow.

Portraiture

Like lithography, which was invented only in 1797, photography met the growing middle-class demand for images of all kinds. By 1850, large numbers of the bourgeoisie were having their likenesses painted, and it was in portraiture that photography found its readiest acceptance. Soon after the daguerreotype was introduced, photographic studios sprang up everywhere, especially in America, and multi-image *cartes de visites*, invented in 1854 by Adolphe Eugène Disdéri, became ubiquitous. Anyone could have a portrait taken cheaply and easily. In the process, the average person became memorable. Photography thus became an outgrowth of the democratic values fostered by the American and French revolutions. There was also keen competition among photographers to get the famous to pose for portraits.

NADAR. Gaspard Félix Tournachon (1820–1910), better known as Nadar, managed to attract most of France's leading lights to his studio. Like many early photographers, he started out as an artist and initially used the camera to capture the likenesses of the 280 sitters whom he caricatured in an enormous lithograph, *Le Panthéon Nadar;* he came to prefer the lens to the brush.

The actress Sarah Bernhardt posed for him several times, and his photographs of her (fig. 905) are the direct ancestors

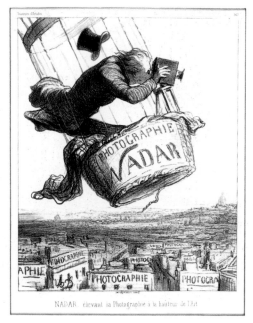

906. HONORÉ DAUMIER. *NADAR ELEVATING PHOTOGRAPHY TO THE HEIGHT OF ART.* 1862. Lithograph.
George Eastman House, Rochester, New York

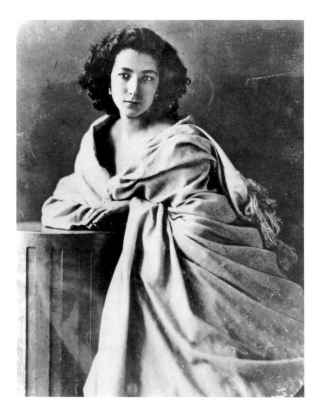

905. NADAR. *SARAH BERNHARDT.* 1859.
George Eastman House, Rochester, New York

of modern glamour photography (compare fig. 1130). With her romantic pose and expression, she is a counterpart to the soulful maidens who inhabit much of nineteenth-century painting. Nadar has treated her in remarkably sculptural terms: indeed, the play of light and sweep of drapery are reminiscent of the sculptured portrait busts that were so popular with collectors at the time.

The Restless Spirit

Early photography reflected the outlook and temperament of Romanticism, and indeed the entire nineteenth century had a pervasive curiosity and an abiding belief that everything could be discovered. While this fascination sometimes manifested a serious interest in science—witness Darwin's voyage on the *Beagle* from 1831 to 1836—it more typically took the form of a restless quest for new experiences and places. Photography had a remarkable impact on the imagination of the period by making the rest of the world widely available, or by simply revealing it in a new way. Sometimes the search for new subjects was close to home; Nadar, for example, took aerial photographs of Paris from a hot-air balloon. This feat was wittily parodied by Daumier (fig. 906), whose caption, "Nadar Elevating Photography to the Height of Art," expresses the prevailing skepticism about the aesthetics of the new medium.

A love of the exotic was fundamental to Romantic escapism, and by 1850 photographers had begun to cart their equipment to faraway places. The same Romantic spirit that we saw in George Caleb Bingham's *Fur Traders Descending the Missouri* (see fig. 884) also drew photographers to the frontier, where they documented the westward expansion of the United States, often for the U.S. Geological Survey, with pictures that have primarily historical interest today.

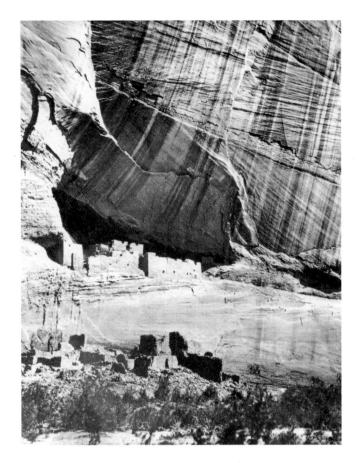

908. *TSAR CANNON OUTSIDE THE SPASSKY GATE, MOSCOW* (cast 1586; world's largest caliber, 890 mm; presently inside Kremlin). Second half 19th century. Stereophotograph (courtesy Culver Photos)

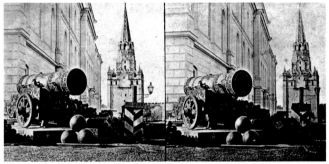

O'SULLIVAN. An exception is the landscape photography of Timothy O'Sullivan (c. 1841–1882), who often preferred scenery that contemporary painters had overlooked. He practically invented his own aesthetic in photographing the *Cañon de Chelle* (fig. 907), for it conforms to no established pictorial type. The view fills the entire photograph, allowing no visual relief and lending it awesome force. The composition is held together by the play of lines of the displaced strata of the rock, which creates a striking abstract design. O'Sullivan's control of tonal relations is so masterful that even color photographs taken since of the same site have far less impact.

Stereophotography

The unquenchable thirst for vicarious experiences accounts for the expanding popularity of stereoscopic daguerreotypes. Invented in 1849, the two-lens camera produced two photographs that correspond to the slightly different images perceived by our two eyes; when seen through a special viewer called a stereoscope, the stereoptic photographs fuse to create a remarkable illusion of three-dimensional depth. Two years later, stereoscopes became the rage at the Crystal Palace exposition in London (see fig. 938). Countless thousands of double views were taken, such as that in figure 908; virtually every corner of the earth became accessible to practically any household, with a vividness second only to being there.

Stereophotography was an important breakthrough, for its binocular vision marked a distinct departure from perspective in the pictorial tradition and demonstrated for the first time photography's potential to enlarge vision. Curiously enough, this success waned, except for special uses: people were simply too habituated to viewing pictures as if with one eye.

Later on, when the halftone plate was invented in the 1880s for reproducing pictures on a printed page, stereophotographs revealed another drawback: as our illustration shows, they were unsuitable for this process of reproduction. From then on, single-lens photography was inextricably linked with the mass media of the day.

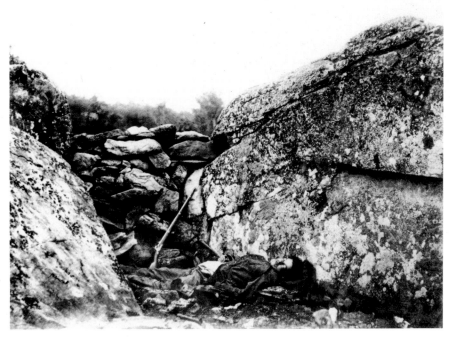

909. ALEXANDER GARDNER. *HOME OF A REBEL SHARPSHOOTER, GETTYSBURG.*
July 1863. Wet-plate photograph. Chicago Historical Society

Photojournalism

Fundamental to the rise of photography was the pervasive nineteenth-century sense that the present was already history in the making. Only with the advent of the Romantic hero did great acts other than martyrdom become popular subjects for contemporary painters and sculptors, and it can hardly be surprising that photography was invented a year after the death of Napoleon, who had been the subject of more paintings than any secular leader ever before.

At about the same time, Géricault's *The Raft of the "Medusa"* (fig. 861) and Delacroix's *The Massacre at Chios* (fig. 866) signaled a decisive shift in the Romantic attitude, toward representing contemporary events. This outlook brought with it a new kind of photography: photojournalism.

BRADY. The first great photojournalist was Mathew Brady (1823–1896), who covered the Civil War. Other wars had already been photographed, but Brady and his twenty assistants (including Timothy O'Sullivan), using cameras too slow and cumbersome to show actual combat, nevertheless brought home its horrors with unprecedented directness.

GARDNER. *Home of a Rebel Sharpshooter* (fig. 909) by Alexander Gardner (1821–1882), who left Brady to form his own team, is a landmark in the history of art, conveying inexorably both the grim reality and the significance of death on the battlefield in a single image. Compared with the heroic act celebrated by Benjamin West (see fig. 840), this tragedy is as anonymous as the slain soldier himself. The photograph is all the more persuasive for having the same harsh realism found in David's *The Death of Marat* (see fig 839), and the limp figure, hardly visible between the rocks framing the scene, is no less poignant. In contrast, the paintings and engravings by the artists—notably Winslow Homer (see page 675)—who illustrated the Civil War for magazines and newspapers were mostly genre scenes that kept the reality of combat safely at arm's length.

CHAPTER TWO
REALISM
AND
IMPRESSIONISM

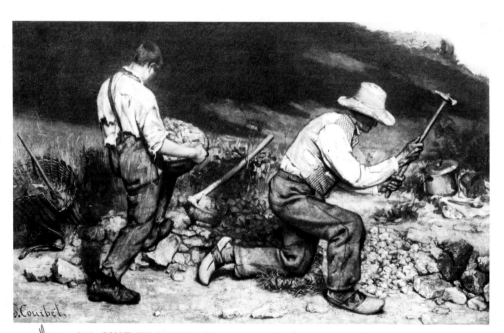

910. GUSTAVE COURBET. *THE STONE BREAKERS.* 1849 (destroyed 1945).
Oil on canvas, 63×102″ (1.6×2.6 m). Formerly Gemäldegalerie, Dresden

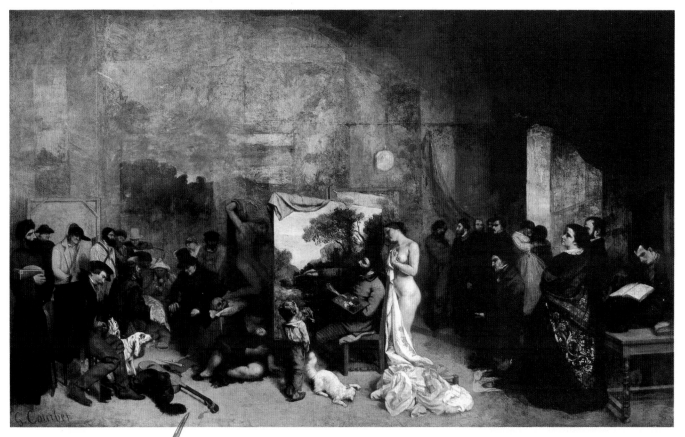

911. GUSTAVE COURBET. *STUDIO OF A PAINTER: A REAL ALLEGORY SUMMARIZING MY SEVEN YEARS OF LIFE AS AN ARTIST.* 1854–55. Oil on canvas, 11'10"×19'7" (3.6×6 m). Musée d'Orsay, Paris

PAINTING

France

"Can Jupiter survive the lightning rod?" asked Karl Marx, not long after the middle of the century. The question, implying that the ancient god of thunder and lightning was now in jeopardy through science, sums up the dilemma we felt in the sculptor Carpeaux's *The Dance.* The French poet and art critic Charles Baudelaire was addressing himself to the same problem when, in 1846, he called for paintings that expressed "the heroism of modern life." At that time only one painter was willing to make an artistic creed of this demand: Baudelaire's friend Gustave Courbet (1819–1877).

COURBET AND REALISM. Proud of his rural background—he was born in Ornans, a village near the French-Swiss border—and a socialist in politics, Courbet had begun as a Neo-Baroque Romantic in the early 1840s; but by 1848, under the impact of the revolutionary upheavals then sweeping over Europe, he had come to believe that the Romantic emphasis on feeling and imagination was merely an escape from the realities of the time. The modern artist must rely on his own direct experience ("I cannot paint an angel because I have never seen one," he said); he must be a Realist. As a descriptive term, "realism" is not very precise. For Courbet, it meant something akin to the "naturalism" of Caravaggio (fig. 739). As an admirer of Louis Le Nain and

Rembrandt he had, in fact, strong links with the Caravaggesque tradition, and his work, like Caravaggio's, was denounced for its supposed vulgarity and lack of spiritual content.

The storm broke in 1849, when he exhibited *The Stone Breakers* (fig. 910), the first canvas fully embodying his programmatic Realism. Courbet had seen two men working on a road, and had asked them to pose for him in his studio. He painted them lifesize, solidly and matter-of-factly, with none of Millet's overt pathos or sentiment: the young man's face is averted, the old one's half hidden by a hat. Yet he cannot have picked them casually: their contrast in age is significant—one is too old for such heavy work, the other too young. Endowed with the dignity of their symbolic status, they do not turn to us for sympathy. Courbet's friend, the socialist Pierre-Joseph Proudhon, likened them to a parable from the Gospels.

During the Paris Exposition of 1855, where works by Ingres and Delacroix were prominently displayed, Courbet brought his pictures to attention by organizing a private exhibition in a large wooden shed and by distributing a "manifesto of Realism." The show centered on a huge canvas, the most ambitious of his career, entitled *Studio of a Painter: A Real Allegory Summarizing My Seven Years of Life as an Artist* (fig. 911). "Real allegory" is something of a teaser (allegories, after all, are unreal by definition); Courbet meant either an allegory couched in the terms of his particular Realism, or one that did not conflict with the "real" identity of the figures or objects embodying it.

The framework is familiar; Courbet's composition clearly belongs to the type of Velázquez' *The Maids of Honor* and Goya's *The Family of Charles IV* (see figs. 799 and 856). But now the artist has moved to the center; his visitors are here his guests, not royal patrons who enter whenever they wish. He has invited them specially, for a purpose that becomes evident only upon thoughtful reflection; the picture does not yield its full meaning unless we take the title seriously and inquire into Courbet's relation to this assembly.

There are two main groups: on the left are "the people"—types rather than individuals, drawn largely from the artist's home environment at Ornans—hunters, peasants, workers, a Jew, a priest, a young mother with her baby. On the right, in contrast, we see groups of portraits representing the Parisian side of Courbet's life—clients, critics, intellectuals (the man reading is Baudelaire). All of these people are strangely passive, as if they were waiting for we know not what. Some are quietly conversing among themselves, others seem immersed in thought; hardly anybody looks at Courbet. They are not his audience, but a representative sampling of his social environment.

Only two people watch the artist at work: a small boy, intended to suggest "the innocent eye," and the nude model. What is her role? In a more conventional picture, we would identify her as Inspiration, or Courbet's Muse, but she is no less "real" than the others here; Courbet probably meant her to be Nature, or that undisguised Truth which he proclaimed to be the guiding principle of his art (note the emphasis on the clothing she has just taken off). Significantly enough, the center group is illuminated by clear, sharp daylight but the background and the lateral figures are veiled in semi-darkness, to underline the contrast between the artist—the active creator—and the world around him that waits to be brought to life.

MANET AND THE "REVOLUTION OF THE COLOR PATCH." Courbet's *Studio* helps us to understand a picture that shocked the public even more: Manet's *Luncheon on the Grass* (see fig. 4), showing a nude model accompanied by two gentlemen in frock coats. Édouard Manet (1832–1883) was the first to grasp Courbet's full importance—his *Luncheon*, among other things, is a tribute to the older artist. He particularly offended contemporary morality by juxtaposing the nude and nattily attired figures in an outdoor setting, the more so since the noncommittal title offered no "higher" significance. Yet the group has so formal a pose (for its classical source, see figs. 5 and 6) that Manet certainly did not intend to depict an actual event. Perhaps the meaning of the canvas lies in this denial of plausibility, for the scene fits neither the plane of everyday experience nor that of allegory.

The *Luncheon*, as a visual manifesto of artistic freedom, is much more revolutionary than Courbet's; it asserts the painter's privilege to combine whatever elements he pleases for aesthetic effect alone. The nudity of the model is "explained" by the contrast between her warm, creamy flesh tones and the cool black-and-gray of the men's attire. Or, to put it another way, the world of painting has "natural laws"

that are distinct from those of familiar reality, and the painter's first loyalty is to his canvas, not to the outside world. Here begins an attitude that was later summed up in the doctrine of Art for Art's Sake and became a bone of contention between progressives and conservatives for the rest of the century (see page 672). Manet himself disdained such controversies, but his work attests to his lifelong devotion to "pure painting"—to the belief that brushstrokes and color patches themselves, not what they stand for, are the artist's primary reality. Among painters of the past, he found that Hals, Velázquez, and Goya had come closest to this ideal. He admired their broad, open technique, their preoccupation with light and color values. Many of his canvases are, in fact, "pictures of pictures"—they translate into modern terms those older works that particularly challenged him. Yet he always took care to filter out the expressive or symbolic content of his models, lest the beholder's attention be distracted from the pictorial structure itself. His paintings, whatever

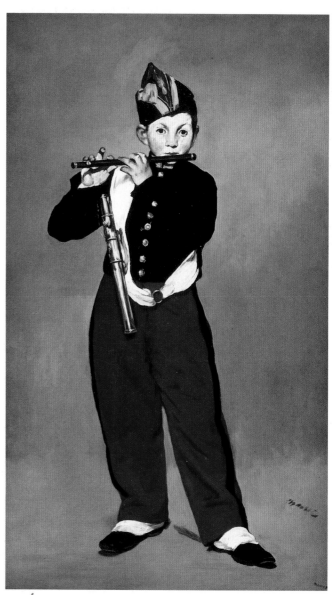

912. ÉDOUARD MANET. *THE FIFER.* 1866. Oil on canvas, 63×38¼" (160×97.5 cm). Musée d'Orsay, Paris

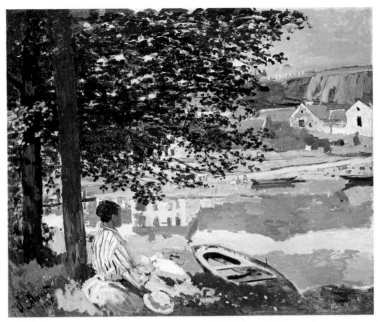

913. CLAUDE MONET. *THE RIVER* (*Au Bord de l'Eau, Bennecourt*). 1868.
Oil on canvas, 32⅛×39⅝″ (81.8×100.5 cm).
The Art Institute of Chicago. Potter Palmer Collection

their subject, have an emotional reticence that can easily be mistaken for emptiness unless we understand its purpose.

Courbet is said to have remarked that Manet's pictures were as flat as playing cards. Looking at *The Fifer* (fig. 912), we can see what he meant. Done three years after the *Luncheon,* it is a painting without shadows (there are a few, actually, but it takes a real effort to find them), hardly any modeling, and no depth. The figure looks three-dimensional only because its contour renders the forms in realistic foreshortening; otherwise, Manet eschews all the methods devised since Giotto's time for transmuting a flat surface into a pictorial space. The undifferentiated light-gray background seems as near to us as the figure, and just as solid; if the fifer stepped out of the picture, he would leave a hole, like the cut-out shape of a stencil.

Here, then, the canvas itself has been redefined—it is no longer a "window," but a screen made up of flat patches of color. How radical a step this was can be readily seen if we match *The Fifer* against Delacroix's *The Massacre at Chios* (fig. 866), and a Cubist work such as Picasso's *Three Dancers* of 1925 (fig. 1014). The structure of Manet's painting obviously resembles that of Picasso's, whereas Delacroix's—or even Courbet's—still follows the "window" tradition of the Renaissance. In retrospect, we realize that the revolutionary qualities of Manet's art were already to be seen, if not yet so obvious, in the *Luncheon*. The three figures lifted from Raphael's group of river gods form a unit nearly as shadowless and stencillike as *The Fifer*; they would be more at home on a flat screen, for the chiaroscuro of their present setting, which is inspired by the landscapes of Courbet, no longer fits them.

MONET AND IMPRESSIONISM. What brought about this "revolution of the color patch"? We do not know, and

Manet himself surely did not reason it out beforehand. It is tempting to think that he was impelled to create the new style by the challenge of photography. The "pencil of nature," then known for a quarter century, had demonstrated the objective truth of Renaissance perspective, but it established a standard of representational accuracy that no hand-made image could hope to rival. Painting needed to be rescued from competition with the camera. This Manet accomplished by insisting that a painted canvas is, above all, a material surface covered with pigments—that we must look *at* it, not *through* it. Unlike Courbet, he gave no name to the style he had created; when his followers began calling themselves Impressionists, he refused to accept the term for his own work.

The word Impressionism had been coined in 1874, after a hostile critic had looked at a picture entitled *Impression: Sunrise* by Claude Monet (1840–1926), and it certainly fits Monet better than it does Manet. Monet had adopted Manet's concept of painting and applied it to landscapes done out-of-doors. Monet's *The River* of 1868 (fig. 913) is flooded with sunlight so bright that conservative critics claimed it made their eyes smart; in this flickering network of color patches, the reflections on the water are as "real" as the banks of the Seine. Even more than *The Fifer*, Monet's painting is a "playing card"; were it not for the woman and the boat in the foreground, the picture would be just as effective upside-down. The mirror image here serves a purpose contrary to that of earlier mirror images (compare fig. 554): instead of adding to the illusion of real space, it strengthens the unity of the actual painted surface. This inner coherence sets *The River* apart from Romantic "impressions" such as Constable's *Hampstead Heath* (see fig. 879), or Corot's *Papigno* (see fig. 872), even though all three share the same on-the-spot immediacy and fresh perception.

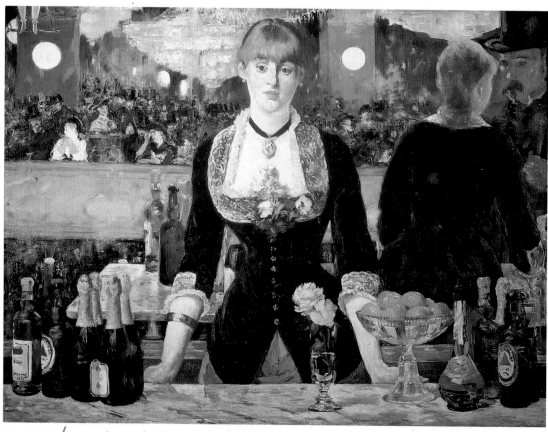

914. ÉDOUARD MANET. *A BAR AT THE FOLIES-BERGÈRES.* 1881–82. Oil on canvas, 37½×51″ (95.3×129.7 cm). Courtauld Institute Galleries, Home House Trustees, London

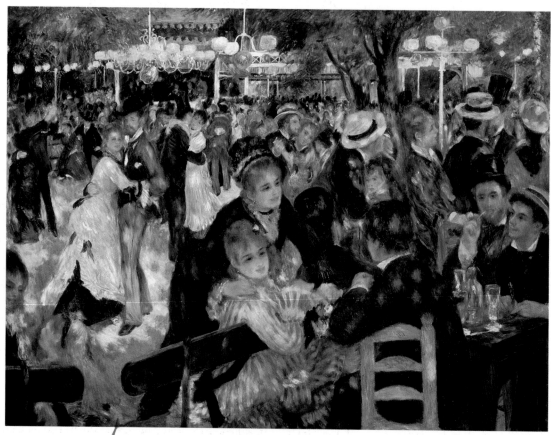

915. AUGUSTE RENOIR. *LE MOULIN DE LA GALETTE.* 1876. Oil on canvas, 51½×69″ (130.7×175.3 cm). Musée d'Orsay, Paris

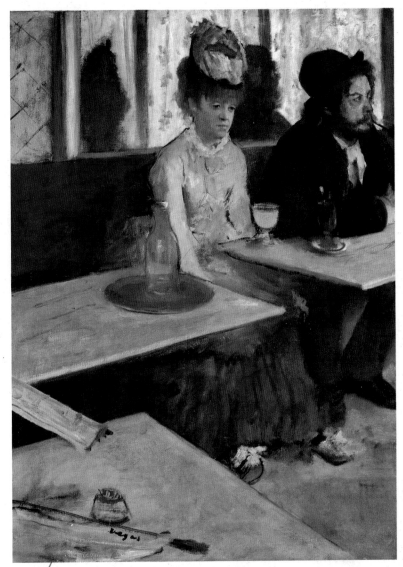

916. EDGAR DEGAS. *THE GLASS OF ABSINTHE.* 1876.
Oil on canvas, 36×27″ (91.3×68.7 cm). Musée d'Orsay, Paris

MANET AND IMPRESSIONISM. These latter qualities came less easily to the austere and deliberate Manet; they appear in his work only after about 1870, under Monet's influence. Manet's last major picture, *A Bar at the Folies-Bergères*, of 1881–82 (fig. 914), shows a single figure as calm—and as firmly set within the rectangle of the canvas—as the fifer, but the background is no longer neutral. A huge shimmering mirror image now fills four-fifths of the picture. The mirror, close behind the barmaid, shows the whole interior of the nightclub, but deprives it of three-dimensionality, in part by taking liberties with the scene (note how the barmaid's reflection is shown off to one side, something that is impossible in reality). The serving girl's attitude, detached and touched with melancholy, contrasts poignantly with the gaiety of her setting, which she is not permitted to share. For all its urbanity, the mood of the canvas reminds us oddly of Daumier's *The Third-Class Carriage* (see fig. 870).

RENOIR. Scenes from the world of entertainment—dance halls, cafés, concerts, the theater—were favorite subjects for Impressionist painters. Auguste Renoir (1841–1919), another important member of the group, filled his work with the *joie de vivre* of a singularly happy temperament. The flirting couples in *Le Moulin de la Galette* (fig. 915), dappled with sunlight and shadow, radiate a human warmth that is utterly entrancing, even though the artist permits us no more than a fleeting glance at any of them. Our role is that of the casual stroller, who takes in this slice of life in passing.

DEGAS. By contrast, Edgar Degas (1834–1917) makes us look steadily at the disenchanted pair in his café scene (fig. 916), but, so to speak, out of the corner of our eye. The design of this picture at first seems as unstudied as a snapshot (indeed Degas practiced photography), yet a longer look shows us that everything here dovetails precisely—that the zigzag

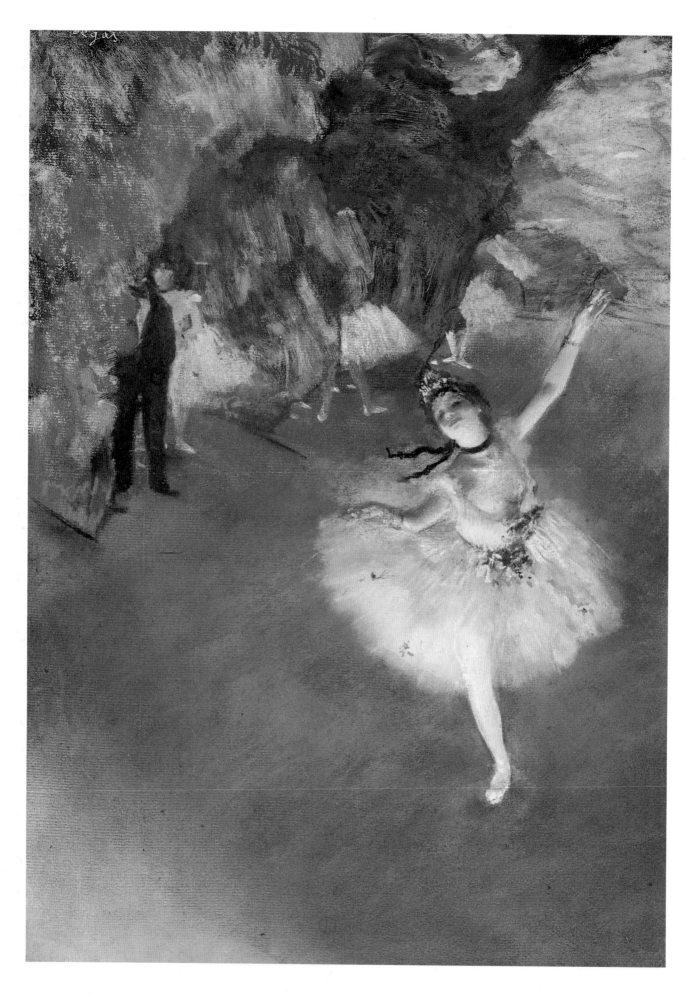

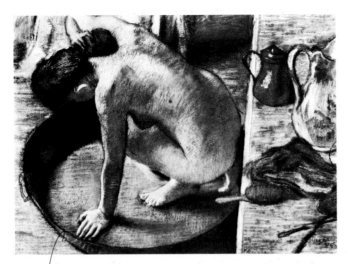

917. (*above*) EDGAR DEGAS. *THE TUB*. 1886. Pastel,
23½×32⅓″ (59.7×82.3 cm). Musée d'Orsay, Paris

918. (*opposite*) EDGAR DEGAS. *PRIMA BALLERINA*. c. 1876.
Oil on canvas, 23×16½″ (58.3×42 cm).
Musée d'Orsay, Paris

of empty tables between us and the luckless couple reinforces their brooding loneliness. Compositions as boldly calculated as this set Degas apart from other Impressionists. A wealthy aristocrat by birth, he had been trained in the tradition of Ingres, whom he greatly admired. Like Ingres, he despised portraiture as a trade but, unlike him, he acted on his conviction and portrayed only friends and relatives—individuals with whom he had emotional ties. His profound sense of human character lends weight even to seemingly casual scenes such as that in *The Glass of Absinthe.*

When he joined the Impressionists, Degas did not abandon his early allegiance to draftsmanship. His finest works were often done in pastel (powdered pigments molded into sticks), a medium that had a strong appeal for him since it yielded effects of line, tone, and color simultaneously. *Prima Ballerina* (fig. 917) well demonstrates this flexible technique. The oblique view of the stage, from a box near the proscenium arch, has been shaped into another deliberately off-center composition; the dancer floats above the steeply tilted floor like a butterfly caught in the glare of the footlights.

A decade later, *The Tub* (fig. 918) is again an oblique view, but now severe, almost geometric in design: the tub and the crouching woman, both vigorously outlined, form a circle within a square, and the rest of the rectangular format is filled by a shelf so sharply tilted that it almost shares the plane of the picture; yet on this shelf Degas has placed two pitchers (note how the curve of the small one fits the handle of the other) that are hardly foreshortened at all. Here the tension between "two-D" and "three-D" surface and depth comes close to the breaking point.

The Tub is Impressionist only in its shimmering, luminous colors. Its other qualities are more characteristic of the 1880s, the first post-Impressionist decade, when many artists showed a renewed concern with problems of form (see Chapter 3).

MORISOT. The Impressionists' ranks included several women of great ability. Berthe Morisot (1841–1895), a member of the group from its inception, was influenced at first by Manet, whose brother she later married, but it is clear that he in turn was affected by her work. Her subject matter was the world she knew: the domestic life of the French upper middle class, which she depicted with sensitive understanding. Morisot's early paintings, centering on her mother and her sister Edma, have a subtle but distinct sense of alienation. Her mature work is altogether different in character. The birth of her daughter in 1878 signaled a change in her art, which reached its height a decade later. Her painting of a little girl reading in a room overlooking the artist's garden (fig. 919) shows a light-filled style of her own making. Morisot applied her virtuoso brushwork with a sketchlike brevity that omits non-essential details yet conveys a complete impression of the scene. The figure is fully integrated within the formal design; its appeal is enhanced by the pastel hues she favored. Morisot's painting radiates an air of contentment free of the sentimentality that often affects genre paintings of the period.

CASSATT. In 1877, the American painter Mary Cassatt (1845–1926) joined the Impressionists, becoming a tireless champion of their work. She had received a standard academic training in her native Philadelphia, but had to struggle to overcome traditional barriers. Like Morisot, she was able to pursue her career as an artist, an occupation regarded as unsuitable for women, because she was independently wealthy. Cassatt was instrumental in gaining early acceptance of Impressionist paintings in the United States through her social contacts with wealthy private collectors. Maternity provided the thematic and formal focus of most of her work. From her mentor Degas, as well as from her thoughtful study of Japanese prints, Cassatt developed an individual

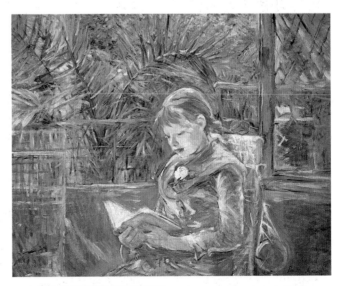

919. BERTHE MORISOT. *LA LECTURE (READING)*. 1888.
Oil on canvas, 29¼×36½″ (74.3×92.7 cm).
Museum of Fine Arts, St. Petersburg, Florida.
Gift of Friends of Art in Memory of Margaret Acheson Stuart

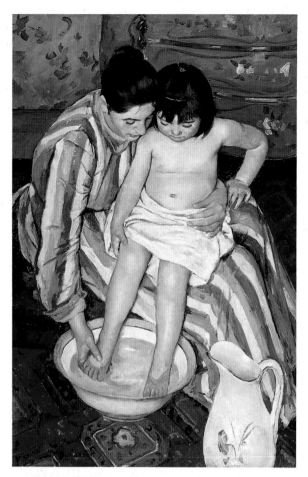

920. MARY CASSATT. *THE BATH*. 1891. Oil on canvas,
39½×26″ (100.3×66 cm). The Art Institute of Chicago.
Robert A. Waller Collection

the artist created a self-contained world for purely personal and artistic purposes. The subjects he painted there are as much reflections of his imagination as they are of reality. Furthermore, they convey a different sense of time. Instead of the single moment captured in *The River*, his *Water Lilies, Giverny* summarizes a shifting impression of the pond in response to the changing water as the breezes play across it.

England

REALISM. By the time Monet came to admire his work, Turner's reputation was at a low ebb in his own country. Toward 1850, when Courbet launched his revolutionary doctrine of Realism, a concern with "the heroism of modern life" asserted itself quite independently in English painting as well, although the movement lacked a leader of Courbet's stature and assertiveness. Perhaps the best-known example of English Realism is *The Last of England* (fig. 922) by Ford Madox Brown (1821–1893), a picture that enjoyed vast popularity throughout the latter half of the century in the English-speaking world. The subject—a group of emigrants as they set out on their long overseas journey—may be less obvious today than it once was, and it does not carry the same emotional charge. Nonetheless, there can be no question that the artist has treated an important theme taken from modern experience, and that he has done so with touching seriousness. If the pathos of the scene strikes us as a bit the-

and highly accomplished style. In its oblique view, simplified color forms, and flat composition, *The Bath* (fig. 920) shows Cassatt at her best and is characteristic of her mature style around 1890.

MONET'S LATER WORKS. Among the major figures of the movement, Monet alone remained faithful to the Impressionist view of nature. Nevertheless, his work became more subjective over time, although he never ventured into fantasy, nor did he abandon the basic approach of his earlier landscapes. About 1890, Monet began to paint pictures in series, showing the same subject under various conditions of light and atmosphere. These tended increasingly to resemble Turner's "airy visions, painted with tinted steam" as Monet concentrated on effects of colored light (see page 644; he had visited London, and knew Turner's work). His *Water Lilies, Giverny* (fig. 921) is a fascinating sequel to *The River* (fig. 913) across a span of almost forty years. The pond surface now takes up the entire canvas, so that the effect of a weightless screen is stronger than ever; the artist's brushwork, too, has greater variety and a more individual rhythm. While the scene is still based on nature, this is no ordinary landscape but one entirely of his making. On the estate at Giverny given to him late in life by the French government,

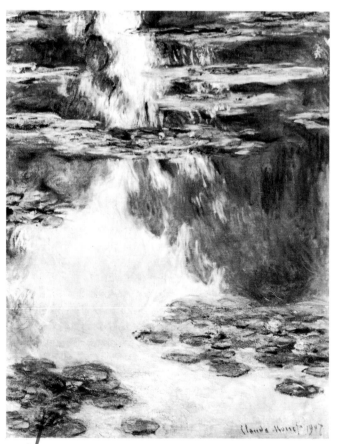

921. CLAUDE MONET. *WATER LILIES, GIVERNY*. 1907.
Oil on canvas, 36½×29″ (92.7×73.7 cm). Private collection

But Rossetti, unlike Brown, was not concerned with social problems; he thought of himself, rather, as a reformer of aesthetic sensibility. His early masterpiece, *Ecce Ancilla Domini* (fig. 923), though naturalistic in detail, is full of self-conscious archaisms such as the pale tonality, the limited range of colors, the awkward perspective, and the stress on the verticals, not to mention the title in Latin. At the same time, this Annunciation radiates an aura of repressed eroticism that became the hallmark of Rossetti's work and exerted a powerful influence on other Pre-Raphaelites.

We can sense it even in the political cartoon (fig. 924) by the illustrator and book designer Walter Crane (1845–1915), which shows another kind of "annunciation": the genius of Liberty, strongly reminiscent of the style of Botticelli (see fig. 635), brings the glad tidings of socialism to a sleeping worker who is being oppressed by capitalism in the shape of a nightmarish vampire. Shades of Henry Fuseli! (Compare fig. 876.)

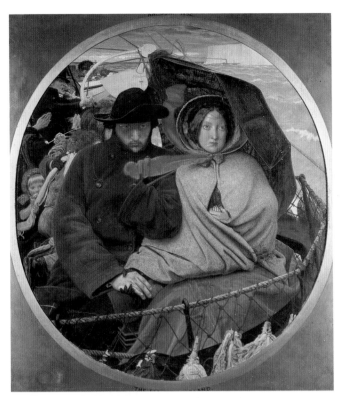

922. FORD MADOX BROWN. *THE LAST OF ENGLAND.*
1852–55. Oil on panel, 32½×29½" (82.5×74.9 cm).
City Museum and Art Gallery, Birmingham, England.
By permission Birmingham Museum and Art Gallery

atrical—note the contrast between the brooding young couple in the foreground and the "good riddance" gesture of the man at the upper left—we recognize its source in the "dumb shows" of Hogarth, whom Brown revered (see fig. 831).

Brown's style, however, has nothing in common with Hogarth's; its impersonal precision of detail strikes us as almost photographic; no hint of subjective "handwriting" is permitted to intervene between us and the scene depicted. Brown had acquired this painstaking technique some years earlier, after he met the Nazarenes, the group of German painters in Rome who practiced what they regarded as a "medieval" style (see page 646). He in turn transmitted it to the painter and poet Dante Gabriel Rossetti (1828–1882), who in 1848 helped to found an artists' society called the Pre-Raphaelite Brotherhood.

THE PRE-RAPHAELITES. Brown himself never actually joined the Pre-Raphaelites, but he shared their basic aim: to do battle against the frivolous art of the day by producing "pure transcripts . . . from nature" and by having "genuine ideas to express." As the name of the Brotherhood proclaims, its members took their inspiration from the "primitive" masters of the fifteenth century; to that extent, they belong to the Gothic revival, which had long been an important aspect of the Romantic movement. What set the Pre-Raphaelites apart from Romanticism pure-and-simple was an urge to reform the ills of modern civilization through their art; thus the emigrants in *The Last of England* dramatize the conditions that made them decide to leave England.

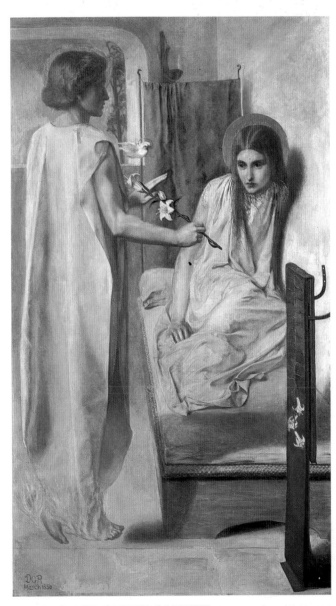

923. DANTE GABRIEL ROSSETTI. *ECCE ANCILLA DOMINI*
(THE ANNUNCIATION). 1849–50. Oil on canvas, 28½×16½"
(72.4×41.9 cm). The Tate Gallery, London

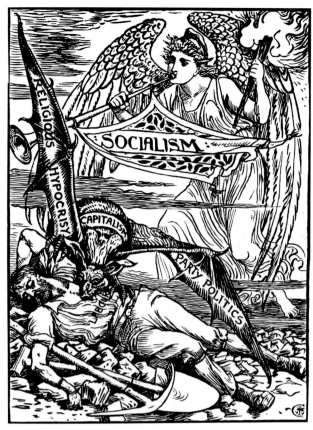

924. WALTER CRANE. Political cartoon from *CARTOONS FOR THE CAUSE*. 1886. Woodcut

MORRIS. The link between Rossetti and Crane's cartoon was William Morris (1834–1896), who started out as a Pre-Raphaelite painter but soon shifted his interest to "art for use"—domestic architecture and interior decoration such as furniture, tapestries, and wallpapers. He wanted to displace the shoddy products of the machine age by reviving the handicrafts of the pre-industrial past, an art "made by the people, and for the people, as a happiness to the maker and the user."

Morris was an apostle of simplicity: architecture and furniture ought to be designed in accordance with the nature of their materials and working processes; surface decoration ought to be flat rather than illusionistic. His interiors (fig. 925) are total environments that create an effect of quiet intimacy. Despite Morris' self-proclaimed championship of the medieval tradition, he never imitated its forms directly but sought to capture its spirit. He invented the first original system of ornament since the Rococo—no small achievement.

Through the many enterprises he sponsored, as well as his skill as a writer and publicist, Morris became a tastemaker without peer in his day. Toward the end of the century, his influence had spread throughout Europe and America. Nor was he content to reform the arts of design alone; he saw them, rather, as a lever by which to reform modern society as a whole. As a consequence, he played an important part in the early history of Fabian socialism (the gradualist variety invented in England as an alternative to the revolutionary socialism of the Continent). Many of his artist friends, including Walter Crane, came to share his convictions, and some contributed their artistic talents to the cause. Such, then, is the background of Crane's cartoon.

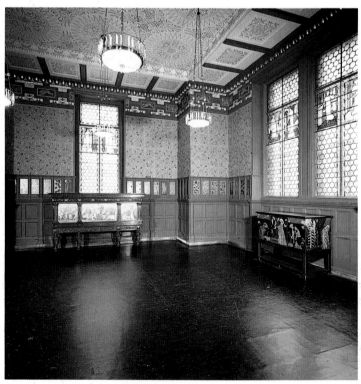

925. WILLIAM MORRIS (MORRIS & CO.). Green Dining Room.
1867. Victoria & Albert Museum, London (Crown copyright reserved)

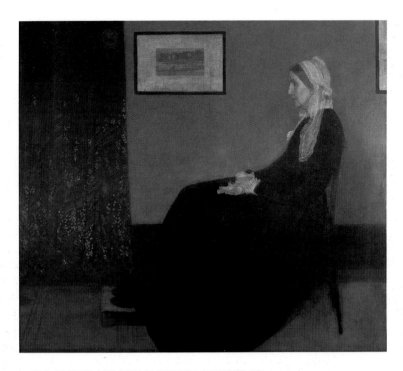

926. JAMES ABBOTT MCNEILL WHISTLER. *ARRANGEMENT IN BLACK AND GRAY: THE ARTIST'S MOTHER.* 1871. Oil on canvas, 57×64½" (144.6×163.8 cm). Musée d'Orsay, Paris

United States

WHISTLER. Courbet, during the later years of his life, enjoyed considerable fame and influence abroad; the Impressionists gained international recognition more slowly. Surprisingly, Americans were their first patrons, responding to the new style sooner than Europeans did. At a time when no French museum would have them, Impressionist works entered public collections in the United States, and American painters were among the earliest followers of Manet and his circle. James Abbott McNeill Whistler (1834–1903) came to Paris in 1855 to study painting; four years later he moved to London to spend the rest of his life, but he visited France during the 1860s and was in close touch with the rising Impressionist movement.

His best-known picture, *Arrangement in Black and Gray: The Artist's Mother* (fig. 926), reflects the influence of Manet in its emphasis on flat areas, and the likeness has the austere precision of Degas' portraits. Its fame as a symbol of our latter-day "mother cult" is a paradox of popular psychology that would have dismayed Whistler: he wanted the canvas to be appreciated for its formal qualities alone.

A witty, sharp-tongued advocate of Art for Art's Sake, he thought of his pictures as analogous to pieces of music, calling them "symphonies" or "nocturnes." The boldest example, painted about 1874, is *Nocturne in Black and Gold: The Falling Rocket* (fig. 927); without an explanatory subtitle, we would have real difficulty making it out. No French painter had yet dared to produce a picture so "non-representational," so reminiscent of Cozens' "blot-scapes" and Turner's "tinted steam" (see figs. 844 and 881). It was this canvas, more than any other, that prompted John Ruskin to accuse Whistler of "flinging a pot of paint in the public's

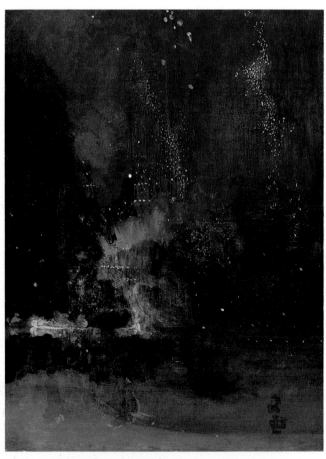

927. JAMES ABBOTT MCNEILL WHISTLER.
NOCTURNE IN BLACK AND GOLD: THE FALLING ROCKET.
c. 1874. Oil on wood panel, 23¾×18⅜" (60.2×46.8 cm).
The Detroit Institute of Arts. Gift of Dexter M. Ferry, Jr.

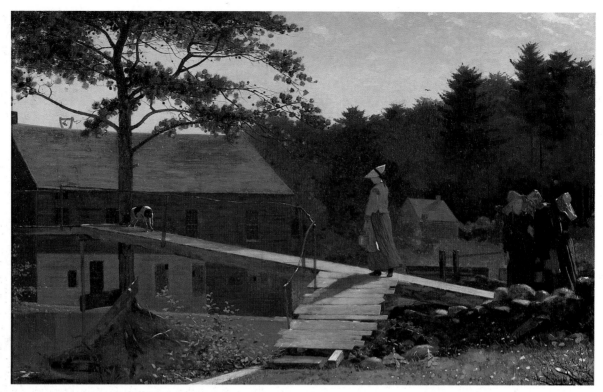

928. WINSLOW HOMER. *THE MORNING BELL.* c. 1870. Oil on canvas, 24×38″ (61×96.7 cm).
Yale University Art Gallery, New Haven, Connecticut. Stephen C. Clark Collection

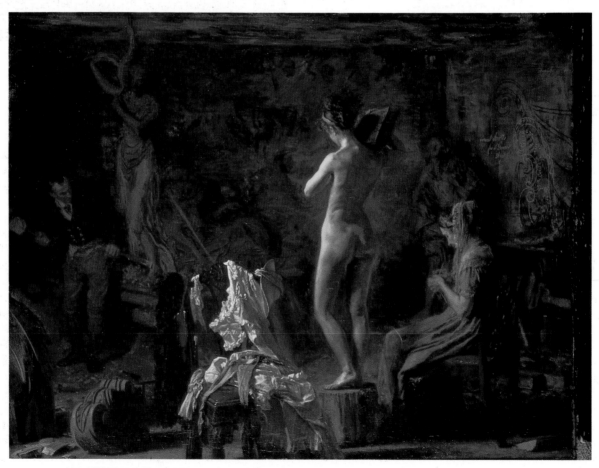

929. THOMAS EAKINS. *WILLIAM RUSH CARVING HIS ALLEGORICAL FIGURE OF THE SCHUYLKILL RIVER.*
1877. Oil on canvas, 20⅛×26½″ (51.1×67.3 cm).
The Philadelphia Museum of Art. Given by Mrs. Thomas Eakins and Miss Mary A. Williams

face." (Since the same critic had highly praised Turner's *The Slave Ship*, we must conclude that what Ruskin really liked was not the tinted steam itself but the Romantic sentiment behind it.)

During Whistler's subsequent suit for libel, he offered a definition of his aims that seems to be particularly applicable to *The Falling Rocket:* "I have perhaps meant rather to indicate an artistic interest alone in my work, divesting the picture from any outside sort of interest . . . . It is an arrangement of line, form, and color, first, and I make use of any incident of it which shall bring about a symmetrical result." The last phrase has special significance, since Whistler acknowledges that in utilizing chance effects, he does not look for resemblances but for a purely formal harmony. While he rarely practiced what he preached to quite the same extent as he did in *The Falling Rocket*, his statement reads like a prophecy of American abstract painting (see fig. 1035).

HOMER. Whistler's gifted contemporary in America, Winslow Homer (1836–1910), also came to Paris as a young man, but left too soon to receive the full impact of Impressionism. He was a pictorial reporter throughout the Civil War and continued as a magazine illustrator until 1875. Yet he did some of his most remarkable paintings in the 1860s. Such a work is *The Morning Bell* (fig. 928); the fresh delicacy of the sunlit scene might be called "pre-Impressionist"—halfway between Corot and Monet (compare figs. 872 and 913). The picture has an extraordinarily subtle design as well: the dog, the center girl, and those at the right turn the footpath into a seesaw, its upward slant balanced by the descending line of treetops. At the same time, the tilted walkway emphasizes the reluctance of the trudging figure, echoed by the little dog, to enter the mill where she will spend the rest of the day. The painting documents the early Industrial Revolution, before the advent of child labor laws, when young people often toiled long hours at difficult jobs.

EAKINS. Thomas Eakins (1844–1916) arrived in Paris from Philadelphia about the time Homer painted *The Morning Bell*; he went home four years later, after receiving a conventional academic training, with decisive impressions of Courbet and Velázquez. Elements from both these artists are combined in *William Rush Carving His Allegorical Figure of the Schuylkill River* (fig. 929; compare figs. 911 and 798). Eakins had encountered stiff opposition for advocating traditional life studies at the Pennsylvania Academy of the Fine Arts. To him, Rush was a hero for basing his 1809 statue for the Philadelphia Water Works on the nude model, though the figure itself was draped in a classical robe. Eakins no doubt knew contemporary European paintings of sculptors carving from the nude; these were related to the theme of Pygmalion and Galatea that was popular at the time among academic artists. Conservative critics nevertheless denounced *William Rush Carving His Allegorical Figure of the Schuylkill River* for its nudity, despite the presence of the chaperon knitting quietly to the right, while to us the painting's declaration of unvarnished truth seems an apposite fulfillment of Baudelaire's demand for pictures that express the heroism of modern life.

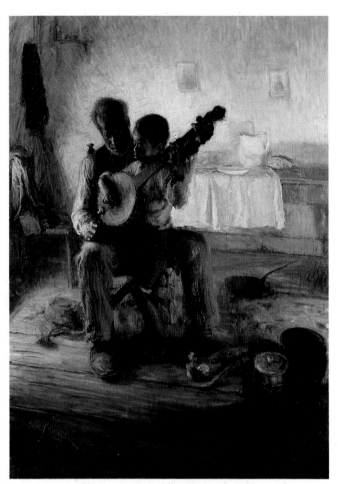

930. HENRY O. TANNER. *THE BANJO LESSON.* c. 1893.
Oil on canvas, 48×35″ (122×89 cm).
Hampton University Museum, Hampton, Virginia

TANNER. Thanks in large part to Eakins' enlightened attitude, Philadelphia became the leading center of minority artists in the United States. Eakins encouraged women and blacks to study art seriously at a time when professional careers were closed to them. African-Americans had no chance to enter the arts before Emancipation, and after the Civil War the situation improved only gradually. Henry O. Tanner (1859–1937), the first important black painter, studied with Eakins in the early 1880s. Tanner's masterpiece, *The Banjo Lesson* (fig. 930), painted after he moved permanently to Paris, bears Eakins' unmistakable impress: avoiding the mawkishness of similar subjects by other American painters, the scene is rendered with the same direct realism as *William Rush Carving His Allegorical Figure of the Schuylkill River.*

SCULPTURE

Impressionism, it is often said, revitalized sculpture no less than painting. The statement is at once true and misleading. Auguste Rodin (1840–1917), the first sculptor of genius since Bernini, redefined sculpture during the same years that Manet and Monet redefined painting; in so doing, however, he did not follow these artists' lead. How indeed could the effect of such pictures as *The Fifer* or *The River* be reproduced in three dimensions and without color?

RODIN. What Rodin did accomplish is already visible in the first piece he tried to exhibit (it was rejected, as we might expect), *The Man with the Broken Nose* of 1864 (fig. 931). Earlier, he had worked briefly under Barye, whose influence may help to explain the vigorously creased surface (compare fig. 890). These welts and wrinkles produce, in polished bronze, an ever-changing pattern of reflections. But is this effect borrowed from Impressionist painting? Does Rodin dissolve three-dimensional form into flickering patches of light and dark? These fiercely exaggerated shapes pulsate with sculptural energy, and they retain this quality under whatever conditions the piece is viewed. For Rodin did not work directly in bronze; he modeled in wax or clay. How could he calculate in advance the reflections on the bronze surfaces of the casts that would ultimately be made from these models?

He worked as he did, we must assume, for an altogether different reason: not to capture elusive optical effects, but to emphasize the process of "growth"—the miracle of dead matter coming to life in the artist's hands. As the color patch for Manet and Monet is the primary reality, so are the malleable lumps from which Rodin builds his forms. Conservative critics rejected *The Man with the Broken Nose* and Impressionist painting on the same grounds—it was "unfinished," a mere sketch.

Sculptors, of course, had always made small, informal

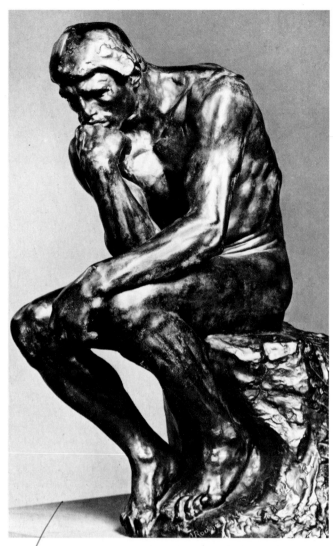

932. AUGUSTE RODIN. *THE THINKER*. 1879–89. Bronze, height 27½" (69.8 cm). The Metropolitan Museum of Art, New York. Gift of Thomas F. Ryan, 1910

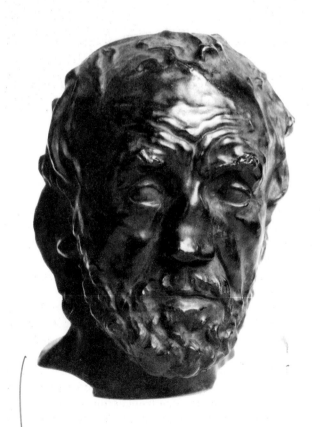

931. AUGUSTE RODIN. *THE MAN WITH THE BROKEN NOSE*. 1864. Bronze, height 9½" (24 cm). Rodin Museum, The Philadelphia Museum of Art

sketches (the plastic counterpart of drawings), but these were for the artist's private use, not for public display. Rodin was the first to make of unfinishedness an aesthetic principle that governed both his handling of surfaces and the whole shape of the work (*The Man with the Broken Nose* is not a bust, but a head "broken off" at the neck). By discovering what might be called the autonomy of the fragment, he rescued sculpture from mechanical verisimilitude just as Manet rescued painting from photographic realism.

This sculptural revolution, proclaimed with such daring by Rodin at twenty-four, did not reach full force until the late 1870s. For his living, the young artist had to collaborate with officially recognized sculptors on their public commissions, mostly memorials and architectural sculpture in the Neo-Baroque style of Carpeaux. In 1880 he was at last entrusted with a major task, the entrance of the École des Arts Décoratifs in Paris.

Rodin elaborated the commission into an ambitious ensemble called *The Gates of Hell*, its symbolic program inspired by Dante's *Inferno*. He never finished the *Gates*, but they served as a matrix for countless smaller pieces that he eventually made into independent works.

The most famous of these autonomous fragments is *The Thinker* (fig. 932), intended for the lintel of the *Gates*, whence the figure was to contemplate the panorama of despair below him. The ancestry of *The Thinker* goes back, indirectly, to the first phase of Christian art (the pensive man seated at the left in the Byzantine ivory in figure 361 reflects an Early Christian source); it also includes the action-in-repose of Michelangelo's superhuman bodies (see figs. 655, 658, and 660), the tension in Puget's *Milo of Crotona* (see fig. 817, especially the feet), and the expressive dynamism of *The Man with the Broken Nose*. Who is *The Thinker*? Partly Adam, no doubt (though there is also a different Adam by Rodin, another "outgrowth" of the *Gates*), partly Prometheus, and partly the brute imprisoned by the passions of the flesh. Rodin wisely refrained from giving him a specific name, for the statue fits no preconceived identity. In this new image of a man, form and meaning are one, instead of cleaving apart as in Carpeaux's *The Dance*. Carpeaux produced naked figures that pretend to be nude, while *The Thinker*, like the nudes of Michelangelo, is free from subservience to the undressed model.

The Kiss (fig. 933), an over-lifesize group in marble, also derives from the *Gates*. Less powerful than *The Thinker*, it exploits another kind of artful unfinishedness. Rodin had been impressed by the struggle of Michelangelo's "Slaves"

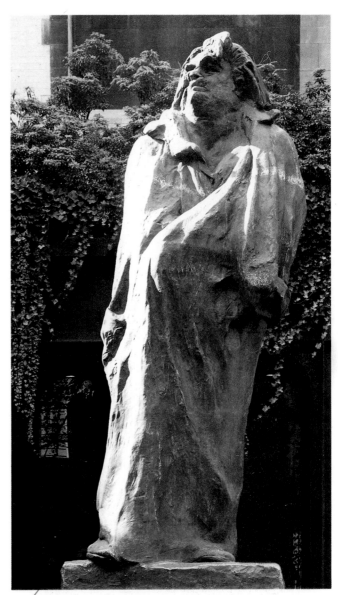

934. AUGUSTE RODIN. *MONUMENT TO BALZAC*. 1897–98.
Bronze (cast 1954), height 8′10″ (2.69 m).
Collection, The Museum of Modern Art, New York.
Presented in memory of Curt Valentin by his friends

against the remnants of the blocks that imprison them; *The Kiss* was planned from the start to include the mass of roughhewn marble to which the lovers are attached, and which thus becomes symbolic of their earthbound passion. The contrast of textures emphasizes the veiled, sensuous softness of the bodies.

But Rodin was by instinct a modeler, not a carver like Michelangelo. His greatest works were intended to be cast in bronze. Even these, however, reveal their full strength only when we see them in plaster casts made directly from Rodin's clay originals. The *Monument to Balzac*, his most daring creation (fig. 934), remained in plaster for many years, rejected by the committee that had commissioned it.

The figure is larger than life, physically and spiritually; it has the overpowering presence of a specter. Like a huge monolith, the man of genius towers above the crowd; he shares "the sublime egotism of the gods" (as the Romantics

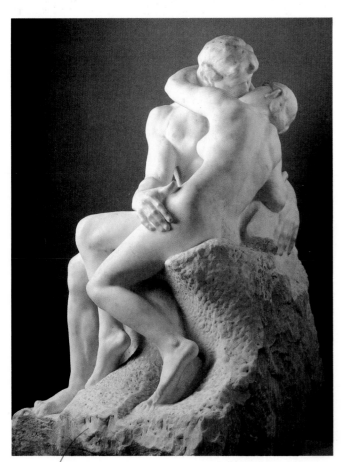

933. AUGUSTE RODIN. *THE KISS*. 1886–98.
Marble, over lifesize. Rodin Museum, Paris

put it). Rodin has minimized the articulation of the body, so that from a distance we see only its great bulk. As we approach, we become aware that Balzac is wrapped in a long, shroudlike cloak. From this mass the head thrusts upward—one is tempted to say, erupts—with elemental force. When we are close enough to make out the features clearly, we sense beneath the disdain an inner agony that stamps *Balzac* as the kin of *The Man with the Broken Nose.*

CLAUDEL. Rodin employed various assistants throughout his career. One of them, Camille Claudel (1864–1943), has emerged as an important artist in her own right. Claudel entered Rodin's studio as a nineteen-year-old and was for many years his collaborator and mistress. Her sculptures are stylistically akin to Rodin's; some of her strongest pieces might be mistaken for his. However, Claudel's lyrical sensibility, which contrasts with Rodin's confident sense of the heroic, is a distinctive hallmark of her work, the subject matter of which is often autobiographical. *Ripe Age* (fig. 935) was begun at the time when she was being replaced in Rodin's affections by another woman, his long-time companion Rose Beuret. It shows Rodin, whose features are clearly recognizable, being led away with apparent reluctance by the other woman, who is portrayed as a sinister, shrouded figure. Claudel adapted this figure from an earlier work showing Clotho, one of the three Fates, ironically caught in the web of life she had woven for herself. The nude figure on the right is a self-portait of the pleading Claudel; this figure, too, evolved from an earlier work, *Entreaty.*

ARCHITECTURE
Industrial Architecture and the Machine Aesthetic

For more than a century, from the mid-eighteenth to the late nineteenth, architecture had been dominated by a succession of "revival styles" (see pages 652–56). This term, we will recall, does not imply that earlier forms were slavish copies; the best work of the time has both individuality and high distinction. Yet the architectural wisdom of the past, however freely interpreted, proved in the long run to be inadequate for the practical demands of the Industrial Age—the factories, warehouses, stores, and city apartments that formed the bulk of building construction. For it is after about 1800, in the world of commercial architecture, that we find the gradual introduction of new materials and techniques that were to have a profound effect on architectural style by the end of the century. The most important was iron, never before used as an actual structural member. Within a few decades of their first appearance, cast-iron columns and arches had become the standard means of supporting roofs over the large spaces required by railroad stations, exhibition halls, and public libraries.

LABROUSTE. A famous early example is the Bibliothèque Ste.-Geneviève in Paris by Henri Labrouste (1801–1875). The exterior (fig. 936) represents the historicism prevailing at mid-century. It is drawn chiefly from Italian Renaissance

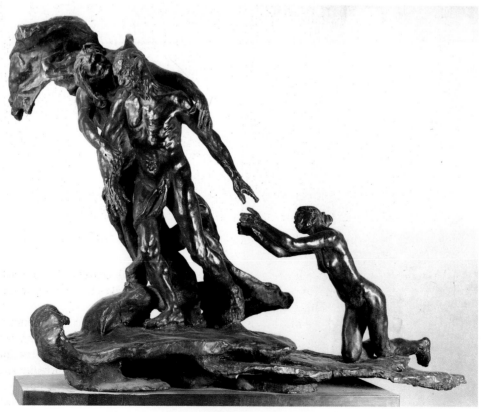

935. CAMILLE CLAUDEL. *RIPE AGE.* c. 1907. Bronze, 34½×20½″ (87.6×21.9 cm). Musée d'Orsay, Paris

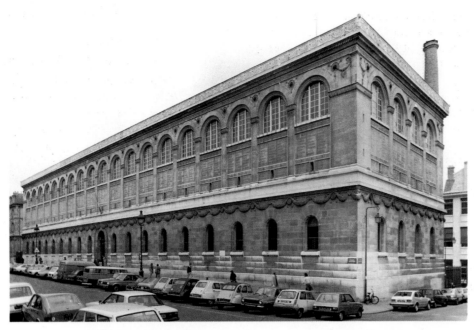

936. HENRI LABROUSTE. Bibliothèque Ste.-Geneviève, Paris. 1843–50

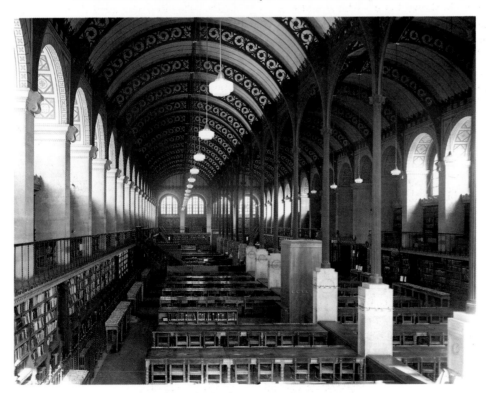

937. HENRI LABROUSTE. Reading Room, Bibliothèque Ste.-Geneviève

banks, libraries, and churches. To identify the building as a library, Labrouste used the simple but ingenious device of inscribing the names of great writers around the façade. The reading room (fig. 937), on the other hand, recalls the nave of a French Gothic cathedral (compare fig. 466). But why did Labrouste choose cast-iron columns and arches, hitherto used exclusively for railroad stations? Cast iron was not necessary to provide structural support for the two barrel roofs—this could have been done using other materials—but to complete the building's symbolic program. The library, Labrouste suggests to us, is a storehouse of something even

more precious and sacred than material wealth: the world's literature, which takes us on a journey not to faraway places but of the mind.

Labrouste chose to leave the interior iron skeleton uncovered and to face the difficulty of relating it to the massive Renaissance revival style of the exterior of the building. If his solution does not fully integrate the two systems, it at least lets them coexist. The iron supports, shaped like Corinthian columns, are as slender as the new material permits; their collective effect is that of a space-dividing screen, belying their structural importance. To make them weightier,

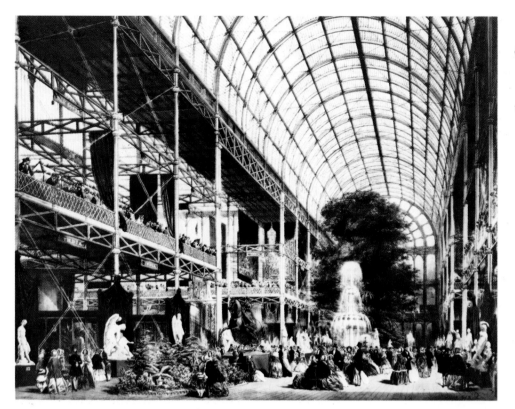

938. SIR JOSEPH PAXTON
The Crystal Palace, London
(interior view looking north). 1851;
reerected in Sydenham 1852;
destroyed 1936
(lithograph by Joseph Nash).
Victoria & Albert Museum, London
(Crown copyright reserved)

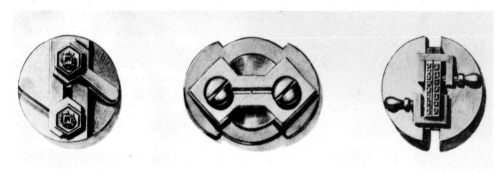

939. STUDIO OF CARL MICHEL
Jewelry designs. c. 1865. Watercolor.
Staatliche Zeichenakademie,
Hanau am Main, Germany

Labrouste has placed them on tall pedestals of solid masonry, instead of directly on the floor. Aesthetically the arches presented greater difficulty, since there was no way to make them look as powerful as their masonry ancestors. Here Labrouste has gone to the other extreme, perforating them with lacy scrolls as if they were pure ornament. This architectural—as against merely technical—use of exposed iron members has a fanciful and delicate quality that links it, indirectly, to the Gothic revival. Later superseded by structural steel and ferroconcrete, it is a peculiarly appealing final chapter in the history of Romantic architecture.

The authority of historic modes had to be broken if the industrial era was to produce a truly contemporary style. It nevertheless proved extraordinarily persistent. Labrouste, pioneer though he was of cast-iron construction, could not think of architectural supports as anything but columns having proper capitals and bases. The "architecture of conspicuous display" espoused by Garnier (see page 655) was divorced, even more than were the previous revival styles, from the needs of the present. It was only in structures that were not considered "architecture" at all that new building materials and techniques could be explored without these inhibitions.

PAXTON. Within a year of the completion of the Bibliothèque Ste.-Geneviève, the Crystal Palace (fig. 938) was built in London. An achievement far bolder in conception than Labrouste's library, the Crystal Palace was designed to house the first of the great international expositions that continue in our day. Its designer, Sir Joseph Paxton (1801–1865), was an engineer and builder of greenhouses; and the Crystal Palace was indeed a gigantic greenhouse—so large that it enclosed some old trees growing on the site—with its iron skeleton freely on display. Still, the notion that there might be beauty, and not merely utility, in the products of engineering made headway very slowly, even though the doctrine "form follows function" found advocates from the mid-nineteenth century on.

OTHER FIELDS. Among the earliest harbingers of the "machine aesthetic" are certain jewelry designs of the 1860s in France and Germany; these are composed of screw heads, nuts, bolts, wrenches, and other symbols of the age (fig. 939). They might have been intended to appeal to prosperous factory owners, since the materials indicated are gold and precious stones (the era of cheap, mass-produced "costume jewelry" was yet to come). Regardless of who they were intended for, these designs have a clean-cut, uncluttered quality that a modernist painter such as Fernand Léger could have liked (see fig. 1016).

GODWIN. In the 1860s the reform ideas of William Morris began to bear fruit in domestic architecture and decoration (see page 672). The boldest innovations, however, came not from members of his immediate circle but from Edward William Godwin (1833–1886), a friend of Whistler, who designed the remarkable sideboard illustrated in figure 940. Godwin had been much impressed with the simplicity of Japanese interior furnishings, which he knew mainly from the colored woodcuts newly available in the West. His sideboard, composed of "boxes" within a framework of straight "sticks," owes its elegance almost entirely to its finely balanced proportions, since applied ornament has been kept to a minimum. At the same time, it has been planned for ease and low cost of manufacture (the material is cheap wood, painted black). In its geometric austerity, it seems prophetic of Rietveld (compare figures 939, 1099, and 1100).

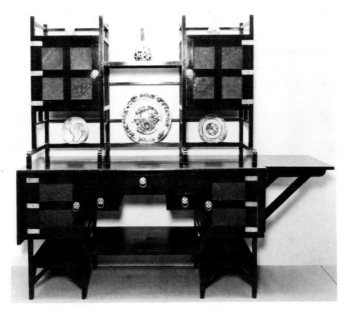

940. EDWARD WILLIAM GODWIN. Sideboard. c. 1867.
Ebonized wood with silver hardware and imitation leather panels,
height 71″ (180.3 cm). Victoria & Albert Museum, London
(Crown copyright reserved)

CHAPTER THREE
POST-IMPRESSIONISM

PAINTING

In 1882, just before his death, Manet was made a chevalier of the Legion of Honor by the French government. Four years later, the Impressionists, who had been exhibiting together since 1874, held their last group show. These two events mark the turn of the tide—Impressionism had gained wide acceptance among artists and the public, but by the same token it was no longer a pioneering movement. The future now belonged to the "Post-Impressionists."

Taken literally, this colorless label applies to all painters of significance since the 1880s; in a more specific sense, it designates a group of artists who passed through an Impressionist phase but became dissatisfied with the limitations of the style and went beyond it in various directions. As they did not share one common goal, it is difficult to find a more descriptive term for them than Post-Impressionists. In any event, they were not "anti-Impressionists." Far from trying to undo the effects of the "Manet Revolution," they wanted to carry it further; Post-Impressionism is in essence just a later stage—though a very important one—of the development that had begun in the 1860s with such pictures as Manet's *Luncheon on the Grass.*

CÉZANNE. Paul Cézanne (1839–1906), the oldest of the Post-Impressionists, was born in Aix-en-Provence, near the Mediterranean coast. A man of intensely emotional temperament, he came to Paris in 1861 imbued with enthusiasm for the Romantics; Delacroix was his first love among painters—he never lost his admiration for him—and he quickly grasped the nature of the "Manet Revolution." After passing through a "Neo-Baroque" phase, Cézanne began to paint bright outdoor scenes, but he never shared his fellow Impressionists' interest in "slice-of-life" subjects, in movement and change. About 1879, when he painted the *Self-Por-*

trait in our figure 941, he had decided "to make of Impressionism something solid and durable, like the art of the museums." His Romantic impulsiveness of the 1860s has now given way to a patient, disciplined search for harmony of form and color: every brushstroke is like a building block, firmly placed within the pictorial architecture; the balance of "two-D" and "three-D" is less harsh than before (note how the pattern of wallpaper in the background frames the rounded shape of the head); and the colors are deliberately controlled so as to produce "chords" of warm and cool tones that reverberate throughout the canvas.

In Cézanne's still lifes, such as *Still Life with Apples* (fig. 942), this quest for the "solid and durable" can be seen even more clearly. Not since Chardin have simple everyday objects assumed such importance in a painter's eye. Again the ornamental backdrop is integrated with the three-dimensional shapes, and the brushstrokes have a rhythmic pattern that gives the canvas its shimmering texture. We also notice another aspect of Cézanne's mature style that is more conspicuous here than in the *Self-Portrait* and may puzzle us at first: the forms are deliberately simplified and outlined with dark contours; and the perspective is "incorrect" for both the fruit bowl and the horizontal surfaces, which seem to tilt upward. The longer we study the picture, the more we realize the rightness of these apparently arbitrary distortions. When Cézanne took these liberties with reality, his purpose was to uncover the permanent qualities beneath the accidents of appearance (all forms in nature, he believed, are based on the cone, the sphere, and the cylinder). This order underlying the external world was the true subject of his pictures, but he had to interpret it to fit the separate, closed world of the canvas.

To apply this method to landscape became the greatest challenge of Cézanne's career. From 1882 on, he lived in isolation near his home town of Aix-en-Provence, exploring its

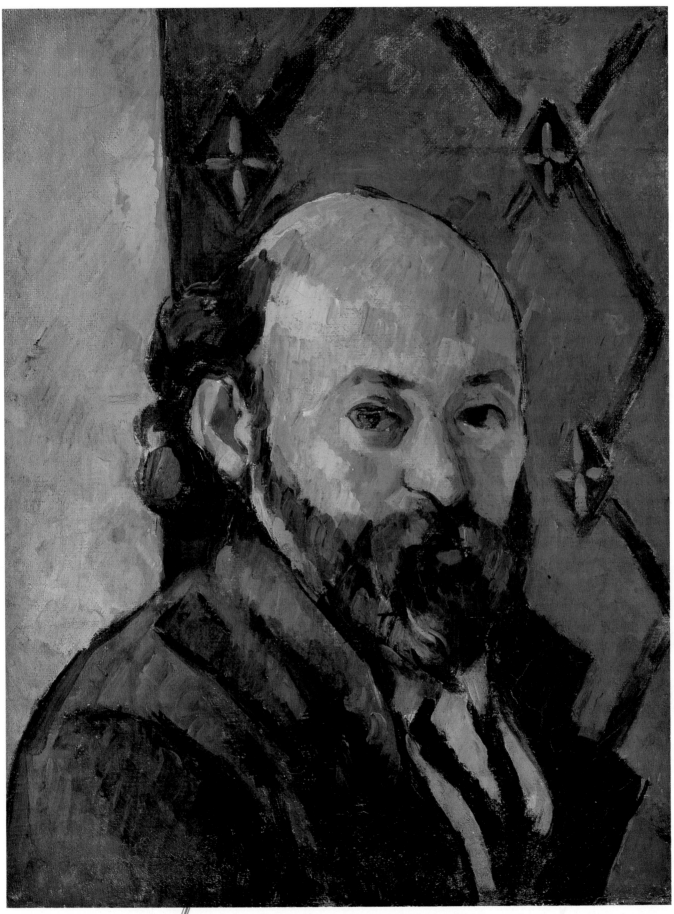

941. PAUL CÉZANNE. *SELF-PORTRAIT*. c. 1879. Oil on canvas,
13¾×10⅝″ (35×27 cm). The Tate Gallery, London

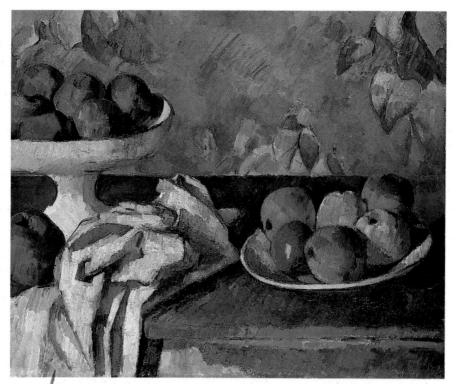

942. PAUL CÉZANNE. *STILL LIFE WITH APPLES*. 1879–82. Oil on canvas,
17⅛×21¼" (43.5×54 cm). Ny Carlsberg Glyptotek, Copenhagen

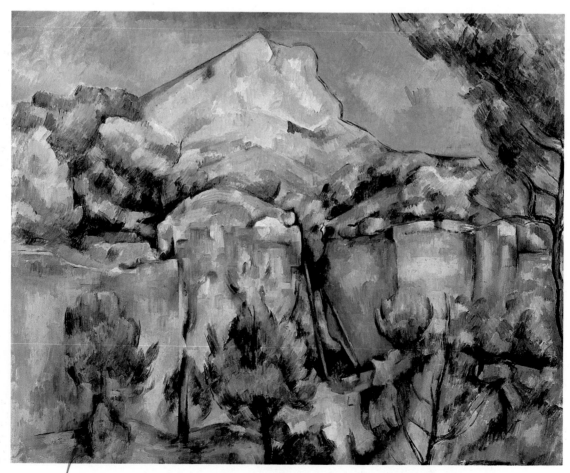

943. PAUL CÉZANNE. *MONT SAINTE-VICTOIRE SEEN FROM BIBÉMUS QUARRY*. c. 1897–1900.
Oil on canvas, 25⅛×32" (63.9×81.3 cm). The Baltimore Museum of Art. The Cone Collection,
formed by Dr. Claribel Cone and Miss Etta Cone of Baltimore, Maryland

environs as Claude Lorraine and Corot had explored the Roman countryside. One motif, the distinctive shape of a mountain called Mont Sainte-Victoire, seemed almost to obsess him; its craggy profile looming against the blue Mediterranean sky appears in a long series of compositions, such as the very monumental late work in figure 943. There are no hints of human presence here—houses and roads would only disturb the lonely grandeur of this view. Above the wall of rocky cliffs that bar our way like a chain of fortifications, the mountain rises in triumphant clarity, infinitely remote yet as solid and palpable as the shapes in the foreground. For all its architectural stability, the scene is alive with movement; but the forces at work here have been brought into equilibrium, subdued by the greater power of the artist's will. This disciplined energy, distilled from the trials of a stormy youth, gives the mature style of Cézanne its enduring strength.

SEURAT. Georges Seurat (1859–1891) shared Cézanne's aim to make Impressionism "solid and durable," but he went about it very differently. His career was as brief as those of Masaccio, Giorgione, and Géricault, and his achievement just as astonishing. Seurat devoted his main efforts to a few very large paintings, spending a year or more on each of them: he made endless series of preliminary studies before

he felt sure enough to tackle the definitive version. This painstaking method reflects his belief that art must be based on a system; like Degas, he had studied with a follower of Ingres, and his theoretical interests came from this experience. But, as with all artists of genius, Seurat's theories do not really explain his pictures; it is the pictures, rather, that explain the theories.

The subject of his first large-scale composition, *The Bathers* of 1883–84 (fig. 944), is of the sort that had long been popular among Impressionist painters. Impressionist, too, are the brilliant colors and the effect of intense sunlight. Otherwise, however, the picture is the very opposite of a quick "impression"; the firm, simple contours and the relaxed, immobile figures give the scene a timeless stability that recalls Piero della Francesca (see fig. 609) and shows a clear awareness of Puvis de Chavannes (see page 690). Even the brushwork demonstrates Seurat's passion for order and permanence: the canvas surface is covered with systematic, impersonal "flicks" that make Cézanne's architectural brushstrokes seem temperamental and dynamic by comparison.

In Seurat's later works such as *Invitation to the Side Show* (*La Parade*; fig. 945), the flicks become tiny dots of brilliant color that were supposed to merge in the beholder's eye and

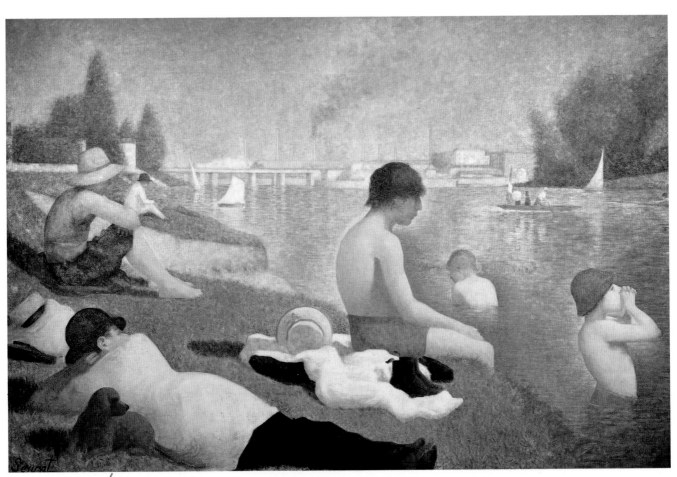

944. GEORGES SEURAT. *THE BATHERS.* 1883–84. Oil on canvas, 79½×118½″ (202×300.3 cm).
The National Gallery, London. Reproduced by courtesy of the Trustees

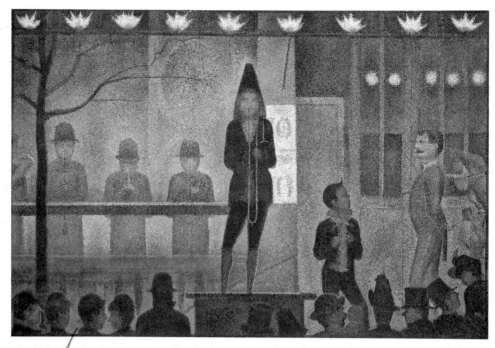

945. GEORGES SEURAT. *INVITATION TO THE SIDE SHOW (LA PARADE)*.
1887–88. Oil on canvas, 39¼×59″ (99.6×150 cm).
The Metropolitan Museum of Art, New York. Bequest of Stephen C. Clark, 1960

produce intermediary tints more luminous than those obtainable from pigments mixed on the palette. This procedure was variously known as Neo-Impressionism, Pointillism, or Divisionism (the term preferred by Seurat). The actual result, however, did not conform to the theory. Looking at *Invitation to the Side Show* from a comfortable distance (seven to ten feet for the original), we find that the mixing of colors in the eye remains incomplete; the dots do not disappear, but are as clearly visible as the tesserae of a mosaic (compare fig. 345). Seurat himself must have liked this unexpected ef-

fect—had he not, he would have reduced the size of the dots—which gives the canvas the quality of a shimmering, translucent screen.

In *Invitation to the Side Show*, the bodies do not have the weight and bulk they had in *The Bathers*; modeling and foreshortening are reduced to a minimum, and the figures appear mostly in either strict profile or frontal views, as if Seurat had adopted the rules of ancient Egyptian art (see page 100). Moreover, he has fitted them very precisely into a system of vertical and horizontal coordinates that holds them in place and defines the canvas as a self-contained rectilinear field. Only in the work of Vermeer have we encountered a similar "area-consciousness" (compare fig. 794).

The machinelike quality of Seurat's forms, achieved through rigorous abstraction, is the first expression of a peculiarly modern outlook leading to Futurism (see page 720). Seurat's systematic approach to art has the internal logic of modern engineering, which he and his followers hoped would transform society for the better. This social consciousness was allied to a form of anarchism descended from Courbet's friend Proudhon, and contrasts with the general political indifference of the Impressionists.

VAN GOGH. While Cézanne and Seurat were converting Impressionism into a more severe, classical style, Vincent van Gogh (1853–1890) pursued the opposite direction. He believed that Impressionism did not provide the artist with enough freedom to express his emotions. Since this was his main concern, he is sometimes called an Expressionist, although the term ought to be reserved for certain later paint-

946. VINCENT VAN GOGH. *THE POTATO EATERS*. 1885.
Oil on canvas, 32¼×45″ (82×114.3 cm).
Rijksmuseum Vincent van Gogh, Amsterdam

ers (see the next chapter). Van Gogh, the first great Dutch master since the seventeenth century, did not become an artist until 1880; as he died only ten years later, his career was even briefer than that of Seurat. His early interests were in literature and religion; profoundly dissatisfied with the values of industrial society and imbued with a strong sense of mission, he worked for a while as a lay preacher among povertystricken coal miners. This same intense feeling for the poor dominates the paintings of his pre-Impressionist period, 1880–85. In *The Potato Eaters* (fig. 946), the last and most ambitious work of those years, there remains a naïve clumsiness that comes from his lack of conventional training, but this only adds to the expressive power of his style. We are reminded of Daumier and Millet (see figs. 870 and 874), and of Rembrandt and Le Nain (see figs. 787 and 801). For this peasant family, the evening meal has the solemn importance of a ritual.

When he painted *The Potato Eaters*, Van Gogh had not yet discovered the importance of color. A year later in Paris, where his brother Theo had a gallery devoted to modern art, he met Degas, Seurat, and other leading French artists. Their effect on him was electrifying: his pictures now blazed with color, and he even experimented briefly with the Divisionist technique of Seurat. This Impressionist phase, however, lasted less than two years. Although it was vitally important for his development, he had to integrate it with the style of his earlier years before his genius could fully unfold. Paris had opened his eyes to the sensuous beauty of the vis-

ible world and had taught him the pictorial language of the color patch, but painting continued to be nevertheless a vessel for his personal emotions. To investigate this spiritual reality with the new means at his command, he went to Arles, in the south of France. It was there, between 1888 and 1890, that he produced his greatest pictures.

Like Cézanne, Van Gogh now devoted his main energies to landscape painting, but the sun-drenched Mediterranean countryside evoked a very different response in him: he saw it filled with ecstatic movement, not architectural stability and permanence. In *Wheat Field and Cypress Trees* (fig. 947), both earth and sky show an overpowering turbulence—the wheat field resembles a stormy sea, the trees spring flamelike from the ground, and the hills and clouds heave with the same undulant motion. The dynamism contained in every brushstroke makes of each one not merely a deposit of color, but an incisive graphic gesture. The artist's personal "handwriting" is here an even more dominant factor than in the canvases of Daumier (compare figs. 870 and 871). Yet to Van Gogh himself it was the color, not the form, that determined the expressive content of his pictures. The letters he wrote to his brother include many eloquent descriptions of his choice of hues and the emotional meanings he attached to them. Although he acknowledged that his desire "to exaggerate the essential and to leave the obvious vague" made his colors look arbitrary by Impressionist standards, he nevertheless remained deeply committed to the visible world.

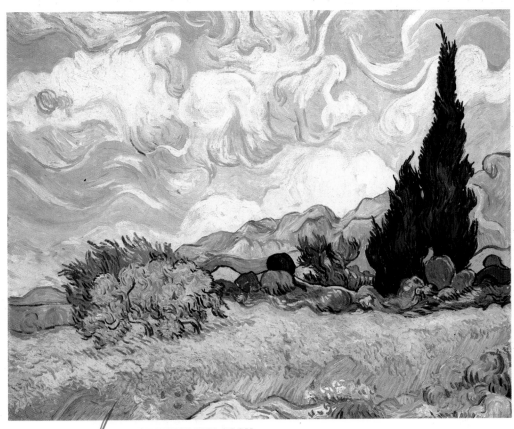

947. VINCENT VAN GOGH. *WHEAT FIELD AND CYPRESS TREES.*
1889. Oil on canvas, 28½×36″ (72.3×91.3 cm).
The National Gallery, London. Reproduced by courtesy of the Trustees

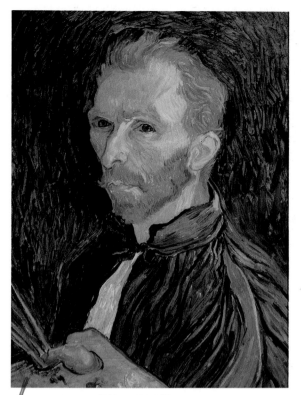

948. VINCENT VAN GOGH. *SELF-PORTRAIT.* 1889.
Oil on canvas, 22½×17″ (57×43.3 cm).
Collection Mrs. John Hay Whitney, New York

Compared to Monet's *The River* (see fig. 913), the colors of *Wheat Field and Cypress Trees* are stronger, simpler, and more vibrant, but in no sense "unnatural." They speak to us of that "kingdom of light" Van Gogh had found in the South, and of his mystic faith in a creative force animating all forms of life—a faith no less ardent than the sectarian Christianity of his early years. The missionary had now become a prophet. We see him in that role in the *Self-Portrait* (fig. 948), his emaciated, luminous head with its burning eyes set off against a whirlpool of darkness. "I want to paint men and women with that something of the eternal which the halo used to symbolize," Van Gogh had written, groping to define for his brother the human essence that was his aim in pictures such as this. At the time of the *Self-Portrait*, he had already begun to suffer fits of a mental illness that made painting increasingly difficult for him. Despairing of a cure, he committed suicide a year later, for he felt very deeply that art alone made his life worth living.

GAUGUIN AND SYMBOLISM. The quest for religious experience also played an important part in the work—if not in the life—of another great Post-Impressionist, Paul Gauguin (1848–1903). He began as a prosperous stockbroker in Paris and an amateur painter and collector of modern pictures. At the age of thirty-five, however, he became convinced that he must devote himself entirely to art; he

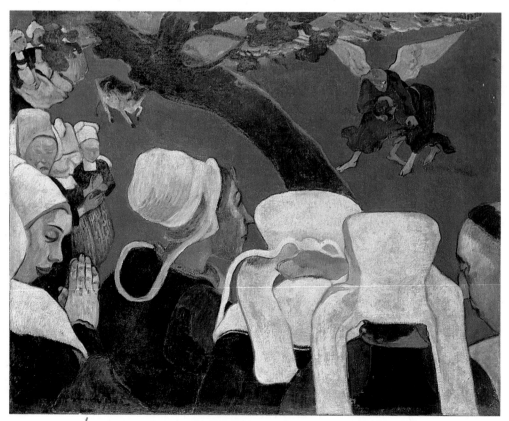

949. PAUL GAUGUIN. *THE VISION AFTER THE SERMON (JACOB WRESTLING WITH THE ANGEL).* 1888. Oil on canvas, 28¾×36½ (73×92.7 cm).
The National Galleries of Scotland, Edinburgh

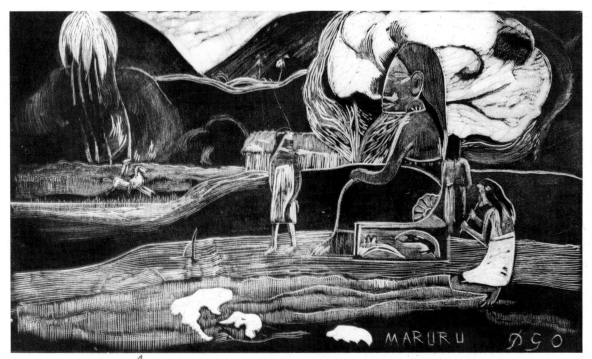

950. PAUL GAUGUIN. *OFFERINGS OF GRATITUDE*, c. 1891–93. Woodcut, 8¹/₁₆×14″ (20.5×35.5 cm).
Collection, The Museum of Modern Art, New York. Lillie P. Bliss Collection

abandoned his business career, separated from his family, and by 1889 was the central figure of a new movement called Synthetism or Symbolism.

Gauguin began as a follower of Cézanne and once owned one of his still lifes. He then developed a style that, though less intensely personal than Van Gogh's, was in some ways an even bolder advance beyond Impressionism. Gauguin believed that Western civilization was "out of joint," that industrial society had forced people into an incomplete life dedicated to material gain, while their emotions lay neglected. To rediscover for himself this hidden world of feeling, Gauguin left Paris for western France to live among the peasants of Brittany. He noticed particularly that religion was still part of the everyday life of the country people, and in pictures such as *The Vision After the Sermon (Jacob Wrestling with the Angel*; fig. 949), he tried to depict their simple, direct faith. Here at last is what no Romantic painter had achieved: a style based on pre-Renaissance sources.

Modeling and perspective have given way to flat, simplified shapes outlined heavily in black, and the brilliant colors are equally "un-natural." This style, inspired by folk art and medieval stained glass, is meant to re-create both the imagined reality of the vision, and the trancelike rapture of the peasant women. Yet we sense that Gauguin, although he tried to share this experience, remains an outsider; he could paint pictures *about* faith, but not *from* faith.

Two years later, Gauguin's search for the unspoiled life led him even farther afield. He voyaged to Tahiti as a sort of "missionary in reverse," to learn from the natives instead of teaching them. Although he spent the rest of his life in the South Pacific (he returned home only once, in 1893–95), none of his Tahitian canvases are as daring as those he had painted in Brittany. His strongest works of this period are woodcuts; *Offerings of Gratitude* (fig. 950) again presents the theme of religious worship, but the image of a local god now replaces the biblical subject of the *Vision*. In its frankly "carved" look and its bold white-on-black pattern, we can feel the influences of the native art of the South Seas and of other non-European styles. The renewal of Western art and Western civilization as a whole, Gauguin believed, must come from "the Primitives"; he advised other Symbolists to shun the Greek tradition and to turn instead to Persia, the Far East, and ancient Egypt.

The idea of primitivism itself was not new. It stems from the Romantic myth of the Noble Savage, propagated by the thinkers of the Enlightenment more than a century before, and its ultimate source is the age-old tradition of an earthly paradise where human societies once dwelled—and might perhaps live again—in a state of nature and innocence. But no one before Gauguin had gone as far to put the doctrine of primitivism into practice. His pilgrimage to the South Pacific had more than a purely private meaning: it symbolizes the end of the four hundred years of colonial expansion which had brought the entire globe under Western domination. The "white man's burden," once so cheerfully—and ruthlessly—shouldered by the empire builders, was becoming unbearable.

THE NABIS. Gauguin's Symbolist followers, who called themselves Nabis (from the Hebrew word for "prophet"), were less remarkable for creative talent than for their ability to spell out and justify the aims of Post-Impressionism in the-

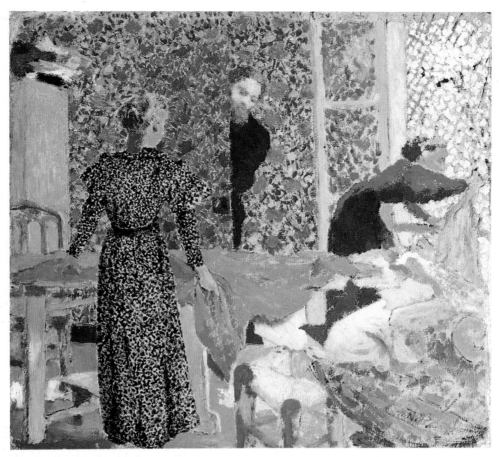

951. ÉDOUARD VUILLARD. *INTERIOR AT L'ETANG-LA-VILLE (THE SUITOR)*. 1893. Oil on millboard panel, 12½×14⅞″ (31.8×36.4 cm). Smith College Museum of Art, Northampton, Massachusetts

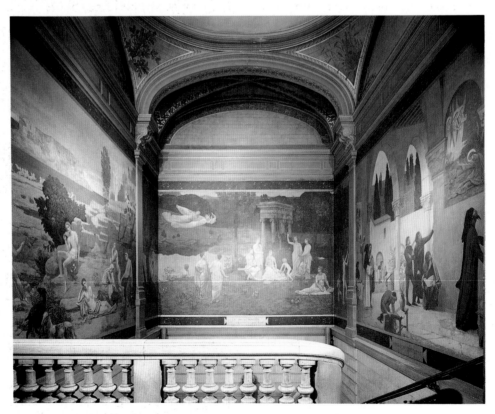

952. PIERRE CÉCILE PUVIS DE CHAVANNES. *THE SACRED GROVE*, c. 1883–84;
VISION OF ANTIQUITY, c. 1888–89; and *CHRISTIAN INSPIRATION*, c. 1888–89 Painting cycle,
grand staircase, Musée des Beaux-Arts, Lyons, France

oretical form. One of them, Maurice Denis, coined the statement that was to become the First Article of Faith for modernist painters of the twentieth century: "A picture—before being a war horse, a female nude, or some anecdote—is essentially a flat surface covered with colors in a particular order."

VUILLARD. Oddly enough, the most gifted member of the Nabis, Édouard Vuillard (1868–1940), was more influenced by Seurat than by Gauguin. In his pictures of the 1890s—mainly domestic scenes, small in scale and intimate in effect, like the *Interior at l'Étang-la-Ville* (fig. 951)—he combines into a remarkable new entity the flat planes and emphatic contours of Gauguin (fig. 949) with the shimmering Divisionist "color mosaic" and the geometric surface organization of Seurat (see fig. 945). This seemingly casual view of his mother's corset-shop workroom has a delicate balance of "two-D" and "three-D" effects and a quiet magic that makes us think of Vermeer and Chardin (compare figs. 794 and 823). Such economy of means became an important precedent for Matisse a decade later (see fig. 989). By then, however, Vuillard's own style had grown more conservative. He never recaptured the delicacy and daring of his early canvases.

PUVIS DE CHAVANNES The Symbolists also discovered that there were some older artists, descendants of the Romantics, whose work, like their own, placed inner vision above the observation of nature. Many of them, as well as other Post-Impressionists, took their inspiration from the classicism of Pierre Puvis de Chavannes (1824–1898), a follower of Ingres who succeeded in becoming the leading muralist of his day. Rejecting academic conventions, he sought a radical simplification of style, which at first seemed anachronistic but was soon hailed by the critics and artists of all persuasions. The effectiveness of the murals he executed in the 1880s for the museum at Lyons (fig. 952) depends in large part on Puvis' formal devices: the compressed space, schematic forms, and restricted palette, which imitates in oil the chalky surface of old frescoes. The anti-naturalism of his style emphasizes the allegorical character of the scene, lending it a gravity and mystery absent from other decorative paintings by his contemporaries. Anecdotal interest is replaced by nostalgia for an idealized, mythical past. The stiff, ritualistic poses serve both to freeze time and to convey a poetry that is at once elegiac and serene. Puvis' economy of means was intended to present his ideas with maximum clarity, but it has just the opposite effect: it heightens their suggestiveness. His popularity resulted precisely from this ambiguity, which permitted a wide variety of interpretation. Symbolists from Gauguin through the young Picasso could thus claim him as one of their own; nevertheless, he vehemently protested any association with the Symbolist movement, although he reciprocated a mutual admiration with the English Pre-Raphaelites (see page 671).

MOREAU. One of the Symbolists, Gustave Moreau (1826–1898), a recluse who admired Delacroix, created a world of personal fantasy that has much in common with the medieval reveries of some of the English Pre-Raphaelites. *The Apparition* (fig. 953) shows one of his favorite themes: the head of John the Baptist, in a blinding radiance of light, appears to the dancing Salome. Her odalisquelike sensuousness, the stream of blood pouring from the severed head, the vast, mysterious space of the setting—suggestive of an exotic temple rather than of Herod's palace—summon up all the dreams of Oriental splendor and cruelty so dear to the Romantic imagination, commingled with an insistence on the reality of the supernatural.

Only late in life did Moreau achieve a measure of recognition; suddenly, his art was in tune with the times. During his last six years, he even held a professorship at the conservative École des Beaux-Arts, the successor of the official art academy founded under Louis XIV (see page 596). There he attracted the most gifted students, among them such future modernists as Matisse and Rouault.

BEARDSLEY. How prophetic Moreau's work was of the taste prevailing at the end of the century is evident from a comparison with Aubrey Beardsley (1872–1898), a gifted

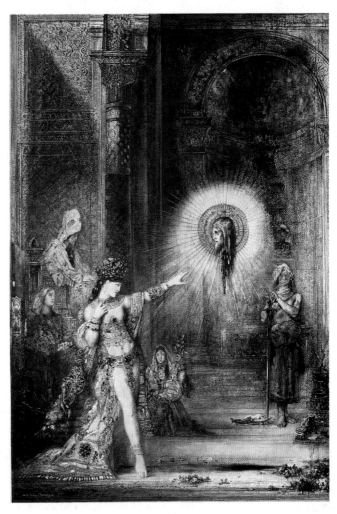

953. GUSTAVE MOREAU. *THE APPARITION (DANCE OF SALOME)*. 1876. Watercolor, 41¾ × 28⅜" (106 × 72 cm). Musée d'Orsay, Paris

young Englishman whose elegantly "decadent" black-and-white drawings were the very epitome of that taste. They include a *Salome* illustration (fig. 954) that might well be the final scene of the drama depicted by Moreau: Salome has taken up John's severed head and triumphantly kissed it. Whereas Beardsley's erotic meaning is plain—Salome is passionately in love with John and has asked for his head because she could not have him in any other way—Moreau's remains ambiguous. Did his Salome perhaps conjure up the vision of the head? Is she, too, in love with John? Nevertheless, the parallel is striking, and there are formal similarities as well, such as the "stem" of trickling blood from which John's head rises like a flower. Yet Beardsley's *Salome* cannot be said to derive from Moreau's. The sources of his style are English—the graphic art of the Pre-Raphaelites (see fig. 924)—with a strong admixture of Japanese influence.

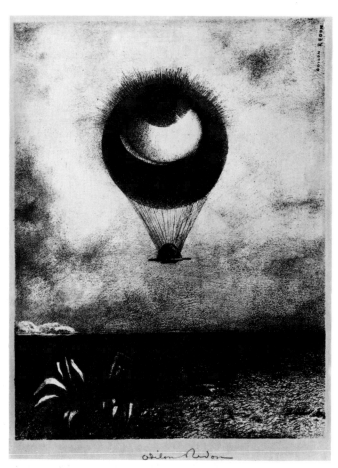

955. ODILON REDON. *THE BALLOON EYE*, from the series *À Edgar Poe*. 1882. Lithograph

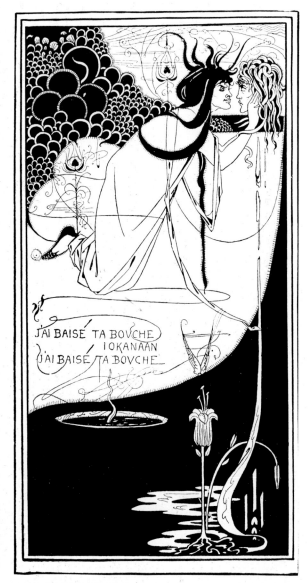

954. AUBREY BEARDSLEY. *SALOME*. 1892. Pen drawing. Princeton University Library, Princeton, New Jersey

REDON. Another solitary artist whom the Symbolists discovered and claimed as one of their own was Odilon Redon (1840–1916). Like Moreau, he had a haunted imagination, but his imagery was even more personal and disturbing. A master of etching and lithography, he drew inspiration from the fantastic visions of Goya (see fig. 858) as well as Romantic literature. The lithograph shown in figure 955 is one of a set he issued in 1882 and dedicated to Edgar Allan Poe. The American poet had been dead for thirty-three years; but his tormented life and his equally tormented imagination made him the very model of the *poéte maudit*, the doomed poet, and his works, excellently translated by Baudelaire and Mallarmé, were greatly admired in France. Redon's lithographs do not illustrate Poe; they are, rather, "visual poems" in their own right, evoking the macabre, hallucinatory world of Poe's imagination. In our example, the artist has revived a very ancient device, the single eye representing the all-seeing mind of God. But, in contrast to the traditional form of the symbol, Redon shows the whole eyeball removed from its socket and converted into a balloon that drifts aimlessly in the sky. Disquieting visual paradoxes of this kind were to be exploited on a large scale by the Dadaists and Surrealists in our own century (see figs. 1010, 1020, and 1023)

TOULOUSE-LAUTREC. Van Gogh's and Gauguin's discontent with the spiritual ills of Western civilization was part of a sentiment widely shared at the end of the nineteenth century. A self-conscious preoccupation with decadence, evil, and darkness pervaded the artistic and literary climate. Even those who saw no escape analyzed their predicament in fascinated horror. Yet, somewhat paradoxically, this very awareness proved to be a source of strength (the truly decadent, we may assume, are unable to realize their plight). The most remarkable instance of this strength was Henri de Toulouse-Lautrec (1864–1901); physically an ugly dwarf, he was an artist of superb talent who led a dissolute life in the night spots of Paris and died of alcoholism.

He was a great admirer of Degas, and his *At the Moulin Rouge* (fig. 956) recalls the zigzag form of Degas' *The Glass of Absinthe* (see fig. 916). Yet this view of the well-known nightclub is no Impressionist "slice of life"; Toulouse-Lautrec sees through the gay surface of the scene, viewing performers and customers with a pitilessly sharp eye for their character (including his own: he is the tiny bearded man next to the very tall one in the back of the room). The large areas of flat color, however, and the emphatic, smoothly curving outlines, reflect the influence of Gauguin. Although Toulouse-Lautrec was no Symbolist, the Moulin Rouge that he shows here has an atmosphere so joyless and oppressive that we have to wonder if the artist did not regard it as a place of evil.

ENSOR. In the art of the Belgian painter James Ensor (1860–1949), this pessimistic view of the human condition reaches obsessive intensity. *The Intrigue* (fig. 957) is a gro-

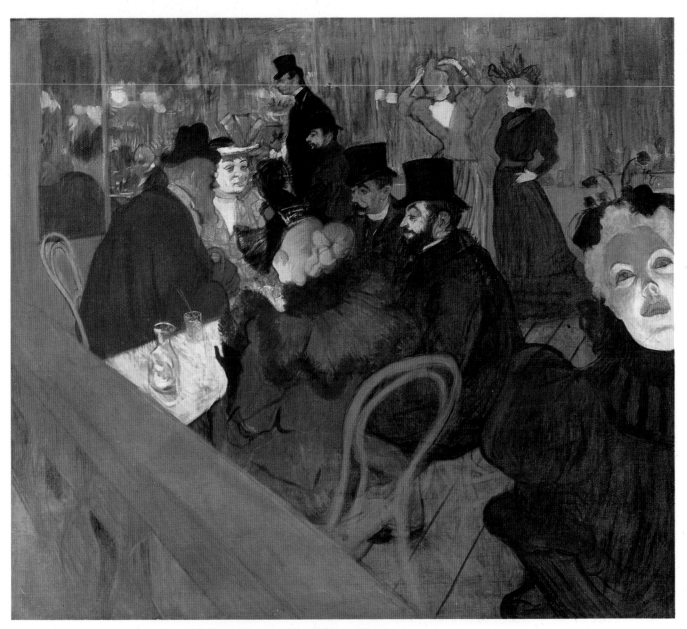

956. HENRI DE TOULOUSE-LAUTREC. *AT THE MOULIN ROUGE*.
1892. Oil on canvas, 48⅜×55¼″ (123×140.5 cm).
The Art Institute of Chicago. Helen Birch Bartlett Memorial Collection

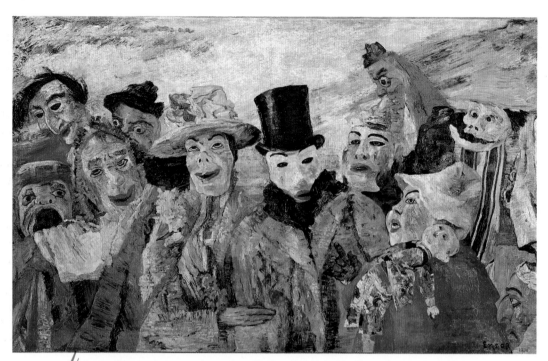

957. JAMES ENSOR. *THE INTRIGUE.* 1890. Oil on canvas, 35½×59″ (90.3×150 cm)
Koninklijk Museum voor Schone Kunsten, Antwerp

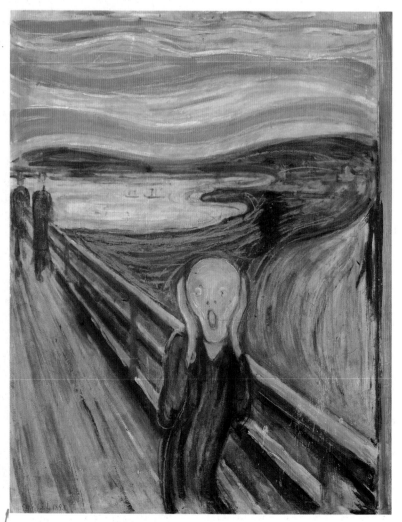

958. EDVARD MUNCH. *THE SCREAM.* 1893. Tempera and casein on cardboard,
36×29″ (91.3×73.7 cm). Nasjonalgalleriet, Oslo

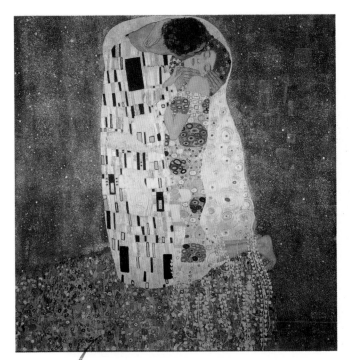

959. GUSTAVE KLIMT. *THE KISS*. 1907–8.
Oil on canvas, 70⅞×70⅞″ (180×180 cm).
Österreichische Galerie, Vienna

tesque carnival, but as we scrutinize these masks we become aware that they are the mummers' true faces, revealing the depravity ordinarily hidden behind the façade of everyday appearances. The demon-ridden world of Bosch and Schongauer has come to life again in modern guise (compare figs. 560 and 571).

MUNCH. Something of the same macabre quality pervades the early work of Edvard Munch (1863–1944), a gifted Norwegian who came to Paris in 1889 and based his starkly expressive style on Toulouse-Lautrec, Van Gogh, and Gauguin. *The Scream* (fig. 958) shows the influences of all three; it is an image of fear, the terrifying, unreasoned fear we feel in a nightmare. Unlike Fuseli and Goya (see figs. 876 and 858), Munch visualizes this experience without the aid of frightening apparitions, and his achievement is the more persuasive for that very reason. The rhythm of the long, wavy lines seems to carry the echo of the scream into every corner of the picture, making of earth and sky one great sounding board of fear.

KLIMT. Munch's works generated such controversy when they were exhibited in Berlin in 1892 that a number of young radicals broke from the artists association and formed the Berlin Secession, which took its name from a similar group that had been founded in Munich earlier that year. The Secession quickly became a loosely allied international movement. In 1897 it spread to Austria, where Gustave Klimt (1862–1918) established the Vienna Secession with the purpose of raising the level of the arts and crafts in Austria through close ties to *Art Nouveau*, called in Germany and Austria *Jugendstil*—literally Youth Style. *The Kiss* (fig. 959) by Klimt expresses a different kind of anxiety from Munch's

The Scream. The image will remind us of Beardsley's *Salome* (fig. 954), but here the barely suppressed eroticism has burst into desire. Engulfed in mosaiclike robes that create an illusion of rich beauty, the angular figures steal a moment of passion whose brevity emphasizes their joyless existence.

PICASSO'S BLUE PERIOD. Pablo Picasso (1881–1974), coming to Paris in 1900, felt the spell of the same artistic atmosphere that had generated the style of Munch. His so-called Blue Period (the term refers to the prevailing color of his canvases as well as to their mood) consists almost exclusively of pictures of beggars and derelicts, such as *The Old Guitarist* (fig. 960)—outcasts or victims of society whose pathos reflects the artist's own sense of isolation. Yet these figures convey poetic melancholy more than outright despair. The aged musician accepts his fate with a resignation that seems almost saintly, and the attenuated grace of his limbs reminds us of El Greco (compare fig. 691). *The Old Guitarist* is a strange amalgam of Mannerism and of the art of Gauguin and Toulouse-Lautrec (note the smoothly curved contours), imbued with the personal gloom of a twenty-two-year-old genius.

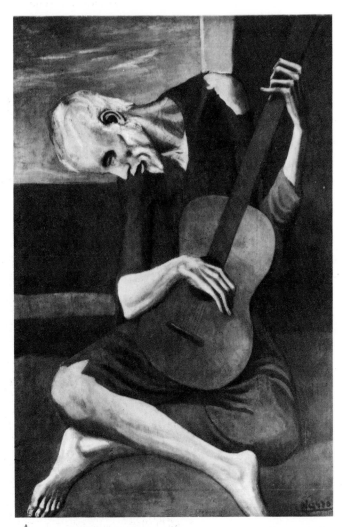

960. PABLO PICASSO. *THE OLD GUITARIST*. 1903. Oil on panel,
47¾×32½″ (121.3×82.7 cm). The Art Institute of Chicago.
Helen Birch Bartlett Memorial Collection

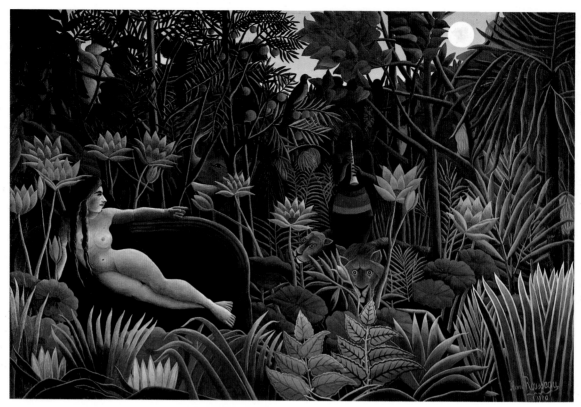

961. HENRI ROUSSEAU. *THE DREAM.* 1910. Oil on canvas, 6'8½"×9'9½" (2×3 m).
Collection, The Museum of Modern Art, New York. Gift of Nelson A. Rockefeller

ROUSSEAU. A few years later, Picasso and his friends discovered a painter who until then had attracted no attention,
although he had been exhibiting his work since 1886. He
was Henri Rousseau (1844–1910), a retired customs collector who had started to paint in his middle age without training of any sort. His ideal—which, fortunately, he never
achieved—was the arid academic style of the followers of
Ingres. Rousseau is that paradox, a folk artist of genius. How
else could he have done a picture like *The Dream* (fig. 961)?
What goes on in the enchanted world of this canvas needs
no explanation, because none is possible. Perhaps for that
very reason its magic becomes believably real to us. Rousseau himself described the scene in a little poem:

> Yadwigha, peacefully asleep
> Enjoys a lovely dream:
> She hears a kind snake charmer
> Playing upon his reed.
> On stream and foliage glisten
> The silvery beams of the moon.
> And savage serpents listen
> To the gay, entrancing tune.

Here at last was an innocent directness of feeling that Gauguin thought was so necessary for the age. Picasso and his
friends were the first to recognize this quality in Rousseau's
work. They revered him as the godfather of twentieth-century painting.

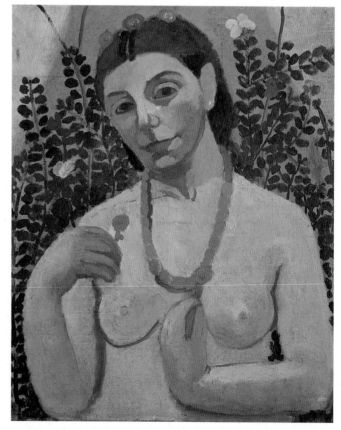

962. PAULA MODERSOHN-BECKER. *SELF-PORTRAIT.* 1906.
Oil on canvas, 24×19¾" (61×50 cm).
Öffentliche Kunstsammlung, Kunstmuseum, Basel

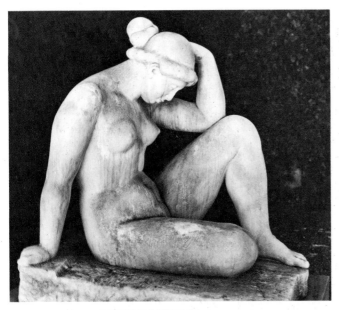

963. ARISTIDE MAILLOL. *SEATED WOMAN*
(*MÉDITERRANÉE*). c. 1901. Stone, height 41″ (104 cm).
Collection Oskar Reinhart, Winterthur, Switzerland

and clearly defined volumes also recall Cézanne's statement that all natural forms are based on the cone, the sphere, and the cylinder. But the most notable quality of the figure is its harmonious, self-sufficient repose, which the outside world cannot disturb.

A statue, Maillol thought, must above all be "static," structurally balanced like a piece of architecture; it must represent a state of being that is detached from the stress of circumstance, with none of the restless, thrusting energy of Rodin's work. In this respect, the *Seated Woman* is the exact opposite of *The Thinker* (see fig. 932). Maillol later gave it the title *Méditerranée*—The Mediterranean—to suggest the source from which he drew the timeless serenity of his figure.

MINNE. *Kneeling Boy* (fig. 964) by the Belgian sculptor George Minne (1866–1941) also shows a state of brooding calm, but the haggard, angular limbs reflect Gothic, not classical, influence, and the trancelike rigidity of the pose suggests religious meditation. The statue became the basis for a fountain design with five kneeling boys grouped around a circular basin as if engaged in a solemn ritual. By treating the figure as an anonymous member of a rhythmically repeated sequence, Minne heightened its mood of ascetic withdrawal.

MODERSOHN-BECKER. The inspiration of primitivism that Gauguin had traveled so far to find was discovered by Paula Modersohn-Becker (1876–1907) in the small village of Worpswede, near her family home in Bremen, Germany. Among the artists and writers who congregated there was the Symbolist lyric poet Rainer Maria Rilke, Rodin's friend and briefly his personal secretary. Rilke had visited Russia and been deeply impressed with what he viewed as the purity of Russian peasant life; his influence on the colony at Worpswede certainly affected Modersohn-Becker, whose last works are direct precursors of modern art. Her gentle and powerful *Self-Portrait* (fig. 962), painted the year before her early death, presents a transition from the Symbolism of Gauguin and his followers, which she absorbed during several stays in Paris, to Expressionism. The color has the intensity of Matisse and the *Fauves* (see pages 711–14). At the same time, her deliberately simplified treatment of forms parallels the experiments of Picasso, which were to culminate in *Les Demoiselles d'Avignon* (fig. 998)

SCULPTURE

MAILLOL. No tendencies to be equated with Post-Impressionism appear in sculpture until about 1900. Sculptors in France of a younger generation had by then been trained under the dominant influence of Rodin, and were ready to go their own ways. The finest of these, Aristide Maillol (1861–1944), began as a Symbolist painter, although he did not share Gauguin's anti-Greek attitude. Maillol might be called a "classic primitivist"; admiring the simplified strength of early Greek sculpture, he rejected its later phases. The *Seated Woman* (fig. 963) evokes memories of the Archaic and Severe styles (compare figs. 167, 179–80 and 201–05) rather than of Phidias and Praxiteles. The solid forms

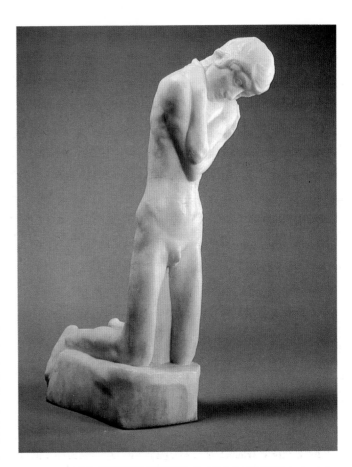

964. GEORGE MINNE. *KNEELING BOY*. 1898.
Marble, height 31″ (78.7 cm).
Museum voor Schone Kunsten, Ghent

emotions—wrath, fear, grief—that seem imposed upon them by invisible presences. When they act, they are like somnambulists, unaware of their own impulses.

Human beings, to Barlach, are humble creatures at the mercy of forces beyond their control; they are never masters of their fate. Characteristically, these figures do not fully emerge from the material substance (often, as here, a massive block of wood) of which they are made; their clothing is like a hard chrysalis that hides the body, as in medieval sculpture. Barlach's art has a range that is severely restricted in both form and emotion, yet its mute intensity within these limits is not easily forgotten.

ARCHITECTURE

The search for a modern architecture began in earnest around 1880. It required wedding the ideas of William Morris and the machine aesthetic, first explored tentatively some fifteen years earlier (see page 672), to new construction materials and techniques. The process itself took several decades, during which architects experimented with a variety of styles. It is significant that the symbol was the skyscraper, and that its first home was Chicago, then a burgeoning metropolis not yet encumbered by allegiance to the styles of the past.

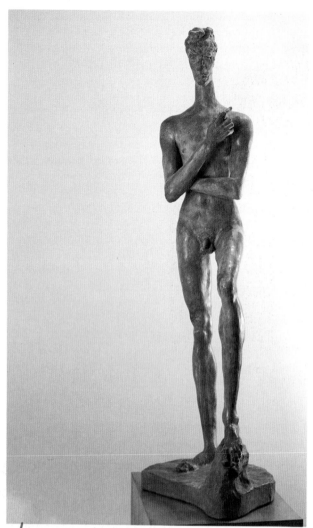

965. WILHELM LEHMBRUCK. *STANDING YOUTH.* 1913.
Cast stone, height 7'8" (2.33 m); base 36×26¾"
(91.3×68 cm). Collection, The Museum of Modern Art,
New York. Gift of Abby Aldrich Rockefeller

LEHMBRUCK. Minne's art attracted little notice in France, but was admired in Germany. His influence is apparent in *Standing Youth* (fig. 965) by Wilhelm Lehmbruck (1881–1919); here a Gothic elongation and angularity are conjoined with a fine balance derived from Maillol's art, and also with some of Rodin's expressive energy. The total effect is a looming monumental figure well anchored in space, yet partaking of that poetic melancholy we observed in Picasso's Blue Period.

BARLACH. Ernst Barlach (1870–1938), another important German sculptor who reached maturity in the years before World War I, seems the very opposite of Lehmbruck; he is a "Gothic primitivist," and more akin to Munch than to the Western Symbolist tradition. What Gauguin had experienced in Brittany and the tropics, Barlach found by going to Russia: the simple humanity of a pre-industrial age. His figures, such as *Man Drawing a Sword* (fig. 966), embody elementary

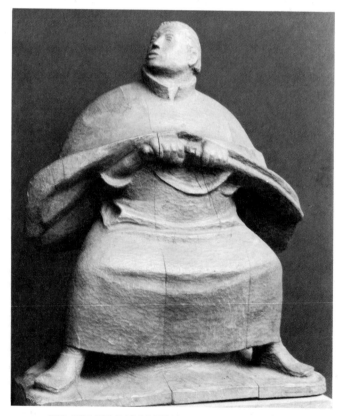

966. ERNST BARLACH. *MAN DRAWING A SWORD.*
1911. Wood, height 31" (78.7 cm).
Private collection

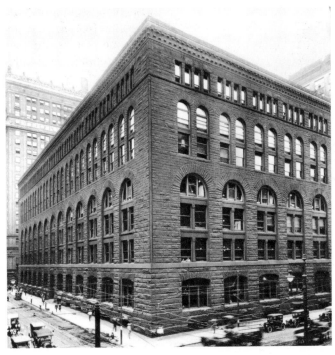

967. HENRY HOBSON RICHARDSON. Marshall Field
Wholesale Store (demolished 1930), Chicago, 1885–87

United States

RICHARDSON. The Chicago fire of 1871 had opened vast
opportunities to architects from older cities such as Boston
and New York. Among them was Henry Hobson Richardson
(1838–1886), who profited as a young man from contact with
Labrouste in Paris (see fig. 937). Most of his work along the
Eastern seaboard shows a massive Neo-Romanesque style.
There are still echoes of this in his last major project for Chicago, the Marshall Field Wholesale Store designed in 1885
(fig. 967). The huge structure filled an entire city block. In
its symmetry and the treatment of masonry, it may remind
us of Italian Early Renaissance palaces (see fig. 597). Yet the
complete lack of ornament proclaims its utilitarian purpose.

Warehouses and factories as commercial building types
had a history of their own going back to the later eighteenth
century. Richardson must have been familiar with this
tradition, which on occasion had produced remarkably impressive "stripped-down" designs such as those of the warehouses on New Quay, Liverpool (fig. 968). In contrast to
these earlier structures, however, the walls of the Marshall
Field Wholesale Store do not present a continuous surface
pierced by windows; except for the corners, which have the
effect of heavy piers, they show a series of superimposed arcades, like a Roman aqueduct (see fig. 261), an impression
strengthened by the absence of ornament and the thickness
of the masonry (note how deeply the windows are recessed).
These arcaded walls are as functional and self-sustaining as
their ancient predecessors. They invest the building with a
strength and dignity unrivaled in any earlier commercial
structure. Behind them is an iron skeleton that actually supports the seven floors, but the exterior does not depend on
it, either structurally or aesthetically.

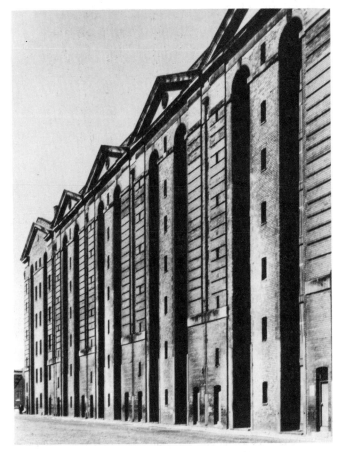

968. Warehouses on New Quay, Liverpool. 1835–40

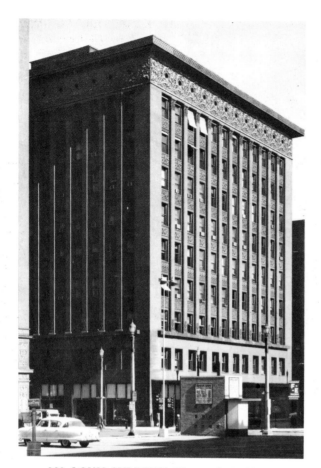

969. LOUIS SULLIVAN. Wainwright Building,
St. Louis, Missouri. 1890–91

SULLIVAN. Richardson's Marshall Field building thus stands midway between the old and the new: it embodies, with utmost severity and logic, a concept of monumentality derived from the past, but its opened-up walls, divided into vertical "bays," look forward to the work of Louis Sullivan (1856–1924). The Wainwright Building in St. Louis (fig. 969), his first skyscraper, is only five years after the Marshall Field Wholesale Store. It, too, is monumental, but in a very untraditional way. The organization of the exterior both reflects and expresses the internal steel skeleton, in the slender, continuous brick piers that rise between the windows from the base to the attic. Their collective effect is that of a vertical grating encased by the corner piers and by the emphatic horizontals of attic and mezzanine.

This is, of course, only one of the many possible "skins" that could be stretched over the structural frame; what counts is that we immediately feel that this wall is derived from the skeleton underneath, that it is not self-sustaining. "Skin" is perhaps too weak a term to describe this brick sheathing; to Sullivan, who often thought of buildings as analogous to the human body, it was more like the "flesh" and "muscle" that are organically attached to the "bone" yet capable of an infinite variety of expressive effects. When he insisted that "form follows function," he meant a flexible relationship, not rigid dependence.

The range of Sullivan's invention becomes evident if we compare the Wainwright Building with his last skyscraper, the department store of Carson Pirie Scott & Company in Chicago, begun nine years later (figs. 970 and 971). The sheathing of white terracotta here follows the grid of the steel frame far more closely, and the over-all effect is one of lightness and crispness rather than of harnessed energy. Yet the contrast between the horizontal continuity of the flanks and the vertical accent at the corner has been subtly calculated.

970. (*left*) LOUIS SULLIVAN. Carson Pirie Scott & Company
Department Store, Chicago. 1899–1904

971. (*below*) Detail of façade, showing Chicago window,
Carson Pirie Scott & Company

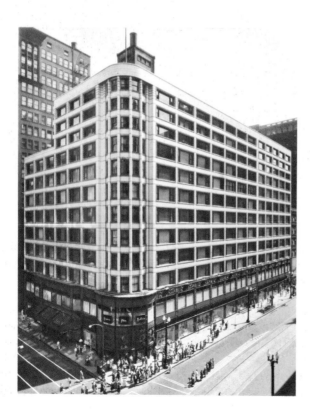

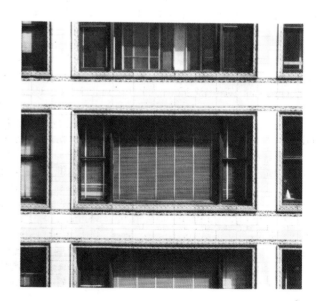

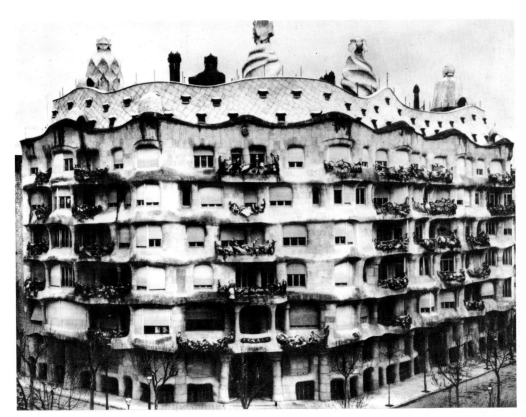

973. (*below*) Floor plan of
typical floor, Casa Milá

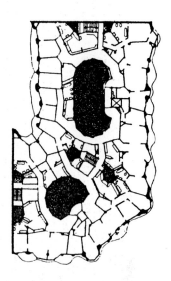

Art Nouveau

In Europe, meanwhile, the authority of the "revival styles" was being undermined by a movement now usually called by its French name, *Art Nouveau*, although it was known by various other names as well. It was primarily a new style of decoration based on linear patterns of sinuous curves that often suggest water lilies. Its ancestor was the ornament of William Morris. It is also related to the styles of such artists as Gauguin, Beardsley, and Munch (see figs. 949, 954, and 958). During the 1890s and early 1900s its pervasive influence on the applied arts may be seen in wrought-iron work, furniture, jewelry, glass, typography, and even women's fashions; it had a profound effect on public taste, but did not lend itself easily to architectural designs on a large scale.

GAUDÍ. The most remarkable instance is the Casa Milá in Barcelona (figs. 972 and 973), a large apartment house by Antoní Gaudí (1852–1926). It shows an almost maniacal avoidance of all flat surfaces, straight lines, and symmetry of any kind, so that the building looks as if it had been freely modeled of some malleable substance. (The material is not stucco or cement, as we might suppose, but cut stone.) The softly rounded openings anticipate the "eroded" shapes of Henry Moore's sculpture (see fig. 1066); the roof has the rhythmic motion of a wave; and the chimneys seem to have been squeezed from a pastry tube. The Casa Milá expresses one man's fanatical devotion to the ideal of "natural" form; it could never be repeated, let alone developed further. Structurally, it is a tour de force of old-fashioned craftsmanship, an attempt at architectural reform from the periphery, rather

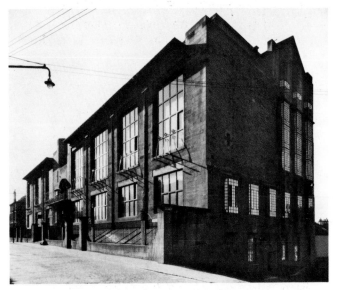

974. CHARLES RENNIE MACKINTOSH. North façade,
Glasgow School of Art, Glasgow, Scotland. 1896–1910

than from the center. Gaudí and Sullivan stand at opposite poles, although both strove for the same goal—a contemporary style independent of the past.

MACKINTOSH. Gaudí represents one extreme of *Art Nouveau* architecture; the Scot Charles Rennie Mackintosh (1868–1928) represents another. His basic outlook is so close to the functionalism of Sullivan that at first glance his work hardly seems to belong to *Art Nouveau* at all. The north façade of the Glasgow School of Art (fig. 974) was designed

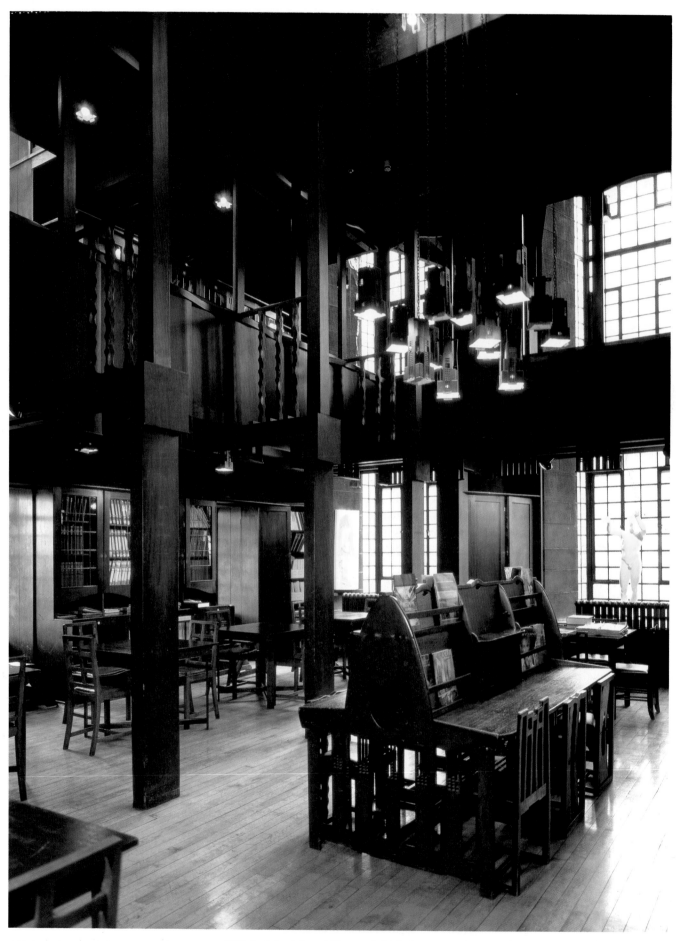

975. Interior, Library, Glasgow School of Art

as early as 1896, but might be mistaken for a building done thirty years later. Huge, deeply recessed studio windows have replaced the walls, leaving only a framework of massive, unadorned cut-stone surfaces except in the center bay; this bay is "sculptured" in a style not unrelated to Gaudí's, despite its preference for angles over curves. Another *Art Nouveau* feature is the wrought-iron grillwork (here with a minimum of ornament).

Even more surprising than the exterior is the two-story library (fig. 975), with its rectangular wooden posts and lintels supporting the balcony. The entire room has been designed in the spirit of Godwin's sideboard (see fig. 940), as it were, but Mackintosh shows an even finer sense of balance in the matching of voids and solids.

VAN DE VELDE. Through architectural magazines and exhibitions, Mackintosh's work came to be widely known abroad. Its structural clarity and force had a profound effect on one of the founding fathers of *Art Nouveau*, the Belgian Henry van de Velde (1863–1957). Trained as a painter, Van de Velde, under the influence of William Morris, had become a designer of posters, furniture, silverware, and glass; after 1900, he worked mainly as an architect. It was he who founded the Weimar School of Arts and Crafts in Germany, which became famous after World War I as the Bauhaus (see page 781). His most ambitious building (figs. 976 and 977), the theater he designed in Cologne for an exhibition sponsored by the Werkbund (arts and crafts association) in 1914, makes a telling contrast with the Paris Opéra (figs. 899 and 900). Whereas the older building tries to evoke the splendors of the Louvre Palace, Van de Velde's exterior is a tautly stretched "skin" that covers—and reveals—the individual units of which the internal space is composed. It seems almost incredible that the Opéra should have been completed only forty years before.

TAUT. The Werkbund exhibition of 1914 was a showcase for a whole generation of young German architects who were to achieve prominence after World War I. Many of the buildings they designed for the fairgrounds anticipate ideas of the 1920s. Among the most adventurous is the staircase of the "Glass House" (fig. 978) by Bruno Taut (1880–1938), made magically translucent by the use of glass bricks, then a novel material. Its structural steel skeleton is as thin and unobtrusive as the great strength of the metal permits. The total effect suggests Stella's Futurist *Brooklyn Bridge* (fig. 1003) translated into three dimensions.

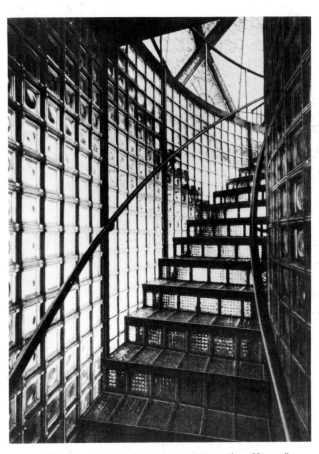

978. BRUNO TAUT. Staircase of the "Glass House," Werkbund Exhibition, Cologne. 1914

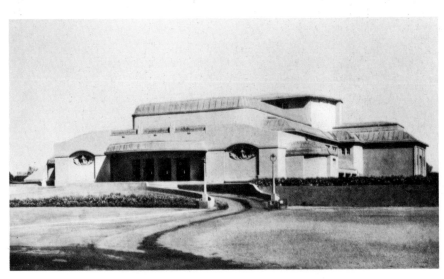

976. HENRY VAN DE VELDE. Theater, Werkbund Exhibition, Cologne (destroyed). 1914

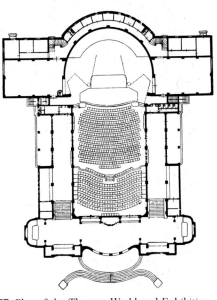

977. Plan of the Theater, Werkbund Exhibition

PHOTOGRAPHY

Documentary Photography

During the second half of the nineteenth century, the press played a leading role in the social movement that brought the harsh realities of poverty to the public's attention. The camera became an important instrument of reform through the photodocumentary, which tells the story of people's lives in a pictorial essay. It responded to the same conditions that had stirred Courbet (see page 663), and its factual reportage likewise fell within the Realist tradition. Before then, photographers had been content to present the romanticized image of the poor like those in genre paintings of the day. The first photodocumentary was John Thomson's illustrated sociological study *Street Life in London*, published in 1877. To get his pictures, he had to pose his figures.

RIIS. The invention of gunpowder flash ten years later allowed Jacob Riis (1849–1914) to rely for the most part on the element of surprise. Riis was a police reporter in New York City, where he learned at first hand about the crimeinfested slums and their appalling living conditions. He kept up a steady campaign of illustrated newspaper exposés, books, and lectures which in some cases led to major revisions of the city's housing codes and labor laws. His photographs' unflinching realism has lost none of its force. Certainly it would be difficult to imagine a more nightmarish scene than *Bandits' Roost* (fig. 979). With good reason we sense a pervasive air of danger in the eerie light. The notorious gangs of New York City's Lower East Side sought their victims by night, killing them without hesitation. The motionless figures seem to look us over with the practiced casualness of hunters coldly sizing up potential prey.

Pictorialism

The raw subject matter and realism of documentary photography had little impact on art and were shunned by most other photographers as well. England, through such organizations as the Photographic Society of London, founded in 1853, became the leader of the movement to convince doubting critics that photography, by imitating painting and printmaking, could indeed be art. To Victorian England, beauty above all meant art with a high moral purpose or noble sentiment, preferably in a classical style.

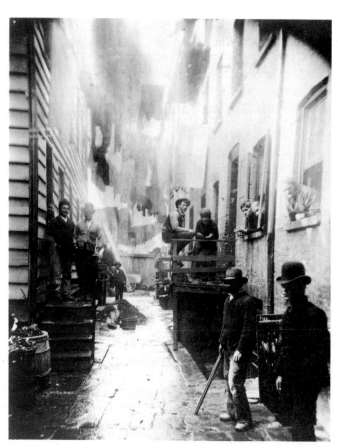

979. JACOB RIIS. *BANDITS' ROOST.* c. 1888. Gelatin-silver print.
Museum of the City of New York

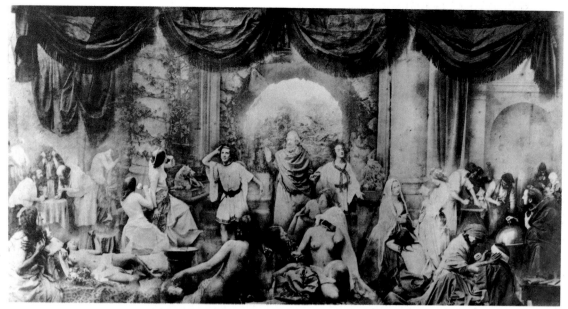

980. OSCAR REJLANDER. *THE TWO PATHS OF LIFE.* 1857.
Combination albumen print, 16×31″ (40.7×78.7 cm).
George Eastman House, Rochester, New York

REJLANDER. *The Two Paths of Life* (fig. 980) by Oscar Rejlander (1818–1875) fulfills these ends by presenting an allegory clearly descended from Hogarth's *Rake's Progress* series (figs. 831 and 832). This tour de force, almost three feet wide, combines thirty negatives through composite printing: a young man (in two images) is choosing between the paths of virtue or of vice, the latter represented by a half dozen nudes. The picture created a sensation in 1857 and Queen Victoria herself purchased a print. Rejlander, however, never enjoyed the same success again. He was the most adventurous photographer of his time and soon turned to other subjects less in keeping with prevailing taste.

ROBINSON. The mantle of art photography fell to Henry Peach Robinson (1830–1901), who became the most famous photographer in the world. He established his reputation with *Fading Away* (fig. 981), which appeared a year after Rejlander's *The Two Paths of Life.* With six lines from Shelley's "Queen Mab" printed below on the mat, it is typical of Robinson's sentimental scenes. Like *The Two Paths of Life*, it is a photomontage, but of only five negatives, and the scene is as carefully staged as any Victorian melodrama. At first Robinson made detailed drawings of his scenes before photographing the individual components; he later renounced multiple-negative photography, but still contrived to imitate contemporary genre painting in his pictures. When treating elevated subject matter he continued to distinguish between fact and truth, which to him was a mixture of the real and the artificial.

CAMERON. The photographer who pursued ideal beauty with the greatest passion was Julia Margaret Cameron

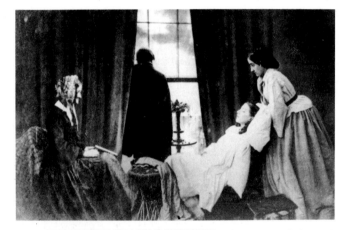

981. HENRY PEACH ROBINSON. *FADING AWAY.* 1858.
Combination print. Royal Photographic Society, London

(1815–1879). An intimate of leading poets, scientists, and artists, she took up photography at age forty-eight when given a camera and went on to create a remarkable body of work. In her own day Cameron was known for her allegorical and narrative pictures, but now she is remembered primarily for her portraits of the men who shaped Victorian England. Many of her finest photographs, however, are of the women who were married to her closest friends. An early study of the actress Ellen Terry (fig. 982) has the lyricism and grace of the Pre-Raphaelite aesthetic that shaped Cameron's style (compare fig. 923).

Naturalistic Photography

EMERSON. The cudgel against art photography was taken up by Peter Henry Emerson (1856–1936), who became Robinson's bitter enemy. Emerson espoused what he called Naturalistic Photography, based on scientific principles and Constable's landscapes. Nevertheless, he too contrasted realism with truth, defining truth in terms of sentiment, aesthetics, and the selective arrangement of nature. Using a single negative, Emerson composed his scenes with the greatest care, producing results that were sometimes similar to Robinson's, though of course he never acknowledged this. Most of Emerson's work was devoted to scenes of rural and coastal life which are not far removed from early documentary photographs.

In his best prints, nature predominates. He was a master at distributing tonal masses across a scene, and his photographs (fig. 983) are equivalent to fine English landscape paintings of the period. Although the effect is rarely apparent in his work, Emerson advocated putting the lens slightly out of focus, in the belief that the eye sees sharply only the central area of a scene. When he gave up this idea a few years later, he decided that photography was indeed science instead of art because it was machine-made, not personal.

Photo-Secession

The issue of whether photography could be art came to a head in the early 1890s with the Secession movement (see page 706), which was spearheaded in 1893 by the founding in London of the Linked Ring, a rival group to the renamed Royal Photographic Society of Great Britain. Stimulated by Emerson's ideas, the Secessionists sought a pictorialism independent of science and technology. They steered a course between academicism and naturalism by imitating every form of late Romantic art that did not involve narrative. Equally antithetical to their aims were Realist and Post-Impressionist painting, then at their zenith. In the group's approach to photography as Art for Art's Sake, the Secession had the most in common with Whistler's aestheticism.

To resolve the dilemma between art and mechanics, the Secessionists tried to make their photographs look as much like paintings as possible. Rather than resorting to composite or multiple images, however, they exercised total control over the printing process, chiefly by adding special materials to their printing paper to create different effects. Pigmented gum brushed on coarse drawing paper yielded a warm-toned, highly textured print that in its way approximated Impressionist painting. Paper impregnated with platinum salts was especially popular among the Secessionists for the clear grays in their prints. Their subtlety and depth lend a remarkable ethereality to *The Magic Crystal* (fig. 984) by Gertrude Käsebier (1854–1934), in which spiritual forces are almost visibly sweeping across the photograph.

STEICHEN. Through Käsebier and Alfred Stieglitz, the Linked Ring had close ties with America, where Stieglitz opened his Photo-Secession gallery in New York in 1905.

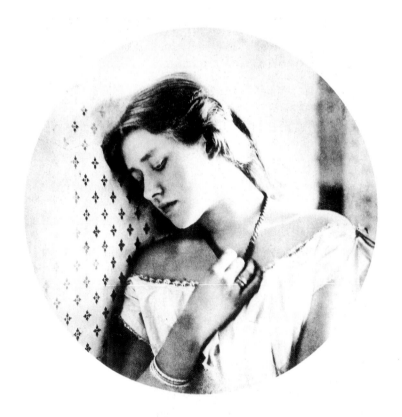

982. JULIA MARGARET CAMERON
PORTRAIT OF ELLEN TERRY. 1863. Carbon, diameter 9⁷⁄₁₆″ (24 cm).
The Metropolitan Museum of Art, New York. The Alfred Stieglitz Collection, 1949

Among his protégés was the young Edward Steichen (1879–1973), whose photograph of Rodin in his sculpture studio (fig. 985) is without doubt the finest achievement of the entire Photo-Secession movement. The head in profile contemplating *The Thinker* expresses the essence of the confrontation between the sculptor and his work of art. His brooding introspection hides the inner turmoil evoked by the ghostlike monument to Victor Hugo which rises dramatically like a genius in the background. Not since *The Creation of Adam* by Michelangelo (fig. 657), who was Rodin's ideal, have we seen a more telling use of space or an image that penetrates the mystery of creativity so deeply.

The Photo-Secession achieved its goal of gaining wide recognition for photography as an art form, but by 1907 its artifices were regarded as stilted. Though the movement lasted for a few more years, it was becoming clear that the future of photography did not lie in the imitation of painting, for painting was then being drastically reformed by modernists (see page 710). Yet the legacy of the Photo-Secession was valuable, its limitations notwithstanding, for it taught photographers much about the control of composition and response to light.

Motion Photography

MUYBRIDGE. An entirely new direction was charted by Eadweard Muybridge (1830–1904), father of motion photography. He wedded two different technologies, devising a set of cameras capable of photographing action at successive points. Photography had grown from such marriages; an-

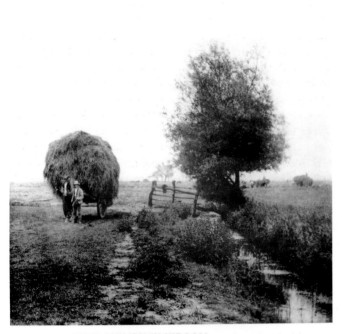

983. PETER HENRY EMERSON. *HAYMAKING IN THE NORFOLK BROADS.* c. 1890. Platinum print. Société Française de Photographie, Paris

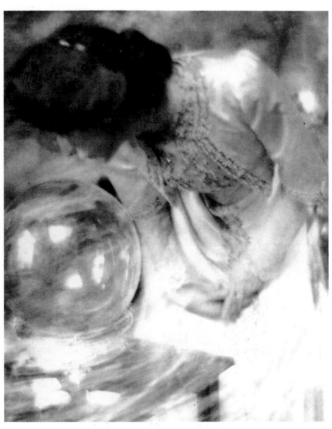

984. GERTRUDE KÄSEBIER. *THE MAGIC CRYSTAL.* c. 1904. Platinum print. Royal Photographic Society, Bath

other instance had occurred earlier when Nadar used a hot-air balloon to take aerial shots of Paris (fig. 906). After some trial efforts, Muybridge managed in 1877 to get a set of pictures of a trotting horse which forever changed artistic depictions of the horse in movement. Of the 100,000 photographs he devoted to the study of animal and human locomotion, the most astonishing were those taken from several vantage points at once (fig. 986). The idea was surely in the air, for the art of the period occasionally shows similar experiments, but Muybridge's photographs must nevertheless have come as a revelation to artists. The simultaneous views present an entirely new treatment of motion across time and space that challenges the imagination. Like a complex visual puzzle, they can be combined in any number of ways that are endlessly fascinating.

Muybridge left it to others to pursue these possibilities further. Much of his later work was conducted at the University of Pennsylvania in Philadelphia with the support of Eakins, then the head of the Academy of the Fine Arts. Eakins was already adept at using a camera, and it provided the subjects for several of his paintings; soon his interest in science led him to take up motion photography. Unlike Muybridge's suc-cession of static images, Eakins' multiple exposures show sequential motion on one plate. In the end, photography for Eakins was simply a means of depicting figures more realistically.

MAREY. It was Étienne-Jules Marey (1830–1904) who developed motion photography into an art. A noted French physiologist, Marey, like Muybridge, with whom he was in direct contact, saw the camera as a tool for demonstrating the mechanics of bodily movement, but he soon began to use it so creatively that his photographs have a perfection not equaled for another sixty years (compare fig. 1142). Indeed, his multiple exposure of a man walking (fig. 987 a, b.) satisfies both scientific and aesthetic truth in a way that Emerson and the Secessionists never imagined.

The photographs of Muybridge and Marey convey a peculiarly modern sense of dynamics reflecting the new tempo of life in the machine age. However, because the gap was then so great between scientific fact on the one hand and visual perception and artistic representation on the other, their far-reaching aesthetic implications were to be realized only by the Futurists (see page 720).

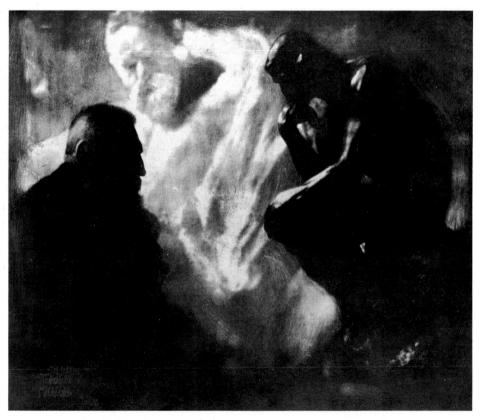

985. EDWARD STEICHEN. *RODIN WITH HIS SCULPTURES "VICTOR HUGO" AND THE "THINKER."* 1902. Gum print. The Art Institute of Chicago. Alfred Stieglitz Collection

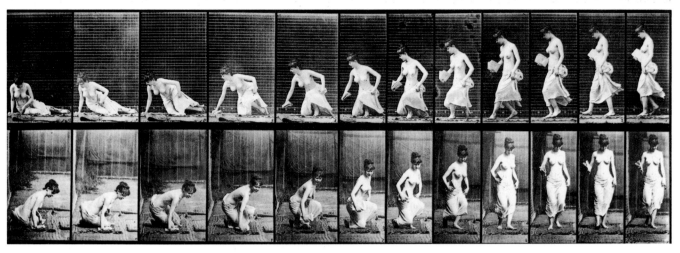

986. EADWEARD MUYBRIDGE. *FEMALE SEMI-NUDE IN MOTION,* from HUMAN AND ANIMAL LOCOMOTION, vol. 2, pl. 271. 1887. George Eastman House, Rochester, New York

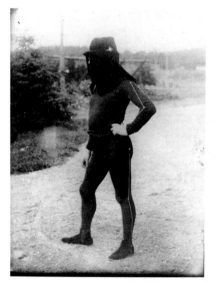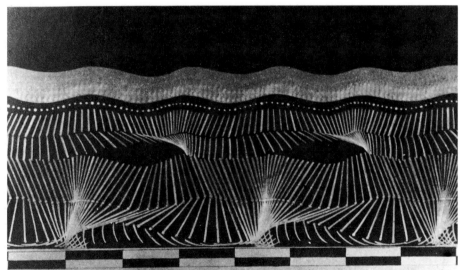

987a, b. ÉTIENNE-JULES MAREY. *MAN IN BLACK SUIT WITH WHITE STRIPES DOWN ARMS AND LEGS, WALKING IN FRONT OF A BLACK WALL.* c. 1884. Chronophotograph

CHAPTER FOUR
TWENTIETH-CENTURY PAINTING

PAINTING BEFORE WORLD WAR I

In our account of art in the modern era, we have already discussed a succession of "isms": Neoclassicism, Romanticism, Realism, Impressionism, Post-Impressionism, Divisionism, Symbolism. There are many more to be found in twentieth-century art—so many, in fact, that nobody has made an exact count. These "isms" can form a serious obstacle to understanding: they may make us feel that we cannot hope to comprehend the art of our time unless we immerse ourselves in a welter of esoteric doctrines. Actually, we can disregard all but the most important "isms"; like the terms we have used for the styles of earlier periods, they are merely labels to help us sort things out. If an "ism" fails the test of usefulness, we need not retain it. This is true of many "isms" in contemporary art; the movements they designate either cannot be seen very clearly as separate entities, or have so little importance that they can interest only the specialist. It has always been easier to invent new labels than to create a movement in art that truly deserves a new name.

Still, we cannot do without "isms" altogether. Since the start of the modern era, the Western world—and, increasingly, the non-Western world—has faced the same basic problems everywhere, and local artistic traditions have steadily given way to international trends. Among these we can distinguish three main currents, each comprising a number of "isms," that began among the Post-Impressionists, and have developed greatly in our own century: Expressionism, Abstraction, and Fantasy.

The primary concern of the Expressionist is the human community; of the Abstractionist, the structure of reality; and of the artist of Fantasy, the labyrinth of the individual human mind. Thus these three currents correspond to general attitudes rather than to specific styles. They are not mutually exclusive by any means. We shall find them interrelated in many ways, and the work of one artist may belong to more than one current. Moreover, each current embraces a wide range of approaches, from the realistic to the completely non-representational (or non-objective). And we shall find that Realism, which is concerned with the appearance of reality, has continued to exist independently of the other three, especially in the United States where art has often pursued a separate course. These currents bear a shifting relation to each other that reflects the complexity of modern life. To be understood, they must be seen in their proper historical context. After 1945, it is no longer meaningful to trace the evolution of these strands separately; the art of our times has become too complex for that.

In addition, we will encounter modernism, a concept peculiar to the twentieth century, though its roots can be traced to Romanticism. To the artist it is a trumpet call that both asserts his freedom to create in a new style and provides him with the mission to define the meaning of his times—and even to reshape society through his art. This is a role for which the problematic term "avant-garde" (literally, vanguard) is hardly sufficient. Of course, artists have always responded to the changing world around them, but rarely have they risen to the challenge as now, or with so fervent a sense of personal cause.

Expressionism

The twentieth century may be said, so far as painting is concerned, to have begun five years late. Between 1901 and 1906, several comprehensive exhibitions of the work of Van Gogh, Gauguin, and Cézanne were held in Paris. Thus, for the first time the achievements of these masters became accessible to a broad public.

THE FAUVES. The young painters who had grown up in the "decadent," morbid mood of the 1890s (see page 692) were profoundly impressed, and several of them developed a radical new style, full of violent color and bold distortions. On their first public appearance, in 1905, they so shocked critical opinion that they were dubbed the *Fauves* (the wild beasts), a label they wore with pride. Actually, it was not a common program that brought them together, but their shared sense of liberation and experiment. As a movement, Fauvism comprised numerous loosely related individual styles, and the group dissolved after a few years.

MATISSE. Its leading member was Henri Matisse (1869–1954), the oldest of the founding fathers of twentieth-century painting. *The Joy of Life* (fig. 988), probably the most important picture of his long career, sums up the spirit of Fauvism better than any other single work. It obviously derives its flat planes of color, heavy undulating outlines, and the "primitive" flavor of its forms from Gauguin (see fig. 949); even its subject suggests the vision of humanity in a state of Nature that Gauguin had pursued in Tahiti (see fig. 950). But we soon realize that these figures are not Noble Savages under the spell of a native god: the subject is a pagan scene in the classical sense—a bacchanal like Titian's (compare fig. 676). Even the poses of the figures have for the most part a classical origin, and in the apparently careless draftsmanship resides a profound knowledge of the human body (Matisse had been trained in the academic tradition). What makes the picture so revolutionary is its radical simplicity, its "genius of omission": everything that possibly can be has been left out or stated by implication only, yet the scene retains the essentials of plastic form and spatial depth.

Painting, Matisse seems to say, is the rhythmic arrangement of line and color on a flat plane, but it is not only that; how far can the image of nature be pared down without destroying its basic properties and thus reducing it to mere surface ornament? "What I am after, above all," he once explained, "is expression . . . [But] . . . expression does not consist of the passion mirrored upon a human face . . . The whole arrangement of my picture is expressive. The placement of figures or objects, the empty spaces around them, the proportions, everything plays a part." But what, we wonder, does *The Joy of Life* express? Exactly what its title says. Whatever his debt to Gauguin, Matisse was never stirred by the same agonized discontent with the "decadence" of our civilization. He had strong feelings about only one thing— the act of painting: this to him was an experience so profoundly joyous that he wanted to transmit it to the beholder.

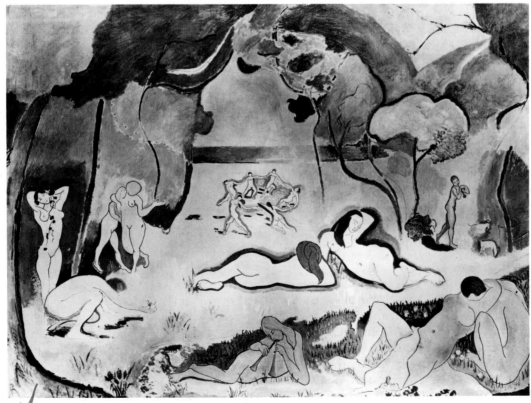

988. HENRI MATISSE. *THE JOY OF LIFE*. 1905–6. Oil on canvas, 68½×93¾″ (171.3×238 cm).
Copyright Barnes Foundation, Merion, Pennsylvania

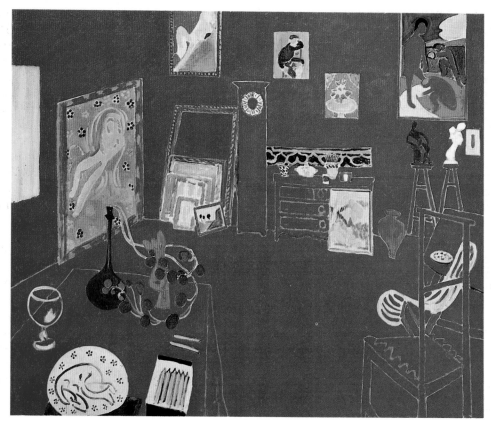

989. HENRI MATISSE. *THE RED STUDIO*. 1911. Oil on canvas, 5'9¼"×7'2¼" (1.81×2.19 m). Collection, The Museum of Modern Art, New York. Mrs. Simon Guggenheim Fund

Matisse's "genius of omission" is again at work in *The Red Studio* (fig. 989). By reducing the number of tints to a minimum, he makes color an independent structural element. The result is to emphasize the radical new balance he struck between the "two-D" and "three-D" aspects of painting. Matisse spreads the same flat red color on the tablecloth and wall as on the floor, yet he distinguishes the horizontal from the vertical planes with complete assurance using only a few lines. Equally bold is Matisse's use of pattern. By repeating a few basic shapes, hues, and decorative motifs in seemingly casual—but perfectly calculated—array around the edges of the canvas, he harmonizes the relation of each element with the rest of the picture. Cézanne had pioneered this integration of surface ornament into the design of a picture (see fig. 941), but Matisse here makes it a mainstay of his composition.

ROUAULT. Another member of the *Fauves*, Georges Rouault (1871–1958), would not have used Matisse's definition of "expression." For him this had still to include, as it had in the past, "the passion mirrored upon a human face"; we need only look at his *Head of Christ* (fig. 990). But the expressiveness does not reside only in the "image quality" of the face. The savage slashing strokes of the brush speak equally eloquently of the artist's rage and compassion. (If we cover the upper third of the picture, it is no longer a recognizable image, yet the expressive effect is hardly dimin-

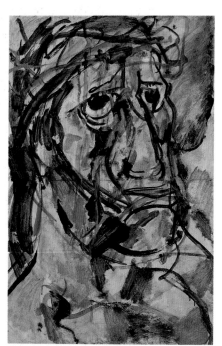

990. GEORGES ROUAULT. *HEAD OF CHRIST*. 1905. Oil on paper, mounted on canvas, 39×25¼" (99.1×64.2 cm). The Chrysler Museum, Norfolk, Virginia. Gift of Walter P. Chrysler, Jr.

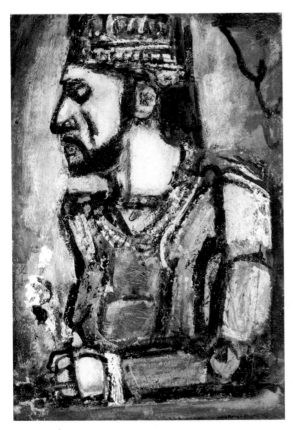

ished.) Rouault is the true heir of Van Gogh's and Gauguin's concern for the corrupt state of the world. He, however, hoped for spiritual renewal through a revitalized Catholic faith. His pictures, whatever their subject, are personal statements of that ardent hope. Trained in his youth as a stained-glass worker, he was better prepared than the other *Fauves* to share Gauguin's enthusiasm for medieval art. Rouault's later work, such as *The Old King* (fig. 991), has glowing colors and compartmented, black-bordered shapes inspired by Gothic stained-glass windows (compare fig. 517). Yet within this framework he retains a good deal of the pictorial freedom we saw in the *Head of Christ*, and the old king's face conveys a mood of resignation and inner suffering that reminds us of Rembrandt and Daumier.

DIE BRÜCKE. It was in Germany that Fauvism had its most enduring impact, especially among the members of *Die Brücke* (The Bridge), a group of like-minded painters who lived in Dresden in 1905. Their early works, such as Ernst Ludwig Kirchner's *Street, Dresden* (fig. 992), not only reflect Matisse's simplified, rhythmic line and loud color, but also clearly reveal the direct influence of Van Gogh and Gauguin. *Street, Dresden* also shows elements derived from Munch (compare fig. 958), who was then living in Berlin and deeply impressed the German Expressionists.

NOLDE. One *Brücke* artist, Emil Nolde (1867–1956), stands somewhat apart; older than the rest, he shared Rouault's predilection for religious themes. The thickly en-

991. GEORGES ROUAULT. *THE OLD KING.* 1916–37.
Oil on canvas, 30¼×21¼" (79.5×54 cm).
Carnegie Institute, Pittsburgh

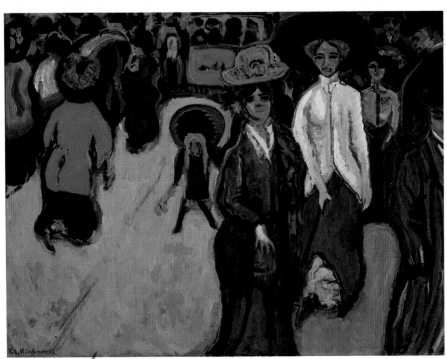

992. ERNST LUDWIG KIRCHNER. *STREET, DRESDEN.*
1908, dated 1907 on painting.
Oil on canvas, 59¼×78⅞" (150.5×200.3 cm).
Collection, The Museum of Modern Art, New York. Purchase

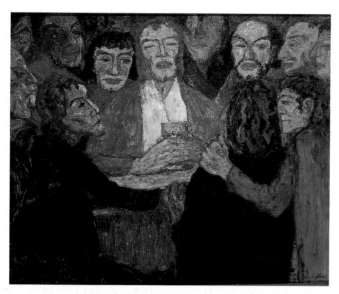

993. EMIL NOLDE. *THE LAST SUPPER.* 1909.
Oil on canvas, 32½×41¾″ (82×106 cm).
Stiftung Seebüll Ada und Emil Nolde,
Neukirchen (Schleswig), Germany

crusted surfaces and deliberately clumsy draftsmanship of his *The Last Supper* (fig. 993) show that Nolde rejected pictorial refinement in favor of a primeval, direct expression inspired by Gauguin. Ensor's grotesque masks, too, come to mind (see fig. 957), as do the mute intensity of Barlach's peasants (see fig. 966).

KOKOSCHKA. Another artist of highly individual talent, related to *Die Brücke* although not a member of it, was the Austrian painter Oskar Kokoschka (1886–1980). His most memorable works are his portraits painted before World War I, such as the moving *Self-Portrait* (fig. 994). Like Van Gogh, Kokoschka sees himself as a visionary, a witness to the truth and reality of his inner experiences (compare fig. 948); the hypersensitive features seem lacerated by a great ordeal of the imagination. It may not be fanciful to find in this tortured psyche an echo of the cultural climate that also produced Sigmund Freud.

KOLLWITZ. The work of Käthe Kollwitz (1876–1945), consists almost exclusively of prints and drawings that parallel those of Kokoschka, whose work she admired. Her graphics had their sources in the nineteenth century. The German artist Max Klinger (1857–1920), Munch, and Klimt were early inspirations, as was her friend Ernst Barlach (see pages 694 and 698). Yet Kollwitz pursued a resolutely independent course, devoting her art to themes of inhumanity and injustice. To articulate her social and ethical concerns, she adopted an intensely expressive, naturalistic style that is as unrelenting in its bleakness as her choice of subjects. Gaunt mothers and exploited workers provided much of Kollwitz's thematic focus, but her most eloquent statements were reserved for war. World War I, which cost her oldest son his life, made her an ardent pacifist. Her lithograph *Never Again War!* (fig. 995) is a visceral image of protest.

KANDINSKY. The most daring and original step beyond Fauvism was taken in Germany by a Russian, Wassily Kandinsky (1866–1944), the leading member of a group of Munich artists called *Der Blaue Reiter* (The Blue Horseman). Kandinsky began to forsake representation as early as 1910 and abandoned it altogether several years later. Using the rainbow colors and the free, dynamic brushwork of the Paris *Fauves*, he created a completely non-objective style. These works have titles as abstract as their forms; our example, one of the most striking, is called *Sketch I for "Composition VII"* (fig. 996).

Perhaps we should avoid the term "abstract," because it is so often taken to mean that the artist has analyzed and simplified the shapes of visible reality (compare Cézanne's dictum that all natural forms are based on the cone, sphere, and cylinder). This was not the method of Kandinsky. His aim was to charge form and color with a purely spiritual meaning (as he put it) by eliminating all resemblance to the physical world. Whistler, too, had spoken of "divesting the picture from any outside sort of interest"; he even anticipated Kandinsky's "musical" titles (fig. 927). But it was the liberating influence of the *Fauves* that permitted Kandinsky to put this theory into practice. The possibility was clearly implicit in Fauvism from the start, as shown in our experiment

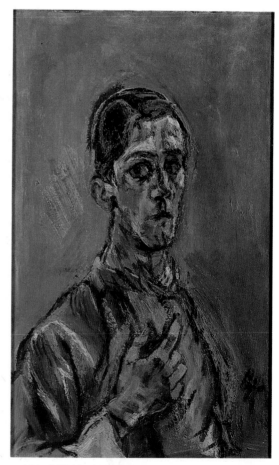

994. OSKAR KOKOSCHKA. *SELF-PORTRAIT.* 1913.
Oil on canvas, 32×19½″ (81.7×49.7 cm).
Collection, The Museum of Modern Art, New York. Purchase

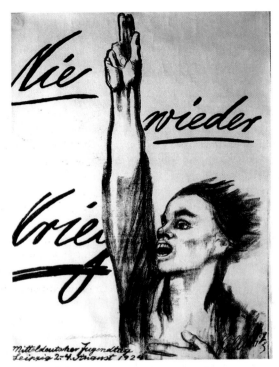

995. KÄTHE KOLLWITZ. *NEVER AGAIN WAR!* 1924.
Lithograph. Courtesy Gallerie St. Etienne, New York

with Rouault's *Head of Christ* (fig. 990): when the upper third of the picture is covered, the rest becomes a non-representational composition strangely similar to Kandinsky's.

How valid is the analogy between painting and music? When a painter like Kandinsky carries it through so uncompromisingly, does he really lift his art to another plane? Or could it be that his declared independence from representational images now forces him instead to "represent music," which limits him even more severely? Kandinsky's advocates like to point out that representational painting has a "literary" content, and they deplore such dependence on another art; but they do not explain why the "musical" content of non-objective painting should be more desirable. Is painting less alien to music than to literature? They seem to think music is a higher art than literature or painting because it is inherently non-representational—a point of view with an ancient tradition that goes back to Plato and includes Plotinus, St. Augustine, and their medieval successors. The attitude of the non-objectivists might thus be termed "secular iconoclasm": they do not condemn images as wicked, but denounce them as non-art.

The case is difficult to argue, and it does not matter whether this theory is right or wrong; the proof of the pudding is in the eating, not in the recipe. Kandinsky's—or any artist's—ideas are not important to us unless we are con-

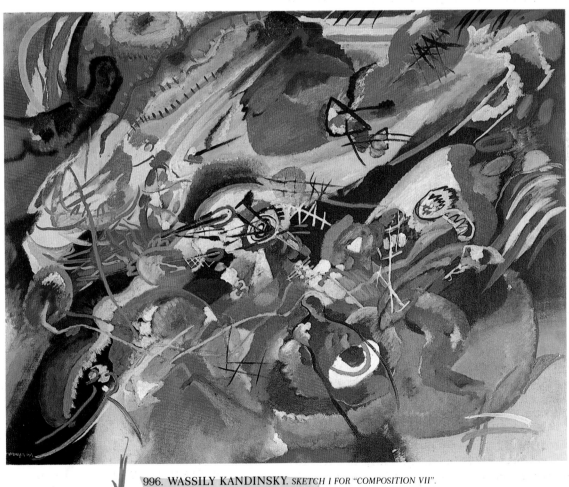

996. WASSILY KANDINSKY. *SKETCH I FOR "COMPOSITION VII"*.
1913. India ink, 30¾×39⅜" (78×100 cm).
Kunstmuseum, Bern, Switzerland. Collection Felix Klee

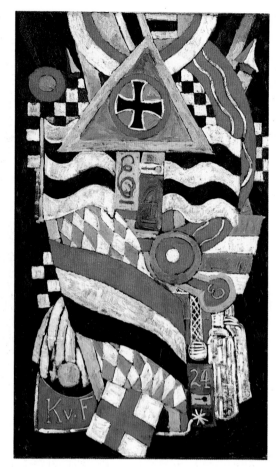

997. MARSDEN HARTLEY. *PORTRAIT OF A GERMAN OFFICER*.
1914. Oil on canvas, 68¼×41⅜" (173.9×105.2 cm).
The Metropolitan Museum of Art, New York.
The Alfred Stieglitz Collection, 1949

the insignia, epaulets, Maltese cross, and other details from an officer's uniform of the day. The result is a compelling testimony to the militarism he encountered everywhere in Germany.

Abstraction

The second of our main currents is the one we call Abstraction. When discussing Kandinsky, we said that the term is usually taken to mean the process (or the result) of analyzing and simplifying observed reality. Literally, it means "to draw away from, to separate." If we have ten apples, and then separate the ten from the apples, we get an "abstract number," a number that no longer refers to particular things. But "apples," too, is an abstraction, since it places ten apples in one class, without regard for their individual qualities. The artist who sets out to paint ten apples will find no two of them alike, yet he cannot possibly take account of all their differences: even the most painstakingly realistic portrayal of these particular pieces of fruit is bound to be some sort of an abstraction. Abstraction, then, goes into the making of any work of art, whether the artist knows it or not. The process was not conscious and controlled, however, until the Early Renaissance, when artists first analyzed the shapes of nature in terms of mathematical bodies (see page 466). Cézanne and Seurat revitalized this approach and explored it further; they are the direct ancestors of the abstract movement in twentieth-century art.

PICASSO'S DEMOISELLES D'AVIGNON. It is difficult to imagine the birth of modern abstraction without Pablo Picasso. About 1905, stimulated as much by the *Fauves* as by the retrospective exhibitions of the great Post-Impressionists, he gradually abandoned the melancholy lyricism of his Blue Period for a more robust style. He shared Matisse's enthusiasm for Gauguin and Cézanne, but he viewed these masters very differently; in 1907 he produced his own counterpart to *The Joy of Life,* a monumental canvas so challenging that it outraged even Matisse (fig. 998). The title, *Les Demoiselles d'Avignon* ("The Young Ladies of Avignon"), does not refer to the town of that name, but to Avignon Street in a notorious section of Barcelona. When Picasso started the picture, it was to be a temptation scene in a brothel, but he ended up with a composition of five nudes and a still life. But what nudes! Matisse's generalized figures in *The Joy of Life* (see fig. 988) seem utterly innocuous compared to this savage aggressiveness.

The three on the left are angular distortions of classical figures, but the violently dislocated features and bodies of the other two have all the barbaric qualities of ethnographic art (compare figs. 57, 58, and 62–65). Following Gauguin's lead, the *Fauves* had discovered the aesthetic appeal of African and Oceanic sculpture and had introduced Picasso to this material; yet it was he, rather than they, who used primitivist art as a battering ram against the classical conception of beauty. Not only the proportions, but the organic integrity and continuity of the human body are denied here, so that the canvas (in the apt description of one critic) "resembles a field of broken glass."

vinced of the importance of his pictures. Did he create a viable style? Admittedly, his work demands an intuitive response that may be hard for some of us, yet the painting reproduced here has density and vitality, and a radiant freshness of feeling that impresses us even though we are uncertain what exactly the artist has expressed.

HARTLEY. Americans became familiar with the *Fauves* through exhibitions from 1908 on. After the pivotal Armory show of 1913, which introduced the latest European art to New York, there was a growing interest in the German Expressionists as well. The driving force behind the modernist movement in the United States was the photographer Alfred Stieglitz (see pages 796–97), who almost single-handedly supported many of its early members. To him, modernism meant abstraction and its related concepts. Among the most significant achievements of the Stieglitz group are the canvases painted by Marsden Hartley in Munich during the early years of World War I under the direct influence of Kandinsky. *Portrait of a German Officer* (fig. 997) is a masterpiece of design from 1914, the year Hartley (1887–1943) was invited to exhibit with *Der Blaue Reiter.* He had already been introduced to Futurism and several offshoots of Cubism (see pages 718–22), which he used to discipline Kandinsky's super-charged surface. The emblematic portrait incorporates

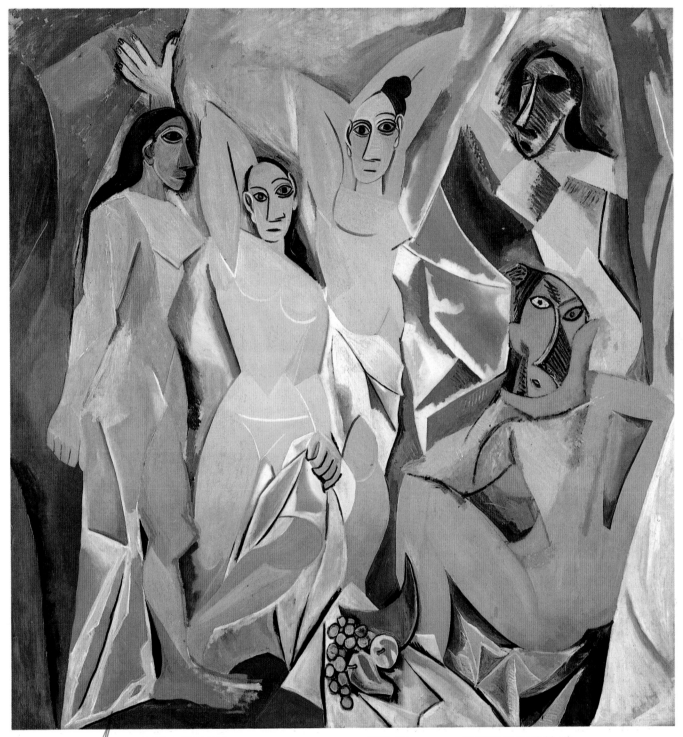

998. PABLO PICASSO. *LES DEMOISELLES D'AVIGNON*. 1907. Oil on canvas, 8′×7′8″ (2.43×2.33 m). Collection, The Museum of Modern Art, New York. Acquired through the Lillie P. Bliss Bequest

Picasso, then, has destroyed a great deal; what has he gained in the process? Once we recover from the initial shock, we begin to see that the destruction is quite methodical: everything—the figures as well as their setting—is broken up into angular wedges or facets; these, we will note, are not flat, but shaded in a way that gives them a certain three-dimensionality. We cannot always be sure whether they are concave or convex; some look like chunks of solidified space, others like fragments of translucent bodies.

They constitute a unique kind of matter, which imposes a new integrity and continuity on the entire canvas. The *Demoiselles*, unlike *The Joy of Life*, can no longer be read as an image of the external world; its world is its own, analogous to nature but constructed along different principles. Picasso's revolutionary "building material," compounded of voids and solids, is hard to describe with any precision. The early critics, who saw only the prevalence of sharp edges and angles, dubbed the new style Cubism.

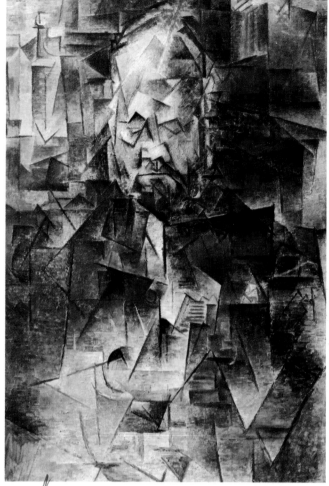

999. PABLO PICASSO. *PORTRAIT OF AMBROISE VOLLARD.*
1910. Oil on canvas, 36¼×25⅝″ (92×65 cm).
The Pushkin State Museum of Fine Arts, Moscow

ANALYTIC CUBISM. That the *Demoiselles* owes anything to Cézanne may at first seem incredible. Nevertheless, Picasso had studied Cézanne's late work (such as fig. 943) with great care, finding in Cézanne's abstract treatment of volume and space the translucent structural units from which to derive the faceted shapes of Analytic (or Facet) Cubism. The link is clearer in Picasso's portrait of Ambroise Vollard (fig. 999), painted three years later; the facets are now small and precise, more like prisms, and the canvas has the balance and refinement of a fully mature style.

Contrasts of color and texture, so pronounced in the *Demoiselles*, are now reduced to a minimum (the subdued tonality of the picture approaches monochrome), so as not to compete with the design. And the structure has become so complex and systematic that it would seem wholly cerebral if the "imprismed" sitter's face did not emerge with such dramatic force. Of the "barbaric" distortions in the *Demoiselles* there is no trace; they had served their purpose. Cubism has become an abstract style within the purely Western sense. But its distance from observed reality has not significantly increased—Picasso may be playing an elaborate game of hide-and-seek with nature, but he still needs the visible world to challenge his creative powers. The nonobjective realm held no appeal for him, then or later.

SYNTHETIC CUBISM. By 1910, Cubism was well established as an alternative to Fauvism, and Picasso had been joined by a number of other artists, notably Georges Braque (1882–1963), with whom he collaborated so intimately that their work at that times is difficult to tell apart. Both of them—it is not clear to whom the chief credit belongs—initiated the next phase of Cubism, which was even bolder than the first. Usually called Synthetic Cubism because it puts forms back together, it is also known as Collage Cubism, after the French word for "paste-up," the technique that started it all. We see its beginnings in Picasso's *Still Life with Chair Caning* of 1912 (fig. 1000). Most of the painting shows the now-familiar facets, except for the letters; these, being already abstract signs, could not be translated into prismatic shapes, but from beneath the still life emerges a piece of imitation chair caning, which has been pasted onto the canvas, and the picture is "framed" by a piece of rope. This intrusion of alien materials has a most remarkable effect: the abstract still life appears to rest on a real surface (the chair caning) as on a tray, and the substantiality of this tray is further emphasized by the rope.

Within a year, Picasso and Braque were producing still lifes composed almost entirely of cut-and-pasted scraps of material, with only a few lines added to complete the design. In *Le Courrier* by Braque (fig. 1001) we recognize strips of imitation wood graining, part of a tobacco wrapper with a contrasting stamp, half the masthead of a newspaper, and a bit of newsprint made into a playing card (the ace of hearts). Why did Picasso and Braque suddenly prefer the contents of the wastepaper basket to brush and paint? Because, wanting to explore the new concept of the picture-as-a-tray, they found the best way was to put real things on the tray. The ingredients of a collage actually play a double role; they have been shaped and combined, then drawn or painted upon to give them a representational meaning, but they do not lose their original identity as scraps of material, "outsiders" in the world of art. Thus their function is both to *represent* (to be a part of an image) and to *present* (to be themselves). In this latter capacity, they endow the collage with a self-sufficiency that no Analytic Cubist picture can have. A tray, after all, is a self-contained area, detached from the rest of the physical world; unlike a painting, it cannot show more than is actually on it.

The difference between the two phases of Cubism may also be defined in terms of picture space: Analytic Cubism retains a certain kind of depth, the painted surface acting as a window through which we still perceive the remnants of the familiar perspective space of the Renaissance. Though fragmented and redefined, this space lies behind the picture plane and has no visible limits; potentially, it may contain objects that are hidden from our view. In Synthetic Cubism, on the contrary, the picture space lies in front of the plane of the "tray"; space is not created by illusionistic devices, such as modeling and foreshortening, but by the actual overlapping of layers of pasted materials. When, as in figure 1001, the apparent thickness of these materials and their distance

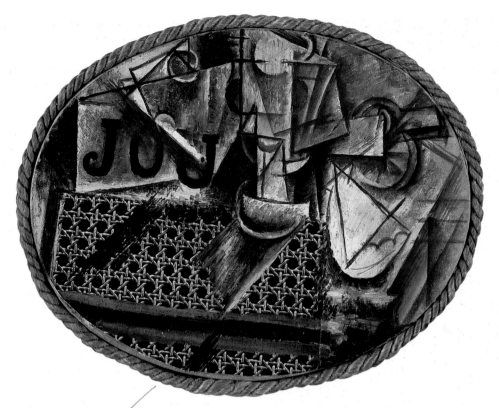

1000. PABLO PICASSO. *STILL LIFE WITH CHAIR CANING.* 1912.
Collage of oil, oilcloth, and pasted paper simulating chair caning on canvas,
10½×13¾″ (26.7×35 cm). Musée Picasso, Paris

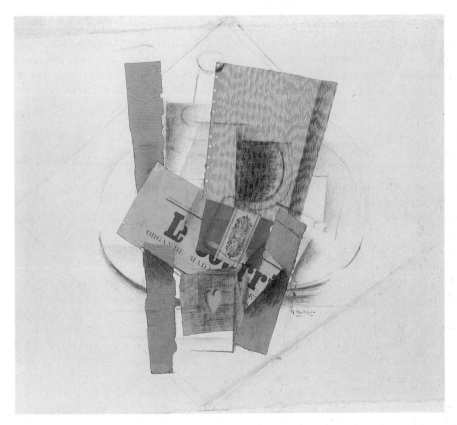

1001. GEORGES BRAQUE. *NEWSPAPER, BOTTLE, PACKET OF
TOBACCO (LE COURRIER).* 1914. Collage of charcoal, gouache, pencil, ink,
and pasted paper on cardboard, 20⅝×25″ (52.4×63.5 cm).
The Philadelphia Museum of Art. A. E. Gallatin Collection

from each other is increased by a bit of shading here and there, this does not affect the integrity of the non-perspective space. Synthetic Cubism, then, offers a basically new space concept, the first since Masaccio: it is a true landmark in the history of painting.

Before long Picasso and Braque discovered that they could retain this new pictorial space without the use of pasted materials; they had only to paint as if they were making collages. World War I, however, put an end to their collaboration and disrupted the further development of Synthetic Cubism, which reached its height in the following decade.

FUTURISM. As originally conceived by Picasso and Braque, Cubism was a formal discipline of subtle balance applied to traditional subjects—still life, portraiture, the nude. Other painters, however, saw in the new style a special affinity with the geometric precision of engineering that made it uniquely attuned to the dynamism of modern life. The short-lived Futurist movement in Italy exemplifies this attitude; in 1909–10 its disciples, led by the poet Filippo Tommaso Marinetti, issued a series of manifestos violently rejecting the past and exalting the beauty of the machine.

At first they used techniques developed from Post-Impressionism to convey in otherwise static compositions, still dependent upon representational images, the surge of industrial society. But by adopting the simultaneous views of Analytic Cubism in *Dynamism of a Cyclist* (fig. 1002), Umberto Boccioni (1882–1916), the most original of the Futurists, was able to communicate the look of furious pedaling across time and space far more tellingly than if he had actually depicted the human figure, which could be seen in only one time and place in traditional art. In the flexible vocabulary provided by Cubism, Boccioni found the means of expressing the twentieth century's new sense of time, space,

and energy that Albert Einstein had defined in 1905 in his Special Theory of Relativity. Moreover, Boccioni suggests the unique quality of the modern experience. With his pulsating movement, the cyclist has become an extension of his environment, from which he is now indistinguishable.

Futurism literally died out in World War I; its leading artists were killed by the same vehicles of destruction they had glorified only a few years earlier in their revolutionary manifesto. But strong echoes of Futurism appear in *Brooklyn Bridge* (fig. 1003), by the Italian-American Joseph Stella (1880–1946), with its maze of luminescent cables, vigorous diagonal thrusts, and crystalline "cells" of space.

CUBO-FUTURISM. As its name implies, Cubo-Futurism, which arose in Russia a few years before World War I as the result of close contacts with the leading European art centers, took its style from Picasso and based its theories on Futurist tracts. The Russian Futurists were above all modernists. They welcomed industry, which was spreading rapidly throughout Russia, as the foundation of a new society and the means for conquering that old Rusian enemy, nature. Unlike the Italian Futurists, however, the Russians rarely glorified the machine, least of all as an instrument of war.

Central to Cubo-Futurist thinking was the concept of *zaum*, a term which has no counterpart in the West: invented by Russian poets, *zaum* was a trans-sense (as opposed to the Dadaists' non-sense; see page 730) language based on new word forms and syntax. In theory, *zaum* could be understood universally, since it was thought that meaning was implicit in the basic sounds and patterns of speech. When applied to painting, *zaum* provided the artist with complete freedom to redefine the style and content of art. The picture surface was now seen as the sole conveyer of meaning through its appearance; hence, the subject of a work of art

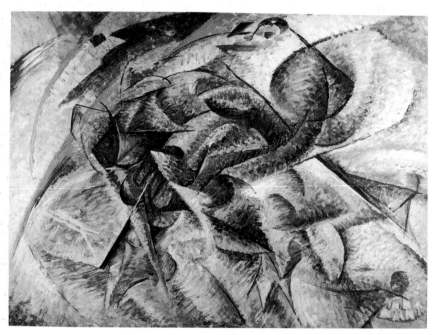

1002. UMBERTO BOCCIONI. *DYNAMISM OF A CYCLIST.* 1913. Oil on canvas,
27⅝×37⅜" (70×95 cm). Collection Gianni Mattioli, Milan

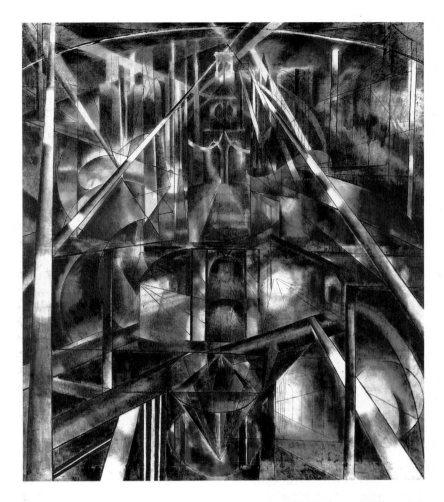

1003. (*above*) JOSEPH STELLA. *BROOKLYN BRIDGE.* 1917.
Oil on bedsheeting, 7′×6′4″ (2.13×1.93 m).
Yale University Art Gallery, New Haven, Connecticut
Gift of Collection Société Anonyme

1004. (*right*) LIUBOV POPOVA. *THE TRAVELER.* 1915.
Oil on canvas, 56×41½″ (142.3×104 cm).
Norton Simon Art Foundation, Pasadena, California

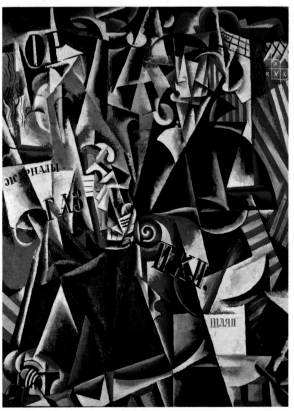

became the visual elements and their formal arrangement.
However, because Cubo-Futurism was concerned with
means, not ends, it failed to provide the actual content that
is found in modernism.

Although the Cubo-Futurists were more important as theorists than artists, they provided the springboard for later
Russian movements. The new world envisioned by the Russian modernists led to a broad redefinition of the roles of man
and woman, and the finest painter of the group was Liubov
Popova (1889–1924). It was then, in Russia, that women
emerged as artistic equals to an extent not achieved in Europe or America until considerably later. Popova studied in
Paris in 1912 and visited Italy in 1914. The combination of
Cubism and Futurism that she absorbed abroad is seen in
The Traveler (fig. 1004). The treatment of forms remains essentially Cubist, but the painting shares the Futurist obses-

1005. KAZIMIR MALEVICH. *BLACK QUADRILATERAL*.
c. 1913–15. Oil on canvas, 24 × 17″ (61 × 43.3 cm).
Art Co. Ltd. (The George Costakis Collection), Athens

black quadrilateral represents the eclipse of the sun of Western painting and of everything based upon it. Further, the work can be seen as the triumph of the new order over the old, the East over the West, humanity over Nature, idea over matter. The black quadrilateral (which is not even a true rectangle) was intended to stand as a modern icon, superseding the traditional Christian trinity and symbolizing a "supreme" reality, because geometry is an independent abstraction in itself: hence the movement's name, Suprematism.

According to Malevich, Suprematism was also a philosophical color system constructed in time and space. His space was an intuitive one, having both scientific and mystical overtones. The flat plane replaces volume, depth, and perspective as a means of defining space; each side or point represents one of the three dimensions, the fourth side standing for the fourth dimension, time. Like the universe itself, the black surface would be infinite were it not delimited by an outer boundary which is the white border and shape of the canvas. *Black Quadrilateral* thus constitutes the first satisfactory redefinition, visually and conceptually, of time and space in modern art. Like Einstein's formula $E=mc^2$ for the theory of relativity, it has an elegant simplicity that belies the intense effort required to synthesize a complex set of ideas and reduce them to a fundamental "law." When it appeared for the first time, Suprematism had much the same impact on Russian artists that Einstein's theory had on scientists: it unveiled a world never seen before, one that was unequivocally modern.

Later, Malevich began to tilt his quadrilaterals and simplify his paintings still further in search of the ultimate work of art. Malevich's efforts culminated in *Suprematist Composition: White on White* (fig. 1006), his most famous compo-

sion with representing dynamic motion in time and space. The jumble of image fragments creates the impression of objects seen in rapid succession; across the plane the furious interaction of forms with their environment threatens to extend the painting into the surrounding space. At the same time, the strong modeling draws attention to the surface, lending it a relieflike quality that is enhanced by the vigorous texture.

SUPREMATISM. The first purely Russian art of the twentieth century, however, was that of Suprematism. In one of the greatest leaps of the symbolic and spatial imagination in the history of art, Kazimir Malevich (1878–1935) invented the *Black Quadrilateral* seen in figure 1005. How is it that such a disarmingly simple image should be so important? By limiting art to a few elements—a single shape repeated in two tones and fixed firmly to the picture plane—he emphasized the painting as a painting even more radically than had his predecessors. At the same time, he transformed it into a concentrated symbol having multiple layers of meaning, thereby providing the content missing from Cubo-Futurism. The inspiration for *Black Quadrilateral* came in 1913 while Malevich was working on designs for the opera *Victory over the Sun*, a production that was one of the important collaborations in the modern era. In the context of the opera, the

1006. KAZIMIR MALEVICH. *SUPREMATIST COMPOSITION: WHITE ON WHITE*. c. 1918. Oil on canvas, 31¼ × 31¼″ (79.4 × 79.4 cm). Collection, The Museum of Modern Art, New York

sition, which limits art to its fewest possible components. It is all too tempting to dismiss such a radical extreme as a *reductio ad absurdum*; seen in person, however, the canvas is surprisingly persuasive. The shapes, created by the subtlest nuances of texture, have a revelatory purity that makes even *Black Quadrilateral* seem needlessly complex.

The heyday of Suprematism was over by the early 1920s. Reflecting the growing diversity and fragmentation of Russian art, its followers defected to other movements, above all to the Constructivism led by Vladimir Tatlin (see page 762).

Fantasy

The third current, which we term Fantasy, follows a course less clear-cut than the other two, since it depends on a state of mind more than on any particular style. The one thing all painters of fantasy have in common is the belief that imagination, "the inner eye," is more important than the outside world. And since every artist's imagination is his own private domain, the images it provides for him are likely to be equally private, unless he subjects them to a deliberate process of selection. But how can such "uncontrolled" images have meaning to the beholder, whose own inner world is not the same as the artist's? Psychoanalysis has taught us that we are not so different from each other in this respect as we like to think. Our minds are all built on the same basic pattern, and the same is true of our imagination and memory. These belong to the unconscious part of the mind where experiences are stored, whether we want to remember them or not. At night, or whenever conscious thought relaxes its vigilance, our experiences come back to us and we seem to live through them again.

However, the unconscious mind does not usually reproduce our experiences as they actually happened. They will often be admitted into the conscious part of the mind in the guise of "dream images"—in this form they seem less vivid, and we can live with our memories more easily. This digesting of experience by the unconscious mind is surprisingly alike in all of us, although the process works better with some individuals than with others. Hence we are always interested in imaginary things, provided they are presented to us in such a way that they *seem* real. What happens in a fairy tale, for example, would be absurd in the matter-of-fact language of a news report, but when it is told to us as it should be told, we are enchanted. The same thing is true of paintings—we recall *The Dream* by Henri Rousseau (see fig. 961).

But why, we may ask, does private fantasy loom so large in twentieth-century art? We saw the trend beginning at the end of the eighteenth century in the art of Fuseli and Goya (see figs. 876 and 858); perhaps they suggest part of the answer. There seem to be several interlocking causes: first, the cleavage that developed between reason and imagination in the wake of rationalism, which tended to dissolve the heritage of myth and legend that had been the common channel of private fantasy in earlier times; second, the artist's greater freedom—and insecurity—within the social fabric, giving him a sense of isolation and favoring an introspective attitude; and, finally, the Romantic cult of emotion that prompted the artist to seek out subjective experience, and to

accept its validity. In nineteenth-century painting, private fantasy was still a minor current. After 1900, it became a major one.

DE CHIRICO. The heritage of Romanticism can be seen most clearly in the astonishing pictures painted in Paris just before World War I by Giorgio de Chirico (1888–1978), such as *Mystery and Melancholy of a Street* (fig. 1007). This deserted square with endless diminishing arcades, nocturnally illuminated by the cold full moon, has all the poetry of Romantic reverie. But it has also a strangely sinister air; this is an "ominous" scene in the full sense of that term—everything here suggests an omen, a portent of unknown and disquieting significance. De Chirico himself could not explain the incongruities in these paintings—the empty furniture van, or the girl with the hoop—that trouble and fascinate us. Later, after he had returned to Italy, he adopted a conservative style and repudiated his early work, as if he were embarrassed at having put his dream world on public display.

CHAGALL. The power of nostalgia, so evident in *Mystery and Melancholy of a Street*, also dominates the fantasies of Marc Chagall (1887–1985), a Russian Jew who came to Paris in 1910. *I and the Village* (fig. 1008) is a Cubist fairy tale, weaving dreamlike memories of Russian folk tales, Jewish proverbs, and the look of Russia into one glowing vision.

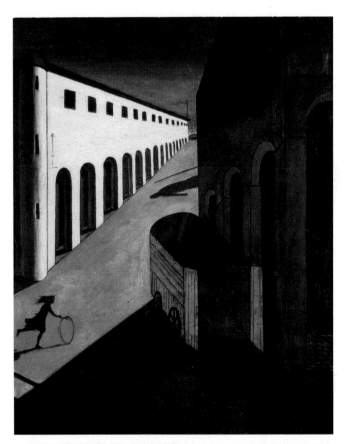

1007. GIORGIO DE CHIRICO. *MYSTERY AND MELANCHOLY OF A STREET.* 1914. Oil on canvas, 34¼×28½″ (88.2×72.3 cm).
Private collection

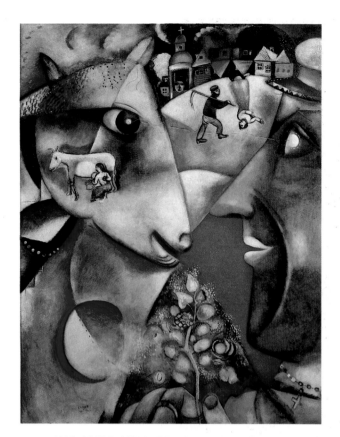

1008. MARC CHAGALL. *I AND THE VILLAGE*. 1911.
Oil on canvas, 75½×59½″ (191.5×151 cm).
Collection, The Museum of Modern Art, New York.
Mrs. Simon Guggenheim Fund

Here, as in many later works, Chagall relives the experiences of his childhood; these were so important to him that his imagination shaped and reshaped them for years without their persistence being diminished.

DUCHAMP. In Paris on the eve of World War I, we encounter yet another artist of fantasy, the Frenchman Marcel Duchamp (1887–1968). After basing his early style on Cézanne, he initiated a dynamic version of Analytic Cubism, similar to Futurism, by superimposing successive phases of movement on each other, as in multiple-exposure photography (see fig. 987a, b). His *Nude Descending a Staircase* (fig. 1009), done in this vein, caused a scandal at the Armory Show of modern art in New York in 1913.

Very soon, however, Duchamp's development took a far more disturbing turn. In *The Bride* (fig. 1010), we will look in vain for any resemblance, however remote, to the human form; what we see is a mechanism that seems part motor, part distilling apparatus; it is beautifully engineered to serve no purpose whatever. Its title, which cannot be irrelevant (Duchamp, by lettering it right onto the canvas, has emphasized its importance), causes us real perplexity. Did he intend to satirize the scientific outlook on humanity by "analyzing" the bride until she is reduced to a complicated piece of plumbing? If so, the picture may be the negative counterpart of the glorification of the machine, so stridently proclaimed by the Futurists.

Realism

THE ASH CAN SCHOOL. In America, the first wave of change was initiated not by the Stieglitz circle but by the Ash Can School, which flourished in New York just before World War I, although it was soon eclipsed by the rush toward a more radical modernism set off by the Armory Show in 1913 (see page 716). Centering on Robert Henri, who had studied with a pupil of Thomas Eakins at the Pennsylvania Academy, and consisting mainly of former illustrators for Philadelphia and New York newspapers, this group of artists was fascinated with the teeming life of the city slums. They found an endless source of subjects in the everyday urban scene, to which they brought the reporter's eye for color and drama. Despite the socialist philosophy that many of them shared, theirs was not an art of social commentary, but one that felt the pulse of city life, discovering in it vitality and richness while ignoring poverty and squalor. To capture

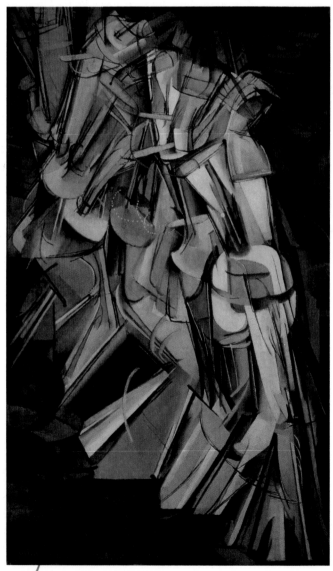

1009. MARCEL DUCHAMP. *NUDE DESCENDING A STAIRCASE
NO. 2*. 1912. Oil on canvas, 58×35″ (147.3×89 cm).
The Philadelphia Museum of Art.
Louise and Walter Arensberg Collection

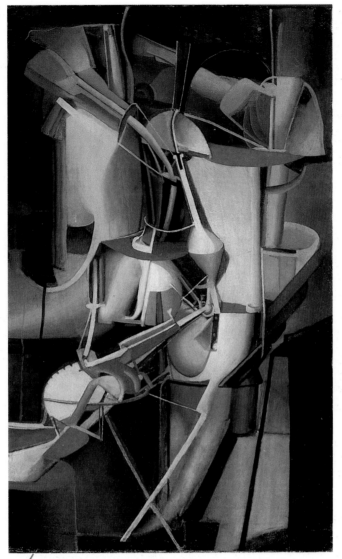

1010. MARCEL DUCHAMP. *THE BRIDE.* 1912. Oil on canvas,
35⅛×21¾″ (89.4×55.2 cm). The Philadelphia
Museum of Art. Louise and Walter Arensberg Collection

these qualities they relied on rapid execution, inspired by Baroque and Post-Impressionist painting, which lends their canvases the immediacy of spontaneous observation.

BELLOWS. Although not a founding member of the Ash Can School, George Bellows (1882–1925) became a leading representative of the group in its heyday. His masterpiece, *Stag at Sharkey's* (fig. 1011), shows why: no painter in America before Jackson Pollock expressed such heroic energy. Yet *Stag at Sharkey's* reminds us of Eakins' *William Rush Carving His Allegorical Figure* (see fig. 929), for it continues the same Realist tradition. Both place us in the scene as if we were present, and both use the play of light to pick out the main figures against a dark background. Bellows' paintings were fully as shocking as Eakins' had been. Most late-nineteenth-century American artists had all but ignored urban life in favor of landscapes, and compared with these, the subjects and surfaces of the Ash Can pictures had a disturbing rawness.

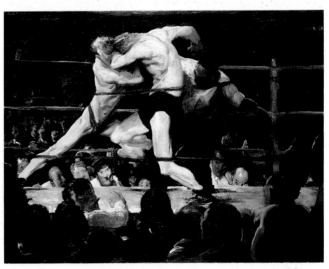

1011. GEORGE BELLOWS. *STAG AT SHARKEY'S.* 1909.
Oil on canvas, 36¼×48¼″ (92.1×122.6 cm).
The Cleveland Museum of Art. Hinman B. Hurlbut Collection

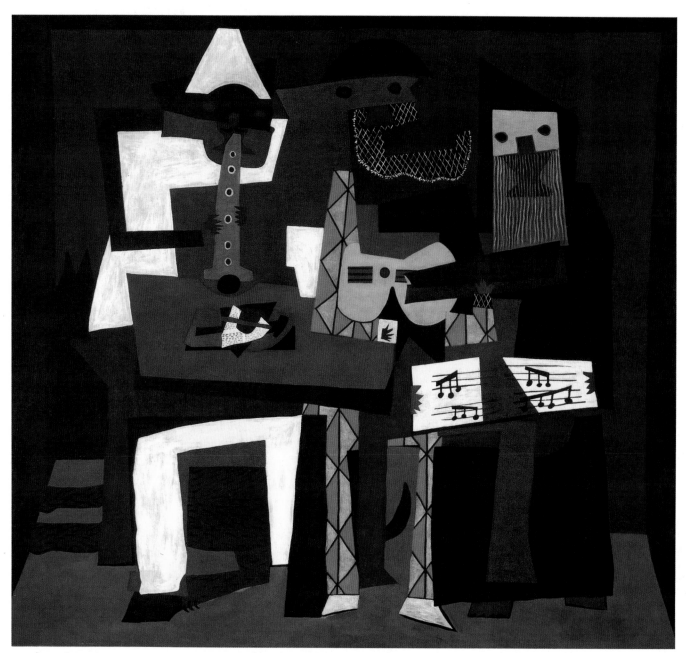

1012. PABLO PICASSO. *THREE MUSICIANS.* Summer 1921.
Oil on canvas, 6'7"×7'3¾" (2×2.23 m).
Collection, The Museum of Modern Art, New York.
Gift of Mrs. Simon Guggenheim Fund

PAINTING BETWEEN THE WARS

PICASSO. The end of World War I unleashed an unprecedented outpouring of art after a four-year creative lull. We begin with Picasso, whose genius towers over all others of the period and transcends categorization. As a Spanish national living in Paris he was not involved in the conflict, unlike many French and German artists who served in the military and even sacrificed their lives. This was a time of quiet experimentation that laid the foundation for Picasso's art over the next several decades. The results did not become

fully apparent, however, until the early 1920s, following a phase of intensive cultivation. *Three Musicians* (fig. 1012) shows the fruit of that labor. It utilizes the "cut-paper style" of Synthetic Cubism so consistently that we cannot tell from the reproduction whether it is painted or pasted.

By now, Picasso was internationally famous. Cubism had spread throughout the Western world; it influenced not only other painters, but sculptors and even architects. Yet Picasso was already striking out in a new direction. Soon after the invention of Synthetic Cubism, he had begun to do drawings in a painstakingly realistic manner reminiscent of Ingres, and by 1920 he was working simultaneously in two quite separate styles: that of the *Three Musicians*, and a Neoclassic style of strongly modeled, heavy-bodied figures such as his *Mother and Child* (fig. 1013). To many of his admirers, this seemed a kind of betrayal, but in retrospect the reason for Picasso's double-track performance is clear: chafing under the limitations of Synthetic Cubism, he needed to resume contact with the classical tradition, the "art of the museums." The figures in *Mother and Child* have a mock-monumental quality that suggests colossal statues rather than flesh-and-blood human beings, yet the theme is treated with surprising tenderness. The forms, however, are carefully dovetailed within the frame, not unlike the way the *Three Musicians* is put together.

A few years later the two tracks of Picasso's style began to converge, making an extraordinary synthesis that was to become the basis of his art. The *Three Dancers* of 1925 (fig. 1014) shows how he accomplished this seemingly impossible feat. Structurally, the picture is pure Synthetic Cubism; it even includes painted imitations of specific materials—patterned wallpaper and samples of various fabrics cut out with pinking shears. But the figures, a wildly fantastic version of

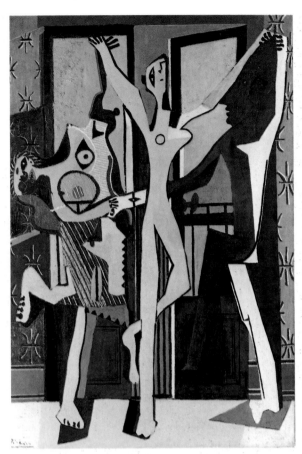

1014. PABLO PICASSO. *THREE DANCERS.* 1925.
Oil on canvas, 84½×56¼″ (214×143 cm).
The Tate Gallery, London

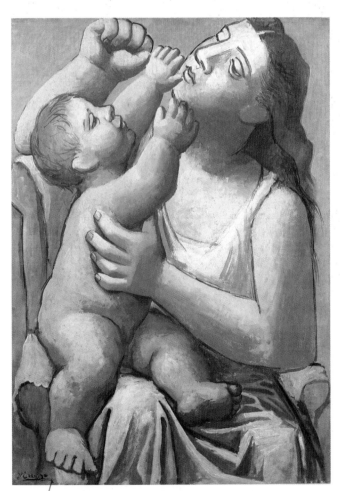

1013. PABLO PICASSO. *MOTHER AND CHILD.* 1921–22.
Oil on canvas, 38×28″ (96.7×71 cm).
The Alex L. Hillman Family Foundation, New York

a classical scheme (compare the dancers in Matisse's *The Joy of Life*, fig. 988), are an even more violent assault on convention than the figures in *Les Demoiselles d'Avignon*. Human anatomy is here simply the raw material for Picasso's incredibly fertile inventiveness; limbs, breasts, and faces are handled with the same sovereign freedom as the fragments of external reality in Braque's *Le Courrier* (fig. 1001). Their original identity no longer matters—breasts may turn into eyes, profiles merge with frontal views, shadows become substance, and vice versa, in an endless flow of metamorphoses. They are "visual puns," offering wholly unexpected possibilities of expression—humorous, grotesque, macabre, even tragic.

Three Dancers marks a transition to Picasso's experiment with Surrealism (see page 731). Because he did not practice automatism, he never developed into a true adherent of the movement. Nevertheless, the impact of his fellow Spaniard Joan Miró (see page 732) can be seen in the biomorphism of his mural *Guernica* (fig. 1015). Picasso did not show any interest in politics during World War I or the 1920s, but the Spanish Civil War stirred him to ardent partisanship with the Loyalists. The mural, executed in 1937 for the Pavilion of the Spanish Republic at the Paris International Exposition, has truly monumental grandeur. It was inspired by the terror-bombing of Guernica, the ancient capital of the

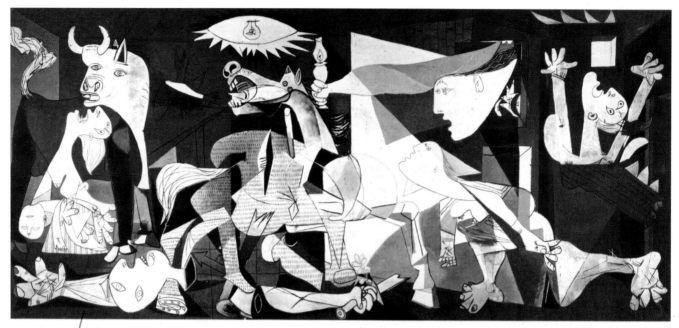

1015. PABLO PICASSO. *GUERNICA*. 1937. Oil on canvas, 11'6"×25'8" (3.5×7.8 m). Museo del Prado, Madrid

Basques in Northern Spain. The painting does not represent the event itself; rather, with a series of powerful images, it evokes the agony of total war.

The destruction of Guernica was the first demonstration of the technique of saturation bombing which was later employed on a huge scale in the course of World War II; the mural was thus a prophetic vision of doom—the doom that threatens us even more in this age of nuclear warfare. The symbolism of the scene resists precise interpretation, despite its several traditional elements: the mother and her dead child are the descendants of the Pietà (see fig. 505), the woman with the lamp recalls the Statue of Liberty, and the dead fighter's hand, still clutching a broken sword, is a familiar emblem of heroic resistance. We also sense the contrast between the menacing, human-headed bull, surely intended to represent the forces of darkness, and the dying horse.

These figures owe their terrifying eloquence to what they *are*, not to what they *mean*; the anatomical dislocations, fragmentations, and metamorphoses, which in the *Three Dancers* seemed willful and fantastic, now express a stark reality, the reality of unbearable pain. The ultimate test of the validity of collage construction (here in superimposed flat "cutouts" restricted to black, white, and gray) is that it could serve as the vehicle of such overpowering emotions.

Abstraction

Picasso's abandonment of strict Cubism signaled the broad retreat of abstraction after 1920 because the utopian ideals associated with it had been largely dashed by "the war to end all wars." The Futurist spirit nevertheless continued to find adherents on both sides of the Atlantic.

LÉGER. Buoyant with optimism and pleasurable excitement, *The City* (fig. 1016) by the Frenchman Fernand Léger (1881–1955) conjures up a mechanized utopia. This beautifully controlled industrial landscape is stable without being static, and reflects the clean geometric shapes of modern machinery. In this instance, the term "abstraction" applies more to the choice of design elements and their manner of combination than to the shapes themselves, since these (except for the two figures on the staircase) are "pre-fabricated" entities.

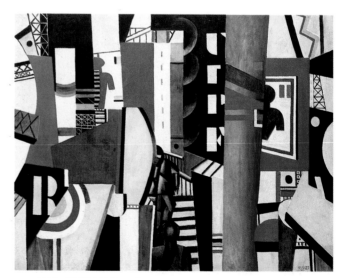

1016. FERNAND LÉGER. *THE CITY.* 1919. Oil on canvas, 7'7"×9'9" (2.31×2.98 m). The Philadelphia Museum of Art. A. E. Gallatin Collection

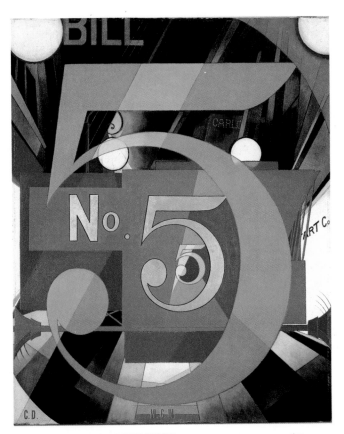

1017. CHARLES DEMUTH. *I SAW THE FIGURE 5 IN GOLD.*
1928. Oil on composition board, 36×29¾″ (91.4×75.6 cm).
The Metropolitan Museum of Art, New York.
The Alfred Stieglitz Collection

that he called Neo-Plasticism (the movement as a whole is also known as *De Stijl*, after the Dutch magazine advocating his ideas). *Composition with Red, Blue, and Yellow* (fig. 1018) shows Mondrian's style at its most severe: he restricts his design to horizontals and verticals and his colors to the three primary hues, plus black and white. Every possibility of representation is thereby eliminated. Yet Mondrian sometimes gave to his works such titles as *Trafalgar Square*, or *Broadway Boogie Woogie* (fig. 14), that hint at some degree of relationship, however indirect, with observed reality. Unlike Kandinsky, Mondrian did not strive for pure, lyrical emotion; his goal, he asserted, was "pure reality," and he defined this as equilibrium "through the balance of unequal but equivalent oppositions."

Perhaps we can best understand what he meant if we think of his work as "abstract collage" that uses black bands and colored rectangles instead of recognizable fragments of chair caning and newsprint. He was interested solely in relationships and wanted no distracting elements or fortuitous associations. But, by establishing the "right" relationship among his bands and rectangles, he transforms them as thoroughly as Braque transformed the snippets of pasted paper in *Le Courrier* (fig. 1001). How did he discover the "right" relationship? And how did he determine the shape and number for the bands and rectangles? In Braque's *Le Courrier*, the ingredients are to some extent "given" by chance; Mondrian, apart from his self-imposed rules, constantly faced the dilemma of unlimited possibilities. He could not change the relationship of the bands to the rectangles without changing the bands and rectangles themselves. When we consider his task, we begin to realize its infinite complexity.

DEMUTH. The modern movement in America proved short-lived. One of the few artists to continue working in this vein after World War I was Charles Demuth (1883–1935). A member of the Stieglitz group (see pages 796–97), he had been friendly with Duchamp and exiled Cubists in New York during World War I. A few years later, under the impact of Futurism, he developed a style known as Precisionism to depict urban and industrial architecture. We can detect influences from all of these movements in *I Saw the Figure 5 in Gold* (fig. 1017), but the dynamic treatment of the background most directly recalls Joseph Stella's *Brooklyn Bridge* (fig. 1003). The title is taken from a poem by Demuth's friend William Carlos Williams, whose name—as "Bill," "Carlos," and "W. C. W."—also forms part of the design. In the poem the figure 5 appears on a red fire truck, while in the painting it has become the dominant feature, thrice repeated to reinforce its echo in our memory as the fire truck rushes on through the night.

MONDRIAN. The most radical abstractionist of our time was a Dutch painter nine years older than Picasso, Piet Mondrian (1872–1944). He came to Paris in 1912 as a mature Expressionist in the tradition of Van Gogh and the *Fauves*. Under the impact of Analytic Cubism, his work soon underwent a complete change, and within the next decade Mondrian developed an entirely non-representational style

1018. PIET MONDRIAN. *COMPOSITION WITH RED, BLUE, AND YELLOW.* 1930. Oil on canvas, 20×20″ (50.3×50.3 cm).
Private collection

Looking again at *Composition with Red, Blue, and Yellow*, we find that when we measure the various units, only the proportions of the canvas itself are truly rational, an exact square; Mondrian has arrived at all the rest "by feel," and must have undergone agonies of trial and error. How often, we wonder, did he change the dimensions of the red rectangle to bring it and the other elements into self-contained equilibrium? Strange as it may seem, Mondrian's exquisite sense for nonsymmetrical balance is so specific that critics well acquainted with his work have no difficulty in distinguishing fakes from genuine pictures. Designers who work with nonfigurative shapes, such as architects and typographers, are likely to be most sensitive to this quality, and Mondrian has had a greater influence on them than on painters (see Chapter 6).

NICHOLSON. Mondrian nevertheless did produce a number of followers among the painters. By far the most original was the English artist Ben Nicholson (1894–1982). A rigorous Abstractionist, he bent Mondrian's rules without breaking them in his painted reliefs (fig. 1019), which also show the inspiration of his wife, the sculptor Barbara Hepworth (see page 760). The overlapping shapes violate the integrity of the rectangle and overcome the tyranny of the grid maintained by Mondrian. The geometry is further enlivened by the introduction of the circle. Yet his work, too, relies on the delicate balance of elements. The effect is enhanced by the subdued palette and matte finish, which create harmonies of the utmost refinement. Indeed, compared to Nicholson's, Mondrian's primary colors seem astonishingly bright and exuberant.

Fantasy

DADA Out of despair over the mechanized mass killing of World War I, a number of artists in New York and Zurich simultaneously launched in protest a movement called Dada

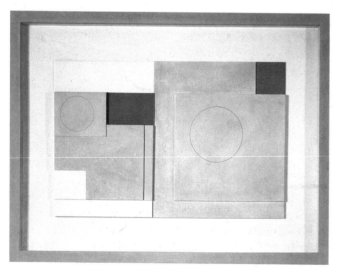

1019. BEN NICHOLSON. *PAINTED RELIEF.* 1939. Synthetic board mounted on plywood, painted, 32⅞×45″ (83.3×114.4 cm).
Collection, The Museum of Modern Art, New York.
Gift of H. S. Ede and the artist (by exchange)

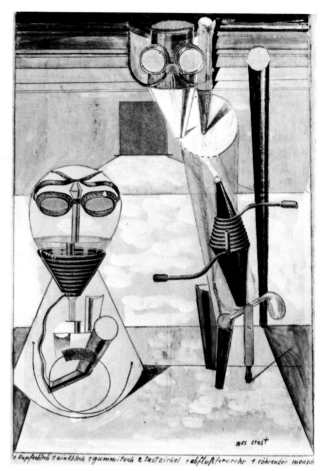

1020. MAX ERNST. *1 COPPER PLATE 1 ZINC PLATE 1 RUBBER CLOTH 2 CALIPERS 1 DRAINPIPE TELESCOPE 1 PIPING MAN.* 1920.
Collage, 12×9″ (30.5×23 cm). Estate of Hans Arp

(or Dadaism), which then spread to other cities in Germany and France. The term, meaning "hobbyhorse" in French, was reportedly picked at random from a dictionary, and as an infantile, all-purpose word, it perfectly fitted the spirit of the movement. Dada has often been called nihilistic, and its declared purpose was indeed to make clear to the public at large that all established values, moral or aesthetic, had been rendered meaningless by the catastrophe of the Great War. During its short life (c. 1915–1922) Dada preached nonsense and anti-art with a vengeance. Marcel Duchamp once "improved" a reproduction of Leonardo's *Mona Lisa* with a mustache and the letters LHOOQ, which when pronounced in French, make an off-color pun. Not even modern art was safe from the Dadaists' assaults; one of them exhibited a toy monkey inside a frame with the title "Portrait of Cézanne." Yet Dada was not a completely negative movement. In its calculated irrationality there was also liberation, a voyage into unknown provinces of the creative mind. The only law respected by the Dadaists was that of chance, and the only reality, that of their own imaginations.

ERNST. Although their most characteristic art form was the ready-made (see page 763), the Dadaists adopted the collage technique of Synthetic Cubism for their purposes: figure 1020 by the German Dadaist Max Ernst (1891–1976), an associate of Duchamp, is largely composed of snippets from illustrations of machinery. The caption pretends to enumerate these mechanical ingredients which include (or add up to?) "1 Piping Man." Actually, there is also a "piping woman." These offspring of Duchamp's prewar *Bride* stare at us blindly through their goggles.

ARP. Hans (Jean) Arp (1887–1966), another early member of the movement, invented a new kind of collage (fig. 1021) whose elements—colored pieces of paper that had been shaped by tearing rather than by cutting—were arranged "according to the laws of chance." Arp started these compositions by dropping the bits of paper on a larger sheet, and then cautiously adjusted this "natural" configuration. The artist's task, he believed, was to "court the Muse of Chance," eliciting from her what he called "organic concretions" (he disliked the term "abstraction," which implies discipline and conscious purpose, not reliance on the happy accident).

SURREALISM. In 1924, after Duchamp's retirement from Dada, a group led by the poet André Breton founded Dada's successor, Surrealism. They defined their aim as "pure psychic automatism . . . intended to express . . . the true process of thought . . . free from the exercise of reason and from any aesthetic or moral purpose." Surrealist theory was heavily

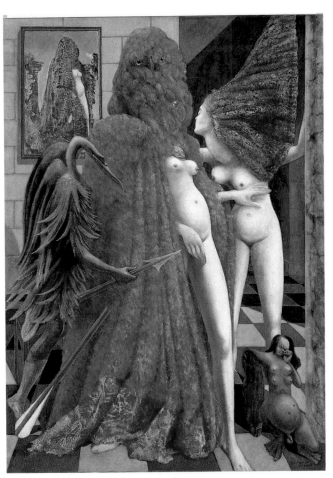

1022. MAX ERNST. *LA TOILETTE DE LA MARIÉE*
(ATTIREMENT OF THE BRIDE). 1940. Oil on canvas, 51×37⅞"
(129.6×96.3 cm). Peggy Guggenheim Collection, Venice

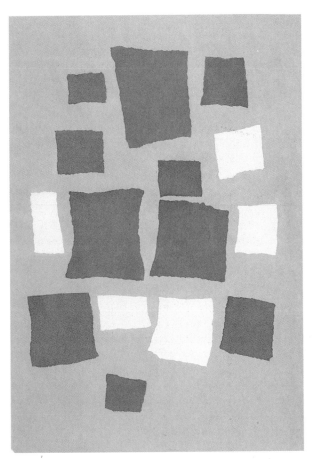

1021. HANS (JEAN) ARP. *COLLAGE WITH SQUARES ARRANGED
ACCORDING TO THE LAWS OF CHANCE.* 1916–17.
Collage of colored papers, 19⅛×13⅝" (48.5×34.5 cm).
Collection, The Museum of Modern Art, New York. Purchase

larded with concepts borrowed from psychoanalysis, and its overwrought rhetoric is not always to be taken seriously. The notion that a dream can be transposed directly from the unconscious mind to the canvas, bypassing the conscious awareness of the artist, did not work in practice: some degree of control was simply unavoidable. Nevertheless, Surrealism stimulated several novel techniques for soliciting and exploiting chance effects.

ERNST'S DECALCOMANIA. Max Ernst, the most inventive member of the group, often combined collage with "frottage" (rubbings from pieces of wood, pressed flowers, and other relief surfaces—the process we all know from the children's pastime of rubbing with a pencil on a piece of paper covering, say, a coin). In *La Toilette de la Mariée* (fig. 1022), he has obtained fascinating shapes and textures by "decalcomania" (the transfer, by pressure, of oil paint to the canvas from some other surface). This procedure is in essence another variant of that recommended by Alexander Cozens (see fig. 844) and Leonardo da Vinci, and Ernst certainly found, and elaborated upon, an extraordinary wealth of images among his stains. The end result does have some of the qualities of a dream, but it is a dream born of a strikingly Romantic imagination.

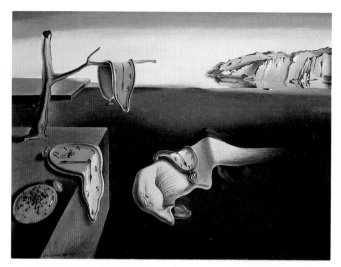

1023. SALVADOR DALI. *THE PERSISTENCE OF MEMORY*. 1931.
Oil on canvas, 9½×13″ (24×33 cm). Collection,
The Museum of Modern Art, New York. Given anonymously

DALI. The same can be said of *The Persistence of Memory* (fig. 1023) by Salvador Dali (1904–1989). The most notorious of the Surrealists, Dali used a meticulous verism to render a "paranoid" dream in which time, forms, and space have been distorted in a frighteningly real way.

MIRÓ. Surrealism, however, has a more boldly imaginative branch: some works by Picasso, such as *Three Dancers* (fig. 1014), have affinities with it, and its greatest exponent was also Spanish, Joan Miró (1893–1983), who painted the striking *Painting* (fig. 1024). His style has been labeled "biomorphic abstraction," since his designs are fluid and curvilinear, like organic forms, rather than geometric. Actually, "biomorphic concretion" might be a more suitable name, for the shapes in Miró's pictures have their own vigorous life. They seem to change before our eyes, expanding and contracting like amoebas until they approach human individuality closely enough to please the artist. Their spontaneous "becoming" is the very opposite of abstraction as we defined it above (see page 716), though Miró's formal discipline is no less rigorous than that of Cubism (he began as a Cubist).

KLEE. The German-Swiss painter Paul Klee (1879–1940), too, had been influenced by Cubism; but ethnographic art, and the drawings of small children, held an equally vital interest for him. During World War I, he molded from these disparate elements a pictorial language of his own, marvelously economical and precise. *Twittering Machine* (fig. 1025), a delicate pen drawing tinted with watercolor, demonstrates the unique flavor of Klee's art: with a few simple lines, he had created a ghostly mechanism that imitates the sound of birds, simultaneously mocking our faith in the mir-

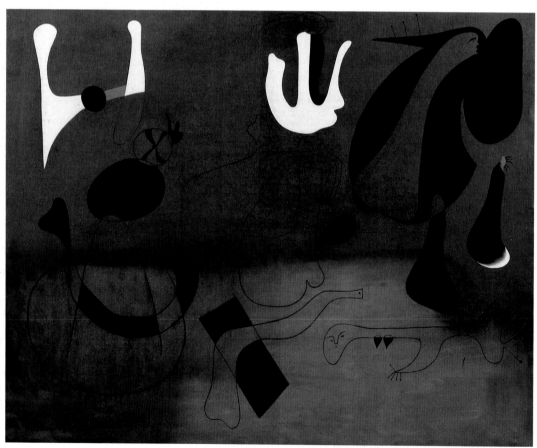

1024. JOAN MIRÓ. *PAINTING*. 1933. Oil on canvas, 51¼×63½″
(130.5×161.3 cm). Wadsworth Atheneum, Hartford, Connecticut.
© Wadsworth Atheneum. Ella Gallup Sumner and Mary Catlin Sumner Collection

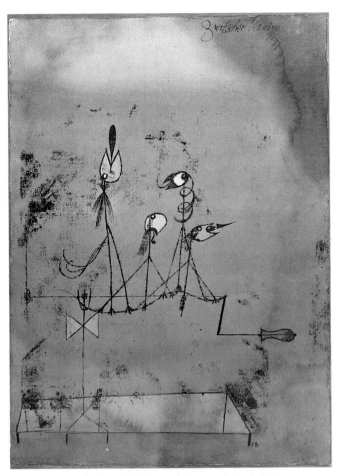

1025. PAUL KLEE. *TWITTERING MACHINE.* 1922.
Watercolor and pen and ink on oil transfer drawing on paper,
mounted on cardboard, 25¼×19″ (64.1×48.2 cm).
Collection, The Museum of Modern Art, New York. Purchase

Toward the end of his life, he immersed himself in the study of ideographs of all kinds, such as hieroglyphics, hex signs, and the mysterious markings in prehistoric caves—"boiled-down" representational images that appealed to him because they had the twin quality he strove for in his own graphic language. This "ideographic style" is very pronounced in figure 1026, *Park near Lu(cerne).* As a lyric poet may use the plainest words, these deceptively simple shapes sum up a wealth of experience and sensation: the innocent gaiety of spring, the clipped orderliness peculiar to captive plant life in a park. Has it not a relationship, in spirit if not in fact, with the Romanesque *Summer Landscape* in the manuscript of *Carmina Burana* (fig. 450)? Shortly before his death, Klee's horror at World War II led him to abandon this light-hearted vein in favor of a bleakly pessimistic manner that drew close to Miró's darkest fantasies of the same time.

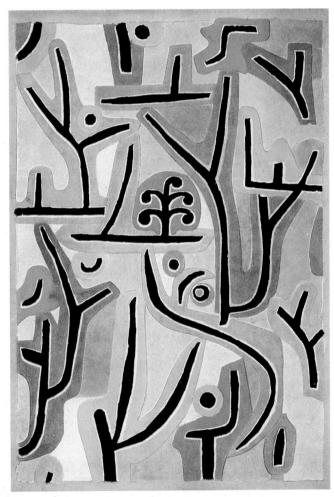

1026. PAUL KLEE. *PARK NEAR LU(CERNE).* 1938.
Oil and newsprint on burlap, 39½×27½″ (100.3×69.7 cm).
Fondation Paul Klee, Musée des Beaux-Arts de Berne,
Bern, Switzerland.
Copyright 1986 COSMOPRESS, Genf

acles of the machine age and our sentimental appreciation of bird song. The little contraption (which is not without its sinister aspect: the heads of the four sham birds look like fishermen's lures, as if they might entrap real birds) thus condenses into one striking invention a complex of ideas about present-day civilization.

The title has an indispensable role; it is characteristic of the way Klee worked that the picture itself, however visually appealing, does not reveal its full evocative quality unless the artist tells us what it means. The title, in turn, needs the picture—the witty concept of a twittering machine does not kindle our imagination until we are shown such a thing. This interdependence is familiar to us from cartoons; Klee lifts it to the level of high art without relinquishing the playful character of these verbal-visual puns. To him art was a "language of signs," of shapes that are images of ideas as the shape of a letter is the image of a specific sound, or an arrow the image of the command, "This way only." But he also realized that in any conventional system the sign is no more than a "trigger"; the instant we perceive it, we automatically invest it with its meaning, without stopping to ponder its shape. Klee wanted *his* signs to impinge upon our awareness as visual facts, yet also to share the quality of "triggers."

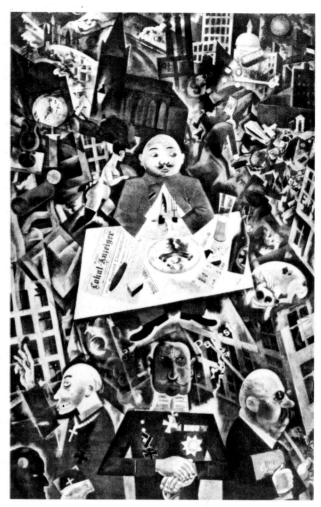

1027. GEORGE GROSZ. *GERMANY, A WINTER'S TALE.* 1918.
Formerly Collection Garvens, Hanover, Germany

Expressionism

GROSZ. The experience of World War I filled German artists with a deep anguish at the state of modern civilization, which found its principal outlet in Expressionism. George Grosz (1893–1959), a painter and graphic artist, studied in Paris in 1913, then joined Dadaism in Berlin after the end of the war. Inspired by the Futurists, he used a dynamized form of Cubism to develop a bitter, savagely satiric style that expressed the disillusionment of his generation. In *Germany, a Winter's Tale* (fig. 1027), the city of Berlin forms the kaleidoscopic—and chaotic—background for several large figures, which are superimposed on it as in a collage: the marionettelike "good citizen" at his table, and the sinister forces that molded him (a hypocritical clergyman, a general, and a schoolmaster).

BECKMANN. Max Beckmann (1884–1950), a robust descendant of the *Brücke* artists, did not become an Expressionist until after he had lived through World War I, which filled him with a deep despair at the state of modern civilization. *The Dream* (fig. 1028) is a mocking nightmare, a tilted, zigzag world crammed with puppetlike figures, as disquieting as those in Bosch's *Hell* (see fig. 559). Its evocatively

powerful symbolism, however, is even more difficult to interpret, since it is necessarily subjective.

How indeed could Beckmann have expressed the chaos in Germany after that war with the worn-out language of traditional symbols? "These are the creatures that haunt my imagination," he seems to say. "They show the true nature of the modern condition—how weak we are, how helpless against ourselves in this proud era of so-called progress." Many elements from this grotesque and sinister sideshow recur more than a decade later in the lateral panels of Beckmann's triptych *Departure* (fig. 1029), completed when, under Nazi pressure, he was on the point of leaving his homeland. In the hindsight of today, the topsy-turvy quality

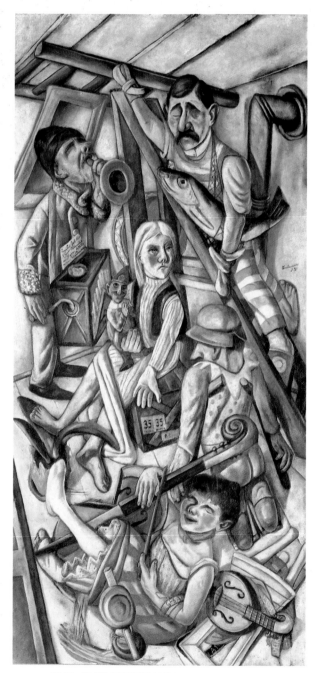

1028. MAX BECKMANN. *THE DREAM.* 1921.
Oil on canvas, 71×35″ (180.3×89 cm).
Collection Morton D. May, St. Louis, Missouri

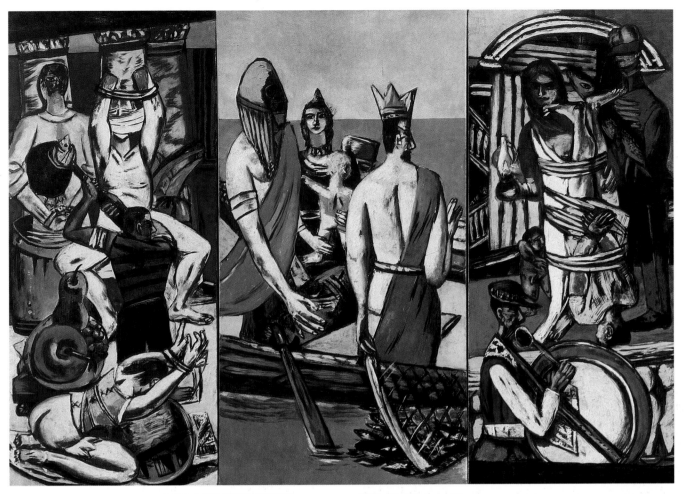

1029. MAX BECKMANN. *DEPARTURE*. 1932–33. Triptych, Oil on canvas,
center panel 84¾ × 45⅜″ (215.3 × 115.5 cm); side panels 84¾ × 99¼″ (215.3 × 99.7 cm).
Collection, The Museum of Modern Art, New York. Given anonymously (by exchange)

of these two scenes, full of mutilations and meaningless rituals, has acquired the force of prophecy. The stable design of the center panel, in contrast, with its expanse of blue sea and its sunlit brightness, conveys the hopeful spirit of an embarkation for distant shores. (After living through World War II in occupied Holland, under the most trying conditions, Beckmann spent the final three years of his life in America.)

DOVE.   After 1920 in the United States, most of the original members of the Stieglitz group concentrated on landscapes, which they treated in representational styles derived loosely from Expressionism. Alone among them, Arthur G. Dove (1880–1946) consistently maintained a form of abstraction based on Kandinsky's expressionistic style. The difference between the two artists is that Dove sought to reveal the inner life of nature, whereas Kandinsky tried to rid his images of readily recognizable subject matter. Dove's paintings possess a monumental spirit that belies their typically modest size. *Foghorns* (fig. 1030) exemplifies the intelligence and economy of his mature landscapes. To evoke the diffusion of sound, Dove utilized the simple but ingenious device of irregular concentric circles of color that grow paler as they radiate outward.

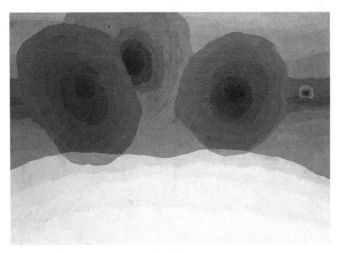

1030. ARTHUR G. DOVE. *FOGHORNS*. 1929.
Oil on canvas, 18×26″ (42.7×66 cm).
Colorado Springs Fine Arts Center. Anonymous gift

OROZCO. During the 1930s, the center of Expressionism in the New World was Mexico. The Mexican Revolution began in 1911 with the fall of the dictator Porfirio Diaz and continued for more than two decades; it inspired a group of young painters to search for a national style incorporating the great native heritage of Pre-Columbian art. They also felt that their art must be "of the people," expressing the spirit of the Revolution in vast mural cycles in public buildings. Although each developed his own distinctive style, they shared a common point of departure: the Symbolist art of Gauguin. This art had shown how non-Western forms could be integrated with the Western tradition, and the flat, decorative quality was moreover particularly suited to murals. The involvement of these artists in the political turmoil of the day often led them to overburden their works with ideological significance.

The artist least subject to this imbalance of form and subject matter was José Clemente Orozco (1883–1949), a passionately independent artist who refused to get embroiled in

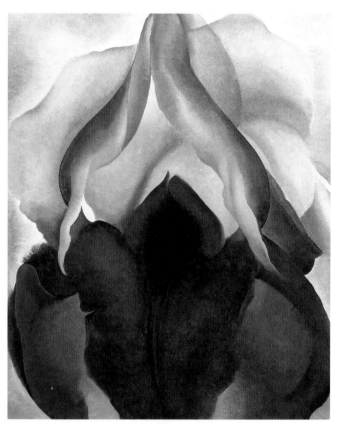

1032. GEORGIA O'KEEFFE. *BLACK IRIS III.* 1926.
Oil on canvas, 36×29⅞″ (91.4×75.9 cm).
The Metropolitan Museum of Art.
The Alfred Stieglitz Collection

factional politics. The detail from the mural cycle at the University of Guadalajara (fig. 1031) illustrates his most powerful trait, a deep humanitarian sympathy with the silent, suffering masses.

Realism

O'KEEFFE. The naturalism that characterized American art as a whole during the 1920s found its most important representative in Georgia O'Keeffe (1887–1986). Throughout her long career, she covered a wide range of subjects and styles. Like Arthur Dove, she practiced a form of organic abstraction indebted to Expressionism; she also adopted the Precisionism of Charles Demuth (see page 729), so that she is sometimes considered an abstract artist. Her work often combines aspects of both approaches; as she assimilated a subject into her imagination, she would alter and simplify it to convey a personal meaning. Nonetheless, she remained a realist at heart. *Black Iris III* (fig. 1032) is the kind of painting for which she is best known. The image is marked by a strong sense of design uniquely her own, yet the flower is deceptive in its decorative treatment. Observed with detachment, it is a thinly disguised symbol of female sexuality.

AMERICAN SCENE PAINTING. The 1930s witnessed an even stronger artistic conservatism than the previous decade's, in reaction to the economic depression and social turmoil that gripped both Europe and the United States.

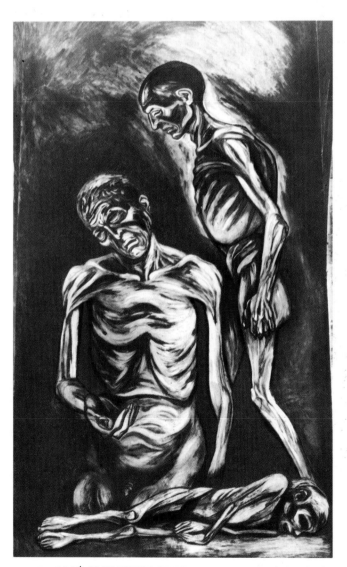

1031. JOSÉ CLEMENTE OROZCO. *VICTIMS.* Detail of fresco cycle. 1936. University of Guadalajara, Mexico

The dominance of realism signaled the retreat of progressive art everywhere. In Germany, where it was known as the New Objectivity, realism was linked to the reassertion of traditional values. Most American artists split into two camps, the Regionalists and the Social Realists. The Regionalists sought to revive idealism by updating the American myth, defined, however, largely in Midwestern terms. The Social Realists, on the other hand, captured in their pictures the dislocation and despair of the Depression era, and were often concerned with social reform. But both movements, although bitterly opposed, drew freely on the Ash Can School (see page 724).

HOPPER. The one artist who appealed to all factions alike, including that of the few remaining modernists, was a former pupil of Robert Henri, Edward Hopper (1882–1967). He focused on what has since become known as the "vernacular architecture" of American cities—store fronts, movie houses, all-night diners—which no one else had thought worthy of an artist's attention. *Early Sunday Morning* (fig. 1033) distills a haunting sense of loneliness from the all-too-familiar elements of an ordinary street. Its quietness, we realize, is temporary; there is hidden life behind these facades. We almost expect to see one of the window shades raised as we look at them. But apart from its poetic appeal, the picture also shows an impressive formal discipline; we note the strategy in placing the fireplug and barber pole, the subtle varia-

tions in the treatment of the row of windows, the precisely calculated slant of sunlight, the delicate balance of verticals and horizontals. Obviously, Hopper was not unaware of Mondrian.

PAINTING SINCE WORLD WAR II

Abstract Expressionism: Action Painting

The term Abstract Expressionism is often applied to the style of painting that prevailed for about a dozen years following the end of World War II. It was initiated by artists living in New York City in reaction to the anxiety brought on by the nuclear age and subsequent Cold War. Under the influence of existentialist philosophy, Action Painters, the first of the Abstract Expressionists, developed from Surrealism a new approach to art. Painting became a counterpart to life itself, an ongoing process in which the artist faces comparable risks and overcomes the dilemmas confronting him through a series of conscious and unconscious decisions in response to both inner and external demands. The Color Field Painters coalesced the frenetic gestures and violent hues of the Action Painters into broad forms of poetic color that partly reflect the spirituality of Oriental mysticism. In a sense, Color Field Painting resolved the conflicts expressed by Action Painting. They are, however, two sides of the same coin, separated by the thinnest differences of approach.

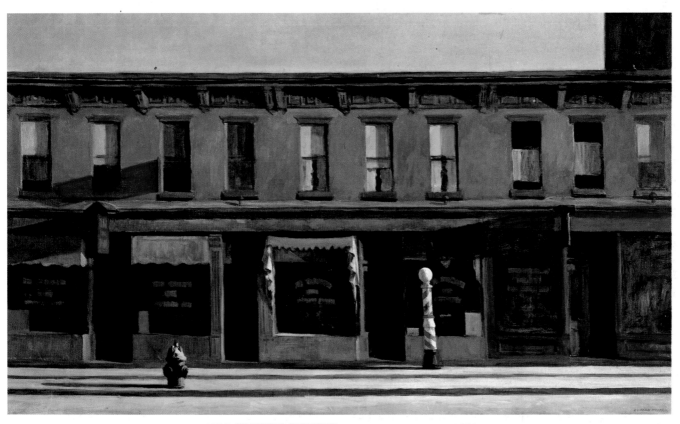

1033. EDWARD HOPPER. *EARLY SUNDAY MORNING.* 1930.
Oil on canvas, 35×60″ (88.9×152.4 cm).
Whitney Museum of American Art, New York

GORKY. Arshile Gorky (1904–1948), an Armenian who came to America at sixteen, was the pioneer of the movement and the single most important influence on its other members. It took him twenty years—painting first in the vein of Cézanne, then in that of Picasso—to arrive at his mature style as we see it in *The Liver Is the Cock's Comb* (fig. 1034). The enigmatic title suggests Gorky's close contact with the poet André Breton and other Surrealists who found refuge in New York during the war, as well as the personal mythology that underlies his work. The treatment, moreover, reflects his own experience in camouflage, gained from a class he conducted earlier. Everything here is in the process of turning into something else. The biomorphic shapes clearly owe much to Miró, while their spontaneous handling and the glowing color reflect Gorky's enthusiasm for Kandinsky (figs. 1024 and 996). Yet the dynamic interlocking of the forms, their aggressive power of attraction and repulsion are uniquely his own.

POLLOCK. The most important of the Action Painters proved to be Jackson Pollock (1912–1956), who in 1950 did the huge and original picture entitled *Autumnal Rhythm: Number 30, 1950* (fig. 1035) mainly by pouring and spattering his colors, instead of applying them with the brush. The result, especially when viewed at close range, suggests both Kandinsky and Max Ernst (compare figs. 996 and 1022).

Kandinsky's non-representational Expressionism and the Surrealists' exploitation of chance effects are indeed the main sources of Pollock's work, but they do not sufficiently account for his revolutionary technique and the emotional appeal of his art. Why did Pollock "fling a pot of paint in the public's face" (as Ruskin had accused Whistler of doing)? Not, surely, to be more abstract than his predecessors, for the strict control implied by abstraction is exactly what Pollock relinquished when he began to dribble and spatter. A more plausible explanation is that he came to regard paint itself not as a passive substance to be manipulated at will but as a storehouse of pent-up forces for him to release.

The actual shapes visible in our illustration are largely determined by the internal dynamics of his material and his process: the viscosity of the paint, the speed and direction of its impact upon the canvas, its interaction with other layers of pigment. The result is a surface so alive, so sensuously rich, that all earlier painting looks pallid in comparison. But when he releases the forces within the paint by giving it a momentum of its own—or, if you will, by "aiming" it at the canvas instead of "carrying" it on the tip of his brush—Pollock does not simply "let go" and leave the rest to chance. He is himself the ultimate source of energy for these forces, and he "rides" them as a cowboy might ride a wild horse, in a frenzy of psychophysical action. He does not always stay in the saddle, yet the exhilaration of this contest, which strains

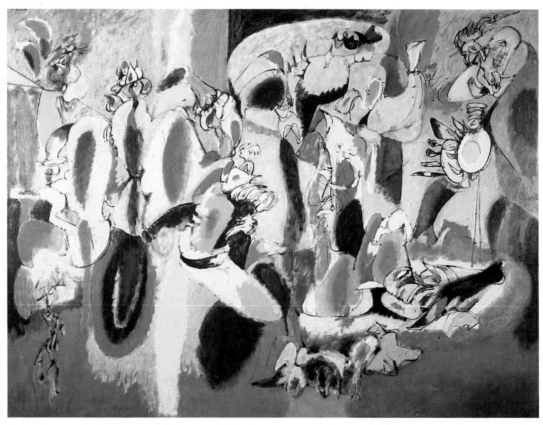

1034. ARSHILE GORKY. *THE LIVER IS THE COCK'S COMB.* 1944.
Oil on canvas, 73¼×98″ (186×249 cm). The Albright-Knox
Art Gallery, Buffalo, New York. Gift of Seymour H. Knox, 1956

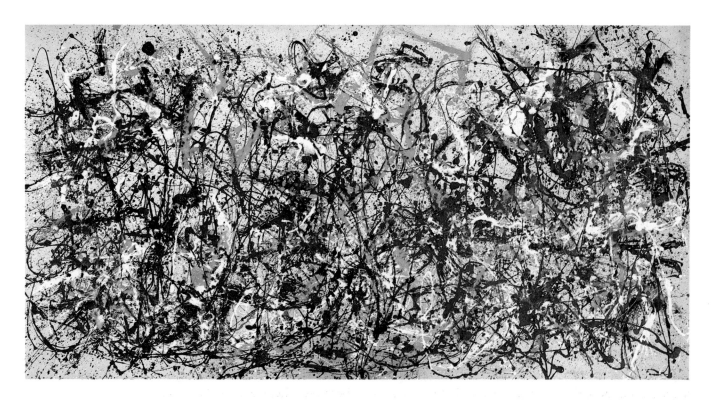

1035. (above) JACKSON POLLOCK
AUTUMNAL RHYTHM: NUMBER 30, 1950.
Oil on canvas, 8'8"×17'3"
(2.66×5.25 m).
The Metropolitan Museum of Art,
New York. George A. Hearn Fund

1036. (right) LEE KRASNER
CELEBRATION. 1959–60.
Oil on canvas, 7'8¼"×16'4½" (2.3×5 m).
Private collection.
Courtesy Robert Miller Gallery, New York

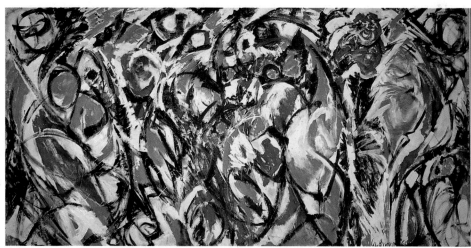

every fiber of his being, is well worth the risk. Our simile, though crude, points up the main difference between Pollock and his predecessors: his total commitment to the *act* of painting. Hence his preference for huge canvases that provide a "field of combat" large enough for him to paint not merely with his arms, but with the motion of his whole body.

The term "Action Painting" conveys its essence far better than does Abstract Expressionism. To those who complain that Pollock was not sufficiently in control of his medium, we reply that this loss is more than offset by a gain—the new continuity and expansiveness of the creative process that gave his work its distinctive mid–twentieth-century stamp. Pollock's drip technique, however, was not in itself essential to Action Painting, and he stopped using it in 1953.

KRASNER. Lee Krasner (1908–1984), who was married to Pollock, never abandoned the brush. Although Krasner and Pollock clearly influenced each other, she struggled to establish her artistic identity, and emerged from his long shadow only after undergoing several changes in direction and destroying much of her early work. After Pollock's death, she succeeded in doing what he had been attempting to do for the last three years of his life: to reintroduce the figure into Abstract Expressionism while retaining its automatic handwriting. The potential had always been there in Pollock's work; in *Autumnal Rhythm*, we can easily imagine wildly dancing people. In *Celebration* (fig. 1036), Krasner defines these nascent shapes from within the tangled network of lines by using the broad gestures of Action Painting to suggest human forms without actually depicting them.

DE KOONING. The work of Willem De Kooning (born 1904), another prominent member of the group and a close friend of Gorky, always retains a link with the world of images, whether or not it has a recognizable subject. In some paintings, such as *Woman II* (fig. 1037), the image emerges from the jagged welter of brushstrokes as insistently as it does in Rouault's *Head of Christ* (see fig. 990). What De Kooning has in common with Pollock is the furious energy of the process of painting, the sense of risk, of a challenge successfully—but barely—met.

Expressionism in Europe

Action Painting marked the international coming-of-age for American art. The movement had a powerful impact on European art, which in those years had nothing to show of com-

parable force and conviction. One French artist, however, was of such prodigal originality as to constitute a movement all by himself: Jean Dubuffet, whose first exhibition soon after the Liberation electrified—and antagonized—the art world of Paris.

DUBUFFET. As a young man Dubuffet (1901–1985) had formal instruction in painting, but he responded to none of the various trends he saw around him nor to the art of the museums; all struck him as divorced from real life, and he turned to other pursuits. Only in middle age did he experience the breakthrough that permitted him to discover his creative gifts: he suddenly realized that for him true art had to come from outside the ideas and traditions of the artistic elite, and he found inspiration in the art of children and of the insane. The distinction between "normal" and "abnor-

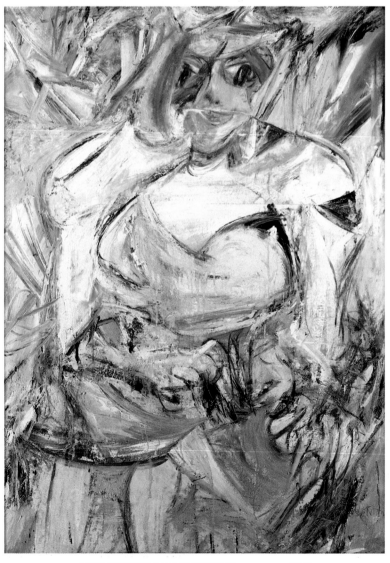

1037. WILLEM DE KOONING. *WOMAN II.* 1952.
Oil on canvas, 59×43″ (150×109.3 cm).
Collection, The Museum of Modern Art, New York.
Gift of Mrs. John D. Rockefeller 3rd

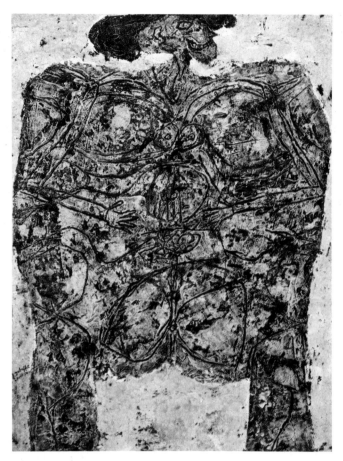

1038. JEAN DUBUFFET. *LE MÉTAFISYX (CORPS DE DAMES)*.
1950. 45¾ × 35¼″ (116.3 × 89.7 cm).
Private collection

mal" struck him as no more tenable than established notions of "beauty" and "ugliness." Not since Marcel Duchamp (see page 724) had anyone ventured so radical a critique of the nature of art.

Dubuffet made himself the champion of what he called *l'art brut*, "art-in-the-raw," but he created something of a paradox besides: while extolling the directness and spontaneity of the amateur as against the refinement of professional artists, he became a professional artist himself. Duchamp's questioning of established values had led him to cease artistic activity altogether, but Dubuffet became incredibly prolific, second only to Picasso in output. Compared with Paul Klee, who had first utilized the style of children's drawings (see pages 732–33), Dubuffet's art is "raw" indeed; its stark immediacy, its explosive, defiant presence, are the opposite of the older painter's formal discipline and economy of means. Did Dubuffet perhaps fall into a trap of his own making? If his work merely imitated the *art brut* of children and the insane, would not these self-chosen conventions limit him as much as those of the artistic elite?

We may be tempted to think so at our first sight of *Le Métafisyx* (fig. 1038) from his *Corps de Dames* series—even De Kooning's wildly distorted *Woman II* (fig. 1037) seems gentle when matched against this shocking assault on our inherited sensibilities. The paint is as heavy and opaque as a rough coating of plaster, and the lines articulating the blocklike body are scratched into this surface like graffiti made by an untrained hand. But appearances can deceive; the fury and concentration of Dubuffet's attack should convince us that his demonic female is not "something any child can do." In an eloquent statement the artist has explained the purpose of images such as this: "The female body . . . has long . . . been associated with a very specious notion of beauty which I find miserable and most depressing. Surely I am for beauty, but not that one . . . I intend to sweep away everything we have been taught to consider—without question—as grace and beauty [and to] substitute another and vaster beauty, touching all objects and beings, not excluding the most despised . . . I would like people to look at my work as an enterprise for the rehabilitation of scorned values, and . . . a work of ardent celebration."

APPEL. *L'art brut* and Abstract Expressionism provided the mainsprings for the COBRA group in Denmark, Belgium, and Holland, which took its name from Copenhagen, Brussels, and Amsterdam, the capitals of those countries. The Dutch artist Karel Appel (born 1921), one of the group's co-founders, soon distinguished himself as the finest pure

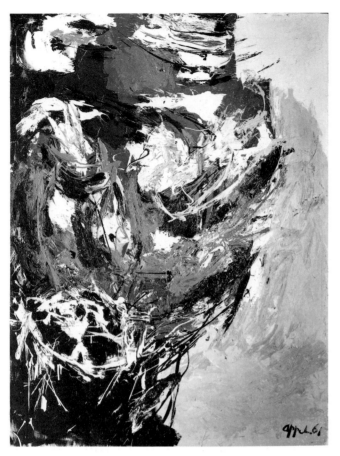

1039. KAREL APPEL. *BURNED FACE.* 1961.
9'10"×6'6¾" (3×2 m). Private collection

painter of his generation in post-war Europe. To the subject matter of Dubuffet he added the slashing brushwork and vivid colors of De Kooning.

In the late 1950s and early 1960s, after several extended visits to the United States, his palette became even more sonorous, the texture more sensuous, and the space more complex, the results of being directly exposed to the Action Painters and inspired by jazz musicians. *Burned Face* (fig. 1039), one of the personages that inhabit Appel's work from that period, is an explosion of color applied with a brilliant technique that at first hides the figural elements lurking within the painting. In maintaining the importance of content while thoroughly integrating it with the style of Abstract Expressionism, Appel established a precedent which was followed by many other European artists, as well as by a number of American painters who have become preoccupied with the same problem.

BACON. The English artist Francis Bacon (1909–1992) is allied not with Abstract Expressionism, though he is clearly related to it, but with the Expressionist tradition. For his power to transmute sheer anguish into visual form he has no equal among twentieth-century artists unless it be Rouault (see pages 712–13). Bacon often derived his imagery from other artists, freely combining several sources while transforming them so as to infuse them with new meaning. *Head Surrounded by Sides of Beef* (fig. 1040) reflects Bacon's obsession with Velásquez' *Pope Innocent X* (compare fig. 798),

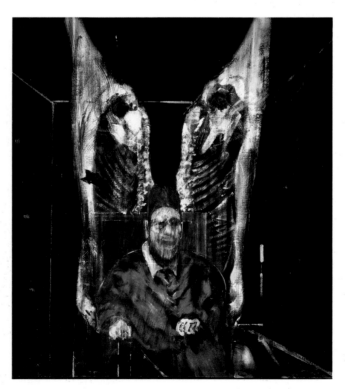

1040. FRANCIS BACON. *HEAD SURROUNDED BY SIDES OF BEEF.*
1954. Oil on canvas, 50¾×48" (129×122 cm).
The Art Institute of Chicago. Harriott A. Fox Fund

1041. MARK ROTHKO. *OCHRE AND RED ON RED.* 1954.
Oil on canvas, 7'8⅝"×5'3¾" (2.35×1.62 m).
The Phillips Collection, Washington, D.C.

a picture that haunted him for some years. It is, of course, no longer Innocent X we see here but a screaming ghost, inspired by a scene from Sergei Eisenstein's film *Alexander Nevsky*, that is materializing out of a black void in the company of two luminescent sides of beef taken from a painting by Rembrandt. Knowing the origin of the canvas does not help us to understand it, however. Nor does comparison with earlier works such as Grünewald's *The Crucifixion*, Fuseli's *Nightmare*, Ensor's *The Intrigue*, or Munch's *The Scream* (see figs. 710, 876, 957, and 958), which are its antecedents. Bacon was a gambler, a taker of risks, in real life as well as in the way he worked; he competed with Velázquez here, but on his own terms, which were to set up an almost unbearable tension between the shocking violence of his vision and the luminous beauty of his brushwork. What he sought were images that, in his own words, "unlock the deeper possibilities of sensation."

Color Field Painting

By the late 1940s, a number of artists began to transform Action Painting into the style called Color Field Painting, in which the canvas is stained with thin, translucent color washes. These may be oil or even ink, but the favored mate-

rial quickly became acrylic, a plastic suspended in a polymer resin, which can be thinned with water so that it flows freely.

ROTHKO. In the mid-1940s Mark Rothko (1903–1970) worked in a style derived from Gorky, yet within less than a decade he subdued the aggressiveness of Action Painting so completely that his pictures breathe the purest contemplative stillness. *Ochre and Red on Red* (fig. 1041) consists of two rectangles with blurred edges—one a rich yellow ochre, the other a clear red—on a dark red ground. The canvas is very large, over seven and one-half feet tall, and the thin washes of paint permit the texture of the cloth to be seen throughout. But to use such bare factual terms to describe what we see hardly touches the essence of the work, or the reasons for its mysterious power to move us. These are to be found in the delicate equilibrium of the shapes, their strange interdependence, the subtle variations of hue (note how the pink "halo" around the lower rectangle seems to immerse it in the red ground, while the yellow rectangle stands out more assertively in front of the red). Not every beholder responds to the works of this withdrawn, introspective artist; for those who do, the experience is akin to a trancelike rapture.

FRANKENTHALER. The stained canvas was also pioneered by Helen Frankenthaler (born 1928), who was inspired by Rothko's example as early as 1952. In *The Bay* (fig. 1042) Frankenthaler uses the same biomorphic forms basic to early Action Painting but eliminates the personal handwriting found in the brushwork of Gorky and De Kooning, with results that are at once more lyrical, more decorative, and just as impressive.

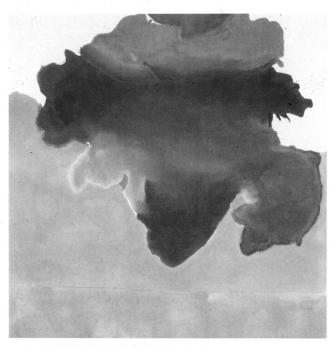

1042. HELEN FRANKENTHALER. *THE BAY.* 1963.
Acrylic on canvas, 6'8¾"×6'9¾" (2.1×2.1 m).
The Detroit Institute of Arts.
Gift of Dr. and Mrs. Hilbert H. DeLawter

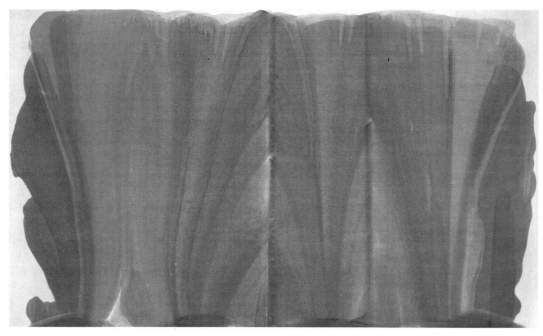

1043. MORRIS LOUIS. *BLUE VEIL.* 1958–59. Acrylic resin paint
on canvas, 8′4½″×12′5″ (2.55×3.75 m).
Fogg Art Museum, Harvard University, Cambridge, Massachusetts.
Gift of Lois Orswell and Gifts for Special Uses Fund

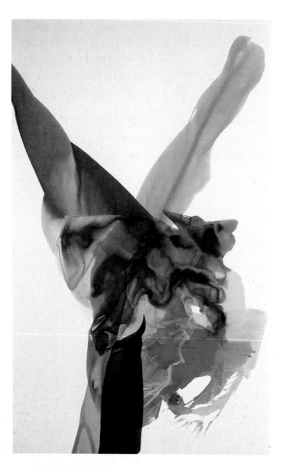

1044. PAUL JENKINS. *PHENOMENA ASTRAL SIGNAL.* 1964.
Acrylic on canvas, 9′8″×6′ (2.9×1.8 m).
Collection Mr. and Mrs. Harry W. Anderson, New York

LOUIS. Among the most gifted of the Color Field painters was Morris Louis (1912–1962). The successive veils of color in *Blue Veil* (fig. 1043) appear to have been "floated on" without visible marks of the brush, mysteriously beautiful like the aurora borealis. It is their harmonious interaction, their delicately shifting balance, that give the picture enduring appeal.

JENKINS. Other artists, such as Paul Jenkins (born 1923), have developed distinctive variations on the theme of Color Field Painting. In *Phenomena Astral Signal* (fig. 1044) the liquid medium has been made to flow in currents of varying speed and density. The resulting veils of color may be gossamer-thin or have the rich depth of stained glass. No spattering, no dribbling betrays the painter's "action"; the forces that give rise to these shapes seem to be of the same kind as those governing the cloud formations in a windswept sky and the pattern of veins in a leaf.

Late Abstract Expressionism

Many artists who came to maturity in the 1950s turned away from Action Painting altogether in favor of hard-edge painting.

KELLY. *Red Blue Green* (fig. 1045) by Ellsworth Kelly (born 1923), an early leader of this tendency, abandons Rothko's impressionistic softness. Instead, flat areas of color are circumscribed within carefully delineated forms as part of the formal investigation of color and design problems for their own sake.

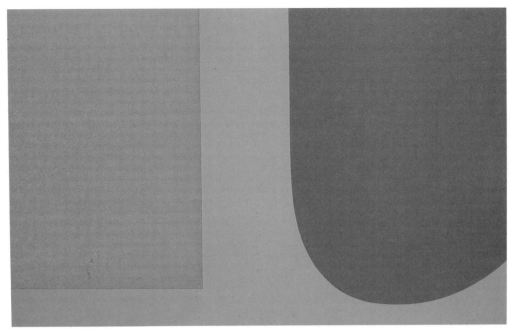

1045. ELLSWORTH KELLY. *RED BLUE GREEN*. 1963.
Oil on canvas, 6′11⅝″ × 11′3⅞″ (2.12 × 3.43 m).
Collection San Diego Museum of Contemporary Art.
Gift of Dr. and Mrs. J. M. Farris

STELLA. The brilliant and precocious Frank Stella (born 1936), having conceived an early enthusiasm for Mondrian, soon evolved a non-figurative style that was even more self-contained; unlike Mondrian (see page 729), Stella did not concern himself with the vertical-horizontal balance that relates the older artist's work to the world of nature. Logically enough, he also abandoned the traditional rectangular format, so as to make quite sure that his pictures bore no resemblance to windows. The shape of the canvas had now become an integral part of the design. In one of his largest works, the majestic *Empress of India* (fig. 1046), this shape is determined by the thrust and counterthrust of four huge chevrons, identical in size and shape but sharply differentiated in color and in their relationship to the whole. The paint, moreover, contains powdered metal which gives it an iridescent sheen—yet another way to stress the impersonal precision of the surfaces and to remove the work from any comparison with the "hand-made" look of easel pictures. In fact, to speak of *Empress of India* as a picture seems decidedly awkward. It demands to be called an object, sufficient unto itself.

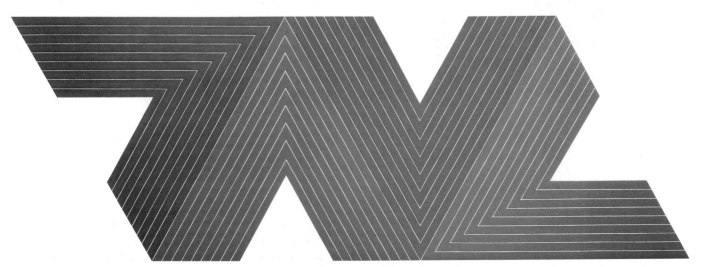

1046. FRANK STELLA. *EMPRESS OF INDIA*. 1965.
Metallic powder in polymer emulsion on shaped canvas, 6′5″ × 18′8″ (1.9 × 5.7 m).
Collection, The Museum of Modern Art, New York. Gift of S. I. Newhouse, Jr.

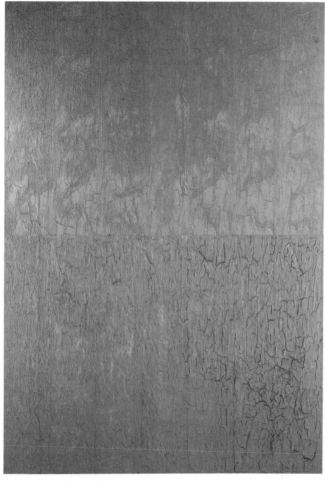

1047. WILLIAM T. WILLIAMS. *BATMAN*. 1979. Acrylic on canvas, 80 × 60″ (203.2 × 152.4 cm). Collection the artist

WILLIAMS. The legacy of the Expressionists can still be seen in the work of William T. Williams (born 1942). Williams is a member of the lyrical Expressionists from the early 1970s whose contribution has been largely overlooked. After a period of intense self-scrutiny, he developed the sophisticated technique seen in *Batman* (fig. 1047). His method can be compared to jazz improvisation, a debt that the artist himself has acknowledged. He interweaves his color and brushwork within a clear two-part structure that permits endless variations on the central theme. Although Williams is concerned primarily with the presentation of the encrusted surface, the patterns, light, and space evoke a landscape. Instead of depicting nature, however, the painting uses color and abstraction to capture an evanescent memory of the artist's past.

Williams belongs to the generation of African-Americans born around 1940 who have brought black painting and sculpture to artistic maturity. In the 1920s, the Harlem Renaissance had produced a cultural revival that unfortunately was short-lived, its promise dashed by the economic catastrophe of the Depression. Following World War II, however, African-Americans began to attend art schools in growing numbers, at the very time that Abstract Expressionism marked the coming of age of American art. The civil rights movement helped them to establish their artistic identities and to find appropriate styles for expressing them. The turning point proved to be the assassinations of Malcolm X in 1965 and of Martin Luther King, Jr., in 1968, which provoked an outpouring of African-American art.

Since then, these artists have pursued three major tendencies. Mainstream Abstractionists, particularly those of the older generation, tend to be concerned primarily with seeking a personal aesthetic, maintaining that there is no such thing as African-American, or black, art, only good art. Consequently, they have been denounced by activist artists who, stirred by social consciousness as well as by political ideology, have adopted highly expressive representational styles as the means for communicating a distinctive black perspective directly to the people in their communities. Mediating between these two approaches is a very decorative form of art that frequently incorporates African, Caribbean, and sometimes Mexican motifs. No hard-and-fast principles separate these alternatives, and aspects of each have been successfully combined into separate individual styles. Abstraction has nevertheless proved the most fruitful path, for it has opened up avenues of expression that allow the black artist, however private his concerns may be, to achieve a universal, not only an ethnic, appeal.

Op Art

A direction that gathered force in the mid-1950s was the trend known as "Op Art" because of its concern with optics (that is, the physical and psychological process of vision). Op Art is devoted primarily to optical illusions. Needless to say, all representational art from the Old Stone Age onward has been involved with optical illusion in one sense or another. What is new about Op Art is that it is rigorously non-representational: it evolved partly from hard-edge abstraction, although its ancestry can be traced back still further to Mondrian (see page 729). At the same time, it seeks to extend the realm of optical illusion in every possible way by taking advantage of the new materials and processes constantly supplied by science, including the latest: laser technology. Much Op Art consists of constructions or "environments" (see page 773) that are dependent for their effect on light and motion and cannot be reproduced satisfactorily in a book.

Because of its reliance on science and technology, Op Art's possibilities appear to be unlimited. The movement nevertheless matured within a decade of its inception and developed little thereafter. The difficulty lies primarily with its subject. Op Art seems overly cerebral and systematic, more akin to the sciences than to the humanities. And although Op Art's effects are undeniably fascinating, they encompass a relatively narrow range of concerns that lie for the most part outside the mainstream of modern art. Only a handful of artists have enriched it with the variety and expressiveness necessary to make it a viable tradition.

VASARELY. Op Art's present development stems largely from the work of Victor Vasarely (born 1908), a Hungarian long domiciled in France, who has been its chief theoretician as well as its most inventive practitioner. Much of his work is in stark black-and-white, such as the large canvas *Vega* (fig. 1048), named after the brightest star in the Lyra constellation. It is a huge checkerboard whose regularity has been disturbed by bending the lines that make the squares. But since many of these squares have been subjected to distortion, their sizes vary considerably. As a consequence, no matter what our viewing distance, our eyes receive contradictory data. The picture thus practically forces us to move back and forth, and as we do so, the field itself seems to move, expanding, undulating, contracting. If *Vega* were a three-dimensional object, the variety of effects would be greater still.

ANUSZKIEWICZ. Op Art, then, involves the beholder with the work of art in a truly novel, dynamic way. Josef Albers, who came to America after 1933, when Hitler closed the Bauhaus school at Dessau (see page 781), became the founding father of another, more austere kind of Op Art based on subtle color relations among simple geometric shapes. His gifted pupil Richard Anuszkiewicz (born 1930) developed his art by relaxing Albers' self-imposed restrictions. In *Entrance to Green* (fig. 1049), the ever-decreasing series of rectangles creates a sense of infinite recession toward the center; this is counterbalanced by the color pattern, which brings the center close to us by the gradual shift from cool

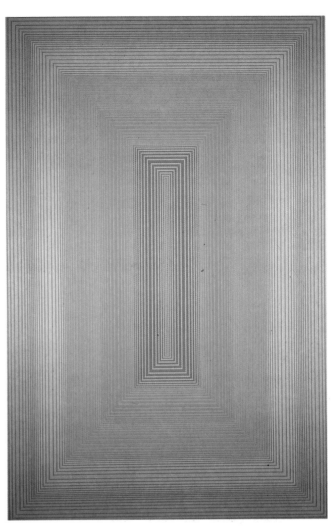

1049. RICHARD ANUSZKIEWICZ. *ENTRANCE TO GREEN.*
1970. Acrylic on canvas, 9′×6′ (2.74×1.83 m).
Collection the artist

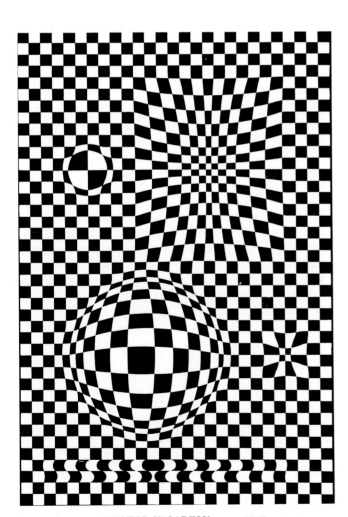

1048. VICTOR VASARELY. *VEGA.* 1957.
77×51″ (195.6×129.5 cm). Collection the artist

to warm tones as we move inward from the periphery. Surprising for such an avowedly abstract work is its expressive intensity. The resonance of the colors within the strict geometry heightens the optical push-pull, producing an almost mystical power. The painting can be likened to a modern icon, capable of providing a deeply moving experience to those attuned to its vision.

Pop Art

Other artists who made a name for themselves in the mid-1950s rediscovered what the layman continued to take for granted despite all efforts to persuade otherwise: that a picture is not "essentially a flat surface covered with colors" (as Maurice Denis had insisted) but an image wanting to be recognized. If art was by its very nature representational, then the modern movement, from Manet to Pollock, was based on a fallacy, no matter how impressive its achievements. Could it be that painting had been on a kind of voluntary starvation diet for the past hundred years, feeding upon itself rather than on the world around us? Wasn't it time to give in to the

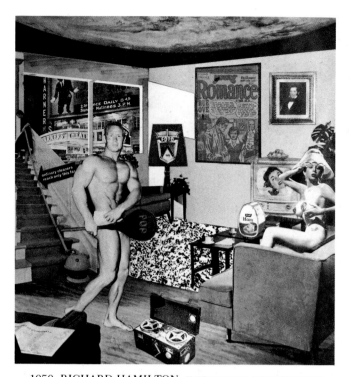

1050. RICHARD HAMILTON. *JUST WHAT IS IT THAT MAKES TODAY'S HOME SO DIFFERENT, SO APPEALING?* 1956. Collage, 10¼ × 9¾″ (26 × 24.8 cm). Kunsthalle Tübingen. Sammlung Zundel

"image-hunger" thus built up—a hunger from which the public at large had never suffered, since its demand for images was abundantly supplied by photography, advertising, magazine illustrations, and comic strips?

The artists who felt this way seized upon these products of commercial art catering to popular taste. Here, they realized, was an essential aspect of our century's visual environment that had been entirely disregarded as vulgar and anti-aesthetic by the representatives of "highbrow" culture, a presence that cried out to be examined. Only Marcel Duchamp and some of the Dadaists, with their contempt for all orthodox opinion, had dared to penetrate this realm (see page 730). It was they who now became the patron saints of "Pop Art," as the new movement came to be called.

HAMILTON. Pop Art actually began in London in the mid-1950s with the Independent Group of artists and intellectuals. They were fascinated by the impact on British life of the American mass media, which had been flooding England ever since the end of World War II. The first work that can be called an unequivocal statement of Pop Art was a small collage (fig. 1050) made in 1956 by Richard Hamilton (born 1922) a follower of Marcel Duchamp, which already incorporates most of the themes that were taken up by later artists.

It is not surprising that the new art had a special appeal for America, and that it reached its fullest development there during the following decade. In retrospect, Pop Art in the

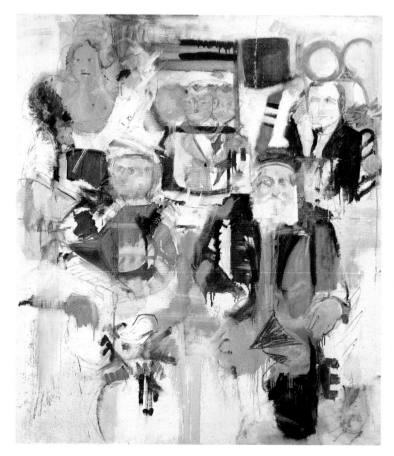

1051. LARRY RIVERS. *EUROPE II.* 1956. Oil on canvas, 54×48″ (137.1×121.9 cm). Private collection

1052. Photograph of great uncle and cousins of Larry Rivers in Poland. c. 1928

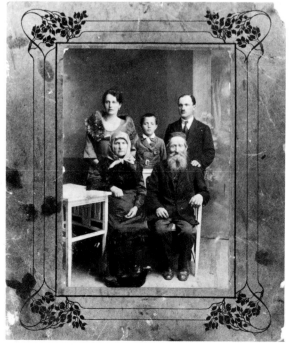

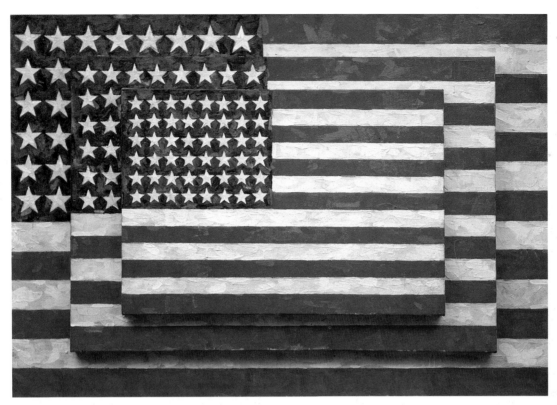

1053. JASPER JOHNS. *THREE FLAGS*. 1958. Encaustic on
canvas, 30⅞×45½×5″ (78.4×115.6×12.7 cm).
Collection, Whitney Museum of American Art, New York

United States was an expression of the optimistic spirit of the 1960s that began with the election of John F. Kennedy and ended at the height of the Vietnam war. Unlike Dada, Pop Art was not motivated by despair or disgust at contemporary civilization; it viewed commercial culture as its raw material, an endless source of pictorial subject matter, rather than as an evil to be attacked. Nor did Pop Art share Dada's aggressive attitude toward the established values of modern art.

RIVERS. The transition from Action Painting to Pop Art in the mid-1950s may be seen in *Europe II* (fig. 1051) by Larry Rivers (born 1923). With its energetic gestures of the brush, its boldly abbreviated shapes, it still speaks a language akin to that of De Kooning. At the same time, however, we sense that the picture is *about* something, that it has been built on an older image that keeps asserting itself underneath. In this instance we happen to know the image: a photograph taken of members of the artist's family in Poland a generation earlier (fig. 1052). Even if we did not know the specific source, we would recognize its kind, for such frontal, stiffly posed pictures have been made ever since photography was invented and form part of everyone's family album. Rivers has taken this visual commonplace seriously; he is moved by its

solemn air commemorating some special occasion, now long forgotten, that momentarily brought these people together. In his painting the group has begun to dissolve, the divergent personalities to regain their separateness; the family icon is about to fall apart. Yet it remains a meaningful whole, a shared experience made new by the painter's intense scrutiny of it.

JOHNS. The work of Jasper Johns (born 1930), one of the pioneers of Pop Art in America, raises questions that go beyond the boundaries of the movement (see page 67). Johns began by painting, meticulously and with great precision, such familiar objects as flags, targets, numerals, and maps (see fig. 26). His *Three Flags* (fig. 1053) presents an intriguing problem: just what is the difference between image and reality? We instantly recognize the Stars and Stripes, but if we try to define what we actually see here, we find that the answer eludes us. These flags behave "unnaturally"—instead of waving or flopping they stand at attention, as it were, rigidly aligned with each other in a kind of reverse perspective. Yet there is movement of another sort: the reds, whites, and blues are not areas of solid color but subtly modulated. Can we really say, then, that this is an image of three flags? Clearly, no such flags can exist anywhere except in the

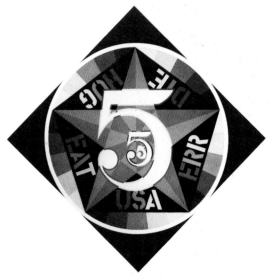

1054. ROBERT INDIANA. *THE DEMUTH FIVE.* 1963.
Oil on composition board, 63″ (160 cm) square.
Collection Mr. and Mrs. Robert C. Scull, New York

artist's head. And we begin to marvel at the picture as a feat of the imagination—probably the last thing we expected to do when we first looked at it.

INDIANA. Revolutionary though it was, Johns' use of flags, numerals, and similar elements as pictorial themes had to some extent been anticipated thirty years before by another American painter, Charles Demuth, in such pictures as *I Saw the Figure 5 in Gold* (fig. 1017). That the canvas was an ancestor of Pop Art is attested to by Robert Indiana (born 1928), who pays homage to it in *The Demuth Five* (fig. 1054). Here, however, the format has been changed to that of a highway sign connoting danger: the numerals have been superimposed on a five-pointed star suggestive of a sheriff's badge, and the pentagonal field behind the star (a reference to the Pentagon in Washington?) carries five "commands" in big stenciled letters—an indictment of American society in capsule form. Such bitter messages are rare in Pop Art.

LICHTENSTEIN. Roy Lichtenstein (born 1923), in contrast, has seized upon comic strips—or, more precisely, upon the standardized imagery of the traditional strips devoted to violent action and sentimental love, rather than those bearing the stamp of an individual creator. His paintings, such as *Girl at Piano* (fig. 1055), are greatly enlarged copies of single frames, including the balloons, the impersonal, simplified black outlines, and the dots used for printing colors on cheap paper.

These pictures are perhaps the most paradoxical in the entire field of Pop Art: unlike any other paintings past or present, they cannot be accurately reproduced in this book, for they then become indistinguishable from the comic strip on which they are based. Enlarging a design meant for an area about six inches square to one no less than 3,264 square inches must have given rise to a host of formal problems that could be solved only by the most intense scrutiny: how, for example, to draw the girl's nose so it would look "right" in comic-strip terms, or how to space the colored dots so they would have the proper weight in relation to the outlines.

Clearly, our picture is not a mechanical copy, but an interpretation which remains faithful to the spirit of the original only because of the countless changes and adjustments of detail that the artist has introduced. How is it possible for images of this sort to be so instantly recognizable? Why are they so "real" to millions of people? What fascinates Lichtenstein about comic strips—and what he makes us see for the first time—are the rigid conventions of their style, as firmly set and as remote from life as those of Byzantine art.

WARHOL. An artist who seized on this very quality was Andy Warhol (1928–1987), who used it in ironic commentaries on modern society. A former commercial artist, he made the viewer consider the aesthetic qualities of everyday images, such as soup cans, that we readily overlook. He did much the same thing with the subject of death, an obsession of his, in silk-screened pictures of electric chairs and gruesome traffic accidents, which demonstrate that dying has been reduced to a banality by the mass media. Warhol had

1055. ROY LICHTENSTEIN. *GIRL AT PIANO.* 1963.
Magna on canvas, 68 × 48″ (172.7 × 121.9 cm).
Private collection

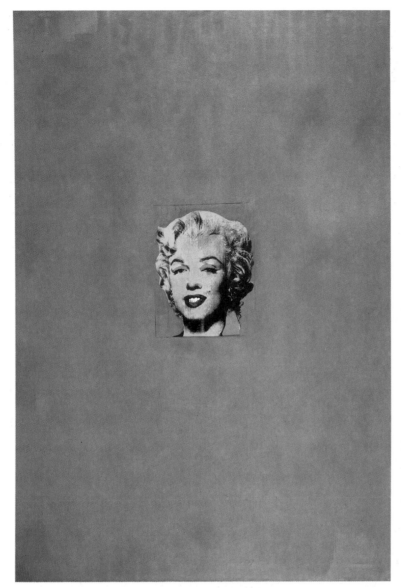

1056. ANDY WARHOL. *GOLD MARILYN MONROE.* 1962.
Synthetic polymer paint, silkscreened, and oil on canvas, 6'11¼"×4'7" (2.1×1.4 m).
Collection, The Museum of Modern Art, New York. Gift of Philip Johnson

an uncanny understanding of how media shape our view of people and events, creating their own reality and larger-than-life figures. He became a master at manipulating the media to project a public persona that disguised his true character. These themes come together in his image of Marilyn Monroe (fig. 1056). Set against a gold background, like a Byzantine icon, she becomes a modern-day Madonna (can it be a co-incidence that a Marilyn look-alike singer has taken Madonna as her stage name?). Yet Warhol conveys a sense of the tragic personality that lay behind the famous movie star's glamorous façade. The color, lurid and off-register like a sleazy magazine reproduction's, makes us realize that she has been reduced to a cheap commodity. Through mechanical means, she is rendered as impersonal as the Virgin that stares out from the thousands of icons produced by hack artists through the ages.

Photorealism

Although Pop Art was sometimes referred to as "the new realism," the term hardly seems to fit the painters we have discussed. They are, to be sure, sharply observant of their sources; but the material chosen—flags, numerals, lettering, signs, badges, comic strips—is itself rather abstract. A more recent offshoot of Pop Art is the trend called Photorealism because of its fascination with camera images. Photographs had been utilized by nineteenth-century painters soon after the "pencil of nature" was invented—one of the earliest to do so, surprisingly, was Delacroix—but they were no more than a convenient substitute for reality. When Larry Rivers used an old family photograph (fig. 1052), he freely translated the camera image into the personal idiom of his brush. For the Photorealists, in contrast, the photograph itself is the reality on which they build their pictures.

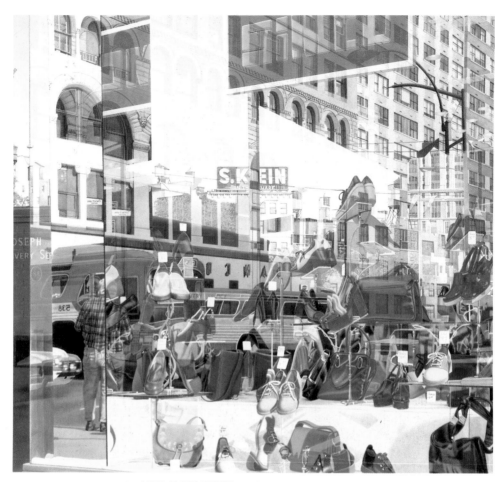

1057. DON EDDY. *NEW SHOES FOR H.* 1973–74.
Acrylic on canvas, 44×48″ (111.7×121.9 cm).
The Cleveland Museum of Art. Purchased with a grant
from the National Endowment for the Arts, matched by gifts from
members of The Cleveland Society for Contemporary Art

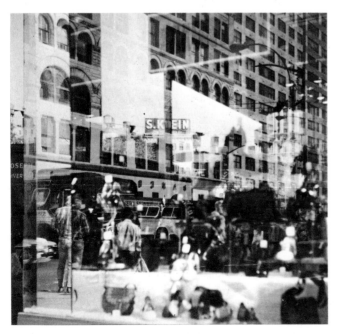

1058. DON EDDY. Photograph for *NEW SHOES FOR H.* 1973–74.
The Cleveland Museum of Art. Gift of the artist

EDDY. At its best, their work, as in *New Shoes for H* by Don Eddy (born 1944), has a visual complexity that challenges the most acute observer. Eddy grew up in southern California; as a teenager he learned to do fancy paint jobs on cars and surfboards with an air brush, then worked as a photographer for several years. When he became a painter, he used both earlier skills. In preparing *New Shoes for H* (fig. 1057), Eddy took a series of pictures of the window display of a shoe store on Union Square in Manhattan. One photograph (fig. 1058) served as the basis for the painting. What intrigued him, clearly, was the way glass filters (and transforms) everyday reality. Only a narrow strip along the left-hand edge offers an unobstructed view: everything else—shoes, bystanders, street traffic, buildings—is seen through one or more layers of glass, all of them at oblique angles to the picture surface. The combined effect of these panes—displacement, distortion, and reflection—is the transformation of a familiar scene into a dazzlingly rich and novel visual experience.

When we compare the painting with the photograph, we realize that they are related in much the same way as Lichtenstein's *Girl at Piano* (fig. 1055) is to the comic-strip

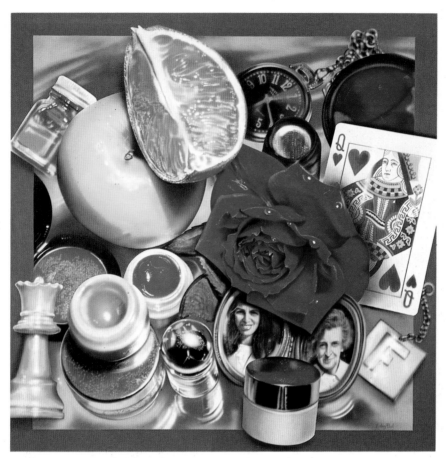

1059. AUDREY FLACK. *QUEEN*. 1975–76. Acrylic on canvas, 6'8" (2.03 m) square.
Private collection. Courtesy Louis K. Meisel Gallery, New York

frame from which it derives. Unlike Eddy's photograph, his canvas shows everything in uniformly sharp focus, articulating details lost in the shadows; most important of all, he gives pictorial coherence to the scene through a brilliant color scheme whose pulsating rhythm plays over the entire surface. At the time he painted *New Shoes for H*, color had become newly important in Eddy's thinking; the H of the title pays homage to Henri Matisse and to Hans Hofmann, the latter a painter linked to Abstract Expressionism whom Eddy had come to admire.

Photorealism was part of a general tendency that marked American painting in the 1970s: the resurgence of realism. It has taken on a wide range of themes and techniques, from the most personal to the most detached, depending on the artist's vision of objective reality and its subjective significance; its flexibility made realism a sensitive vehicle for the feminist movement that came to the fore in the same decade. Beyond the organizing of groups dedicated to a wider recognition for women artists, feminism in art has shown little of the unity that characterizes the social movement. Many feminists, for example, turned to "traditional" women's crafts, particularly textiles, or incorporated crafts into a collage approach known as Pattern and Decoration. In painting, however, the majority have pursued different forms of realism for a variety of ends.

FLACK. Women artists such as Audrey Flack (born 1931) have used realism to explore the world around them and their relation to it from a personal as well as a feminist viewpoint. Like most of Flack's paintings, *Queen* (fig. 1059) is an extended allegory. The queen is the most powerful figure on the chessboard yet she remains expendable in defense of the king. Equally apparent is the meaning inherent to the queen of hearts, but here the card also refers to the passion for gambling in members of Flack's family, who are present in the locket with photos of the artist and her mother. The contrast of youth and age is central to *Queen:* the watch is a traditional emblem of life's brevity, and the dewy rose stands for transience of beauty, which is further conveyed by the makeup on the dressing table. The suggestive shapes of the bud and fruits can also be taken as symbols of feminine sexuality.

Queen is successful not so much for its provocative statement, however, as for its compelling imagery. Flack creates a purely artistic reality by superimposing two separate photographs. Critical to the illusion is the gray border, which acts as a framing device and also establishes the central space and color of the painting. The objects that seem to project from the picture plane are shown in a different perspective from those on the tilted tabletop behind. The picture space is made all the more active by the play of its colors within the neutral gray.

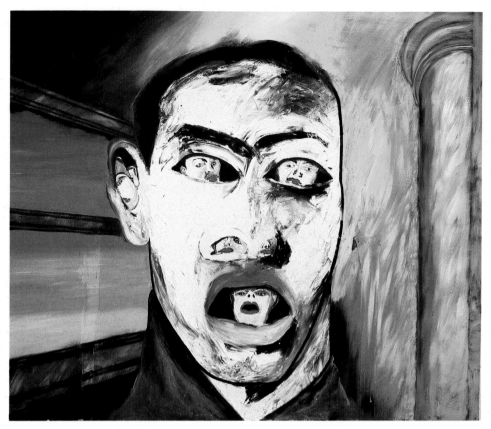

1060. FRANCESCO CLEMENTE. *UNTITLED.* 1983.
Oil and wax on canvas, 6'6"×7'9" (1.98×2.36 m).
Courtesy Thomas Ammann, Zurich

Painting in the 1980s

Art since 1980 has been called Post-Modern. The term itself is anomalous: modernity can never be outdated, because it is simply whatever is contemporary. The word nevertheless suggests the paradoxical nature of Post-Modernism, which seeks out incongruity. Post-Modernism is marked by an abiding skepticism that rejects modernism as an ideal defining twentieth-century culture as we have known it. In challenging tradition, however, Post-Modernism resolutely refuses to define a new meaning or impose an alternative order in its place. It represents a generation consciously *not* in search of its identity. Hence, it is not a coherent movement at all, but a loose collection of tendencies which, all told, reflect a new sensibility.

We are, in a sense, the new Victorians. A century ago, Impressionism underwent a like crisis, from which Post-Impressionism emerged as the direction for the next twenty years. Behind its elaborate rhetoric, Post-Modernism can be seen as a strategem for sorting through the past while making a decisive break with it that will allow new possibilities to emerge. Having received a rich heritage, artists are faced with a wide variety of alternatives. The principal features of the new art are a ubiquitous eclecticism and a bewildering array of styles. Taken together, these pieces provide a jig-saw puzzle of our times. Another indication of the state of flux is the emergence of many traditional European and regional American art centers.

From all the recent ferment, a new direction of art has begun to appear, at least for the time being. Much recent art has been concerned with Appropriation and Deconstruction. Appropriation looks back self-consciously to earlier art, both by imitating previous styles and by taking over specific motifs or even entire images. Artists, of course, have always borrowed from tradition, but rarely so systematically as now. Such plundering is nearly always a symptom of deepening cultural crisis, suggesting bankruptcy. The first sign of this historicism actually occurred in the early 1970s with the widespread use of "Neo-" to describe the latest tendencies. Unbound as it is to any system, Post-Modernism is free not only to adopt earlier imagery but also to radically alter its meaning through Deconstruction by placing it in a new context. The traditional importance assigned to the artist and the object he or she creates is de-emphasized in this approach, which stresses process over content. Hence, Performance Art (which is discussed with sculpture on pages 778–79) is perhaps the most characteristic art form to emerge in the 1980s.

CLEMENTE. The Italian Francesco Clemente (born 1952) is symptomatic in many respects of his artistic generation. His association with the *Arte Povera* ("Poor Art") movement in Italy led him to develop a potent Neo-Expressionism. His career took a decisive turn in 1982 when he decided to come to New York in order "to be where the great painters have been," but he also spends much of his time in India, where he has been inspired by Hinduism. His canvases and wall paintings sometimes have an ambitiousness that can assume the form of allegorical cycles addressed directly to the Italian painters who worked on a grand scale, starting with Giotto. His most compelling works, however, are those having as their subject matter the artist's moods, fantasies, and appetites. Clemente is fearless in recording urges and memories that the rest of us repress. Art becomes for him an act of cathartic necessity that releases, but never resolves, the impulses that assault his acute self-awareness. His self-portraits (fig. 1060) suggest a soul bombarded by drives and sensations that can never be truly enjoyed. Alternately fascinating and repellent, his pictures remain curiously unsensual, yet their expressiveness is riveting. Since his work responds to fleeting states of mind, Clemente utilizes whatever style or medium seems appropriate to capturing the transient phenomena of his inner world. He is unusual among Italians in being influenced heavily by Northern European Symbolism and Expressionism with an occasional reminiscence of Sur-

realism. Here indeed is his vivid nightmare, having the masklike features of Ensor, the psychological terror of Munch, and the haunted vision of De Chirico.

KIEFER. The German artist Anselm Kiefer (born 1945) is the direct heir to Northern Expressionism, but rather than investigating personal moods he confronts moral issues posed by Nazism that have been evaded by other post-war artists in his country. By exploring from a modern perspective the major themes of German Romanticism, he has attempted to reweave the threads broken by history. That tradition, which began as a noble ideal based on a similar longing for the mythical past, ended as a perversion at the hands of Hitler and his followers because it lent itself readily to abuse.

To the Unknown Painter (fig. 1061) is a powerful statement of the human and cultural catastrophe presented by World War II. Conceptually as well as compositionally it was inspired by the paintings of Caspar David Friedrich (see page 646), of which it is a worthy successor. To express the tragic proportions of the Holocaust, Kiefer works on an appropriately epic scale. Painted in jagged strokes of predominantly earth and black tones, the charred landscape is made tangible by the inclusion of pieces of straw. Amid this destruction stands a somber ruin: it is shown in woodcut to proclaim Kiefer's allegiance to the German Renaissance and to Ex-

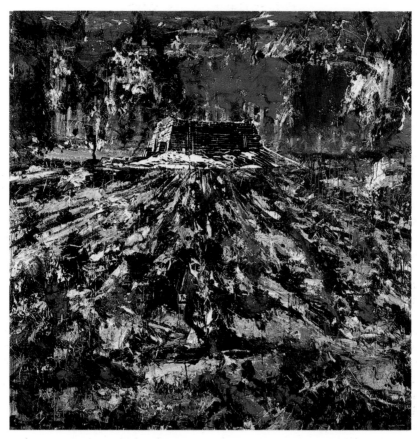

1061. ANSELM KIEFER. *TO THE UNKNOWN PAINTER*. 1983.
Oil, emulsion, woodcut, shellac, latex, and straw on canvas, 9′2″ (2.8 m) square.
Carnegie Museum of Art, Pittsburgh. Richard M. Scaife Fund; A. W. Mellon Acquisition Endowment Fund

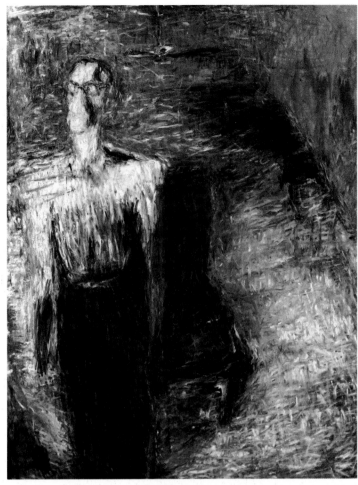

1062. SUSAN ROTHENBERG. *MONDRIAN*. 1983–84.
Oil on canvas, 9'1"×7' (2.8×2.1 m).
Private collection, Courtesy Sperone Westwater Gallery, New York

pressionism. Recalling the tombs and temples of ancient civilizations (see figs. 77 and 109), the fortresslike structure is a suitable monument for heroes. But instead of being dedicated to soldiers who died in combat, it is a memorial to the painters whose art was equally a casualty of Fascism.

ROTHENBERG. Neo-Expressionism has found its most gifted American representative in Susan Rothenberg (born 1945). In the mid-1970s the contours of the horse seen in profile provided a thematic focus and personal emblem for her highly formal paintings, but toward the end of the decade she turned to more emotive subjects. The sheer beauty of the surface in *Mondrian* (fig. 1062) belies the intensity of her vision. The figure emerges from the welter of feathery brushstrokes like an apparition from a nightmare. The face, which bears Mondrian's unmistakable features, conjures up a vision of madness. We have seen its like before in Bacon's *Head Surrounded by Sides of Beef* (fig. 1040). The picture,

then, announces Rothenberg's allegiance to Expressionism and constitutes a highly charged commentary on Mondrian, whose rigorous discipline is so antithetical to her painterly freedom.

MURRAY. Neo-Expressionism has a counterpart in Neo-Abstraction, which has yielded less impressive results thus far. The greatest success in the Neo-Abstractionist vein has been achieved by those artists seeking to infuse their formal concerns with the personal meaning of Neo-Expressionism. Elizabeth Murray (born 1940) has emerged since 1980 as the leader of this cross-over style in America. *More Than You Know* (fig. 1063) makes a fascinating comparison with Audrey Flack's *Queen* (fig. 1059), for both are replete with autobiographical references. While it is at once simpler and more abstract than Flack's, Murray's composition seems about to fly apart under the pressure of barely contained emotions. The table will remind us of the one in Picasso's

Three Musicians (fig. 1012), a painting she has referred to in other works from the same time. The contradiction between the flattened collage perspective of the table and chair and the allusions to the distorted three-dimensionality of the surrounding room establishes a disquieting pictorial space. The more we look at the painting, the more we begin to realize how eerie it is. Indeed, it seems to radiate an almost unbearable tension. The table threatens to turn into a figure surmounted by a skull-like head, which moves with the explosive force seen in Picasso's *Three Dancers* (fig. 1014). What was Murray thinking of? She has said that the room reminds her of the place where she sat with her ill mother. At the same time, the demonic face was inspired by Munch's *The Scream* (fig. 958), while the sheet of paper recalls Vermeer's paintings of women reading letters (fig. 794), which to her express a combination of serenity and anxiety.

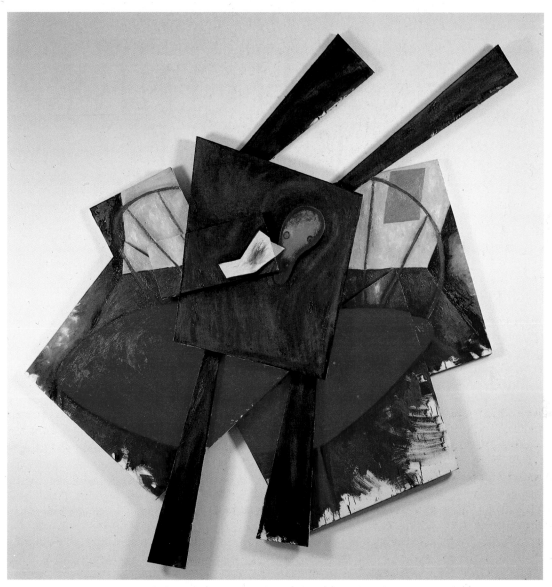

1063. ELIZABETH MURRAY. *MORE THAN YOU KNOW.* 1983.
Oil on ten canvases, 9'3"×9'×8" (281.9×274.3×20.3 cm).
The Edward R. Broida Trust,
Courtesy Paula Cooper Gallery, New York

CHAPTER FIVE
TWENTIETH-CENTURY SCULPTURE

SCULPTURE BEFORE 1945

The three main currents we followed in painting before 1945—Expressionism, Abstraction, and Fantasy—may be found also in sculpture. They are present, however, in different measure. While painting has been the richer and more adventurous of the two arts, sculpture has challenged its leadership by often following a separate path of development. For that reason, the parallelism between them should not be overstressed.

BRANCUSI. Expressionism, for instance, is a much less important current in sculpture than in painting—which is rather surprising, since the rediscovery of ethnographic sculpture by the *Fauves* might have been expected to evoke a strong response among sculptors. Only one important sculptor shared in this rediscovery: Constantin Brancusi (1876–1957), a Romanian who came to Paris in 1904. But he was more interested in the formal simplicity and coherence of primitive carvings than in their savage expressiveness: this is evident in *The Kiss* (fig. 1064), executed in 1909 and now placed over a tomb in a Parisian cemetery.

The compactness and self-sufficiency of this group is a radical step beyond Maillol's *Seated Woman* (see fig. 963), to which it is related much as are the *Fauves* to Post-Impressionism. Brancusi has a "genius of omission" not unlike Matisse's; to him, a monument is an upright slab, symmetrical and immobile—a permanent marker, like the steles of the ancients—and he disturbs this basic shape as little as possible. The embracing lovers are differentiated just enough to be separately identifiable, and seem more primeval

than primitive. They are a timeless symbol of generation, innocent and anonymous—the exact opposite of Rodin's *The Kiss* (see fig. 933), where the contrast of flesh and stone mirrors the dualism of guilt and desire.

MOORE. Brancusi's "primevalism" was the starting point of a sculptural tradition that still continues today. It has appealed particularly to English sculptors, as we may see in the early works of Henry Moore (1898–1986); his majestic *Two Forms* of 1936 (fig. 1065) are, as it were, the second-generation offspring of Brancusi's *The Kiss*. More abstract and subtle in shape, they are nevertheless "persons," even though they can be called "images" only in the metaphoric sense. This family group—the forked slab evolved from the artist's studies of the mother-and-child theme—is mysterious and remote like the monoliths of Stonehenge, which greatly impressed the sculptor (see fig. 52). His *Recumbent Figure* (fig. 1066) retains both a classical motif—one thinks of a reclining river god—and a primeval look, as if the forms had resulted from slow erosion over a thousand years. The design of the figure is in complete harmony with the natural striations of the stone.

HEPWORTH. Barbara Hepworth (1903–1975), for long the preeminent woman sculptor of modern times, was closely associated with Moore during the early 1930s; they became leaders of the modern movement in England and influenced one another. Like Moore's, her sculpture had a biological foundation, but it began to change after her marriage to the abstract painter Ben Nicholson (see page 730), her association with the Constructivist Naum Gabo, and her contact in

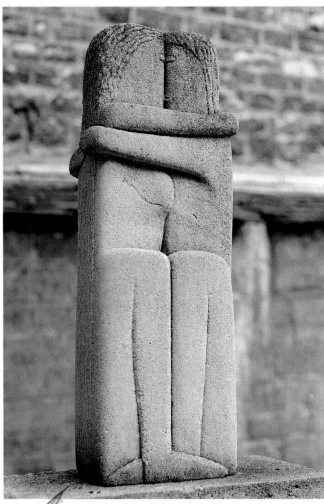

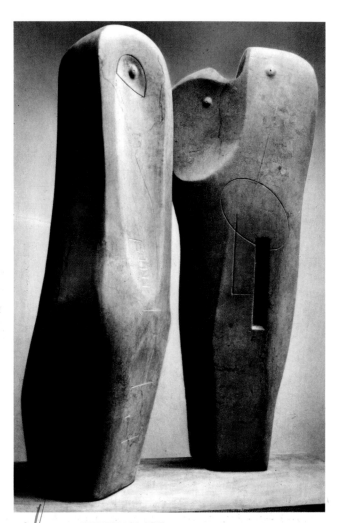

1064. CONSTANTIN BRANCUSI. *THE KISS.* 1909. Stone,
height 35¼″ (89.5 cm). Tomb of T. Rachevskaia,
Montparnasse Cemetery, Paris

1065. HENRY MOORE. *TWO FORMS.* 1936. Stone,
height c. 42″ (106.7 cm). Philadelphia Museum of Art.
Gift of Mrs. H. Gates Lloyd

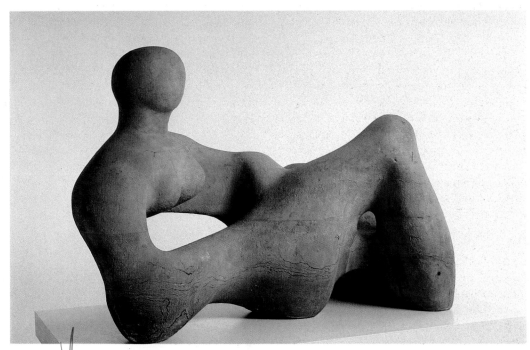

1066. HENRY MOORE. *RECUMBENT FIGURE.* 1938. Green Hornton stone,
length c. 54″ (137.2 cm). The Tate Gallery, London

Paris with Arp (see page 731) and Brancusi. For a time she was practicing several modes at once under these influences. With the beginning of World War II, however, she initiated an individual style that emerged fully in 1943. *Sculpture with Color (Oval Form)* flawlessly synthesizes painting and sculpture, Surrealist biomorphism and organic abstraction, and the molding of space and shaping of mass (fig. 1067). Carved from wood and immaculately finished, Hepworth's sculpture reduces the natural shape of an egg to a timeless ideal that has the lucid perfection of a classical head, yet the elemental expressiveness of the face of a primitive mask (compare fig. 68). The colors accentuate the play between the interior and exterior of the hollowed-out form, the strings seeming to suggest a life force within.

BRANCUSI'S BIRD IN SPACE. Hepworth's egg undoubtedly owes something to Brancusi, although their work is very different in appearance. Brancusi's work had taken another daring step in about 1910, when he began to produce non-representational pieces in marble or metal. (He reserved his "primeval" style for wood and stone.) The former fall into two groups: variations on the egg shape, with such titles as *The Newborn* or *The Beginning of the World*; and soaring, vertical "bird" motifs, (*Bird in Space*, figure 1068, is one of these).

Because he concentrated on two basic forms of such uncompromising simplicity, Brancusi has at times been called the Mondrian of sculpture; this comparison is misleading, however, for Brancusi strove for essences, not for relationships. He was fascinated by the antithesis of life as potential and as kinetic energy—the self-contained perfection of the egg, which hides the mystery of all creation, and the pure dynamics of the creature released from this shell. *Bird in Space* is not the abstract image of a bird; rather, it is flight itself, made visible and concrete. Its disembodied quality is emphasized by the high polish that gives the surface the reflectivity of a mirror, and thus establishes a new continuity between the molded space within and the free space without.

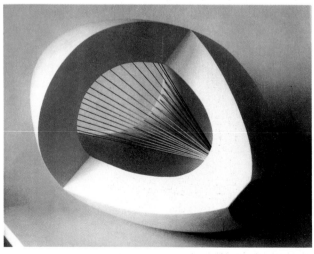

1067. BARBARA HEPWORTH. *SCULPTURE WITH COLOR (OVAL FORM), PALE BLUE AND RED.* 1943. Wood with strings, length 18″ (45.7 cm). Private collection

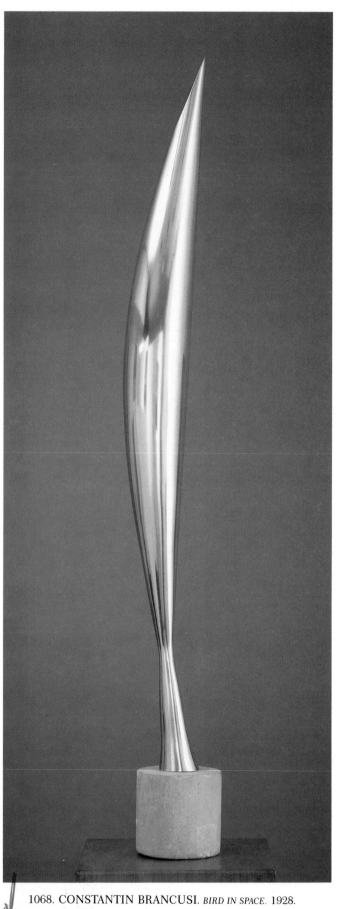

1068. CONSTANTIN BRANCUSI. *BIRD IN SPACE.* 1928. Bronze (unique cast), 54×8½×6½″ (137.2×21.6×16.5 cm). Collection, The Museum of Modern Art, New York. Given anonymously

BOCCIONI. Other sculptors in the first decade of the century were tackling the problem of body-space relationships with the formal tools of Cubism. The running figure entitled *Unique Forms of Continuity in Space* (fig. 1069), by the Futurist Umberto Boccioni (see page 720), is as breathtaking in its complexity as *Bird in Space* is simple. Boccioni has attempted to represent not the human form itself, but the imprint of its motion upon the medium in which it moves; the figure remains concealed behind its "garment" of aerial turbulence. The statue recalls the famous Futurist statement that "the roaring automobile is more beautiful than the Winged Victory," although it obviously owes more to the Winged Victory (the *Nike of Samothrace*, fig. 229) than to the design of motor cars (fins and streamlining, in 1931, were still to come). Or perhaps Boccioni's source of inspiration was closer at hand—he could have seen the work of Niccoló dell'Arca (compare fig. 627).

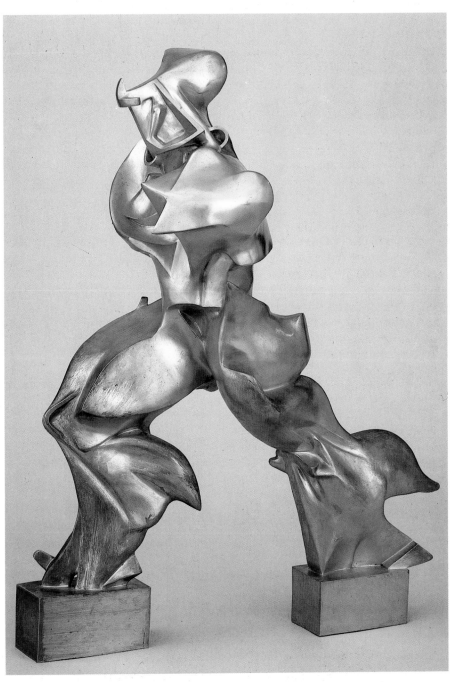

1069. UMBERTO BOCCIONI. *UNIQUE FORMS OF CONTINUITY IN SPACE.*
1913. Bronze (cast 1931), 43⅞×34⅞×15¾″ (111.5×88.6×40 cm).
Collection, The Museum of Modern Art, New York.
Acquired through the Lillie P. Bliss Bequest

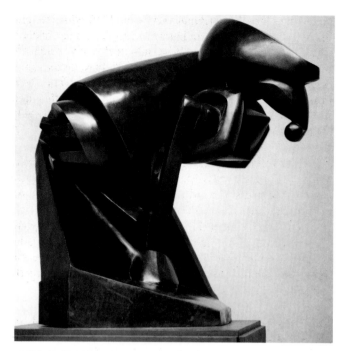

1070. RAYMOND DUCHAMP-VILLON. *THE GREAT HORSE*. 1914.
Bronze, height 39⅜″ (100 cm). The Art Institute of
Chicago. Gift of Miss Margaret Fisher

Revolution temperament of Russia, when great deeds, not great thoughts, were needed.

Cut off from artistic contact with Europe during World War I, Constructivism developed into a uniquely Russian art that was little affected by the return of some of the country's most important artists, such as Kandinsky and Chagall. The Revolution galvanized the modernists, who celebrated the overthrow of the old regime with a creative outpouring throughout Russia. Tatlin's model for a *Monument to the Third International* (fig. 1071) captures the dynamism of the technological utopia envisioned under communism: pure energy is expressed as lines of force that establish new time-space relationships as well. The work also implies a new social structure, for the Constructivists believed in the power of art literally to reshape society. This extraordinary tower revolving at three speeds was conceived on a monumental scale, complete with Communist Party offices; like other such projects, it was wildly impractical in a society still recovering from the ravages of war and revolution and was never built.

Constructivism subsequently proceeded to a Productivist phase, which ignored any contradiction between true artistic creativity and purely utilitarian production. After the move-

DUCHAMP-VILLON. Raymond Duchamp-Villon (1876–1916), an elder brother of Marcel Duchamp, achieved a bolder solution in *The Great Horse* (fig. 1070). He began with abstract studies of the animal, but his final version is an image of "horsepower," wherein the body has become a coiled spring and the legs resemble piston rods. Because of this very remoteness from their anatomical model, these quasi-mechanical shapes have a dynamism that is more persuasive—if less picturesque—than that of Boccioni's figure.

CONSTRUCTIVISM. In Analytic Cubism, we recall, concave and convex were postulated as equivalents; all volumes, whether positive or negative, were "pockets of space." The Constructivists, a group of Russian artists led by Vladimir Tatlin, applied this principle to sculpture and arrived at what might be called three-dimensional collage.

TATLIN. Eventually the final step was taken of making the works free-standing. According to Tatlin (1895–1956) and his followers, these "constructions" were actually four-dimensional: since they implied motion, they also implied time. Suprematism (see page 722) and Constructivism were therefore closely related, and in fact overlapped, for both had their origins in Cubo-Futurism; but they were nonetheless separated by a fundamental difference in approach. For Tatlin, art was not the Suprematists' spiritual contemplation but an active process of formation that was based on material and technique. He believed that each material dictates specific forms that are inherent in it, and that these must be followed if the work of art was to be valid according to the laws of life itself. In the end, Constructivism won out over Suprematism because it was better suited to the post-

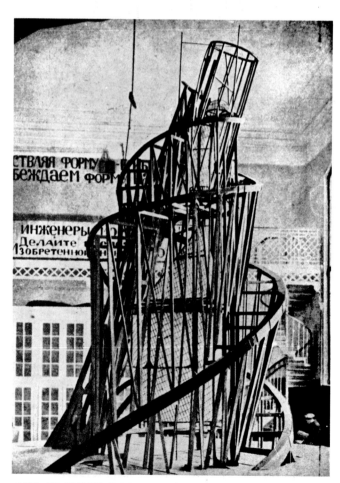

1071. VLADIMIR TATLIN. Project for *MONUMENT TO THE THIRD INTERNATIONAL*. 1919–20. Wood, iron, and glass, height 20′ (6.1 m). Destroyed; contemporary photograph "re-created" the lost original version of 1915 with this one made in 1945. Some of Duchamp's examples consist of combinations of found objects: these "assisted" ready-mades approach the status of constructions or of three-dimensional collage. This technique, later baptized "assemblage" (see pages 770–72), proved to have unlimited possibilities, and numerous younger artists have explored it since, especially in junk-ridden America (see fig. 1086).

SURREALISM. The Surrealist contribution to sculpture is harder to define: it was difficult to apply the theory of "pure psychic automatism" to painting, but still harder to live up to it in sculpture. How indeed could solid, durable materials be given shape without the sculptor being consciously aware of the process? Thus, apart from the devotees of the ready-made, few sculptors were associated with the movement, and the effect produced by those who were cannot be directly compared with Surrealist painting.

GIACOMETTI. One of the exceptions is The Palace at 4 A.M. (fig. 1073), by Alberto Giacometti (1901–1966), a Swiss sculptor and painter who lived in Paris. The materials—wood, glass, wire, and string—suggest Constructivism, but Giacometti's concern is not with structural problems. This airy cage is the three-dimensional equivalent of a Surrealist picture; unlike earlier pieces of sculpture, it creates its own spatial environment that clings to it as though this eerie miniature world were protected from everyday reality by an invisible glass bell. The space thus trapped is mysterious and corrosive, and gnaws away at the forms until only their skeletons are left; and even they, we feel, will disappear before long.

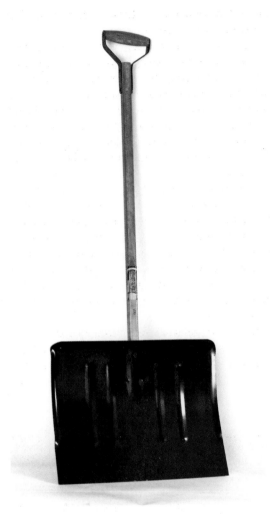

1072. MARCEL DUCHAMP. *IN ADVANCE OF THE BROKEN ARM.* 1945, from the original of 1915. Snow shovel, length 46¾" (121.3 cm). Yale University Art Gallery, New Haven, Connecticut. Gift of Katherine S. Dreier for the Collection Société Anonyme

ment had been suppressed as "bourgeois formalism," some of its members emigrated to the West and joined forces with the Dutch group, *De Stijl* (see page 729).

DADA. As it did in the other arts, Dada uncompromisingly rejected formal discipline in sculpture—perhaps even more so, since only three-dimensional objects could become ready-mades, the sculpture of Dada. Ready-mades are certainly extreme demonstrations of a principle. But the principle itself—that artistic creation depends neither on established rules nor on manual craftsmanship—was an important discovery.

DUCHAMP. Playfulness and spontaneity are the impulses behind the ready-mades of Marcel Duchamp (see pages 724 and 763), which the artist created by shifting the context of the objects from the utilitarian to the aesthetic. He would put his signature, and a provocative title, on ready-made objects such as bottle racks and snow shovels and exhibit them as works of art. *In Advance of the Broken Arm* (fig. 1072) pushed the spirit of ready-mades to a new height; Duchamp

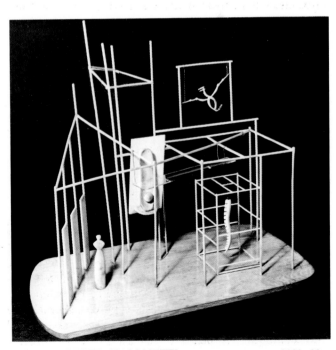

1073. ALBERTO GIACOMETTI. *THE PALACE AT 4 A.M.* 1932–33. Construction in wood, glass, wire, and string, 25×28¼×15¾" (63.5×71.8×40 cm). Collection, The Museum of Modern Art, New York. Purchase

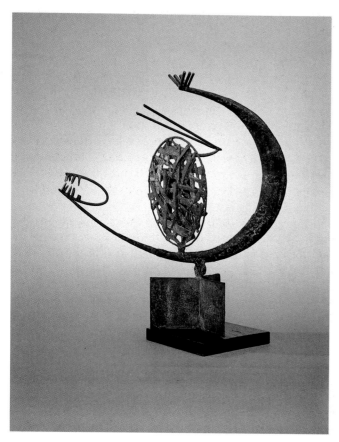

GONZALEZ. Surrealism may also have contributed to the astonishing sculptural imagination of Julio Gonzalez (1872–1942). Trained as a wrought-iron craftsman in his native Catalonia, Gonzalez had come to Paris in 1900. Although he was a friend of both Brancusi and Picasso, he produced little of consequence until the 1930s, when his creative energies suddenly came into focus. It was Gonzalez who established wrought iron as an important medium for sculpture, taking advantage of the very difficulties that had discouraged its use before. *Head* (fig. 1074) combines extreme economy of form with an aggressive reinterpretation of anatomy that is derived from Picasso's work after the mid-1920s (see fig. 1014, especially the head of the figure on the left): the mouth is an oval cavity with spikelike teeth, the eyes two rods that converge upon an "optic nerve" linking them to the tangled mass of the "brain." Similar gruesomely expressive metaphors have since been created by a whole generation of younger sculptors in wrought iron and welded steel, as if the violence of their working process mirrored the violence of modern life.

CALDER. The early 1930s, which brought Giacometti and Gonzalez to the fore, produced still another important development, the mobile sculpture—mobiles, for short—of the American Alexander Calder (1898–1976): these are delicately balanced constructions of metal wire, hinged together and weighted so as to move with the slightest breath of air. They may be of any size, from tiny tabletop models to the huge *Lobster Trap and Fish Tail* (fig. 1075). Kinetic sculpture had been conceived by the Constructivists, and their

1074. JULIO GONZALEZ. *HEAD*. c. 1935.
Wrought iron, 17¾×15¼″ (45.1×38.7 cm).
Collection, The Museum of Modern Art, New York. Purchase

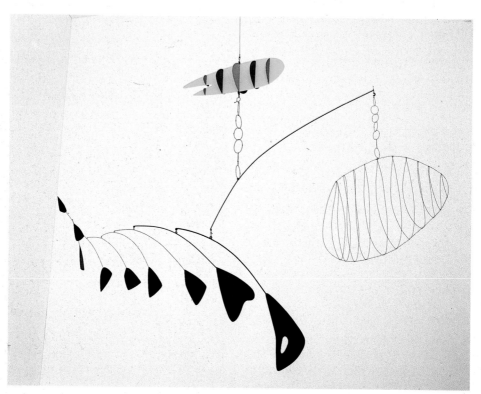

1075. ALEXANDER CALDER. *LOBSTER TRAP AND FISH TAIL*.
1939. Painted steel wire and sheet aluminum, c. 8′6″×9′6″ (2.6×2.9 m).
Collection, The Museum of Modern Art, New York.
Commissioned by the Advisory Committee for the stairwell of the Museum

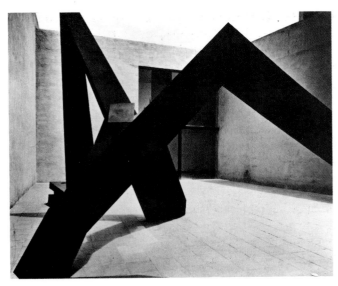

1076. MATHIAS GOERITZ. *STEEL STRUCTURE.*
1952–53. Height 14′9″ (4.5 m).
The Echo (Experimental Museum), Mexico City

influence is evident in Calder's earliest mobiles; these were motor-driven, and tended toward abstract geometric configurations. Calder was also affected early on by Mondrian, but it was his contact with Surrealism that made him realize the poetic possibilities of "natural" rather than fully controlled movement; he borrowed biomorphic shapes from Miró and began to think of mobiles as similes of organic structures—owers on flexible stems, foliage quivering in the breeze, marine animals floating in the sea. Such mobiles are infinitely responsive to their environment. Unpredictable and ever-changing, they incorporate the fourth dimension as an essential element of their structure. Within their limited sphere, they are more truly alive than any fabricated thing.

SCULPTURE SINCE 1945

Primary Structures
and Environmental Sculpture

Like painting, sculpture since 1945 has been notable for its epic proportions. Indeed, scale assumed fundamental significance for a sculptural movement that extended the scope—indeed, the very concept—of sculpture in an entirely new direction. "Primary Structure," the most suitable name suggested for this type, conveys its two salient characteristics: extreme simplicity of shapes and a kinship with architecture. The radical abstraction of form is known as Minimalism, which implies an equal reduction of content. Another term, "Environmental Sculpture" (not to be confused with the mixed-medium "environments" of Pop), refers to the fact that many Primary Structures are designed to envelop the beholder, who is invited to enter or walk through them. It is this space-articulating function that distinguishes Primary Structures from all previous sculpture and relates them to architecture. They are the modern successors, in structural

steel and concrete, to such prehistoric monuments as Stonehenge (see figs. 52 and 53).

GOERITZ. The first to explore these possibilities was Mathias Goeritz (born 1915), a German working in Mexico City. As early as 1952–53, he established an experimental museum, The Echo, for the display of massive geometric compositions, some of them so large as to occupy an entire patio (fig. 1076). His ideas have since been taken up on both sides of the Atlantic. Often, these sculptors limit themselves to the role of designer and leave the execution to others, to emphasize the impersonality and duplicability of their invention.

BLADEN. If no patron is found to foot the bill for carrying out these very costly structures, they remain on paper—like unbuilt architecture—but sometimes such works reach the mock-up stage. *The X* (fig. 1077), by the Canadian Ronald Bladen (1918–1988), was originally built with painted wood substituting for metal for an exhibition inside the two-story hall of the Corcoran Gallery in Washington, D.C. Its commanding presence, dwarfing the Neoclassic colonnade of the hall, seems doubly awesome in such a setting.

SMITH. Not all Primary Structures are Environmental Sculptures, of course. Most are free-standing works independent of the sites that contain them. (Bladen's *The X*, for example, was later constructed of painted steel as an outdoor

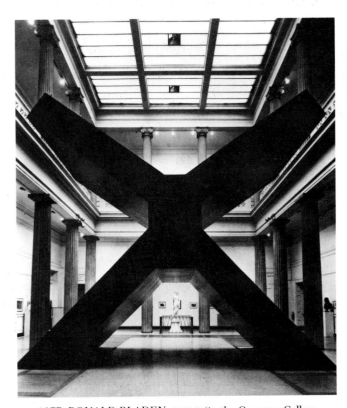

1077. RONALD BLADEN. *THE X* (in the Corcoran Gallery, Washington, D.C.). 1967. Painted wood, later constructed in steel, 22′8″ × 24′6″ × 12′6″ (6.9 × 7.3 × 3.8 m).
Courtesy Fischbach Gallery, New York

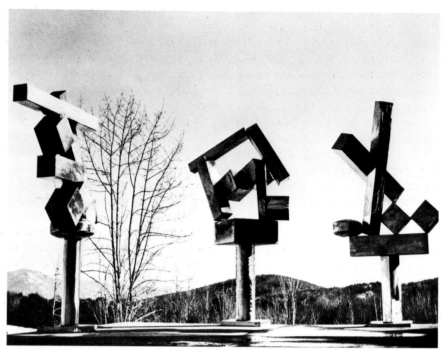

1078. DAVID SMITH. *CUBI* Series. Stainless steel. (left) *CUBI XVIII.* 1964. Height 9' 8" (2.9 m). Museum of Fine Arts, Boston; (center) *CUBI XVII.* 1963. Height 9' (2.7 m). Dallas Museum of Fine Arts; (right) *CUBI XIX.* 1964. 9' 5" (2.9 m). The Tate Gallery, London

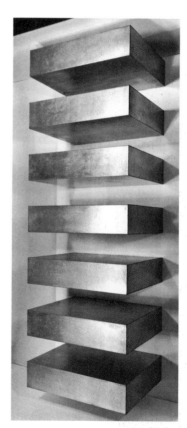

1079. DONALD JUDD. *UNTITLED.* 1965.
Galvanized iron, seven boxes,
each 9×40×31" (22.9×101.6×78.7 cm).
9" or (22.9 cm) between each box.
Gordon Locksley-Shea Gallery, Minneapolis

sculpture.) They nevertheless share the same monumental scale and economy of form. The artist who played the most influential role in defining their character was David Smith (1906–1965). His earlier work had been strongly influenced by the wrought-iron constructions of Julio Gonzales (fig. 1074), but he evolved during the last years of his life a singularly impressive form of Primary Structure in his *Cubi* series. Figure 1078 shows three of these against the open sky and rolling hills of the artist's farm at Bolton Landing, New York (all are now in major museums). Only two basic components are employed—cubes (or multiples of them) and cylinders—yet Smith has created a seemingly endless variety of configurations. The units that make up the structures are poised one upon the other as if they were held in place by magnetic force, so that each represents a fresh triumph over gravity. Unlike the younger members of the Primary Structure movement, Smith executed these pieces himself, welding them of sheets of stainless steel whose shiny surfaces he finished and controlled with exquisite care. As a result, his work displays an "old-fashioned" subtlety of touch that reminds us of the polished bronzes of Brancusi.

JUDD. Donald Judd (born 1928) carries the implications of Primary Structures to their logical conclusion. Unlike Environmental Sculpture, his works serve to articulate interior space without shaping it. In search of the ultimate unity, he separated Smith's *Cubi* into its two components, reducing the geometry to a single cube or cylinder. Judd established the proportions through precise mathematical formulas and eliminated any hint of personal intervention by contracting the work out to industrial fabricators. Having gained total control over all his elements, he soon began to elaborate on them. The most involved pieces produce a decorative opulence by repeating the shape serially at set intervals and adding an intense primary color to one or more sides (fig. 1079). Judd's strict guidelines permit few variations, only greater refinement, but within these limitations the results are often impressive. Why this should be so is not easily explained, although the artist is an eloquent spokesman. In the end, the success of his work depends on its subtle proportions and flawless finish, which enable him to attain a degree of perfection shared by few other Minimalists. Minimalism was a quest for basic elements representing the fundamental aesthetic values of art, without regard to issues of content. At its most extreme, it reduced art not to an eternal essence but to an arid simplicity.

OLDENBURG. On a large scale, Primary Structures are obviously monuments. But just as obviously they are not monuments commemorating or celebrating anything except their designer's imagination. To the uninitiated, they offer no ready frame of reference, nothing to be reminded of, even though the original meaning of "monument" is "a reminder." Presumably, monuments in this traditional sense died out when contemporary society lost its consensus of what ought to be publicly remembered. Yet the belief in the possibility of such monuments has not been abandoned altogether. The

Pop Artist Claes Oldenburg (born 1929) has proposed a number of unexpected and imaginative solutions to the problem of the monument; he is, moreover, an exceptionally precise and eloquent commentator on his ideas. All his monuments are heroic in size, though not in subject matter; all share one common feature, their origin in humble objects of everyday use.

In 1969 Oldenburg conceived and executed a work shaped like a gigantic ice bag (fig. 1080) with a mechanism inside to make it move—movements caused by an invisible hand," as the artist described them. For a piece of outdoor sculpture he wanted a form that combined hard and soft and did not need a base. An ice bag met these demands, so he bought one and started playing with it. He soon realized, he says, that the object was made for manipulation, "that movement was part of its identity and should be used." He sent the *Giant Ice Bag* to the U.S. Pavilion at EXPO 70 in Osaka, Japan, where crowds were endlessly fascinated to watch it heave, rise, and twist like a living thing, then relax with an almost audible sigh.

What do such monuments celebrate? What is the secret of their appeal? Part of it, which they share with ready-mades and Pop Art, is that they reveal the aesthetic potential of the ordinary and all-too-familiar. But they also have an undeniable grandeur.

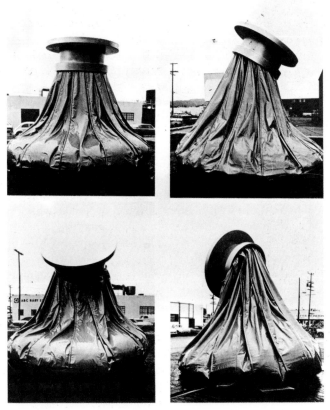

1080. CLAES OLDENBURG. *ICE BAG–SCALE B.* 1970.
Programmed kinetic sculpture of polyvinyl, fiberglass,
wood, and hydraulic and mechanical movements.
16 × 18 × 18′ (4.9 × 5.5 × 5.5 m).
Collection National Gallery of Art, Washington, D.C.

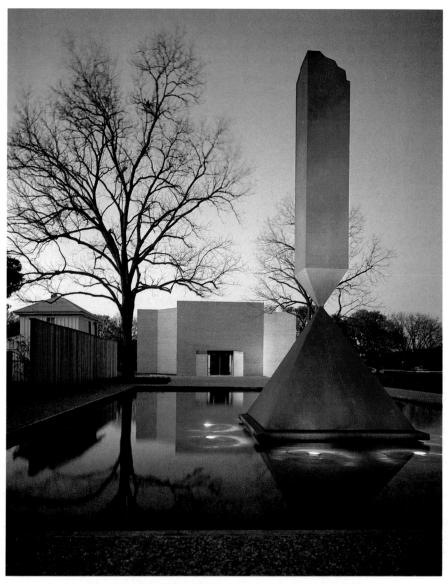

1081. BARNETT NEWMAN. *BROKEN OBELISK.* 1963–67.
Steel, height 25'1" (7.7 m). Rothko Chapel, Houston

NEWMAN. There is one dimension, however, that is missing in Oldenburg's monuments. They delight, astonish, amuse—but they do not move us. Wholly secular, wedded to the here and now, they fail to touch our deepest emotions. In our time, one monument has been successful in this: *Broken Obelisk* (fig. 1081) by Barnett Newman (1905–1970). An artist beset by profound religious and philosophical concerns, which he struggled throughout his life to translate into visual form, Newman conceived *Broken Obelisk* in 1963 but could not have it executed until four years later, when he found the right steel fabricator. It consists of a square base plate beneath a four-sided pyramid whose tip meets and supports that of the up-ended broken obelisk.

Obelisks are slender, four-sided pillars of stone erected by the ancient Egyptians. The Romans brought many obelisks to Italy (one marks the center of the colonnaded piazza of St. Peter's; see fig. 747), and these inspired a number of later monuments in Europe and America. The two tips have exactly the same angle (53 degrees, borrowed from that of the Egyptian pyramids, which had long fascinated the artist) so that their juncture forms a perfect **X**. Why this monument has such power to stir our feelings is difficult to put into words. Is it the daring juxtaposition of two age-old shapes that have contrary meanings, the one symbolizing timeless stability, the other a thrust toward the heavens? Surely—but what if the obelisk were intact? Would that not reduce the whole to an improbable balancing feat? The brokenness of the obelisk, then, is essential to the pathos of the monument. It speaks to us of our unfulfilled spiritual yearnings, of a quest for the infinite and universal that persists today as it has for thousands of years.

KELLY. The spiritual restlessness of Newman's *Broken Obelisk* seems to find a resolution in the timeless serenity of Ellsworth Kelly's sculpture. An early leader of hard-edge Color Field Painting, Kelly (born 1923) began with sculp-

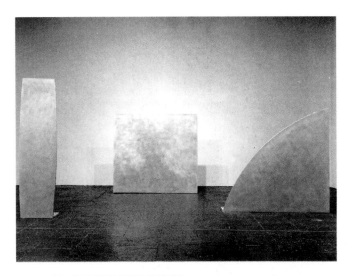

1082. ELLSWORTH KELLY. *UNTITLED*. 1982. Aluminum,
1″ (2.5 cm) thick; (left) 105×29¾″ (266.7×75.6 cm);
(center) 85×93½″(216×237.5 cm);
(right) 85×89¼″ (216×226.7 cm).
Blum Helman Gallery, New York

tures which adopted the same geometric shapes and primary hues. After moving to shaped canvases to escape the limitations of the rectangular format, he became interested in the two-dimensional plane as object, freed from the wall, and he largely abandoned color in favor of polished metal surfaces. His achievement is clear in the sculptural group shown in figure 1082. Surprisingly, it centers on a true rectangle, whose straight edges, however, seem to bend in response to the curves of the totemic "Venus figure," as he calls it, and the finlike quarter-circle on either side. In itself, each piece is strikingly beautiful for a subtlety and elegance equaling Brancusi's. The perfection of Kelly's contours reveals his obsession with edges and how they cut into space. When juxtaposed, the forms further articulate their surroundings; at the same time, they are transformed from monolithic slabs into mythological presences. Like Henry Moore's *Two Forms* (fig. 1065), they seem almost preternaturally alive, but the air of mute expectancy recalls statues from Tell Asmar (fig. 111).

SMITHSON. The ultimate medium for Environmental Sculpture is the earth itself, since it provides complete freedom from the limitations of the human scale. Some designers of Primary Structures have, logically enough, turned to "Earth Art," inventing projects that stretch over many miles. These latter-day successors to the mound-building Indians of Neolithic times have the advantage of modern earth-moving machinery, but this is more than outweighed by the problem of cost and the difficulty of finding suitables sites on our crowded planet.

The few projects of theirs that have actually been carried out are mostly found—and the finding is itself often difficult enough—in remote regions of western America. *Spiral Jetty*, the work of Robert Smithson (1938–1973), jutted out into Great Salt Lake in Utah (fig. 1083) and is now partly submerged. Its appeal rests in part on the Surrealist irony of the

concept: a spiral jetty is as self-contradictory as a straight corkscrew. But it can hardly be said to have grown out of the natural formation of the terrain like the Great Serpent Mound (see fig. 54). No wonder it has not endured long, nor was it intended to—the process by which nature is reclaiming *Spiral Jetty*, already twice submerged, was integral to Smithson's design from the start. The project nevertheless lives on in photographs.

CHRISTO. By way of contrast, the projects of Christo (Christo Javacheff, born 1935), who specializes in wrapping things, are deliberately short-lived; they enhance the environment only temporarily instead of altering it permanently. *Surrounded Islands, Biscayne Bay, Miami* (fig. 1084), his most satisfying project to date, was installed for all of two weeks in the spring of 1983. Part Conceptual Art, part Happening (see pages 776–78), this ambitious repackaging of nature was a public event involving a small army of assistants. While the emphasis was on the campaign itself, the outcome was a triumph of epic fantasy.

Photographs hardly do justice to the results. Our collage of Christo's drawings, an aesthetic object in its own right,

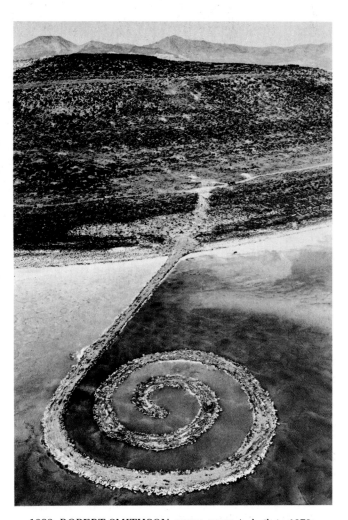

1083. ROBERT SMITHSON. *SPIRAL JETTY*. As built in 1970.
Total length 1,500′ (457.2 m); width of jetty 15′ (4.6 m).
Great Salt Lake, Utah

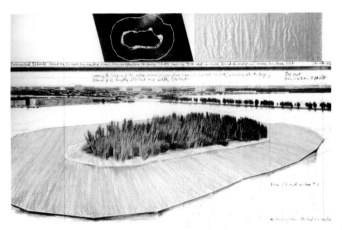

1084. CHRISTO (CHRISTO JAVACHEFF). *SURROUNDED ISLANDS,
BISCAYNE BAY, MIAMI.* 1983. Mixed mediums,
upper, 15×95⅝″ (38×243 cm). Private collection

gives a clearer picture of the artist's intention by presenting the project in different ways and conveying the complexity of the experience it provided. In effect, Christo turned the islands into inverse lily pads of pink fabric. If Smithson's *Spiral Jetty* suggests the futility of grandiose undertakings, Christo's visual pun is as festive and decorative as Monet's water-lily paintings (fig. 921), an inspiration the artist has acknowledged.

Constructions and Assemblage

Constructions present a difficult problem. If we agree to restrict the term "sculpture" to objects made of a single substance, then we must put "assemblages" (that is, constructions using mixed mediums) in a class of their own—probably a useful distinction, because of their kinship with ready-mades. But what of Picasso's *Bull's Head* (fig. 2)? Is it not an instance of assemblage, and have we not called it a piece of sculpture? Actually, there is no inconsistency here; the *Bull's Head* is a bronze cast, even though we cannot tell this by looking at a photograph of it. Had Picasso wished to display the actual handlebars and bicycle seat, he would surely have done so. If he chose to have them cast in bronze, this must have been because he wanted to "dematerialize" the ingredients of the work by having them reproduced in a single material. Apparently he felt it necessary to clarify the relation of image to reality in this way—the sculptor's way—and the same procedure was his general custom whenever he utilized ready-made objects.

Nevertheless, we must not apply the "single-material" rule too strictly. Calder's mobiles, for instance, often combine metal, string, wood, and other substances, yet they do not strike us as being assemblages, because these materials are not made to assert their separate identities. Conversely, an object may deserve to be called an assemblage even though composed of essentially homogeneous material. Such is often true of works known as "junk sculpture," made of fragments of old machinery, parts of wrecked automobiles, and similar discards, which constitute a broad class that can be called sculpture, assemblage, or environment, depending on the work itself.

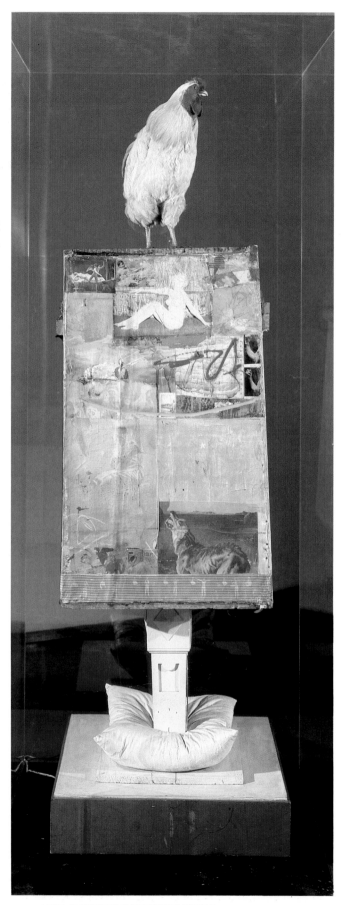

1085. ROBERT RAUSCHENBERG. *ODALISK.* 1955–58.
Construction, 81×25×25″ (205.7×63.5×63.5 cm).
Museum Ludwig, Cologne

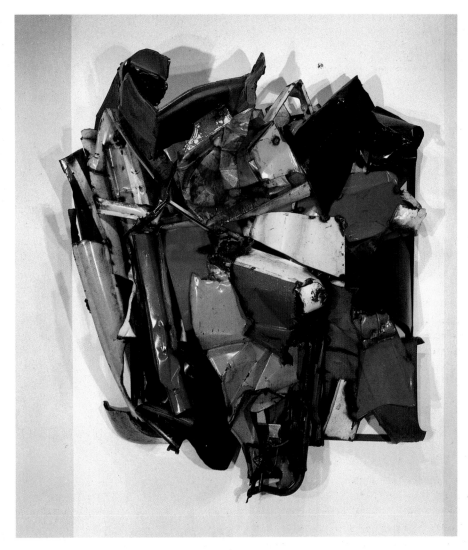

1086. JOHN CHAMBERLAIN. *ESSEX*. 1960.
Automobile body parts and other metal,
9′×6′8″×43″ (2.7×2.0×1.1 m).
Collection, The Museum of Modern Art, New York.
Gift of Mr. and Mrs. Robert C. Scull and Purchase

RAUSCHENBERG. Robert Rauschenberg (born 1925) pioneered assemblage as early as the mid-1950s. Like a composer making music out of the noises of everyday life, he constructed works of art from the trash of urban civilization. *Odalisk* (fig. 1085) is a box covered with a miscellany of pasted images—comic strips, photos, clippings from picture magazines—held together only by the skein of brushstrokes the artist has superimposed on them; the box perches on a foot improbably anchored to a pillow on a wooden platform and is surmounted by a stuffed chicken.

The title, a witty blend of "odalisque" and "obelisk," refers both to the nude girls among the collage of clippings (for the original meaning of "odalisque," see page 635) and to the shape of the construction as a whole: the box shares its verticality and slightly tapering sides with real obelisks. Rauschenberg's unlikely "monument" has at least some elements in common with its predecessors: compactness and

self-sufficiency. We will recognize in this improbable juxtaposition the same ironic intent as the ready-mades of Duchamp, whom Rauschenberg had come to know well in New York.

CHAMBERLAIN. A most successful example of junk sculpture—and a puzzling borderline case—is *Essex* (fig. 1086) by John Chamberlain (born 1927). The title refers to a make of car that has not been on the market for many years, suggesting that the object is a kind of homage to a vanished species. But we may well doubt that these pieces of enameled tin ever had so specific an origin. They have been carefully selected for their shape and color, and composed in such a way that they form a new entity, evoking Duchamp-Villon's *The Great Horse* (fig. 1070) rather than the crumpled automobiles to which they once belonged. Whether we prefer to call *Essex* assemblage or sculpture is of little importance, but in trying to reach a decision we gain a better insight into the qualities that constitute its appeal.

NEVELSON. Although it is almost always made entirely of wood, the work of Louise Nevelson (1900–1988) must be classified as assemblage, and when extended to a monumental scale, it acquires the status of an environment. Before Nevelson, there had not been important women sculptors in twentieth-century America. Sculpture had traditionally been reserved for men because of the manual labor involved. Thanks to the women's suffrage movement in the second half of the nineteenth century, Harriet Hosmer (1830–1908) and her "White Marmorean Flock" (as the novelist Henry James called her and her followers in Rome) had succeeded in legitimizing sculpture as a medium for women. This school of sculpture lapsed, however, when the sentimental, idealizing Neoclassical style fell out of favor after the Philadelphia Centennial of 1876.

Nevelson, rejecting external reality, began in the 1950s to construct her separate realities, using her collection of found pieces of wood, both carved and rough. These self-contained realms were at first miniature cityscapes; they soon grew into large environments of free-standing "buildings," encrusted with decorations that were inspired by the sculpture on Mayan ruins. Nevelson's work generally took the form of large wall units that flatten her architecture into reliefs (fig. 1087). Assembled from individual compartments, the whole is always painted a single color, usually a matte black to suggest the shadowy world of dreams. Each compartment is elegantly designed and is itself a metaphor of thought or experience. While the organization of the ensemble is governed by an inner logic, the whole statement remains an enigmatic monument to the artist's fertile imagination.

GRAVES. Nevelson's success has encouraged other American women to become sculptors, including the versatile Nancy Graves (born 1940), who often incorporates bits and pieces of found objects into her work. The playful fantasy of *Trace* (fig. 1088), however, is the very opposite of Nevelson's solemn grandeur. The ribbonlike boughs of this seemingly elastic tree support a lacy foliage of steel mesh. Caught in its "leaves" are a brightly colored ladder, kite frame, streamers, and ropes, which complete the gaily elegant effect.

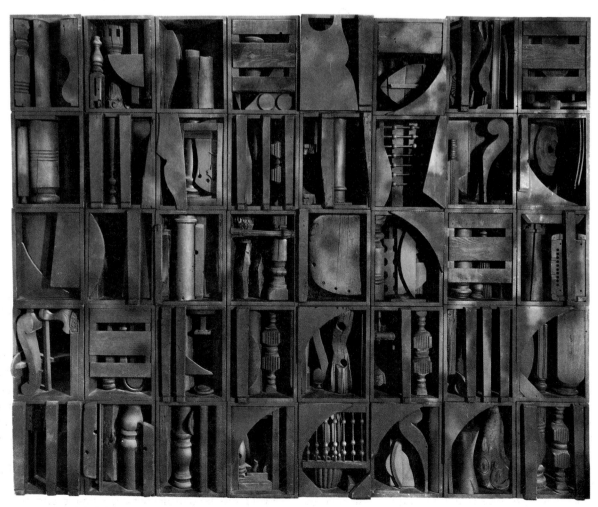

1087. LOUISE NEVELSON. *BLACK CORD.* 1964. Painted wood, 8′ × 10′ × 11½″ (2.44 m × 3.05 m × 29.2 cm).
Whitney Museum of American Art. Gift of Anne and Joel Ehrenkranz

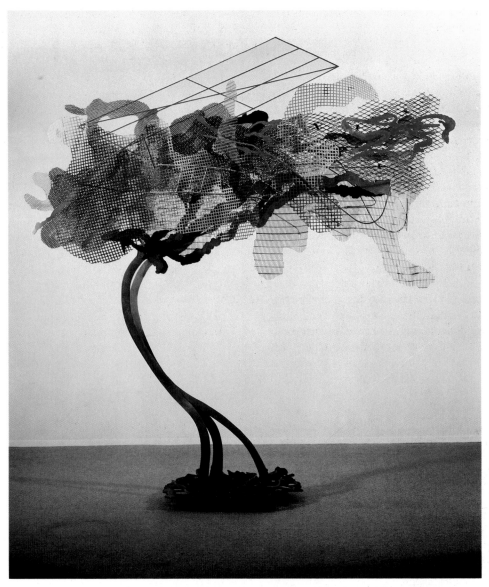

1088. NANCY GRAVES. *TRACE.* 1979–80.
Bronze, steel, patina, and paint,
107×115×59″ (271.8×292.1×149.7 cm).
Collection Mr. and Mrs. Graham Gund

Environments and Installations

A number of artists associated with Pop Art have also turned to assemblage because they find the flat surface of the canvas too confining; in order to bridge the gap between image and reality, they often introduce three-dimensional objects into their pictures. Some even construct full-scale models of everyday things and real-life situations, utilizing every conceivable kind of material in order to embrace the entire range of their physical environment, including the people, in their work. These "environments" combine the qualities of painting, sculpture, collage, and stagecraft. Being three-dimensional, they can claim to be considered sculpture, but the claim rests on a convention which Pop Art itself has helped to make obsolete. According to this convention, a work of art consisting of a flat or smoothly curved surface covered with colors is a painting (or, if the surface is not covered, a draw-

ing), while sculpture is everything else, whether or not the surface is colored and regardless of the material, size, or degree of relief (unless we can enter it, in which case we call it architecture).

Our habit of using "sculpture" in this sense is only a few hundred years old. Antiquity and the Middle Ages had separate terms to denote various kinds of sculpture according to the materials and working processes involved, but no single term that covered them all. Maybe it is time to revive such distinctions and to modify the all-too-inclusive definition of sculpture by acknowledging "environments" as a separate category, distinct from both painting and sculpture in its use of heterogeneous materials ("mixed mediums") and its blurring of the borderline between image and reality. The differences are underscored by "installations," which are expansions of environments into room-size settings.

SEGAL. George Segal (born 1924) creates lifesize three-dimensional pictures showing people and objects in everyday situations, such as *Cinema* (fig. 1089). The subject is ordinary enough to be instantly recognizable: a man changing the letters on a movie theater marquee. Yet the relation of image and reality is far more subtle and complex than the obvious authenticity of the scene suggests. The man's figure is cast from a live model by a technique of Segal's invention and retains its ghostly white plaster surface. Thus it is one crucial step removed from our world of daily experience, and the neon-lit sign has been carefully designed to complement and set off the shadowed figure. Moreover, the scene is brought down from its natural context, high above the entrance to the theater where we might have glimpsed it in passing, and is presented at eye-level, in isolation, so that we grasp it completely for the first time.

HANSON. Stunningly realistic figures have been cast from models by Duane Hanson (born 1925), using a similar technique in painted polyester and fiberglass. His subjects, however, are types of people so familiar that we take them for granted. Be they satires of tourists in gaudy attire (fig. 1090) or sympathetic renderings of elderly persons or of workers, Hanson's sculptures, taken collectively, represent the failure

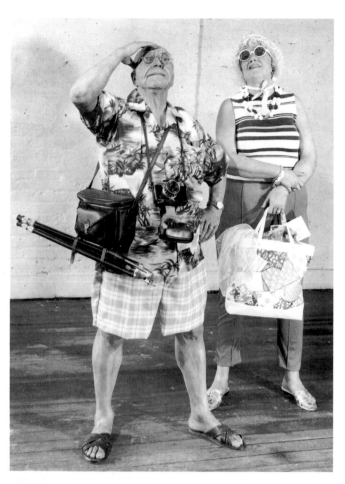

1090. DUANE HANSON. *TOURISTS*. 1970. Fiberglass and polychromed polyester, 64×65×67″ (162.6×165×170.2 cm). Glasgow Art Gallery, Glasgow, Scotland

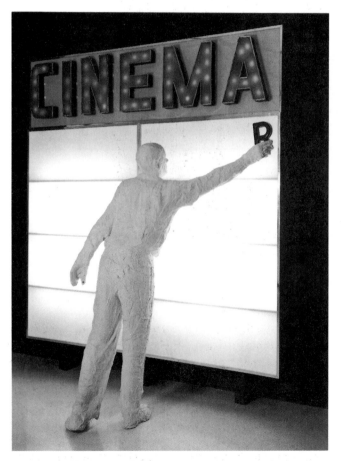

1089. GEORGE SEGAL. *CINEMA*. 1963. Plaster, metal, Plexiglas, and fluorescent light, 9′10″×8′×3′3″ (3.0×2.4×1.0 m). The Albright-Knox Art Gallery, Buffalo, New York. Gift of Seymour H. Knox

of the American dream. But by isolating them from their usual contexts he makes us see—and understand—their condition in life as if for the first time.

DE ANDREA. Hanson's main disciple, John De Andrea (born 1941), pursues very different ends. Though his sculptures sometimes create a certain tension through the choice of sitter, pose, and expression, *The Artist and His Model* (fig. 7) is more typical of the subtle content and composition of his work. This conceptual integrity and almost classical purity make him a worthy successor to Antonio Canova, but with a difference (see pages 648–50). Here the Romantic sculptor's dilemma of representation versus duplication is reversed: without confusing the two, De Andrea's hyper-realism expresses an ideal, while leaving us in just enough doubt to make the illusion convincing.

KIENHOLZ. Some "environments" can have a shattering impact on the beholder. This is certainly true of *The State Hospital* (fig. 1091) by the West Coast artist Edward Kienholz (born 1927), which shows a cell in a ward for senile patients with a naked old man strapped to the lower bunk. He is the victim of physical cruelty—his body is little more than a skeleton covered with leathery, discolored skin—which has reduced what little mental life he had in him al-

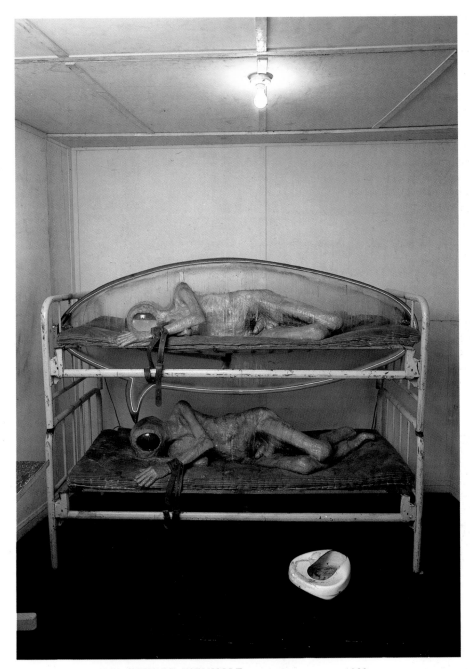

1091. EDWARD KIENHOLZ. *THE STATE HOSPITAL.* 1966.
Mixed mediums, 8×12×10′ (2.4×3.7×3.1 m).
Moderna Museet, Stockholm

most to the vanishing point: his head is a glass bowl with live goldfish, of whom we catch an occasional glimpse. The horrifying realism of the scene even has an olfactory dimension: when the work was displayed at the Los Angeles County Museum, it exuded a sickly hospital smell. But what of the figure in the upper bunk? It almost duplicates the one below, with one important difference: it is a mental image, since it is enclosed in the outline of a comic-strip balloon rising from the goldfish bowl. It represents, then, the patient's awareness of himself. The abstract devices of the balloon and the metaphoric goldfish bowl are both alien to the realism of the scene as a whole, yet they play an essential part in it, for they help to break the grip of horror and pity—

they make us think as well as feel. Kienholz' means may be Pop, but his aim is that of Greek tragedy. As a witness to the unseen miseries beneath the surface of modern life, he has no equal today.

PFAFF. The installations of Judy Pfaff (born 1946) can be likened to exotic indoor landscapes. The inspiration of nature is apparent in the junglelike density of *Dragons* (fig. 1092), aptly named for its fiery forms and colors. Pfaff uses painting together with sculptural and other materials to activate architectural space. The treatment of the wall surface will remind us of the collage in *Odalisk* (fig. 1085), but Pfaff's playfulness is closer to Graves' whimsy (fig. 1088) than to Rauschen-

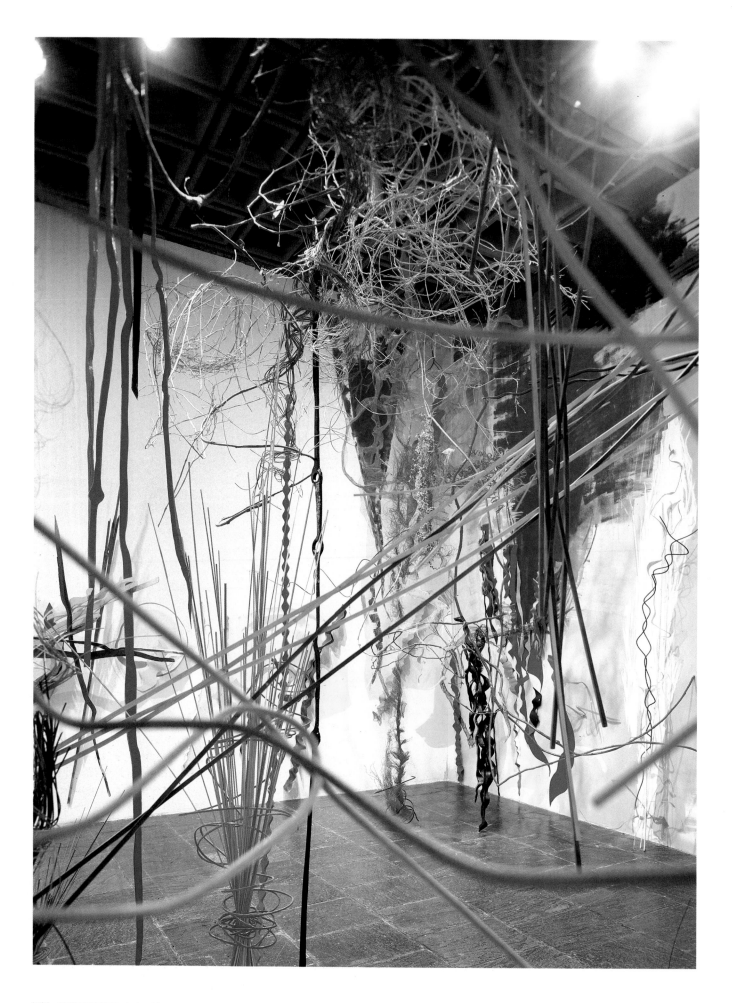

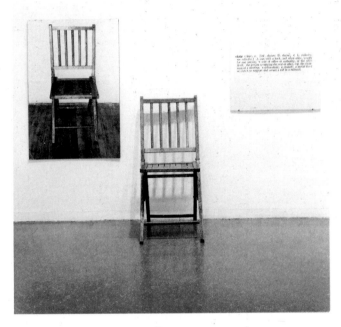

1093. JOSEPH KOSUTH. *ONE AND THREE CHAIRS.* 1965.
Photograph of chair, 36×24⅛″ (91.4×61.7 cm);
wood folding chair, 32⅜×14⅞×20⅞″ (82.3×37.8×52.8 cm);
photographic enlargement of dictionary definition
of chair, 24⅛×24½″ (61.7×62.2 cm).
Collection, The Museum of Modern Art, New York.
Larry Aldrich Foundation Fund

berg's ironic wit. The nearest equivalent to Pfaff's spontaneous energy is the Action Painting of Jackson Pollock. It is as if the poured paint had been released from the canvas and left free to roam in space. The swirling profusion around the viewer makes for an experience that is at once pleasurable and vertiginous.

Conceptual Art

Conceptual Art has the same "patron saint" as Pop Art: Marcel Duchamp. It arose during the 1960s out of the Happenings staged by Alan Kaprow, in which the event itself became the art. Conceptual Art challenges our definition of art more radically than Pop, insisting that the leap of the imagination, not the execution, is art. Since the works of art are incidental by-products of the imaginative leap, they can be dispensed with altogether; so too can galleries and, by extension, even

1092. (*opposite*) JUDY PFAFF. *DRAGONS.* Installation at the Whitney Biennial, February–April 1981. Mixed mediums. Whitney Museum of American Art, New York. Courtesy Holly Solomon Gallery, New York

the artist's public. The creative process need only be documented in some way—sometimes in verbal form, but more often by still photography, video, or cinema displayed within an installation.

Conceptual Art, we will recognize, is akin to Minimalism as a phenomenon of the 1960s, but instead of abolishing content, it eliminates aesthetics from art. This deliberately anti-art approach, stemming from Dada (see page 730), poses a number of stimulating paradoxes. As soon as the documentation takes on visible form, it begins to come perilously close to more traditional forms of art (especially if it is placed in a gallery where it can be seen by an audience), since it is impossible fully to divorce the imagination from aesthetic matters.

KOSUTH. We see this in *One and Three Chairs* (fig. 1093) by Joseph Kosuth (born 1945), which is clearly indebted to Duchamp's ready-mades (fig. 1072): it "describes" a chair by combining in one installation an actual chair, a full-scale photograph of that chair, and a printed dictionary definition of a chair. Whatever the Conceptual artist's intention, this making of his work of art, no matter how minimal the proc-

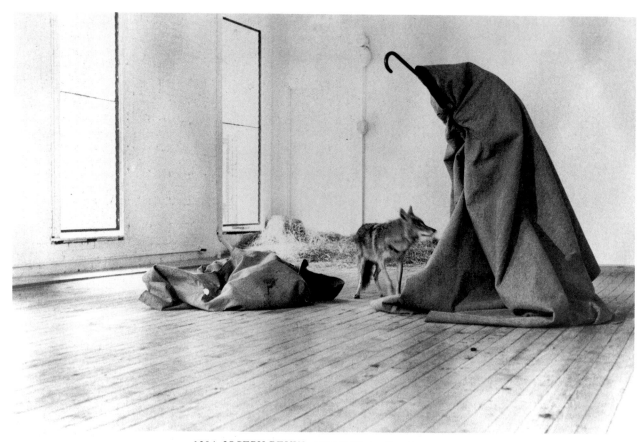

1094. JOSEPH BEUYS. *COYOTE*. Photo of performance at
Rene Block Gallery, New York, 1974. Photo: Copyright 1974 Caroline Tisdall,
Courtesy Ronald Feldman Fine Arts, New York

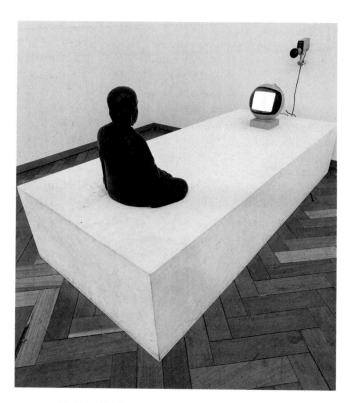

1095. NAM JUNE PAIK. *TV BUDDHA*. 1974. Video
installation with statue. Stedelijk Museum, Amsterdam

ess, is as essential as it was for Michelangelo (see page 47). In the end, all art is the final document of the creative process, because without execution, no idea can ever be fully realized. Without such "proof of performance," the Conceptual artist becomes like the emperor wearing new clothes that no one else can see. And, in fact, Conceptual Art has embraced all of the mediums in one form or another.

Performance Art

Performance art, which originated in the early decades of this century, belongs to the history of theater, but the form that arose in the 1970s combined aspects of Happenings and Conceptual Art with installations. In reaction to Minimalism, the artist now sought to assert his presence once again by becoming, in effect, a living work of art. The results, however, relied mainly on the shock value of irreverent humor or explicit sexuality.

BEUYS. The German artist Joseph Beuys (1921–1986) managed to overcome these limitations, though he, too, was a controversial figure who incorporated an element of parody into his work. Life, for Beuys, was a creative process in which everyone is an artist. He assumed the guise of a modern-day shaman intent on healing the spiritual crisis of contemporary life caused by the rift between the arts and sciences. To find the common denominator behind such

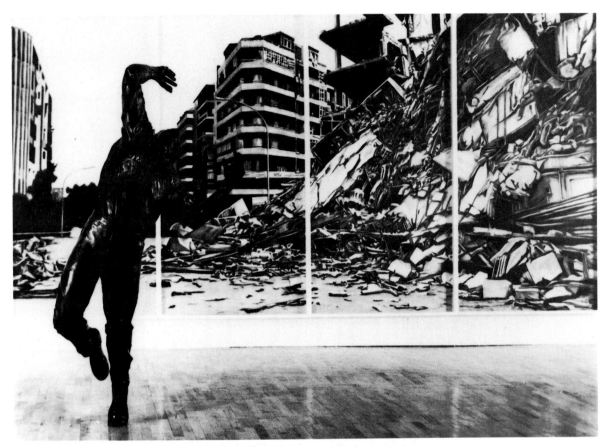

1096. ROBERT LONGO. *NOW EVERYBODY (FOR R. W. FASSBINDER)*.
1982–83. Charcoal, graphite, and ink on paper.
96 × 192″ (244 × 488 cm); cast bronze, 79 × 28 × 45″ (201 × 71 × 114 cm).
National Gallery, Budapest

polarities, he created objects and scenarios which, though often baffling at face value, were meant to be accessible to the intuition. In 1974, Beuys spent one week caged up in a New York gallery with a coyote (fig. 1094)—an animal sacred to the American Indian but persecuted by the white man. His objective in this "dialogue" was to lift the trauma caused to an entire nation by the schism between the two opposing world views.

PAIK. The notes and photographs that document Beuys' performances hardly do them justice. His chief legacy today lies perhaps in the stimulation he provided his many students, including Anselm Kiefer (see page 755) and collaborators, among them Nam June Paik (born 1932). The sophisticated video displays of the Korean-born Paik fall outside the scope of this book; but his installation with a Buddha contemplating himself on television (fig. 1095) is a memorable image uniquely appropriate to our age, in which the fascination with electronic media has replaced transcendent spirituality as the focus of modern life.

LONGO. The work of Robert Longo (born 1953) is the direct outgrowth of his experience in performance art. Longo addresses disturbing issues in his large tableaux. These usually consist of wall pieces incorporating a variety of mediums, sometimes even sound, but may extend into space as well,

so that they fall somewhere between assemblage and environments. Notable for their formal elegance, they are produced with the aid of collaborators, though the conception remains his. The effect produced by these conflicting elements can be unsettling, in keeping with the provocative subject matter. Longo's characteristic theme is violence and alienation in the artificial world of the urban middle class. The figure in *Now Everybody* (fig. 1096) is seen in a pose inspired by discothèques that, upon closer inspection, is strangely contorted, as if he had been shot or struck by an unseen force. He is engaged, we realize, in the universal dance of death that belies his sheltered life.

CHAPTER SIX
TWENTIETH-CENTURY ARCHITECTURE

The technical and aesthetic basis for a truly modern architecture was laid by the eve of World War I. Much of twentieth-century architecture is distinguished by an aversion to decoration for its own sake. Instead, it favors a clean functionalism announced by Taut's staircase for the "Glass House" (fig. 978) of 1914, which expresses the machine age with its insistent rationalism. Yet modern architecture demanded far more than a reform of architectural grammar and vocabulary: to take advantage of the expressive qualities of the new building techniques and materials that the engineer had placed at his disposal, the architect needed a new philosophy. The leaders of modern architecture have characteristically been vigorous and articulate thinkers, in whose minds architectural theory is closely linked with ideas of social reform to meet the challenges posed by industrial civilization. To them, architecture's ability to shape human experience brings with it the responsibility to play an active role in molding modern society for the better.

WRIGHT. The first indisputably modern architect was Frank Lloyd Wright (1867–1959), Louis Sullivan's great disciple. If Sullivan, Gaudí, Mackintosh, and Van de Velde could be called the Post-Impressionists of architecture, Wright took architecture to its Cubist phase. This is certainly true of his brilliant early style, between 1900 and 1910, which had broad international influence. (For an example of his late work, see the Introduction, pages 64–5.) In the beginning Wright's main activity was the design of suburban houses in the upper Midwest; these were known as Prairie School houses, because their low, horizontal lines were meant to blend with the flat landscape around them.

Frank Lloyd Wright's last, and his most accomplished, example in this series is the Robie House of 1909 (figs. 1097 and 1098). The exterior, so unlike anything seen before, instantly proclaims the building's modernity. However, its "Cubism" is not merely a matter of the clean-cut rectangular elements composing the structure, but of Wright's handling of space. It is designed as a number of "space blocks" around a central core, the chimney; some of the blocks are closed and others are open, yet all are defined with equal precision. Thus the space that has been architecturally shaped includes the balconies, terrace, court, and garden, as well as the house itself. Voids and solids are regarded as equivalents, analogous in their way to Analytic Cubism in painting, and the entire complex enters into active and dramatic relationship with its surroundings.

Wright did not aim simply to design a house, but to create a complete environment. He even took command of the details of the interior and designed stained glass, fabrics, and furniture. The controlling factor here was not so much the individual client's special wishes as Wright's conviction that buildings have a profound influence on the people who live, work, or worship in them, making the architect, consciously or unconsciously, a molder of people.

RIETVELD. The work of Frank Lloyd Wright had attracted much attention in Europe by 1914. Among the first to recognize its importance were some young Dutch architects who, a few years later, joined forces with Mondrian in the *De Stijl* movement (see page 729). Among their most important experiments is Schröder House, designed by Gerrit Rietveld (1888–1964) in 1924. The façade of Schröder House looks like a Mondrian painting transposed into three dimensions, for it utilizes the same rigorous abstraction and refined geometry (fig. 1100). The lively arrangement of floating panels and intersecting planes is based on Mondrian's principle of dynamic equilibrium—achieved through the balance of unequal but equivalent oppositions, which expresses the mystical harmony of humanity with the universe. Steel beams, rails, and other elements are painted in bright, primary colors to articulate the composition. Unlike a painting by Mondrian, the parts look as if they can be shifted at will, though in fact they fit as tightly as interlocking pieces of a jig-saw puzzle; not a single element could be moved without destroying the delicate balance of the whole.

Rietveld's approach to the interior (figs. 1099 and 1101), which reveals his background as a cabinetmaker, recalls Godwin's sideboard (see fig. 940) in its use of unadorned "boxes" of space. However, the upper story can be left open or configured into different work and sleeping areas through a system of sliding partitions that fit neatly together when moved out of the way. While this flexible treatment of the living quarters was devised with the owner, herself an artist, to suit her individual lifestyle, the decentralized plan also incorporates a continuous, "universal" space which is given a linear structure by the network of panel dividers.

Despite the fact that it retains an allegiance to traditional materials and craftsmanship, which were equated by *De Stijl* with the self-indulgent materialism of the past, Schröder House proclaims a utopian ideal widely held in the early twentieth century. The machine would hasten our spiritual development by liberating us from nature, with its conflict and imperfection, and by leading us to the higher order of beauty reflected in the architect's clean, abstract forms. The harmonious design of Schröder House owes its success to the insistent logic of this aesthetic, which we respond to intuitively even without being aware of its ideology. Yet the design, far from being impersonal, is remarkably intimate.

International Style

THE BAUHAUS. Schröder House was recognized immediately as one of the classic statements of modern architecture. The *De Stijl* architects represented the most advanced ideas in European architecture in the early 1920s. They had a decisive influence on so many architects abroad that the movement soon became international. The largest and most complex example of this International Style of the 1920s is the group of buildings created in 1925–26 by Walter Gropius (1883–1969) for the Bauhaus in Dessau, the famous German art school of which he was the director. (Its curriculum embraced all the visual arts, linked by the root concept of "structure," *Bau*.) The plan consists of three major blocks (fig.

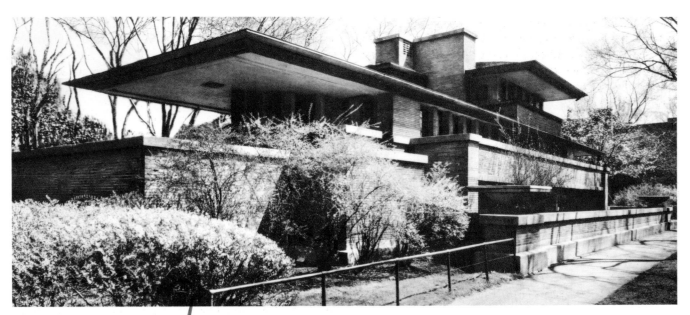

1097. FRANK LLOYD WRIGHT. Robie House, Chicago. 1909

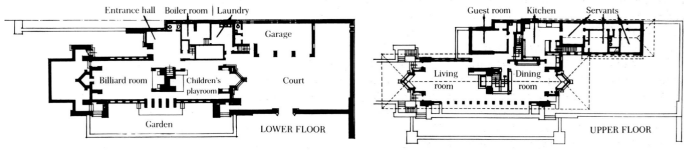

1098. Plan of the Robie House

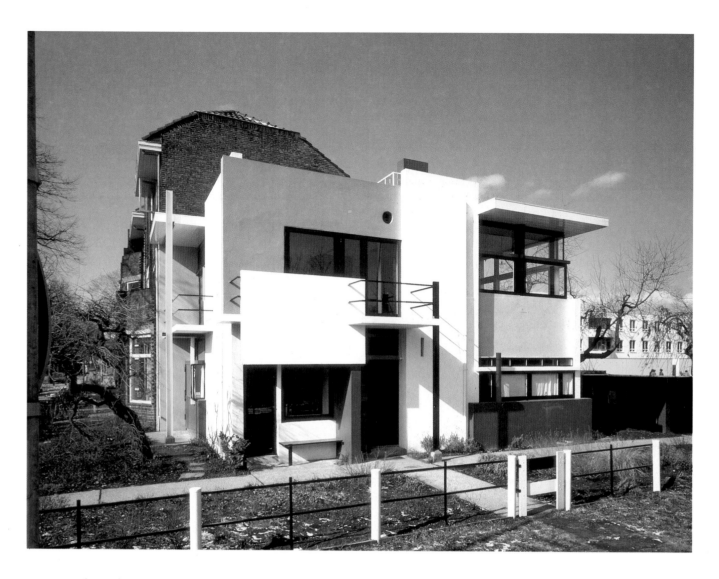

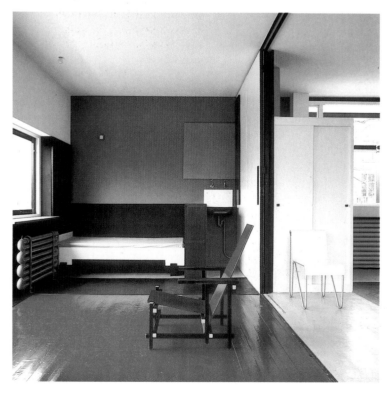

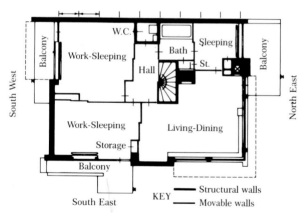

1099. (*above*) Plan of the Schröder House

1100. (*top*) GERRIT RIETVELD.
Schröder House, Utrecht. 1924

1101. (*left*) Interior, Schröder House

1102) for classrooms, shops, and studios, the first two linked by a bridge of ferroconcrete containing offices (fig. 1103, extreme left).

The most dramatic is the shop block, a four-story box with walls that are a continuous surface of glass. This radical step had been possible ever since the introduction of the structural steel skeleton several decades before, which relieved the wall of any load-bearing function; Sullivan had approached it in the Carson Pirie Scott & Company store (fig. 970), but he could not yet free himself from the traditional notion of the window as a "hole in the wall." Gropius frankly acknowledged, at last, that in modern architecture the wall is no more than a curtain or climate barrier, which may consist entirely of glass if maximum daylight is desirable.

A quarter-century later, the same principle was used on a much larger scale for the two main faces of the great slab that houses the Secretariat of the United Nations (fig. 1104). The effect is rather surprising: since such walls reflect as well as transmit light, their appearance depends on the interplay of these two effects. They respond, as it were, to any change of conditions without and within, and thus introduce a strange quality of life into the structure. (The mirrorlike finish of Brancusi's *Bird in Space* serves a similar purpose.)

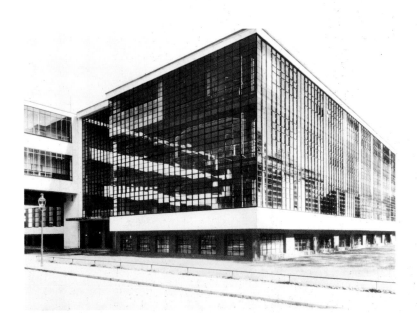

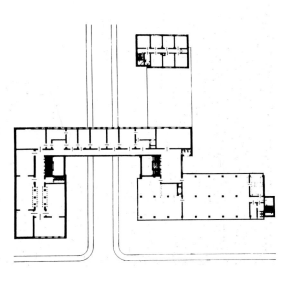

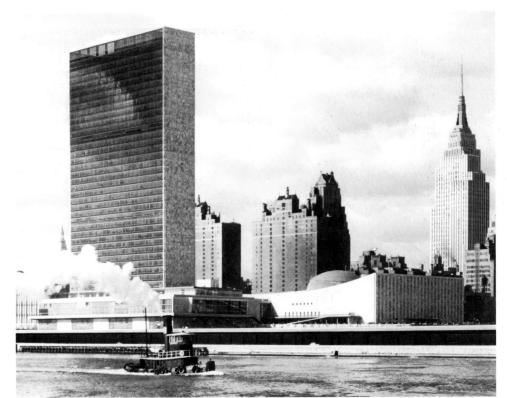

1102. (*above left*)
WALTER GROPIUS
Shop Block, the Bauhaus,
Dessau, Germany. 1925–26

1103. (*above*)
Plan of the Bauhaus

1104. (*left*)
WALLACE K. HARRISON
and an International Advisory
Committee of Architects
(LE CORBUSIER,
OSCAR NIEMEYER, and others).
United Nations Building,
New York. 1949–51

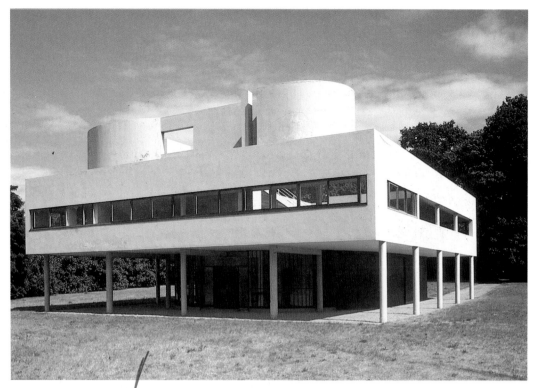

1105. LE CORBUSIER. Savoye House, Poissy-sur-Seine,
France, 1929–30

LE CORBUSIER'S EARLY WORK. In France, the most distinguished representative of the International Style during the 1920s was the Swiss-born architect Le Corbusier (Charles Édouard Jeanneret, 1886–1965). At that time he built only private houses—from necessity, not choice—but these are as important as Wright's Prairie School houses. Le Corbusier called them *machines à habiter* (machines to be lived in), a term intended to suggest his admiration for the clean, precise shapes of machinery, not a desire for "mechanized living." (The paintings of his friend Fernand Léger during those years reflect the same attitude; see fig. 1016.) Perhaps he also wanted to imply that his houses were so different from conventional homes as to constitute a new species.

Such is indeed our impression as we approach the most famous of them, the Savoye House at Poissy-sur-Seine (fig. 1105): it resembles a low, square box resting on stilts—pillars of reinforced concrete that form part of the structural skeleton and reappear to divide the "ribbon windows" running along each side of the box. The flat, smooth surfaces, denying all sense of weight, stress Le Corbusier's preoccupation with abstract "space blocks."

In order to find out how the box is subdivided, we must enter it (fig. 1106): we then realize that this simple "package" contains living spaces that are open as well as closed, separated by glass walls. Within the house, we are still in communication with the outdoors (views of the sky and the surrounding terrain are everywhere to be seen). Yet we enjoy complete privacy, since an observer on the ground cannot see us unless we stand next to a window. The functionalism of the Savoye House thus is governed by a "design for living," not by mechanical efficiency.

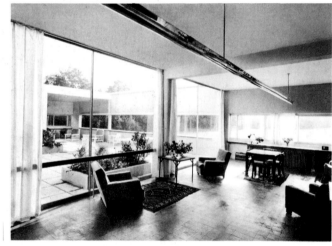

1106. Interior, Savoye House

AALTO. Although its style and philosophy were codified around 1930 by an international committee of Le Corbusier and his followers, the International Style was by no means monolithic; soon, all but the most purist among them began to depart from this standard. One of the first to break ranks was the Finnish architect Alvar Aalto (1898–1976), whose Villa Mairea (figs. 1107 and 1108) reads at first glance like a critique of Le Corbusier's Savoye House of a decade earlier. Like Rietveld's Schröder House, Villa Mairea was designed for a woman artist; her second-story studio, covered with wood slats, dominates the view of the house from three directions. This time, however, the architect was given a free hand by his patron, and the building is a summation of ideas

Aalto had been developing for nearly ten years. He adapted the International Style to the traditional architecture, materials, lifestyle, and landscape of Finland. Aalto took the opposite approach of Le Corbusier's in order to arrive at a similar end. Aalto's primary concern was human needs, both physical and psychological, which he sought to harmonize with functionalism. The modernist heritage, extending back to Wright, is unmistakable in his vocabulary of forms and massing of elements; yet everywhere there are romantic touches that add a warmth absent from Savoye House. Wood, brick, and stone are employed in various combinations throughout the interior and exterior, in pointed contrast to Le Corbusier's pristine classicism. Free forms are introduced at several places to inject an element of playfulness, as well as to break up the cubic geometry and smooth surfaces favored by the International Style. Aalto's importance is undeniable, but his place in twentieth-century architecture remains unclear. His infusion of nationalist elements in Villa Mairea has been interpreted both as a rejection of modernism and as a fruitful regional variation on the International Style. Today he can be seen as a direct forerunner of Post-Modern architecture (see pages 789–90).

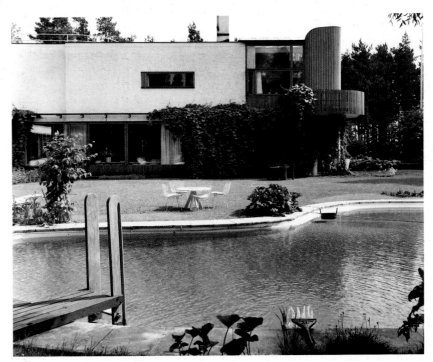

1107. ALVAR AALTO. Villa Mairea. 1937–38. Noormarkku, Finland

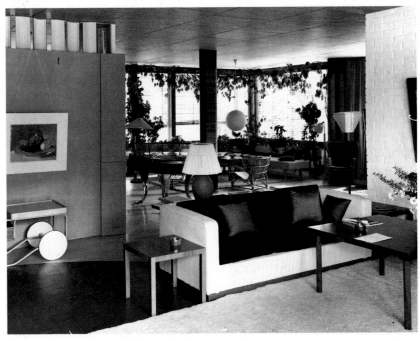

1108. Interior, Villa Mairea

Post-War Architecture

UNITED STATES. America, despite its early position of leadership, did not share the exciting growth that took place in European architecture during the 1920s. The impact of the International Style did not begin to be felt on its side of the Atlantic until the very end of the decade. A pioneer example is the Philadelphia Savings Fund Society Building of 1931–32 (fig. 1109) by George Howe (1886–1954) and William E. Lescaze (1896–1969), a skyscraper in the tradition of Sullivan that incorporates in its design many features evolved in Europe after the end of World War I.

MIES VAN DER ROHE. During the following years, the best German architects, whose work Hitler condemned as "un-German," came to this country and greatly stimulated the development of American architecture. Gropius, who was appointed chairman of the architecture department at Harvard University, had an important educational influence; Ludwig Mies van der Rohe (1886–1969), his former colleague at Dessau, settled in Chicago as a practicing architect. The Lake Shore Drive apartment houses (fig. 1110), two severely elegant slabs placed at right angles to each other, exemplify Mies van der Rohe's dictum that "less is more." Here is the great spiritual heir of Mondrian among contemporary designers, possessed of the same "absolute pitch" in determining proportions and spatial relationships.

LE CORBUSIER'S LATER WORK. Abandoning the abstract purism of the International Style, Le Corbusier's postwar work shows a growing preoccupation with sculptural, even anthropomorphic, effects. Thus the Unité d'Habitation,

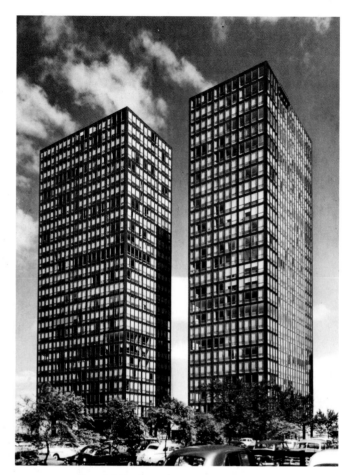

1110. LUDWIG MIES VAN DER ROHE
Lake Shore Drive Apartment Houses, Chicago. 1950–52

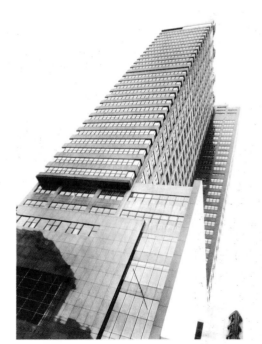

1109. GEORGE HOWE and WILLIAM E. LESCAZE
Philadelphia Savings Fund Society Building,
Philadelphia. 1931–32

a large apartment house in Marseilles (fig. 1111), is a "box on stilts" like the Savoye House, but the pillars are not thin rods; their shape now expresses their muscular strength in a way that makes us think of Doric columns. The exposed staircase on the flank, too, is vigorously sculptural, and the flat plane of the all-glass façade has a honeycomb screen of louvers and balconies that forms a sun-break but also enhances the three-dimensional quality of the structure. This projecting screen has proved to be an invention of great importance, practically and aesthetically; it is now a standard feature of modern architecture throughout the tropics (Le Corbusier himself introduced it in India and Brazil).

The most revolutionary building of the mid-twentieth century, however, is Le Corbusier's church of Notre-Dame-du-Haut at Ronchamp in eastern France (figs. 1112–14). Rising like a medieval fortress from a hillcrest, its design is so irrational that it defies analysis, even with the aid of perspective diagrams. The play of curves and countercurves is here as insistent as in Gaudí's Casa Milá, though the shapes are now simple and more dynamic: the massive walls seem to obey an unseen force that makes them slant and curl like paper; and the overhanging roof suggests the brim of an enormous hat, or the bottom of a ship split lengthwise by the sharp-edged buttress from which it is suspended. If the Casa Milá brings to mind the "eroded" softness of Henry Moore's *Re-*

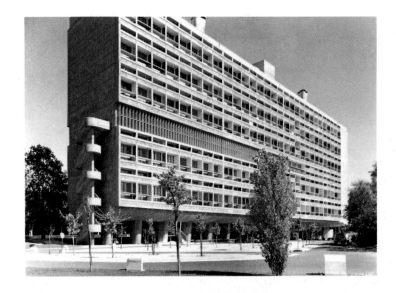

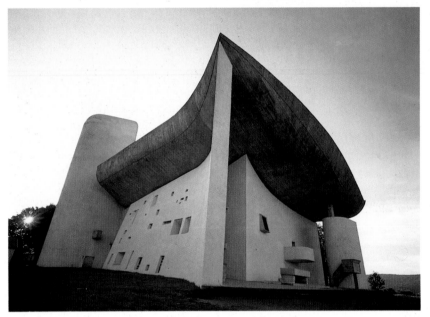

1112. (*left*) LE CORBUSIER
Notre-Dame-du-Haut (from the southeast).
Ronchamp, France. 1950–55

1113. (*below left*) Interior, Notre-Dame-du-Haut

1114. (*below*) Bird's-eye perspective diagram of
Notre-Dame-du-Haut (from the northeast)

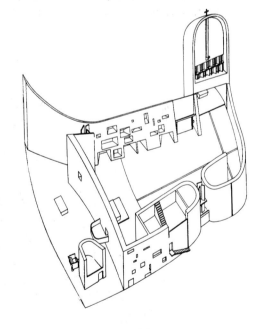

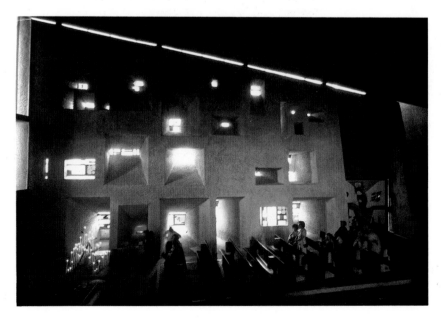

cumbent Figure, Ronchamp has the megalithic quality of the same artist's *Two Forms* (see figs. 1066 and 1065).

This evocation of the dim, prehistoric past is quite intentional: asked to create a sanctuary on a hilltop, Le Corbusier must have felt that this was the primeval task of architecture, placing him in a direct line of succession with the builders of Stonehenge, the ziggurats of Mesopotamia, and the Greek temples. Hence, he also consciously avoids any correlation between exterior and interior. The doors are concealed: we must seek them out like clefts in a hillside, and to pass through them is much like entering a secret—and sacred—cave.

Only inside do we sense the specifically Christian aspect of Ronchamp. The light, channeled through stained-glass windows so tiny that they seem hardly more than slits or pinpricks on the exterior, cuts widening paths through the thickness of the wall, and thus becomes once more what it had been in medieval architecture—the visible counterpart of the Light Divine. There is true magic in the interior of Ronchamp, but also a strangely disquieting quality, a nostalgia for the certainties of a faith that is no longer unquestioned. Ronchamp mirrors the spiritual condition of the modern age—which is a measure of its greatness as a work of art.

URBAN PLANNING. Le Corbusier belongs to the same heroic generation as Gropius and Mies van der Rohe, both born in the 1880s. It was these men who in the course of their long, fruitful careers coined the language of twentieth-century architecture. Their successors continue to use many aspects of its vocabulary in new building types and materials, and they do not forget its fundamental logic.

To some younger architects, the greatest challenge is not the individual structure but urban design: replacing the slums of our decaying cities with housing that will provide a socially healthful environment for very large numbers of people. Urban planning is probably as old as civilization itself (which, we recall, means "city life"). We have caught only occasional glimpses of it in this book (see pages 214, 220, and 402), since its history is difficult to trace by direct visual evidence: cities, like living organisms, are ever-changing, and to reconstruct their pasts from their present appearances is a laborious task. With the advent of the industrial era two centuries ago, cities began to grow explosively, and have continued to do so ever since.

Much of this growth was uncontrolled, beyond the laying out of a network of streets; housing standards were poor or poorly enforced. The unfortunate result can be seen in the overcrowded, crumbling apartment blocks that are the blight of vast urban areas everywhere. They were taken over by the poor, while those who could afford it fled to the dormitory towns of suburbia. This exodus, accelerated by the automobile, has produced the dangerous tensions that lend urgency to the cry for urban renewal today. Such renewal, needless to say, must involve the political, social, and economic resources of an entire society, rather than the architect alone. Yet the architect has an essential role in the process, that of translating the schemes of the planning agencies into reality.

One particularly thorny problem is how to develop an alternative to the conventional high-rise apartment block in densely populated areas: a housing pattern that will be less deadeningly uniform (but no more expensive), and provide more light and air, safer access, and a multitude of other de-

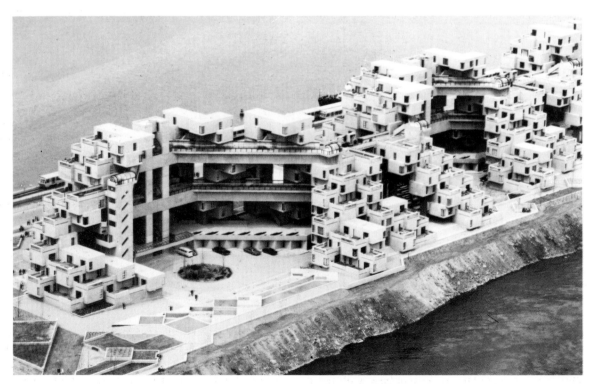

1115. MOSHE SAFDIE and others. Habitat, EXPO 67, Montreal. 1967

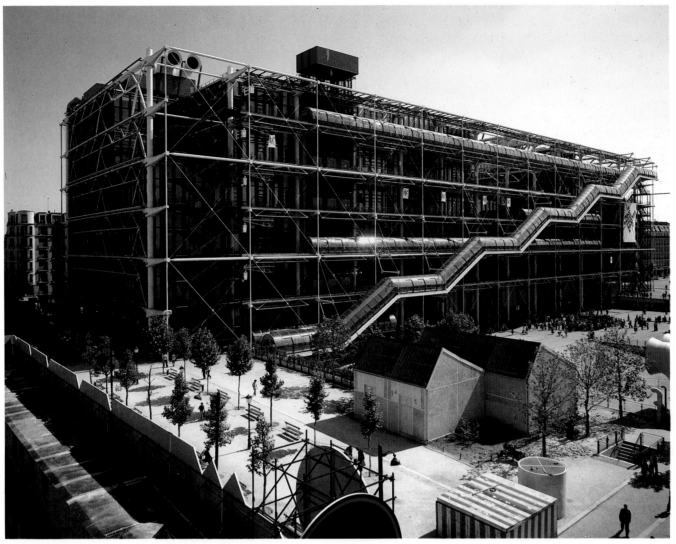

1116. RENZO PIANO and RICHARD ROGERS. Centre National d'Art et de Culture Georges Pompidou, Paris. 1971–77

sirable features. A promising solution, by the Israeli architect Moshe Safdie (born 1938) and his associates (fig. 1115), was demonstrated in the Habitat complex at the Montreal EXPO 67. The individual apartments consist of prefabricated "boxes" that can be combined into units of several sizes and shapes, attached to a zigzagging concrete framework that can be extended to fit any site.

POST-MODERNISM. Spurred by more radical social theories, Post-Modernism—as its misleading name implies (see page 789)—constitutes a broad repudiation of the mainstream of twentieth-century architecture. It represents an attempt to reinstate meaning in architecture, as against the self-contained designs espoused by the modern tradition. Post-Modernism rejects not only the vocabulary of Gropius and his followers, but also the social and ethical ideals implicit in their lucid proportions. As in the visual arts, Post-Modernism includes a variety of tendencies, but acquires a subtly different meaning when applied to architecture.

One approach is to repudiate the formal beauty of the International Style. Among the freshest, as well as most con-

troversial, results is the Centre Georges Pompidou, the national arts and cultural center in Paris (fig. 1116). Selected in an international competition, the design by the Anglo-Italian team of Renzo Piano (born 1937) and Richard Rogers (born 1933) looks like the Bauhaus (fig. 1102) turned inside-out. The architects have eliminated any trace of Le Corbusier's elegant façades (fig. 1105), exposing the building's inner mechanics while disguising the underlying structure. The interior itself has no fixed walls, so that temporary dividers can be arranged to meet any need. This stark utilitarianism reflects a populist sentiment current in France. Yet it is enlivened by eye-catching colors, each keyed to a different function. The festive display is as vivacious and imaginative as Léger's *The City* (fig. 1016), which, with Paris' Eiffel Tower, can be regarded as the Pompidou Center's true ancestor.

The Pompidou Center represents a reaction against the International Style without abandoning its functionalism. Other Post-Modernist buildings seek to create more human environments by reverting to what can only be called Pre-Modernist architecture: their chief means of introducing

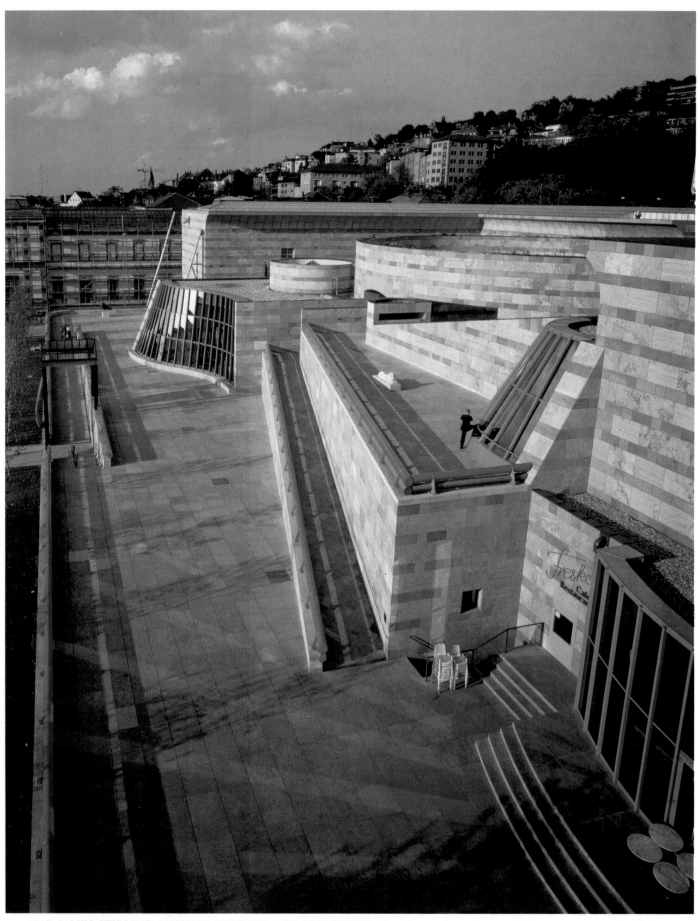

1117. JAMES STIRLING, MICHAEL WILFORD AND ASSOCIATES. Neue Staatsgalerie, Stuttgart, West Germany. Completed 1984.
© Timothy Hursley, courtesy *House and Garden* (The Arkansas Office)

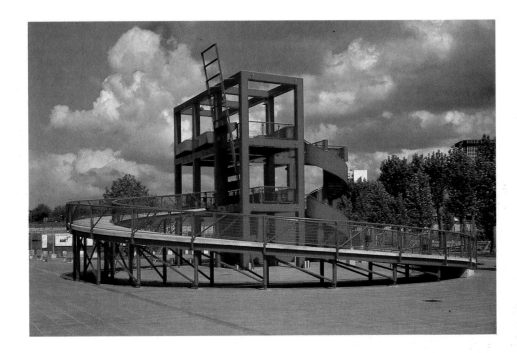

greater expressiveness has been to adopt elements from historical styles rich with association. The Neue Staatsgalerie in Stuttgart (fig. 1117) has the grandiose scale befitting a "palace" of the arts, but instead of the monolithic cube of the Pompidou Center, English architect James Stirling (born 1926) incorporates more varied shapes within more complex spatial relationships. There is, too, an overtly decorative quality that will remind us, however indirectly, of Garnier's Paris Opéra (fig. 899). The similarity does not stop there. Stirling has likewise invoked a form of historicism through paraphrase that is far more subtle than Garnier's opulent revivalism, but no less self-conscious. The primly Neoclassical masonry façade, for example, is punctured by a narrow arched window recalling the Italian Renaissance (compare fig. 613) and by a rusticated portal that has a distinctly Mannerist look. This eclecticism is more than a veneer—it lies at the heart of the building's success. The site, centering on a circular sculpture court, is designed along the lines of ancient temple complexes from Egypt through Rome, complete with a monumental entrance stairway. This plan enables Stirling to solve a wide range of practical problems with ingenuity and to provide a stream of changing vistas which fascinate and delight the visitor.

DECONSTRUCTIVISM. Historicism addresses only the decorative veneer of the International Style, but Deconstructivism, another tendency that has been gathering momentum since 1980, goes much farther in challenging its substance. It does so, paradoxically enough, by returning to one of the earliest sources of modernism: the Russian avant-garde. The Russian experiment in architecture proved short-lived, and few of its ideas ever made it beyond the laboratory stage. Recent architects, inspired by the bold sculpture of the Constructivists and the graphic designs of the Suprematists, seek to violate the integrity of modern architecture by subverting its internal structure, which the Russians themselves did little to undermine. Nevertheless, Deconstructivism does not abandon modern architecture and its principles altogether. Unlike some other avant-garde investigations that seek a decisive break with tradition, it remains an architecture of the possible based on structural engineering. As the term suggests, Deconstructivism dismantles modern architecture, then puts it back together again in new ways.

Although Deconstructivist designs have won major awards, their experimental approach and ambitious scale have discouraged their actual construction. Among the most advanced designs to get off the drawing board is the Parc de La Villette in Paris, an ensemble of brightly colored structures designed by Bernard Tschumi (born 1944). The geometry of Parc de La Villette is derived from the most basic shapes laid out on a simple grid, but broken up and rearranged by Tschumi to create highly unorthodox relationships both between and within the elements—relationships that give the park a disquieting sense of instability. The individual buildings resemble large-scale sculptures extended almost to the breaking point (fig. 1118). Yet the tension between the reality of the built structures and their "impossibility" results in an architectural vitality that is unprecedented.

Clearly such buildings push modern architecture to its practical limits. This sort of questioning has gone on before. It happened, for example, under Mannerism when architects introduced an element of decadence into the classical vocabulary inherited from the Renaissance. Repeatedly, architects, like artists, have plundered the past in search of fresh ideas. Deconstructivism is no mere historicism, however, but a transition much like *Art Nouveau* at the turn of the century, which provided the foundation for modern architecture. It is a necessary part of the process that will redefine architecture as we have come to know it.

CHAPTER SEVEN
TWENTIETH-CENTURY PHOTOGRAPHY

THE FIRST HALF CENTURY

During the nineteenth century, photography struggled to establish itself as art but failed to find an identity. Only under extraordinary conditions of political upheaval and social reform did it address the most basic subject of art, which is life itself. In developing an independent vision, photography would combine the aesthetic principles of the Secession and the documentary approach of photojournalism with lessons learned from motion photography. At the same time, modern painting, with which it soon became allied, forced a decisive change in photography by undermining its aesthetic assumptions and posing a new challenge to its credentials as one of the arts. Like the other arts, photography responded to the three principal currents of our time: Expressionism, Abstraction, and Fantasy. But because it has continued to be devoted for the most part to the world around us, modern photography has adhered largely to realism and, hence, has followed a separate development. We must therefore discuss twentieth-century photography primarily in terms of different schools and how they have dealt with those often-conflicting currents.

The course pursued by modern photography was facilitated by technological advances. It must be emphasized, however, that these have enlarged but never dictated the photographer's options. George Eastman's invention of the hand-held camera in 1888 and the advent of 35mm photography with the Leica camera in 1924 simply made it easier to take pictures that had been difficult but by no means impossible to take with the traditional view camera.

Surprisingly, even color photography did not have such revolutionary importance as might be expected. It began in 1907 with the introduction of the "autochrome" by Louis Lumière (1864–1948). The autochrome was a glass plate covered with grains of potato starch dyed in three colors which acted as color filters, over which was applied a coating of silver bromide emulsion; it yielded a positive color transparency upon development and was not superseded until Kodak began to make color film in 1932, using the same principles but more advanced materials. The autochrome was based on the color theories used by Seurat and even achieved Divisionist effects, as we can see if we look hard enough at *Young Lady with an Umbrella* (fig. 1119), an early effort. Except for its color, the picture differs little from photographs by the Photo-Secessionists, who were the first to turn to the new process. Color, in fact, had relatively little impact on the content, outlook, or aesthetic of photography, even though it removed the last barrier cited by nineteenth-century critics of photography as an art.

The School of Paris

ATGET. Modern photography began quietly in Paris with Eugène Atget, who turned to the camera only in 1898 at the age of forty-two. From then until his death in 1927, he toted his heavy equipment around Paris, recording the city in all its variety. Atget was all but ignored by the art photographers, for whom his commonplace subjects had little interest. He himself was a humble man whose studio sign read simply, "Atget—Documents for Artists," and, indeed, he was patronized by the fathers of modern art—Braque, Picasso, Duchamp, and Man Ray, to name only the best known. It is no accident that these artists were also admirers of Henri Rousseau, for Rousseau and Atget had in common a naïve vision, though Atget found inspiration in unexpected corners of his environment rather than in magical realms of the imagination.

Atget's pictures are marked by a subtle intensity and technical perfection that heighten the reality, and hence the significance, of even the most mundane subject. Few photographers have equaled his ability to compose simultaneously in two- and three-dimensional space. Like *Pool, Versailles* (fig. 1120), his scenes are often desolate, bespeaking a strange and individual outlook. The viewer has the haunting sensation that time has been transfixed by the stately composition and the photographer's obsession with textures. While Atget's work is marginally in the journalistic tradition of Nadar, Brady, and Riis (see pages 659, 661, and 704), its distinct departure from that earlier photography can only be explained in relation to late–nineteenth-century art. His pictures of neighborhood shops and street vendors, for example, are virtually identical with slightly earlier paintings by minor realists whose names are all but forgotten. Moreover, his photographs are directly related to a strain of magic realism that was a forerunner of Surrealism. Atget has been called a Surrealist, and while this characterization is misleading, one can easily understand why he was rediscovered by Man Ray, the Dada and Surrealist artistphotographer, and championed by Man Ray's assistant, Berenice Abbott (see page 805). As a whole, however, Atget's work is simply too varied to permit convenient classification.

KERTÉSZ. Atget's direct successors were two East Europeans. The older of them, André Kertész (1894–1985), began photographing in his native Hungary as early as 1915, and his style was already defined when he came to Paris ten years later. *Blind Musician* (fig. 1121), made in Hungary in 1921, is the kind of picture Atget sometimes took, and it uses much the same devices, above all the careful composition that isolates the subject within just enough of its surroundings to set the scene.

BRASSAÏ The photographic style of Gyula Halasz, known simply as Brassaï (1899–1984), Atget's other successor, was also conditioned by Paris, its views and its habits. He was born in Transylvania and studied art in Budapest, but was a Frenchman at heart even before arriving in Paris in 1923. Several years later, while working there as a journalist, he borrowed a camera from Kertész and took a series of evocative photographs of the city by night. He soon turned to the

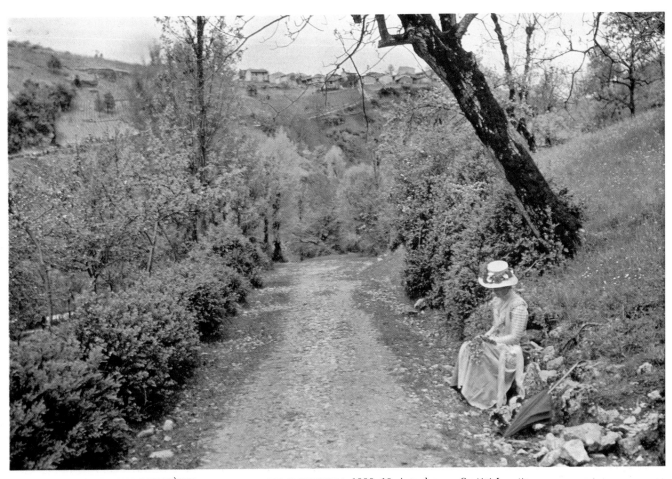

1119. LOUIS LUMIÈRE. *YOUNG LADY WITH AN UMBRELLA*. 1906–10. Autochrome. Société Lumière

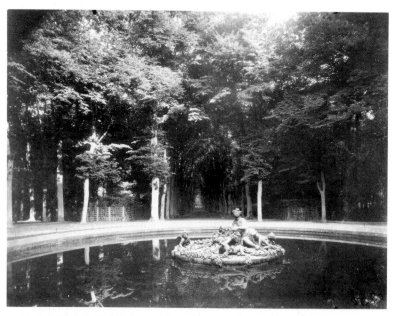

1120. EUGÈNE ATGET. *POOL, VERSAILLES*. 1924. Gold-toned printing-out paper,
7×9⅜″ (17.8×23.8 cm). Collection, The Museum of Modern Art, New York.
The Abbott-Levy Collection. Partial Gift of Shirley C. Burden

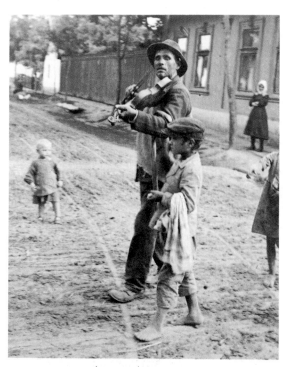

1121. ANDRÉ KERTÉSZ. *BLIND MUSICIAN*. 1921.
Gelatin-silver print, 16⅜×13¼″ (41.6×33.7 cm).
Collection, The Museum of Modern Art, New York.
Gift of the artist

nightlife of the Parisian cafés, where he had an unerring eye for the exotic characters who haunt them. *"Bijou" of Montmartre* (fig. 1122) shows the same sense of the typically aberrant as *At the Moulin Rouge* (see fig. 956) by Toulouse-Lautrec, whose art certainly influenced him.

CARTIER-BRESSON. The culmination of this Paris school is no doubt Henri Cartier-Bresson (born 1908), the son of a wealthy thread manufacturer. He studied under a Cubist painter in the late 1920s before taking up photography in 1932. Strongly affected at first by Atget, Man Ray (see page 804), Kertész, and even by the cinema, he soon developed into the most influential photojournalist of his time, and he still thinks of himself primarily as one. His purpose and technique are nevertheless those of an artist.

Cartier-Bresson is the master of what he has termed "the decisive moment." This to him means the instant recognition and visual organization of an event at the most intense moment of action and emotion in order to reveal its inner meaning, not simply to record its occurrence. Unlike other members of the Paris school, he seems to feel at home anywhere in the world and always to be in sympathy with his subjects, so that his photographs have a nearly universal appeal. His work is distinguished by an interest in composition for its own sake, derived from modern abstract art. He also has a particular fascination with motion, which he invests with all the dynamism of Futurism and the irony of Dada.

The key to his work is his use of space to establish relations that are suggestive and often astonishing. Indeed, although he deals with reality, Cartier-Bresson is a Surrealist at heart and has admitted as much. The results can be disturbing, as in *Mexico, 1934* (fig. 1123). By omitting the man's face, Cartier-Bresson prevents us from identifying the meaning of the gesture, yet we respond to its tension no less powerfully.

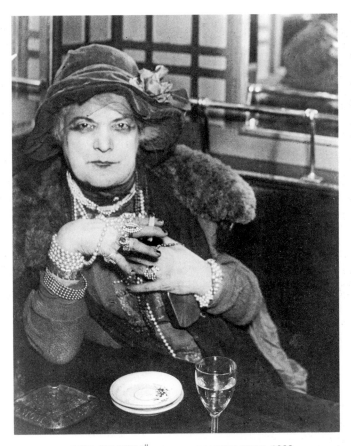

1122. BRASSAÏ. *"BIJOU" OF MONTMARTRE.* 1933.
11⅞×9¼″ (30.2×23.5 cm).
Collection, The Museum of Modern Art, New York.
The Ben Schultz Memorial Collection. Gift of the artist

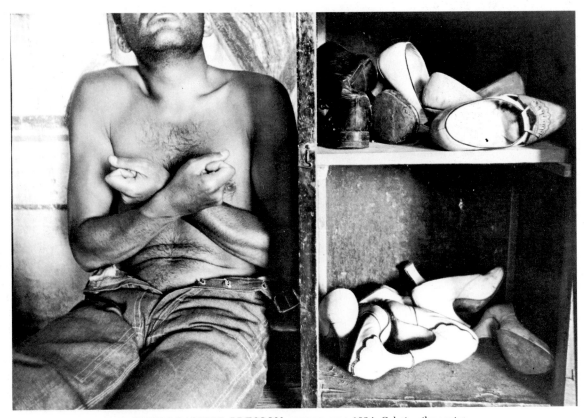

1123. HENRI CARTIER-BRESSON. *MEXICO, 1934.* 1934. Gelatin-silver print

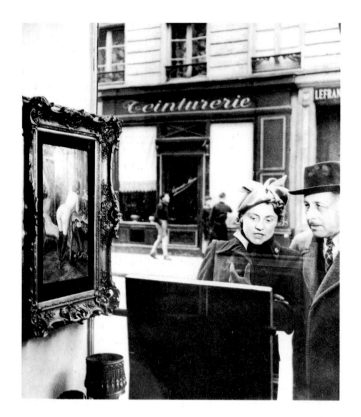

DOISNEAU. If Cartier-Bresson has a peer in any area, it is in the ironic wit of Robert Doisneau (born 1912). His subject matter is human foibles, which he unmasks with the best of humor. Who has not seen the man in *Side Glance* (fig. 1124), sneaking a glimpse of the voluptuous nude while his wife comments on the more serious painting before them.

The Stieglitz School

STIEGLITZ. The father of modern photography in the United States was Alfred Stieglitz, whose influence continued dominant throughout his life (1864–1946). From his involvement with the Photo-Secession (see page 706), he was a tireless spokesman for photography-as-art, although he defined this more broadly than did other members of the movement. He backed his words by publishing the magazine *Camera Work* and supporting the other pioneers of American photography through exhibiting their work in his New York galleries, especially the first one, known as "291." The bulk of his early work adheres to Secessionist conventions, treating photography as a pictorial equivalent to painting. During the mid-1890s, however, he took some pictures of street scenes that are harbingers of his mature photographs.

His classic statement, and the one he regarded as his finest photograph, is *The Steerage* (fig. 1125), taken in 1907 on a trip to Europe. Like Ford Madox Brown's *The Last of*

1124. (*above*) ROBERT DOISNEAU
SIDE GLANCE. 1953.
Gelatin-silver print

1125. (*right*) ALFRED STIEGLITZ
THE STEERAGE. 1907.
The Art Institute of Chicago.
Alfred Stieglitz Collection

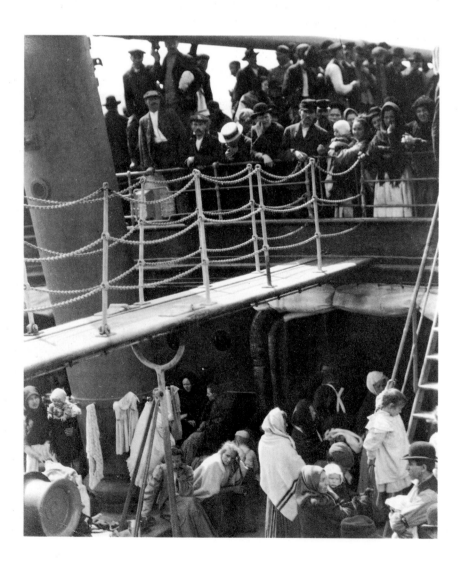

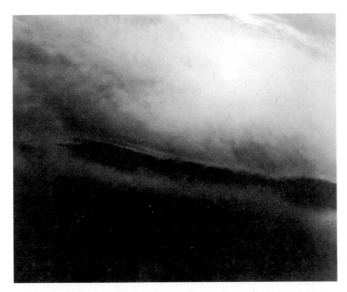

1126. ALFRED STIEGLITZ. *EQUIVALENT.* 1930. Chloride print.
The Art Institute of Chicago, Alfred Stieglitz Collection

England (see fig. 922), painted more than a half-century earlier, it captures the feeling of a voyage, but does so by letting the shapes and composition tell the story. The gangway bridge divides the scene visually, emphasizing the contrasting activities of the people below in the steerage, which was reserved for the cheapest fares, and the observers on the upper deck. If the photograph lacks the obvious sentiment of Brown's painting, it possesses an equal drama by remaining true to life.

This kind of "straight" photography is deceptive in its simplicity, for the image mirrors the feelings that stirred Stieglitz. For that reason, it marks an important step in his evolution and a turning point in the history of photography. Its importance emerges only in comparison with earlier photographs such as Steichen's *Rodin* (see fig. 985) and Riis' *Bandits' Roost* (see fig. 979). *The Steerage* is a pictorial statement independent of painting on the one hand and free from social commentary on the other. It represents the first time that documentary photography achieved the level of art in America.

Stieglitz' "straight" photography formed the basis of the American school. It is therefore ironic that it was Stieglitz, with Steichen's encouragement, who became the champion of abstract art against the urban realism of the Ash Can School (see page 724), whose paintings were at face value often similar in content and appearance to his photographs. The resemblance is misleading; for Stieglitz, photography was less a means of recording things than of expressing his experience and philosophy of life, much as a painter does.

This attitude culminated in his "Equivalents"; in 1922 Stieglitz began to photograph clouds to show that his work was independent of subject and personality. A remarkably lyrical cloud photograph from 1930 (fig. 1126) corresponds to a state of mind waiting to find full expression rather than merely responding to the moonlit scene. The study of clouds is as old as Romanticism itself, but no one before Stieglitz had made them a major theme in photography. As in Käse-

bier's *The Magic Crystal* (see fig. 984), unseen forces are evoked that make *Equivalent* a counterpart to Kandinsky's "*Composition VII*" (see fig. 996).

WESTON. Stieglitz' concept of the Equivalent opened the way to "pure" photography as an alternative to "straight" photography. The leader of this new approach was Edward Weston (1886–1958), who, although not Stieglitz' protégé, was decisively influenced by him. During the 1920s he pursued abstraction and realism as separate paths, but by 1930 he fused them both in images that are wonderful in their design and miraculous for their detail.

Pepper (fig. 1127) is a splendid example that is anything but a straightforward record of this familiar fruit. Like Stieglitz' clouds, Weston's photography makes us see the mundane with new eyes. The pepper is shown with preternatural sharpness and so close up that it seems larger than life. Thanks to the tightly cropped composition, we are forced to contemplate the form, whose every undulation is revealed by the dramatic lighting. *Pepper* has the sensuousness of O'Keeffe's *Black Iris III* (see fig. 1032) that lends the Equivalent a new meaning. Here the shapes are intentionally suggestive of the photographs of the female nude that Weston also pioneered.

ADAMS. To achieve uniform detail and depth, Weston worked with the smallest possible camera lens openings, and

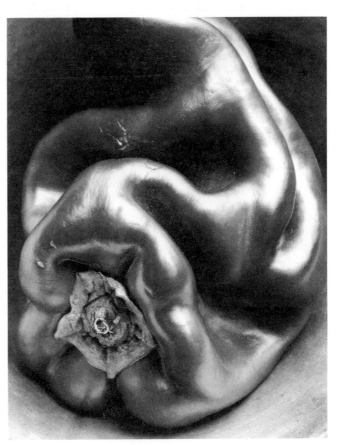

1127. EDWARD WESTON. *PEPPER.* 1930.
Center for Creative Photography, Tucson, Arizona

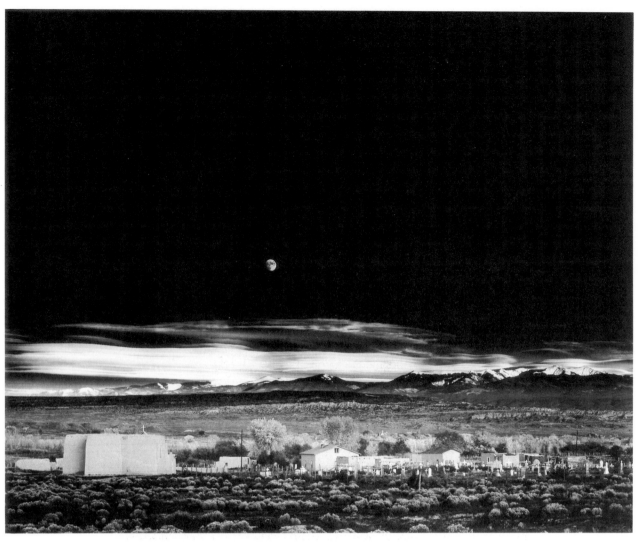

1128. ANSEL ADAMS. *MOONRISE, HERNANDEZ, NEW MEXICO.* 1941. Gelatin-silver print,
15×18½″ (38.1×47 cm). Collection, The Museum of Modern Art, New York. Gift of the artist

his success led to the formation, in 1932, of the West Coast society known as Group f/64, for the small lens opening. Among the founding members was Ansel Adams (1902–1984), who soon became the foremost nature photographer in America. He can rightly be regarded as the successor to O'Sullivan (see fig. 907), for his landscapes hark back to nineteenth-century American painting and photography.

Adams was a meticulous technician, beginning with the composition and exposure and continuing through the final printing. His justifiably famous work *Moonrise, Hernandez, New Mexico* (fig. 1128) came from pure serendipity which could never be repeated, a perfect marriage of straight and Equivalent photography. As in all of Adams' pictures, there is a full range of tonal nuances, from clear whites to inky blacks. The key to the photograph lies in the low cloud that divides the scene into three zones, so that the moon appears to hover effortlessly in the early evening sky.

BOURKE-WHITE. Stieglitz was among the first to photograph skyscrapers, the new architecture that came to dominate the horizon of America's growing cities. In turn, he

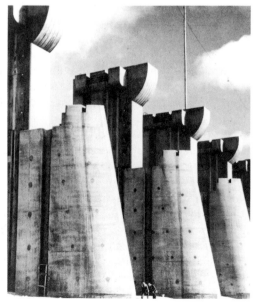

1129. MARGARET BOURKE-WHITE. *FORT PECK DAM, MONTANA,* 1936. Time Warner, Inc.

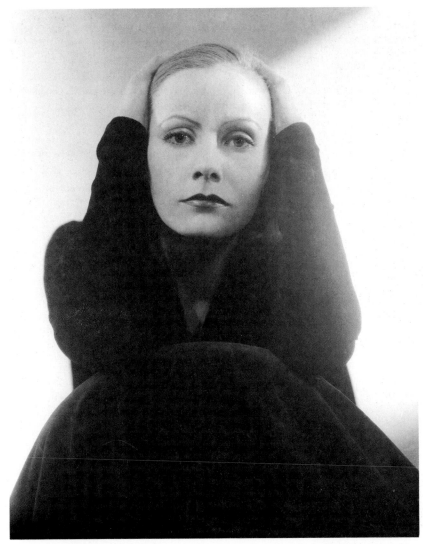

1130. EDWARD STEICHEN. *GRETA GARBO*. 1928 (for *Vanity Fair* magazine).
Collection, The Museum of Modern Art, New York. Gift of the artist

championed the Precisionist painters (see page 729) who, inspired by Futurism, began to depict urban and industrial architecture around 1925. Several of them soon took up the camera as well. Thus, painting and photography once again became closely linked. Both were responding to the revitalized economy after World War I which led to an unprecedented industrial expansion on both sides of the Atlantic. During the subsequent Depression, industrial photography continued surprisingly to grow with the new mass-circulation magazines that ushered in the great age of photojournalism and, with it, of commercial photography. In the United States, most of the important photographers were employed by the leading journals and corporations.

Margaret Bourke-White (1904–1971) was the first staff photographer hired by *Fortune* magazine and then by *Life* magazine, both published by Henry Luce; her cover photograph of Fort Peck Dam in Montana for *Life*'s inaugural issue on November 23, 1936, remains a classic example of the new photojournalism (fig. 1129). The decade was witnessing enormous building campaigns, and with her keen eye for compositions, Bourke-White drew a visual parallel between

the dam and the massive constructions of ancient Egypt (compare fig. 95), an idea that had already appeared in a painting of 1927 by Charles Demuth, *My Egypt* (see page 729). In addition to their architectural power, Bourke-White's columnar forms have a remarkable sculptural quality and an almost human presence, looming like colossal statues at the entrance to a temple. But unlike the pharaohs' passive timelessness, these "guardian figures" have the spectral alertness of Henry Moore's abstract monoliths (see fig. 1065). Bourke-White's rare ability to suggest multiple levels of meaning made this cover and her accompanying photo essay an astonishing revelation.

STEICHEN. The flourishing magazine business also gave rise to fashion and glamour photography, which was developed into an art in its own right by Edward Steichen, America's most complete photographer to date. Steichen's talent for portraiture, seen in his early Photo-Secession photograph of Rodin (see fig. 985), makes *Greta Garbo* (fig. 1130) a worthy successor to Nadar's *Sarah Bernhardt* (see fig. 905). The young film actress would have her picture

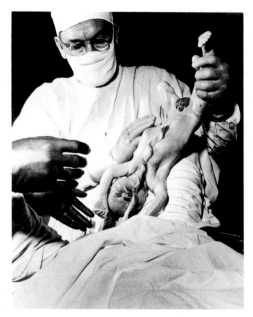

1131. WAYNE MILLER. *CHILDBIRTH.*
"Family of Man" exhibition. 1955

taken countless times, despite her desire "to be alone," but none captures better the magnetic presence and complex character seen in her movies. The photograph owes much to its abstract black-and-white design, which focuses attention on her wonderfully expressive face. But Steichen's stroke of genius was to have Garbo put her arms around her head in order to suggest her enigmatic personality.

MILLER. One of Steichen's contributions to photography was to organize the "Family of Man" exhibition, which opened in New York in 1955. Wayne Miller's picture of childbirth (fig. 1131) from this epoch-making show captures the miracle of life in one dramatic image. It records with shocking honesty the newborn infant's abrupt entry into the world we all share. At the same time, the hands that reach out to help him are a moving affirmation of human existence.

VAN DER ZEE. The nature of the Harlem Renaissance, which flourished in the 1920s (see page 746), was hotly debated by black critics even in its own day. While its achievement in literature is beyond dispute, the photography of

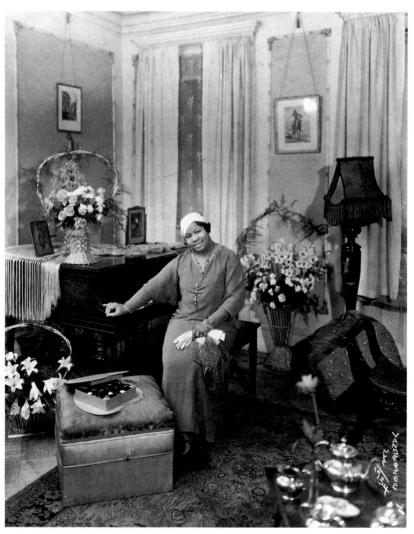

1132. JAMES VAN DER ZEE. *THE WIFE OF THE REVEREND BECTON,*
PASTOR OF SALEM METHODIST CHURCH. 1934. James Van Der Zee Estate

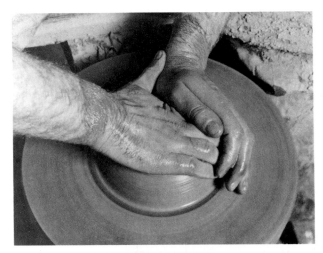

1133. ALBERT RENGER-PATZSCH. *POTTER'S HANDS.*
1925, Gelatin-silver print, 15⅛×11¾″ (38.2×29.8 cm).
Collection, The Museum of Modern Art, New York.
Gift of the artist

James Van Der Zee (1886–1983) is often regarded today as its chief contribution to the visual arts. Much of his work is commercial and variable in quality, yet it remains of great documentary value and, at its best, provides a compelling portrait of the era. Van Der Zee had an acute understanding of settings as reflections of people's sense of place in the world, which he used to bring out a sitter's character and dreams. Though posed in obvious imitation of fashionable photographs of white society, his picture of the wife of the Reverend George Wilson Becton (fig. 1132), taken two years after the popular pastor of the Salem Methodist Church in Harlem was murdered, shows Van Der Zee's unique ability to capture the pride of African-Americans during a period when their aspirations seemed on the verge of being realized.

Germany

With the New Objectivity movement in Germany during the late 1920s and early 1930s (see page 737), photography achieved a degree of excellence that has never been surpassed. Fostered by the invention of superior German cameras and the boom in publishing everywhere, this German version of straight photography emphasized materiality at a time when many other photographers were turning away from the real world. The intrinsic beauty of things was brought out through the clarity of form and structure in their photographs. This approach accorded with Bauhaus principles except with regard to function (see page 781).

RENGER-PATZSCH. *Potter's Hands* (fig. 1133) by Albert Renger-Patzsch (1897–1966), New Objectivity's leading exponent, is a marvel of technique and design that deliberately avoids any personal statement by reducing the image to an abstraction; the content lies solely in the cool perfection of the presentation and the orderly world it implies.

SANDER. When applied to people rather than things, the New Objectivity could have deceptive results. August Sander (1876–1964), whose *Face of Our Time* was published in

1929, concealed the book's intentions behind a disarmingly straightforward surface; the sixty portraits provide a devastating survey of Germany during the rise of the Nazis, who later suppressed the book. Clearly proud of his position, Sander's *Pastry Cook, Cologne* (fig. 1134) is the very opposite of the timid figure in George Grosz' *Germany, a Winter's Tale* (see fig. 1027); despite their curious resemblance, this "good citizen" seems oblivious to the evil that Grosz has depicted so vividly. While the photograph passes no individual judgment, the subject's unconcern stands as a strong indictment, particularly in light of later history.

The Heroic Age of Photography

CAPA. The years from 1930 to 1945 can be called the heroic age of photography for its photographers' notable response to the challenges of their times. Their physical bravery was exemplified by the combat photographer Robert Capa (1913–1954), who covered wars around the world for twenty years before being killed by a land mine in Vietnam. While barely adequate technically, his picture of a Loyalist soldier being shot during the Spanish Civil War (fig. 1135) captures fully

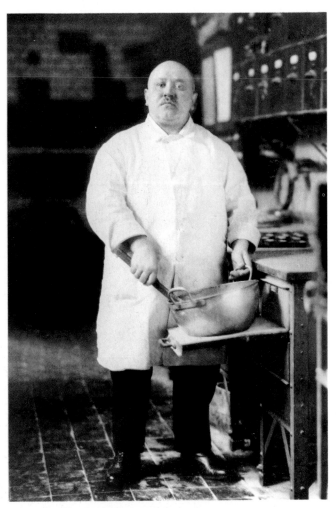

1134. AUGUST SANDER. *PASTRY COOK, COLOGNE.*
1928. Courtesy of August Sander Archive and
Sander Gallery, Inc., New York

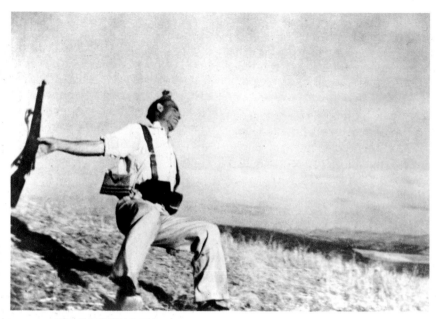

1135. ROBERT CAPA. *DEATH OF A LOYALIST SOLDIER.* September 5, 1936

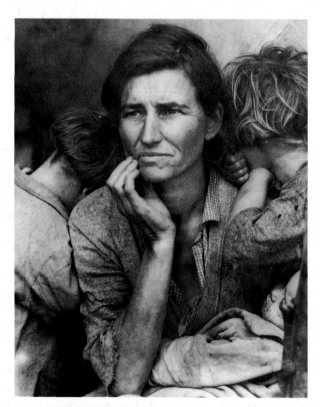

1136. DOROTHEA LANGE. *MIGRANT MOTHER, CALIFORNIA.*
February 1936. Gelatin-silver print.
Library of Congress, Washington, D.C.

the horror of death at the moment of impact. Had it been taken by someone else, it might seem a freak photograph, but it is altogether typical of Capa's battle close-ups; he was as fearless as Civil War photographer Mathew Brady.

LANGE. Photography in those difficult times demonstrated moral courage as well. Under Roy Stryker, staff photographers of the Farm Security Administration compiled a comprehensive photodocumentary archive of rural America during the Depression. While the FSA photographers presented a balanced and objective view, most of them were also reformers whose work responded to the social problems they confronted daily in the field. The concern of Dorothea Lange (1895–1965) for people and her sensitivity to their dignity made her the finest documentary photographer of the time in America.

At a pea-pickers' camp in Nipomo, California, Lange discovered 2,500 virtually starving migrant workers and took several pictures of a young widow with her children, much later identified as Florence Thompson; when *Migrant Mother, California* (fig. 1136) was published in a news story on their plight, the government rushed in food, and eventually migrant relief camps were opened. More than any Social Realist or Regionalist painting (see page 736), *Migrant Mother, California* has come to stand for that entire era. Unposed and uncropped, this photograph has an unforgettable immediacy no other medium can match.

Fantasy and Abstraction

"Impersonality," the very liability that had precluded the acceptance of photography in the eyes of many critics, became a virtue in the 1920s. Precisely because photographs are produced by mechanical devices, the camera's images now seemed to some artists the perfect means for expressing the modern era. This change in attitude did not stem from the Futurists who, contrary to what might be expected, never fully grasped the camera's importance for modern art, despite Marey's influence on their paintings (see page 708). The new view of photography arose as part of the Berlin Dadaists' assault on traditional art.

Toward the end of World War I, the Dadaists "invented" the photomontage and the photogram, although these completely different processes had been practiced early in the history of photography. In the service of anti-art they lent themselves equally well to fantasy and to abstraction, despite the apparent opposition of the two modes.

PHOTOMONTAGE. Photomontages are simply parts of photographs cut out and recombined into new images. Composite negatives originated with the art photography of Rejlander and Robinson (see page 705), but by the 1870s they were already being used in France to create witty impossibilities that are the ancestors of Dada photomontages. Like *1 Piping Man* (see fig. 1020) by Max Ernst (who, not surprisingly, became a master of the genre), Dadaist photomontages utilize the techniques of Synthetic Cubism to ridicule social and aesthetic conventions.

These imaginative parodies destroy all pictorial illusionism and therefore stand in direct opposition to straight photo-

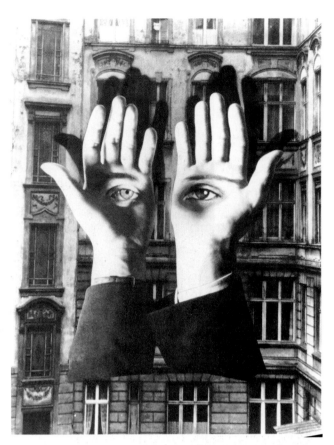

1138. HERBERT BAYER. *LONELY METROPOLITAN.* 1932.
Photomontage, 14×11″ (35.6×28 cm).
Collection the artist (copyright)

graphs, which use the camera to record and probe the meaning of reality. Dada photomontages might be called "ready-images," after Duchamp's ready-mades. Like other collages, they are literally torn from popular culture and given new meaning. Although the photomontage relies more on the laws of chance (see page 730), the Surrealists later claimed it to be a form of automatic handwriting on the grounds that it responds to a stream of consciousness.

Most Surrealist photographers have been influenced by the Belgian painter René Magritte, whose mystifying fantasies (fig. 1137) are treated with a magic realism that is the opposite of automatic handwriting. Since Magritte's pictorial style was already highly naturalistic, he only experimented with the camera. His impact on photography was nevertheless considerable, because his illusionistic paradoxes can be readily emulated in photographs, such as the photomontage *lonely metropolitan* (fig. 1138) by Herbert Bayer (born 1900, in Germany). The purpose of such visual riddles is to challenge our conception of reality, showing up the discrepancy between our perception of the world and our irrational understanding of its significance.

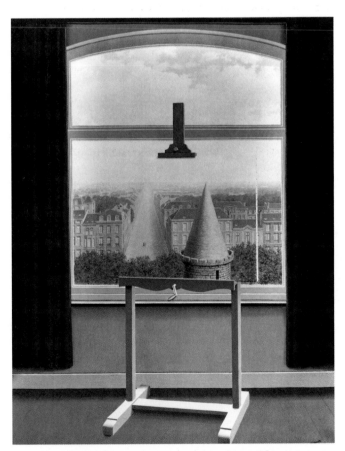

1137. RENÉ MAGRITTE. *LES PROMENADES D'EUCLID.*
1935. Oil on canvas, 64⅛×51⅛ (163×130 cm).
The Minneapolis Institute of Arts.
The William Hood Dunwoody Fund

POSTERS. Photomontages were soon incorporated into carefully designed posters as well. In Germany, posters became a double-edged sword in political propaganda, used by Hitler's sympathizers and enemies alike. The most acerbic

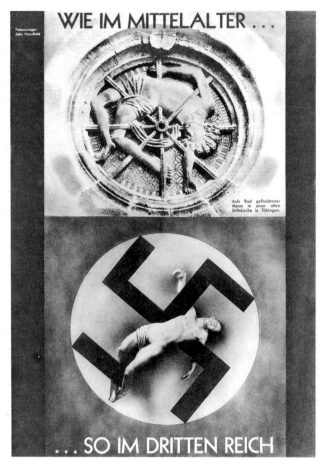

WIE IM MITTELALTER...

...SO IM DRITTEN REICH

1139. JOHN HEARTFIELD. *AS IN THE MIDDLE AGES,
SO IN THE THIRD REICH.* 1934. Poster, photomontage.
Akademie der Künste, Heartfield Archiv, Berlin

anti-Nazi commentaries were provided by John Heartfield (1891–1968), who changed his name from the German Herzfeld as a sign of protest. His horrific poster (fig. 1139) of a Nazi victim crucified on a swastika appropriates a Gothic image of humanity punished for its sins on the wheel of divine judgment. Obviously, Heartfield was not concerned about misinterpreting the original meaning in his montage, which communicates its new message to powerful effect.

PHOTOGRAMS. The photogram does not take pictures but makes them; objects are placed directly onto photographic paper and exposed to light. This technique, too, was not new; Fox Talbot (see page 658) had used it to make negative images of plants which he called "photogenic drawings." The Dadaists' photograms, however, like their photomontages, were intended to alter nature's forms, not to record them, and to substitute impersonal technology for the work of the individual. Since the results in the photogram are so unpredictable, making one involves even greater risks than does a photomontage.

Man Ray (1890–1976), an American working in Paris, was not the first to make photograms, but his name is the most closely linked to them through his "Rayographs." Fittingly enough, he discovered the process by accident. The amusing face in figure 1140, like Arp's *Collage with Squares* (see fig.

1021), was made according to the laws of chance by dropping a string, two strips of paper, and a few pieces of cotton onto the photographic paper, then coaxing them here and there before exposure. The resulting image is a witty creation that shows the playful, spontaneous side of Dada and Surrealism as against Heartfield's grim satire.

THE CONSTRUCTIVISTS. Because the Russian Constructivists had a comparably mechanistic conception of society, they soon followed Dada's lead in using photograms and photomontages as a means to integrate industry and art, albeit for quite different purposes. László Moholy-Nagy (1895–1946), a Hungarian teaching at the Bauhaus who was deeply affected by Constructivism, successfully combined the best features of both approaches. By removing the lens to make photograms, he transformed his camera from a reproductive into a productive instrument; photography could now become, in theory if not in practice, a technological tool for fostering creativity in mass education.

Like many of the Russian artists in the 1920s, Moholy-Nagy also saw light as the embodiment of dynamic energy in space. The effects conjured up by the superimposition and interpenetration of forms in his photographs are fascinating (fig. 1141). We feel transported in time and space to the edges of the universe, where the artist's imagination gives shape to the play of cosmic forces created by a supreme cosmic will.

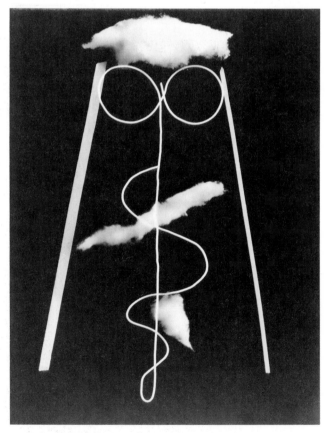

1140. MAN RAY. *RAYOGRAPH 1928.* 1928. Gelatin-silver print,
15½×11⅝" (39.4×29.5 cm). Collection, The Museum of
Modern Art, New York. Gift of James Thrall Soby

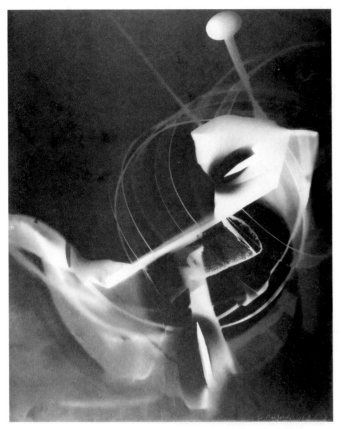

1141. LÁSZLÓ MOHOLY-NAGY. *UNTITLED.*
Photogram, silver bromide print, 19½×15¾″ (49.5×40 cm).
The Art Institute of Chicago. Gift of George Bancroft, 1968

ABBOTT. One of the principal educational purposes of Moholy-Nagy's images was to extend sense perception in new ways. Similar goals have been achieved by taking pictures through microscopes and telescopes. Such photographs have helped to open our eyes to the invisibly small and the infinitely far. Wondrous scientific photographs were taken from 1939 to 1958 by Berenice Abbott (born 1898), Man Ray's former pupil and assistant, to demonstrate the laws of physics (fig. 1142). Like Marey's motion photographs of fifty years earlier (see fig. 987a, b), they are arresting images, literally and visually. Their formal perfection makes them aesthetically compelling and scientifically valid, and they have proved to be even more educational than Moholy-Nagy's photograms.

PHOTOGRAPHY SINCE 1945

Abstraction

SISKIND. Photography after World War II was marked by abstraction for nearly two decades, particulary in the United States. Aaron Siskind (born 1903), a close friend of the Abstract Expressionist painters, recorded modern society's debris and decaying signs. Hidden in these details he discovered cipherlike figures (fig. 1143) that are ironically similar to the ideographs of some forgotten civilization no longer intelligible to us.

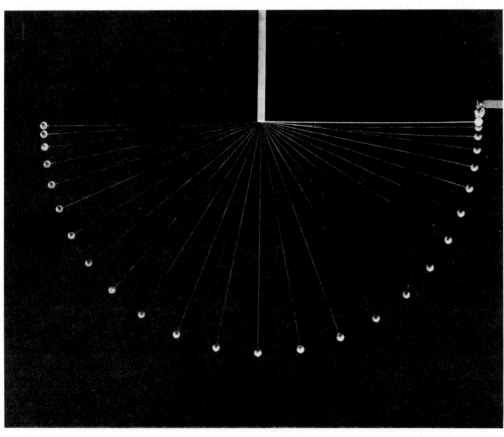

1142. BERENICE ABBOTT. *TRANSFORMATION OF ENERGY.* 1939–58. Courtesy Parasol Press

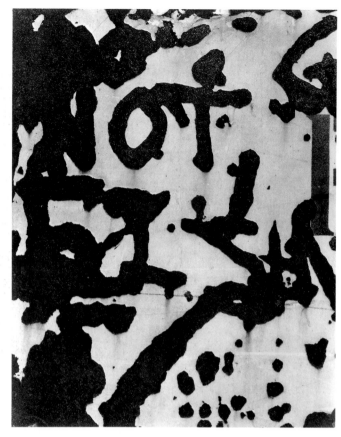

1143. AARON SISKIND. *NEW YORK 2.* 1951. Collection the artist

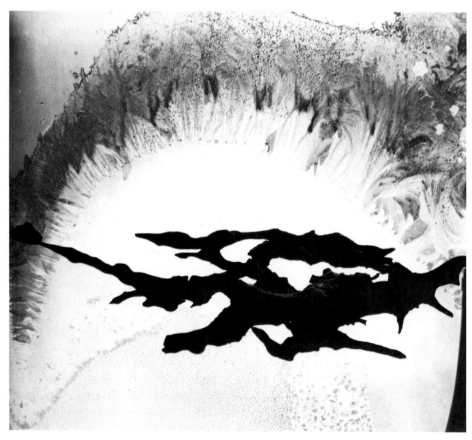

1144. MINOR WHITE. *RITUAL BRANCH.* 1958. Gelatin-silver print, 10⅜×10⅝″ (26.3×27 cm).
Collection of the International Museum of Photography at George Eastman House, Rochester, New York.

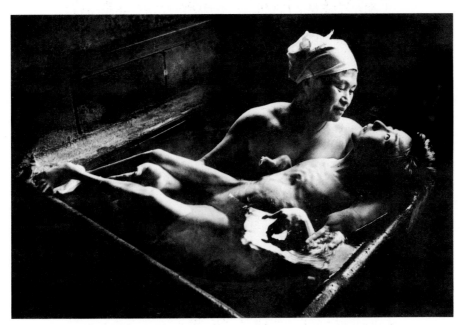

1145. W. EUGENE SMITH. *TOMOKO IN HER BATH*. December 1971.
Gelatin-silver print. Aileen and W. Eugene Smith—Black Star

WHITE. Minor White (1908–1976) approached even closer to the spirit of Abstract Expressionism. An associate of Adams and Weston, he was decisively influenced by Stieglitz' concept of the Equivalent. During his most productive period, from the mid-1950s to the mid-1960s, he worked in a highly individual style, using the alchemy of the darkroom to transform reality into a mystical metaphor. His *Ritual Branch* (fig. 1144) evokes a primordial image: what it shows is not as important as what it stands for, and the meaning that we sense there remains elusive.

Documentary Photography

SMITH. The continuing record of misery that photography provides has often been the vehicle for making strong personal statements. W. Eugene Smith (1918–1978), the foremost photojournalist of our time, was a compassionate cynic who commented on the human condition with "reasoned passion," as he put it. *Tomoko in Her Bath* (fig. 1145), taken in 1971 in the Japanese fishing village of Minamata, shows a child crippled by mercury poisoning being bathed by her mother. Not simply the subject itself but Smith's treatment of it makes this an intensely moving work. The imagery lies deep in our heritage: the mother holding her child's body goes back to the theme of the German Gothic Pietà (see fig. 505), while the dramatic lighting and vivid realism recall a painting of another martyr in his bath, Jacques-Louis David's *The Death of Marat* (see fig. 839). But what engages our emotions above all in making the photograph memorable is the infinite love conveyed by the mother's tender expression.

FRANK. The birth of a new form of straight photography in the United States was largely the responsibility of one man, Robert Frank (born 1924). His book *The Americans*, compiled from a cross-country odyssey in 1955–56, created a sensation upon its publication in 1959, for it expressed the same restlessness and alienation as *On the Road* by his traveling companion, the Beat poet Jack Kerouac, published in 1957. This friendship suggests that words have an important role in Frank's photographs, which are as loaded in their meaning as are Demuth's and Indiana's paintings (figs. 1017 and 1054), yet Frank's social point of view is often hidden behind a façade of disarming neutrality. It is with shock that we finally recognize the ironic intent of *Santa Fe, New Mexico* (fig. 1146): the gas pumps face the sign SAVE in the barren landscape like members of a religious cult vainly seeking salvation at a revival meeting. Frank, who subsequently turned to film, holds up an image of American culture that is as sterile as it is joyless. Even spiritual values, he tells us, become meaningless in the face of vulgar materialism.

Fantasy

Fantasy gradually reasserted itself on both sides of the Atlantic in the mid-1950s. Photographers first manipulated the camera for the sake of extreme visual effects by using special lenses and filters to alter appearances, sometimes virtually beyond recognition. Since about 1970, however, they have employed mainly printing techniques, with results that are frequently even more startling.

BRANDT. Manipulation of photography was pioneered by Bill Brandt (1904–1983). Though regarded as the quintessential English photographer, he was born in Germany and did not settle in London until 1931. He decided on a career in photography during psychoanalysis and was apprenticed briefly to Man Ray. Consequently, Brandt remained a Surrealist who manipulated visual reality in search of a deeper one, charged with mystery. His work was marked consistently by a literary, even theatrical, cast of mind which drew on the cinema for some of its effects. His early photodocumentaries were often staged as re-creations of personal experience for the purpose of social commentary based on Victorian models. Brandt's fantasy images manifest a strikingly romantic imagination. *London Child* (fig. 1147) has the haunting mood of novels by the Brontës. At the same time, this is a classic dream image fraught with troubling psychological overtones. There is an oppressive anxiety that is implicit in his landscapes, portraits, and nudes. The spatial dislocation, worthy of De Chirico, expresses the malaise of a person who is alienated from both himself and the world.

UELSMANN. The American Jerry Uelsmann (born 1934), a more recent leader of this movement, was inspired by Oscar Rejlander's multiple-negative photographs, as well as by Stieglitz' Equivalents. While Uelsmann's work has a playful side close to Pop Art, for the most part he involuntarily expresses archetypal images from deep within the subconscious. The nude lying within the earth in *Untitled* (fig. 1148) seemingly conveys a dream in which the psyche retreats into the womblike sanctuary of primal nature. Each part of the photograph is a faithful record; it is their juxtaposition that gives the image a new reality.

Uelsmann once participated in one of White's classes, and their photographs are not as far removed visually or expressively from each other's as they might seem. The principal difference lies in their approach to the Equivalent as a means of achieving a poetical inner truth: White, like Stieglitz, recognizes his symbols in nature, whereas Uelsmann creates his symbols from his imagination. Paradoxically, it is Uelsmann's untitled print, not *Ritual Branch*, that is instantly recognizable, but neither yields an ultimate meaning.

LEONARD. Photographers have increasingly turned to fantasy as autobiographical expression. Both the image and the title of *Romanticism Is Ultimately Fatal* (fig. 1149) by Joanne Leonard (born 1940) suggest a meaning that is personal in its reference. We will recognize in this disturbing vision something of the tortured eroticism of Fuseli's *The Nightmare* (see fig. 876). The clarity of the presentation turns the apparition at the window into a real and terrifying personification of despair. This is no romantic knight in shining armor, but a grim reaper whose ancestors can be found in Dürer's woodcut *The Four Horsemen of the Apocalypse* (see fig. 714).

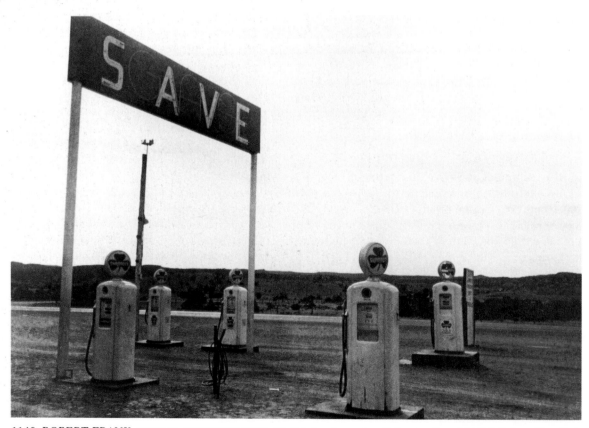

1146. ROBERT FRANK. *SANTA FE, NEW MEXICO.* 1955–56. Gelatin-silver print. Collection Pace-MacGill Gallery, New York

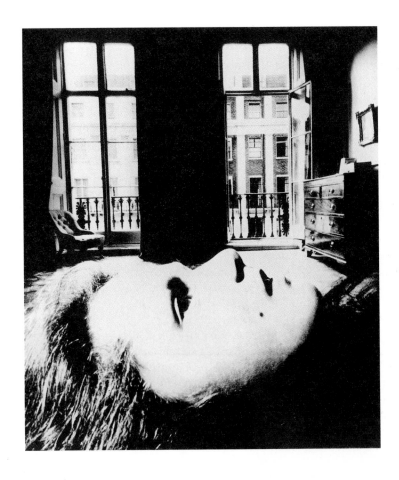

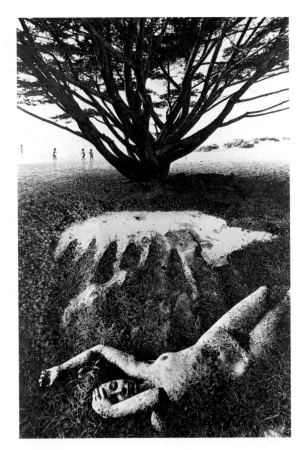

1147. (*above*) BILL BRANDT
LONDON CHILD 1955.
Copyright Mrs. Noya Brandt.
Courtesy Edwynn Houk Gallery, Chicago

1148. (*above right*) JERRY UELSMANN
UNTITLED. c. 1972.
Collection the artist

1149. (*right*) JOANNE LEONARD
ROMANTICISM IS ULTIMATELY FATAL,
from "Dreams and Nightmares." 1982.
Positive transparency selectively
opaqued with collage,
9¾×9¼″ (24.8×23.5 cm).
Collection M. Neri, Benicia, California

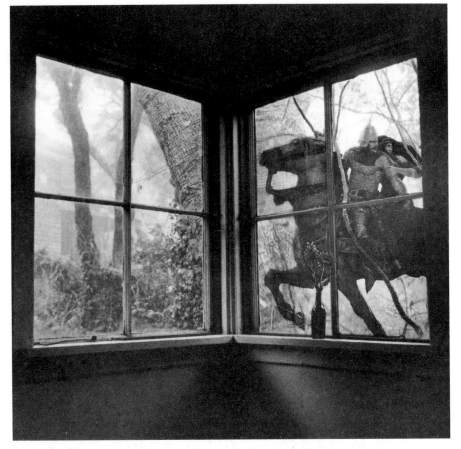

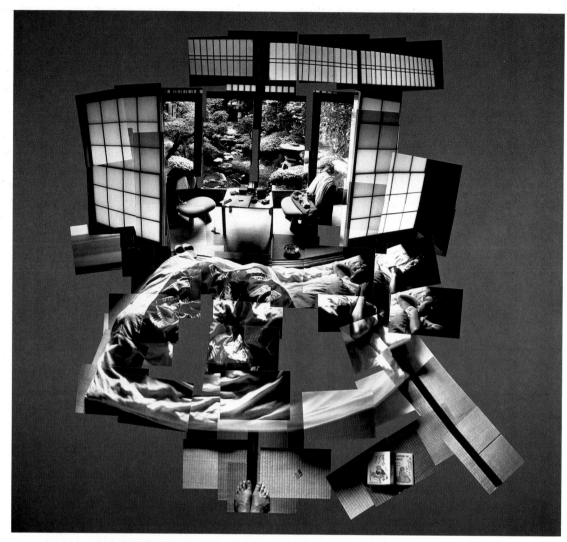

1150. DAVID HOCKNEY. *GREGORY WATCHING THE SNOW FALL, KYOTO, FEB. 21, 1983.*
Photographic collage, 43½×46½″ (110.5×118 cm). Collection the artist. © David Hockney, 1983

Artists as Photographers

HOCKNEY. The most recent demonstrations of photography's power to extend our vision have come, fittingly enough, from artists. The photographic collages that the English painter David Hockney (born 1937) has been making since 1982 are like revelations that overcome the traditional limitations of a unified image, fixed in time and place, by closely approximating how we actually see. In *Gregory Watching the Snow Fall, Kyoto, Feb. 21, 1983* (fig. 1150), each frame is analogous to a discrete eye movement containing a piece of visual data that must be stored in our memory and synthesized by the brain. Just as we process only essential information, so there are gaps in the matrix of the image, which becomes more fragmentary toward its edge, though without the loss of acuity experienced in vision itself. The resulting shape of the collage is a masterpiece of design. The scene appears to bow curiously as it comes toward us. This ebb and flow is more than simply the result of optical physics. In the perceptual process, space and its corollary, time, are not linear, but fluid. Moreover, by including his own feet as reference points to establish our position clearly, Hockney

helps us to realize that vision is less a matter of looking outward than an egocentric act that defines the viewer's visual and psychological relationship to the surrounding world. The picture is as expressive as it is opulent. Hockney has recorded his friend several times to suggest his reactions to the serene landscape outside the door.

Hockney's approach is embedded in the history of modern painting, for it shows a self-conscious awareness of earlier art. It combines the faceted views of Picasso (see fig. 999) and the sequential action of Duchamp (see fig. 1009) with the dynamic energy of Popova (see fig. 1004). *Gregory Watching the Snow Fall* is nonetheless a distinctly contemporary work, for it incorporates the fascinating effects of Photorealism and the illusionistic potential of Op Art (see fig. 1048). Hockney has begun to explore further implications inherent in these photo collages, such as continuous narrative. No doubt others will be discovered as well. Among these is the possibility of showing an object or scene simultaneously from multiple vantage points to let us see it completely for the first time.

LEMIEUX. Unlike Hockney, most artists do not take their own photographs but appropriate them from other mediums. Because their pictures are intended as counterparts to paintings, they are enlarged on an unprecedented scale, using commercial processes developed for advertisements, which may also serve as sources. Many of these re-photographers are conceptual artists, such as Annette Lemieux (born 1957), whose work conveys a message, served with the aid of texts. Her themes are thoughtprovoking. Centering on social issues, they address the human condition without engaging in polemic. Lemieux has a gift for perceiving new possibilities of meaning in old photographs and illustrations. *Truth* (fig. 1151) is an image about sound—or, rather, the lack of it. The photograph, derived from a book on the history of radio, is a visual counterpart to the saying, "Hear no evil, speak no evil, see no evil." Transferred to canvas, it acquires a very different meaning in its new context, a process known as deconstruction. Stenciled in bold letters is the Russian proverb, "Eat bread and salt but speak the truth," which means roughly, "Be frank when accepting someone's hospitality." The lettering transforms the image from an amusing publicity photograph into an ominous-looking propaganda poster. Contrary to initial impressions, the issue is neither Russia nor communism—the photograph features the famous American entertainer Jack Benny—but the role of the media in modern life. They enter our homes as guests without being candid: here the performer covers his mouth in order to speak no evil. Shielded by the medium itself, he distorts truth by selectively concealing information, not by telling a deliberate falsehood. Truth emerges as a matter of relative perspective, determined as much by who controls it as by who hears it.

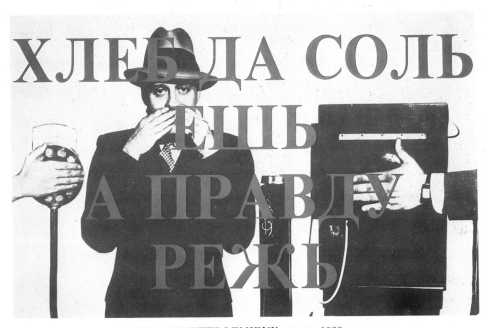

1151. ANNETTE LEMIEUX. *TRUTH*. 1989.
Latex and acrylic on canvas, 84×133×1½" (213.4×337.8×3.8 cm).
Josh Baer Gallery, New York

ILLUSTRATED TIME CHART IV

Edmund Burke, English reformer
  (1729–97)

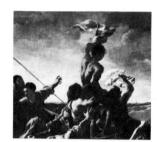

Géricault, *Raft of the "Medusa"*

Gray's *Elegy* 1750
Benjamin Franklin's experiments
  with electricity c. 1750
Diderot, *Encyclopedia* 1751–72
Johnson, *Dictionary* 1755
Winckelmann, *Thoughts on Greek Art* 1755
Rousseau, *Social Contract* and *Emile* 1762
Mechanization of textile spinning 1764–69
Priestley discovers oxygen 1774
Goethe, *Sorrows of Young Werther* 1774
Coke-fed blast furnaces for iron smelting
  perfected c. 1760–75

1775

American Revolution 1775–85; Constitu-
  tion adopted 1789
French Revolution 1789–1802; Louis
  XVI beheaded, Reign of Terror under
  Robespierre 1793
Consulate of Napoleon 1799–1804

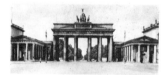

Langhans, Brandenburg Gate, Berlin

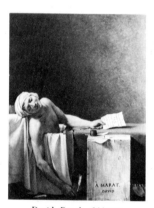

David, *Death of Marat*

Gibbon, *Decline and Fall of the
  Roman Empire* 1776–87
Adam Smith, *Wealth of Nations* 1776
Kant, *Critique of Pure Reason* 1781
Crossing of English Channel in hydrogen-
  filled balloon 1785
Paine, *The Rights of Man* 1790
Power loom 1785; cotton gin 1793
Lavoisier, French chemist (1743–94)
Hutton, *Theory of the Earth* 1795
Laplace's nebular hypothesis 1796
Jenner's smallpox vaccine 1796
Wordsworth and Coleridge,
  Lyrical Ballads 1798

1800

First child labor laws 1802
Jefferson negotiates Louisiana Purchase
  1803
Napoleon (1769–1821) crowns himself
  emperor 1804; fails in Russian campaign 1812; exiled to Elba 1814; defeated at Waterloo, exiled to St.
  Helena 1815
War of 1812
Congress of Vienna, 1814–15
Bolivar leads revolution in Latin America, six countries gain independence 1822
Greeks declare independence
  from Turks 1822
Monroe Doctrine proclaimed
  by U.S. 1823

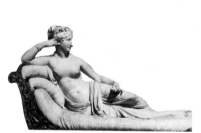

Canova, *Pauline Borghese*

Volta invents electric battery 1800
Lewis and Clark expedition
  to Pacific 1803–6
First voyage of Fulton's steamship 1807;
  first Atlantic crossing 1819
Hegel, *Phenomenology of Mind* 1807
Goethe, *Faust*: Part I, 1808; Part II, 1833
Byron, *Childe Harold's Pilgrimage* 1812–18
Saint-Simon's ideals for the reorganization
  of European society 1814
Stephenson's first steam locomotive 1814
Cuvier's work on paleontology 1815
Shelley, *Prometheus Unbound* 1820
Faraday discovers principle of electric
  dynamo 1821
Keats (1795–1821) dies in Rome
Walter Scott, Waverley novels 1814–25

1825

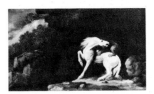

Stubbs, *Lion Attacking Horse*

Horace Walpole, Strawberry Hill
Soufflot, Panthéon
Greuze, *The Village Bride*
West, *Death of General Wolfe*
Stubbs, *Lion Attacking Horse*
Robert Adam, Landsdowne
   House, London

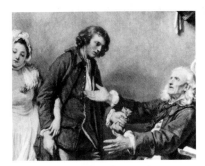

Greuze, *The Village Bride*

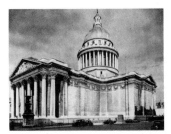

Soufflot, Panthéon, Paris

Jefferson, Monticello,
   Charlottesville
Copley, *Watson and the Shark*
Houdon, *Voltaire*
Cozens, *A New Method...*
Fuseli, *The Nightmare*
David, *Death of Socrates*
Langhans, Brandenburg
   Gate, Berlin
Houdon, *George Washington*
David, *Death of Marat*
Blake, *The Ancient of Days*
Gros, *Napoleon at Arcole*
Canova, Tomb of Maria
   Christina, Vienna

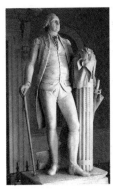

Houdon,
George Washington

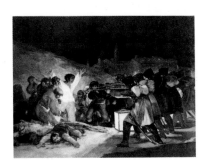

Goya, *Third of May ... 1808*

Goya, *Family of Charles IV*
Latrobe, Catholic Cathedral,
   Baltimore
Canova, *Pauline Borghese*
Géricault, *Mounted Officer*
Ingres, *Odalisque*
Goya, *Third of May... 1808*
Nash, Brighton Pavilion
Géricault, *Raft of the "Medusa"*
Delacroix, *Massacre at Chios*
Friedrich, *Polar Sea*

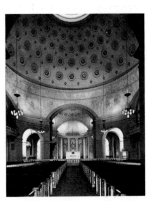

Latrobe, Catholic Cathedral,
Baltimore

1825

July Revolution of 1830 in France

Political and social reforms in England 1832–35

France conquers Algeria 1830–47

Queen Victoria crowned 1837

British win Hong Kong 1841

Oregon Trail opens western settlement 1842

U.S. treaty with China opens ports 1844

U.S. annexes western land areas 1845–60

Famine in Ireland, mass emigration 1845

Proudhon founds anarchism 1846

Parliament repeals Corn Laws 1846

Marx and Engels, *Communist Manifesto* 1848

Revolution of 1848: fails in Germany, Hungary, Austria, Italy; France sets up Second Republic (Louis Napoleon)

Gold discovered in California 1848

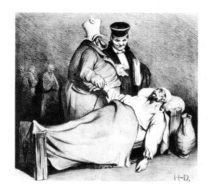

Daumier, *It's Safe to Release This One!*

Erie Canal opened 1825

First railroad in England 1825; in U.S. 1829

Pushkin, *Eugene Onegin* 1825–31

Lyell, *Principles of Geology* 1830

Stendhal, *The Red and The Black* 1831

McCormick invents reaper 1831; John Deere perfects steel plow 1837

Balzac writes the 92 novels and stories that comprise *La Comédie Humaine* 1832–50

Gogol's satirical drama *The Inspector General* 1836

Dickens, *Oliver Twist* 1838

Daguerre's process of photography, Fox Talbot's negative-positive process 1839

Emerson, *Essays* 1841, 1844

Kierkegaard, *Either/Or* 1843

Morse perfects telegraphy 1844

A. Dumas, *The Three Musketeers* 1844

Poe, *The Raven and Other Poems* 1845

Elias Howe invents sewing machine 1846

Morton demonstrates ether anaesthesia 1846

Joule formulates First Law of Thermodynamics 1847

Margaret Fuller, American writer and lecturer (1810–50)

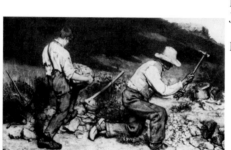

Courbet, *Stone Breakers*

1850

Louis Napoleon takes title of Napoleon III 1852

Crimean War 1853–55; England and France halt Russia's advance into Balkans

Commodore Perry opens Japan 1854

Unification of Italy by Garibaldi 1860–70

Russia abolishes serfdom 1861

Frederick Douglass (c. 1817–95) becomes American abolitionist leader

Civil War (1861–65) ends slavery in U.S.; Lincoln assassinated 1865

Russia sells Alaska to U.S. 1867

Canada granted dominion status 1867

Marx, *Das Kapital* 1867–94

Susan B. Anthony (with Elizabeth Cady Stanton) organizes National Woman Suffrage Association 1869

Franco-Prussian War 1870–71; Third Republic in France; Bismarck becomes first chancellor of German empire

Disraeli, British prime minister 1874–80

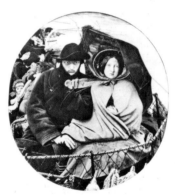

Brown, *The Last of England*

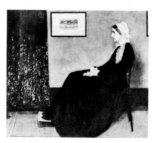

Whistler, *The Artist's Mother*

Stowe, *Uncle Tom's Cabin* 1851

Lord Kelvin states Second Law of Thermodynamics 1851

Melville, *Moby Dick* 1851

Thoreau, *Walden* 1854

Whitman, *Leaves of Grass* 1855

Flaubert, *Madame Bovary* 1856

Baudelaire, *Les Fleurs du Mal* 1857

First transatlantic cable laid 1858–66

Darwin, *Origin of Species* 1859

First oil well drilled (Pennsylvania) 1859

Bessemer patents tilting converter for steel manufacture 1860

Victor Hugo, *Les Misérables* 1862

Pasteur develops germ theory 1864

Tolstoy, *War and Peace* 1864–69

Mendel publishes first experiments in genetics 1865

Lewis Carroll, *Alice in Wonderland* 1865

Dostoyevsky, *Crime and Punishment* 1867

Nobel invents dynamite 1867

First transcontinental railroad in U.S. 1869

Suez Canal opened 1869

Celluloid, first plastic, discovered c. 1869

Mendelijeff's periodic law of elements 1869

Schliemann excavates at Troy 1872

Maxwell, *Electricity and Magnetism* 1873

1875

Corot, *Papigno*
Daumier, *It's Safe to
    Release This One!*
Ingres, *Louis Bertin*
Préault, *Slaughter*
Rude, *La Marseillaise*
Barry and Pugin, Houses of
    Parliament, London
Constable, *Hampstead Heath*
Turner, *Slave Ship*
Daguerre, *Still Life*
Labrouste, Bibliothèque
    Ste.-Geneviève, Paris
Bingham, *Fur Traders*
Bonheur, *Plowing in the Nivernais*
Courbet, *Stone Breakers*
Rossetti, *Ecce Ancilla Domini*
Delacroix, *Odalisque*
Fox Talbot, *Sailing Craft*

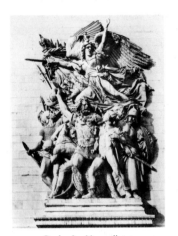
Rude, *La Marseillaise*

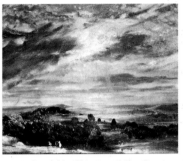
Constable, *Hampstead Heath*

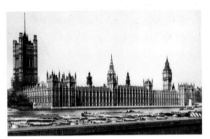
Barry and Pugin, Houses of Parliament

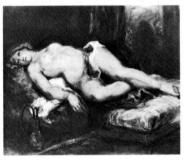
Delacroix, *Odalisque*

———— 1850

Millet, *The Sower*
Barye, *Jaguar Devouring a Hare*
Paxton, Crystal Palace, London
Brown, *The Last of England*
Courbet, *Studio of a Painter...*
Rude, *Marshal Ney*
Nadar, *Sarah Bernhardt*
Rejlander, *Two Paths of Life*
Garnier, Opèra, Paris
Carpeaux, *The Dance*
Daumier, *Third-Class Carriage*
Manet, *Luncheon on the Grass*
Rodin, *Man with Broken Nose*
Julia Cameron, *Portrait of Ellen Terry*
Monet, *The River*
Morisot, *La Lecture*
Whistler, *The Artist's Mother*

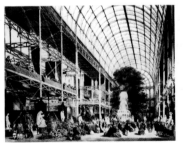
Paxton, Crystal Palace

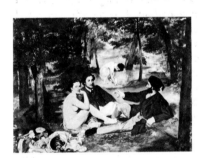
Manet, *Luncheon on the Grass*

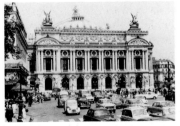
Garnier, Opéra, Paris

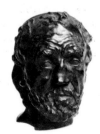
Rodin, *Man with Broken Nose*

———— 1875

1875

Peak of colonialism worldwide 1876–1914

First pogroms in Russia 1881–82

Labor unrest in U.S.: Haymarket riot, Chicago 1886; Carnegie steel strike, Homestead, Pa. 1892

"Dreyfus affair" (false treason charge), France, 1894–1906

First Zionist Congress called by Theodor Hertzl 1897

Spanish-American War 1898; U.S. gains Philippines, Guam, Puerto Rico, annexes Hawaii

Boxer Rebellion, China, against Western interests 1899–1900

Boer War, British defeat South Africans, 1899–1902

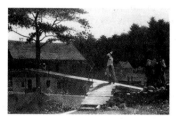
Homer, *Morning Bell*

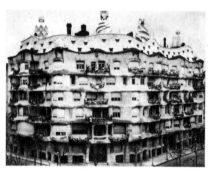
Seurat, *Bathers*

Bell patents the telephone 1876

Mark Twain, *Tom Sawyer* 1876

Ibsen, *A Doll's House* 1879

Edison invents phonograph 1877; incandescent bulb 1879

Zola, *Nana* 1880

Henry James, *Portrait of a Lady* 1881

Internal combustion engines for gasoline 1885

Research on germ-caused diseases at Pasteur Institute, Paris (founded 1888); at Robert Koch's Institute of Infectious Diseases, Berlin (1891)

Emily Dickinson (1830–86), poetry published 1890, 1891

Oscar Wilde, *Lady Windermere's Fan* 1892

Edison invents motion picture 1894

Roentgen discovers X-rays 1895

Marconi invents wireless telegraphy (precursor of radio) 1895

G. B. Shaw, *Plays Pleasant and Unpleasant* 1898

Pierre and Marie Curie discover radium 1898

Anton Chekhov, *Uncle Vanya* 1899

1900

8,800,000 immigrate to U.S., 1901–10

Theodore Roosevelt (pres. 1901–9) attacks trusts, promotes Panama Canal (opened 1914)

William James, *The Varieties of Religious Experience* 1902

Internal strife, reforms in Russia 1905

Revolution in China, republic led by Sun Yat-sen set up 1911

First World War 1914–18; U.S. enters 1917

Bolshevik Revolution in Russia 1917

Armistice signed 1918; League of Nations founded in Geneva 1919

Woman suffrage enacted in U.S. 1920; in England 1928; in France 1945

Poland, Czechoslovakia, Austria, Germany become republics 1918; Finland 1919; Irish Free State 1921; Turkey 1923; Lebanon 1926

Gandhi leads Indian National Congress 1920s

Mussolini's Fascists seize Italian government 1922

Adolf Hitler writes *Mein Kampf* 1924

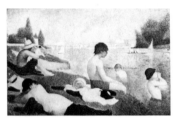
Gaudí, Casa Milá, Barcelona

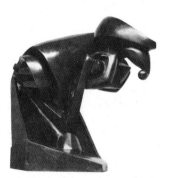
Duchamp-Villon, *Great Horse*

Planck formulates quantum theory 1900

Freud, *Interpretation of Dreams* 1900

Pavlov experiments with conditioned reflexes in dogs 1900

Nobel Prizes initiated 1901

Walter Reed pinpoints mosquito in spread of yellow fever 1901

Maxim Gorky, *Lower Depths* 1902

Wright brothers' first flight 1903

Einstein's relativity theory, $E = mc^2$, 1905

Ford begins assembly-line automobile manufacture 1909

Gertrude Stein, *Three Lives* 1909

Russell and Whitehead, *Principia Mathematica* 1910–13

Rutherford's theory of positively charged atomic nucleus 1911

D. H. Lawrence, *Sons and Lovers* 1913

Marcel Proust, *Remembrance of Things Past* 1913–27

James Joyce, *Ulysses* 1914–21

Margaret Sanger leads birth-control movement c. 1915

John Dewey (1859–1952), philosopher, influences progressive education

First regular radio station broadcasts 1920

Sinclair Lewis, *Main Street* 1920

Maria Montessori (1870–1952) pioneers in children's education

Insulin developed by Banting and Best 1921–22

T. S. Eliot, *The Waste Land* 1922

1925

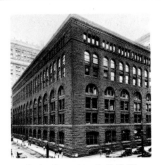

Richardson, Marshall Field
Wholesale Store

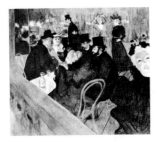

Toulouse-Lautrec, *Moulin Rouge*

Homer, *Morning Bell*
Eakins, *William Rush Carving...*
Moreau, *The Apparition*
Renoir, *Moulin de la Galette*
Degas, *Glass of Absinthe*
Cézanne, *Mont Sainte-Victoire*
Redon, *À Edgar Poe*
Seurat, *Bathers*
Marey, *Man in Black Suit...*
Richardson, Marshall Field Wholesale
   Store, Chicago
Muybridge, *Human and Animal Locomo-*
   tion
Gauguin, *Vision After the Sermon*
Riis, *Bandits' Roost*
Van Gogh, *Self-Portrait*
Ensor, *The Intrigue*
Sullivan, Wainwright Building, St. Louis
Cassatt, *The Bath*
Toulouse-Lautrec, *Moulin Rouge*
Beardsley, *Salome*
Rodin, *Balzac*
Munch, *The Scream*
Tanner, *The Banjo Lesson*
Mackintosh, Glasgow School of Art
Vuillard, *Interior*

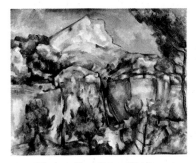

Cézanne, *Mont Sainte-Victoire*

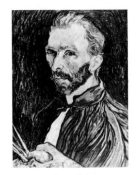

Van Gogh, *Self-Portrait*

1900

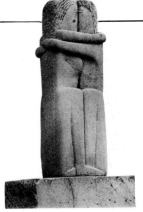

Brancusi, *The Kiss*

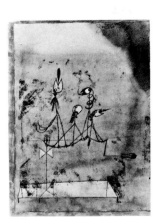

Klee, *Twittering Machine*

Steichen, *Rodin with His Sculptures*
Matisse, *Joy of Life*
Lumière, *Young Lady with an Umbrella*
Gaudí, Casa Milá, Barcelona
Stieglitz, *The Steerage*
Picasso, *Les Demoiselles d'Avignon*
Brancusi, *The Kiss*
Nolde, *Last Supper*
Bellows, *Stag at Sharkey's*
Rousseau, *The Dream*
Chagall, *I and the Village*
Barlach, *Man Drawing Sword*
Duchamp, *The Bride*
Kandinsky, *Sketch I for Composition VII*
Malevich, *Black Quadrilateral*
Boccioni, *Unique Forms...*
Popova, *The Traveler*
De Chirico, *Mystery and Melancholy...*
Duchamp-Villon, *Great Horse*
Arp, *Collage with Squares...*
Stella, *Brooklyn Bridge*
Tatlin, Project for *Monument to the*
   Third International
Léger, *The City*
Brancusi, *Bird in Space*
Kertész, *Blind Musician*
O'Keeffe, *Black Iris III*
Ernst, *1 Copper Plate...*
Klee, *Twittering Machine*
Atget, *Pool, Versailles*
Rietveld, Schröder House, Utrecht

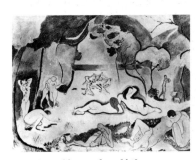

Matisse, *Joy of Life*

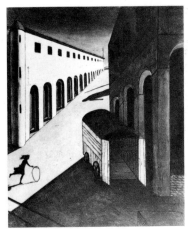

De Chirico, *Mystery and Melancholy...*

1925

1925

Chiang Kai-shek unites Nationalist
China 1927–28

Stock-market crash in U.S. 1929; worldwide economic depression

Japan invades Manchuria 1931

Spain becomes republic 1931

Hitler seizes power in Germany 1933

Roosevelt proclaims New Deal 1933

Spanish Civil War 1936–39; won by Franco

Hitler annexes Austria 1938; seizes
Czechoslovakia, signs nonaggression
pact with Russia 1939

Germany invades Poland, initiating
World War II 1939

Japan bombs Pearl Harbor: U.S. enters
World War II 1941

Atomic bomb dropped on Hiroshima 1945

United Nations Charter signed 1945

Philippine independence 1946

British rule ends in India 1947

U.S. starts Marshall Plan 1947

Apartheid becomes government policy in
South Africa 1948

Israel achieves nationhood 1948

NATO founded 1949

West Germany becomes Federal Republic 1949

People's Republic of China founded 1949

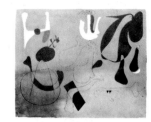

Miró, *Composition*

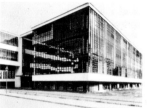

Gropius, Bauhaus, Dessau

Ezra Pound, *Cantos* 1925–72

Lindbergh flies solo, nonstop from New
York to Paris 1927

Berthold Brecht, *Three-Penny Opera* 1928

Margaret Mead, *Coming of Age in
Samoa* 1928

Ernest Hemingway, *A Farewell to Arms* 1929

William Faulkner, *Sanctuary* 1931

Eugene O'Neill, *Mourning Becomes Electra* 1931

Radar developed, Watson-Watt 1934–35

C. F. Richter devises scale for measuring
earthquakes 1935

DDT invented 1939; banned 1972

Antibiotics discovered: penicillin 1939;
streptomycin 1944

First large-scale atomic explosion (fis-
sion), Los Alamos 1943

Jean-Paul Sartre formulates existential-
ism, *Being and Nothingness* 1943

Computer technology developed 1944

Television licensed for commercial use 1945

Xerography invented 1946; commercial
use 1958

Dead Sea scrolls discovered 1947

Norman Mailer, *The Naked and the Dead* 1948

Alfred Kinsey, *Sexual Behavior in the
Human Male* 1948; *Female* 1953

1950

Korean War 1950–53

U.S. Supreme Court outlaws racial seg-
regation in public schools 1954

Warsaw pact signed by East European
countries 1955

Common Market in Europe 1957

U.S. tests first ICBM 1957

Castro takes over Cuba 1959

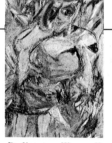

De Kooning, *Woman II*

Rachel Carson, *The Sea Around Us* 1951

First hydrogen bomb (atomic fusion) 1952

Samuel Beckett, *Waiting for Godot* 1952

Double helix of DNA established 1953;
genetic code determined

Sputnik, first satellite, launched 1957

Jack Kerouac, *On the Road* 1957

Vladimir Nabokov, *Lolita* 1958

Jet planes adopted commercially 1959

1960

Sit-ins protest racial discrimination 1960

17 African countries independent 1960

Berlin Wall built 1961

John F. Kennedy assassinated 1963

U.S. intervention in Vietnam begins
1965

Martin Luther King assassinated 1968

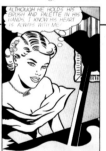

Lichtenstein, *Girl at Piano*

Oral birth-control pill 1960

Laser device invented in U.S. 1960

Weather and communications satellites
launched 1960–61

First manned space flight 1961

Rise of the Beatles 1963

Planetary probes begin with Mars, 1965;
five probed, more planned

First manned moon landing 1969

1970

Nixon opens relations with People's Republic of China 1972

Supreme Court legalizes abortion 1973

Vietnam war ends 1973

Nixon resigns presidency 1974

Margaret Thatcher elected British Prime
Minister 1979

Ayatollah Khomeini proclaims Islamic
republic in Iran 1979

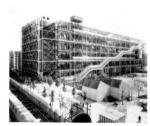

Piano and Rogers, Pompidou Center

Three "test tube" babies born in England 1973

Eudora Welty, *The Optimist's Daughter*
1973

Viking II lands on Mars 1976

Saul Bellow, *Humboldt's Gift* 1976

Personal computers become available
1978

1980

Socialization of French banks 1981

Lech Walesa, Polish Solidarity leader,
wins Nobel Peace Prize 1983

Space shuttle initiated by U.S. 1981

First artificial heart implanted 1982

Alice Walker, *The Color Purple* 1983

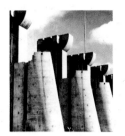

Bourke-White, *Fort Peck Dam*

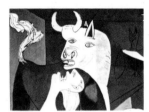

Picasso, *Guernica*

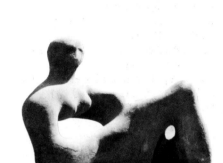

Hopper, *Early Sunday Morning*

Picasso, *Three Dancers*
Gropius, Bauhaus, Dessau
Demuth, *I Saw the Figure 5 in Gold*
Sander, *Pastry Cook, Cologne*
Le Corbusier, Savoye House, Poissy
Howe and Lescaze, Philadelphia Savings
    Fund Society Building
Hopper, *Early Sunday Morning*
Giocometi, *Palace at 4 A.M.*
Picasso, *Girl Before a Mirror*
Brassaï, *"Bijou" of Montmartre*
Miró, *Composition*
Heartfield, *As in the Middle Ages...*
González, *Head*
Moore, *Two Forms*
Bourke-White, *Fort Peck Dam*
Capa, *Death of a Loyalist Soldier*
Picasso, *Guernica*
Moore, *Recumbent Figure*
Abbott, *Transformation of Energy*
Calder, *Lobster Trap and Fish Tail*
Hepworth, *Oval Form*
A. Adams, *Moonrise...*
Gorky, *The Liver is the Cock's Comb*
Mondrian, *Composition*
Harrison, U.N. Buildings, New York
Siskind, *New York 2*

Moore, *Recumbent Figure*

1950

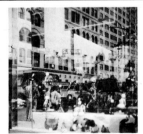

Rauschenberg, *Odalisk*

Pollock, *Autumnal Rhythm*
Dubuffet, *Le Metafisyx*
Mies van der Rohe, Lake Shore
    Drive Apartments, Chicago
Le Corbusier, Notre-Dame-
    du-Haut, Ronchamp
De Kooning, *Woman II*

Rothko, *Ochre and Red on Red*
Frank, *Santa Fe...*
Rauschenberg, *Odalisk*
Vasarely, *Vega*
Johns, *Three Flags*
Appel, *Burned Face*
Krasner, *Celebration*

1960

Warhol, *Gold Marilyn Monroe*
Lichtenstein, *Girl at Piano*
George Segal, *Cinema*
Barnett Newman, *Broken Obelisk*
D. Smith, *Cubi* series
Nevelson, *Black Chord*
Kosuth, *One and Three Chairs*
Kienholz, *State Hospital*

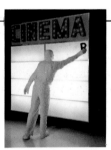

George Segal, *Cinema*

1970

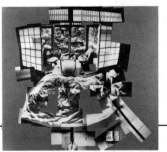

Hockney, *Gregory Watching...*

Hanson, *Tourists*
Piano and Rogers, Pompidou Center
W. E. Smith, *Tomoko in Her Bath*
Eddy, *New Shoes for H*
Paik, *TV Buddha*
Flack, *Queen*

Eddy, *New Shoes for H*

1980

Graves, *Trace*
Rothenberg, *Mondrian*
Hockney, *Gregory Watching...*
Murray, *More Than You Know*

BOOKS FOR FURTHER READING

This list includes standard works and the most recent and comprehensive books in English. Books with material relevant to several chapters are cited only under the first heading. Many authors cited have written other works on their fields. Two useful series, not all volumes of which are cited here, are the *Pelican History of Art* and the *World of Art* series. Two excellent general bibliographies are *Guide to the Literature of Art History* by E. Arntzen and R. Rainwater (American Library Association, 1980) and *Art Books: A Basic Bibliography* by E. L. Lucas (New York Graphic Society, 1968). Many libraries now have access to electronic data bases, such as *Art Bibliographies Modern* and *RLIN*, which can help you find other works. A useful guide to art historical research is *Art Information: Research Methods and Resources* by L. S. Jones (3d ed., Kendall/Hunt Publishing Co., c. 1990). Asterisks (*) indicate titles available in paperback; for publishers, distributors, and the like, see *Paperbound Books in Print* (R.R. Bowker, annual).

INTRODUCTION

*ARNHEIM, R., *Art and Visual Perception*, 2d ed., Univ. of California Press, Berkeley, 1974
*_____, *Visual Thinking*, Univ. of California Press, Berkeley, 1970
BAUMGART, F., *A History of Architectural Styles*, Praeger, N.Y., 1970
BERNHEIMER, R., *The Nature of Representation*, New York Univ. Press, 1961
CAHN, W., *Masterpieces: Chapters on the History of an Idea*, Princeton Univ. Press, 1979
DICKIE, G., *Art and the Aesthetic: An Institutional Analysis*, Cornell Univ. Press, Ithaca, 1974
*DIENHARD, H., *Meaning and Expression: Toward a Sociology of Art*, Beacon Press, Boston, 1970
*ELSEN, A. E., *Purpose of Art*, 3d ed., Holt, Rinehart, Winston, N.Y., 1972
*FEIBELMAN, J. K., *The Quiet Rebellion: The Making and Meaning of the Arts*, Horizon, N.Y., 1972
*FINN, D., *How to Look at Sculpture*, Abrams, N.Y., 1989
*GOMBRICH, E. H., *Art and Illusion*, 4th ed., Pantheon Books, N.Y., 1972
_____, *Ideals and Icons: Essays on Value in History and in Art*, Phaidon, Oxford, 1979
*_____, *The Sense of Order, a Study in the Psychology of Decorative Art*, Cornell Univ. Press, Ithaca, N.Y., c. 1979, 1984
*HOLT, E. G., *A Documentary History of Art*, 2d ed., 2 vols., Doubleday, Garden City, 1981
KEPES, G., ed., *The Man-Made Object*, Braziller, N.Y., 1966
*KUBLER, G., *The Shape of Time*, Yale Univ. Press, New Haven, 1962
LANG, B., ed., *The Concept of Style*, Univ. of Pennsylvania Press, Philadelphia, 1979
*PANOFSKY, E., *Meaning in the Visual Arts*, Doubleday, Garden City, 1955; reprint, Overlook Press, Woodstock, 1974
PODRO, M., *The Manifold in Perception: Theories of Art from Kant to Hildebrand*, Clarendon Press, Oxford, 1972
READ, H. E., *Art and Alienation: The Role of the Artist in Society*, Horizon, N.Y., 1967
_____, *Icon and Idea*, Schocken, N.Y., 1965
*ROSENBERG, H., *The Anxious Object: Art Today and Its Audience*, 2d ed., Horizon, N.Y., 1966
SIRCELLO, G., *Mind and Art*, Princeton Univ. Press, 1972
*TAYLOR, J. C., *Learning to Look: A Handbook for the Visual Arts*, 2d ed., Univ. of Chicago Press, 1981

PART THREE
THE RENAISSANCE, MANNERISM, AND THE BAROQUE
1. "LATE GOTHIC" PAINTING, SCULPTURE, AND THE GRAPHIC ARTS

BLUM, S. N., *Early Netherlandish Triptychs: A Study in Patronage*, Univ. of California Press, Berkeley, 1969
CHÂTELET, A., *Early Dutch Painting*, Rizzoli, N.Y., 1981
*CUTTLER, C. D., *Northern Painting: From Pucelle to Bruegel*, Holt, Rinehart & Winston, N.Y., 1968
DAVIES, M., *Rogier van der Weyden, an Essay with a Critical Catalogue of Paintings*, Phaidon, N.Y., 1972
DHANENS, E., *Hubert and Jan van Eyck*, Alpine Fine Arts Collection, N.Y., 1980
EICHENBERG, F., *The Art of the Print: Masterpieces, History, and Techniques*, Abrams, N.Y., 1976
FRAENGER, W., *Hieronymus Bosch*, 1st Amer. ed., Putnam, N.Y., 1983
FRIEDLÄNDER, M. J., *Early Netherlandish Painting*, 14 vols., Praeger, N.Y., 1967–73
_____, *From Van Eyck to Bruegel: Early Netherlandish Painting*, Phaidon, N.Y., 1969
FRINTA, M. S., *The Genius of Robert Campin*, Mouton & Co., The Hague, 1966
GIBSON, W. S., *Hieronymus Bosch*, Praeger, N.Y., 1973
*HIND, A. M., *History of Engraving and Etching*, 3d ed. rev., Houghton Mifflin, Boston, 1923
_____, *An Introduction to a History of Woodcut*, 2 vols., Houghton Mifflin, Boston, 1935
*IVINS, W. M., JR., *How Prints Look*, Metropolitan Museum of Art, N.Y., 1943
MEISS, M., *French Painting in the Time of Jean de Berry: The Limbourgs and Their Contemporaries*, 2 vols., Braziller, N.Y., 1974
MULLER, T., *Sculpture in the Netherlands, Germany, France and Spain, 1400–1500*, Pelican History of Art, Penguin, Harmondsworth, Baltimore, 1966
*PANOFSKY, E., *Early Netherlandish Painting*, 2 vols., Harvard Univ. Press, Cambridge, 1958
PURTLE, C. J., *The Marian Painting of Jan van Eyck*, Princeton Univ. Press, 1982
PUYVELDE, VAN, *Flemish Painting from the van Eycks to Metsys*, McGraw-Hill, N.Y., 1970
SNYDER, J., *Northern Renaissance Art*, Abrams, N.Y., 1985

2. THE EARLY RENAISSANCE IN ITALY

*ALAZARD, J., *The Florentine Portrait*, Schocken, N.Y., 1969
*ALBERTI, L. B., *On Painting and On Sculpture*, Phaidon, N.Y., 1972
*_____, *Ten Books on Architecture*, ed. J. Rykwert, Tiranti, London, 1955
*ANTAL, F., *Florentine Painting and Its Social Background*, Boston Book & Art Shop, 1965
ARGAN, G. C., *The Renaissance City*, Braziller, N.Y., 1969
*AVERY, C., *Florentine Renaissance Sculpture*, Harper & Row, N.Y., 1970
BATTISTI, E., *Brunelleschi: The Complete Work*, Rizzoli, N.Y., 1981
*BAXANDALL, M., *Painting and Experience in Fifteenth-Century Italy*, Clarendon Press, Oxford, 1972
*BECK, J., *Italian Renaissance Painting*, Harper & Row, N.Y., 1981
BERENSON, B., *The Drawings of the Florentine Painters*, 3 vols. (reprint, 1938 ed.), Univ. of Chicago Press, 1973
*_____, *Italian Painters of the Renaissance*, rev. ed., Phaidon, London, 1967
_____, *Italian Pictures of the Renaissance: Central and North Italian Schools*, 3 vols., Phaidon, London, 1968
_____, *Italian Pictures of the Renaissance: Florentine School*, 2 vols., Phaidon, London, 1963
*BLUNT, A., *Artistic Theory in Italy, 1450–1600*, Oxford Univ. Press, N.Y., 1956
*BURCKHARDT, J. C., *The Civilization of the Renaissance in Italy*, 3d ed., rev., Phaidon, London, 1950
CHASTEL, A., *The Age of Humanism: Europe, 1480–1530*, McGraw-Hill, N.Y., 1964
_____, *Studios and Styles of the Italian Renaissance, 1460–1500*, Braziller, N.Y., 1971
CLARK, K. M., *Piero della Francesca*, 2d ed., Phaidon, London, 1969
COLE, B., *Masaccio and the Art of Early Renaissance Florence*, Indiana Univ. Press, Bloomington, 1980
EDGERTON, S. Y., JR., *The Renaissance: Rediscovery of Linear Perspective*, Basic Books, N.Y., 1975
EISLER, C., *The Genius of Jacopo Bellini: The Complete Drawings and Paintings*, Abrams, N.Y., 1989
FINE, E. H., *Women and Art: A History of Women Painters and Sculptors from the Renaissance to the 20th Century*, Allanheld & Schram, Montclair, 1978
GILBERT, C., *History of Renaissance Art Throughout Europe: Painting, Sculpture, Architecture*, Abrams, N.Y., 1973
*_____, *Italian Art, 1400–1500: Sources and Documents*, Prentice-Hall, Englewood Cliffs, 1980
GOMBRICH, E. H., *The Heritage of Apelles: Studies in the Art of the Renaissance*, Phaidon, Oxford Univ. Press, 1976
*_____, *Norm and Form: Studies in the Art of the Renaissance*, Phaidon, London, 1966
GREENHALGH, M., *Donatello and His Sources*, Duckworth, London, 1982
HARTT, F., *History of Italian Renaissance Art*, 3d ed., Abrams, N.Y., 1987
HENDY, P., *Piero della Francesca and the Early Renaissance*, Macmillan, N.Y., 1968
HERSEY, G. L., *Pythagorean Palaces: Magic and Architecture in the Italian Renaissance*, Cornell Univ. Press, Ithaca, 1976
HEYDENREICH, L. H., & W. LOTZ, *Architecture in Italy, 1400–1600*, Pelican History of Art, Penguin, Harmondsworth, Baltimore, 1974
JANSON, H. W., *The Sculpture of Donatello*, 2 vols., Princeton Univ. Press, 1957
KATZ, M. B., *Leon Battista Alberti and the Humanist Theory of the Arts*, Univ. Press of America, Washington, D.C., 1978
*LEE, R. W., *Ut Pictura Poesis: The Humanistic Theory of Painting*, Norton, N.Y., 1967
*LEVEY, M., *Early Renaissance*, Penguin, Harmondsworth, Baltimore, 1967
*LOWRY, B., *Renaissance Architecture*, Braziller, N.Y., 1962
MANETTI, A. de T., *The Life of Brunelleschi*, Pennsylvania State Univ. Press, University Park, 1970
*MURRAY, P., *Renaissance Architecture*, Abrams, N.Y., 1976
*PANOFSKY, E., *Renaissance and Renascences in Western Art*, Humanities Press, N.Y., 1970
POPE-HENNESSY, J., *Fra Angelico*, Phaidon, London, 1952
_____, *Italian Renaissance Sculpture*, Phaidon, N.Y., 1971
_____, *Paolo Uccello: Complete Edition*, 2d ed., Phaidon, N.Y., 1969
SEYMOUR, C., JR., *Sculpture in Italy, 1400–1500*, Pelican History of Art, Penguin, Baltimore, 1966
*SEZNEC, J., *The Survival of the Pagan Gods*, reprint by Bollingen Foundation & Pantheon Books, Princeton Univ. Press, 1972
STEINBERG, R. W., *Fra Girolamo Savonarola, Florentine*

Art and Renaissance Historiography, Ohio Univ. Press, Athens, 1977

TURNER, A. R., *The Vision of Landscape in Renaissance Italy*, Princeton Univ. Press, 1974

VASARI, G., *The Lives of the Painters, Sculptors and Architects*, tr. by Gaston Du C. De Vere, 4 vols., Abrams, N.Y., 1977

WACKERNAGEL, M., *The World of the Florentine Renaissance Artist: Projects and Patrons, Workshop and Art Market*, Princeton Univ. Press, 1981

WILDE, J., *Venetian Art from Bellini to Titian*, Clarendon Press, Oxford, 1974

*WITTKOWER, R., *Architectural Principles in the Age of Humanism*, 3d ed., Random House, N.Y., 1965

3. THE HIGH RENAISSANCE IN ITALY

*ACKERMAN, J. S., & J. NEWMAN, *The Architecture of Michelangelo, With a Catalogue of Michelangelo's Works*, Penguin, Harmondsworth, Baltimore, 1971

BECK, J. H., *Raphael*, Abrams, N.Y., 1976

BRUSCHI, A., *Bramante*, Thames & Hudson, London, 1977

CLARK, K. M., *Leonardo da Vinci*, rev. ed., Penguin, Baltimore, 1967

DE TOLNAY, C., *Michelangelo*, 5 vols. 2d ed., rev., Princeton Univ. Press, 1969–71

FISCHEL, O., *Raphael*, Spring Books, London, 1964

*FREEDBERG, S. J., *Painting in Italy, 1500–1600*, 1st rev. ed., Pelican History of Art, Penguin, Harmondsworth, Baltimore, 1975

———, *Painting of the High Renaissance in Rome and Florence*, 2 vols., Harvard Univ. Press, Cambridge, 1961

HARTT, F., *Michelangelo*, 3 vols., Abrams, N.Y., 1965–76

*HIBBARD, H. *Michelangelo*, new ed., Penguin, Harmondsworth, Baltimore, 1978

*KLEIN, R., & H. ZERNER, *Italian Art, 1500–1600: Sources and Documents*, Prentice-Hall, Englewood Cliffs, 1966

*LEVEY, M., *High Renaissance*, Style and Civilization, Penguin, Baltimore, 1975

MURRAY, L., *The High Renaissance and Mannerism: Italy, the North and Spain, 1500–1600*, Oxford Univ. Press, N.Y., 1977 (published in 1967 under two titles: *The High Renaissance* and *The Late Renaissance and Mannerism*)

PANOFSKY, E., *Problems in Titian, Mostly Iconographic*, New York Univ. Press, 1969

*———, *Studies in Iconology: Humanistic Theories in the Art of the Renaissance*, Harper & Row, N.Y., 1972

PIGNATTI, T., *Giorgione*, Phaidon, N.Y., 1971

POPE-HENNESSY, J., *Italian High Renaissance and Baroque Sculpture*, 3 vols., Phaidon, London, 1963

PORTOGHESI, P., *Rome of the Renaissance*, Phaidon, London, 1972

ROSAND, D., *Painting in Cinquecento Venice: Titian, Veronese, Tintoretto*, Yale Univ. Press, New Haven, London, 1982

———, *Titian*, Abrams, N.Y., 1978

WETHEY, H. E., *The Paintings of Titian*, 2 vols., Phaidon, London, 1969–71

*WÖLFFLIN, H., *Classic Art: An Introduction to the Italian Renaissance*, 3d ed., Phaidon, N.Y., 1968

4. MANNERISM AND OTHER TRENDS

*ACKERMAN, J. S., *Palladio*, Penguin, Harmondsworth, Baltimore, 1966

BOSQUET, J., *Mannerism, the Painting and Style of the Late Renaissance*, Braziller, N.Y., 1964

*CELLINI, B., *Autobiography*, ed. by J. Pope-Hennessy, Phaidon, London, 1960

*FRIEDLAENDER, W. F., *Mannerism and Anti-Mannerism in Italian Painting*, Columbia Univ. Press, N.Y., 1957

GUDIOL, J., *Domenikos Theotokopoulos, El Greco, 1541–1614*, Viking, N.Y., 1973

HARRIS, A. S., & L. NOCHLIN, *Women Artists, 1550–1950*, Knopf, N.Y., 1976

*HOLT, E. G., ed., *A Documentary History of Art*, Vol. II, *Michelangelo and the Mannerists: The Baroque and the Eighteenth Century*, 2d ed., Doubleday, Garden City, 1957

*SHEARMAN, J. K. G., *Mannerism*, Style and Civilization, Penguin, Baltimore, 1967

SMYTH, C. H., *Mannerism and Maniera*, Augustin, Locust Valley, N.Y., 1963

VALCANOVER, F., & T. PIGNATTI, *Tintoretto*, Abrams, N.Y., 1984

WETHEY, H. E., *El Greco and His School*, 2 vols., Princeton Univ. Press, 1962

WÜRTENBERGER, F., *Mannerism, the European Style of the Sixteenth Century*, Holt, Rinehart & Winston, N.Y., 1963

5. THE RENAISSANCE IN THE NORTH

*BENESCH, O., *The Art of the Renaissance in Northern Europe*, rev. ed., Phaidon, London, 1965

*BLUNT, A., *Art and Architecture in France, 1500–1700*, 4th ed., Pelican History of Art, Penguin, Harmondsworth, N.Y., 1981

CHRISTENSEN, C. C., *Art and the Reformation in Germany*, Ohio Univ. Press, Athens, 1979

GANZ, P., *The Paintings of Hans Holbein the Younger*, 1st comp. ed., Phaidon, London, 1956

GIBSON, W. S., *Bruegel*, Oxford Univ. Press, N.Y., 1977

LEYMARIE, J., *Dutch Painting*, Skira, Geneva, 1956

OSTEN, G. VON DER, & H. VEY, *Painting and Sculpture in Germany and the Netherlands, 1500–1600*, Pelican History of Art, Penguin, Baltimore, 1969

PANOFSKY, E., *The Life and Art of Albrecht Dürer*, 4th ed., Princeton Univ. Press, 1955

PEVSNER, N., & M. MEIER, *Gruenewald*, Abrams, N.Y. 1958

STECHOW, W., *Northern Renaissance Art, 1400–1600: Sources and Documents*, Prentice-Hall, Englewood Cliffs, 1966

*———, *Pieter Bruegel the Elder*, Abrams, N.Y., 1969

STRIEDER, P., *Albrecht Dürer: Paintings, Prints, Drawings*, Eng. ed., Abaris, N.Y., 1982

*WATERHOUSE. E. K., *Painting in Britain, 1530–1790*, 4th ed., Pelican History of Art, Penguin, Baltimore, 1978

6. THE BAROQUE IN ITALY AND GERMANY

*ARGAN, G. C., *The Baroque Age*, Rizzoli, N.Y., 1989

CONNORS, J., *Borromini and the Roman Oratory: Style and Society*, MIT Press, Cambridge, Architectural History Foundation, N.Y., 1980

ENGASS, R., & J. BROWN, *Italy and Spain, 1600–1750: Sources and Documents*, Prentice-Hall, Englewood Cliffs, 1970

FREEDBERG, S. J., *Circa 1600: A Revolution of Style in Italian Painting*, Harvard Univ. Press, Cambridge, 1983

*FRIEDLAENDER, W. F., *Caravaggio Studies*, Princeton Univ. Press, 1955

HASKELL, F., *Patrons and Painters: A Study in the Relations Between Italian Art and Society in the Age of the Baroque*, rev. & enl. ed., Yale Univ. Press, New Haven, 1980

HELD, J., & D. POSNER, *Seventeenth and Eighteenth Century: Baroque Painting, Sculpture, Architecture*, Abrams, N.Y., 1971

HEMPEL, E., *Baroque Art and Architecture in Central Europe*, Pelican History of Art, Penguin, Baltimore, 1977

*HIBBARD, H., *Carlo Maderno and Roman Architecture: 1580–1630*, Pennsylvania State Univ. Press, University Park, 1971

HITCHCOCK, H.-R., *Rococo Architecture in Southern Germany*, Phaidon, London, 1968

MAGNUSON, T., *Rome in the Age of Bernini*, Alqvist & Wiksell, Stockholm; Humanities Press, Atlantic Highlands, 1982

*MILLON, H. A., *Baroque and Rococo Architecture*, Braziller, N.Y., 1961

MOIR, A., *Caravaggio*, Abrams, N.Y., 1982

———, *The Italian Followers of Caravaggio*, 2 vols., Harvard Univ. Press, Cambridge, 1967

MORASSI, A., *Complete Catalogue of the Paintings of G. B. Tiepolo*, Phaidon, London, 1962

NORBERG-SCHULTZ, C., *Baroque Architecture*, Abrams, N.Y., 1971

*———, *Late Baroque and Rococo Architecture*, Abrams, N.Y., 1983

PORTOGHESI, P., *Roma Barocca: The History of an Architectonic Culture*, MIT Press, Cambridge, 1970

POSNER, D., *Annibale Carracci*, 2 vols., Phaidon, London, 1971

SPEAR, R. E., *Domenichino*, 2 vols., Yale Univ. Press, New Haven, 1982

*WITTKOWER, R., *Art and Architecture in Italy, 1600–1750*, 3d rev. ed., with corrections and augmented bibliography, Pelican History of Art, Penguin, Harmondsworth, N.Y., 1980

———, *Gian Lorenzo Bernini: The Sculptor of the Roman Baroque*, 3d rev. ed., Cornell Univ. Press, Ithaca, 1981

7. THE BAROQUE IN FLANDERS, HOLLAND, AND SPAIN

BAARD, H. P., *Frans Hals*, Abrams, N.Y., 1981

BAUDOUIN, F., *Pietro Paolo Rubens*, Abrams, N.Y., 1977

BROWN, J., *Francisco de Zurbarán*, Abrams, N.Y., 1974

GÁLLEGO, J., & J. GUDIOL, *Zurbarán, 1598–1664: Biography and Critical Analysis*, Rizzoli, N.Y., 1977

GERSON, H., & E. H. TER KUILE, *Art and Architecture in Belgium, 1600–1800*, Pelican History of Art, Penguin, Baltimore, 1978

HAAK, B., *The Golden Age: Dutch Painters of the Seventeenth Century*, Abrams, N.Y., 1984

KAHR, M. M., *Velazquez: The Art of Painting*, Harper & Row, N.Y., 1976

KUBLER, G. A., & M. SORIA, *Art and Architecture in Spain and Portugal and Their American Dominions, 1500–1800*, Pelican History of Art, Penguin, Baltimore, 1959

LÓPEZ-REY, J., *Velazquez' Work and World*, New York Graphic Society, Greenwich, 1968

NASH, J. M., *The Age of Rembrandt and Vermeer: Dutch Painting in the Seventeenth Century*, Holt, Rinehart & Winston, N.Y., 1972

NICOLSON, B., *Hendrick Terbrugghen*, Lund Humphries, London, 1958

*ROSENBERG, J., *Rembrandt, Life and Work*, rev. ed., Cornell Univ. Press, Ithaca, 1980

ROSENBERG, J., S. SLIVE, & E. H. TER KUILE, *Dutch Art and Architecture, 1600–1800*, 3d (2d integrated) ed., Pelican History of Art, Penguin, Harmondsworth, N.Y., 1977

SÉRULLAZ, M., & C. POUILLON, *Velazquez*, Abrams, N.Y., 1981

SLATKES, L. J., *Vermeer and His Contemporaries*, Abbeville, N.Y., 1981

SLIVE, S., *Frans Hals*, 3 vols., Phaidon, N.Y., 1970–74

———, *Jacob Van Ruisdael*, Abbeville, N.Y., 1981

*STECHOW, W., *Dutch Landscape Painting of the Seventeenth*

Century, reprint of 1966 ed., Cornell Univ. Press, Ithaca, 1980

WHEELOCK, A. K., Jan Vermeer, Abrams, N.Y., 1981

WHITE, C., Rembrandt as an Etcher, 2 vols., Pennsylvania State Univ. Press, University Park, 1969

8. THE BAROQUE AND ROCOCO IN FRANCE AND ENGLAND

BLUNT, A., Nicolas Poussin, 2 vols., Bollingen Foundation & Pantheon Books, Princeton Univ. Press, 1967

FRIEDLAENDER, W. F., Nicolas Poussin, A New Approach, Abrams, N.Y., 1966

GAUNT, W., The Great Century of British Painting: Hogarth to Turner, Phaidon, London, 1971

GOULD, C. A. M., Bernini in France, Princeton Univ. Press, 1982

HERRMANN, L., British Landscape Painting of the 18th Century, Oxford Univ. Press, N.Y., 1974

*KALNEIN, W. GRAF, & M. LEVEY, Art and Architecture of the Eighteenth Century in France, Pelican History of Art, Penguin, Harmondsworth, Baltimore, 1972

*LEVEY, M., Rococo to Revolution: Major Trends in Eighteenth Century Painting, Oxford Univ. Press, N.Y., 1977

NICOLSON, B., & C. WRIGHT, Georges de La Tour, Phaidon, London, 1974

PARRY, E., The Image of the Indian and the Black Man in American Art, 1590–1900, new ed., Braziller, N.Y., 1974

PAULSON, R., Hogarth, His Life, Art and Times, 2 vols., Yale Univ. Press, New Haven, 1971

POSNER, D., Antoine Watteau, Cornell Univ. Press, Ithaca, 1984

RÖTHLISBERGER, M., Claude Lorrain: The Paintings, 2 vols., Yale Univ. Press, New Haven, 1961

SCHÖNBERGER, A., & H. SOEHNER, The Rococo Age: Art and Civilization of the 18th Century, McGraw-Hill, N.Y., 1960

*SUMMERSON, J. N., Architecture in Britain, 1530–1830, 6th rev. ed., Pelican History of Art, Penguin, Baltimore, 1977

WILDENSTEIN, G., & D., Chardin, rev. & enl. ed., New York Graphic Society, Greenwich, 1969

———, The Paintings of Fragonard: Complete Edition, Phaidon, London, 1960

PART FOUR
THE MODERN WORLD
1. NEOCLASSICISM AND ROMANTICISM

BOIMÉ, A., The Academy and French Painting in the 19th Century, Phaidon, N.Y., 1970

BROWN, M. W., American Art to 1900, Abrams, N.Y., 1977

BUCKLAND, G., Fox Talbot and the Invention of Photography, Godine, Boston, 1980

*CLARK, K. M., The Gothic Revival, Humanities Press, N.Y., 1970

———, The Romantic Rebellion: Romantic Versus Classical, Harper & Row, N.Y., 1974

CRAVEN, W., Sculpture in America, Crowell, N.Y., 1968

CROOK, J.M., The Dilemma of Style: Architectural Ideas from the Picturesque to the Post Modern, Univ. of Chicago Press, 1987

DAVAL, J. L., Photography: History of an Art, Skira/Rizzoli, N.Y., 1982

DAVIS, L. G., & J. SIMS, Black Artists in the United States: An Annotated Bibliography of Books, Articles and Dissertations on Black Artists, 1779–1979, Greenwood Press, Westport, Connecticut, 1980

*DIXON, R., & S. MUTHESIUS, Victorian Architecture, Oxford Univ. Press, N.Y., 1978

DRISKELL, D. C., Two Centuries of Black American Art, Los Angeles County Museum of Art/Knopf, N.Y., 1976

EITNER, L. E., Géricault: His Life and Works, Cornell Univ. Press, Ithaca, 1982

*———, Neoclassicism and Romanticism, 1750–1850: Sources and Documents, 2 vols., Prentice-Hall, Englewood Cliffs, 1970

ESSICK, R. N., William Blake, Printmaker, Princeton Univ. Press, 1980

FINBERG, A. J., The Life of J. M. W. Turner, R.A., 2d rev. ed., Clarendon Press, Oxford, 1961

*FRIEDLAENDER, W. F., From David to Delacroix, Harvard Univ. Press, Cambridge, 1952

GAUNT, W., The Restless Century: Painting in Britain, 1800–1900, Phaidon, London, 1972

GERNSHEIM, H., Julia Margaret Cameron, Her Life and Photographic Work, 2d ed., Aperture, Millerton, N.Y., 1975

GERNSHEIM, H. & A., The History of Photography from the Camera Obscura to the Beginning of the Modern Era, 2d ed., McGraw-Hill, N.Y., 1969

———, L. J. M. Daguerre: The History of the Diorama and the Daguerreotype, Dover, N.Y., 1968

GOSLING, N., Nadar, Knopf, N.Y., 1976

GUDIOL, J., Goya, Abrams, N.Y., 1965

HAMILTON, G. H., Nineteenth and Twentieth Century Art: Painting, Sculpture, Architecture, Abrams, N.Y., 1970

HERRMANN, L., Turner: Paintings, Watercolors, Prints and Drawings, New York Graphic Society, Boston, 1975

*HITCHCOCK, H.-R., Architecture: Nineteenth and Twentieth Centuries, 2d ed., Pelican History of Art, Penguin, Baltimore, 1971

*HONOUR, H., Neoclassicism, Style and Civilization, Penguin, Harmondsworth, Baltimore, 1968

*———, Romanticism, Icon Ed., Harper & Row, N.Y., 1979

JANSON, H. W., 19th Century Sculpture, Abrams, N.Y., 1985

*JEFFREY, I., Photography: A Concise History, Oxford Univ. Press, N.Y., 1982

JOHNSON, L., The Paintings of Eugène Delacroix: A Critical Catalogue, 1816–1831, 2 vols., Clarendon Press, Oxford, 1981

LAFUENTE-FERRARI, E. L., ed., Goya: His Complete Etchings, Aquatints, and Lithographs, Abrams, N.Y., 1962

LENNOX-BOYD, A., et al, Traditional English Gardens, Rizzoli, N.Y., 1986

LICHT, F., Canova, Abbeville, N.Y., 1983

*———, Goya: The Origins of the Modern Temper in Art, Icon Ed., Harper & Row, N.Y., 1983

———, Sculpture, 19th and 20th Century, New York Graphic Society, Greenwich, 1967

MC CARTHY, M. J., The Origins of the Gothic Revival, Yale Univ. Press/Paul Mellon Center for Studies in British Art, New Haven, 1987

MC COUBREY, J., American Art, 1700–1960: Sources and Documents, Prentice-Hall, Englewood Cliffs, 1965

MAISON, K. E., Honoré Daumier: Catalogue Raisonné of the Paintings, Watercolors and Drawings, 2 vols., New York Graphic Society, Greenwich, 1968

*MIDDLETON, R., & D. WATKIN, Neoclassical and Nineteenth Century Architecture, Abrams, N.Y., 1980

*NANTEUIL, L. DE, David, Abrams, N.Y., 1985

*NEWHALL, B., The History of Photography from 1830 to the Present Day, 5th rev. ed., New York Graphic Society, Greenwich, 1982

*NOVOTNY, F., Painting and Sculpture in Europe, 1780–1880, Pelican History of Art, Penguin, Baltimore, 1971

*PIERSON, W., & W. H. JORDY, American Buildings and Their Architects, 4 vols., Doubleday, Garden City, 1970-78

PINGEOT, A. et al., Sculpture: The Adventure of Modern Sculpture in the Nineteenth and Twentieth Centuries, Rizzoli, N.Y., 1986

*POLLACK, P., Picture History of Photography, rev. ed., Abrams, N.Y., 1970

REYNOLDS, G., Constable, the Natural Painter, Schocken, N.Y., 1969

*———, Turner, World of Art, Thames & Hudson; distr. by Norton, N.Y., 1985

ROSEN, C., & H. ZERNER, Romanticism and Realism: The Mythology of Nineteenth-Century Art, Viking, N.Y., 1984

ROSENBLUM, R., Jean-Auguste-Dominique Ingres, new ed., Abrams, N.Y., 1985

*———, Transformations in Late Eighteenth Century Art, Princeton Univ. Press, 1967

ROSENBLUM, R., & H. W. JANSON, 19th-Century Art, Abrams, N.Y., 1984

*SCHAPIRO, M., Modern Art: Nineteenth and Twentieth Centuries, 2 vols., Braziller, N.Y. 1982

SNYDER, J., American Frontiers: The Photographs of Timothy H. O'Sullivan, 1867–1874, Aperture, Millerton, N.Y., 1981

*STAROBINSKI, J., The Invention of Liberty, Rizzoli, N.Y., 1986

TURNER, T., English Garden Design: History and Styles Since 1650, Antique Collectors' Club, Woodbridge, Suffolk, 1986

VIDLER, A., The Writing on the Walls, Princeton Architectural Press, Princeton, 1987

VINCENT, H. P., Daumier and His World, Northwestern Univ. Press, Evanston, 1968

WELLING, W., Photography in America: The Formative Years, 1839–1900, Crowell, N.Y., 1978

WILDENSTEIN, G., Ingres, 2d rev. ed., Phaidon, London, 1956

WILTON, A., J. M. W. Turner: His Life and Art, Rizzoli, N.Y., 1979

2. REALISM AND IMPRESSIONISM

BREESKIN, A. D., Mary Cassatt: A Catalogue Raisonné of the Oils, Pastels, Watercolors and Drawings, National Gallery of Art, Washington, D.C., 1970

*CLARK, T. J., The Painting of Modern Life: Paris in the Art of Manet and His Followers, Princeton Univ. Press, 1984

*DENVIR, B., The Impressionists: A Documentary Study, Thames & Hudson, N.Y., 1986

ELSEN, A. E., Origins of Modern Sculpture: Pioneers and Premises, Braziller, N.Y., 1974

*———, Rodin, Doubleday, Garden City, for The Museum of Modern Art, N.Y., 1963

FLEMING, G. H., Rossetti and the Pre-Raphaelite Brotherhood, Hart-Davies, London, 1967

GOODRICH, L., Thomas Eakins, 2 vols., Harvard Univ. Press, Cambridge, for the National Gallery of Art, Washington, D.C., 1982

GORDON, R. & A. FORGE, Monet, Abrams, N.Y., 1983

GREENFIELD, H., The Impressionist Revolution, Doubleday, Garden City, 1972

HANSEN, A. C., Manet and the Modern Tradition, Yale Univ. Press, New Haven, 1977

HENDRICKS, G., The Life and Work of Winslow Homer, Abrams, N.Y., 1979

HERBERT, R. L., Impressionism: Art, Leisure and Parisian Society, Yale Univ. Press, New Haven, 1988

*HILTON, T., The Pre-Raphaelites, Abrams, N.Y., 1971

KELDER, D., The French Impressionists and Their Century, Praeger, N.Y., 1970

*KLINGENDER, F. D., Art and the Industrial Revolution, Rev. & enl. ed., Evelyn, Adams & MacKay, Chatham, 1968

NICOLL, J., Dante Gabriel Rossetti, 1st Amer. ed., Macmillan, N.Y., 1976, c. 1975

*NOCHLIN, L., Impressionism and Post-Impressionism, 1874–1904: Sources and Documents, Prentice-Hall, Englewood Cliffs, 1976

*———, Realism, Style and Civilization, Penguin, Harmondsworth, Baltimore, 1972

*———, Realism and Tradition in Art, 1848–1900: Sources and Documents, Prentice-Hall, Englewood Cliffs, 1966

REWALD, J., The History of Impressionism, 4th rev. ed., New York Graphic Society, Greenwich, for The Museum of Modern Art, N.Y., 1973

REYNOLDS, G., Victorian Painting, Macmillan, N.Y., 1966

WEISBERG, G. P., The Realist Tradition: French Painting and Drawing, 1830–1900, Cleveland Museum of Art, 1981

WHITE, B. E., Renoir, His Life, Art, and Letters, Abrams, N.Y., 1984

*WILMERDING, J., American Art, Pelican History of Art, Penguin, Harmondsworth, Baltimore, 1976

3. POST-IMPRESSIONISM

ALLAND, A., SR., Jacob A. Riis, Photographer and Citizen Aperture, Millerton, N.Y., 1974

BADT, K., The Art of Cézanne, Univ. of California Press, Berkeley, 1965

BUNNELL, P., ed., A Photographic Vision: Pictorial Photography 1889–1923, Peregrine Smith, Salt Lake City, 1980

CHASSÉ, C., The Nabis and Their Period, Praeger, N.Y., 1969

*CHIPP, H. B., Theories of Modern Art, Univ. of California Press, Berkeley, 1968

*DELEVOY, R. L., Symbolists and Symbolism, Rizzoli, N.Y., 1982

DOTY, R., Photo-Secession: Stieglitz and the Fine Arts Movement in Photography, Dover, N.Y., 1978

GIBSON, M., The Symbolists, Abrams, N.Y., 1988

HAAS, R. B., Muybridge, Man in Motion, Univ. of California Press, Berkeley, 1976

*HAMILTON, G. H., Painting and Sculpture in Europe, 1880–1940, 3d ed., Pelican History of Art, Penguin, Harmondsworth, Baltimore, 1981

*HODIN, J. P., Edvard Munch, Praeger, N.Y., 1972

HOMER, W. I., Seurat and the Science of Painting, MIT Press, Cambridge, 1964

HUISMAN, P., & M. G. DORTU, Toulouse-Lautrec, Doubleday, Garden City, 1973

HULSKER, J., The Complete Van Gogh, Abrams, N.Y., 1980

JAWORSKA, W., Gauguin and the Pont-Aven School, New York Graphic Society, Greenwich, 1972

JOHNSON, D. C., American Art Nouveau, Abrams, N.Y., 1979

JONES, E. Y., Father of Art Photography: O. E. Rejlander, 1813–1875, New York Graphic Society, Greenwich, 1973

*MADSEN, S. T., Art Nouveau, McGraw-Hill, N.Y., 1967

REWALD, J., Post-Impressionism: From Van Gogh to Gauguin, 2d ed., The Museum of Modern Art, N.Y., 1962

*ROOKMAAKER, H. R., Gauguin and 19th Century Art Theory, Swets & Zeitlinger, Amsterdam, 1972

ROSKILL, M., Van Gogh, Gauguin, and the Impressionist Circle, New York Graphic Society, Greenwich, 1970

RUBIN, W., ed., Cézanne: The Late Work–Essays, New York Graphic Society, Boston, for The Museum of Modern Art, N.Y., 1977

SCHAPIRO, M., Paul Cézanne, 3d ed., Abrams, N.Y., 1965

———, Van Gogh, rev. ed., Abrams, N.Y., 1982

SCHARF, A., Art and Photography, Penguin, Baltimore, 1974

SCHMUTZLER, R., Art Nouveau, Abrams, N.Y., 1962

SELZ, P., Art in Our Times: A Pictorial History 1890–1980, Abrams, N.Y., 1981

SUTTER, J., ed., The Neo-Impressionists, New York Graphic Society, Greenwich, 1970

4. TWENTIETH-CENTURY PAINTING

ADES, D., et al., *In the Mind's Eye: Dada and Surrealism*, Abbeville, N.Y., 1986
*ALLOWAY, L., *Roy Lichtenstein*, Abbeville, N.Y., 1983
ARGAN, G. C., *Henry Moore*, Abrams, N.Y., 1973
ARNASON, H. H., *History of Modern Art: Painting, Sculpture, Architecture, Photography*, 3d ed., Abrams, N.Y., 1986
ARP, H., *Arp on Arp, Poems, Memories, Essays*, Viking, N.Y., 1972
BAKER, K., *Minimalism*, Abbeville, N.Y., 1989
BARR, A. H., JR. ed., *Cubism and Abstract Art*, reprint of 1936 ed. of The Museum of Modern Art, Arno Press, N.Y., 1966
______, *Fantastic Art, Dada, Surrealism*, reprint of 1936 ed. of The Museum of Modern Art, Arno Press, N.Y., 1969
______, *Matisse, His Art and His Public*, reprint of 1951 ed. of The Museum of Modern Art, Arno Press, N.Y., 1966
______, *Picasso, Fifty Years of His Art*, reprint of 1946 ed. of The Museum of Modern Art, Arno Press, N.Y., 1966
*BARRON, S., & M. TUCHMAN, eds., *Avant-Garde in Russia, 1910–1930: New Perspectives*, MIT Press, Cambridge, 1980
*BATTCOCK, G., *Idea Art: A Critique*, new ed., Dutton, N.Y., 1973
*______, *Minimal Art: A Critical Anthology*, Dutton, N.Y., 1968
*______, *The New Art: A Critical Anthology*, rev. ed., Dutton, N.Y., 1973
*______, *Superrealism: A Critical Anthology*, Dutton, N.Y., 1975
*______, *Why Art: Casual Notes on the Aesthetics of the Immediate Past*, Dutton, N.Y., 1977
BOWNESS, A., *Modern European Art*, Harcourt, Brace, Jovanovich, N.Y., 1972
BRAUN, E., ed., *Italian Art in the 20th Century*, Prestel-Verlag, Munich, 1989
*BROUDE, N., & M. D. GARRARD, eds., *Feminism and Art History: Questioning the Litany*, Harper & Row, N.Y., 1982
BROWN, M. W., *The Story of the Armory Show*, updated ed., Abbeville, N.Y., 1988
*CALAS, N. & E., *Icons and Images of the Sixties*, Dutton, N.Y., 1971
*CELANT, G., *Unexpressionism: Art Beyond the Contemporary*, Rizzoli, N.Y., 1988
CORK, R., *Vorticism and Abstract Art in the First Machine Age*, 2 vols., Univ. of California Press, Berkeley, 1976–77
CRANE, D., *The Transformation of the Avant-Garde: The New York Art World, 1940–1985*, Univ. of Chicago Press, 1987
CRESPELLE, J.-P., *The Fauves*, New York Graphic Society, Greenwich, 1962
CRICHTON, M., *Jasper Johns*, Abrams, N.Y., for the Whitney Museum of American Art, N.Y., 1977
DAIX, P., *Cubists and Cubism*, Rizzoli, N.Y., 1982
**Deconstruction: The Omnibus Volume*, ed. by A. Papadakes, et al., Rizzoli, N.Y., 1989
DE FRANCIA, P., *Fernand Léger*, Yale Univ. Press, New Haven, 1983
DOESBURG, T. VAN, *Principles of Neo-Plastic Art*, New York Graphic Society, Greenwich, 1968
DOTY, R., ed., *Contemporary Black Artists in America*, Whitney Museum of American Art, N.Y., 1971
DUBE, W.-D., *Expressionists and Expressionism*, Rizzoli, N.Y., 1983
*DUTHUIT, G., *The Fauvist Painters*, Wittenborn, Schultz, N.Y., 1950
*FINCH, C., *Pop Art: The Object and the Image*, Dutton, N.Y., 1968
FINE, E. H., *The Afro-American Artist: A Search for Identity*, Holt, Rinehart & Winston, N.Y., 1973
FLACK, A., *Audrey Flack on Painting*, Abrams, N.Y., 1981
*FRANCIS, R. H., *Jasper Johns*, Abbeville, N.Y., 1984
*FRANK, E., *Jackson Pollock*, Abbeville, N.Y., 1983
*GELDZAHLER, H., *American Painting in the Twentieth Century*, Metropolitan Museum of Art, N.Y., 1965
GIBIAN, C., & H. W. TJALSMA, eds., *Russian Modernism: Culture and the Avant-Garde, 1900–1930*, Cornell Univ. Press, Ithaca, 1976
GODFREY, T., *The New Image: Painting in the 1980s*, Abbeville, N.Y., 1986
*GOLDING, J., *Cubism: A History and an Analysis, 1907–1914*, 3d ed., Harvard Univ. Press, Cambridge, 1988
*GOLDWATER, R., *Primitivism in Modern Art*, rev. ed., Vintage, N.Y., 1967
*GOWING, L., *Matisse*, Oxford Univ. Press, N.Y., 1979
*GRAY, C., *The Russian Experiment in Art, 1863–1922*, Abrams, N.Y., 1970
GREEN, C., *Cubism and Its Enemies: Modern Movements and Reaction in French Art, 1916–1928*, Yale Univ. Press, New Haven, 1987
______, *Léger and the Avant Garde*, Yale Univ. Press, New Haven, 1976
GROHMANN, W., *Paul Klee*, Abrams, N.Y., 1955
*HERBERT, R. L., ed., *Modern Artists on Art*, Prentice-Hall, Englewood Cliffs, 1965
HOMER, W. I., & V. ORGAN, *Robert Henri and His Circle*, Cornell Univ. Press, Ithaca, 1969
HUNTER, S., & J. JACOBUS, *American Art of the Twentieth Century: Painting, Sculpture, Architecture*, Abrams, N.Y., 1974
JAFFE, H. L. C., *De Stijl, 1917–1931: Visions of Utopia*, Abbeville, N.Y., 1982
______, *Piet Mondrian*, Abrams, N.Y., 1970
KAHNWEILER, D.-H., *Juan Gris: His Life and Work*, rev. ed., Abrams, N.Y., 1969
*KRAUSS, R. E., *The Originality of the Avant-Garde and Other Modernist Myths*, MIT Press, Cambridge, 1986
LALIBERTE, N., & A. MOGELSON, *Collage, Montage, Assemblage: History and Contemporary Techniques*, Van Nostrand-Reinhold, N.Y., 1972
LAMBERT, J.-C., *Cobra*, Abbeville, N.Y., 1984
LANDAU, E., *Jackson Pollock*, Abrams, N.Y., 1989
LEVIN, G., *Edward Hopper, The Art and the Artist*, Whitney Museum of American Art, N.Y., 1980
*LEYMARIE, J., *Fauves and Fauvism*, Rizzoli, N.Y., 1987
*LIPPARD, L. R., *Dadas on Art*, Prentice-Hall, Englewood Cliffs, 1971
*______, *From the Center: Feminist Essays on Women's Art*, Dutton, N.Y., 1976
*______, *Pop Art*, Praeger, N.Y., 1966
*______, *Surrealists on Art*, Prentice-Hall, Englewood Cliffs, 1970
LODDER, C., *Russian Constructivism*, Yale Univ. Press, New Haven, 1983
LUCIE-SMITH, E., *Art Now*, Morrow, N.Y., 1977
*______, *Late Modern: The Visual Arts Since 1945*, Oxford Univ. Press, N.Y., 1975
MAHSUN, C. A. R., ed., *Pop Art: The Critical Dialogue*, UMI, Ann Arbor, 1989
MARTIN, M. W., *Futurist Art and Theory, 1909–1915*, Clarendon Press, Oxford, 1968
MATTHEWS, J. H., *An Introduction to Surrealism*, Pennsylvania State Univ. Press, University Park, 1965
MEISEL, L. K., *Photorealism*, Abrams, N.Y., 1989
*MONTE, J. K., *22 Realists*, Whitney Museum of American Art, N.Y., 1970
*MOTHERWELL, R., ed., *The Dada Poets and Painters: An Anthology*, 2d ed., Harvard Univ. Press, Cambridge, 1989
*MULLER, J.-E., *Fauvism*, Praeger, N.Y., 1967
MUNRO, E., *Originals: Women Artists*, Simon & Schuster, N.Y., 1979
*NADEAU, M., *History of Surrealism*, Harvard Univ. Press, Cambridge, 1989
*O'KEEFFE, G., *Georgia O'Keeffe*, Viking, Penguin, N.Y., 1977
Phaidon Dictionary of Twentieth-Century Art, Phaidon, N.Y., 1973
*PINCUS-WITTEN, R., *Postminimalism into Maximalism: American Art, 1966–1986*, UMI, Ann Arbor, 1987
POPPER, F., *Origins and Development of Kinetic Art*, New York Graphic Society, Greenwich, 1968
*RAABE, P., ed., *The Era of German Expressionism*, Overlook Press, Woodstock, N.Y., 1985
RICHTER, H., *Dada: Art and Anti-Art*, McGraw-Hill, N.Y., 1965
RICKEY, G., *Constructivism: Origins and Evolution*, Braziller, N.Y., 1967
ROETHEL, H. K., *The Blue Rider...in the Municipal Gallery, Munich*, Praeger, N.Y., 1971
*ROSE, B., *American Art Since 1900*, rev. ed., Praeger, N.Y., 1975
______, *Jackson Pollock: Drawing into Painting*, The Museum of Modern Art, N.Y., 1980
ROSENBERG, H., *The De-Definition of Art: Action Art to Pop to Earthworks*, Horizon, N.Y., 1972
*ROSENBLUM, R., *Cubism and Twentieth-Century Art*, rev. ed., Abrams, N.Y., 1976
*______, *Modern Painting and the Northern Tradition: Friedrich to Rothko*, Harper & Row, N.Y., 1975
*ROSENTHAL, N., *Robert Rauschenberg*, Abbeville, N.Y., 1984
ROTERS, E., *Painters of the Bauhaus*, Praeger, N.Y., 1969
RUBIN, W., *Dada and Surrealist Art*, Abrams, N.Y., 1968
______, ed., *Pablo Picasso, A Retrospective*, New York Graphic Society, Greenwich, for The Museum of Modern Art, N.Y., 1980
RUDENSTINE, A. Z., ed., *Russian Avant-Garde Art: The George Costakis Collection*, Abrams, N.Y., 1981
*SCHNEEDE, U. M., *Surrealism*, Abrams, N.Y., 1974
SCHNEIDER, P., *Matisse*, Rizzoli, N.Y., 1984
*SPIES, W., *Max Ernst*, Abrams, N.Y., 1969
______, *Vasarely*, Abrams, N.Y., 1969
STIEGLITZ, A., *Georgia O'Keeffe: A Portrait*, Viking, N.Y., 1979
*VERGO, P., *Art in Vienna, 1898–1918: Klimt, Kokoschka, Schiele and Their Contemporaries*, Cornell Univ. Press, Ithaca, 1981
VOGT, P., *Contemporary Painting*, Abrams, N.Y., 1981
______, *Expressionism: German Painting, 1905–1920*, Abrams, N.Y., 1980
WALDMAN, D., *Mark Rothko, 1903–1970: A Retrospective*, Abrams, N.Y., 1978
WERNER, A., *Chaim Soutine*, Abrams, N.Y., 1977

5. TWENTIETH-CENTURY SCULPTURE

ARGAN, G. C., *Henry Moore*, Abrams, N.Y., 1973
*BURNHAM, J., *Beyond Modern Sculpture*, Braziller, N.Y., 1968
*______, *Great Western Saltworks: Essays on the Meaning of Post-Formalist Art*, Braziller, N.Y., 1974
GEIST, S., *Brancusi: The Sculpture and Drawings*, Abrams, N.Y., 1975
*GOLDBERG, R. L., *Performance Art from Futurism to the Present*, rev. & enl. ed., Abrams, N.Y., 1988
HAMMACHER, A. M., *Modern Sculpture: Tradition and Innovation*, Abrams, N.Y., 1988
KRAUSS, R. E., *Terminal Ironworks: The Sculpture of David Smith*, MIT Press, Cambridge, 1971
KULTERMANN, U., *The New Sculpture, Environments and Assemblages*, Praeger, N.Y., 1968
MARCUS, S. E., *David Smith: The Sculptor and His Work*, Cornell Univ. Press, Ithaca, 1983
MELVILLE, R., *Henry Moore: Sculpture and Drawings, 1921–1969*, Abrams, N.Y., 1970
TRIER, E., *Form and Space: The Sculpture of the Twentieth Century*, rev. ed., Praeger, N.Y., 1968
WITHERS, J., *Julio Gonzalez, Sculpture in Iron*, New York Univ. Press, 1978

6. TWENTIETH-CENTURY ARCHITECTURE

BANHAM, R., *Theory and Design in the First Machine Age*, 2d ed., Praeger, N.Y., 1960
*BAYER, H., *Bauhaus 1919–1928*, New York Graphic Society, Greenwich, for The Museum of Modern Art, N.Y., 1976
BRANZI, A., *The Hot House, Italian New Wave Design*, MIT Press, Cambridge, 1984
BUSH-BROWN, A., *Louis Sullivan*, Braziller, N.Y., 1960
*COLE, D., *From Tipi to Skyscraper: A History of Women in Architecture*, MIT Press, Cambridge, 1978
COLLINS, G., *Antonio Gaudi*, Braziller, N.Y., 1960
*DAL CO, F., *Figures of Architecture and Thought: German Architectural Culture, 1890–1920*, Rizzoli, N.Y., 1986
*DREXLER, A. L., *Ludwig Mies van der Rohe*, Braziller, N.Y., 1960
*______, *Transformations in Modern Architecture*, New York Graphic Society, Greenwich, 1980
**Encyclopedia of 20th-Century Architecture*, rev. ed., Abrams, N.Y., 1985
FITCH, J. M., *American Building*, 2d ed., 2 vols., Houghton Mifflin, Boston, 1966–72
*______, *Walter Gropius*, Braziller, N.Y., 1960
FRAMPTON, K., *Modern Architecture, 1851–1945*, 2 vols., Rizzoli, N.Y., 1983
GIEDION, S., *Space, Time and Architecture*, 5th rev. & enl. ed., Harvard Univ. Press, Cambridge, 1967
*HITCHCOCK, H.-R., & P. C. JOHNSON, *The International Style*, Norton, N.Y., 1966
JENCKS, C., *Post-Modernism: The New Classicism in Art and Architecture*, Rizzoli, N.Y., 1987
JOHNSON, P. C., *Mies van der Rohe*, 3d ed., rev., New York Graphic Society, Greenwich, for The Museum of Modern Art, N.Y., 1978
*KALLIR, J. *Viennese Design and the Wiener Werkstätte*, Braziller, N.Y., 1986
KLOTZ, H., *History of Postmodern Architecture*, MIT Press, Cambridge, 1988
OCHSNER, J. K., *H. H. Richardson: Complete Architectural Works*, MIT Press, Cambridge, 1982
*PEVSNER, N., *The Sources of Modern Architecture and Design*, Oxford Univ. Press, N.Y., 1977
*PORTOGHESI, P., *Postmodern: The Architecture of the Post-Industrial Society*, Rizzoli, N.Y., 1983
PULOS, A. J., *The American Design Adventure, 1940–1975*, MIT Press, Cambridge, 1988
*______, *The American Design Ethic: A History of Industrial Design*, MIT Press, Cambridge, 1986
RISEBERO, B., *Modern Architecture and Design: An Alternative History*, MIT Press, Cambridge, 1983
RUSSELL, J., *Art Nouveau Architecture*, Rizzoli, N.Y., 1979
SCULLY, V. J., *Modern Architecture*, rev. ed., Braziller, N.Y., 1974
SHARP, D., *Modern Architecture and Expressionism*, Braziller, N.Y., 1966
______, *The Rationalists: Theory and Design in the Modern Movement*, Architectural Press, London, 1979
TAFURI, M., *Contemporary Architecture*, Abrams, N.Y., 1977
______, *Modern Architecture*, 2 vols., Rizzoli, N.Y., 1986

THACKARA, J., ed., *Design After Modernism: Beyond the Object*, Thames & Hudson, N.Y., 1988

*TROY, N. J., *The De Stijl Environment*, MIT Press, Cambridge, 1983

TUNNARD, C., *The City of Man*, 2d ed., Scribner, N.Y., 1970

7. TWENTIETH-CENTURY PHOTOGRAPHY

ADES, D., *Photomontage*, Pantheon Books, N.Y., 1976

August Sander: Photographs of an Epoch, 1904–1959, Preface by Beaumont Newhall, commentary by Robert Kramer, Aperture, Millerton, N.Y., 1980

BERNARD, B., *Photodiscovery: Masterworks of Photography 1840–1940*, Abrams, N.Y., 1980

BUCKLAND, G., *Reality Recorded: Early Documentary Photography*, New York Graphic Society, Greenwich, 1974

CALLAHAN, S., ed., *The Photographs of Margaret Bourke-White*, New York Graphic Society, Greenwich, 1972

CARTIER-BRESSON, H., *The Decisive Movement*, Simon & Schuster, N.Y., 1952

COKE, V. D., *The Painter and the Photograph from Delacroix to Warhol*, rev. ed., Univ. of New Mexico Press, Albuquerque, 1972

FREUND, G., *Photography and Society*, Godine, Boston, 1980

GIDAL, T. N., *Modern Photojournalism: Origins and Evolution 1910–33*, Macmillan, N.Y., 1973

GOLDBERG, V., ed., *Photography in Print*, Simon & Schuster, N.Y., 1981

GREEN, J., *American Photography: A Critical History, 1945 to the Present*, Abrams, N.Y., 1984

GREENOUGH, S., et al, *On the Art of Fixing a Shadow*, Bullfinch, 1989; distr. by Little Brown, Boston

HAUS, A., *Moholy-Nagy: Photographs and Photograms*, Pantheon, N.Y., 1980

HEARTFIELD, J., *Photomontages of the Nazi Period*, Universe Books, N.Y., 1977

HOMER, W. I., *Alfred Stieglitz and the American Avant-Garde*, New York Graphic Society, Greenwich, 1977

HURLEY, F. J., *Portrait of a Decade: Roy Stryker and the Development of Documentary Photography in the Thirties*, Louisiana State Univ. Press, Baton Rouge, 1972

Life Library of Photography, 17 vols., rev. ed., Time-Life Books, Alexandria, Va., 1983

LYONS, N., ed., *Aaron Siskind Photographer*, George Eastman House, Rochester, N.Y., 1965

MADDOW, B., *Edward Weston, His Life and Photographs*, rev. ed., Aperture, Millerton, N.Y., 1979

MARZONA, E. & R. FRICKE, *Bauhaus Photography*, MIT Press, Cambridge, 1987

METZKER, M., *Dorothea Lange, A Photographer's Life*, Farrar, Straus & Giroux, N.Y., 1978

NAEF, W. J., *The Collection of Alfred Stieglitz: Fifty Pioneers of Modern Photography*, Metropolitan Museum of Art/ Viking, N.Y., 1979

NEWHALL, N., *Ansel Adams: The Eloquent Light*, Aperture, Millerton, N.Y., 1980

Paul Strand: Sixty Years of Photographs, profile by Calvin Tompkins, Aperture, Millerton, N.Y., 1976

PETRUCK, P. R., ed., *The Camera Viewed: Writings on Twentieth-Century Photography*, 2 vols., Dutton, N.Y., 1979

*PHILLIPS, C., ed., *Photography in the Modern Era: European Documents and Critical Writings, 1913–1940*, Metropolitan Museum of Art, N.Y., 1989

Photographs by Man Ray: 1920 Paris 1934, 1935, reprint, Dover, N.Y., 1979

SIPLEY, L. W., *A Half Century of Color*, Macmillan, N.Y., 1951

SOUTHALL, T. W., *Diane Arbus: Magazine Work*, Aperture, Millerton, N.Y., 1984

STEICHEN, E., *A Life in Photography*, Doubleday, Garden City, 1984

STRYKER, R., & N. WOOD, *In This Proud Land: America 1935–43 as Seen in the FSA Photographs*, New York Graphic Society, Greenwich, 1973

SZARKOWSKI, J., *Mirrors and Windows: American Photography Since 1960*, The Museum of Modern Art, N.Y., 1978

SZARKOWSKI, J. & M. M. HAMBOURG, *The Work of Atget*, 4 vols., The Museum of Modern Art, N.Y., 1981–84

GLOSSARY

ABACUS. A slab of stone at the top of a classical CAPITAL, just beneath the ARCHITRAVE.

ABBEY. 1) A religious community headed by an abbot or abbess. 2) The buildings which house the community. An abbey church often has an especially large CHOIR to provide space for the monks or nuns.

ACADEMY. A place of study, the word coming from the Greek name of a garden near Athens where Plato and, later, Platonic philosophers held philosophical discussions from the 5th century B.C. to the 6th century A.D. The first academy of fine arts, properly speaking, was the Academy of Drawing founded 1563 in Florence by Giorgio Vasari. Important later academies were the Royal Academy of Painting and Sculpture in Paris, founded 1648, and the Royal Academy of Arts in London, founded 1768. Their purpose was to foster the arts by systematic teaching, exhibitions, discussion, and occasionally by financial assistance.

ACANTHUS. 1) A Mediterranean plant having spiny or toothed leaves. 2) An architectural ornament resembling the leaves of this plant, used on MOLDINGS, FRIEZES, and Corinthian CAPITALS.

ACRYLIC. A plastic binder MEDIUM for PIGMENTS that is soluble in water. Developed about 1960 (figs. 1042, 1044).

AERIAL PERSPECTIVE. See PERSPECTIVE.

AISLE. See SIDE AISLE.

ALLA PRIMA. A painting technique in which PIGMENTS are laid on in one application with little or no UNDERPAINTING.

ALLAH. The unique and personal God of the MOSLEM faith.

ALTAR. 1) A mound or structure on which sacrifices or offerings are made in the worship of a deity. 2) In a Catholic church, a table-like structure used in celebrating the Mass.

ALTARPIECE. A painted or carved work of art placed behind and above the ALTAR of a Christian church. It may be a single panel (fig. 44) or a TRIPTYCH or a POLYPTYCH having hinged wings painted on both sides (figs. 547, 551). Also called a reredos or retable.

AMBULATORY. A covered walkway. 1) In a BASILICAN church, the semicircular passage around the APSE. 2) In a CENTRAL-PLAN church, the ring-shaped AISLE around the central space (fig. 757). 3) In a CLOISTER the covered COLONNADED or ARCADED walk around the open courtyard.

ANNULAR. From the Latin word for ring. Signifies a ring-shaped form, especially an annular barrel VAULT.

APOCALYPSE. The Book of Revelation, the last book of the New Testament. In it St. John the Evangelist describes his visions, experienced on the island of Patmos, of heaven, the future of mankind, and the Last Judgment.

APOSTLE. One of the twelve disciples chosen by Christ to accompany him in his lifetime, and to spread the GOSPEL after his death. The traditional list in Matt. 10:1-4 includes Andrew, Bartholomew, James the Greater (son of Zebedee), James the Less (son of Alphaeus), John, Judas Iscariot, Matthew, Peter, Philip, Simon the Canaanite, Thaddeus (or Jude), and Thomas. In art, however, the same twelve are not always represented since "apostle" was sometimes applied to other early Christians, such as St. Paul.

APSE. 1) A semicircular or polygonal niche terminating one or both ends of the NAVE in a Roman BASILICA. 2) In a Christian church, it is usually placed at the east end of the nave beyond the TRANSEPT or CHOIR (figs. 706, 828); it is also sometimes used at the end of transept arms.

AQUATINT. A print processed like an ETCHING, except that the ground or certain areas are covered with a solution of asphalt, resin, or salts which, when heated, produces a granular surface on the plate and rich gray tones in the final print (fig. 844). Etched lines are usually added to the plate after the aquatint ground is laid.

AQUEDUCT. Latin for duct of water. 1) An artificial channel or conduit for transporting water from a distant source. 2) The overground structure which carries the conduit across valleys, rivers, etc.

ARCADE. A series of ARCHES supported by PIERS or COLUMNS (fig. 589). When attached to a wall, these form a blind arcade.

ARCH. A curved structure used to span an opening. Masonry arches are built of wedge-shaped blocks, called voussoirs, set with their narrow side toward the opening so that they lock together. The topmost voussoir is called the keystone. Arches may take different shapes, as in the pointed Gothic arch (fig. 897), or the rounded classical arch (fig. 896), but all require support from other arches or BUTTRESSES.

ARCHBISHOP. The chief BISHOP of an ecclesiastical district.

ARCHITRAVE. The lowermost member of a classical ENTABLATURE, i.e., a series of stone blocks that rest directly on the COLUMNS (figs. 704, 705, 853).

ARCHIVOLT. A molded band framing an ARCH, or a series of such bands framing a TYMPANUM, often decorated with sculpture (fig. 634).

ARRICCIO. See SINOPIA.

ATMOSPHERIC PERSPECTIVE. See PERSPECTIVE.

ATRIUM. 1) The central court of an ancient Roman house, or its open entrance court. 2) An open court, sometimes COLONNADED or ARCADED, in front of a church.

ATTIC. A low upper story placed above the main CORNICE or ENTABLATURE of a building, and often decorated with windows and PILASTERS (fig. 666).

AUTOCHROME. A color photograph invented by Louis Lumière in 1903, using a glass plate covered with grains of starch dyed in three colors to act as filters, then a silver bromide emulsion (fig. 1119).

BACCHANT (fem. BACCHANTE). A priest or priestess of the wine god, Bacchus (in Greek mythology, Dionysus), or one of his ecstatic female followers, who were sometimes called maenads (fig. 676).

BALUSTRADE. A railing supported by short pillars called balusters (fig. 661). Occasionally applied to a low parapet (fig. 647).

BAPTISTERY. A building or a part of a church, often round or octagonal, in which the sacrament of baptism is administered. It contains a baptismal font, a receptacle of stone or metal which holds the water for the rite.

BARREL VAULT. See VAULT.

BASE. 1) The lowermost portion of a COLUMN or PIER, beneath the SHAFT. 2) The lowest element of a wall, DOME, or building, or occasionally of a statue or painting (see PREDELLA).

BASILICA. 1) In ancient Roman architecture, a large, oblong building used as a hall of justice and public meeting place, generally having a NAVE, SIDE AISLES, and one or more APSES. 2) In Christian architecture, a longitudinal church derived from the Roman basilica, and having a nave, apse, two or four side aisles or side chapels, and sometimes a NARTHEX (fig. 590). 3) One of the seven main churches of Rome (St. Peter's, St. Paul Outside the Walls, St. John Lateran, etc.), or another church accorded the same religious privileges.

BATTLEMENT. A parapet consisting of alternating solid parts and open spaces designed originally for defense and later used for decoration (fig. 892).

BAY. A subdivision of the interior space of a building, usually in a series bounded by consecutive architectural supports.

BISHOP. The spiritual overseer of a number of churches or a diocese. His throne, or cathedra, placed in the principal church of the diocese, designates it as a cathedral.

BLIND ARCADE. See ARCADE.

BLOCK BOOKS. Books, often religious, of the 15th century, containing WOODCUT prints in which picture and text were usually cut into the same block (compare fig. 570).

BOOK. A written work of some length on consecutive sheets of PAPER, PARCHMENT, etc., fastened or bound together in a volume. See CODEX.

BOOK COVER. The stiff outer covers protecting the bound pages of a BOOK. In the medieval period, frequently covered with precious metal and elaborately embellished with jewels, embossed decoration, etc.

BOOK OF HOURS. A private prayer book containing the devotions for the seven canonical hours of the Roman Catholic church (matins, vespers, etc.), liturgies for local saints, and sometimes a calendar (fig. 43). They were often elaborately ILLUMINATED for persons of high rank, whose names are attached to certain extant examples.

BRACKET. A stone, wooden, or metal support projecting from a wall and having a flat top to bear the weight of a statue, CORNICE, beam, etc. The lower part may take the form of a SCROLL: it is then called a scroll bracket (fig. 568).

BROKEN PEDIMENT. See PEDIMENT.

BRONZE. An alloy of copper and tin, used since early times for sculpture. See CIRE-PERDU.

BRUSH DRAWING. See DRAWING.

BURIN. See ENGRAVING.

BUTTRESS. 1) A projecting support built against an external wall, usually to counteract the lateral THRUST of a VAULT or ARCH within (fig. 709). 2) FLYING BUTTRESS. An arched bridge above the aisle roof that extends from the upper nave wall, where the lateral thrust of the main vault is greatest, down to a solid pier.

BYZANTIUM. City on the Sea of Marmara, founded by the ancient Greeks and renamed Constantinople in 330 A.D. Today called Istanbul.

CAESAR. The surname of the Roman dictator, Caius Julius Caesar, subsequently used as the title of an emperor; hence the German *Kaiser*, and the Russian *czar* (*tsar*).

CALVARY. The hill originally outside Jerusalem where Christ was crucified, the name being taken from the Latin word *calvaris*, meaning skull (Golgotha is the Greek transliteration of skull in Aramaic). The hill was thought to be the spot where Adam was buried, and was thus traditionally known as "the place of the skull."

CAMERA OBSCURA. Latin for dark room. A darkened enclosure or box with a small opening or lens on one wall through which light enters to form an inverted image on the opposite wall. The principle had long been known, but was not used as an aid in picture making until the 16th century.

CAMPAGNA. Italian word for countryside. When capitalized, it usually refers to the countryside near Rome.

CAMPANILE. From the Italian word *campana*, meaning bell. A bell tower, either round or square in plan, and sometimes freestanding (fig. 705).

CAMPOSANTO. Italian word for holy field. A cemetery near a church, and often enclosed.

CANOPY. In architecture, an ornamental, roof-like projection or cover above a statue or sacred object (fig. 748).

CAPITAL. The uppermost member of a COLUMN or PILLAR supporting the ARCHITRAVE.

CARDINAL. In the Roman Catholic church, a member of the Sacred College, the ecclesiastical body which elects the pope and constitutes his advisory council.

CARTOON. From the Italian word *cartone*, meaning cardboard. 1) A full-scale DRAWING for a picture or design intended to be transferred to a wall, panel, tapestry, etc. (fig. 643). 2) A drawing or print, usually humorous or satirical, calling attention to some action or person of popular interest (fig. 869).

CARVING. 1) The cutting of a figure or design out of a solid material such as stone or wood, as contrasted to the additive technique of MODELING. 2) A work executed in this technique (figs. 654, 655).

CASTING. A method of duplicating a work of sculpture by pouring a hardening substance such as plaster or molten metal into a mold. See CIRE-PERDU.

CAST IRON. A hard, brittle iron produced commercially in blast furnaces by pouring it into molds where it cools and hardens. Extensively used as a building material in the early 19th century (figs. 937, 938), it was superseded by STEEL and FERROCONCRETE.

CATHEDRA, CATHEDRAL. See BISHOP.

CELLA. 1) The principal enclosed room of a temple, to house an image. Also called the naos. 2) The entire body of a temple as distinct from its external parts.

CENTERING. A wooden framework built to support an ARCH, VAULT, or DOME during its construction.

CENTRAL-PLAN CHURCH. 1) A church having four arms of equal length. The CROSSING is often covered with a DOME (figs. 618–20). Also called a Greek-cross church. 2) A church having a circular or polygonal plan (fig. 648).

CHALK. Calcium carbonate, either natural or artificially prepared, finely ground to make a white substance used in GESSO. It may be pressed in sticks and used in its white form, or mixed with colored pigments to make PASTELS.

CHANCEL. See CHOIR.

CHAPEL. 1) A private or subordinate place of worship (figs. 591–94). 2) A place of worship that is part of a church, but separately dedicated (figs. 608, 656).

CHASING. 1) A technique of ornamenting a metal surface by the use of various tools. 2) The procedure used to finish a raw bronze cast.

CHÂTEAU (pl. CHÂTEAUX). French word for castle, now used to designate a large country house as well (fig. 731).

CHIAROSCURO. Italian word for light and dark. In painting, a method of modeling form primarily by the use of light and shade (figs. 640, 676, 739).

CHOIR. In church architecture, a square or rectangular area between the APSE and the NAVE or TRANSEPT. It is reserved for the clergy and the singing choir, and is usually marked off by steps, a railing, or a CHOIR SCREEN. Also called the chancel. See PILGRIMAGE CHOIR.

CHOIR SCREEN. A screen, frequently ornamented with sculpture, separating the CHOIR of a church from the NAVE or TRANSEPT.

CIRE-PERDU PROCESS. The lost-wax process of CASTING. A method in which an original is MODELED in wax or coated with wax, then covered with clay. When the wax is melted out, the resulting mold is filled with molten metal (often BRONZE) or liquid plaster.

CITY-STATE. An autonomous political unit comprising a city and the surrounding countryside.

CLERESTORY. A row of windows in the upper part of a wall that rises above an adjoining roof; built to provide direct lighting, as in a BASILICA or church (fig. 589).

CLOISTER. 1) A place of religious seclusion such as a monastery or nunnery. 2) An open court attached to a church or monastery and surrounded by a covered ARCADED walk or AMBULATORY. Used for study, meditation, and exercise.

CODEX (pl. CODICES). A manuscript in BOOK form made possible by the use of PARCHMENT instead of PAPYRUS. During the 1st to 4th centuries A.D., it gradually replaced the ROLL or SCROLL previously used for written documents.

COFFER. 1) A small chest or casket. 2) A recessed, geometrically shaped panel in a ceiling. A ceiling decorated with these panels is said to be coffered (figs. 756, 760, 896).

COLLAGE. A composition made of cut and pasted scraps of materials, sometimes with lines or forms added by the artist (figs. 1001, 1021).

COLONNADE. A series of regularly spaced COLUMNS supporting a LINTEL or ENTABLATURE (fig. 647).

COLOSSAL ORDER. COLUMNS, PIERS, or PILASTERS which extend through two or more stories (figs. 614, 665).

COLUMN. An approximately cylindrical, upright architectural support, usually consisting of a long, relatively slender SHAFT, a BASE, and a CAPITAL (fig. 589). When imbedded in a wall, it is called an engaged column (fig. 614). Columns decorated with spiral RELIEFS were used occasionally as free-standing commemorative monuments (fig. 765).

COMPOUND PIER. See PIER.

CONCRETE. A mixture of sand or gravel with mortar and rubble, invented in the ancient Near East and further developed by the Romans. Largely ignored during the Middle Ages, it was revived by Bramante in the early 16th century for St. Peter's (fig. 650). Reinforced concrete: see FERROCONCRETE.

CONFRATERNITY. See SCUOLA.

CONTRAPPOSTO. Italian word for set against. A method developed by the Greeks to represent freedom of movement in a figure. The parts of the body are placed asymmetrically in opposition to each other around a central axis, and careful attention is paid to the distribution of the weight (fig. 586).

CORINTHIAN ORDER. See ORDER, ARCHITECTURAL.

CORNICE. 1) The projecting, framing members of a classical PEDIMENT, including the horizontal one beneath and the two sloping or "raking" ones above (fig. 616). 2) Any projecting, horizontal element surmounting a wall or other structure, or dividing it horizontally for decorative purposes (fig. 597).

COUNTER REFORMATION. The movement of self-renewal and reform within the Roman Catholic church following the Protestant REFORMATION of the early 16th century, and attempting to combat its influence. Also known as the Catholic Reform. Its principles were formulated and adopted at the Council of Trent, 1545–63.

CRENELATED. See BATTLEMENT.

CROSSHATCHING. See HATCHING.

CROSSING. The area in a church where the TRANSEPT crosses the NAVE, frequently emphasized by a DOME (fig. 595), or crossing tower.

CROSS SECTION. See SECTION.

CRYPT. In a church, a VAULTED space beneath the CHOIR, causing the floor of the choir to be raised above the level of that of the NAVE.

DAGUERREOTYPE. Originally, a photograph on a silver-plated sheet of copper which had been treated with fumes of iodine to form silver iodide on its surface and, after exposure, was developed by fumes of mercury. The process, invented by L. J. M. Daguerre and made public in 1839 (fig. 903), was modified and accelerated as daguerreotypes gained worldwide popularity.

DEËSIS. From the Greek word for entreaty. The representation of Christ enthroned between the Virgin Mary and St. John the Baptist, frequent in Byzantine MOSAICS and depictions of the Last Judgment (fig. 548); refers to the roles of the Virgin Mary and St. John as intercessors for mankind.

DIPTYCH. 1) Originally a hinged two-leaved tablet used for writing. 2) A pair of ivory CARVINGS or PANEL paintings, usually hinged together.

DOME. 1) A true dome is a VAULTED roof of circular, polygonal, or elliptical plan, formed with hemispherical or ovoidal curvature (figs. 647, 756). May be supported by a circular wall or DRUM, and by PENDENTIVES or related constructions. Domical coverings of many other sorts have been devised (figs. 594, 762).

DONOR. The patron or client at whose order a work of art was executed; the donor may be depicted in the work (figs. 547, 562).

DORIC ORDER. See ORDER, ARCHITECTURAL.

DRAWING. 1) A work in pencil, pen and ink, charcoal, etc., often on paper (fig. 954). 2) A similar work in ink or WASH, etc., made with a brush and often called a brush drawing (fig. 805). 3) A work combining these or other techniques.

A drawing may be large or small, a quick sketch or an elaborate work. Among its various forms are: a record of something seen (figs. 643, 682); a study for all or part of another work (figs. 631, 865; see also OIL SKETCH; SINOPIA); an illustration associated with a text (fig. 645); a technical aid.

DRUM. 1) A section of the SHAFT of a COLUMN. 2) A wall supporting a DOME (fig. 666).

DRYPOINT. See ENGRAVING.

ELEVATION. 1) An architectural drawing presenting a building as if projected on a vertical plane parallel to one of its sides. 2) Term used in describing the vertical plane of a building.

ENAMEL. 1) Colored glassy substances, either opaque or translucent, applied in powder form to a metal surface and fused to it by firing. Two main techniques developed: "champlevé" (from the French for raised field), in which the areas to be treated are dug out of the metal surface; and "cloisonné" (from the French for partitioned), in which compartments or "cloisons" to be filled are made on the surface with thin metal strips. 2) A work executed in either technique (fig. 698).

ENGAGED COLUMN. See COLUMN.

ENGRAVING. 1) A means of embellishing metal surfaces or gem stones by incising a design on the surface. 2) A PRINT made by cutting a design into a metal plate (usually copper) with a pointed steel tool known as a burin. The burr raised on either side of the incised line is removed; ink is then rubbed into the V-shaped grooves and wiped off the surface; the plate, covered with a damp sheet of paper, is run through a heavy press (fig. 571). The image on the paper is the reverse of that on the plate (figs. 831, 832). When a fine steel needle is used instead of a burin and the burr is retained, a drypoint engraving results, characterized by a softer line (fig. 572). 3) These

techniques are called respectively engraving and drypoint.

ENTABLATURE. 1) In a classical order, the entire structure above the COLUMNS; this usually includes ARCHITRAVE, FRIEZE, and CORNICE. 2) The same structure in any building of a classical style (fig. 849).

ENTASIS. A swelling of the SHAFT of a COLUMN.

ETCHING. 1) A PRINT made by coating a copper plate with an acid-resistant resin and drawing through this ground, exposing the metal with a sharp instrument called a STYLUS. The plate is bathed in acid, which eats into the lines; it is then heated to remove the resin, and finally inked and printed on paper (figs. 687, 785). 2) The technique itself is also called etching.

EUCHARIST. 1) The sacrament of Holy Communion, the celebration in commemoration of the Last Supper (fig. 611). 2) The consecrated bread and wine used in the ceremony.

EVANGELISTS. Matthew, Mark, Luke, and John, traditionally thought to be the authors of the GOSPELS, the first four books of the New Testament, which recount the life and death of Christ. They are usually shown with their symbols, which are probably derived from the four beasts surrounding the throne of the Lamb in the Book of Revelation (4:7) or from those in the vision of Ezekiel (1:4-14): a winged man or angel for Matthew (fig. 695), a winged lion for Mark, a winged ox for Luke, and an eagle for John. These symbols may also represent the Evangelists.

FAÇADE. The principal face or the front of a building.

FERROCONCRETE. Reinforced CONCRETE, strengthened by STEEL rods and mesh placed in it before hardening. Introduced in France c. 1900, and widely used today (figs. 1102, 1105, 1113, 1115).

FIBULA. A clasp, buckle, or brooch, often ornamented.

FINIAL. A relatively small, decorative element terminating a GABLE, PINNACLE, or the like (fig. 730).

FLUTING. In architecture, the ornamental grooves channeled vertically into the SHAFT of a COLUMN or PILASTER (fig. 623). They may meet in a sharp edge as in the Doric ORDER, or be separated by a narrow strip or fillet, as in the Ionic, Corinthian, and Composite orders.

FLYING BUTTRESS. See BUTTRESS.

FONT. See BAPTISTERY.

FORESHORTENING. A method of reducing or distorting the parts of a represented object which are not parallel to the PICTURE PLANE, in order to convey the impression of three dimensions as perceived by the human eye (figs. 803, 864).

FRESCO. Italian word for fresh. 1) True fresco is the technique of painting on moist plaster with PIGMENTS ground in water so that the paint is absorbed by the plaster and becomes part of the wall itself (fig. 39). Fresco secco is the technique of painting with the same colors on dry plaster. 2) A painting done in either of these techniques.

FRIEZE. 1) A continuous band of painted or sculptured decoration (fig. 925). 2) In a classical building, the part of the ENTABLATURE between the ARCHITRAVE and the CORNICE. A Doric frieze consists of alternating TRIGLYPHS and METOPES, the latter often sculptured. An Ionic frieze is decorated with continuous RELIEF sculpture.

FROTTAGE. See RUBBING.

GABLE. 1) The triangular area framed by the CORNICE or eaves of a building and the sloping sides of a pitched roof. In classical architecture, it is called a PEDIMENT. 2) A decorative element of similar shape, such as the triangular structures above the PORTALS of a Gothic church.

GALLERY. A second story placed over the SIDE AISLES of a church and below the CLERESTORY, or, in a church with a four-part ELEVATION, below the TRIFORIUM and above the NAVE ARCADE which supports it on its open side.

GENIUS (pl. GENII). A winged semi-nude figure, often purely decorative (fig. 623) but frequently representing the guardian spirit of a person or place, or personifying an abstract concept (fig. 887).

GENRE. French word for kind or sort. A work of art, usually a painting, showing a scene from everyday life that is represented for its own sake (fig. 823).

GESSO. A smooth mixture of ground CHALK or plaster and glue, used as the basis for TEMPERA PAINTING and for OIL PAINTING on PANEL.

GILDING. 1) A coat of gold or of a gold-colored substance that is applied mechanically or chemically to surfaces of a painting, sculpture, or architectural decoration (figs. 587, 769). 2) The process of applying same.

GISANT. From the French verb gésir, meaning to lie helpless or dead. A recumbent statue on a tomb (fig. 737).

GLAZE. 1) A thin layer of translucent oil color applied to a painted surface or to parts of it in order to modify the tone. 2) A glassy coating applied to a piece of ceramic work before firing in the kiln, as a protective seal and often as decoration.

GLORIOLE or GLORY. The circle of radiant light around the head or figures of God, Christ, the Virgin Mary, or a saint. When it surrounds the head only, it is called a halo or nimbus (fig. 41); when it surrounds the entire figure with a large oval, it is called a mandorla (the Italian word for almond). It indicates divinity or holiness, though originally it was placed around the heads of kings and gods as a mark of distinction.

GOLD LEAF, SILVER LEAF. 1) Gold beaten into very thin sheets or "leaves," and applied to ILLUMINATED MANUSCRIPTS and PANEL paintings (fig. 587), to sculpture or to the back of the glass TESSERAE used in MOSAICS. 2) Silver leaf is also used, though ultimately it tarnishes. Sometimes called gold foil, silver foil.

GOLGOTHA. See CALVARY.

GOSPEL. 1) The first four books of the New Testament. They tell the story of Christ's life and death, and are ascribed to the EVANGELISTS Matthew, Mark, Luke, and John. 2) A copy of these, usually called a Gospel Book, often richly ILLUMINATED.

GREEK-CROSS CHURCH. See CENTRAL-PLAN CHURCH.

GROIN VAULT. See VAULT.

GROUND PLAN. An architectural drawing presenting a building as if cut horizontally at the floor level.

HALL CHURCH, HALL CHOIR. See HALLENKIRCHE.

HALLENKIRCHE. German word for hall church. A church in which the NAVE and the SIDE AISLES are of the same height. The type was developed in Romanesque architecture, and occurs especially frequently in German Gothic churches.

HALO. See GLORIOLE.

HATCHING. A series of parallel lines used as shading in PRINTS and DRAWINGS (fig. 631). When two sets of crossing parallel lines are used, it is called crosshatching (fig. 719).

HIGH RELIEF. See RELIEF.

HÔTEL. French word for hotel, but used also to designate an elegant town house (fig. 820).

ICON. From the Greek word for image. A PANEL painting of one or more sacred personages such as Christ, the Virgin (fig. 34), a saint, etc., particularly venerated in the ORTHODOX Catholic church.

ICONOSTASIS. See CHOIR SCREEN.

ILLUMINATED MANUSCRIPT. A MANUSCRIPT decorated with drawings or with paintings in TEMPERA colors.

ILLUSIONISM. In artistic terms, the technique of manipulating pictorial or other means in order to cause the eye to perceive a particular reality. May be used in architecture (fig. 762) and sculpture (figs. 750, 751), as well as in painting (figs. 745, 753).

IMPASTO. From the Italian word meaning "in paste." Paint, usually OIL PAINT, applied very thickly (figs. 799, 947).

IONIC ORDER. See ORDER, ARCHITECTURAL.

ISLAM. The religion of the MOSLEMS, based on the submission of the faithful to the will of ALLAH as this was revealed to the Prophet MOHAMMED and recorded in the KORAN. The adjectival form is Islamic.

JAMBS. The vertical sides of an opening. In Romanesque and Gothic churches, the jambs of doors and windows are often cut on a slant outward, or "splayed," thus providing a broader surface for sculptural decoration.

JESUIT ORDER. The "Society of Jesus" was founded in 1540 by Ignatius Loyola (1491–1556), and especially devoted to the service of the pope. The order was a powerful influence in the struggle of the Catholic COUNTER REFORMATION with the Protestant REFORMATION, and also very important for its missionary work, disseminating Christianity in the Far East and the New World. The mother church in Rome, Il Gesù (figs. 707–9), conforms in design to the preaching aims of the new order.

KEYSTONE. See ARCH.

KORAN. The scriptures of the MOSLEMS, revealed by ALLAH to MOHAMMED at Mecca and Medina, and transcribed by the Prophet himself, or by one of his associates. The text was established 651–52 A.D.

LABORS OF THE MONTHS. The various occupations suitable to the months of the year. Scenes or figures illustrating these were frequently represented in ILLUMINATED manuscripts (fig. 43); sometimes with the symbols of the ZODIAC signs, CARVED around the PORTALS of Romanesque and Gothic churches.

LANTERN. A relatively small structure crowning a DOME, roof, or tower, frequently open to admit light to an enclosed area below (fig. 666).

LAPIS LAZULI. From the Latin for stone of blue. A deep-blue stone used first for ornamental purposes, or, after the 12th century, for preparing the blue PIGMENT known as ultramarine.

LAY BROTHER. One who has joined a monastic ORDER but has not taken monastic vows, and therefore belongs still to the people or laity, as distinguished from the clergy or religious.

LIBERAL ARTS. Traditionally thought to go back to Plato, they comprised the intellectual disciplines considered suitable or necessary to a complete education, and included grammar, rhetoric, logic, arithmetic, music, geometry, and astronomy. During the Middle Ages and the Renaissance, they were often represented allegorically in painting, engravings, and sculpture.

LINTEL. See POST AND LINTEL.

LITHOGRAPH. A PRINT made by drawing a design with an oily crayon or other greasy substance on a porous stone or, later, a metal plate; the design is then fixed, the entire surface is moistened, and the printing ink which is applied adheres only to the oily lines of the drawing. The design can then be transferred easily in a press to a piece of paper. The technique was invented c. 1796 by Aloys Senefelder, and quickly became popular (figs. 869, 955). It is also widely used commercially, since many impressions can be taken from a single plate.

LOGGIA. A covered GALLERY or ARCADE open to the air on at least one side. It may stand alone or be part of a building (figs. 690, 701).

LONGITUDINAL SECTION. See SECTION.

LOUVERS. One slat or a series of overlapping boards or slats which can be opened to admit air, but are slanted so as to exclude sun and rain (fig. 1111).

LOW RELIEF. See RELIEF.

LUNETTE. 1) A semicircular or pointed wall area, as under a VAULT or above a door or window (fig. 852). When it is above the PORTAL of a medieval church, it is called a TYMPANUM (fig. 31). 2) A painting (fig. 746), relief sculpture (fig. 622), or window of the same shape (fig. 847).

MAESTÀ. Italian word for majesty, applied in the 14th and 15th centuries to representations of the Madonna and Child enthroned, and surrounded by her celestial court of saints and angels (fig. 35).

MAGNA. Paint in the form of PIGMENT ground in an ACRYLIC resin with solvents and plasticizer (fig. 1055).

MAGUS (pl. MAGI). 1) A member of the priestly caste of ancient Media and Persia. 2) In Christian literature (Matt. 2:1–12), one of the three Wise Men or Kings who came from the East bearing gifts to the newborn Jesus (fig. 44).

MANDORLA. See GLORIOLE.

MANUSCRIPT. From the Latin word for handwritten. 1) A document, scroll, or book written by hand, as distinguished from such a work in print (i.e., after c. 1450). 2) A book produced in the Middle Ages, frequently ILLUMINATED.

MAUSOLEUM. 1) The huge tomb erected at Halicarnassus in Asia Minor in the 4th century B.C. by King Mausolus and his wife Artemisia. 2) A generic term for any large funerary monument.

MEANDER. From the name Maeander (modern Menderes), a winding river in western Turkey that flows into the Aegean Sea. A decorative motif of intricate, rectilinear character, applied to architecture and sculpture.

MEDIUM (pl. MEDIUMS). 1) The material or technique in which an artist works. 2) The vehicle in which PIGMENTS are carried in PAINT, PASTEL, etc.

METOPE. In a Doric FRIEZE, one of the panels, either decorated or plain, between the TRIGLYPHS. Originally it probably covered the empty spaces between the ends of the wooden ceiling beams.

MINIATURE. 1) A single illustration in an ILLUMINATED manuscript. 2) A very small painting, especially a portrait on ivory, glass, or metal (fig. 563).

MINOTAUR. In Greek mythology, a monster having the head of a bull and the body of a man, who lived in the Labyrinth of the palace of Knossos on Crete.

MODEL. 1) The preliminary form of a sculpture, often finished in itself but preceding the final CASTING or CARVING (figs. 815, 816, 891). 2) Preliminary or reconstructed form of a building, made to scale. 3) A person who poses for an artist.

MODELING. 1) In sculpture, the building up of a figure or design in a soft substance such as clay or wax (fig. 821). 2) In painting and drawing, producing a three-dimensional effect by changes in color, the use of light and shade, etc.

MOHAMMED (also Muhammad). Arab prophet and the founder of ISLAM (c. 570–632). His first revelations were c. 610 and continued throughout his lifetime; collected and recorded, these form the basis of the KORAN. Mohammed was forced to flee from Mecca, his birthplace, to Medina in 622; the date of this "Hegira" marks the beginning of the Islamic calendar.

MOLDING. In architecture, any of various long, narrow, ornamental bands having a distinctive profile, which project from the surface of the structure and give variety to the surface by means of their patterned contrasts of light and shade (figs. 623, 634).

MOSAIC. Decorative work for walls, VAULTS, ceilings, or floors, composed of small pieces of colored materials (called TESSERAE) set in plaster or CONCRETE. The Romans, whose work was mostly for floors, used regularly shaped pieces of marble in its natural colors. The early Christians used pieces of glass whose brilliant hues, including gold, and slightly irregular surfaces produced an entirely different, glittering effect. See also GOLD LEAF.

MOSLEM (also Muslim). 1) One who has embraced ISLAM: a follower of MOHAMMED. 2) An adjective for the religion, law, or civilization of ISLAM.

MURAL. From the Latin word for wall, *murus*. A large painting or decoration, either executed directly on a wall (FRESCO) or done separately and affixed to it (fig. 952).

MUSES. In Greek mythology, the nine goddesses who presided over various arts and sciences. They are led by Apollo as god of music and poetry, and usually include Calliope, Muse of Epic Poetry; Clio, Muse of History; Erato, Muse of Love Poetry; Euterpe, Muse of Music; Melpomene, Muse of Tragedy; Polyhymnia, Muse of Sacred Music; Terpsichore, Muse of Dancing; Thalia, Muse of Comedy; and Urania, Muse of Astronomy.

NARTHEX. The transverse entrance hall of a church, sometimes enclosed but often open on one side to a preceding ATRIUM.

NAVE. 1) The central aisle of a Roman BASILICA, as distinguished from the SIDE AISLES. 2) The same section of a Christian basilican church extending from the entrance to the APSE or TRANSEPT (fig. 589).

NIKE. The ancient Greek goddess of victory, often identified with Athena, and by the Romans with Victoria. She is usually represented as a winged woman with windblown draperies.

NIMBUS. See GLORIOLE.

OBELISK. A tall, tapering, four-sided stone shaft with a pyramidal top. First constructed in an-ancient Egypt; certain examples since exported to other countries (figs. 747, 759).

ODALISQUE. Turkish word for a harem slave girl or concubine (figs. 863, 867).

OIL. In art, the MEDIUM for pigments used in OIL PAINTING. Among numerous vegetable oils, the traditional favorite is refined linseed oil, which dries to a tough, solid film.

OIL PAINTING. 1) A painting executed with PIGMENTS mixed with OIL, first applied ei-ther to a panel prepared with a coat of GESSO (as also in TEMPERA PAINTING), later to a stretched canvas primed with a coat of white paint and glue. The latter method has been usual since the late 15th century. Oil painting also may be executed on paper, parchment, copper, etc. 2) The technique of executing such a painting.

OIL SKETCH. A work in oil painting of an infor-mal character, sometimes preparatory to a fin-ished work (figs. 774, 879).

ORDER, ARCHITECTURAL. An architectural system based on the COLUMN and its EN-TABLATURE, in which the form of the ele-ments themselves (CAPITAL, SHAFT, BASE, etc.) and their relationships to each other are specifically defined. The five classical orders are the Doric, Ionic, Corinthian, Tuscan, and Composite. See also COLOSSAL ORDER, SUPERIMPOSED ORDER.

ORDER, MONASTIC. A religious society whose members live together under an established set of rules. See JESUIT, THEATINE.

ORTHODOX. From the Greek word for right in opinion. The Eastern Orthodox church, which split from the Western Catholic church during the 5th century A.D. and transferred its allegiance from the pope in Rome to the Byz-antine emperor in Constantinople and his ap-pointed patriarch. Sometimes called the Byzantine church.

PAINT. See ACRYLIC, ENCAUSTIC, FRES-CO, MAGNA, OIL PAINTING, TEMPERA PAINTING, WATERCOLOR.

PALAZZO (pl. PALAZZI). Italian word for pal-ace (in French, *palais*). Refers either to large, official buildings (fig. 665), or to important pri-vate town houses (fig. 597).

PALETTE. 1) A thin, usually oval or oblong board with a thumb hole at one end, used by painters to hold and mix their colors. 2) The range of colors used by a particular painter. 3) In Egyptian art, a slate slab, usually decorated with sculpture in low RELIEF.

PANEL. 1) A wooden surface used for painting, usually in TEMPERA, and prepared before-hand with a layer of GESSO. Large ALTAR-PIECES require the joining together of two or more boards (fig. 564). 2) Recently panels of Masonite or other composite materials have come into use (fig. 1055).

PANTHEON. A temple dedicated to all the gods, or housing tombs of the illustrious dead of a nation, or memorials to them (fig. 850).

PAPER. General name for a writing material made from various fibrous substances. Invent-ed in China in the 2nd century A.D., it was known in Europe in the Middle Ages, but its possibilities as a cheap substitute for PARCH-MENT were not fully realized until the devel-

opment of printing in northern Europe in the 15th century.

PARCHMENT. From Pergamum, the name of a Greek city in Asia Minor where parchment was invented in the 2nd century B.C. 1) A paper-like material made from thin bleached animal hides, used extensively in the Middle Ages for MANUSCRIPTS. Vellum is a superior type of parchment, made from calfskin. 2) A docu-ment or miniature on this material.

PASSION. 1) In ecclesiastic terms, the events of Christ's last week on earth. 2) The representa-tion of these events in pictorial, literary, theat-rical, or musical form (figs. 555, 611, 680, 773).

PASTEL. 1) A color of a soft, subdued shade. 2) A drawing stick made from PIGMENTS ground with CHALK and mixed with gum water. 3) A drawing executed with these sticks (fig. 918).

PEDESTAL. An architectural support for a stat-ue, vase, column, etc.

PEDIMENT. 1) In classical architecture, a low GABLE, typically triangular, framed by a hori-zontal CORNICE below and two raking cor-nices above; frequently filled with relief sculpture (fig. 850). 2) A similar architectural member, either round or triangular, used over a door, window, or niche (fig. 660). When pieces of the cornice are either turned at an an-gle or broken, it is called a broken pediment (fig. 661).

PENDENTIVE. One of the spherical triangles which achieve the transition from a square or polygonal opening to the round BASE of a DOME or the supporting DRUM (fig. 620).

PERIPTERAL. An adjective describing a build-ing surrounded by a single row of COLUMNS or COLONNADE.

PERISTYLE. 1) In an ancient Roman house, an open garden court surrounded by a COLON-NADE. 2) A colonnade around a building or court (fig. 648).

PERSPECTIVE. A technique for representing spatial relationships and three-dimensional ob-jects on a flat surface so as to produce an effect similar to that perceived by the human eye. In "atmospheric" or aerial perspective, this is ac-complished by a gradual decrease in the inten-sity of local color and in the contrast of light and dark, so that everything in the far distance tends toward a light bluish-gray tone (fig. 548). In one-point linear perspective, developed in Italy in the 15th century, a mathematical system is used, based on orthogonals (all lines receding at right angles to the picture plane) that converge on a single vanishing point on the ho-rizon. Since this presupposes an absolutely sta-tionary viewer and imposes rigid restrictions on the artist, it is seldom applied with complete consistency (figs. 581, 610).

PHOTOGRAM. A shadow-like photograph made without a camera by placing objects on light-sensitive paper and exposing them to a light source (fig. 1140).

PHOTOGRAPH. The relatively permanent or "fixed" form of an image made by light that passes through the lens of a camera and acts upon light-sensitive substances. Often called a PRINT.

PHOTOJOURNALISM. Journalism in which written copy is subordinate to photography.

PHOTOMONTAGE. A photograph in which prints in whole or in part are combined to form a new image (fig. 1139). A technique much practiced by the Dada group in the 1920s.

PIAZZA (pl. PIAZZE). Italian word for public square (in French, *place*; in German, *Platz*).

PICTURE PLANE. The flat surface on which a picture is painted.

PICTURESQUE. Visually interesting or pleas-ing, as if resembling a picture (fig. 849).

PIER. An upright architectural support, usually rectangular, and sometimes with CAPITAL and BASE. When COLUMNS, PILASTERS, or SHAFTS are attached to it, as in many Romanesque and Gothic churches, it is called a compound pier.

PIETÀ. Italian word for both pity and piety. A rep-resentation of the Virgin grieving over the dead Christ. When used in a scene recording a specific moment after the Crucifixion, it is usu-ally called a "Lamentation."

PIGMENT. Colored substances found in organic and inorganic sources; many are now prepared synthetically. 1) Pigment finely divided and suspended in a liquid medium becomes a paint, ink, etc. See ACRYLIC, OIL PAINTING, TEMPERA PAINTING, WATERCOLOR, FRESCO. 2) Pigment suspended in a solid me-dium becomes CRAYON, PASTEL, etc.

PILASTER. A flat, vertical element projecting from a wall surface, and normally having a BASE, SHAFT, and CAPITAL. It has general-ly a decorative rather than structural purpose (figs. 616, 618).

PILGRIMAGE CHOIR. The unit in a Roman-esque church composed of the APSE, AMBU-LATORY, and RADIATING CHAPELS.

PILLAR. A general term for a vertical architec-tural support which includes COLUMNS, PIERS, and PILASTERS.

PINNACLE. A small, decorative structure cap-ping a tower, PIER, BUTTRESS, or other ar-chitectural member, and used especially in Gothic buildings.

PLAN. See GROUND PLAN.

PODIUM. 1) The tall base upon which rests a temple. 2) The ground floor of a building made to resemble such a base (fig. 808).

POLYPTYCH. An ALTARPIECE or devotional work of art made of several panels joined to-gether (fig. 549), often hinged.

PORCH. General term for an exterior appendage to a building which forms a covered approach to a doorway. See PORTICO for porches con-sisting of columns.

PORTA. Latin word for door or gate.

PORTAL. A door or gate, usually a monumental one with elaborate sculptural decoration.

PORTICO. A porch supporting a roof or an EN-TABLATURE and PEDIMENT, often ap-proached by a number of steps (fig. 847). It provides a monumental covered entrance to a building, and a link with the space surround-ing it.

POST AND LINTEL. A basic system of con-struction in which two or more uprights, the "posts," support a horizontal member, the "lin-tel." The lintel may be the topmost element or support a wall or roof (fig. 975).

PREDELLA. The base of an ALTARPIECE, of-ten decorated with small scenes which are re-lated in subject to that of the main panel or panels (fig. 44).

PRINT. A picture or design reproduced, usually on paper and often in numerous copies, from a prepared wood block, metal plate, or stone slab, or by photography. See AQUATINT, EN-GRAVING, ETCHING, LITHOGRAPH, PHO-TOGRAPH, WOODCUT.

PSALTER. 1) The book of Psalms in the Old Tes-tament, thought to have been written in part by David, king of ancient Israel. 2) A copy of the Psalms, sometimes arranged for liturgical or devotional use, and often richly ILLUMI-NATED.

PULPIT. A raised platform in a church from which the clergyman delivers a sermon or con-ducts the service. Its railing or enclosing wall may be elaborately decorated.

PUTTO (pl. PUTTI). A nude, male child, usually

winged, often represented in classical and Renaissance art (fig. 628). Also called a cupid or *amoretto* when he carries a bow and arrow and personifies Love (figs. 673, 775).

PYLON. Greek word for gateway. 1) The monumental entrance building to an Egyptian temple or forecourt, consisting either of a massive wall with sloping sides pierced by a doorway, or of two such walls flanking a central gateway. 2) A tall structure at either side of a gate, bridge, or avenue, marking an approach or entrance.

QUATREFOIL. An ornamental element composed of four lobes radiating from a common center.

RADIATING CHAPELS. Term for CHAPELS arranged around the AMBULATORY (and sometimes the TRANSEPT) of a medieval church.

REFECTORY. 1) A room for refreshment. 2) The dining hall of a monastery, college, or other large institution.

REFORMATION. The religious movement in the early 16th century which had for its object the reform of the Catholic Church, and led to the establishment of Protestant churches. See also COUNTER REFORMATION.

REINFORCED CONCRETE. See FERROCONCRETE.

RELIEF. 1) The projection of a figure or part of a design from the background or plane on which it is CARVED or MODELED. Sculpture done in this manner is described as "high relief" or "low relief" depending on the height of the projection. When it is very shallow, it is called *schiacciato*, the Italian word for flattened out (fig. 579). 2) The apparent projection of forms represented in a painting or drawing.

RESPOND. 1) A half-PIER, PILASTER, or similar element projecting from a wall to support a LINTEL, or an ARCH whose other side is supported by a free-standing COLUMN or pier, as at the end of an ARCADE. 2) One of several pilasters on a wall behind a COLONNADE (fig. 589) which echo or "respond to" the columns, but are largely decorative. 3) One of the slender shafts of a COMPOUND PIER in a medieval church which seems to carry the weight of the VAULT.

RIB. A slender, projecting archlike member which supports a VAULT either transversely or at the GROINS, thus dividing the surface into sections. In late Gothic architecture, its purpose is often primarily ornamental.

RIBBED VAULT. See VAULT.

ROLL. A long sheet of PAPYRUS or PARCHMENT with a written text, sometimes illustrated, used as a book before the introduction of the CODEX. Also called a SCROLL, and, in Latin, a *rotulus*.

ROOD SCREEN. See CHOIR SCREEN.

RUBBING. A reproduction of a relief surface made by covering it with paper and rubbing with pencil, chalk, etc. Also called "frottage."

RUSTICATION. A masonry technique of laying beveled stones with sharply indented joints (figs. 597, 702).

SACRA CONVERSAZIONE. Italian for holy conversation. A composition of the Madonna and Child with Saints in which the figures all occupy the same spatial setting, and appear to be conversing or communing with each other (figs. 634, 677).

SACRISTY. A room near the main altar of a church, or a small building attached to a church, where the vessels and vestments required for the service are kept. Also called a vestry.

SALON. 1) A large, elegant drawing or reception room in a palace or a private house (fig. 820). 2) Official government-sponsored exhibition of paintings and sculpture by living artists held in the Louvre at Paris, first biennially, then annually. 3) Any large public exhibition patterned after the Paris Salon.

SANCTUARY. 1) A sacred or holy place or building. 2) An especially holy place within a building, such as the CELLA of a temple, or the part of a church around the altar.

SANGUINE. A reddish-brown CHALK stick used for DRAWING (fig. 682).

SARCOPHAGUS (pl. SARCOPHAGI). A large stone coffin usually decorated with sculpture and/or inscriptions. The term is derived from two Greek words meaning flesh and eating, which were applied to a kind of limestone in ancient Greece, since the stone was said to turn flesh to dust.

SATYR. One of a class of woodland gods thought to be the lascivious companions of Dionysus, the Greek god of wine (or of Bacchus, his Roman counterpart). They are represented as having the legs and tail of a goat, the body of a man, and a head with horns and pointed ears. A youthful satyr is also called a faun (fig. 636).

SCRIPTORIUM (pl. SCRIPTORIA). A workroom in a monastery reserved for copying and illustrating MANUSCRIPTS.

SCROLL. 1) An architectural ornament with the form of a partially unrolled spiral, as on the CAPITALS of the Ionic and Corinthian ORDERS. 2) A form of written text: see ROLL.

SCROLL BRACKET. See BRACKET.

SCUOLA. Italian word for school. In Renaissance Venice it designated a fraternal organization or confraternity, dedicated to good works, usually under ecclesiastical auspices.

SECTION. An architectural drawing presenting a building as if cut across the vertical plane, at right angles to the horizontal plane. Cross section: a cut along the transverse axis. Longitudinal section: a cut along the longitudinal axis.

SEXPARTITE VAULT. See VAULT.

SFUMATO. Italian word meaning gone up in smoke, used to describe very delicate gradations of light and shade in the MODELING of figures; applied especially to the work of Leonardo da Vinci and his followers (fig. 644).

SHAFT. In architecture, the part of a COLUMN between the BASE and the CAPITAL.

SIBYLS. In Greek and Roman mythology, any of numerous women who were thought to possess powers of divination and prophecy. They appear in Christian representations, notably in Michelangelo's Sistine Ceiling, because they were believed to have foretold the coming of Christ.

SIDE AISLE. A passageway running parallel to the NAVE of a Roman BASILICA or Christian church, separated from it by an ARCADE or COLONNADE (fig. 757). There may be one on either side of the nave, or two, an inner and outer.

SILENI. A class of minor woodland gods in the entourage of the wine god, Dionysus (or Bacchus). Like Silenus, the wine god's tutor and drinking companion, they are thick-lipped and snub-nosed, and fond of wine. Similar to SATYRS, they are basically human in form except for horse's tails and ears.

SILVER LEAF. See GOLD LEAF.

SILVER SALTS. Compounds of silver—bromide, chloride, and iodide—which are sensitive to light and are used in the preparation of photographic materials. This sensitivity was first observed by Johann Heinrich Schulze in 1727.

SINOPIA (pl. SINOPIE). Italian word taken from Sinope, the ancient city in Asia Minor which was famous for its brick-red PIGMENT. In FRESCO paintings, a full-sized, preliminary sketch done in this color on the first rough coat of plaster or "arriccio."

SKENE. See THEATER.

SKETCH. See DRAWING, OIL SKETCH.

SPANDREL. The area between the exterior curves of two adjoining ARCHES, or, in the case of a single arch, the area around its outside curve from its springing to its keystone (fig. 677).

SPHINX. 1) In ancient Egypt, a creature having the head of a man, animal, or bird, and the body of a lion; frequently sculpted in monumental form. 2) In Greek mythology, a creature usually represented as having the head and breasts of a woman, the body of a lion, and the wings of an eagle. It appears in classical, Renaissance, and Neoclassical art.

STANZA (pl. STANZE). Italian word for room.

STEEL. Iron modified chemically to have qualities of great hardness, elasticity, and strength. For use in sculpture, see figs. 1078, 1081. For architectural use, see STRUCTURAL STEEL.

STELE. From the Greek word for standing block. An upright stone slab or pillar with a CARVED commemorative design or inscription.

STEREOBATE. The substructure of a classical building, especially a Greek temple.

STEREOSCOPE. An optical instrument which enables the user to combine two pictures taken from points of view corresponding to those of the two eyes into a single image having the depth and solidity of ordinary binocular vision (fig. 908). First demonstrated by Sir Charles Wheatstone in 1838.

STILTS. Term for pillars or posts supporting a superstructure; in 20th-century architecture, these are usually of FERROCONCRETE (figs. 1105, 1111). Stilted, as in stilted arches, refers to tall supports beneath an architectural member.

STRUCTURAL STEEL. STEEL used as an architectural building material either invisibly (fig. 969) or exposed (figs. 978, 1104). See FERROCONCRETE.

STUCCO. 1) A CONCRETE or cement used to coat the walls of a building. 2) A kind of plaster used for architectural decorations such as CORNICES, MOLDINGS, etc. (fig. 820), or for sculptured RELIEFS (fig. 699).

STUDY. See DRAWING.

STYLOBATE. A platform or masonry floor above the STEREOBATE forming the foundation for the COLUMNS of a classical temple.

STYLUS. From the Latin word *stilus*, the writing instrument of the Romans. 1) A pointed instrument used in ancient times for writing on tablets of a soft material such as clay. 2) The needle-like instrument used in drypoint or etching. See ENGRAVING, ETCHING.

SUPERIMPOSED ORDERS. Two or more rows of COLUMNS, PIERS, or PILASTERS placed above each other on the wall of a building (fig. 701).

TABERNACLE. 1) A place or house of worship. 2) A CANOPIED niche or recess built for an image (fig. 577). 3) The portable shrine used by the Jews to house the Ark of the Covenant.

TEMPERA PAINTING. 1) A painting made with PIGMENTS mixed with egg yolk and water. In the 14th and 15th centuries, it was applied to PANELS which had been prepared with a coating of GESSO; the application of GOLD LEAF and of underpainting in green or brown preceded the actual tempera painting (fig. 38). 2) The technique of executing such a painting.

TERRACOTTA. Italian word for cooked earth. 1) Earthenware, naturally reddish-brown but often GLAZED (fig. 622) in various colors and fired. Used for pottery, sculpture (fig. 627), or as a building material or decoration. 2) An object made of this material. 3) Color of the natural material.

TESSERA (pl. TESSERAE). A small piece of colored stone, marble, glass, or gold-backed glass used in a MOSAIC.

THEATINE ORDER. Founded in Rome in the 16th century by members of the recently dissolved Oratory of Divine Love. Its aim was to reform the Catholic church, and its members were pledged to cultivate their spiritual lives and to perform charitable works.

THRUST. The lateral pressure exerted by an ARCH, VAULT, or DOME, which must be counteracted at its point of greatest concentration either by the thickness of the wall or by some form of BUTTRESS.

TOTEM. Among the Indians of North America, a natural object or animal assumed as the emblem of a tribe or family, or the representation of it, such as those CARVED on the posts or "totem poles" in front of their dwellings.

TRACERY. 1) Ornamental stone work in Gothic windows. 2) Similar ornamentation using various materials and applied to walls, shrines, etc. (fig. 567).

TRANSEPT. A cross arm in a BASILICAN church, placed at right angles to the NAVE, and usually separating it from the CHOIR or APSE.

TREE OF KNOWLEDGE. The tree in the Garden of Eden from which Adam and Eve ate the forbidden fruit which destroyed their innocence (Gen. 2:9, 17).

TREE OF LIFE. A tree in the Garden of Eden whose fruit was reputed to give everlasting life; in medieval art it was frequently used as a symbol of Christ (Gen. 2:9; 3:22).

TRIFORIUM. The section of a NAVE wall above the ARCADE and below the CLERESTORY. It frequently consists of a BLIND ARCADE with three openings in each bay. When the GALLERY is also present, a four-story ELEVATION results, the triforium being between the gallery and clerestory. It may also occur in the TRANSEPT and the CHOIR walls.

TRIGLYPH. The element of a Doric FRIEZE separating two consecutive METOPES, and being divided by channels (or glyphs) into three sections. Probably an imitation in stone of wooden ceiling beam ends.

TRIPTYCH. An ALTARPIECE or devotional picture, either CARVED or painted, with one central panel and two hinged wings (fig. 559).

TRIUMPHAL ARCH. 1) A monumental ARCH, sometimes a combination of three arches, erected by a Roman emperor in commemoration of his military exploits, and usually decorated with scenes of these deeds in RELIEF sculpture. 2) The great transverse arch at the eastern end of a church which frames ALTAR and APSE and separates them from the main body of the church. It is frequently decorated with MOSAICS or MURAL paintings.

TROPHY. 1) In ancient Rome, arms or other spoils taken from a defeated enemy and publicly displayed on a tree, PILLAR, etc. 2) A representation of these objects, and others symbolic of victory, as a commemoration or decoration.

TRUSS. A triangular wooden or metal support for a roof which may be left exposed in the interior, or be covered by a ceiling.

TURRET. 1) A small tower, part of a larger structure. 2) A small tower at an angle of a building, frequently beginning some distance from the ground.

TYMPANUM. 1) In classical architecture, the recessed, usually triangular area, also called a PEDIMENT, often decorated with sculpture. 2) In medieval architecture, an arched area between an ARCH and the LINTEL of a door or window, frequently carved with RELIEF sculpture (fig. 31).

UNDERPAINTING. See TEMPERA PAINTING.

VAULT. An arched roof or ceiling usually made of stone, brick, or CONCRETE. Several distinct varieties have been developed; all need BUTTRESSING at the point where the lateral THRUST is concentrated. 1) A barrel vault is a semicylindrical structure made up of successive ARCHES. It may be straight or ANNULAR in plan. 2) A groin vault is the result of the intersection of two barrel vaults of equal size which produces a BAY of four compartments with sharp edges, or "groins," where the two meet. 3) A ribbed groin vault is one in which RIBS are added to the groins, for structural strength and for decoration. When the diagonal ribs are constructed as half circles, the resulting form is a domical ribbed vault. 4) Sexpartite vault: a ribbed groin vault in which each bay is divided into six compartments by the addition of a transverse rib across the center. 5) The normal Gothic vault is quadripartite with all the arches pointed to some degree. 6) A fan vault is an elaboration of a ribbed groin vault, with elements of TRACERY using cone-like forms. It was developed by the English in the 15th century, and was employed for decorative purposes.

VELLUM. See PARCHMENT.

VESTRY. See SACRISTY.

VICES. Often represented allegorically in conjunction with the seven VIRTUES, they include Pride, Avarice, Wrath, Gluttony, Unchastity (Luxury), Folly, and Inconstancy, though others such as Injustice are sometimes substituted.

VILLA. Originally a large country house (fig. 704), but in modern usage, also a detached house or suburban residence.

VIRTUES. The three theological virtues, Faith, Hope, and Charity, and the four cardinal ones, Prudence, Justice, Fortitude, and Temperance, were frequently represented allegorically, particularly in medieval manuscripts and sculpture.

VOLUTE. A spiral architectural element found notably on Ionic and Composite CAPITALS, but also used decoratively on building FAÇADES and interiors (fig. 709).

VOUSSOIR. See ARCH.

WASH. A thin layer of translucent color or ink used in WATERCOLOR PAINTING and BRUSH DRAWING (fig. 805), and occasionally in OIL PAINTING.

WATERCOLOR PAINTING. Painting, usually on paper, in PIGMENTS suspended in water (figs. 713, 1025).

WING. The side panel of an ALTARPIECE which is frequently decorated on both sides, and also hinged, so that it may be shown either open or closed (figs. 549, 551).

WOODCUT. A PRINT made by carving out a design on a wood block cut along the grain, applying ink to the raised surfaces which remain, and printing from those (figs. 569, 714, 924).

WROUGHT IRON. A comparatively pure form of iron which is easily forged and does not harden quickly, so that it can be shaped or hammered by hand (fig. 1074), in contrast to molded CAST IRON.

ZODIAC. 1) An imaginary belt circling the heavens, including the paths of the sun, moon, and major planets, and containing twelve constellations and thus twelve divisions called signs, which have been associated with the months. The signs are: Aries, the ram; Taurus, the bull; Gemini, the twins; Cancer, the crab; Leo, the lion; Virgo, the virgin; Libra, the balance; Scorpio, the scorpion; Sagittarius, the archer; Capricorn, the goat; Aquarius, the water-bearer; and Pisces, the fish. They are frequently represented around the PORTALS of Romanesque and Gothic churches in conjunction with the LABORS OF THE MONTHS.

INDEX

Works ascribed to a specific artist are indexed under the artist's name, shown in CAPITAL letters. Insofar as possible, unascribed works, including buildings and archaeological remains, are indexed by site. *See* references (e.g., *Bull's Head, see* Picasso; Colosseum, *see* Rome) are provided to assist in finding the correct name or site. Illustration references, shown in *italic* type, are to *figure numbers* rather than page numbers; but when a figure is also shown on a color plate page, that page number is given with the figure number (e.g., *673* and p. 20).

AALTO, ALVAR, 784–85; Villa Mairea, Noormarkku, 784–85; *1107, 1108*
ABBOTT, BERENICE, 793, 805; *Transformation of Energy*, 708, 805; *1142*
Abstract Expressionism, 57, 737–40, 741, 742, 744–46, 805, 807; *see also* Action Painting
Abstraction/Abstractionism, 466, 675, 710, 716–23, 728–30, 746, 802–3, 805–7
academic painters, 49; *see also* art academies
acrylic, 743
Action Painting, 737, 739, 740, 742, 743, 744, 749, 777; *see also* Abstract Expressionism
ADAM, ROBERT, 623, 653, room from Lansdowne House, London, 629, 653; *852*
Adam, from *Ghent Altarpiece, see* Eyck
Adam, sculpture, *see* Rodin
Adam and Eve, see Dürer
Adam in Paradise, Early Christian ivory, 452; *585*
ADAMS, ANSEL, 797–98, 807; *Moonrise, Hernandez, New Mexico*, 798; *1128*
Adoration of the Magi, see Gentile da Fabriano
Adoration of the Magi, unfinished panel, *see* Leonardo da Vinci
Aegina, Greece, Late Archaic sculpture, 626
AERTSEN, PIETER, 542–43, 582; *The Meat Stall*, 542–43, 579; *726*
aesthetics, defined, 42; *see also* machine aesthetic
African-American artists, 675, 746, 800–801
African art, 716
Agra, India, Taj Mahal, 653
ALBERS, JOSEF, 747
ALBERTI, LEONE BATTISTA, 452, 456, 469–72, 474, 495, 526; Palazzo Rucellai, Florence, 469, 470, 501, 546, 791; *613*; S. Andrea, Mantua, 470–71, 474, 503, 527–28, 529; *616, 617*; S. Francesco, Rimini, 469–70; *614, 615*; *Treatise on Architecture*, 456, 471–72, 486
Alexander Nevsky (film; Eisenstein), 743
Alexander the Great, 538
Alfred the Great, 627
Alkestis Leaving Hades, see Ephesus
all'antica, 419
Altarpiece of the Four Latin Fathers, see Pacher
altarpieces: Antwerp Cathedral, *see* Rubens; of

the Four Latin Fathers, see Pacher; Florence, *see* Gentile da Fabriano; Geneva Cathedral, *see* Witz; *Ghent, see* Eyck; *Isenheim, see* Grünewald; *Merode, see* Master of Flémalle; *Portinari, see* Goes; *St. Wolfgang, see* Pacher
ALTDORFER, ALBRECHT, 538–39, 540; *The Battle of Issus*, 538–39; *721*
alto (high) relief, 61
American art, *see* Colonial America; Pre-Columbian art; United States
American Revolution, 615, 619, 647, 659
Americans (Frank), 807
AMMANATI, BARTOLOMMEO, 526; courtyard, Palazzo Pitti, Florence, 526, 546; *702*
Amorgos, Cyclades, Greece: *Harpist* (Orpheus), 43–44; *1*; idol from, p. 5
Amsterdam, The Netherlands, 741
Analytic Cubism, 718, 720, 724, 729, 762, 780
Ancient Near East, 439
Ancient of Days, see Blake
Ancient Ruins in the Cañon de Chelle, N.M., in a Niche 50 Feet Above the Present Cañon Bed, see O'Sullivan
Andachtsbild (Bonn *Pietà*) 454, 531
Andrews, Mr. and Mrs. Robert, portrait of, *see* Gainsborough
ANGELICO, FRA, 464; *The Annunciation*, S. Marco monastery, Florence, 464; *606*
Anghiari, Battle of, 492; *see also* Leonardo da Vinci
ANGUISSOLA, SOFONISBA, 516; *Portrait of the Artist's Sister Minerva*, 516; *687*
Annunciation (by Daret?), detail from, *see* Woodcut of St. Christopher
Annunciation, Dijon, *see* Broederlam
Annunciation (*Ecce Ancilla Domini*), *see* Rossetti
Annunciation, from *Isenheim Altarpiece, see* Grünewald
Annunciation, St. Lorenz, Nuremberg, *see* Stosz
Annunciation, S. Marco, Florence, *see* Angelico
Annunciation of the Death of the Virgin, Siena, *see* Duccio
Antwerp, Belgium, 568, 572; Cathedral altarpiece, *see* Rubens
ANUSZKIEWICZ, RICHARD, 747; *Entrance to Green*, 747; *1049*
apartment houses: Casa Milà, Barcelona, *see* Gaudí; Lake Shore Drive, Chicago, *see* Mies van der Rohe; Unité d'Habitation, Marseilles, *see* Le Corbusier
Apollo and Daphne, see Bernini
Apollo Belvedere, Graeco-Roman, 622, 625, 626
Apparition, see Moreau
APPEL, KAREL, 741–42; *Burned Face*, 742; *1039*
applied arts, defined, 49
Appropriation, 754
Arabs, 439
Arc de Triomphe, Paris, sculpture, *see* Rude
Archaic smile, 493

Archaic style, Greek, 626, 697; Kore, p. 5
architectural proportions, 456, 471
architecture: as applied art, 49; classical orders, 456; construction in concrete, 495; industrial, 678–81; and sculpture, 765, 773; and space, 62–64
Arch of Constantine, *see* Rome
Arena Chapel, Padua, murals, *see* Giotto
Arezzo, Italy, 474; S. Francesco frescoes, *see* Piero della Francesca
Aristotle, 505
Armory Show (New York, 1913), 716, 724
Arnolfini family, 430
ARP, HANS (JEAN), 731, 760; *Collage with Squares Arranged According to the Laws of Chance*, 731, 804; *1021*
Arrangement in Black and Gray: The Artist's Mother, see Whistler
art: introduction to, 42–69; market forces, 572; and photography, 657; Renaissance view, 445
art brut, 741
Artemis, Temple of, *see* Ephesus
Arte Povera, 755
Art for Art's Sake doctrine, 664, 673, 706
Arthur, king of the Britons, 629
Artist and His Model, see De Andrea
Artist in the Character of Design Listening to the Inspiration of Poetry, see Kauffman
artists: earliest, 43–44; as photographers, 810–11; Renaissance view of, 445, 488
Art Nouveau, 695, 701–3, 791
Ascension of Mohammed, The, Islamic, p. 10
Ash Can School, 724–25, 737, 797
As in the Middle Ages, So in the Third Reich, see Heartfield
assemblages, 763, 770–72, 773
Assumption, Basilica of, Baltimore, *see* Latrobe
Assumption, see Nanni di Banco
Assumption of the Virgin, see Correggio
ATGET, EUGÈNE, 792–93, 794; *Pool, Versailles*, 793; *1120*
Athens, Greece, 445; Acropolis, 445, 629; Propylaea, 629
atmospheric perspective, 426
At the Moulin Rouge, see Toulouse-Lautrec
Attirement of the Bride (La Toilette de la Mariée), see Ernst
Au Bord de l'Eau, Bennecourt (The River), see Monet
Augsburg, Germany, 540
Augustine, Saint, 425, 485, 519, 715; portrait of, *see* Pacher
Augustinerkirche, Vienna, Tomb of the Archduchess Maria Christina, *see* Canova
Aurora, Casino Rospiglioso, Rome, *see* Reni
Aurora, Villa Ludovisi, Rome, *see* Guercino
Austria, 564–65, 695
autochrome, 792
Autumnal Rhythm: Number 30, 1950, see Pollock

Two Forms, see Moore
"291" Gallery, New York, 796
Two Paths of Life, see Rejlander

UCCELLO, PAOLO, 467–68, 479; *Battle of San Romano*, 467–68, 492; *610*
UELSMANN, JERRY, 808; untitled photograph, 808; *1148*
Uffizi Palace, Florence, *see* Vasari
Ulu Mosque, *see* Erzurum
Umbria, Italy, 486
Unique Forms of Continuity in Space, see Boccioni
Unité d'Habitation Apartment House, Marseilles, *see* Le Corbusier
United Nations Secretariat Building, New York, *see* Harrison
United States: Impressionism, 669, 673–75; Post-Impressionism, 699–700; Romanticism, 647–48; 20th-century art, 710, 724, 735, 736–37, 748–50, 786; *see also* Colonial America
University of Pennsylvania, 708
Ur (El Muqeiar), Iraq, *Ram and Tree*, p. 4
urban planning, 788–89
Urban VIII, Pope, *Glorification of Reign of, see* Cortona; *Visiting Il Gesù, see* Sacchi
Urbino, Italy, 486
U.S. Geological Survey, 659
ut pictura poesis, 423, 590
Utrecht, The Netherlands, Schröder House, *see* Rietveld
Utrecht School, 572, 581

VAN, names with *van, van de,* or *van der* are listed under next element of name (e.g., VAN GOGH, *see* Gogh)
VANBRUGH, SIR JOHN, 603, 652; Blenheim Palace, Woodstock, 603, 604, 626; *830*
VASARELY, VICTOR, 746–47; *Vega*, 746–47, 810; *1048*
VASARI, GIORGIO, 501, 513, 514, 526; Palazzo degli Uffizi, Florence, 526, 529; Loggia of, 526; *701*
Vatican Palace, *see* Rome
vault, one-piece, 456
Vauxhall Gardens, London, Handel statue, *see* Roubiliac
Vecchio Palace, *see* Florence
Vega, see Vasarely
VELÁZQUEZ, DIEGO, 582–84, 631, 664, 675, 743; *The Maids of Honor*, 584, 631, 664; *799; Pope Innocent X*, 582, 675, 742–43; *798; The Water Carrier of Seville*, 582, 588; *797*
VELDE, HENRY VAN DE, 703, 780; Theater, Werkbund Exhibition (1914), Cologne, 703; *976, 977*
VENEZIANO, *see* Domenico Veneziano
Venice, Italy, 79, 454, 478, 479, 481, 508, 516–20, 522, 531; Campo SS. Giovanni e Paolo, Colleoni monument, *see* Verrocchio; S. Giorgio Maggiore, *see* Palladio; *Last Supper* in, *see* Tintoretto; S. Zaccaria, panel, *see* Bellini; Scuolo di San Rocco, *Christ Before Pilate, see* Tintoretto
Venus, Temple of, *see* Baalbek
VERMEER, JAN, 66, 574, 580–81, 584, 600, 686, 691, 757; *The Letter*, 580–81, 686, 691, 757; *794* and p. 23; *Woman Holding a Balance (The Pearl Weigher; The Gold Weigher)*, 66–67, 580; *25*
Verona, Italy, 522; *Equestrian Statue of Can Grande della Scala*, 454, 479–80
VERONESE, PAOLO, 522–23, 525, 567; *Christ in the House of Levi*, 523; *696*
VERROCCHIO, ANDREA DEL, 477–79, 486, 489, 490; *Equestrian Monument of Colleoni,*

Venice, 478–79; 629; *Putto with Dolphin*, Palazzo Vecchio, 478; *628*
Versailles, France, 598; Palace of, 587, 592–95; *812; see also* Hardouin-Mansart; Lebrun; Le Vau; gardens, *see* Le Nôtre
Vicenza, Italy, Villa Rotunda, *see* Palladio
Victims, see Orozco
Victoria, queen of England, 705
Victory over the Sun (opera), 722
VIEN, JOSEPH-MARIE, 619, 646
Vienna, Austria: St. Charles Borromaeus, *see* Fischer von Erlach; Tomb of the Archduchess Maria Christina, Augustinerkirche, *see* Canova
Vienna Secession, 695
Vietnam war, 749, 801
View from His Window at Le Gras, see Niépce
VIGÉE-LEBRUN, MARIE-LOUISE-ELIZA-BETH, 600; *The Duchesse de Polignac*, 600, 607; *825*
VIGNOLA, GIACOMO, 528; Il Gesù, Rome, 528–29, 556; *707, 708*
Village Bride, see Greuze
Villani, Filippo, 445
villas: Farnesina, Rome, fresco, *see* Raphael; Ludovisi, Rome, ceiling fresco, *see* Guercino; Mairea, Noormarkku, Finland, *see* Aalto; Rotunda, Vicenza, 626; *see also* Palladio
Virgin and Child with Angels, see Grünewald
Virgin of the Rocks, see Leonardo da Vinci
Vision after the Sermon, see Gauguin
Vision of Antiquity, see Puvis de Chavannes
Visitation, Dijon, *see* Broederlam
Visitation, Reims Cathedral, *see* Reims
VISPRÉ, FRANCIS XAVIER, *Portrait of Louis-François Roubiliac* (attr.), 69, 607; *29*
Vollard, Ambroise, *Portrait of, see* Picasso
Voltaire, 607, 619, 626; portrait of, *see* Houdon
VUILLARD, ÉDOUARD, 691; *Interior at l'Etang-la-Ville (The Suitor)*, 691; *951*

Wainwright Building, St. Louis, *see* Sullivan
WALPOLE, HORACE, with WILLIAM ROBINSON and others, Strawberry Hill, Twickenham, 653; *892, 893*
warehouses, 699
WARHOL, ANDY, 750–51; *Gold Marilyn Monroe*, 751; *1056*
Washington, George, portrait of, *see* Houdon
Water Carrier of Seville, see Velázquez
Water Lilies, Giverny, see Monet
Watson and the Shark, see Copley
WATTEAU, JEAN-ANTOINE, 597–98, 599, 604, 605; *Gilles and Four Other Characters from the Commedia dell'Arte (Pierrot)*, 598; *819* and p. 24; *A Pilgrimage to Cythera*, 597–98, 600, 605; *818*
Wedding Portrait, see Eyck, J.
Weimar, Germany, School of Arts and Crafts, 703; *see also* Bauhaus
Werkbund Exhibition (1914), *see* Cologne
WEST, BENJAMIN, 619, 622, 623, 642, 647; *The Death of General Wolfe*, 622, 623, 661; *840*
WESTON, EDWARD, 797, 807; *Pepper*, 797; *1127*
WEYDEN, ROGIER VAN DER, 430–33, 438, 443; *Descent from the Cross*, 430–32, 439; *555; Francesco d'Este*, 432–33; *556*
Wheat Field and Cypress Trees, see Gogh, V.
WHISTLER, JAMES ABBOTT MCNEILL, 673–75, 681, 706, 714, 738; *Arrangement in Black and Gray: The Artist's Mother*, 673; *926; Nocturne in Black and Gold: The Falling Rocket*, 673–75, 714; *927*
WHITE, MINOR, 807, 808; *Ritual Branch*, 807, 808; *1144*
Whitehall Palace, London, Banqueting House, *see* Jones

"Wies, Die," Upper Bavaria, *see* Zimmermann
"White Marmorean Flock," 772
Wife of the Reverend Becton, Pastor of Salem Methodist Church, see Zee
WILFORD, MICHAEL, Neue Staatsgalerie, Stuttgart, *see under* Stirling
William Rush Carving His Allegorical Figure of the Schuykill River, see Eakins
Williams, William Carlos, 729
WILLIAMS, WILLIAM T., 746; *Batman*, 746; *1047*
Winckelmann, Joachim, 619, 623, 625
WITZ, CONRAD, 436–37, 442; *The Miraculous Draught of Fishes*, Geneva Cathedral altarpiece, 436–37, 665; *561*
Wolfe, General, 622; *Death of, see* West
Woman Holding a Balance, see Vermeer
Woman II, see De Kooning
Woman with a Veil, see Pompeii
women artists, 516, 549–51, 574, 600, 623, 640, 669–70, 675, 678, 721, 753, 772
Women Regents of the Old Men's Home at Haarlem, see Hals
Woodcut of St. Christopher, detail from an *Annunciation* by Daret (?), 442; *570*
woodcuts, 49, 441–42, 514, 534–35
Woodstock, England, Blenheim Palace, *see* Vanbrugh
Wordsworth, William, 629
World War I, 714, 716, 720, 730, 734, 762
World War II, 728, 733, 735, 755
WREN, SIR CHRISTOPHER, 602–3, 652; St. Paul's Cathedral, London, 602–3, 627; *827, 828, 829*
WRIGHT, FRANK LLOYD, 780, 784, 785; Robie House, Chicago, 780; *1097, 1098*; Solomon R. Guggenheim Museum, 64; *23, 24*
wrought iron, 764
Würzburg, Germany, Episcopal Palace, Kaisersaal, *see* Neumann; frescoes, *see* Tiepolo

X, *see* Bladen

Young Lady with an Umbrella, see Lumière
Young Man Among Roses, see Hilliard

zaum, 720
ZEE, JAMES VAN DER, 800–801; *The Wife of the Reverend Becton, Pastor of Salem Methodist Church*, 801; *1132*
ziggurats, 788
ZIMMERMANN, DOMINIKUS, 567; Die Wies, Upper Bavaria, 567; *771, 772*
ZUCCARI, TADDEO, *The Conversion of St. Paul*, 643; *878*
Zuccone (Prophet), see Donatello
ZURBARÁN, FRANCISCO DE, 582; *St. Serapion*, 582, 622; *796*
Zurich, Switzerland, 730

LIST OF CREDITS

The author and publisher wish to thank the libraries, museums, galleries, and private collectors named in the picture captions for permitting the reproduction of works of art in their collections and for supplying the necessary photographs. Photographs from other sources are gratefully acknowledged below. Plates in the Key Monuments section are indicated by the word "page" preceding the number; all other references are to figure numbers.

ACL (copyright), Brussels: 570, 773, 871; Agence Rapho, Paris: 1124; Alinari, Florence: 573, 577, 579, 580, 583, 585, 591, 597, 613, 621, 628, 630, 659, 660, 674, 678, 679, 701, 702, 754, 756, 890; Wayne Andrews, Grosse Pointe, Michigan: 759, 853; Art Resource, New York: 923, 1066; Artothek, Peissenberg: page 22, 568, 715, 718, 721, 774, 784; Arts Council of Great Britain, London: 921; Copyright Herbert Bayer, Montecito, California: 1138; Biblioteca Laurenziana, from Christian Huelsen, *Il Libro di Giuliano da Sangallo:* 594; Bildarchiv Foto Marburg, Marburg/Lahn: 653, 655, 730; Bildarchiv Preussischer Kulturbesitz, Berlin: page 3, 562, 575, 780; Paul Bitjebier, Brussels: 999; Ferdinand Boesch, New York: 1087; Dr. Gerhard Bott, Darmstadt: 939; Copyright Alan Bowness, London: 1067; Brera Gallery, Milan: 642; The Bridgeman Art Library, London: 914; The British Tourist Authority, New York: 894; F. Bruckmann, Munich: 910; Bryan and Shear, Glasgow: 974; Ets. J. E. Bulloz, Paris: 734, 735, 862, 865, 888, 889; Caisse Nationale de Monuments Historiques et des Sites, Paris: 654, 736, 837, 891; Cameraphoto, Piero Codato, Venice: 677, 696; Ludovico Canali, Rome: page 8, page 12, page 20, 21, 30, 32, 35, 38, 39, 40, 557, 581, 592, 598, 605, 608, 618, 622, 623, 627, 638, 640, 647, 661, 666, 671, 673, 681, 686, 688, 689, 693, 723, 729, 738, 739, 741, 743, 744, 745, 746, 748, 750, 752, 878, 886; Canali/B & M: 614; Canali/Bertoni: page 14, 44, 578, 579, 606, 607, 625, 652, 670; Canali/Codato: 588, 629, 634; Eugenio Cassin, Florence: 582; Cinémathèque Française, Paris: 987a, b; Colorphoto Hans Hinz, SWB, Alschwil-Basel: page 2, 962; *Country Life,* England, Copyright: 893; Eric De Maré Copyright Gordon Fraser Gallery, Ltd., London: 968; Deutscher Kunstverlag, Munich: 855; *Du-Antlantis,* Sept. 1965, Zurich: 924; Etienne Du Cerceau, *Les Plus Excellents Batiments...:* 732; Eeva-Inkeri, New York: page 31, 1063; Bill Eng-

dahl: 1110; Lee Fatherree: 1044; Fischbach Gallery, New York: 1077; Fondazione Giorgio Cini, Istituto di Storia dell'Arte (Foto Rossi), Venice: 706; Foto Positiv Bildagentur, Vienna: 768; Fotocielo, Rome: 747; Fotostudio Schoenen & Junger, Aachen: 1096; Fototeca Unione, Rome: 798; John R. Freeman, Ltd., London: 631; Gabinetto Fotografico Nazionale, Rome: 668, 742, 749, 815; Gabinetto Nazionale delle Stampe, Rome: 663, 708; G.E.K.S., New York: 22, 24, 758, 760, 1107, 1108, 1111; Gemini Gel, Los Angeles: 1080; German Archaeological Institute, Rome: 6; Geymüller (after): 649; Graphische Sammlung Albertina, Vienna: 757; Hedrich-Blessing, Chicago, Illinois: 1097; Lucien Hervé, Paris: 1106, 1112; from H. R. Hitchcock, *Architecture: Nineteenth and Twentieth Centuries:* 900, 973; *Jahrbuch des Deutschen Werkbundes* (1915): 976, 978; H. W. Janson, New York: 599; Bruno Jarret/ADAGP: 933, 935; A. F. Kersting, London: 826, 827, 850, 892; from *Key Monuments in the History of Art,* Abrams, New York: 589, 615, 667, 977; Nikos Kontos, Athens: page 5 (right), 1; Balthazar Korab, Troy, Michigan: 1081; Bernd Kuhnert, Berlin: 1139; Kurt Lange, Oberdorf/Allgau: 574; Jacques Lathion, Oslo: page 28, 958; Galerie Louise Leiris, Paris: 2; William Lescaze, New York: 1109; Jannes Linders, Rotterdam: 1100, 1101; Juan Arauz Lomeli, Guadalajara, courtesy Laurence Schmeckebier, Syracuse, New York: 1031; Magnum Photos, Inc., New York: 1123, 1131, 1135; Marlborough Gallery, New York: 1078; Maryland Historical Society, Baltimore, Maryland: 897; Peter Mauss/Esto: page 32, 1118; Rollie McKenna, Stonington, Connecticut: 595, 616, 703; The Metropolitan Museum of Art, New York: 5, 714, 719; Henry Millon, from *Key Monuments in the History of Architecture,* Abrams, New York: 651, 761; Ministry of Works, London, Crown Copyright: 847, 848; Henry Moore: 1065; Christof Müller, Nuremberg: 566; National Buildings Record, London, Copyright F. H. Crossley 898; Otto Nelson, New York: 1047; Richard Nickel, Chicago, Illinois: 969, 970, 971; Nippon Television Network Corporation: 10, 656, 657, 658; Robert Perron, New York: 1115; from N. Pevsner, *Outline of European Architecture:* 596, 814; Photographie Giraudon, Paris, France: pages 18–19, 641, 643, 646, 710, 711, 712, 733, 736, 837, 845, 864, 866, 899; Photo MAS, Barcelona: 676, 691, 799, 856, 869, 972; Photo Meyer, Vienna: 567; Eric Pollitzer, New York: 948; Antonio Quattrone, Florence (Courtesy of Olivetti): 600, 601, 602, 603; Mario Quattrone, Florence:

page 21, 522, 529, 635, 684; R.M.N., Paris: page 7, page 24, page 26, page 27, 4, 563, 564, 637, 644, 722, 724, 777, 800, 801, 817, 818, 819, 822, 823, 859, 860, 861, 863, 868, 875, 911, 912, 915, 916, 918, 926, 1000; Rijksmuseum, Amsterdam: 572; Carl Riter: 764; Larry Rivers, New York: 1052; Roger-Viollet, Paris: 731, 901; Routhier, Paris: 804; Armando Salas, Portugal: 1076; Scala, Florence: 37, 609, 639, 672, 675; Helga Schmidt-Glassner, Stuttgart: 766, 767; Marco and Toni Schneiders, Lindau: 770, 771; Count Antoine Seilern, London: 565; Edwin Smith, Saffron Walden: 829; Halldor Soehner, Pinakothek, Munich: 690; Soprintendenza alle Galerie, Florence: 576, 682; A. Stratton, from *Life...Wren:* 828; Adolph Studly, Pennsburg, Pennsylvania: 966; Wim Swaan, New York: page 13, 3, 700, 753, 762, 765, 809, 810, 811, 820; Marvin Trachtenberg, New York: 704, 705, 769, 813, 936, 1105, 1112, 1113; Peter Trowles, Glasgow: 975; United Nations, New York: 1104; Victoria and Albert Museum, London: 885; Robert Villani, Merrick, New York: 1099; John B. Vincent, Berkeley, California: 707, 709; Denise Walker, Baltimore, Maryland: 895, 896; Etienne Weill, Jerusalem: 1064, 1116; Whitaker Studios, Richmond, Virginia: 846; David Wilkins, Pittsburgh, Pennsylvania: page 17, 586, 652; A. Zwemmer, Ltd., London, from J. S. Ackerman, *The Architecture of Michelangelo:* 662

Illustration copyrights: Copyright by the Trustees of the Ansel Adams Publishing Rights Trust. All Rights Reserved, 1991: 1128; Copyright, ARS, N.Y., 1991: 1034, 1035, 1036, 1041, 1046, 1056; Copyright, ARS, N.Y./ADAGP, 1991: 26, 920, 990, 991, 996, 998, 999, 1000, 1009, 1010, 1024, 1038, 1064, 1068, 1072, 1073, 1074, 1075, 1122, 1140; Copyright, ARS, N.Y./Cosmopress, 1991: 994, 1021, 1025, 1026, 1137; Copyright, ARS, N.Y./ Les Heritiers Matisse, Paris, 1991: 988, 989; Copyright, ARS, N.Y./Pro Litteris, Zurich, 1991: 1008; Copyright, ARS, N.Y./ SPADEM, 1991: page 28, 2, 12, 913, 921, 935, 960, 963, 1012, 1013, 1014, 1015, 1016, 1020, 1022, 1048, 1120; Copyright, Beeldrecht/VAGA, N.Y., 1991: 14, 1018, 1100, 1101; Copyright, Bild-Kunst/VAGA, N.Y., 1991: 995, 1027, 1028, 1029, 1094, 1138, 1139; Copyright, Demart Pro Arte, Paris u. Genfe, 1991: 1023; Copyright, SIAE/VAGA, N.Y., 1991: 1007; Copyright, VAGA, N.Y., 1991: page 29, 1037, 1049, 1051, 1053, 1055, 1078, 1085, 1088, 1089

The text of this book was set in 9½-point Primer,
a typeface designed in 1949 by the American artist and
designer Rudolf Rudzicka (1883–1978) for the Mergenthaler
Linotype Company and made fully available in 1954.
Primer is a refinement of Century Schoolbook, an eminently
legible face designed by Morris Fuller Benton,
which reflects his studies of reading comprehension; it was
released in 1920 by American Type Founders. Display type is
Arrow, condensed 20 percent. The book was printed and
bound in Japan; the paper is 104 GSM (grams per square meter)
Royal coat. Color illustrations are printed in four-color offset;
black-and-white illustrations are printed in duotone offset.

AH - I1
CC-102 B5
CC-104 B6 LAB L6
ENG - M2